THE GUINNESS
BOOK OF

CLASSIC BRITISH TV

2nd edition

Paul Cornell
Martin Day
and
Keith Topping

GUINNESS PUBLISHING

Editor: Anne Marshall
Design: Vox Inc, Steeple Ashton, Wilts

First published in 1996 by Guinness Publishing Ltd
Reprint 10 9 8 7 6 5 4 3 2 1 0

Printed and bound in Great Britain by The Bath Press

A catalogue record for this book is available from the British Library

ISBN 0-85112-628-6

Picture Acknowledgements
BBC Television 31, 48, 58, 63, 68, 70, 77, 84, 89, 95, 103, 109, 116, 123, 137, 141, 165, 225, 255, 281, 296, 305, 310, 315, 361, 371, 375, 379, 381, 387; Carlton Television 271; Central Television 168, 172, 207; Channel 4 53, 184; Granada Television Ltd 25, 244, 285; Hulton Deutsch 16, 73, 82, 132, 195, 330, 331, 337, 348; LWT 367; Thames Television 114, 204, 238; Yorkshire Television 45, 99

The Authors

Paul Cornell is author of several novels, a small volume of Isaac Asimov criticism (published in Spain), and a TV play mentioned in this book. Martin Day has written music and TV reviews for various magazines, including the *NME*, and a *Doctor Who* novel. Keith Topping is a civil servant. Cornell, Day and Topping are joint authors of three other TV-related books.

Contents

Acknowledgements

We would like to thank the following for their help, suggestions and corrections:

Ian and Janet Abrahams, Ian Atkins, Ian Barnwell, Keith G. Barrett, Julie Barter at Cosgrove Hall Films, Elizabeth Braithwaite, Colin Brockhurst, Anthony Brown, Paul Brown, Paul Burgin, Paul Cockburn, Christopher Cornwell, Andrew Cowper, Mark Cullen, Tony Darbyshire, Helen Day, Helen Dixon (*Emmerdale* Archivist), Lissa Evans at Hat Trick Productions, Karen Frederickson, Graham Howard, David J. Howe, David Hughes, Janice Jacobson, Sue Jenkins, Adam Jezard, Robert Kitching, Jerry Kohl, Alan Lamb, Andy Lane, John Lavalie, Peter Lawrie, Penny List, Sandra Loosemore, Steve Lyons, Donald McFarlan (without whom *none* of this would have been possible), David McKinlay, John McLaughlin, James Masterton, Steven Moffat, Alan Morton, Carrie O' Grady, Oliver Postgate and Peter Firmin at Smallfilms, Darren Page, Len Palace, Andrew Pixley, Ian Potter at the Bradford National Museum of Film and Television, Steve Purcell, Gareth Roberts, Stephen Roddam, Dave Rogers, Sylvia Rothwell, John Smith, Michael Taylor, Colin, Maureen, Alyson and Graeme Topping, Stephen James Walker, Jo Ware, David Whitby, Mark Whitney, Peter and Sonia Wickham, Norma Widdowsen, Martin J. Wiggins, Carmel Wilson. We also wish to thank the staff of Birmingham, Leeds, Newcastle upon Tyne and Westminster libraries, and the staff of the BFI library in London and St Bernard's Hospital in Gibraltar. We gratefully acknowledge the wide range of newspapers and magazines that have supplied valuable information, quotations and comment, particularly the following: *Broadcast*, *Circus*, *DWB/Dreamwatch*, *In-Vision*, *Laugh*, *The Listener*, *Media Week*, *New Musical Express* (principally Len Brown, David Quantick and Gavin Martin), *Primetime*, *Sight and Sound*, *Star Begotten/625*, *Starburst*, *Television Today*, *Televisual*, *Theatre Facts*, *Time Out*, *Time Screen*, *TV Zone*, *The Viewer*, and, especially, the *Radio Times* and *TV Times*.

Special thanks to Simon Coward, Richard Down, Chris Perry, Adrian Petford and everyone else at Kaleidoscope, the classic TV organization, for *British Television Drama Research Guide 1950-1995* and *British Television Comedy and Light Entertainment Research Guide 1950-1995*, and for invaluable help with the factual information in this book.

We owe a huge debt of gratitude to Ian Beard, Alex Briggs, P.R. Jackson and Stephen Poppitt for incredibly detailed comments and corrections.

Special thanks also to Nick Cooper for his invaluable contributions to the Drama, Telefantasy, and Soaps chapters.

Dedicated to our mums and dads

Preface

Classic British TV came into being because of a shared love of British TV drama. We hope that this new, revised edition will inform, bring back memories, and encourage an appreciation of the 20th century's most pervading artform.

In Britain 60 years of television has produced a staggering array of programmes, ranging from the popular and populist to the controversial and the critically championed. All of these have, in some way, contributed to the high regard with which British television is held throughout the world. According to Anthony Davis, *The Boys from the Blackstuff* has been transmitted in the Soviet Union, ***Yes, Minister*** in Dubai, *Tenko* in Malaysia, and *Some Mothers Do 'Ave 'Em* in Turkey. *The Muppet Show* is the most widely viewed programme in the world, with an estimated audience of 235 million people in 106 countries. And, long before the advent of colour television, there was a time when everyone standing at the bus queue would be talking about last night's episode of ***Quatermass***.

This book is a celebration of the very best of British television drama, the sort of series that are held in fond regard by millions of viewers: ***Coronation Street***, ***Z Cars***, ***Steptoe and Son***, ***Doctor Who***. Our selection criteria are wide (see the Introductory Notes that follow), but really we're just talking about different ways of assessing greatness (or 'so-bad-they're-great'-ness).

For decades, though, few saw any value in the TV archives. Repeats were no more than filler material during the summer, and millions of hours of television were wiped in the 70s. Perhaps even those entrusted with this precious resource felt that the medium was unimportant, mere prole entertainment and not worthy of serious study.

The massive success of ***Blackadder***, ***The Magic Roundabout***, ***Steptoe and Son***, and the like, on video has exposed this short-sighted cultural vandalism. We should not be surprised when we hear of such videos outselling Hollywood blockbusters or when we realize that some of ***Porridge***'s largest viewing figures were gained during a repeat run. Channel 4's *TV Heaven* season, BBC2's discovery of 'cult television', and the popularity of the satellite stations UK Gold and Bravo, at last show television developing a respect for its past. One can but hope that, by analysing the past, it will be easier for television to plot a course for the future.

Too much nostalgia can also be a bad thing, and television must always be striving to create contemporary 'classics'. We feature up-to-date programmes in *Classic British TV* for the simple reason that we don't believe that the 'Golden Age of Television' is dead.

In the first edition of this book, published in 1993, we expressed our hope that the BBC would abandon 'producer choice' and market forces and return to what it does best: producing challenging, front-line comedy and bold, relevant drama as new expressions of the corporation's great tradition of public service broadcasting, whether or not the public want or, indeed, deserve it. It is easy to criticize the BBC, especially when television stands at a crossroads. However, the corporation - a unique institution, as our book will hopefully show - cannot afford to enter the next century grovelling to business and government. As Steven Barnett and Andrew Curry commented in their book *The Battle for the BBC*, 'a deep-seated sense of affection and concern for the institution... extends way beyond the United Kingdom to almost every country in the world where the BBC can still sit comfortably alongside Manchester United, the Beatles and William Shakespeare as one of Britain's cultural icons.'

There have been some positive signs in recent years (Alan Yentob's quality revolution is, we hope, finally having an effect), and of course ITV has its role to play. But it is deeply distressing to find the BBC - once the trailblazer that others followed - producing such bland television-by-numbers as *The Vet*, *Dangerfield* and *Keeping Up Appearances*.

To reflect the constantly changing face of TV, this second edition of *Classic British TV* includes eight brand new entries (***Brookside***, ***One Foot in the Grave***, ***Absolutely Fabulous***, Harry Enfield, ***Between the Lines***, ***The Bill***, ***Cracker*** and ***Poldark***). The drama chapter has been completely rewritten and is now some 60 per cent longer, and much of the rest of this book has been revised in one way or another, with errors corrected and, wherever possible, extra factual information supplied.

Sadly, a handful of programmes (*Some Mothers Do 'Ave 'Em*, *Rumpole of the Bailey*, *Alas Smith and Jones*, *Carrott's Lib*, *The Comic Strip Presents...*, *The New Statesman*, *Captain Pugwash* and *Count Duckula*) have been 'devolved' into the chapter introductions or other entries to make room for the new material. This is not to imply that these particular programmes have fallen out of favour, but rather fulfils our aim that *Classic British TV* should evolve dynamically, with the contents of this edition complementing the first.

Despite our best efforts, there will still be omissions, of course, and doubtless we will get letters from readers asking 'Why didn't you include... [insert name of some Third Division sitcom from the 70s, or Beazer Homes League drama series that only three people remember]?' Don't worry, you are not alone in your obsessions (our own families do this to us, hence the references to *Spy-Catcher* - a series that even the people who made it have probably forgotten).

Although we have endeavoured to double-check all the information in this book, we are, as ever, grateful to receive corrections and comments from readers.

Introduction

Classic British TV is an encyclopedia of the best British TV drama programmes from the mid-50s to date. Some programmes are clearly only partly-British (a problem that will doubtless increase as co-production deals become more common), in which case (***The Magic Roundabout***, for instance) we often feel that the British input justifies inclusion.

We have concentrated on drama at the expense of non-fiction programmes in order to give us a manageable, slightly homogenous sphere of interest. It is obvious from the contents of this book that our definition of the term 'drama' is, however, somewhat unusual. Common usage would probably hint at *Play for Today* or the BBC 'Classics', while we take the word in its widest sense, implying that it is virtually synonymous with 'fiction' or, indeed, dramatic story-telling. We deal with comedy, particularly where comic sketches are used, but exclude factual programmes: documentaries, sports and arts programmes, quiz shows, and the like. Whilst episodes of *Life on Earth*, *Panorama*, *Top of the Pops* and *Match of the Day* have (rightly) gone down in television history, people tend not to be 'fans' of these programmes. Fan devotion and public recollection (pub conversations beginning 'Do you remember the episode where...?') point to the lasting impact of television fiction, and are two of our criteria for inclusion.

Other criteria cover subjective feelings of quality (always the most difficult and potentially controversial reason for inclusion), and importance in terms of the development of the medium. Thus, while *Bread* had many more viewers than ***The Young Ones***, we find the former to be a poor example of popular television, whereas the latter is influential and controversial, and will be remembered for many years to come.

What this means in practice is that of the many programmes that we deal with, around one hundred are 'main entries', featuring analysis and production information. These entries form the bulk of this book. The Drama chapter is divided into sections for the various auteurs.

Other programmes are mentioned at relevant points in main entries (e.g. *Going Straight* under ***Porridge***) or in the introductory essays to the various chapters, which give brief overviews of the development of the genre in question. References to main programme entries are indicated by bold italics, other programmes are in standard italics.

In the production credits we stress writers (and, to a lesser extent, directors) because they provide the spark that brings the medium to life. As noted by Melvyn Bragg, when presenting the 1992 BAFTA Writer's Award, writing is the craft that elevates British television above that of the rest of the world.

The following general conventions are used for the factual sections of main entries:

Title
- **Production company and channel**
- **Colour; B&W**
- **Number of episodes (and episode lengths)**
- **Dates of run at a glance, if not indicated above**
- **Creator or original source**
- **Writers**
- **Directors**
- **Producers**

Cast

Listings, season by season (detailed dates)
Episode or story titles, if available

Writers, directors, producers and cast are given in approximate chronological order. When it is impossible to feature all writers and directors in these lists we have tried to select individuals on the grounds of the importance of their contribution to that particular programme or to television drama as a whole. Although we have tried to list all episode titles, in three cases (namely ***The Bill, Dixon of Dock Green*** and ***Z Cars***) the sheer number of titles makes this prohibitive.

Episode titles given are those shown on-screen, or printed in the *Radio Times* or *TV Times*, or as used by the production team. Where there is a clash between information printed in the press and that held by the production company we occasionally list alternative titles. 'Unofficial' titles are given in (single) quotation marks, although normally – where no consensus exists - untitled episodes are listed as such.

When no episode length is given in the season breakdown, the 'standard length' indicated in the summary is intended. Sheer practicality means that the episode lengths specified actually refer to the approximate 'slot' a programme is given on British television. This is particularly important with regard to ITV where, as a rule of thumb, there are five minutes of adverts, trailers, etc. per half hour. Thus, while ***Inspector Morse*** has a 120-minute slot, the episodes actually tend to be around 100 minutes in length.

In the first edition we attempted to make a distinction between sitcom pilots and anthology episodes that were later turned into series, but in this edition all such episodes are listed in the production details. It should also be noted that the distinction between a 'normal' episode and a Christmas special is a reasonably arbitrary one, as is the delineation into seasons. Clearly, the on-going and lengthy 'seasons' of ***Emmerdale***, ***Z Cars*** and ***The Bill*** bear no relation to the recording blocks or other demarcations. Our priority is that of the programmes as they appear on screen, so occasionally a 'season divide' might reflect (say) a bank holiday rather than a gap as envisaged by the production team. However, where there is a major discrepancy between intended and actual running order, this will tend to be indicated by a footnote.

It should be stressed that we normally use the term 'season' to mean a block of episodes, preferring not use the more ambiguous 'series'. We also tend not to differentiate between a 'series' (featuring self-contained storylines) and a 'serial' (with an on-going storyline), feeling that in a non-technical book such as this these terms are virtually synonymous as distinct 'types' of programme (we use both terms interchangeably), and that we would employ 'season' in place of 'series' in a phrase such as 'the new series of ***Casualty***'.

The book is split up into a number of largely self-explanatory chapters, within which the main entries are arranged chronologically. One word that we have used that might be confusing is 'telefantasy', a more general and accurate phrase to reflect what is often called 'science fiction'. We feel that this term is a suitably wide title to cover a whole range of sub-genres, including horror, the supernatural and surrealism. 'Soaps' we take to cover any form of on-going drama that would not fit into any other chapter - see the introduction to this chapter for further comments.

A Brief Technical History

Television technology had only existed for 14 years when the British Broadcasting Company began transmission on 2 November 1936. Although a primitive broadcasting service had been running for some months in Nazi Germany, the BBC is proud of its achievement in producing the world's first high-definition service. John Logie Baird, who invented television in the 20s, had originally used a system that scanned mechanically, rather than electronically, although by the time that the BBC began transmission both Marconi and EMI had experimented with early forms of the present system. However, there was no way of preserving live broadcasts and the only examples of television from the pre-war era which have survived are 'demonstration films' to advertise the BBC's fledgling service.

After 1945, certain live performances were recorded for posterity. In *The Television Heritage*, TV historian Steve Bryant notes that 'the sort of material most likely to be recorded was that of an obviously newsworthy or historic nature, such as the 1953 Coronation, or various television "firsts", particularly in the outside broadcast field'. The same applied to drama, so that whilst many early Nigel Kneale works were telerecorded, only a handful of ***Dixon of Dock Green*** episodes were captured. *The Grove Family*, the first TV soap, fared even worse, with only two examples now in existence.

Telerecording required an adapted film camera to shoot the picture on a flat TV monitor. At this stage, the picture consisted of 405 horizontal lines (all transmissions by BBC1 and ITV prior to 1968 used 405 lines). BBC2, which began in 1964, experimented with the technically-superior 625-line system (which had the effect of making the picture less 'grainy' and reduced flickering) and, by 1969, the two main channels had also switched to 625. The various methods of recording also changed; at first, all recordings were done on film (35 mm for pre-recording, 16 mm for preservation and overseas sales). However, by the late 60s this had been largely replaced by 2-inch video tape.

Colour television became a reality in 1967 (again, BBC2 was the initial recipient), and within two years almost all new television programmes were being made in colour, despite the fact that most sets still only received monochrome. Colour meant a massive leap forward in recording techniques, and everything from ***Doctor Who*** and ***Monty Python's Flying Circus*** to weather broadcasts benefited from technical developments such as colour separation overlay (CSO), which allowed the simple mixing of two separate images.

In the early 70s, due to space restrictions and the cost of maintaining a large archive of recordings, the BBC (and, to a lesser extent, the independent companies) embarked upon a misguided and, with hindsight, unforgivable purge of their back catalogues. The losses that television suffered during this period have been well documented, but some specific cases deserve to be highlighted. As Steve Bryant notes, of the three black-and-white seasons of ***Till Death Us Do Part*** ('a milestone in television comedy, a critical reference point in the debate on "taste" and a social document in its own right'), only three episodes remain, together with a ten-minute fragment of another and a *Late Night Line-Up* documentary on Johnny Speight which includes several clips. 'Enough to make a point,' notes Bryant, sadly, 'but scarcely what one might hope to find.'

Other notable losses include several plays by David Mercer and Dennis Potter, James Burke and Patrick Moore's presentation of the first moon landing, Kenneth Tynan's infamous use of the 'f word' in an episode of *BBC3*, large chunks of ***The Likely Lads***, over 100 episodes of ***Doctor Who***, and over 200 episodes of ***Z Cars***.

Many artists were dismayed by the purge. Dudley Moore used an appearance on *Parkinson* to flay the BBC's junking of ***Not Only... But Also...***. Critics such as Séan Day-Lewis and Peter Fiddick called for an accessible national television archive, and Howard Schuman, whilst criticizing the 'ephemeral nature of television' in an issue of *The Listener*, acknowledged the 'tremendous psychological difference if a writer knew his work would be available for showings and re-evaluation well after its initial transmission'.

The ability to directly manipulate video has, at last, given the medium an advantage over film, although film is still used on 'prestige' series, and rightly so. Television companies have become sensitive to further criticism of neglect in recent years and, with the boom in home video and the need to fill increased hours of scheduling, television archives have been raided more than ever before.

Television technology continues to evolve, with CD-quality NICAM stereo sound and digital, wide screen and high-definition television either with us or on the immediate horizon. Despite this, the beauty of watching television is that it remains as simple as sitting still.

Defined by Hilary Kingsley in *Soap Box* as a story that has 'no beginning and no end', the soap opera is the narrative style of television that is most discussed and most criticized. To fans of the genre, soaps are an extension of their own lives and, as Kingsley notes, 'At the centre of all soap operas there must be the family. Sometimes, as in ***Crossroads***, the family can be a social group... It is this feeling of closeness that matters most in soap.'

The soap opera began on American radio during the 1920s. Daily serials, reflecting the lives of 'ordinary people', became immensely popular and, because many of these were sponsored by soap companies, the term 'soap opera' was used to describe stories of this kind.

In Britain, the first long-running family sagas were also radio series (*The Robinsons, Mrs Dale's Diary, The Archers*). Television's trailblazing serial during the early 50s was *The Appleyards*, a popular children's series that ran for over four years, although one newspaper described it as being 'more a documentary on the chores of family life'.

The style of the soap opera was established by *The Grove Family*. The Groves were a plummy lower-middle-class couple with four children who lived in Hendon. They represented the kind of British family that few recognized but all aspired to be. In many ways *The Grove Family* says more about 50s Britain than a plethora of documentaries ever could. Writer Michael Pertwee created the series with his father, Roland, as a 20-minute Friday night 'filler' in 1954; it starred Edward Evans and Ruth Dunning as Mr and Mrs Grove (and a young Christopher Beeny as one of the children). The series was among the most popular of its era (with audiences pushing nine million), and it only ended because of the mistaken belief that its popularity was on the wane. It came as no surprise when Independent Television, in the shape of ATV, began its own soap in 1957.

By experimenting with form (using characters associated with a particular working environment in place of the family), ATV produced the first occupational soap, *Emergency – Ward 10*, beginning a fascination for hospitals that remains to this day. Created by Tessa Diamond as a six-week serial, it eventually lasted for ten years and over 900 episodes. It wasn't well thought-of by everyone, however. A Manchester St John Ambulance Brigade commissioner forbade his cadets to watch it, saying that nurses were being portrayed as 'feather-headed flibbertigibbets'. Nevertheless, *Ward 10* pushed many of its doctors (Charles Tingwell, John Alderton, Ray Barrett and John Carlisle) towards stardom. Albert Finney and Ian

Hendry had small roles as patients, and the series caused a stir in 1964 when British TV's first 'multi-racial kiss', between a Jamaican nurse (Joan Hooley) and a white Doctor (John White), was dropped by nervous ATV executives, although it was finally shown some months later.

Ward 10 ended in April 1967, the result of falling ratings, although its legacy lived on, with ATV boss Lew Grade (a man loath to admit errors of judgement) calling his decision to ditch the series 'one of the two biggest mistakes I have ever made'. ATV eventually created *General Hospital* as a look-alike replacement and, although the 70s series also proved popular, it too ended on the whim of the ATV chiefs.

The BBC's first stab at recreating the success of *The Grove Family*, *Compact*, began in 1962. The series was created by Hazel Adair as she sat waiting to deliver an article to *Woman's Own*, and was written in collaboration with Peter Ling (the pair would later create ***Crossroads***). The story centred on the 'talented and temperamental people' who worked on a 'topical magazine for busy women'. Critics called the show 'worthless', 'empty-headed' and 'hollow', but, as with *Ward 10*, it was massively popular, and it dealt with some quite controversial subject matter for the early 60s (marital discord and unmarried mothers, for example). *Compact* starred Jean Harvey, Moray Watson, Monica Evans, and Ronald Allen as heart-throb Ian Harmon. Producer Morris Barry tried to liven things up in 1965 with an episode showing two youths being

Richard Thorp (seated, second from left) played Dr John Rennie in *Emergency – Ward 10* some 25 years before finding further fame as Alan Turner in *Emmerdale Farm*

offered reefers, but *Compact* never progressed much beyond the superficial and glossy world featured in the magazines themselves. Hazel Adair has always claimed that that was what they set out to do in the first place.

Compact was British television's first 'avarice soap', designed to appeal to viewers because it represented a glitzy world far removed from reality. This would lead to *Hadleigh*, *Howards' Way*, *Trainer*, and many others.

Of the next two BBC soaps, both begun in 1965, *United!* was the most interesting and, at the same time, the most ridiculous, a twice-weekly saga of life at second division football club Brentwich. Devised by Anthony Cornish and written by Brian Hayles, *United!* had a superb cast, led by David Lodge, Bryan Marshall, George Layton, Stephen Yardley and Arthur Pentelow. The football sequences were filmed at Stoke City, with then Coventry City manager (and later TV icon) Jimmy Hill as the series' football advisor. Several clubs (notably Wolves, then going through something of a crisis) complained that the plot lines had been based on them, but most viewers felt the series was too unrealistic. After the sacking of manager Lodge, Ronald Allen replaced him, but the series remained in the second division of the ratings league and was dropped after 18 months. A pity, as it would be another 20 years before TV would again attempt a football drama series, with Channel 4's superior *The Manageress*.

The Newcomers was the other new BBC soap. Created by Colin Morris, the series was an attempt to match ***Coronation Street*** in realism, taking a group of London families and relocating them in a Suffolk dormitory town. *The Newcomers* had a lot going for it, including a teenage sex-symbol in Judy Geeson and a strong supporting cast that included Alan Browning and Wendy Richard. Some of the plotlines were daring for their time, including an expose on witchcraft, but, significantly, Mary Whitehouse considered the series 'morally sound'. Possibly that was its death-knell.

Morris tried again, in 1969, with *The Doctors*, a strong, gritty series that attracted writers like Fay Weldon and Elaine Morgan. *The Doctors* was an attempt at soap without love-triangles or sentimentality. The series starred John Barrie, Richard Leach, Nigel Stock (whose character later had a spin-off series in *Owen MD*) and Justine Lord as Liz MacNiel (dubbed 'the sexiest woman on television' by one critic). Despite good audience figures, it ended in 1971, to be replaced by one of the great cult series of the 70s, *The Brothers*. Norman Crisp and producer Gerard Glaister created the series which concerned a haulage firm run by a family of back-stabbing kin (and their manipulative mother, a wonderful hard-faced performance by Jean Anderson). What made *The Brothers* so attractive was its sheer capitalist narcissism. Robin Chadwick, Glyn Owen and Richard Easton played the Hammond brothers (Owen was replaced by Patrick O'Connell after a season), whilst the real stars of the show were Gabrielle Drake as Chadwick's wife, who was written out of the series in a car crash (to viewer outrage), Hilary Tindall as Anne, the classic 70s bitch and, later, Colin Baker and Kate O'Mara. Baker's Paul Merroney was a ruthless whiz-kid who had 'a face like a baby's bottom and morals to match', and soon gained the title 'The Nastiest Man on TV'. His later double act with O'Mara (an equally ruthless air freight magnate) was something to behold. Early episodes revolved around the family's snobbery towards Old Man Hammond's mistress (Jennifer Wilson) and her illegitimate daughter, mixing boardroom squabbling with suppressed sexuality in equal doses. Hugely popular for seven seasons and over 90 episodes, the series ended in 1976, when *Dallas* was but a gleam in Aaron Spelling's eye. Glaister went on to create Britain's first Thatcherite soap, *Howards' Way*, with writer Allan Prior (basically *The Brothers* Mark II, but not as much fun). Andrea Newman's

Bouquet of Barbed Wire, with Frank Finlay and Susan Penhaligon, matched *The Brothers* in nihilism and was just as sexually provocative. Another middle-class couple in crisis were Peter Barkworth and Hannah Gordon in *Telford's Change*. Howard Schuman's *Rock Follies* saw Rula Lenska, Julie Covington and Charlotte Cornwall as the Little Ladies, a female rock group constantly manipulated by the male music industry.

By the 80s, with the established soaps (***Coronation Street, Crossroads*** and ***Emmerdale Farm***) seemingly untouchable in terms of popularity and ratings, attempts such as Scottish TV's Glendarroch fable, *Take the High Road*, Granada's brave but disastrous *Albion Market* and the BBC's watchword for planning madness *Triangle* all failed to significantly effect the genre. 1992's much-hyped *Eldorado*, despite Jesse Birdsall at his snarling best, seemed doomed from day one. Criticized mainly for its excessive cost, the series that Julia Smith proudly boasted would contain 'sun, sex and sangria' was cancelled after 150 episodes.

Programmes such as ***Casualty***, ***The Troubleshooters*** and ***All Creatures Great and Small*** might not, at first glance, seem to have much in common with the year-round half-hour slices of life that we associate with the term 'soap'. However, we have not relegated otherwise worthy programmes to this chapter: rather, we define the soap opera as a primitive exercise in grand storytelling which, due to its themes, tends to focus not on the elite in society, but on the masses.

Soap opera is the people's theatre.

Coronation Street

- **Granada** (ITV) ◆ B&W (1960-69); Colour (1970 to date)
- **Standard episode length:** 30 minutes
- **Creator:** Tony Warren
- **Writers include:** Tony Warren, Harry Kershaw, Cyril Abraham, Jack Rosenthal, Adele Rose, Vince Powell, Harry Driver, John Finch, Peter Eckersley, Jim Allen, Geoffrey Lancashire, Malcolm Lynch, Bernard Aspen, Susan Pleat, Julian Roach, Brian Finch, Barry Hill, John Stevenson, Leslie Duxbury, Peter Tonkinson, Esther Rose, Paula Milne, Peter Whalley, Tony Perrin, Tom Elliott, Kay Mellor, James Robson, Frank Cottrell Boyce, Paul Abbott
- **Directors include:** Derek Bennett, Michael Scott, Howard Baker, Roland Joffe, Michael Apted, Mike Newall, Brian Armstrong, Pauline Shaw, Ken Grieve, Oliver Horsburgh, June Wyndham Davies, Bill Gilmour, Matthew Robinson, Jeremy Summers, Malcolm Taylor, Brian Mills, Nicholas Ferguson, Kenny McBain, Gareth Morgan, Mervyn Cumming, John Michael Phillips
- **Producers:** Stuart Latham, Derek Granger, H.V. Kershaw, Margaret Morris, Tim Aspinall, Howard Baker, Peter Eckersley, Jack Rosenthal, Michael Cox, Richard Everitt, Richard Doubleday, John Finch, June Howson, Brian Armstrong, Eric Prytherch, Leslie Duxbury, Susi Hush, Bill Podmore, Pauline Shaw, Mervyn Watson, John G. Temple, Carolyn Reynolds, Sue Pritchard
- **Executive producers:** Harry Elton, H.V. Kershaw, Bill Podmore, David Liddiment, Carolyn Reynolds

At over 35 years of age, *Coronation Street* is the world's longest-running fictional television series. It occupies a place in the hearts of millions of viewers, generations of whom were brought up on its gritty yet charming snapshots of northern life. *Coronation Street* is the most important television series ever made.

Tony Warren was 23 when he created *Coronation Street* in 1960. He was working on adaptations of W.E. Johns's *Biggles* stories for Granada and was desperate to move on. Writing the first episode of a new drama series, under the title of *Florizel Street*, overnight, he submitted the idea to Granada who employed him at £30 a week to develop it into an on-going serial.

Warren's vision was of something that would explore 'the driving forces behind life in a working-class street in the north of England. The purpose... [was] to examine a community of this kind and to entertain.' In creating the backdrop as a bleak fictitious district of Manchester (Weatherfield), Warren was working on similar themes to many contemporary theatre and cinema excursions (e.g. *Saturday Night and Sunday Morning* (GB 60), *A Taste of Honey* (GB 61)) into the world of the working class. However, it hadn't really been done on television before: everyone spoke 'as if they had lovely homes in the Thames Valley'. (It is hardly surprising, therefore, that the early episodes have been compared to the TV work of Mercer, Potter and Alun Owen.)

With the aid of the show's first producer, Stuart Latham, and a team of scriptwriters, including John Finch and Harry Kershaw (who would be associated with the series, as writer, producer – in three spells – or executive producer for most of its first 20 years), a series of marvellously realistic characters were created. With casting under the direction of Margaret Morris and Jose Scott, things fell into place with remarkable ease.

The cast was made up of elderly unknowns, many in the twilight of obscure careers in rep, and an equally obscure young element, mainly from genuine north-west backgrounds. Tony Warren knew several of the actresses he wanted, having worked previously with Doris Speed, Violet Carson and Pat Phoenix. Thus three of the most important characters in the history of television – Annie Walker, Ena Sharples and Elsie Tanner – could almost be said to have been specifically written for the actresses who played them.

The part of Elsie's teenage tearaway son Dennis (TV's original 'Dirty Den') went to Mancunian Philip Lowrie, although another *enfant terrible*, Kenneth Farrington (who played Annie Walker's son, Billy) also screen-tested for the role. Jack Howarth, already a 64-year-old veteran, was the perfect choice for the cantankerous Albert Tatlock, TV's oldest and best 'nasty old man'. William Roache and Alan Rothwell, two young Mancunians, were cast as the Barlow boys, Ken and David. Roache is still in the series today, over 3000 episodes later, and insists that if he had known that *Coronation Street* would last for 30 years he would never have taken the role.

The first episode was broadcast live on Friday 9 December 1960 from the Granada studios to most ITV regions (ATV Midland and Tyne Tees refused to take the programme at first, but quickly backed down when it became apparent that something big was taking place). Ken Irwin, the critic for the *Daily Mirror*, declared after the first episode: 'The programme is doomed ... with its dreary signature tune and grim scenes of a row of terraced houses and smoking chimneys.' However, the much more intuitive *Guardian* TV critic predicted that the series would 'run forever'.

Starring: Violet Carson (Ena Sharples) • Doris Speed (Annie Walker) • Arthur Leslie (Jack Walker) • Pat Phoenix (Elsie Tanner/Howard) • Philip Lowrie (Dennis Tanner) • Frank Pemberton (Frank Barlow) • William Roache (Ken Barlow) • Alan Rothwell (David Barlow) • Lynne Carol (Martha Longhurst) • Margot Bryant (Minnie Caldwell) • Ivan Beavis (Harry Hewitt) • Christine Hargreaves (Christine Hardman/Appleby) • Jack Howarth (Albert Tatlock) • Betty Alberge (Florrie Lindley) • Arthur Lowe (Leonard Swindley) • Doreen Keogh (Concepta Riley/Hewitt/Regan) • Jennifer Moss (Lucille Hewitt) • Eileen Derbyshire (Emily Nugent/Bishop) • Peter Adamson (Len Fairclough) • Jack Watson (Bill Gregory) • Anne Reid (Valerie Tatlock/Barlow) • Graham Haberfield (Jerry Booth) • Susan Jameson (Myra Dickinson/Booth) • Kenneth Cope (Jed Stone) • Gordon Rollings (Charlie Moffitt) • Jean Alexander (Hilda Ogden) • Bernard Youens (Stan Ogden) • Sandra Gough (Irma Ogden/Barlow) • Neville Buswell (Ray Langton) • Paul Maxwell (Steve Tanner) • Susan Patterson/Katie Heanus/Wendy Jane Walker (Susan Barlow/Baldwin) • Bryan Mosley (Alf Roberts) • Irene Sutcliffe (Maggie Clegg/Cooke) • John Sharp (Les Clegg) • Betty Driver (Betty Turpin) • Stephen Hancock (Ernest Bishop) • Alan Browning (Alan Howard) • Julie Goodyear (Bet Lynch/Gilroy) • Barbara Mullaney/Knox (Rita Bates/Littlewood/Fairclough/Sullivan) • Thelma Barlow (Mavis Riley) • Anne Kirkbride (Deirdre Hunt/Langton/Barlow/Rachio) • Geoffrey Hughes (Eddie Yates) • Fred Feast (Fred Gee) • Peter Baldwin (Derek Wilton) • Helen Worth (Gail Potter/Tilsley/Platt) • Johnny Briggs (Mike Baldwin) • Cheryl Murray (Suzie Birchall) • Madge Hindle (Renee Bradshaw/Roberts) • Lynne Perrie (Ivy Tilsley/Brennan) • Christopher Quentin (Brian Tilsley) • George Waring (Arnold Swain) • Warren Jackson (Nicky Tilsley/Platt) • Bill Waddington (Percy Sugden) • Elizabeth Dawn (Vera Duckworth) • William Tarmey (Jack Duckworth) • Nigel Pivaro (Terry Duckworth) • Kevin Kennedy (Norman 'Curly' Watts) • Michael Le Vell (Kevin Webster) • Sally Ann Matthews (Jenny Bradley) • Mark Eden (Alan Bradley) • Sally Whittaker (Sally Seddon/Webster) • Sean Wilson (Martin Platt) • Amanda Barrie (Alma Sedgewick/Baldwin) • Roy Barraclough (Alec Gilroy) • Michelle Holmes (Tina Fowler) • Philip Middlemass (Des Barnes) • Amelia Bullimore (Steph Barnes) • Rita Wolf (Felicity 'Flick' Khan) • Sarah Lancashire (Raquel Wolstenhulme) • Eva Pope (Tanya Poolley)

When viewed today, that first episode, with its establishing shots of back-to-back brick terraces, sends a shiver of nostalgia down the spine. Ena Sharples's first appearance in the corner shop recently taken over by Florrie Lindley – 'Are you a widder woman? Ah'll have a packet of bakin' powder' – is the stuff of which TV legends are made.

Within weeks, with the format established, new characters were being introduced. Leonard Swindley, the gentle, teetotal owner of the local drapery shop, was portrayed by Arthur Lowe. He was soon joined by the bashful Emily Nugent as his business partner, another member of the cast who has lasted through purges and decades of new ideas. Liverpudlian actor Ivan Beavis was cast as Harry Hewitt, the shy and darkly handsome widower whose wayward rebel daughter, Lucille (played by 15-year-old Wigan schoolgirl, Jennifer Moss), became the series' first, and best-loved, teenage sex symbol. The episode in 1962 in which Lucille turned up at school with dyed-blonde hair, wearing a tattoo, has become something of a camp classic amongst older viewers.

Ena Sharples was given the companionship of Minnie Caldwell and Martha Longhurst, to form the ultimate triumvirate of gossiping old women, whilst possibly the most important addition was Peter Adamson's immortal Len Fairclough, the hard man of the Street. Len's young son, Stanley, was portrayed initially by future Herman's Hermits star Peter Noone. (Another future pop star, Davy Jones, five years before he achieved television immortality as a member of The Monkees, also appeared in several early episodes as Ena Sharples's grandson Colin.)

In February 1961, a major storyline involved a broken gas main, causing the evacuation of the entire street to the Mission Hall. This brilliant ploy was used to deepen characterizations of many of the series' regulars, and the viewers showed their appreciation when ratings soared. The first romantic plot of the series concluded in October of that year, when Harry Hewitt proposed to barmaid, Concepta Riley. The marriage, in November 1961, became the first of many to capture the imagination of the nation, and the first of several to spill from the screen into real life.

One of the most memorable early-running themes involved the rather bookish and arrogant Ken Barlow (how little things change in 30 years) and his attempts to better himself. Ken's dissatisfaction with the Street led to the publication of a patronizing article in the *Manchester Evening News* entitled 'Life in a Northern Back Street', which raised the hackles of just about everybody. In a memorable episode climax, Len Fairclough did the whole nation a favour by punching Ken on the jaw in Jack and Annie Walker's pub, the Rovers Return. Ken's reputation improved some months later when he was mainly responsible for talking down potential suicide victim Christine Hardman from the roof of the raincoat factory, whilst his marriage to Valerie Tatlock in 1962 was another celebration of *Coronation Street*'s ability to put on a nice wedding.

This was an era of stability in the street, mirroring the early 60s fixation with family life and safety in numbers. People were born, grew up, lived, worked, drank, grew old and died in *Coronation Street*. As much as it was a part of everyday life, everyday life was a part of the appeal of the series. The sudden arrival of new characters was handled, as in life, in a very abstract manner. One day they weren't there, then they were, propping up the bar in the Rovers Return. There were no applauded introductions on *Coronation Street*, simply a feeling of endless continuity.

Jerry Booth, played sympathetically by Graham Haberfield, was to be the street's first quasi-tragic hero, a figure of immense kindness and charm, whose relationships seemed to be dogged by a horrible feeling of impending doom. This was especially evident after the collapse of his marriage to Myra. Haberfield's sudden death in 1975, after he had recently returned to the series, is still mourned by a legion of fans who remember the youthful Jerry Booth with an affection matched by only a select handful of perennial stars.

One of the arguable weaknesses of *Coronation Street* is its use of archetypes to convey a certain message about the continuity of attitudes from one generation to the next. There has always been 'the gossip', 'the nasty old man', 'the slob', etc. One of the most important of these archetypes was the role of 'the bad lad', the black sheep of the extended family with a heart of gold but feet of clay. Dennis Tanner was the original shady character, and throughout the series' history there has always been at least one morally questionable element. One of the best arrived in April 1961 with the debut of Jed Stone, played with comic brilliance by Kenneth Cope. He was Minnie Caldwell's lodger, who entered into *Coronation Street* folklore in his opening scene when, upon being pinned to a wall by Ena Sharples, he said, cheekily, 'Give 'is a kiss!' Cope's character was a semi-regular throughout the mid-60s, and few viewers will forget his harebrained schemes to make a quick packet.

1963 was the year in which *Coronation Street* first began to explore aspects of black comedy, as in the episode where Albert Tatlock and Alf Roberts had a drunken night out with the Rovers' darts team and ended up in the cells after assaulting a policeman. There was also the introduction of deliberately comic characters, such as Charlie Moffitt, balanced by the more serious storyline of the on–off relationship between Len and Elsie, a 'match made in heaven' which never quite seemed to get much beyond wishful thinking on everyone's part.

The following year, however, was to be one of the most traumatic of the series' history. A young producer named Tim Aspinall was brought in. His period in charge was short (a matter of months), but the impact of Aspinall's changes was to be far-reaching. Aspinall decided, possibly correctly, that the main thing *Coronation Street* needed was an injection of youth (he certainly wouldn't be the last *Coronation Street* producer to come to this conclusion), though the way in which he went about it left a bad taste for years afterwards.

In May, Frank Barlow had a £5000 win on the premium bonds and decided to sell his shop and move out of the area. Frank Pemberton, the genial, staunchly working-class actor who had played him, suddenly found himself on the dole. He, like many after him, was to discover that life outside *Coronation Street* could be unforgiving. But this was merely the tip of an iceberg that rapidly become known as 'the great purge of '64'. At Frank's celebration party in the Rovers Return, Martha Longhurst died from a heart attack in the snug.

There were protests from the cast, Peter Adamson refusing to say the line 'She's dead' throughout rehearsals on the assumption that some kind of stay of execution would arrive. For possibly the first time in television history a regularly returning character in a long-running series died on-screen. With a pathos and poignancy that stunned the viewing audience, the final credits rolled, without Eric Spear's now-legendary theme music, signalling the end of Lynne Carol's contribution to *Coronation Street*. Although the episode is one of most well-remembered of the programme's history, reaction to the death was not positive and within weeks Tim Aspinall was privately admitting that he'd made a terrible mistake.

However, the purge didn't end there. Harry and Concepta left for a new life in Ireland. Then, in July, the potential 'wedding of the year', between Emily Nugent and Leonard Swindley, was scuppered at the last moment when the bride got cold feet. Arthur Lowe left the series soon afterwards for fame elsewhere (initially taking the Swindley character with him in a series called *Pardon the Expression* in 1966), whilst poor Emily remained *Coronation Street*'s lovelorn spinster for a few more years.

9 Dec 60
to date

2000th
episode
transmitted on
2 Jun 1980

Despite the departures, however, 1964 will also be remembered for two major new arrivals at number 13, Stanley and Hilda Ogden. They were to become known as 'the most perfect double act on television', on a par with Morecambe and Wise. For 20 years Stanley Ogden was, in the words of Hilary Kingsley, 'the uncrowned king of the non-working classes', whilst the Stan Ogden Appreciation Society of Newton Abbot hailed him as 'the greatest living Englishman'. Youens himself would later say, 'He is my creation and I'm proud of him.' Hilda, on the other hand, took some time to move from being a rather irritating nosy gossip to the Boadicea-like warrior who would become Britain's best-loved housewife.

The cult of Hilda Ogden (which included such notable catches as Sir John Betjeman, Russell Harty and Michael Parkinson) owed everything to the extraordinary performance of Jean Alexander. Her 23 years on the series earned her a Royal Television Society 'Performance of the Year' award in 1988.

An early Ogden plot concerned Tickler Murphy (Patrick McAlinney) persuading Stan to become a wrestler and take on a formidable opponent at the Viaduct Sports Club, run by Laurie Frazer (Ray Brooks). It ended, of course, with Stan being thrown out of the ring. When David Barlow married the Ogdens' daughter, Irma, at Christmas 1965, it seemed that *Coronation Street* was running out of things to say, but, as in life, events such as marriage, birth and death were just bookends to everyday drama. If *Coronation Street* often seemed obsessed with the mundane or at least trivial, so it mirrored reality.

Unlike other soaps, *Coronation Street*'s episode endings seldom rest on a life-or-death scenario. Rather, they tend to concern themselves with relationships, and, by extension, with change. Tony Warren commented later that 'the stories were harder, grittier then because life was harder. *Coronation Street* didn't go soft – life did.' Thus in 1966, the programme reflected the country's general optimism. However, the marvellous episode in which Stan, on the dole for some weeks, thinks he's won the pools, only to find that Hilda hadn't posted his coupon, showed the negative side of materialism. There remained much that was both surprising and dark in the series.

Lucille Hewitt was now 15 and growing fast. In reality, Jennifer Moss was 21. Ever since the character first appeared, she had been forced to wrap herself in bandages to conceal her breasts. Jennifer had celebrated Lucille's 14th birthday by wearing a bra for the first time. In 1966 she entered into her first affair with another of the 'bad lads', Ray Langton. In May, Lucille and Irma began work at the raincoat factory alongside a new arrival in the area, a tarty blonde called Bet Lynch whom Annie Walker decided was 'rather common'. The 'Swinging 60s' had arrived in Weatherfield.

The Christmas 1966 episode, featuring a fancy dress party thrown by Ken and Val Barlow at the Mission, is still well-remembered, notably for Len and Jerry dressed as Batman and Robin, and Annie Walker's triumphant Elizabeth I costume.

By 1967 *Coronation Street* was an established part of everyday British life, especially in the North. It had developed a huge following, with audience figures regularly topping ten million. Future Prime Minister James Callaghan publicly called Pat Phoenix 'the sexiest woman on TV'. At the turn of the year, writer Jack Rosenthal took over as the series' producer. Although his stay on the series was just a few months, before giving way to another of Granada's young up-and-coming producers, Michael Cox, Rosenthal steered the series through what many viewers regard as one of its golden eras.

The year began with comic brilliance as Irma and Val Barlow were chatted up by a group of young men in the Rovers. One was Ben Kingsley, a decade before he starred in *Gandhi* (GB/USA/India 82). The episode was one of many that year directed by Michael Apted, who would later become part of another television legend as producer/director of the 'real-life soap opera' *Seven Up*. The year ended with Dennis Tanner's flat becoming a temporary home to a group of hippies. The young leader with the Jimi Hendrix haircut was a pre-***Professionals*** Martin Shaw. In between came the episode in which a goods train ploughed through the viaduct parapet and plunged into the Street, apparently burying Ena Sharples until she was pulled from the rubble by David Barlow and Jerry Booth.

The marriage of '67 was Elsie Tanner tying the knot with her wartime sweetheart, US Army Sergeant Steve Tanner (no relation!), which was watched by an audience in excess of 20 million. The episode climaxed with Harry Hewitt crushed to death under Len Fairclough's van as a jack collapsed. Of course, Elsie's marriage was doomed to failure, and she returned to the Street within two months. Her husband soon joined the growing ranks of unwanted *Coronation Street* characters killed off for no adequately explained reason (it turned out to be a murder, although that's another story).

The following couple of years saw many of the stalwarts of the 60s disappear from the series. David and Irma emigrated to Australia, Alan Rothwell's career eventually turning full circle when, 20 years later, he would return to soap opera as drug addict Nicholas Black in ***Brookside***. Dennis Tanner married and moved to London, Philip Lowrie apparently tired of 'mucking around pulling funny faces'. Even Violet Carson was forced to drop out of the series for a few months due to ill health. Les and Maggie Clegg took over the corner shop, whilst new characters like Betty Turpin, Ernest Bishop and Alan Howard all arrived. Bet Lynch became the new barmaid at the Rovers.

Christmas 1969 saw a two-hour ITV extravaganza entitled *All Star Comedy Carnival* in which *Coronation Street* was, somewhat surprisingly (given Granada's fierce stand against trivialization of the series), represented by a special 15-minute Ron McDonnell script, set in the Rovers. It appeared alongside such standard LWT fare as *Doctor in the House*, *On the Buses*, *Please Sir!*, *The Dustbinmen* (Jack Rosenthal's post-*Street* stumble into sitcom), and *Never Mind the Quality, Feel the Width*.

More traditional episodes, however, were still gripping (Val Barlow held hostage by an escaped convict), conventionally comedic (Stan Ogden taking up sculpting), or epic (the November 1969 Rovers outing to the Lakes ended with a bus crash). Ray Langton's hospital rehabilitation seemed to take up most of the next few months (the doctor who treated him was a young Paul Darrow). A shadow was cast over the entire series in 1970, however, when Arthur Leslie, the genial and dignified Jack Walker, suddenly died. The death was written into the series in the same month that Elsie Tanner married yet again, this time to Geordie businessman Alan Howard.

In January 1971 a then record audience of 22 million viewers saw Valerie Barlow die after being electrocuted by a faulty hairdryer plug. The roots of this lay in Anne Reid's decision to leave the series, which was reportedly not taken kindly by the producers, who chose to make her departure as permanent as possible. Jennifer Moss, the victim of a broken marriage and a miscarriage, and Peter Adamson, with severe alcohol problems, were both given extended leaves of absence.

The early 70s saw a marked increase in the series' popularity abroad, especially the sale of the first 1142 episodes to a Canadian television station in 1972, a feat that achieved an entry in *The Guinness Book of Records*. The nation heaved a huge sigh of relief when its favourite spinster, Emily Nugent, married Ernest Bishop. Among the important characters to first appear in the early years of the decade were Ivy Tilsley, Rita Littlewood, Deirdre Hunt, Mavis Riley and Vera Duckworth. Gail Potter, Fred Gee, Derek Wilton and Suzie Birchall arrived in the mid-70s, Derek beginning his courtship of Mavis, one of the longest-running and most frustrating in TV history.

Coronation Street still had the ability to get to the future stars first. In 1973, Ken Barlow had a brief affair with Elaine Perkins, the daughter of the headmaster of the school where he taught. Joanna Lumley still regards this as one of her most memorable performances. In 1974, Joanne Whalley made her screen debut in an episode, playing the young daughter of Muriel Graham (Anna Fox). Several episodes that year were directed by Roland Joffe, who 13 years later would be the creative force behind *The Mission*.

The most important new additions to the cast in the 70s, however, were two further examples of 'the bad lad'. The first could at least claim direct lineage since Eddie Yates was supposed to be Jed Stone's cell-mate from Walton jail. The 16-stone, gap-toothed Scouser became one of the series' best-loved characters, as the

The cast from the first episode, featuring all those characters you grew to know and love. And Ken Barlow

Ogdens' more-or-less permanent lodger. No one who watched the now legendary 'CB affair' in which Eddie ('Slim Jim') met his future wife Marion ('Stardust Lil'), played by Veronica Doran, will ever be able to forget it. At the other end of the scale, by the mid-70s the 'real' villains in life were often being portrayed on television as dodgy employers, back-street cowboys who made their money from the poor and the needy. *Coronation Street* had flirted with a few such characters – notably Reginald Marsh as Dave Smith – but it got its own immortal in the field the day the producers cast Johnny Briggs as Mike Baldwin.

Briggs, a veteran of *No Hiding Place* and character parts in just about every important long-running series of the 60s, was a natural in the role of the smoothy who has, as TV critic Hilary Kingsley notes, 'a second-hand Jaguar and a cheap line in small talk that usually ensnares gullible females into a corny candle-lit dinner for two with soft music and low lights ...'. Perhaps it was this aspect of the brash cockney that most appealed to his many (mostly female) fans. His affairs, the long-running feud with Ken Barlow (which reached epic proportions in 1983) and his many financial disasters, only add to the mythical nature of Mike Baldwin, last of the great lovers.

The classic marriages of the 70s began in 1975 with Ray Langton marrying Deirdre. It lasted a year, producing one daughter (Tracy) and repercussions that are felt to this day. In 1977 Len Fairclough finally lost the 'most eligible bachelor' tag to Mike Baldwin, marrying Rita. Alf Roberts decided to share his corner shop with Renee Bradshaw. All this reached a climax at the end of the decade when the Street celebrated the nuptials of Brian Tilsley and Gail Potter. But perhaps the best celebration of the era was of the programme itself. The Christmas 1975 episode was written by Harry Kershaw and featured the regular cast reminiscing about Christmases past. It was the only time that *Coronation Street* ever allowed itself the luxury of delving into the Granada archives. The flashback sequence, so beloved in most other types of TV drama, exposed all of the old ghosts to a willing audience.

Of course, there was tragedy too. Ernie Bishop, employed as wages clerk in Mike Baldwin's factory, was murdered by masked gunmen during an armed robbery in 1978. (Legend has it that this was caused by Stephen Hancock's attempt to hold a one-man pay revolt against Granada.) The disaster plot was used to good effect again in 1979, when a lorry ploughed through the front of the Rovers, injuring Alf Roberts, Mike Baldwin and Len Fairclough. Renee Roberts died in a car crash in 1980, and Emily Bishop, still grieving over the death of Ernest, had her hopes for a quiet life smashed when the new man in her life, Arnold Swain, turned out to be a bigamist. That same year also saw what, for many, was the end of an era, with the final appearance of Violet Carson.

The early 80s were bad years for the series. Bernard Youens died in 1984 and Stan Ogden was gracefully written out, allowing Jean Alexander a couple of weeks' worth of episodes in which her acting touched even the hardest hearts. Stan's place as the nation's favourite layabout was smoothly taken by William Tarmey's equally workshy Jack Duckworth. Doris Speed was forced to retire from the series through ill health in 1983, and Jack Howarth died in 1984. Pat Phoenix left the series, Elsie running off to Portugal with her old flame, Bill Gregory. The actress had hoped to find some life away from Elsie Tanner, which she did briefly before lung cancer robbed the world of her wit and charm in 1986.

To complete a traumatic couple of years, Peter Adamson, for so long one of the best reasons for watching the series, was charged with indecent assault and involved in a lengthy media trial. Although acquitted in court, Granada declined to renew his contract. Len Fairclough died, off-screen, in a car crash, three months after his alter-ego had left the series for the last time.

The story of 1983, in *Coronation Street* and elsewhere, was the Deirdre–Ken–Mike saga that seemed to occupy more tabloid front pages than Margaret Thatcher, Dennis Nilsen and the Hitler Diaries put together. Ken Barlow and Deirdre Langton had married in 1981. For both it was a chance to forget their tragic pasts. They seemed perfectly matched, but by 1983 the marriage had begun to go wrong and Deirdre began an extended affair with Mike Baldwin. Suddenly, everybody was taking sides. Sir John Betjeman knew whose side he was on when he announced: 'Ken's a nice man; he deserves better.' On the night of 22 February 1983, almost 20 million people watched the final showdown between the protagonists when Deirdre made her decision and chose between Ken and Mike. The press coverage rivalled the BBC's 'Who Shot JR?' hype. Council meetings up and down the country finished early so that everyone could get home to watch the episode. *The Sun* reported that the Queen, on a state visit to Mexico, had rung Buckingham Palace with instructions for the episode to be taped and flown to her. At Old Trafford, Manchester United were playing Arsenal in the semi-final of the Milk Cup. Midway through the first half, the 56,000 crowd were treated to the following message on the electronic scoreboard: 'Deirdre and Ken reunited. Read tomorrow's *Daily Mail* for an action-replay ...' There are some who insist the message got a bigger cheer from the Stretford End than United's first goal.

A new producer, Mervyn Watson, took over the running of the programme in mid-1983. During the next 2½ years he, and his team, had more than a few headaches to contend with. The exodus of the old guard was heralded by some as the death knell of the *Street*. Additionally, 1985 saw the debut of the BBC's long-awaited 'southern answer', ***EastEnders***. For the first time there was a serious rival to *Coronation Street*'s crown.

Granada's response was two-fold. Firstly, they followed ***EastEnders***' example of creating an omnibus Sunday repeat of the week's two episodes (and, in 1989, increased this to a third weekly episode on Friday nights – the first change in programme planning for the *Street* since April 1961). Secondly, they put their faith for the future of the series in the hands of what soon became dubbed as 'the brat pack', a loosely-formed collection of young actors and actresses, many of whom hadn't even been born when the series began. Executive Producer David Liddiment justified the changes by saying, 'The *Street* had been around for 25 years and a lot of its audience had grown up with it. So I was conscious of the need to appeal to a younger audience.' Amongst the new wave of characters were

Kevin Webster and Sally Seddon, Terry Duckworth, Curly Watts, Jenny Bradley, Tina Fowler, Martin Platt, Flick Khan and Des and Steph Barnes.

Not all of the new faces were young, however. The traditional archetypes were maintained. Albert Tatlock's place as the Rovers' most permanently dissatisfied customer was taken by Bill Waddington as Percy Sugden. Amanda Barrie did a very good job fitting into Pat Phoenix's shoes as the Street's resident vamp, Alma Sedgewick.

By one means and another, *Coronation Street* climbed back to the top of the ratings. It was helped by some excellent storylines, like the Rita Fairclough/Alan Bradley saga which ran for 18 months and included situations as diverse as adultery, embezzlement, attempted murder and ultimately Bradley dying under a Blackpool tram whilst trying to put an end to Rita. Bet Lynch, meanwhile, after nearly two decades of serving in the Rovers, finally took over the pub, and got herself a husband into the bargain in the shape of slimy Alec Gilroy. Roy Barraclough, for many years Les Dawson's straight man, holds some kind of record for having appeared in the *Street* as no less than five characters over the years, Alec being the latest.

Ken Barlow and Mike Baldwin hadn't finished their epic battle either. No sooner had Deirdre decided that her future lay with Ken, than his daughter, Susan, also wound up in Mike's bed. This led to marriage, pregnancy, abortion and divorce. Even ***EastEnders*** hadn't 'done' abortion before.

1987 saw Alf Roberts's frighteningly realistic heart-attack, from which he was, thankfully, allowed to recover. Nicky Tilsley was kidnapped by his father Brian, recently separated from Gail. They were soon to remarry, but in 1989 Brian, having been told that Gail wanted a second divorce, was stabbed to death by a bunch of yobs outside a night-club. There was also the horrifying episode in which Hilda Ogden, housekeeping for a doctor and his wife, was brutally assaulted during a robbery. The year ended with Jean Alexander leaving the *Street* with only William Roache and Eileen Derbyshire remaining as links to a long gone era.

Today, perhaps more than ever, *Coronation Street* maintains its grip on those who follow its every twist and turn. It is the ultimate cult TV series, largely because it is so ingrained in British consciousness that it is perceived by many to be – like television itself – a necessity rather than a luxury. On its 30th anniversary, producer Mervyn Watson commented, 'When the *Street* first hit the screens in 1960, its impact derived from the honest representation of working-class people and their lives. A lot has changed, but that representation retains its original honesty and commitment, so *Coronation Street* remains true, and constant ...'

Coronation Street has, of course, attracted its critics, ranging from Roy Hattersley, attacking the show's portrayal of 'contemporary reality', to Phil Redmond, calling it a 'caricature of the North West' (although, to be fair, he can hardly be described as an impartial commentator). Even ex-Granada boss David Plowright admitted that it might be guilty of perpetuating images of a 'steam-age' vision of the North.

Most worrying of all, perhaps, is the programme's unconscious racism. Richard Everitt, wanting to reflect actual trends in Salford, was prevented from introducing an Indian family in the late-60s; Susi Hush, in the mid-70s, was similarly opposed when she wanted to introduce a black family. In the latter case, it was decided that because so few non-white characters had even been seen in *Coronation Street* before, the attitudes of the regulars would have to be explored, resulting in characters such as Stan Ogden being portrayed as racist. Instead, the viewers are asked to accept as 'real' a Manchester suburb with a non-existent ethnic community. Critics have claimed that whilst apartheid has gone from Pretoria, it is still alive and kicking in Weatherfield.

The fans defend the show by claiming that it's just a fictional representation of reality; others claim that the 'social realism' of *Coronation Street* has become comic nostalgia, suggesting that under Bill Podmore it virtually became a sitcom, with its 'boat opera' reminiscent of *Terry and June*.

In the 90s, *Corry* has become a cultural icon, watched and referred to by everybody. The new girl on the street is Raquel Wolstenhulme, already a linchpin and cult figure, as played by Sarah Lancashire. Her attempts to learn French were particularly memorable. On New Year's Eve 1991, Ken Barlow contemplated suicide, but that one original cast member hangs on. Subsequent storylines of note included Tracy Barlow's bad Ecstasy experience and the death of Deirdre's Moroccan boyfriend Samir (he was going to die following an organ transplant to Tracy, but when donor groups objected, he was conveniently mugged instead), and Mavis and Derek's sweetly comic relationship. Rovers barmaid Tanya Poolley caused intrigue with her affair with Raquel's boyfriend Des Barnes. The biggest shock was 1995's departure of Julie Goodyear. In December of that year, to mark the programme's 35th anniversary, an hour-long episode featured Curly and Raquel's marriage. A video-only feature-length special showed their honeymoon cruise.

Although the show has remained much the same, the surrounding merchandise has proliferated, with the Granada studio tour, a magazine and even a line of frozen food. Rumours of a move to satellite television were swiftly dispelled after cries of public indignation, and, far from vanishing into space, the series will gain a fourth, Sunday night, episode in 1996. There now seems no reason to believe that it will not go on into the next century. Perhaps, when *The Guardian* reviewer said that the series would 'run forever', he was closer to the truth than he could possibly have imagined.

Doctor Finlay's Casebook

- **BBC Television** (BBC1) ◆ B&W (1962–69); Colour (1970–71)
- **191 episodes** (50 minutes)
- **Adapted from:** stories by A. J. Cronin
- **Writers include:** Elaine Morgan, Jan Read, Donald Bull, John Lucarotti, Vincent Tilsley, Harry Green, Dick Sharples, John Pennington, N.J. Crisp, Pat Dunlop, Anthony Steven, Robert Holmes
- **Directors include:** Julia Smith, William Slater, Prudence Fitzgerald, Paul Ciappessoni, Laurence Bourne, Tina Wakerell
- **Producers:** Campbell Logan, Andrew Osborn, Gerard Glaister, Douglas Allen, Royston Morley, John Henderson

Regular cast: Andrew Cruickshank (Dr Angus Cameron) • Barbara Mullen (Janet) • Bill Simpson (Dr Alan Finlay)

With: Eric Woodburn (Dr Snoddie) • Effie Morrison (Mistress Niven) • Tracy Reed (Barbara Davidson) • James Copeland ('Hooky' Buchanan) • Geraldine Newman (Mary) • Fulton Mackay (Jamie) • Anthony Valentine (Bruce Cameron) • John Humphrey (Dr Maddock) • Duncan Macrae (Cogger) • Wilfred Pickles (Mr Finlay)

1962 was a vintage year for television doctors. *Doctor Kildare* had finished its first series, and *Emergency – Ward 10* was in full swing. Not oblivious to this trend, the BBC presented a home-grown medical series that August which was to outlast all its contemporaries.

Doctor Finlay's Casebook began as a series of six adaptations of A.J. Cronin's *The Adventures of a Black Bag*, reportedly commissioned in a hurry to fill a gap in the BBC's schedule. However, the audience reaction to the initial six was so positive that a further six were commissioned instantly, the original three-man writing team doing a further batch of adaptations as the first episodes were being screened.

The series concerned the young Alan Finlay, played by ex-newsreader Bill Simpson. He was a junior doctor with radical ideas, who entered the cosy practice of Arden House in the little Scottish town of Tannochbrae in 1928. The practice belonged to Dr Angus Cameron, played by veteran character actor Andrew Cruickshank. A man who did not take to new ideas easily, and a confirmed bachelor to boot, Cameron was the series' best-loved character. The Tannochbrae trio was

First season
(16 Aug–1 Nov 62)
1 It's All in the Mind
2 A Taste of Dust
3 The Quack
4 Conduct Unbecoming
5 What Money Can't Buy
6 Cough Mixture
7 Carver Tam
8 What Women Will Do
9 Snap Diagnosis
10 The Dragon Plate
11 A Spotless Reputation
12 Behind Closed Doors

Second season
(5 Sep 63–28 June 64)
13 A Time for Laughing
14 Clean Sweep
15 The Heat of the Moment
16 Cup, Hand or Cards?
17 A Time for Discretion
18 Alice, Where Art Thou?
19 Ride in a Wheelchair
20 A Questionable Practice
21 Odds on Johnny
22 The Face Saver
23 Room for Doubt
24 Possessed of Devils
25 Cry Wolf
26 The Deep End
27 The Polygraph
28 A Present from Father
29 A Test of Intelligence
30 Charlie is My Darlin'
31 My Late Dear Husband
32 The White Hunter
33 The Whole Truth
34 A Shot in the Arm
35 A Matter of Proof
36 A Call from Cogger
37 A Man May Drink
38 The Big Fight
39 Stranger in Town
40 The Yellow Streak
41 Without the City
42 The Aristocrats
43 The Spirit of Dr McGregor
44 Mortal Sin
45 The Hallelujah Stakes
46 Short of a Miracle
47 The True Lochiel
48 The Old Indomitable
49 The Red Herring
50 The Confrontation
51 Dear Doctor
52 The Doctor Cried

Third season
(3 Jan–27 Jun 65)
53 The Control Group
54 The Raiders
55 The Eternal Spring
56 A Right to Live
57 The Bull Calf
58 Devils Dozen
59 Charity, Dr Finlay
60 Laughing Gas
61 The Gate of the Year
62 Off the Hook
63 The Next Provost But One
64 Soon or Late
65 The Good Fisherman
66 A Little Learning
67 Belle
68 In Committee
69 Another Opinion
70 The Spinster
71 Medical Finance
72 Beware of the Dog
73 Doctor's Lines
74 The Deceivers
75 The End of the Season
76 A Woman's Work
77 The Immortal Memory
78 An Evening Out

Fourth season
(21 Nov 65–15 May 66)
79 The Phantom Piper of Tannochbrae
80 The Champion
81 The Draper of Dumfries
82 The Longest Visit
83 Body and Soul
84 The Vision
85 Miss Letitia
86 They Do It in Africa
87 The Anxious Man
88 Hear No Evil
89 The General
90 Free Medicine
91 The Seniority Rule
92 A Matter of Confidence
93 For Services Rendered
94 To Err is Human
95 Better Safe Than Sorry
96 O Sole Mio
97 No Subsidy for Sin
98 Kate and Robert
99 Written with the Left Hand
100 A Settled Man
101 Crusade
102 Legacy
103 The Decision
104 The Uninvited Guest

Fifth season
(25 Dec 66–14 May 67)
105 The Gifts of the Magi
106 Resolution
107 The Comical Lad
108 Under the Hammer
109 The Masterpiece
110 Who Made You?
111 Bird Seed and Begonias
112 The Greatest Burden
113 The Forgotten Enemy
114 Possessed
115 Life of a Salesman
116 Over My Dead Body
117 A Penny Saved
118 Call in Cameron
119 The Sons of the Hounds
120 A Question of Conflict
121 Advertising Matter
122 A Happy Release
123 Safety in Numbers

Sixth season
(2 Oct 67–24 Mar 68)
124 Criss-Cross
125 The Emotional Factor
126 Come Back, Little Willie
127 Time Past – Time Future
128 Buy Now – Pay Later
129 Accidents Never Happen
130 Random Sample
131 Tell Me True
132 Persons Unknown
133 It's the System
134 Death is a Colony
135 The McTavish Bequest
136 Unfit to Marry
137 The Public Patient
138 A Moral Problem
139 The Cheats
140 Conscience Clause
141 The Dynamizer
142 The North Side of Ben Vorlich
143 Out of the Blue
144 The Equilibrium
145 'Is There Anybody There?' Said the Traveller
146 For Richer, For Poorer
147 Sweet Sorrow
148 Scots Wha Hae
149 To Janet – A Son

completed by Janet, the redoubtable housekeeper. She balanced the two doctors' personalities, and was so down to earth that in one episode it proved impossible to hypnotize her when her mind was on making supper. Other recurring characters included Mistress Niven, the superstitious local midwife and gossip, who was Cameron's nemesis, and the rather unlikeable Dr Snoddie.

When asked why the Finlay formula was so successful, producer Campbell Logan said, 'Its popularity is built on good character drawing, on good psychology, on sentiment which never turns into sentimentality.' Generally, Finlay would get into trouble with his newfangled methods, and Cameron would get him out of it, but not without learning something in the process. A typical episode featured a moral problem in the community, like that of Meg, the faithful wife who, having failed to have a son for 11 years, finds that the village tinker, Tim O'Shea, provides a solution ('A Time for Laughing').

In 1964, Cronin, then 67, declared that he wanted the series to end. He would cease to approve scripts, since they were going too far from his original concept. He was persuaded to change his mind, but at the start of the third season the credit on the show changed to 'created by' and no longer claimed his indirect authorship. The biggest changes occurred in the seventh season, when, in an attempt to inject some life into the unchanging community, the writers had Finlay run for election as the local MP, fail, and, disgusted, leave with the love of his life (Barbara Davidson) to practice in London. He was back after six episodes, fed up with the hypochondria of the metropolis, the romance over.

The Barbara Davidson episodes displayed the continuity which gave *Casebook* much of its flavour. Finlay had first met Barbara a whole season earlier – rescuing her from a stampede of highland cattle – and Tannochbrae had the atmosphere of a real place because the same faces kept appearing. Filmed by BBC Scotland around the village of Callader in Perthshire, the series, as *Not So Much a Programme, More a Way of Life* pointed out, 'offered employment to hundreds of starving Scottish actors'. Prominent amongst these regular faces was Duncan Macrae, who played Cogger, the epitome of the canny Scotsman, of whom Janet once said, 'He must be upset. I've never known him go to the expense of telephoning when a note would do as well.' James Copeland, who portrayed 'Hooky' Buchanan, the old soldier with a hook for a hand, also wrote several episodes. Patrick Troughton seemed to make a habit of appearing on the show, taking on several roles, the most memorable being Miller, the schoolteacher who wore a bulky hearing aid. Such famous Scottish actors as John Laurie, Graham Crowden, Andrew Keir, Fulton Mackay, Gordon Jackson and James Robertson-Justice all took on roles, and were joined south of the border by Anthony Valentine as Finlay's would-be London partner, Bruce Cameron. The familiar feeling of the series' location and characters surely played a big part in its success, based as it was on the Kailyard (or 'cabbage patch') style of Scottish tale,

Janet and Drs Finlay and Cameron from the episode 'A Late Spring'

where home and hearth always emerge triumphant. The summit of this style was doubtless reached in the 1966 Christmas Day episode 'The Gifts of the Magi', where Cameron was called upon to play Santa. No wonder Mary Whitehouse went on record saying that *Finlay* was one of her favourite programmes.

However, *Doctor Finlay's Casebook* wasn't entirely based on cosy familiarity. The series never shied away from important issues, Finlay's crusading spirit finding much rotten in Tannochbrae. The show dealt with back-street abortion and incest, silicosis and the emergence of Communism (miner Willie Gallagher telling an entranced Janet about meeting Lenin in 'Dust'), and mass hysteria (Finlay causing panic at a girls' school in 'The Visitation').

At its height, in 1965, an episode of *Finlay* would be seen by 14 million viewers and Finlay's 1913 Sunbeam (which, in yet another piece of superb continuity, was originally driven by Dr Cameron) could be seen driving about the crofts of Tannochbrae long after the other TV doctors had packed their black bags and gone home.

In 1993, *Doctor Finlay* returned on ITV with new actors and personnel but an old belief in the power of pastoral fantasy, and the social context that had encouraged *The Darling Buds of May* proved almost as supportive of the new *Finlay*.

Seventh season
(9 Mar–31 Aug 69)
150 The Visitation
151 The Honours List
152 The Times We Live In
153 Pastures New
154 The Greatest of These is Charity
155 A Man of Parts
156 A Dove in the Nest
157 Big Ben
158 The Barrier
159 The Rat Race
160 Put Your Cross Here
161 The Stick of the Rocket
162 Fresh Worlds
163 Conquest
164 The Facts of Life
165 Single or Return
166 Oak, Mahogany or Walnut
167 The Call
168 Lack of Communication
169 Monstrous Regiment
170 Blood and State
171 Action, Dr Cameron
172 The Will to Live
173 The Evangelist
174 The Cheap Departed
175 Opportunity and Inclination

Eighth season
(13 Sep 70–3 Jan 71)
176 A Late Spring
177 Dead Fall
178 Comin' Thro' the Rye
179 The Builders
180 Not Qualified
181 Snares and Pitfalls
182 Dorrity
183 Winter's Traces
184 The Honeypot
185 Made for Each Other
186 A Good Prospect
187 Responsibilities
188 Dust
189 Itself and Friend
190 A Question of Values
191 The Burgess Ticket

[Scottish TV's *Doctor Finlay* premiered on 5 Sep 1993 with a six-episode season. Subsequent seasons ran from 18 Mar 94 (six episodes), 27 Jan 95 (seven episodes) and 31 Mar 96 (seven episodes).]

Crossroads/Crossroads, King's Oak

- **ATV Midland/Central** (ITV) ◆ B&W (1964–69); Colour (1970–88)
- **4510 episodes** (30 minutes)
- **Creators:** Hazel Adair, Peter Ling
- **Writers include:** Hazel Adair, Peter Ling, Malcolm Hulke, Keith Mills, Paul Erickson, Roy Russell, Don Houghton, Norma Turner, David Whitaker, Terrance Dicks, Derrick Sherwin, Michael Crees, Ivor Jay, Wendy Greengross, Paula Milne, William Emms, Bill Lyons, David Garfield, Jack Turner, Ian Scrivens, Jon Rollason, Arthur Schmidt, Anne Valery, Raymond Bowers, Lew Schwarz, Gerald Kelsey, Lewis Griefer, Ted Rhodes, Ben Steed, Leslie Thomas, Kate Henderson, Margaret Simpson, Veronica Henry, Julian Spilsbury, Joanne Toye, Diane Culverhouse
- **Directors include:** Eric Price, Michael Hart, Malcolm Taylor, Alan Bromley, John Scolz-Conway, Brian Morgan, Tony Virgo, Nicholas Prosser
- **Producers:** Reg Watson, Pieter Rogers, Jack Barton, Philip Bowman, William Smethurst, Michele Buck

Most television programmes are fondly remembered by someone. Those that are held in high regard and acquire some sort of fan following usually do so on the strength and quality of their production: ***Coronation Street*** thrives because it is, for the most part, well-written, well-acted and well-produced. The same can be said about 95 per cent of the programmes covered in this book. There is, however, one outstanding exception to this rule. If *Crossroads* is fondly remembered – and it is by an enormous number of viewers – then these memories are normally triggered for exactly the wrong kind of reason.

When Radio Rentals brought out an advertisement for their new-fangled videorecorders in the late 1970s, they promised that they could 'take sixteen episodes of *Crossroads* ... If you can!' A generation of British comedians had been raised on the simple notion that mentioning *Crossroads* guaranteed a quick laugh. As TV critic Hilary Kingsley noted, the series never failed to 'provide its critics with ammunition. Some of the acting would have disgraced the humblest of village halls; many of the plots were so farcical they could have been written in a bad dream, and much of the dialogue was pathetic, like the hackneyed arresting line once used by a policeman to Benny: "Come along now, lad. Let's be 'aving you."' *Crossroads* was the series that no one seemed to love. Yet, at its peak, it was watched by more viewers than any other soap except ***Coronation Street***.

The series began in 1964, after producer Reg Watson (the man later responsible for the equally infamous Australian soap *Neighbours*) persuaded Lew Grade, the head of ATV Midland, to begin a soap opera along the lines of the daily series that had become popular in America during the late 1950s. The project was developed by Hazel Adair and Peter Ling, who had previously created the BBC primetime soap, *Compact*. Their working title was *The Midland Road*. It was seen at the time as a Birmingham version of ***Coronation Street***, and was scheduled to last for about 13 weeks. The theme tune was written by Tony Hatch and would be a constant irritant to millions of viewers for the next 24 years (especially after 1975 when the tinny original orchestral version was replaced by Paul McCartney and Wings's awful, guitar-laden adaptation from their *Venus and Mars* LP).

The story centred on a motel run by glamorous widow Meg Richardson (Noele Gordon) and her two young children. For many people, Noele Gordon *was* *Crossroads*. An actress of slender natural ability, Noele was, nevertheless, the most popular woman in the soaps for close on 20 years. When she was axed from the programme by Charles Denton, the Director of Programmes at Central, in 1981, it was the beginning of the end for the series. Over the years, Meg was married three times (one husband tried to murder her) and widowed twice. She was imprisoned for dangerous driving, suffered from amnesia, and finally sailed off on the *QE2* after, apparently, dying in a fire.

Her children didn't fare much better. Jill – who uttered those immortal first words on the programme, 'Crossroads Motel. Can I help you?' – was also married three times (once bigamously), had two miscarriages, became a drug-addict, then an alcoholic, had a child by her step-brother and remained with the series until the bitter end. *Crossroads* also had the distinction of presenting the world's first-ever 11-month pregnancy. This happened when Jane Rossington and her character both became pregnant at the same time. Sadly, Jane had a miscarriage, but producer Jack Barton asked her if she wouldn't mind being padded up as they were getting such good viewer response to Jill's pregnancy. Jane agreed, and two months later, she again became pregnant. So Jill's pregnancy had to continue as well, in all for 11 months. 'Strangely,' remembered Jane Rossington, 'hardly anyone noticed!' It could only happen on *Crossroads*.

Meg's son, Sandy, was played by Roger Tonge, one of the better actors on the series. Before his tragic death from cancer in 1981, at the age of 34, Tonge had become soap opera's first paraplegic. This occurred in 1972 when Sandy was crippled in a car accident. For once, fiction pre-empted fact in a most horrible way when Tonge learned to act in a wheelchair only to discover, a couple of years later, that he would need one in real life. Sandy was the most sympathetic character in *Crossroads*, and his passing away was a devastating blow to the series, although the manner in which it was handled was typically botched. Roger Tonge left the series in early 1981, when he had become too ill to carry on. It was stated that Sandy had gone on holiday. Over a year later, when everyone had almost forgotten the character, a minor member of the cast casually mentioned that Sandy was dead.

The early days on the show, when it was being recorded as a five-days-a-week series, were particularly hectic for the cast. The show was done virtually live, as Anthony Morton, who played the Spanish chef Carlos Raphael until 1969, recalled: 'It was all done on videotape, but only very rarely was there a retake. If you had to do a scene again you felt as though the sword of Damocles was hanging over your head.' At first the series wasn't networked. It was popular in the Midlands and the south-east, but was totally ignored in the North. Tyne Tees didn't begin showing the programme until 1972. In many areas, when it was shown, it was scheduled at 4.35 p.m., leading to worried complaints from parents who objected to an adult series being transmitted in the traditional children's slot. The series' greatest protector was Sir Lew Grade who overruled successive heads of production at ATV who wanted to ditch the series, especially Bill Ward, who didn't like the fact that critics tended to compare the series unfavourably with ATV's other long-running soap, *Emergency – Ward 10*. In the end, of course, *Crossroads* outlived *Ward 10* by nearly 20 years.

Starring: Noele Gordon (Meg Richardson/Ryder/Mortimer) • Jane Rossington (Jill Richardson/Harvey/Chance) • Roger Tonge (Sandy Richardson) • Susan Hanson (Diane Lawton/Parker/Hunter) • Peter Brookes (Vince Parker) • Sue Nicholls/Nadine Hanwell (Marilyn Gates/Hope) • Ann George (Amy Turtle) • Elisabeth Croft (Miss Tatum) • David Davenport (Malcolm Ryder) • Ronald Allen (David Hunter) • Janet Hargreaves (Rosemary Hunter) • Freddie Foot/Stephen Hoye (Chris Hunter) • Gretchen Franklin (Myrtle Cavendish) • Johnny Briggs (Clifford Leyton) • Angus Lennie (Shughie McFee) • John Bentley (Hugh Mortimer) • Sandor Elès (Paul Ross) • Paul Henry (Benny Hawkins) • Kathy Staff (Doris Luke) • Pamela Vezey (Kath Brownlow) • Peter Hill (Arthur Brownlow) • Lynette McMorrough (Glenda Brownlow/Banks) • David Moran (Kevin Banks) • Carl Andrews (Joe MacDonald) • Tony Adams (Adam Chance) • Sue Lloyd (Barbara Brady/Hunter) • Dee Hepburn (Anne-Marie Wade) • Claire Faulkenbridge (Miranda Pollard) • Gabrielle Drake (Nicola Freeman) • Terence Rigby (Tommy 'Bomber' Lancaster) • Philip Goodhew (David Freeman)

Unlike ***Coronation Street***, the early years of *Crossroads* are not packed with memorable characters and incidents, except for the arrival, in 1964, of Ann George and her remarkable Amy Turtle, next to Meg (and possibly Benny) the most cherished *Crossroads* character. Ann was a perfect symbol of everything that was shambolic and unintentionally hilarious about the early days of *Crossroads:* she forgot her lines with monotonous regularity, fluffed cues, and generally acted in a manner that suggested that she was making it all up as she went along. The viewers loved her.

If that takes some believing, then some of the storylines that the writers dreamed up for her are even harder to swallow. In one absurd plot she was accused of being a Russian spy, Amelia Turtlovski. Amy was on the series for 12 years until she was written out in 1976, after being accused of shoplifting. However, Ann was invited back on to the series for a few guest appearances in late 1987 by new producer William Smethurst. When she walked on to the set for the first time in 12 years she was given a standing ovation by the cast and crew.

Sue Nicholls was another important member of the early cast. She played the dizzy brummie waitress, Marilyn Gates, who, in 1969, left the motel to become a pop singer. By the time the character returned she was being played by a different actress.

1965 saw the arrival of Diane Lawton, the immortal 'Miss Diane' who would rise over the years from being a humble waitress to occupying a place in middle-management. Diane was with the programme until 1987, when Susan Hanson was involved in a payment squabble with William Smethurst which ended in the character suddenly dying of a brain haemorrhage, proving once and for all that although *Crossroads* might have been an incompetent imitation of ***Coronation Street***, it could, at times, be equally ruthless.

However, whereas ***Coronation Street*** had a tight, often suffocating, continuity, *Crossroads* would drop characters left right and centre without the slightest hint of where they had gone or why. Benny Wilmott was a case in point. Wilmott was the young manager of the local coffee bar, an obvious concession to the youth market, played by Deke Arlen. One day, in 1967, he left the motel kitchen to fetch some sugar and was never seen (or even mentioned) again. As Hilary Kingsley notes, 'other characters would go missing for months on end and would always be in the next room, on the other end of the phone, or, better still, just their back leg would be seen going out of the door'.

1967 was an important year for *Crossroads.* Firstly, the producers decided to cut the number of episodes broadcast per week from five to four (this was further reduced in 1979 to three on the instructions of the Independent Broadcasting Authority, which had some very harsh things to say about the standard of the programme). The year's big storyline was the discovery of an old wartime bomb which exploded, destroying much of the motel. The reason behind this lay in a move of studios and Reg Watson's wish to upgrade the sets. The following year, the London area stopped transmitting the series, leading to a massive campaign to 'Give Us Our *Crossroads* Back' which featured such notable converts as Mary Wilson, the Prime Minister's wife. Eventually the region complied, but episodes were now being shown six months behind the rest of the country (or at least, the rest of the country that was taking the show in the first place; Granada, Yorkshire and Tyne Tees were still holding out), and they took another eight years to catch up.

The addition to the cast of matinee-idol Ronald Allen, in 1969, as the dour David Hunter, Meg's new partner in the motel, was a shot in the arm for the series' viewing figures. Allen, a soap veteran with previous runs on *Compact* and the football soap *United!*, has been described as an actor 'with the charisma of an ashtray', but he was a vital linchpin in the series' 'golden age' – the mid-70s. His death, in 1990, was mourned by his many admirers. David Hunter's life, as with those around him, was a catalogue of misfortune: his wife, Rosemary, was a neurotic, alcoholic shoplifter who attempted to kill David in 1975. His son, Chris, was an international terrorist who was partly responsible for the death of Meg's third husband, Hugh Mortimer.

David tried to combat his problems by becoming a compulsive gambler. He had a fling with a journalist (played by Justine Lord) but didn't find true happiness until he met novelist Barbara Brady (Sue Lloyd). Allen and Lloyd (an off-screen couple also) were sacked from the show in 1985 as one of the first dramatic acts of new producer Philip Bowman.

For most fans of the soap, this mid-70s 'golden age' of *Crossroads* coincided with the appointment of Jack Barton as producer, taking over from Reg Watson. Barton, also one of the show's most prolific directors, is proud of his work on *Crossroads* and, perhaps rightly, points to the series' success in tackling several controversial subjects, such as rape, bigamy, test-tube pregnancies, physical handicap and Down's Syndrome (a heart-rending storyline featuring a real Down's Syndrome child, Nina Weill). Joe MacDonald was the first regular black character in a soap. Never mind that some of these important themes were handled in a very naive and cosy way; *Crossroads* touched on subjects that other series steered well clear of and, for that reason if nothing else, it deserves recognition.

The characters regularly seen in the motel during this period also included Scottish chef Shughie McFee, nasty old battleaxe Doris Luke, Diane's postman husband Vince Parker, slimy French restaurant manager Paul Ross and the equally slimy financial wizard Adam Chance, and podgy teenage runaway Glenda Brownlow and her sour-faced father Arthur and mother Kath. Both Diane Keen and Elaine Paige made their TV debuts on *Crossroads,* whilst the future star of *A Clockwork Orange* (GB 71), Malcolm McDowell, appeared briefly as PR man Crispin Ryder.

Celebrities queued up to appear in *Crossroads,* including Ken Dodd, Bob Monkhouse, Max Wall and singer Stephanie de Sykes, whose 1974 number two hit 'Born with a Smile on My Face' was featured heavily in *Crossroads* for a few weeks. The character she was playing, pop singer Holly Brown, was staying at the motel (suffering from a nervous breakdown and severe lack of talent). The trick was repeated in 1981, when actress and comedienne Kate Robbins recorded a rather awful ditty entitled 'More Than in Love' whilst appearing in the series. The series hyped it all the way to number two in the charts. Larry Grayson appeared twice in the series, firstly in the Boxing Day 1973 episode, as an irate customer, and secondly in 1975, in the episode in which Meg married Hugh Mortimer, chauffeuring their wedding car.

And then, of course, there was Benny. The cult of the bobble-hat began as a one-episode joke in 1975 when 'Miss Diane' went to visit her uncle's farm and was introduced to a slightly sinister and obviously retarded half-wit. It was a joke that was to run for 12 years and make its object of ridicule, actor Paul Henry, the highest-paid star at Central Television.

Benny followed 'Miss Diane' back to the motel whereupon he continued in regular employment, despite a series of storylines that made Meg and Jill's misfortunes seem mild by comparison. Firstly, he was sent to an open prison for causing an accident to a local landowner who had upset him. Then, on the morning that he was due to marry beautiful gypsy girl, Maureen Flynn, she fell off her bicycle and died. Later, he was falsely accused of murdering Lynda Welsh and spent a long period on the run. There was, somewhat inevitably, a 'Benny is Innocent' campaign in a national newspaper. In 1981, he was temporarily blinded by a hit-and-run driver, whilst his most heart-breaking moment was finding his beloved Miss Diane dead in her bed.

Paul Henry, a respected actor with a fine reputation in serious theatre, regarded Benny as 'a child, someone who took each emotion to the limit. People loved him. Women wanted to mother him, men wanted to feel superior to him.' Paul recorded a song, 'Benny's Theme', in 1977, which sold moderately well but earned him a rebuke from ATV bosses as the lyrics revealed the outcome of Benny's doomed romance with Maureen. Henry would regularly take a break of up to six months each year to tour with a play or appear in panto. During one such sabbatical, Benny went off to look for a spanner and wasn't seen again for six months.

2 Nov 64–4 Apr 88

The *Crossroads, King's Oak* title was introduced in 1987

In 1984, the producer Jack Barton finally left the series and was replaced by brash young Australian Philip Bowman. Bowman, a former associate producer on ***Minder,*** introduced a more stylish type of programme. Hilary Kingsley notes that Bowman 'took cameras outside, introduced action and glamour. The viewing figures rose; *The Times* gave him a good review. He was hated for it!'

Bowman's brief, as he saw it, was to clear out the dead wood and make the programme watchable again. He was responsible for the departures of Glenda and her new husband Kevin Banks, Doris Luke, Paul Ross and, most importantly, David and Barbara Hunter, for which he received numerous death-threats. His introduction of classical actress Gabrielle Drake, as Nicola Freeman, in 1985 was one of his better moves. Bowman himself saw this casting as vital to his long-term plans for the series. 'Once I'd got my Queen in position, everything else fell into place. Being an Australian, I knew that once you're on the horse you've gotta ride it. You know you'll come out covered in shit or glory.' Bowman also introduced glamorous receptionist Anne-Marie Wade, horsey Miranda Pollard and others, but he left the series before his work was completed when, in 1986, his relationship with script-editor Kate Henderson (whom he later married) gave the series some uncomfortable publicity.

The replacement producer was William Smethurst, former producer of the BBC Radio saga *The Archers*. Smethurst wanted to change the corny old working-class, middle-aged *Crossroads* into a sharp, witty, middle-class soap called *Crossroads, Kings Oak*. According to Hilary Kingsley he 'declared war with glee, slaughtered holy cows and male stars, too. He changed writers, sets, the music, the name. It should have worked, given time ...'

Smethurst himself is unrepentant. 'When I was brought in the viewing figures were gently declining, the audience was older than for any of the other soaps and *Crossroads* still had the most awful reputation for shoddy quality. This wasn't really fair, because Philip Bowman had made amazing changes ... Perhaps I was naive to think that if I improved the quality of the scripts, improved the acting, I'd get a higher-quality product.' The series became interested in internal politics and the machinations of new owner Tommy 'Bomber' Lancaster and the scheming Daniel Freeman, Nicola's wicked stepson. Jill Richardson and Adam Chance were reduced to minor supporting characters, and there was no room in the new 'yuppified' motel for a half-wit like Benny.

'We had the old characters dropping out at the rate of one a week,' said Smethurst. 'I'm convinced it was the only way to do it. We had some terrific new writers and new characters. But then we did a survey of what newspapers *Crossroads* viewers read. It was depressing. More of them read the *Daily Star*, which was going through its *Daily Bonk* phase, than the numbers who ever saw any of the quality papers. I realized there was no point in clever, funny writing if no one would appreciate it. But we had to try to attract them. We went ahead with our new pub set, our new landlord and new opening credits and title, *Crossroads, King's Oak*. We were working in the studio when we heard we'd been chopped.'

The decision to end the series was taken by Andy Allan, Director of Programmes at Central, in September 1987. *Crossroads* would have to go since it used up around 20 per cent of Central's studios, though no one was prepared to say what they were planning to use the studio space for. Smethurst was upset. 'Over the last few months, the ratings recovered, the audience profile changed and I really do believe we had a literate, amusing programme.' But the decision to end the series wasn't reversed, and on Easter Monday 1988 the 4510th and final episode of *Crossroads* was broadcast.

By the end, *Crossroads* had become a victim of its own, often ludicrous, success. It could never change sufficiently to erase the past, and there were enough people who didn't want the past erased anyway to resist William Smethurst's attempts to update the concept. It has been suggested that maybe *Crossroads* just wasn't awful enough to be good any more.

The Troubleshooters (originally Mogul)

- **BBC Television** (BBC1) ◆ B&W (1965-69); Colour (1970-72)
- **136 episodes** (50 minutes)
- **Creator:** John Elliot
- **Writers include:** John Elliot, Kenneth Ware, James Mitchell, John Lucarotti, David Weir, Anthony Read, Ian Kennedy Martin, Eve Martell, Roy Clarke, Roy Russell, David Fisher, George Byatt
- **Directors include:** Michael Hayes, Shaun Sutton, Terence Dudley, James Gateward, Max Varnel, Brian Parker, Roger Jenkins, Moira Armstrong, Ian MacNaughton, Viktor Ritelis, Alan Gibson, Ray Menmuir, Ridley Scott, Ron Craddock, Robert Tronson, Lennie Mayne, Frank Cox, Douglas Camfield
- **Producers:** Peter Graham Scott, Anthony Read
  Associate producer: Michael Glynn

Regular cast: Geoffrey Keen (Brian Stead) • Philip Latham (Willy Izzard) • Ray Barrett (Peter Thornton) • Robert Hardy (Alec Stewart)

With: Barry Foster (Robert Driscoll) • Ronald Hines (Derek Prentice) • Justine Lord (Steve Thornton) • Phillippa Gail (Jane Webb) • Deborah Stanford (Roz Stewart) • Michael Hawkins (John Stead) • Virginia Wetherall (Julie Serres) • David Baron (Mike Szabo) • Isobel Black (Eileen O'Rourke) • Edward de Souza (Charles Grandmercy) • Camilla Brockman (Claire Cook) • Jayne Sofiano (Ginny Vickers) • Jennifer Wright (Mrs George) • Barbara Shelley (Letz Perez) • John Carson (James Langely) • Anna Matisse (Britte Langely)

In the 70s, American television produced a series about the jet-set world of the oil industry, mixing power politics, wheeler-dealing and lots of sex. It was called *Dallas* and it is estimated that it has been watched by 65 per cent of the world's population. However, over a decade before, a British series dealt with similar themes and, although it would be impossible to claim that *The Troubleshooters* was an influence on the American series, it was a useful pointer to the viewer as to what lay ahead.

The Troubleshooters began life under a different name, *Mogul* – the name of the oil company central to the plot – and was created by John Elliot, an ex-BBC producer and veteran of the two *Andromeda* series. He researched his subject first-hand by travelling to Nigeria, the Sahara, Greece and Syria, and the series flaunted its location filming, taking the camera far beyond the studio. However, *Mogul* was a company like any other, with offices and pension schemes, and much of the material would concentrate on the boardroom politics involved in corporate big business. (Corporate soap was very popular in the 60s, with ATV producing *The Power Game* – originally *The Plane Makers* – starring Patrick Wymark.)

The cast was impressive: Geoffrey Keen played Stead, director of operations and Philip Latham was Izzard, company secretary. Australian actor Ray Barrett portrayed Thornton, Mogul's troubleshooter. Barry Foster and Ronald Hines appeared as Mogul personnel, whilst Justine Lord played Thornton's wife, 'Steve', and Phillippa Gail, Stead's secretary.

Each episode began with Tom Springfield's strident title music – brass and percussion to the fore – and a memorable set of opening credits, mixing images of the oil business with the Mogul logo and shots of the three male leads.

Early stories dealt with realistic themes. 'Kelly's Eye' concerned industrial espionage and 'Safety Man' included a notable performance from Edward

Woodward as a Mogul safety officer whose erratic behaviour almost brings about a disaster during a royal tour of inspection. In the same week that 'The Schloss Belt' was broadcast, an entire episode of the science programme *Tomorrow's World* was devoted to North Sea drilling. In another episode, Mogul took over a chemical firm just four days before BP did so in reality. This was the first of many such coincidences.

By this time, it was felt necessary to create another central character; one who could hold his own with Ray Barrett – another troubleshooter. To this end, Robert Hardy was cast in the role of Stead's assistant, and the series was renamed. *The Troubleshooters* and *Mogul* were quite different series. *Mogul* had tended to concentrate on internal politics at the expense of the actual workings of the company. Its successor rectified this, taking the cameras off around the world to show Mogul in the field. In 'Thea' many of the carnival scenes in Trinidad were filmed in real West Indian locations. The air disaster in 'Birdstrike' was shot with the aid of a BEA flight-simulator. The series was accepted as accurate by many people in the industry, a Shell executive commenting, '*The Troubleshooters* is extremely good. I am staggered how accurate they are in technical matters. Of course, in real life, we don't have blondes lying about on beds. We miss that facility.' Another source was satisfied with the technical accuracy but had reservations about the picture of management the series presented. 'As far as I can see, Mogul is run by Stead, Izzard and Thornton single-handed. I've got six thousand people working in this building alone. No doubt the Mogul boys are smarter than we are!'

Geoffrey Keen actually received an invitation to an Oil Industry Club dinner. 'Everyone nodded to me, or shook my hand,' he said, 'as though they recognized me as an oil man but nobody could quite remember to which company I belonged!' Finally, someone asked him and he replied 'Mogul!' 'Ah yes,' replied the questioner, 'how silly of me to forget', and went away satisfied.

John Lucarotti's 'This is Where I Came In' placed Thornton in a new Asian state as his marriage is breaking up. Elliot's 'Operation Saigon' was years ahead of its time, set against the background of the Vietnam War; James Mitchell's 'Do Your Best for the Lads' was about industrial relations and featured guest performances from Joss Ackland and Nigel Stock; whilst 'A Run for their Money' concerned local opposition to a Mogul refinery in Wales. An unusual episode was 'Out of your Evil Dream', which asked ethical questions about the periphery of the oil business when one of Mogul's chemical offshoots develops a new crop spray which has deadly side-effects.

MOGUL
First season
(7 Jul–29 Sep 65)
1 Kelly's Eye
2 Young Turk
3 Safety Man
4 Wildcat
5 Tosh and Nora
6 The Schloss Belt
7 Out of Range
8 The Way it Crumbles
9 A Job for Willy
10 Meet Miss Mogul
11 Stoneface
12 Driver of the Year
13 Borrowed Time

THE TROUBLESHOOTERS
Second season
(30 Apr–22 Oct 66)
14 Is that Tiger, Man
15 When You Gotta Go
16 Thea
17 If You Can't Lick 'Em
18 This is Where I Came In
19 Birdstrike
20 The Fires of Hell
21 Wingless Wonder
22 Cablegrams Come Home
23 Operation Saigon
24 Baptism of Fire
25 Join the Club
26 Do Your Best for the Lads
27 Someone's Head Has to Roll
28 Troubled Waters
29 What's Yours is Mine
30 The Bigger They Are
31 Some Wet Night in Sauchiehall Street
32 Error of Judgement
33 They're Probably Drilling for Oil
34 A Run for their Money
35 Happy Landings
36 There's Nothing Like the Great Outdoors
37 Out of your Evil Dream
38 Four Cheers for Geoffrey
39 No Such Thing as Bad Luck

Third season
(30 Jan–1 May 67)
40 Words are Softer than Oil
41 A Damn Great Lump of Iron
42 My Daughter Knows Her Way Around
43 Home and Dry
44 We're None of Us Perfect
45 Think Big
46 Some Days You Just Can't Win
47 Nothing to Do with Mogul
48 No Sentiment in Business
49 Journey from the Interior
50 Long Knives Cut Deep
51 Women and Business Never Did Mix
52 There's Always Next Time

Fourth season
(13 Oct 67–3 May 68)
53 Dragon by the Tail
54 The Daring Young Men
55 When the Carpet Ends
56 Winner Lose All
57 A Nice White Girl – Is she for Sale?
58 Mr Know How
59 And the Walls Came Tumbling Down

For the third season, there was a sequel to 'Do your Best for the Lads' in 'A Damn Great Lump of Iron', at the same Teesside shipyard, and a tense John Lucarotti story entitled 'Some Days You Just Can't Win', set in the midst of political turmoil in Rhodesia and guest-starring John Le Mesurier.

Hardy left as a full-time member at the end of the season. His replacement for the fourth season was played by David Baron, whilst a position was created for Isobel Black as Stead's new public relations officer. Both played prominent roles in an unusual episode, 'A Nice White Girl – Is she for Sale?', which cast a very dismissive eye over Islamic culture. 'And the Walls Came Tumbling Down', in which Thornton is caught up in a Moroccan earthquake, had a great impact. Kenneth Kendall appeared as a newsreader informing viewers of the tragedy. Coincidentally, the night on which the episode was recorded actually saw an earthquake and the night it was transmitted saw another.

Other fourth season episodes included 'Good Lord, No, It's Illegal!' about the Singapore drug trade, and 'The Deeper You Dig', in which Thornton becomes entangled in a party political row over the plans for a channel tunnel (the part of Joan Marple, an MP reportedly based on Margaret Thatcher, was taken by Barbara Shelley). 'Just a Bunch of Arabs in Kilts' had a similar plot to the Bill Forsyth film *Local Hero* (GB 83) – it even featured Fulton Mackay. In 'Stop It, You're Breaking My Heart', Barrett's involvement in the story had to be drastically rewritten when he broke his arm on holiday in Spain. John Lucarotti and Anthony Read quickly redrafted the story, including a new character, played by Brian Blessed, as a younger version of Thornton.

The series also took time to confront its own somewhat uncomfortable position on sexism in 'A Girl to Warm Your Feet On'. In John Lucarotti's 'The Day the Sea Caught Fire', Mogul once again got in ahead of real life by a matter of weeks. The story concerned a blow-out on a rig in the Mediterranean. No sooner had the script been delivered than a gas bubble exploded in the North Sea, and the RAF set fire to a section of oil-slicked ocean. Every national newspaper knew *The Troubleshooters*' reputation for forecasting similar events.

By 1969, Mogul had a rival in the world of TV oil, Zenith, as represented by Stead and Thornton's counterparts (Bernard Hepton and Bruce Boa). Anthony Read had taken over as producer at a time when the BBC seemed keen to cash in on one of their most successful series. A four-page article in the *Radio Times* looked back on the first five years of the show, voicing the opinion that 'when *Mogul* struck North Sea oil two months before anyone else, you sensed this was something more than an adventure series'. John Lucarotti was interviewed exten-

60 Good Lord, No, It's Illegal!
61 Thanks for Nothing
62 Rest You Merry
63 Who Buys Who?
64 The Deeper You Dig
65 Kitchener Knew It Well
66 The Sharp End of the Wedge
67 Just a Bunch of Arabs in Kilts
68 Not for My Friend – He's Driving
69 Stop It, You're Breaking My Heart
70 A Girl to Warm Your Feet On
71 Give Me the Simple Life
72 A Slight Problem with the Press
73 Never the Twain
74 Cut Off Whose Nose?
75 The Day the Sea Caught Fire
76 The Dispossessed
77 The Wrecking of the Sierra Nevada
78 The Minister of The Crown... And the Very Compromising Photograph

[Episode 71 was originally scheduled for transmission between episodes 67 and 68.]

Fifth season
(6 Jan–14 Jul 69)

79 A Dirty Old Man and a Rare Bird
80 Twenty Years is No Time At All
81 How Much is One Man Worth?
82 If He Hollers Let Him Go
83 A Very Special Relationship
84 There's a Nasty Word – Love
85 You're Not Going to Believe This, But ...
86 Take-Over is Two Four-Letter Words
87 Everybody is That Kind of Man
88 So You Think You're One of Us
89 They've More Than Their Assets Frozen
90 There's This Bird, See ...
91 You Want a Clockwork Nightingale
92 Don't Ask – Take
93 Dr Liebling, I Presume
94 You Can't Trust Women
95 Really She Did, Really She Did
96 Some of the Mud is Bound to Stick
97 Lord, What a Tangled Web
98 And One Wise Man Came Out from the East
99 Let's All Drop Out Together
100 She'll Be Right Mate
101 It's a Very Bad Day for Travelling
102 This Place is a Paradise, Mister
103 They Call Me Israel
104 Over the Hill

Sixth season
(18 May–7 Sep 70)
105 The Slick and the Dread
106 A Pig in a Pipe
107 Camelot on a Clear Day
108 Who Did You Say Inherits the Earth?
109 The Price of a Bride
110 Operation Black Gold
111 We Also Need Experts
112 I'm Glad I'm Just an Oilman …
113 Boys and Girls Come Out to Play
114 The Dangerous Green Impala
115 A Truly Exotic Development
116 That's Africa, Baby
117 They Shall Not Pass
118 Let's See the Colour of Your Money
119 Hey We've Got a Problem Here
120 The Order of the Good Time
121 Injury to the Nation

Seventh season
(13 Sep 71–3 Jan 72)
122 Pie in the Sea (part 1)
123 Pie in the Sea (part 2)
124 It's Thumbs Down for You Pizarro!
125 In the Shade of the Old Oak Tree
126 The Bent Bonanza
127 A Touch of the Nelsons
128 The One with the Waggly Tail
129 Shangri-la and All That Jazz
130 Monopoly with Real Money
131 Personally I Think He Looks Like Me
132 Pretend it Never Happened
133 Weekends are for Taking Off
134 Tapu
135 We and Them
136 Whatever Became of theYear 2000?

sively, explaining that the episode 'Some of the Mud is Bound to Stick', in which Alec Stewart is arrested at Algiers airport as a suspected spy, was based on Lucarotti's own humiliating experiences of being strip-searched at gunpoint. Richard Attenborough watched the spectacular Alaskan episode 'They've More than their Assets Frozen' (three days before transmission, BP announced its first Alaskan strike) and then rang his brother David at the BBC to ask how large the budget had been, only to discover that the episode had, in fact, been filmed in ***Doctor Who***'s gravel pit near Gerrards Cross.

John Elliot, still an important voice on the series, was full of praise for his fellow writers, acknowledging the work of John Lucarotti, David Weir and David Fisher. Elliot, however, was dismayed by what he saw as a 'snobbery working against the series' within the BBC. 'There's a gap between series and drama, so that one is supposed to be popular entertainment whereas plays are something else. People tend to think of series as being just pulp for the masses. They forget that big audiences can enjoy a good human story in the foreground but appreciate more sophisticated overtones and undertones. I think we're doing something fairly exciting in bridging the gap.'

These efforts included 'You're Not Going to Believe This, But …', focusing on racial tension between Malays and Chinese in Kuala Lumpur, and 'Take-Over is Two Four-Letter Words', where Mogul are, for once, portrayed as uncaring and money-grabbing. David Fisher, the newest member of the writing team, caused a great stir with his first script, 'You Want a Clockwork Nightingale'. In July 1969 the fifth season ended with 'Over the Hill', a powerful John Elliot story concentrating on the breakdown of the lives of the four main characters. With Stead suffering his third heart-attack in five years, it seemed as though Mogul was ready for the biggest take-over of all, but the BBC kept faith, and *The Troubleshooters* returned in 1970, in colour. The two colour seasons are generally considered to have been less successful than their monochrome predecessors, although both contained good episodes. New characters were introduced, and the series ended in January 1972 with an episode fittingly written by the series' creator, John Elliot. Most of the production team went on to *The Lotus Eaters*.

At its best, *The Troubleshooters* certainly lived up to John Elliot's boast that the series was bridging a gap between 'quality' drama and popular entertainment. It had the freshness of approach of a limited serial, but maintained a continuous narrative structure that kept the series within the boundaries of the soap opera.

The Forsyte Saga

- **BBC Television** (BBC2) ◆ B&W
- **26 episodes** (50 minutes) ◆ 1967
- **Adapted from:** novels by John Galsworthy
- **Writers:** Donald Wilson, Constance Cox, Laurie Craig, Vincent Tilsley, Anthony Steven
- **Directors:** David Giles, James Cellan Jones
- **Producer:** Donald Wilson

Regular cast: Kenneth More (Jolyon Forsyte) • Nyree Dawn Porter (Irene) • Eric Porter (Soames Forsyte) • Joseph O'Conor (Old Jolyon) • Susan Hampshire (Fleur) • Martin Jarvis (Jon)

With: Terence Alexander (Montague Dartie) • Nicholas Pennell (Michael Mont) • Margaret Tyzack (Winifred) • Michael York (Jolly)

The BBC production of *The Forsyte Saga* was, basically, one man's dream, but it was a dream that the BBC was to use to great advantage. Producer Donald Wilson had been passionately interested in John Galsworthy's series of novels since 1928, and had spent 11 years actively seeking the rights, which were held by MGM. He managed to convince the film company to put their interests in a television version, but first he had to persuade the then head of drama at the BBC, Sydney Newman, that costume drama would hold viewer interest. Newman was dubious until Wilson produced a list of stars that had already shown an interest in appearing in such a production. Kenneth More was at the top of the list. The 50-year-old actor had made few television appearances, and his career was at a low ebb. His enthusiasm for the project matched Wilson's. The deal went ahead.

1967 was to be the centenary of Galsworthy's birth, but another birth had recently taken place. The BBC had launched their second channel, BBC2, in 1964. To receive the new channel, TV sets had to be specially adjusted, an expensive process. It was felt that, much in the same way as the Coronation had boosted television sales, an event of some sort was required to stimulate interest in the new channel. For the first time, a drama was to become a media event. It was announced that *The Forsyte Saga*, the BBC's most heavily-publicized product (and, at £250,000, its most expensive drama to date) was only to be broadcast on BBC2. A future repeat on BBC1 was not, at that time, being considered.

The *Saga* itself was the story of an upwardly-mobile family of the late-Victorian era. Jolyon wishes to abandon his bourgeois lifestyle as an underwriter to become an artist. His cousin, Soames, is exactly the opposite, a cold, somewhat harsh, lawyer, tolerating an unconsummated marriage to Irene. The rape of Irene by her husband, late in the series, set the nation alight, and was widely considered to be far too violent, particularly since Galsworthy had covered the matter in one sentence. Jo married three times, initially to Frances (Ursula Howells), who disapproved of his aversion to property. His second marriage produced the ill-fated 'Jolly' Jolyon who married the aptly-named Holly. Jo's third stab at matrimony was with Irene herself, whom he won from Soames. Their son, Jon, nearly tied up the saga in Brontë-esque fashion by having an affair with Fleur, Soames's daughter by his second marriage, but it was not to be, the two lovers returning to their respective spouses in typically tragic fashion.

Production was mounted swiftly, the last 13 episodes being filmed as the first 13 were screened. This led to some precarious moments, such as when

7 Jan–1 Jul 67
1 A Family Festival
2 A Family Scandal
3 The Pursuit of Happiness
4 Dinner at Swithin's
5 A Man of Property
6 Decisions
7 Into the Dark
8 Indian Summer of a Forsyte
9 In Chancery
10 The Challenge
11 In the Web
12 Birth of a Forsyte
13 Encounter
14 Conflict
15 To Let
16 A Family Wedding
17 The White Monkey
18 Afternoon of a Dryad
19 No Retreat
20 A Silent Wooing
21 Action for Libel
22 The Silver Spoon
23 Strike
24 Afternoon at Ascot
25 Portrait of Fleur
26 Swan Song

Eric Porter got appendicitis, thus having to do a large number of his scenes in a block towards the end of filming. Wilson and his writing team had constructed the first three episodes of the *Saga* out of past references found throughout the Galsworthy books, beginning eight years before the first, *The Man of Property*. The time span was to be vast, stretching from 1879 to 1926, and, at one point, covering 21 years in one episode. A chart of 150 characters and their relation to each other took up one wall of Wilson's office. Even with a cliffhanger at the end of each episode, could the audience be expected to retain their interest?

Well, yes, to some extent they could. Out of the 8.5 million people with BBC2-adapted sets, six million watched the show. Three times more people had the adaptation made in January 1967 than the previous month.

If, as has been claimed, *The Forsyte Saga* was the *Twin Peaks* of its day, then the reaction to it was remarkably similar. Most critics shared the opinion of that of the *Morning Star*, who said that the series was 'Authentic, brilliant, but far too long.' The illicit romance of Fleur and Jon wasn't as compelling as the intrigue of the early episodes, and every time a major character died (Old Jolyon in March, young Jo himself in April) ratings fell with them. Still, most viewers were still there when the acquisitive and flawed Soames was struck down by a falling picture whilst saving Fleur from a collapsing beam. He died looking into camera, the culmination of a performance that earned Eric Porter an award from the Guild of TV Producers and Directors. Wilson received the Royal Television Society Silver Medal for his achievement, and the Writer's Guild honoured the script team.

Writing about his fascination with the Forsytes in the *Radio Times*, Wilson stated that 'Although no branch of the family has any real affection for any other, tribal loyalty is intense, and at any threat from outside they collect together in a defensive circle like cattle menaced by a wolf.' The theme of the series, and a neat summation of Galsworthy's long-term view of changing times (ironically, times that many viewers expressed a wish to return to) was, according to Wilson, 'Disturbing Beauty impinging on a possessive world.'

Beginning on 8 September 1968, the series was repeated on BBC1, where it gathered 18 million viewers. Church services were rescheduled to avoid clashing with the broadcasts, and in the Netherlands, where the BBC could be received, sports events were rearranged so that nobody would miss this foreign-language drama. In the States, 165 local stations affiliated with National Educational Television ran it in 1969, to a more muted reaction. The strangest thing of all was that Galsworthy's ironies at the expense of the chattering classes appealed to the Soviets, who bought the show in 1971. The books were back on the bestseller lists, Susan Hampshire became a star, and, for the first time, British television *knew* what audiences liked. 'Pure soap opera', as the *New York Times* said.

Exactly.

Emmerdale Farm/Emmerdale

- **Yorkshire Television** (ITV) ◆ Colour
- **Standard episode length**: 30 minutes ◆ 1972 to date
- **Creator:** Kevin Laffan
- **Writers include**: Kevin Laffan, Anthony Couch, David Crane, Neville Siggs, Tim Vaughan, Michael Russell, Andrew Holden, Bill Lyons, Kathleen Potter, Andy Lynch
- **Directors include**: Tristan de Vere Cole, Michael Snow, David Green, David Reynolds, Paddy Russell, Mervyn Cumming, Len Lurcuck, Mike Gibbon, Fiona Cumming, Darrol Blake, Christopher Lovett, Colin Cant, Garth Tucker
- **Producers**: David Goddard, Robert D. Cardona, Michael Glynn, Anne W. Gibbons, Richard Handford, Michael Russell, Stuart Doughty, Morag Bain, Nicholas Prosser, Mervyn Watson
- **Executive producers**: Peter Holmans, David Cunliffe, Michael Glynn, Keith Richardson

In the early 70s, 24-hour television seemed as remote a possibility as the collapse of the Berlin Wall. ITV's coverage tended to begin at about 2.00 or 3.00 p.m., the programmes showing few signs of effort or originality. One gets the impression that putting out quality programmes in the afternoon was regarded as a waste of time: after all, men were at work, and women had better things to do than watch television.

Someone must have seen through these sexist assumptions, realizing the huge untapped potential of 'proper' afternoon television. In November 1972, ITV launched a new package of programmes, with schools programmes leading up to *Rainbow* at 12.05 p.m. The bulk of the programming that followed came in the form of new drama serials from ITV's main programme producers: Yorkshire's *Emmerdale Farm* on Mondays and Tuesdays, Thames's *Harriet's Back in Town* on Tuesdays and Wednesdays, ATV's *General Hospital* on Thursdays and Fridays, and Granada's *Crown Court* on Wednesdays, Thursdays, and Fridays. (If all this wasn't enough to prompt millions to turn the television on at previously unheard-of times, the masterstroke was a new game show, *Mr and Mrs*, featuring questions such as 'Which leg does your husband put into his pyjamas first?')

The *TV Times* breathlessly exclaimed that 'Afternoon viewing is now on ITV every day of the week. The house-wife, the child, the shift worker, the pensioner, the sick or disabled, all those at home during the day can now find more than twenty extra hours of television entertainment every week.'

Yorkshire's *Emmerdale Farm* was, from the start, different from many of its contemporaries and peers, being the first attempt to move away from the urban hegemony of TV soap and towards the rarefied rustic atmosphere of *The Archers*. The first episode was redolent with a slow, retrospective acceptance, concentrating on the funeral of Jacob Sugden. 'In the beginning is the end', announced the *TV Times*, echoing T. S. Eliot.

The early conflicts and passions soon fell into place as Jack Sugden returned from Rome (and an implausibly successful writing career) to inherit

First season
(16 Oct 72–20 May 75)
Second season
(13 Oct 75–18 May 76)
Third season
(3 Jan–25 Aug 77)
Fourth season
(6 Sep–15 Dec 77)
Fifth season
(10 Jan–29 Jun 78)
Sixth season
(5 Sep–14 Dec 78)
Seventh season
(3 Jan–5 Jul 79)
Eighth season
(8 Jan–17 Jul 80)
Ninth season
(2 Sep–18 Dec 80)
Tenth season
(6 Jan–25 Jun 81)
Eleventh season
(8 Sep–5 Nov 81)
Twelth season
(12 Jan–10 Jun 82)
Thirteenth season
(14 Sep 82–16 Jun 83)
Fourteenth season
(13 Sep 83–14 Jun 84)
Fifteenth season
(11 Sep 84–6 Aug 85)
Sixteenth season
(3 Sep 85 to date)

Starring: Sheila Mercier (Annie Sugden/Kempinski) • Andrew Burt/Clive Hornby (Jack Sugden) • Frazer Hines (Joe Sugden) • Toke Townley (Sam Pearson) • Jo Kendall (Peggy Skilbeck) • Frederick Pyne (Matt Skilbeck) • Ronald Magill (Amos Brierly) • Arthur Pentelow (Henry Wilks) • Gail Harrison (Marian Wilks) • Hugh Manning (Revd Donald Hinton) • Lesley Manville (Rosemary Kendall) • Lynn Dalby (Ruth Merrick) • David Hill/Edward Peel/Jack Carr (Tom Merrick) • Katharine Barker/Jean Rogers (Dolly Arcaster/Skilbeck) • Max Wall (Arthur Braithwaite) • Helen Weir (Pat Merrick/Sugden) • Ian Sharrock (Jackie Merrick) • Jane Hutcheson (Sandie Merrick) • Stan Richards (Seth Armstrong) • Martin Dale (Sgt. MacArthur) • Richard Thorp (Alan Turner) • Diana Davies (Caroline Bates) • Cy Chadwick (Nick Bates) • Peter Alexander (Phil Pearce) • Tony Pitts (Archie Brooks) • Johnny Caesar (Bill Middleton) • Christopher Chittell (Eric Pollard) • Malandra Burrows (Kathy Bates/Merrick/Tate) • Craig McKay (Mark Hughes) • Glenda McKay (Rachel Hughes) • Madeleine Howard/Alyson Spiro (Sarah Connolly/Sugden) • Gregory Floy (Stephen Fuller) • Annie Hulley (Karen Moore) • Naomi Lewis (Elsa Feldmann) • Matthew Vaughan (Michael Feldmann) • Kate Dove (Elizabeth Feldmann/Pollard) • Peter Amory (Christopher Tate) • Norman Bowler (Frank Tate) • Claire King (Kim Tate/Barker) • Leah Bracknell (Zoe Tate) • Stephen Rashbrook (Revd Tony Charlton) • Carl Rigg (Richard Anstey) • Mamta Kaash (Sita Sharma) • Sally Knyvette (Kate Hughes/Sugden) • Fionnuala Ellwood (Lynn Whiteley) • Philomena McDonagh (Carol Nelson) • Bernard Archard (Leonard Kempinksi) • Alun Lewis (Vic Windsor) • Deena Payne (Viv Windsor) • Toby Cockerell (Scott Windsor) • Adele Silva (Kelly Windsor) • Sophie Jeffrey (Donna Windsor) • Rachel Davies (Shirley Foster/Turner) • Brendan Price (Bernard McAllister) • Amanda Wenban (Angharad McAllister) • Camilla Power (Jessica McAllister) • Noah Huntley (Luke McAllister) • Paula Tilbrook (Betty Eagleton) • Michelle Holmes (Britt Woods) • Billy Hartman (Terry Woods) • Christopher Smith (Robert Sugden) • Sandra Gough (Nellie Dingle) • Paul Loughran (Butch Dingle) • James Hooton (Sam Dingle) • Jacqueline Pirie (Tina Dingle) • Steve Halliwell (Zak Dingle) • Johnny Leeze (Ned Glover) • Roberta Kerr (Jan Glover) • Nicky Evans (Roy Glover) • Ian Kelsey (Dave Glover) • Tonicha Jeronimo (Linda Glover) • Tony Barton (Des Burtenshaw) • Stuart Wade (Biff Fowler) • Rachel Ambler (Emma Nightingale) • Matthew Marsden (Daniel Weir) • Samantha Hurst (Dolores Sharp)

Emmerdale Farm after Jacob's death. Jack faced opposition from his tough elder sister, Peggy Skilbeck, angry that the farm had not been left to her, and from Joe, who saw his brother as an interloping prodigal son. Things improved when he encountered retired businessman Henry Wilks and his horse-riding daughter Marian, although Jack's old flame, Ruth, was trapped in a dull marriage.

From the outset, the loves, relationships and affairs of the Sugden family – and the people of Beckindale in general – were played out against the fascinating backdrop of the farming community and the problems of 'everyday life'. Although *Emmerdale* has had more than its fair share of love triangles and illicit meetings, the series is unique in featuring the joys of sheepdog trials, the annual cricket match against Robblesfield, and the problems of farming equipment, pot-holing and sheep-rustling.

2000th episode transmitted on 17 Aug 1995

Emmerdale Farm became *Emmerdale* in 1989

Emmerdale Farm was not networked until 5 Jan 88

This has helped to make *Emmerdale* popular in the farming community, but cannot in itself explain its success. The agricultural environment of *Emmerdale* is alien to most people – certainly more so than working-class life in the East End or Greater Manchester. One of the reasons for *Emmerdale*'s popularity is the beauty of the countryside and the thrill of escapism. And yet, if anything, Kevin Laffan, the show's creator, wanted to demythologize the countryside, noting of the farmer that 'sustaining and destroying life is his business'. *Emmerdale* can claim to be the most literary, spiritual or even 'earthy' soap, Laffan commenting that 'Real country folk are fundamentalists. They accept all the facts of life (and all encompasses much more than the limited and boring gymnastics of procreation) without worrying over niceties of social etiquette.'

However, its introspection has always been matched by drama. Original producer David Goddard said, 'We are not going for straw-sucking yokels or farming notes. The interest comes from the conflicts and relationships of families at the farm. Like *A Family at War*, good, strong, dramatic stories.'

The fact that *Emmerdale Farm* was the slowest-moving and the most philosophical of the soaps made its success all the more surprising. In addition, *Emmerdale* is the most-moved major soap, in terms of both day and time (lunch time, mid-afternoon, evening) of transmission. In the past it was treated with scant disregard by the programme planners: if a programme had to be dropped from the schedules for a week, it was almost always *Emmerdale Farm*. It was often treated with similar disdain by the *TV Times*: while ***Coronation Street*** was always taken with absolute seriousness, some of the reporting on *Emmerdale Farm* made Amos's articles for the *Hotten Courier* seem like Pulitzer Prize material. For example, an interview in 1975 with Lesley Manville (who played the Sugden's 16-year-old cousin, Rosemary), promoted the actress as being 'fed up to her navy-blue knickers with playing schoolgirl parts'.

Such contempt would have killed off a lesser programme, but the very fact that *Emmerdale* is different from its peers has ensured its success. Although some-

The cast in 1995. Richard Thorp (centre, in the open necked shirt), some years earlier, played Dr John Rennie in *Emergency – Ward 10*

times serious to the point of over-earnestness, it has always retained a lightness of touch and a humour that was warm and familiar ('Nay, nay, Mr Wilks!' is the closest a soap has ever come to a catch phrase).

However, Kevin Laffan turned his back on *Emmerdale Farm* in 1985, complaining of an unwarranted increase in 'sex, sin and sensationalism'. Without doubt the programme was striving to modernise its appeal. The infamous Hotten Hotel affair between Jack Sugden and Karen Moore was not just the final straw for Laffan: Mary Whitehouse dubbed the programme 'a den of vice' soon afterwards. This more overt sexuality – and the ensuing brawl between Jack and Tom Merrick – were perhaps less at odds with Laffan's honest look at life than the gratuitous gore when Jackie Merrick was knocked off his motorbike.

Laffan was probably right to imply that it would be foolish for *Emmerdale* to try to tackle ***EastEnders*** at its own game, but change and sensationalism can become habit-forming. The Christmas 1993 Phil Redmond storyline saw a plane crashing on Beckindale, which was followed less than five months later by a traumatic Post Office siege. More than ever before the programme is a patchwork, striving to hold on to what once made the show popular while searching for a new audience with a shorter attention span.

One final point in its favour: *Emmerdale* is the greenest soap, and is therefore, despite its age, well-suited to the 90s. Laffan has commented that 'from the start [it was] about the cruelty of man to nature. The opening had references to the pollution of the rivers by manufacturers, fish dying off – generally issues of conservation ... Jack left because he disagreed with battery hens.' In 1987, Beckindale villagers battled against a planned nuclear dump (and won), a storyline based on real-life incidents at Fulbeck, Lincolnshire.

Emmerdale – the first eco-political soap?

All Creatures Great and Small

- **BBC Television** (BBC1) ◆ Colour
- **90 episodes** (standard length: 50 minutes) ◆ 1978–90
- **Adapted from:** novels by James Herriot
- **Writers include:** Brian Finch, Anthony Steven, Johnny Byrne, Michael Russell
- **Directors include:** Terence Dudley, Peter Moffatt, Christopher Barry, Michael Hayes, Michael Brayshaw, Tony Virgo
- **Producer:** Bill Sellars

Regular cast: Christopher Timothy (James Herriot) • Robert Hardy (Siegfried Farnon) • Peter Davison (Tristan Farnon) • Carol Drinkwater/Lynda Bellingham (Helen Alderson/Herriot) • John McGlynn (Calum Buchanan)

With: Mary Hignett (Mrs Hall) • Margaretta Scott (Mrs Pumphrey) • Judy Wilson (Mrs Greenlaw) • Andrea Gibb (Deirdre McEwan) • Teddy Turner (Hodgekin) • John Sharp (Biggins) • Jean Heywood (Mrs Alton) • James Grout (Granville Bennett)

A small pre-war car transports a medical man across a beautiful landscape to a jaunty signature tune. We've seen it before; this is the BBC resurrecting one of its most successful formats. Not ***Doctor Finlay's Casebook***, but certainly 'son of', and this time the patients aren't even human.

James Herriot's semi-autobiographical memoirs of his life as a vet in the Yorkshire Dales were already popular, and so, for the first three seasons, *All Creatures Great and Small* wisely concentrated on adapting existing material. James arrives at Skeldale House in Darrowby to become the partner of the tempestuous Siegfried Farnon, and his feckless younger brother, Tristan. He meets the love of his life, Helen Alderson, and, in the first few episodes, has to deal with a bull with sunstroke, a local Lord's terminally-ill horse, and, of course, Tricki-Woo, the hypochondriacal lap-dog of the barmy Mrs Pumphrey. There was even a cook, Mrs Hall: more shades of ***Doctor Finlay***. The characters quickly settled down: Siegfried, like a stouter Dr Cameron, would be planning some sound scheme to advance the practice, Tristan would be chatting up a local girl and getting drunk with the bell-ringers, and James would wander through it all, offering a sort of long-suffering middle path of common sense. Amongst the famous faces visiting Darrowby were Patrick Troughton, Michael Sheard, Pamela Salem, Geoffrey Bayldon, Brian Glover, Frank Windsor and Thora Hird.

Eddie Stratton was the first veterinary advisor to the series, a man who had once worked with the real Herriot. He supervised the renowned 'hand up a cow's bottom' scenes, and produced a series of genuine cases from the village of Askrigg that the actors would pretend to handle, or in some cases actually handle.

James's romance with Helen was gently developed, with them marrying her at the end of episode nine. The humour was gentle too, poking fun at the vets' attempts to deal with various animal problems (the impotent bull and the exploding cow spring to mind), but never at the people in the community. Perhaps a goat would eat Helen's laundry, or Tristan would answer the phone in an outrageous German accent to avoid his latest paramour, but there was a sense of love, rather than slapstick, running through the comedy. Shades of country lore ran through the series, as when James, having delivered a calf, was called upon to eat a breakfast of pork fat and piccalilli.

First season
(8 Jan–16 Apr 78)
1 Horse Sense
2 Dog Days
3 It Takes All Kinds ...
4 Calf Love
5 Out of Practice
6 Nothing Like Experience
7 Golden Lads and Girls
8 Advice and Consent
9 The Last Furlong
10 Sleeping Partners
11 Bulldog Breed
12 Practice Makes Perfect
13 Breath of Life

Second season
(23 Sep–24 Dec 78)
14 Cats and Dogs
15 Attendant Problems
16 Fair Means and Fowl
17 The Beauty of the Beast
18 Judgement Day
19 Faint Hearts
20 Tricks of the Trade
21 Pride of Possession
22 The Name of the Game
23 Puppy Love
24 Ways and Means
25 Pups, Pigs and Pickle
26 A Dog's Life
27 Merry Gentlemen

Third season
(29 Dec 79–5 Apr 80)
28 Plenty to Grouse About
29 Charity Begins at Home
30 Every Dog Has His Day
31 Hair of the Dog
32 If Wishes Were Horses
33 Pig in the Middle
34 Be Prepared
35 A Dying Breed
36 Brink of Disaster
37 Home and Away
38 Alarms and Excursions
39 Matters of Life and Death
40 Will to Live
41 Big Steps and Little 'Uns

Christmas special
(25 Dec 83, 90 minutes)
42 The Lord God Made Them All (part 1)

Christmas special
(25 Dec 85, 90 minutes)
43 The Lord God Made Them All (part 2)

Fourth season
(17 Jan–20 Mar 88)
44 One of Nature's Little Miracles
45 Barks and Bites
46 The Bull with the Bowler Hat

In 1980 it all ended. The final episode gained 16 million viewers. In its time the show had risen to the ratings top ten, seeing off opposition like *Bruce Forsyth's Big Night*. However, the series came to a halt with no great outcry. There weren't many stories left to adapt, and James and Siegfried had gone off to join the RAF as war began. Davison and Hardy continued with their successful careers. Timothy, however, found himself hopelessly typecast, and the media was interested only in his affair with Carol Drinkwater.

The BBC tried to use a similar format again, to no great success, in three seasons of the 'zoo vet' stories *One By One*, with *All Creatures* regular Johnny Byrne script-editing. If any one thing brought *All Creatures* back, it was the 'comfiness factor' that had so pervaded ***Doctor Finlay***. Viewers were used to Darrowby,

The star of *All Creatures Great and Small*... And Robert Hardy, Christopher Timothy and Peter Davison

47 The Pig Man Cometh
48 Hail Caesar!
49 Only One Woof
50 Ace, King, Queen, Jack
51 The Healing Touch
52 City Slicker
53 For Richer, for Poorer

Fifth season
(3 Sep–19 Nov 88)
54 Against the Odds
55 Place of Honour
56 Choose a Bright Morning
57 The Playing Field
58 When Dreams Come True
59 A New Chapter
60 A Present from Dublin
61 The Salt of the Earth
62 Cheques and Balances
63 Female of the Species
64 The Jackpot
65 Two of a Kind

Sixth season
(2 Sep–18 Nov 89)
66 Here and There
67 The Course of True Love
68 The Call of the Wild
69 The Nelson Touch
70 Blood and Water
71 Where Sheep May Safely Graze
72 The New World
73 Mending Fences
74 Big Fish, Little Fish
75 In Whom We Trust
76 The Rough and the Smooth
77 The Best Time

Seventh season
(1 Sep–17 Nov 90)
78 The Prodigal Returns
79 Knowin' How to Do It
80 If Music Be the Food of Love
81 A Friend for Life
82 Spring Fever
83 Out with the New
84 Food for Thought
85 A Cat in Hull's Chance
86 A Grand Memory for Forgetting
87 Old Dogs, New Tricks
88 Hampered
89 Promises to Keep

Christmas special
(24 Dec 90, 90 minutes)
90 Brotherly Love

where things changed slowly. They liked the fact that, as in Tannochbrae, familiar faces would pop up every now and then (such as the sophisticated small animal vet Granville Bennett, the sardonic Angus Grier and the awesomely efficient student vet Richard Carmody), and that the drama, while concerned with suffering, always had a homespun solution.

A Christmas special was the most obvious next step – after all, the second season had closed with a Christmas episode. The 90-minute special, in 1983, was a direct adaptation of the remaining book, *The Lord God Made Them All*, and was set after the war. The vets returned to their practice, Helen and James having had a son, Jimmy.

The experiment was successful, and was repeated two years later. It was only a matter of time before public pressure demanded the series return as a regular fixture. Herriot had some unpublished diaries to offer the BBC and the scriptwriters had a freer hand with the material. Real history was to impinge on Darrowby, the characters grappling with the death of the King and the advent of television. Since Davison's commitments elsewhere prevented him from making more than the occasional appearance, a new character was introduced, Calum Buchanan, a prototypical 'green' vet from Glasgow. Calum had a pet badger, and would sneak out in the night to sabotage a hunt (very subversive for 1950). He was also Tristan's great rival in love, winning from him Deidre McEwan, whom he married in the sixth season.

The stories became a little more adventurous, James skiing across the snowbound Dales to help dying piglets in a cut-off farm, and Siegfried attempting to artificially inseminate an angry cow. Both of the senior vets moved away from Skeldale House, Siegfried (who was always dallying with more mature ladies) having also married. James now had a daughter, Rosie, though viewers might have been puzzled by the change in her mother, as Lynda Bellingham took over the part of Helen.

John McGlynn left the series, worried that his part was too limited, and Peter Davison returned. The final season celebrated the comfiness of the format more than any other had. Although James's beloved labrador Dan was dead, Tricki-Woo survived, despite his infirmities. The series ended in 1990, as it should, with Tristan battling over who should be in the bell-ringing squad, in yet another Christmas special.

Brookside

- **Mersey Television for Channel 4** (C4) ◆ **Colour**
- **Standard episode length:** 30 minutes ◆ **1982 to date**
- **Creator:** Phil Redmond
- **Writers include:** Phil Redmond, Frank Cottrell Boyce, Jimmy McGovern, Helen J. Wilson, Valerie Windsor, Maurice Bessman, Chris Curry, John Oakden, Peter Cox, Joe Ainsworth, Andy Lynch, Kathleen Potter, Allan Swift, Shaun Duggan, Barry Woodward, Susan Pleat, Nick Saltrese
- **Directors include:** Richard Standeven, Chris Clough, Peter Boisseau, Eszter Nordin, Barry Letts, Chris Johnston, Andrew Higgs, Bob Carlton, Ken Horn, Brian Morgan, Patrick Tucker, Darrol Blake, Misha Williams, Danny Hiller, Jeff Naylor, Sue Butterworth, David Innes Edwards, Jeremy Summers, Richard Kelly, Nicholas Prosser, Jo Johnson, Stephen Garwood
- **Producers:** Stuart Doughty, Nicholas Prosser, Vanessa Whitburn, Mal Young
- **Executive producer:** Phil Redmond

In 1980, founding Channel 4 Chief Executive Jeremy Isaacs chaired a public meeting and was asked, if the new service was to be innovative and different, could they have programmes with teenagers swearing at 8 p.m.? 'If the context is right', Isaacs replied, and found himself in conversation with his questioner, Phil Redmond. Redmond suggested a twice-weekly soap opera set on a new housing estate, and, mindful of Redmond's success with ***Grange Hill,*** Isaacs commissioned it. An important factor was that Redmond had devised a way to make what would become *Brookside* on the cheap. Other soaps largely used backlot sets or real buildings for exterior scenes, with interiors shot in the studio. As a former quantity surveyor, Redmond knew that it would be cheaper to buy an entire cul-de-sac of new houses for use in all the recording, rather than paying six months' rent. Coupled with Redmond's policy of hiring relatively unknown actors (early bit-part players Margi Clarke and Letitia Dean would go on to greater things), it would also mean an unparalleled sense of reality. Deciding to make the series in Liverpool, Redmond secured a suitable site and chose the type of houses to be built. Three detached houses, two semis and a bungalow were chosen to fit the characters Redmond intended to use, although in the first episode, on the opening night of Channel 4, only two of them were occupied, with a third family moving in that day.

Coronation Street and ***EastEnders,*** being set in working class areas, never convincingly integrated middle-class characters, while ***Crossroads*** was the opposite, with subservient workers tending to their white-collar clientele. *Brookside* featured a socio-economic mix, reflected in the first episode. Roger Huntington and wife Heather were young professionals on their way up. Redundant manager Paul Collins was on his way down, much to the discomfort of wife Annabelle. Factory worker Bobby Grant had got as far as he would on the housing ladder, which pleased wife Sheila, although their children Karen and Damon missed friends from the council estate. Reasonably indifferent was eldest son Barry, who had plans – not all legal – of his own, usually involving his mate Terry Sullivan. Over the years this mix was maintained and whilst at times it seemed like Brookside Close was becoming yuppiefied by the likes of Max and Patricia Farnham, there was always Ron and D-D Dixon to balance the tone.

Reflecting Redmond's teen-drama successes ***Grange Hill*** and *Going Out*, the younger characters had problems of their own. Of the Collins's children, Gordon had come off best, the sale of their previous house financing his private schooling, much to the chagrin of his sister Lucy who had to make do with Brookside Comprehensive. Karen and Damon Grant grew up against a strict Roman Catholic background: Damon didn't like going to church, while Karen's objections centred more on sexual freedom and contraception. Damon's mates

Gizzmo and Ducksie were regular visitors to the Close, and it was their mild bad language in the first episode which led to the infamous 'Channel Swore' headline in the *Daily Express* the next morning.

2 Nov 82 to date
1000th episode transmitted on 9 Oct 1991

Redmond wanted to deal with important issues realistically, and it is largely *Brookside's* treatment of such issues that has courted controversy. Before its first anniversary the series had dealt with attempted rape, politics, and race in a manner worthy of *Play for Today*. One of television's great taboos, sexual assault, was first treated obliquely, with Karen escaping from the clutches of an impatient boyfriend, but her mother was less fortunate. Attacked by a mystery assailant, she became pregnant, also having to cope with the suicide of her friend, Teresa Nolan, following the wrongful arrest of her husband Matty as a suspect (the culprit eventually proved to be an unknown taxi driver). More recently, Peter Harrison was tried for the rape of Diana Corkhill at a party, she having willingly gone to his bedroom, but he was acquitted. It was difficult to establish what point

Starring: Jim Wiggins (Paul Collins) • Doreen Sloane (Annabelle Collins) • Nigel Crowley/Mark Burgess (Gordon Collins) • Katrin Cartlidge/Maggie Saunders (Lucy Collins) • Sue Johnston (Sheila Grant/Corkhill) • Ricky Tomlinson (Bobby Grant) • Paul Usher (Barry Grant) • Simon O'Brien (Damon Grant) • Shelagh O'Hara (Karen Grant) • Amanda Burton (Heather Huntington/Haversham/Black) • Rob Spendlove (Roger Huntington) • Alexandra Pigg (Petra Taylor) • Brian Regan (Terry Sullivan) • Tony Scoggo (Matty Nolan) • Bill Dean (Harry Cross) • Gladys Ambrose (Julia Brogan) • Cliff Howells (George Jackson) • Anna Keaveney (Marie Jackson) • Allan Patterson (Gary Jackson) • Tracey Jay (Michelle Jones) • Ann Hadyn Edwards (Teresa Nolan) • Dicken Ashworth (Alan Partridge) • Dinah May (Samantha Partridge) • Betty Alberge (Edna Cross) • David Easter (Pat Hancock) • Ray Dunbobbin (Ralph Hardwick) • Malcolm Tierney (Tommy McArdle) • Sheila Grier (Sandra Maghie) • Sharon Rosita (Kate Moses) • Michael Starke (Thomas 'Sinbad' Sweeney) • Mark Birch (Ducksie Brown) • Robert Smith (Gizzmo Hawkins) • William Maxwell (Jack Sullivan) • John McArdle (Billy Corkhill) • Kate Fitzgerald (Doreen Corkhill) • Jason Hope (Rod Corkhill) • Justine Kerrigan (Tracy Corkhill) • Robert Pugh (John Clarke) • Dean Sullivan (Jimmy Corkhill) • Alan Rothwell (Nick Black) • Joanne Black (Kirsty Brown) • Rachel Lindsay (Sammy Rogers/Daniels) • Steven Pinner (Jonathan Gordon-Davies) • Jane Cunliffe (Laura Gordon-Davies) • Annie Miles (Sue Harper/Sullivan) • Gillian Kearney (Debbie McGrath) • Eithne Browne (Chrissy Rogers) • Peter Christian (Frank Rogers) • Kevin Carson/Stephen Walters (Geoff Rogers) • Debbie Reynolds/Diane Burke (Katie Rogers) • Jennifer Calvert (Cheryl Boyanowsky) • Daniel Webb (Gavin Taylor) • Danny McCall (Owen Daniels) • David Yip (Michael Choi) • Sarah Lam (Caroline Choi) • Anna Sung (Jessica Choi) • Vince Earl (Ron Dixon) • Irene Marot (D-D Dixon) • Alexandra Fletcher (Jacqui Dixon) • Paul Byatt (Mike Dixon) • Gerard Bostock/Mark Lennock (Tony Dixon) • Cheryl Maiker (Marcia Barrett) • Steven Pinder (Max Farnham) • Gabrielle Glaister (Patricia Farnham) • Nichola Stephenson (Margaret Clemence) • Suzanne Packer (Josie Johnson) • Louis Emerick (Mick Johnson) • Sue Jenkins (Jackie Corkhill) • Paula Frances (Diana Spence/Corkhill) • Francis Johnson (Ellis Johnson) • Naomi Kamanga (Gemma Johnson) • Leeon Sawyer (Lee Johnson) • Angela Morant (Barbara Harrison) • Geoffrey Leesley (John Harrison) • Clive Moore (Derek O'Farrell) • Julie Peasgood (Fran Pearson) • Karen Drury (Susannah Farnham) • David Banks (Graham Curtis) • Robert Beck (Peter Harrison) • Jodie Hanson (Marianne Dwyer) • Sharon Power (Lyn McLoughlin/Matthews/Rogers) • Kazia Pelka (Anna Wolska) • John Burgess (David Crosbie) • Marcia Ashton (Jean Crosbie) • Mary Tamm (Penny Crosbie) • Stephen Donald (Carl Banks) • Paul Broughton (Eddie Banks) • Matthew Lewney (Lee Banks) • Susan Twist (Rosie Banks) • Andrea Marshall (Sarah Banks) • Sarah White (Bev McLoughlin) • Lee Hartney (Simon Howe) • Sandra Maitland (Mandy Jordache) • Anna Friel (Beth Jordache) • Tiffany Chapman (Rachel Jordache) • Bryan Murray (Trevor Jordache) • Gillian Hanna (Brenna Jordache) • Tina Malone (Mo McGee) • Kate Beckett (Jenny Swift)

Damon and Debbie
(4–18 Nov 87)
Three 50-minute episodes
South
(14–21 Mar 88)
Two 25-minute episodes

the production team were trying to make, other than to reflect the complexity of 'date rape'.

The closure of Bobby's factory reflected what had happened so often on Merseyside, whilst through Paul Collins the writers demonstrated that management's fate could be just as bleak. Bobby eventually got a union job, while Paul's spell managing a YTS project contrasted with Damon's experiences on the scheme. In later years, the threat of unemployment would hang over many and varied characters.

Brookside contained television's first AIDS storyline, when Bobby helped a union member with the condition fighting unfair dismissal, although the series has been more circumspect in the inclusion of a regular gay character: it was unfortunate that it was Gordon Collins, with his public school background, pandering somewhat to stereotyping. Only marginally less contentious with the viewers, lesbianism (Beth Jordache and Margaret Clemence's relationship) was treated with sensitivity. Lucy Collins' brief flirtation with Bobby's black colleague Jonah Jones brought racial issues to the fore, and while ***EastEnders*** has been accused of including token black, Asian and Jewish characters who have no identity beyond their ethnicity, *Brookside* has taken a more realistic line. Mick Johnson, for example, works entirely contrary to offensive black male stereotypes, being a good father, hard-working and honest.

The writing-by-numbers pitfalls other series fall into were also avoided with substance abuse. Heather's architect second husband Nick Black underlined this, having the funds to feed his heroin addiction while appearing outwardly ordinary. Similarly, Jimmy Corkhill's addiction was spread over months, by which time he had killed Frank Rogers in a hit-and-run accident hours after his wedding. Perversely, this was condemned because Jimmy was shown to enjoy his drug habit. Such criticism aside, this is one of many examples of long-running storylines which, in other series, would have been unconvincingly introduced, dealt with and finished within weeks. An example of this was the slow descent to suicide taken by Petra Taylor after the death of her husband Gavin. After her suicide, Petra's insensitive sister Marie Jackson inherited the house, but her fireman husband George was implicated in a robbery by Barry's gangster associate Tommy McArdle. George's remand, trial and conviction followed an accurate time-scale and – against all the rules of popular drama – he was imprisoned, leading to a lengthy 'George Jackson is innocent' campaign.

Despite the high body-count over the years (25 unnatural deaths so far), ex-railwayman Harry Cross chose Brookside Close for his retirement home. Harry found fault in almost everybody, and always wanted to know what everyone else was up to. When a stroke forced him to move into the bungalow at No. 6 and rent out No. 7 to nurses Kate and Sandra and hospital porter Pat, Harry often let himself in with his own key to check they weren't up to anything immoral. A fate worse than Harry was reserved for them, being held hostage by the crazed John Clarke. 'The Siege of Brookside Close' – one of the series' first high-profile storylines – ended with Kate and Clarke dead.

Marriages are popular ratings-grabbers, but *Brookside* specializes in its own brand of nuptialis interruptus. Alan 'Ace' Partridge was jilted at the altar, whilst PC Rod 'The Plod' Corkhill's attempt at marrying Diana ended with him unconscious in a public toilet after trying to save a rent boy from a beating. Mick Johnson and Marianne Dwyer had their ceremony interrupted when he was arrested, wrongly accused of armed robbery, and Frank Rogers's second wedding day was disrupted by his death. Although it lasted slightly longer, Jonathan and Laura Gordon-Davies's union was also doomed, Laura electrocuted by a faulty light switch. Other marriages were usually severed in the more conventional way, with Bobby and Sheila Grant, and Doreen and Billy Corkhill, spiralling towards divorce at the same time, although Billy and Sheila later went off to Ireland together. This aside, second marriages in *Brookside* are invariably rocky, Patricia Farnham having to keep a constant eye on Max lest he succumb to the attentions of first wife Susannah.

One relationship that has been through many ups and downs is that of Barry Grant and Terry Sullivan. First introduced in the sixth episode, Terry was an accomplice to Barry's dodgy money-making schemes. He was always expected to comply, regardless of risk, and only occasionally refused (like Barry's illegal warehouse party venture). After Terry married Sue Harper, Barry not only slept with her, but later pushed her and her son Danny from the scaffolding on the parade of shops he was building behind the Close. Terry ploughed the insurance money into a pizza shop, but was too drunk to run it and sold out to Mick. When the Farnham's Polish nanny, Anna, agreed to marry Terry, Barry reported her as an illegal immigrant and she fled the country. Sobering up and getting a job managing the petrol station (replacing white supremacist George Webb), Terry fell under the influence of the religious cult led by Simon Howe, based in Katie Rogers's house in the absence of her stepmother. Katie, vulnerable after her father's death, was also indoctrinated into the cult, although like Terry her faith fell short of obeying Simon's order that the two should sleep together. Barry bought the house from Lyn Rogers, but the cult remained, so he broke in, and, in another hostage saga, Simon was seriously injured by his own bomb. Rather than come to his senses, Terry (by now as mad as toast dipped in scouse) blamed Barry. He was eventually saved, ironically by Barry, from a double suicide with his guru, whom Barry left to die. The losses haven't all been Terry's: when Barry let Terry move into his flat, his posh girlfriend Penny Crosbie said it was him or her and Barry, inevitably, chose Terry!

Not so long-running, but more coherent, was the Jordache saga, a triumph of meticulously planned narrative. In late 1992, 10 Brookside Close was sold to the mysterious Shackletons, but it was Mandy Jordache and her daughters Beth and Rachel who eventually moved in. It turned out that No. 10 was being used as a safe house, Mandy having been beaten by her husband Trevor, who also raped Beth. Released, Trevor tracked his family down and tried to re-establish his hold over Mandy and Beth and have his wicked way with Rachel. Mandy and Beth tried to poison him, but when he found them grinding up tablets to lace his whisky, he attacked Beth. Mandy stabbed him and they buried the body in the garden, telling Rachel he had left. When a badly decomposed body was found in woods nearby, Mandy iden-

Sheila and Bobby Grant

tified the effects as Trevor's and had 'him' buried, but after the funeral Trevor's sister asked for his signet ring. Beth started to dig up the body, but the stench of the decomposition forced her to stop. Sympathetic window cleaner Sinbad Sweeney found her, retrieved the ring and re-buried the body. He then laid a patio over it.

Over the next year-and-a-half, Mandy, Beth and Sinbad kept the secret of the hidden body, although there were dicey moments, such as Mr Shackleton putting the house up for sale, and when Rachel took up shoplifting and hid stolen goods under another part of the patio. After a disastrous relationship with Peter Harrison, Beth found herself attracted to the Farnhams's new nanny, Margaret, herself on the rebound from D-D Dixon's brother Derek. Hesitant at first, Margaret began a relationship with her, but eventually broke it off when she became jealous of Beth's friendship with a university lecturer, who later dumped her when Mandy threatened to inform her superiors.

Beth started a new relationship with Viv, but the crunch came in January 1995 when flooding in the garden led to the discovery of the body, by which time Sinbad, Mandy and the girls had fled to Ireland. Captured and returned to Liverpool, each confessed to killing Trevor on their own, but Sinbad's account didn't match the forensic evidence and Mandy and Beth were charged with the murder. At the trial Rachel denied Trevor had raped her (after telling the press about Beth's lesbian tendencies), and despite a sympathetic summing up by the judge they were found guilty. As an appeal was planned, Beth died from a previously undetected heart condition on the morning of the hearing, while Mandy, pregnant by Sinbad, was released ...

Like no other *Brookside* storyline before, the Jordache saga was able to bring to the public attention an issue of continuing concern. Battered wives charities praised the realism of Mandy's plight, although opinion was split over the verdict: some said it was realistic because it demonstrated the injustice of the law, others argued that it inferred that women who defended themselves would end up in prison. Beth Jordache also became an icon for many lesbians, as well as incest survivors, but the character was also criticized because she seemed to adhere to the stereotype that lesbians become lesbians because they have had a hard time with men, and her untimely death was seen by many as a betrayal.

The series originally went out twice a week, and this was later increased to three episodes. In 1988, five episodes were stripped across one week following the story of Billy and Sheila finally getting together, a trick repeated with the episodes concerning the discovery of Trevor's body and then the trial of Mandy and Beth. The flexibility of Channel 4, which allows *Brookside* to experiment, is something which no other terrestrial channel can offer.

In 1987, a spin-off series, *Damon and Debbie*, had the youngest Grant running away with his girlfriend, while *South* in 1988 saw Tracy Corkhill and boyfriend Jamie Henderson escaping to London to look for fame and fortune. They found only grim reality, but if the producers wanted to make the point that it was grim down south as well, it was perhaps not a good idea to have them step straight off the train and unrealistically bump into Morrissey. Happy with its pop-culture credentials *(Brookie* being the *NME*'s favourite TV show), several Liverpool bands (notably the Farm) have appeared.

Guest appearances are not uncommon in *Brookside*, with Sarah Greene, Michael Parkinson, Paula Yates, Lily Savage and Loyd Grossman all turning up, although this does beg a perennial question. It is often said that the unrealistic thing about soaps is that nobody ever talks about watching the telly. Brookside solved this by incorporating Mersey Television's local education initiative *Meadowcroft Park* (where students script and record their own programmes) into the series as the soap some of the characters watch, whilst a recent addition has been *Sunset Bay*. *The X-Files* and ***Coronation Street*** have both been referred to. Most notably, at the time of the air-crash storyline in ***Emmerdale*** (which Redmond himself devised), Mick Johnson was seen reading a newspaper with the headline 'Air Crash Latest – Village Mourns as Many Die'.

But then, what is reality anyway?

EastEnders

- **BBC Television** (BBC1) ◆ Colour
- **Standard episode length:** 30 minutes ◆ 1985 to date
- **Creators:** Julia Smith, Tony Holland
- **Writers include:** Gerry Huxham, Jane Hollowood, Bill Lyons, Rosemary Mason, Gilly Fraser, Michael Robartes, Juliet Ace, Tony McHale, Liane Aukin, Peter Batt, Charlie Humphreys, Tony Jordan, P.J. Hammond, Debbie Cook, Ashley Pharoah, Susan Boyd, Jeff Povey, Matthew Graham, Len Collin, Joanne Maguire
- **Directors include:** Matthew Robinson, Sue Butterworth, Antonia Bird, Mike Gibbon, Robert Gabriel, William Slater, Chris Clough, Mike Lloyd, Peter Moffatt, Garth Tucker, Alan Wareing, Nicholas Prosser, Mervyn Cumming, Steve Goldie, Philip Draycott, Barry Letts
- **Producers:** Julia Smith, Tony Virgo, Mike Gibbon, Michael Ferguson, Corinne Hollingworth, Richard Bramall, Pat Sandys, Leonard Lewis, Helen Greaves, Barbara Emile, Diana Kyle, Mike Hudson, Jane Fallon, Nicholas Hicks-Beach, Jane Harris, Josephine Ward

EastEnders, like no programme before, was a product of market research and, quite simply, televisual need. The BBC had to create a popular programme, and *EastEnders* was treated like a commercial product, rigorously researched and promoted. However, the initial response to the idea of a new soap was not enthusiastic by any means, and the BBC could hardly claim a track record of success in the area. Although *The Brothers* and *Angels* had been well-received in the 70s, the BBC hadn't tried a 52-week-a-year soap since the 60s, and of *Compact*, *United!*, and *The Newcomers*, only the former was especially popular. And yet, unless the BBC responded to the triple attractions of ***Coronation Street***, ***Crossroads*** and ***Emmerdale Farm***, it would always be open to the accusation of being 'too highbrow' and of being a waste of the majority of licence-payers' money, criticisms that a Conservative government with a passing dislike for the Corporation might well be keen to act upon.

Julia Smith, who had worked on ***Doctor Finlay's Casebook***, *The Newcomers*, ***Z Cars*** and *The Railway Children*, and had directed, then produced, *Angels*, was initially approached in 1983. She quickly roped in Tony Holland, with whom she had worked frequently since ***Z Cars***. Initial ideas – including a longer version of *Angels* (which normally ran for 13 weeks), and new soaps involving a shopping arcade and a mobile-trailer park – were dropped for logistical reasons. The final format was conventional, with many apparent similarities to ***Coronation Street***. The added ingredient was a real social bite. Eschewing the comfortable and aged familiarity of its northern rival, *EastEnders* went for the jugular, embracing the sordid and the depressing as positive dramatic virtues. It had young characters, almost immediate 'bad' publicity (Leslie Grantham's criminal record was dragged up by the gutter press), and it was soon attacked by Mary Whitehouse as being a cynical violation of family viewing time.

Granada launched a new soap – *Albion Market* – shortly after the debut of *EastEnders*, but it struggled to find an audience, partly because of poor scheduling. Michael Grade – controller of BBC1 when *EastEnders* was finally transmitted – was, if nothing else, a master at playing the scheduling game. Grade was initially banking on the usual ***Emmerdale Farm*** summer recess to give 'his' soap time to gain more viewers. When this did not happen, he knew that he had to change the transmission time of the programme to 7.30. Mary Whitehouse's protests gave him an excellent excuse.

Although the figures are open to dispute (a repeat showing had never before boosted audiences to so great an extent), by early 1986 *EastEnders* was the most popular programme on British television, regularly reaching over 23 million

19 Feb 85 to date

1000th episode transmitted on 12 Jul 1994

viewers. Although *EastEnders* needed to be popular, few expected it to take such a hold of the public imagination. (Smith had expected a similar audience rating – say 13 million viewers – to *Angels*.) Thanks also to *Wogan* (which benefited from the *EastEnders* slot on Mondays, Wednesdays and Fridays), the BBC experienced a remarkable upsurge in popularity.

EastEnders began, not surprisingly, with a dead body. The initial scene saw Den Watts kicking down the door of Reg Cox's flat. The first year featured the mixture of the tragic (baby Hassan Osman died in June) and the warmly human (Martin Fowler was born in July) that was to become its hallmark. Strangely, it was like a breath of fresh air.

EastEnders is frequently criticized for being 'depressing', which is not an inaccurate assessment. Yet this is also its most exciting characteristic. The air of inner-city neglect (the wonderfully realistic Elstree set) and family strife that permeates the programme at all levels shows that *EastEnders* is concerned, first and foremost, with drama. Each character's life has a fine vein of tragedy running through it: even a semi-comic, wholly likeable character like Nigel seemed doomed to lose his wife, adopted child and job in the space of a few short months. And one only has to think of Bill Treacher's moving performance as Arthur during his nervous breakdown in 1986 to realize that we witnessed one of the most genuinely dramatic sequences of television shown that year. Arthur had always defined himself in terms of providing for his family, and, when that was no longer possible, his life lost all meaning. Week after week the viewers watched his mental decline, a hunched figure in front of the television. Unable to find the money for his own daughter's wedding, he stole the Christmas Club money, but was too addled to do it properly. When Arthur retreated to his allotment, a nation followed him in sadness. Almost as moving was its effect on Bill Treacher, who

Starring: Anna Wing (Lou Beale) • Wendy Richard (Pauline Fowler) • Bill Treacher (Arthur Fowler) • Susan Tully (Michelle Fowler) • David Scarboro/Todd Carty (Mark Fowler) • Peter Dean (Pete Beale) • Gillian Taylforth (Kathy Beale) • Adam Woodyatt (Ian Beale) • Leslie Grantham (Den Watts) • Anita Dobson (Angie Watts) • Letitia Dean (Sharon Watts) • Gretchen Franklin (Ethel Skinner) • Leonard Fenton (Dr Legg) • John Altman (Nick Cotton) • Sandy Ratcliff (Sue Osman) • Nejdet Salih (Ali Osman) • Andrew Johnson (Saeed Jeffery) • Shreela Ghosh (Naima Jeffery) • Tom Watt (George 'Lofty' Holloway) • Linda Davidson (Mary Smith) • Oscar James (Tony Carpenter) • Paul J. Medford (Kelvin Carpenter) • Shirley Cheriton (Debbie Wilkins) • Ross Davidson (Andy O'Brien) • June Brown (Dot Cotton) • Nick Berry (Simon Wicks) • William Boyde (James Wilmott-Brown) • Michael Cashman (Colin Russell) • Pam St Clements (Pat Wicks/Butcher) • Christopher McHallem (Rod Norman) • Judith Jacob (Carmel Roberts) • Gary Hailes (Barry Clark) • Matilda Ziegler (Donna Ludlow) • Mike Reid (Frank Butcher) • Michelle Collins (Cindy Beale) • Sophie Lawrence (Diane Butcher) • Ross Kemp (Grant Mitchell) • Steve McFadden (Phil Mitchell) • Michael Melia (Eddie Royle) • Jacquetta May (Rachel Kominski) • Daniella Westbrook (Sam Butcher) • Edna Doré (Mo Butcher) • Sid Owen (Ricky Butcher) • Nicola Stapleton (Mandy Salter) • Sean Maguire (Aidan Maguire) • Elizabeth Power (Christine Hewitt) • Sue Dawson (Gill Fowler) • Paul Bradley (Nigel Bates) • Deepak Verma (Sanjay Kapoor) • Shobu Kapoor (Gita Kapoor) • Tommy Eytle (Jules Tavernier) • Michelle Gayle (Hattie Tavernier) • Steven Woodcock (Clyde Tavernier) • Nicola Duffett (Debbie Tyler/Bates) • Mark Monero (Steve Elliot) • Ian Reddington (Richard Cole) • Martine McCutcheon (Tiffany Raymond) • Patsy Palmer (Bianca Jackson) • Elizabeth Kelly (Nellie Ellis) • Lindsey Coulson (Carol Jackson) • Howard Anthony (Alan Jackson) • Sudha Bhuchar (Meena Mackenzie) • David Roper (Geoff Barnes) • Sophie Langham (Binnie Roberts) • Michelle Joseph (Della Alexander) • Lucy Speed (Natalie Price) • Dean Gaffney (Robbie Jackson) • Mona Hammond (Blossom Jackson) • Michael French (David Wicks) • Caroline Paterson (Ruth Aitken/Fowler) • Barbara Windsor (Peggy Mitchell) • Tony Caunter (Roy Evans) • Brian Croucher (Ted Hills)

played Arthur. He found it impossible to entirely leave Arthur behind: 'I once started crying while I was sitting at home in my armchair. I had to tell my wife that it wasn't me who was crying – it was Arthur.'

In one sense, of course, *EastEnders* is not true to life, any more than ***Grange Hill*** can be said to depict the average school, but it does try to assimilate and portray the common experiences and fears of many. This has made it controversial. When Angie tried to commit suicide in February 1986, the press reported with glee a number of 'copycat' cases that followed (as they did when a girl died after allegedly imitating Lofty's stag-night drink). And yet such criticism shows that *EastEnders* can scratch where people painfully itch. Charity and medical organizations can often reach and educate people on a wide variety of matters (teenage pregnancy, abortion, cancer, AIDS, etc.) far more effectively via an *EastEnders* plotline than through other means. Then Junior Health Minister, Edwina Currie, praised the show for its sensitive handling of Sue Osman's suspected breast cancer; Sir Donald Acheson, former Chief Medical Officer, claimed that it was no coincidence that, since Mark Fowler's HIV test, many more people had come forward for such testing.

Julia Smith specifically wanted *EastEnders* to deal with 'homosexuals, rape, unemployment, racial prejudice', and didn't want to 'fudge any issues except politics and swearing'. Both Jonathan Powell and Michael Grade used similar approaches to refute the other early criticism of *EastEnders*, that it was a concession to the lowest common denominator, allowing the BBC to get on with its 'real job' of producing quality television.

From the outset, Smith ruled the show with a rod of iron. The cast were not allowed to change the scripts, and had to ask for permission before being interviewed by the press. The character sketches that she and Holland had produced during a working holiday in Lanzarote would be rigorously adhered to, although some of the names changed before the characters reached the screen. Tracy (Michelle) would get pregnant; Jack Parker (Den) would be a 'Jack the Lad' character.

These early strands (Michelle's pregnancy and the strained marriage of Den and Angie) were by far the most engaging and compelling in the show, and the media quickly took hold of this. As interviews were rarely possible, the press had to resort to 'exclusives' concerning the private lives of the stars, or (almost invariably bogus) revelations of future storylines. Written by Holland and directed by Smith, the 1985 episode that revealed the identity of the father of Michelle's child was a classic of contemporary populist drama. The structure is superb, the three main 'suspects' (Tony Carpenter, Ali Osman and Den) seen leaving the Square after Michelle has arranged a secret meeting. The question that taxed a nation was finally answered when we glimpsed Den's poodle Roly being taken for a walk. The rest of the episode – uninterrupted dialogue between Michelle and Den – showed just how radical, and minimalist, a soap *EastEnders* can be.

True two-handers and one-scene episodes soon followed, including Den and Angie discussing their problems in 1986, Dot and Ethel 'remembering the war' the following year, Michelle revealing who Vicki's father was to Sharon in 1989, and Nick's bogus conversion to Christianity in 1990. In 1992, two episodes dealt with Kathy coming to terms with her rape by James Wilmott-Brown and the after-effects of Phil and Sharon sleeping together. In 1994 – after one of the best, most tortuously-extended threads of narrative in the programme's history, as a drunken Michelle and Sharon discussed the latter's adulterous fling with Phil – it was the turn of the Mitchell brothers in hospital. One-room drama doesn't come any better than this – and drama-as-social-commentary can rarely have equalled the harrowing power of the flashback episodes in 1990, detailing Diane Butcher's plight as a down-and-out.

If Sharon was transformed from sexpot wife to full-fledged tragedy queen – as Julie Burchill described the evolving Sharon-Phil-Grant love/hate-triangle – it was not

Christmas special
(22 Dec 88, 60 minutes)
Civvy Street

Written by Tony Holland
Directed and produced by Julia Smith
Starring: Gary Olsen (Albert Beale), Karen Meagher (Lou Beale), Alison Bettles (Ethel)

Nick Cotton, a 'lank-haired Satan on drugs'

dissimilar from the difficult 'evolution' of Michelle. Until her contrived departure to America in 1995, Michelle – never less than well-played by Susan Tully – was in many ways the lead character, struggling with a young child and a seemingly unquenchable desire for older men and unsuitable younger partners. She jilted Lofty at the altar in September 1986, which prompted Tully to call Tony Holland a murderer (it did seem rather like kicking a poor defenceless puppy), but actually Michelle had made the right decision. They were married in secret in November, and it was a disaster.

Michelle aborted Lofty's child without consulting him, saw Den just before his death, had an affair with a married man, sheltered Clyde when accused of the murder of Eddie Royle, and started studying for a degree. After a one-night stand and the kidnap of Vicki it seemed that Geoff, her tutor, could offer her some much-needed stability, but she felt unable to settle down – especially as it would involve moving to Scotland – and instead tried to instigate an affair with her boss at work. Thanks to her new qualification she was working for the housing department, but she came to realize that she was impotent to execute the wide-ranging social changes that she so deeply desired. A job opportunity in the States seemed to offer her the chance to both find herself away from Walford and engage in work amongst the poor. An involved discussion with Grant of all people led to her sleeping with him and, more to the point, becoming pregnant. But nothing could now stand in the way of Michelle's flight from the East End: not even Pauline's increasingly desperate attempts at emotional manipulation.

It is almost impossible to separate the problems of the Fowler clan from reality (just as Sandy Ratcliff's heroin addiction added a layer of tragic realism to the character of Sue Osman). Mark Fowler was originally played by David Scarboro (who, like Susan Tully, had first appeared in ***Grange Hill***), and his character was that of the sad rebel, starved of love, hanging out with the bad boys (especially Nick Cotton). Mark left home, but was tracked down to Southend by Arthur and Pauline. Scarboro himself had experience of leaving home, but it didn't stop there. The strain of being in *EastEnders* took its toll, and pushed the 20-year-old actor into a nervous breakdown. Continually hounded by the tabloid press, he eventually committed suicide at Beachy Head in April 1988.

The character of Mark had a slightly happier ending (at least until he learned that he was HIV positive). Todd Carty, the most famous young ***Grange Hill*** actor, took on the part, and has made it his own. Mark is now much more likeable; indeed, it wouldn't be too far from the truth to say that Tucker Jenkins lives on beyond ***Grange Hill*** and *Tucker's Luck*.

Angie and Den didn't have a particularly good time of it either (although they did give the makers of the programme an excuse to go to Venice to shoot their 'second honeymoon'). Anita Dobson sang on the first *EastEnders* single ('Anyone Can Fall in Love'), a dreadful version of the theme tune, which was followed by 'Every Loser Wins' by Nick Berry and 'Something Outta Nothing' by the Banned. Somehow, Berry got to number one; the Banned did not.

The Watts's marriage degenerated before our eyes. We sympathized with Angie, but Den was a thoroughly likeable bastard. The programme lost something when Grantham and Dobson finally left the show, although it did allow Den to get involved in some seriously shady goings-on. Den met a sticky end (off-screen, on the insistence of Jonathan Powell, Controller of BBC1), as did Andy O'Brien, the first of the yuppies to come to Albert Square. Ross Davidson dared to provoke the wrath of Julia Smith, and his character was knocked down whilst saving a child's life.

O'Brien's heroics were worlds apart from the evil deeds of Nick Cotton, Albert Square's proverbial bad penny. There was no one in the world he wouldn't try to rip off or abuse, even his mum, the daft pseudo-Christian bigot Dot. When he was in the show, Nick dominated it, a dark, lank-haired Satan on drugs. It came as no great surprise when he was accused of being Eddie Royle's murderer, although he escaped imprisonment.

A number of elements help differentiate *EastEnders* from the other on-going soaps. It positively encourages new writers and directors, much as ***Coronation Street*** did in the 60s, and, increasingly, as ***Emmerdale Farm*** once did, gives them a block of episodes to work on. In its ability to appeal to men and teenagers in a way that ***Coronation Street*** often found so difficult, it became the ubiquitous soap of the 80s, and despite the upheavals that come with the passing of time its popularity seems undiminished in the 90s. The unfolding revelation that David Wicks is Bianca's father, Bianca's on-again off-again relationship with Ricky (and the memorable departure of Natalie), and the reintroduction of Ricky's former-wife Sam, seem guaranteed to enthral viewers of all ages for some time to come. And if we were in any doubt that the Mitchells are a cuddlier version of the Krays, 1994's introduction of Barbara Windsor as their mum, Peggy, completed the picture. The critics still tend to be somewhat condescending about the programme, Mark Lawson of *The Independent* criticizing Grant Mitchell for oscillating between sinister quasi-thug and charming help-grannies-across-the-street normal bloke, implying that characters in soap operas should be starkly-defined black and white, not grey and complex as in 'proper drama'.

EastEnders is also quite happy to leave the East End behind, most notably during Wicksy and Cindy's troublesome holiday in Devon in 1990 and the farcical Spanish shenanigans during the summer of '95. Its treatment of gay characters has integrity (witness what has been called 'television's most controversial kiss'), although for a while black actors had a habit of leaving the show, accusing the BBC of racism.

If its portrayal of ethnic minorities is sometimes suspect (although at least it tries), the other major accusation that can be levelled at *EastEnders* is that its humour contrasts too markedly with the grave nature of the rest of the programme. Sometimes it works – as in Arthur's appearance on the quiz show *Cat and Mouse* – but often it threatens to upset the delicate balance that characterizes the programme's tone. One thinks particularly of the ridiculously malaproprian Ethel Skinner, with her pug 'Little Willy'. Compared to the dank goings on around her, it is as if Mrs Slocombe or a *Carry On* film extra has wandered on to the set.

Maybe, though, even *EastEnders* can only handle so much doom and gloom at one time.

Casualty

- **BBC Television** (BBC1) ◆ Colour
- **176 episodes** (c. 50 minutes) ◆ 1986-96
- **Creators:** Jeremy Brock, Paul Unwin
- **Writers include:** Wally K. Daly, Ray Brennan, Lise Mayer, David Ashton, Ginnie Hole, Bill Gallagher, Sam Snape, Barry Purchese, Ben Aaronovitch, Ian Briggs, Robin Mukherjee, Rona Munro, Christopher Penfold, Stephen Wyatt, Barbara Machin, Helen Greaves, Andrew Holden, Lisa Evans, Nick McCarty, Tony McHale
- **Directors include:** Frank W. Smith, Antonia Bird, Renny Rye, Jan Sargeant, Michael Brayshaw, Alan Wareing, Sharon Miller, Christopher Menaul, Michael Owen Morris, Andrew Morgan, Steve Goldie, Jim Hill, Richard Bramall, Matthew Evans, David Innes Edwards, Chris Clough, Diana Patrick
- **Producers:** Geraint Morris, Peter Norris, Michael Ferguson, Corinne Hollingworth

From *Emergency – Ward 10* to *Angels*, the hospital drama had proved itself to be an effective and popular soap sub-genre. In 1986, *Casualty* kicked some politics into its inert form, and a new BBC saviour was created. By 1991, when the BBC was scrabbling for a new twice-weekly soap, and buffeted by endless bad news, critics were united in pointing to *Casualty* as a hope for the corporation, its audience of 15 million regularly embarrassing the opposition. Channel 4 head, Michael Grade (who had commissioned the show during his BBC days), was vocal in calling for it to be given an on-going 'soap' slot: an interesting reminder of the show's importance.

Only now as *Casualty* approaches its tenth birthday does it begin to show signs of its age: a victim, perhaps, of its own success, and the cowardice of the BBC in seeking to dilute the strength and passion of the original concept. They didn't, in the end, turn it into an on-going soap – which would have killed the programme overnight – but seem to have done the next best thing.

Back at the beginning, though, *Casualty* was rooted in the realities of hospital life, the initial outline created by Jeremy Brock and Paul Unwin, two former BBC script editors who had witnessed at first hand the 'comedy and heroics' of everyday life in the NHS. Their series would be based around the A&E department 'because that's when a city chucks up its worst oddities. And we wanted to deal as grittily as possible with reality because, in the past, hospital series have been

First season
(6 Sep–27 Dec 86)
1 Gas
2 Hide and Seek
3 Runners
4 Jump Start
5 Blood Brothers
6 High Noon
7 Professionals
8 Crazies
9 Moonlight Becomes You...
10 Teeny Poppers
11 Drunk
12 Quiet
13 No Future
14 Survival
15 Closure

Second season
(12 Sep–19 Dec 87)
16 A Little Lobbying
17 A Drop of the Hard Stuff
18 Shades of Love
19 Cry for Help
20 Anaconda
21 Lifelines
22 The Raid
23 Cross Fingers
24 Seeking Heat
25 Rock-a-Bye Baby
26 Hooked
27 Fun Night
28 'Peace, Brother'
29 Burning Cases
30 These Things Happen

Third season
(9 Sep–4 Nov 88)
31 Welcome to Casualty
32 Desperate Odds
33 Drake's Drum
34 Absolution
35 Burn Out
36 A Quiet Night
37 A Wing and a Prayer
38 Living Memories
39 Inferno
40 Caring

Fourth season
(8 Sep–1 Dec 89)
41 Chain Reaction
42 Accidents Happen
43 A Grand in the Hand
44 Day Off
45 Vital Spark
46 Charity
47 Victim of Circumstances
48 Deluge
49 Union
50 Taking Stock
51 Banking for Beginners
52 Hanging On

Fifth season
(7 Sep–7 Dec 90)
53 Penalty
54 Results
55 Close to Home
56 Street Life
57 Hiding Place
58 Salvation
59 Say it with Flowers
60 Love's a Pain
61 A Will to Die
62 Big Boys Don't Cry
63 Remembrance
64 All's Fair
65 A Reasonable Man

Starring: Derek Thompson (Charlie Fairhead) • Catherine Shipton (Lisa Duffin) • Brenda Fricker (Megan Roach) • Bernard Gallagher (Ewart Plimmer) • Christopher Rozycki (Kuba Trzcinski) • George Harris (Clive King) • Debbie Roza (Susie Mercier) • Robert Pugh (Andrew Ponting) • Julia Watson (Barbara 'Baz' Samuels/Hayes) • Maureen O'Brien (Elizabeth Straker) • Helena Little (Mary Tomlinson) • Lisa Bowerman (Sandra Mute) • Nigel Anthony (Ted Roach) • Karen O'Malley (Katie Hardie) • Ella Wilder (Shirley Franklin) • Eddie Nestor (Cyril James) • Paul Lacoux (David Rowe) • Susan Franklyn (Valerie Sinclair) • Carol Leader (Sadie Tomkins) • Geoffrey Leesley (Keith Cotterill) • Tam Hoskyns (Lucy Perry) • Vivienne McKone (Julie Stevens) • Belinda Davison (Alex Spencer) • Robson Green (Jimmy Powell) • William Gaminara (Andrew Bower) • Mamta Kaash (Beth Ramanee) • Nigel Le Vailant (Julian Chapman) • Eamon Boland (Tony Walker) • Patrick Robinson (Martin Ashford) • Maggie McCarthy (Helen Green) • Adie Allen (Kelly Liddle) • Anne Kristen (Norma Sullivan) • Maria Friedman (Patricia Baynes) • Ian Bleasdale (Josh Griffiths) • Caroline Webster (Jane Scott) • Jason Riddlington (Rob Khalefa) • Joanna Foster (Kate Miller) • Emma Bird (Maxine Price) • Maureen Beattie (Sandra Nicholl) • Robert Daws (Simon Eastman) • Clive Mantle (Mike Barrett) • Christopher Guard (Ken Hodges) • Doña Croll (Adele Beckford) • Suzanna Hamilton (Karen Goodliffe) • Samantha Edmonds (Helen Chatsworth) • David Ryall (Tom Harley) • Tara Moran (Mary Skillett) • Naoko Mori (Mie Nishi-Kaewa) • Steven O'Donnell (Frankie Drummer) • Jane Gurnett (Rachel Longworth) • Sorcha Cusack (Kate Wilson) • Lisa Coleman (Jude Kocarnik) • Jason Merrells (Matt Hawley) • Joan Oliver (Eddie Gordon) • Steven Brand (Adam Cook) • Sue Devaney (Liz Harker) • Lizzy McInnerny (Laura Milburn) • Craig Kelly (Daniel Perryman) • Robert Duncan (Peter Hayes)

too smooth and silky.' The city in question is the fictional Holby, although it is often obvious that this is Bristol (with occasional accents to match).

Casualty was always going to be a very different beast from *Angels*, which gained its viewers through its atmosphere of cosy familiarity and its traditional soap conventions. In *Casualty* the private lives of the staff were (realistically, given the pressure of the work) sidelined by those of the A&E patients. Indeed, *Casualty's* mixture of often funny, everyday incidents and 'big themes' mirrors American series such as *St Elsewhere*, where the major plot is always diluted by a funnier, warmer sub-plot. In *Casualty* it is not unusual for lives to be saved whilst an escaped pet snake is pursued or some form of bizarre family dispute is resolved.

The impressive trio of Charlie, Megan and Duffy was crafted with such love that the end result was characters that other soaps would have killed for. Charlie, the charge nurse, is boss of the night shift in all but title: motivated and a superb manager of people, with the sort of dry humour that is an asset when death and injury

Sixth season
(6 Sep–13 Dec 91)
66 Humpty Dumpty
67 Judgement Day
68 Dangerous Games
69 Hide and Seek
70 Joy Ride
71 Something to Hide
72 Beggars can't be Choosers
73 Living in Hope
74 Making the Break
75 Sins of Omission
76 The Last Word
77 Pressure! What Pressure?
78 Facing Up
79 Allegiance
80 Cascade

Seventh season
(12 Sep 92–27 Feb 93)
81 Rates of Exchange
82 Cry Wolf
83 Body Politic
84 Will You Still Love Me?
85 Cherish
86 Profit and Loss
87 One Step Forward
88 Body and Soul
89 Tender Loving Care
90 Money Talks
91 Making Waves
92 If it isn't Hurting ...
93 Act of Faith
94 Point of Principle
95 Silent Night
96 The Ties That Bind
97 Life in the Fast Lane
98 Everybody Needs Something
99 Getting Involved
100 Dividing Loyalties
101 Family Matters
102 Child's Play
103 No Cause for Concern
104 Boiling Point

Eighth season
(18 Sep 93–26 Feb 94)
105 Cat in Hell
106 Riders on the Storm
107 The Final Word
108 No Place to Hide
109 Sunday, Bloody Sunday
110 Good Friends
111 Kill or Cure
112 Born Loser
113 High Roller
114 Deceptions
115 Give Us This Day
116 Wild Card
117 The Good Life
118 Out to Lunch
119 Comfort and Joy
120 Family Ties
121 United We Fall
122 Tippers
123 Value for Money
124 Care in the Community
125 Signed, Sealed, Delivered
126 Relations
127 Grand Rational
128 Hidden Agendas

[Episode 37 was not shown in the first run of the third season due to the death of the guest star Roy Kinnear. It was eventually transmitted (as part of a repeat season) on 19 Aug 89. Episode 80 was postponed from its intended 20 Dec 91 transmission date due to the anniversary of the Lockerbie disaster, and was eventually screened on 27 Feb 92.]

are an everyday occurrence. Derek Thompson (previously seen as an IRA terrorist in Channel 4's *The Price*) created a character who has been described as television's first 'new man'. Charlie, the only original cast member still in the show, has been through hell and back over the past ten years: alcoholism, a breakdown, a couple of love affairs, a platonic relationship with a gay nurse, and even a brief flirtation with the administration of a management system that he despises.

Megan was the mother-figure, her shoulder being the first stop for any worried person, but her own marriage to Ted, a taxi driver, was always under stress. During one memorable episode, she broke down, belittling her 'Mrs Reliable, Mother-soddin'-Earth' image. No one on this side of the Atlantic was surprised at Brenda Fricker's deserved Oscar for her performance in *My Left Foot*.

Duffy, the senior nurse, was the opposite of Megan. Although more than capable professionally, she never exhibited qualms about expressing feelings openly. Her private life, too, was tinted with tragedy and unhappiness as she attempted to juggle the pressures of work and single parenthood.

The other major early figure was Ewart Plimmer, the former surgeon who managed the night shift. His character and his conflicts with authority were crucial to the programme's early notoriety, as he plunged himself headlong into negotiations with the NHS hierarchy in an attempt to avert cutbacks in staff and finance. Edwina Currie called *Casualty* left-wing propaganda, claiming that no real A&E department was that busy; a Conservative Central Office spokesman said that the programme looked like 'a Labour Party meeting'. *Casualty* was discussed in the House of Commons, but many viewers recognized the true face of the NHS.

Ewart was loyal, dedicated to his staff, and well-loved, and, when he collapsed at the end of an episode, millions of viewers were genuinely shocked by his sudden, realistic heart attack. The way this scene was handled – as in real life, unannounced, unheralded – showed *Casualty's* commitment to drama, unencumbered by the expectations of the audience. Plimmer died, despite the character's popularity on both sides of the screen, and the subsequent scenes of the staff struggling with their own grief and yet knuckling down to the job at hand were a poignant joy to behold.

Casualty has never treated death lightly. When it comes, it is terrible and frightening and often lonely, and its effects on the staff run deep. In 1991, Peggy Mount starred as a popular and seemingly reasonably well patient who died without warning. It was a while before the body was discovered: Ash frantically and angrily tried to do something, but it was much too late, and he carried a sense of personal failure with him for some time afterwards.

Mount's appearance reminds us that there is always comedy to balance the pathos, often involving such notable guest stars as Roy Kinnear (his final BBC performance) and Jimmy Jewell. The staff themselves, however, provided the majority of the humour, ranging from the eccentric, romantic Polish hospital porter Kuba in the early seasons, to his future replacement, the Geordie Jimmy. Although gleefully displaying a photograph of the young Martin Ash

Ninth season
(17 Sep 94–25 Mar 95)
129 Blood's Thicker
130 First Impressions
131 Keeping it in the Family
132 Chasing the Dragon
133 Love and Affection
134 Negative Equity
135 A Breed Apart
136 In the Black
137 Crossing the Line
138 Only the Lonely
139 The Facts of Life
140 Under the Weather
141 Talking Turkey
142 End of the Road
143 Learning Curve
144 Stitching the Surface
145 Heartbreak Hotel
146 Trials and Tribulations
147 Out of Time
148 Branded
149 Exiles
150 Nobody's Perfect
151 Not Waving but Drowning
152 Duty of Care

Tenth seson
(16 Sep 95–24 Feb 96)
153 Family Values
154 Money for Nothing
155 Sacrifice
156 Outside Bulawayo
157 Halfway House
158 Compensation
159 Turning Point
160 Battling On
161 Hit and Run
162 When All Else Fails
163 Release
164 Bringing It All Back Home
165 All is Fair
166 Shame the Devil
167 Lost Boys
168 Castles in the Air
169 We Shall Overcome
170 Land of Hope
171 For Your Own Good
172 Asking for Miracles
173 Subject to Contract
174 Cheatin' Hearts
175 That Way Lies Ruin
176 Night Moves

The only known photograph of Charlie smiling

and larking about with 'problem' nurse Kelly, Jimmy's function in the series was much more than a mere comic feed. In one episode, he befriended a down-and-out who was impersonating a porter from a base in the cellars, and ended up taking him home. His relationship with Kelly developed and strengthened as the newly-qualified nurse became more and more unhappy with her job and Duffy's constant criticisms. It all culminated with a lingering shot over her flat where she had already consumed a drink and drugs cocktail: another episode to end in death.

Kelly's suicide was well-signposted, but still shocking,

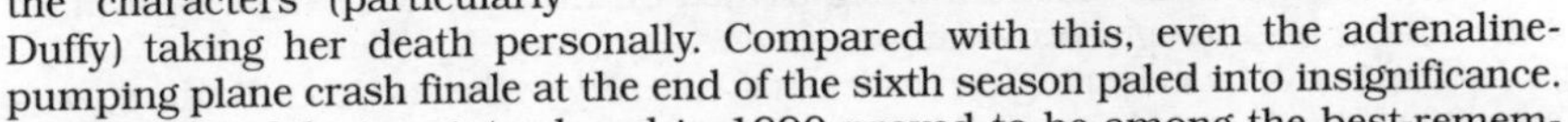

the characters (particularly Duffy) taking her death personally. Compared with this, even the adrenaline-pumping plane crash finale at the end of the sixth season paled into insignificance.

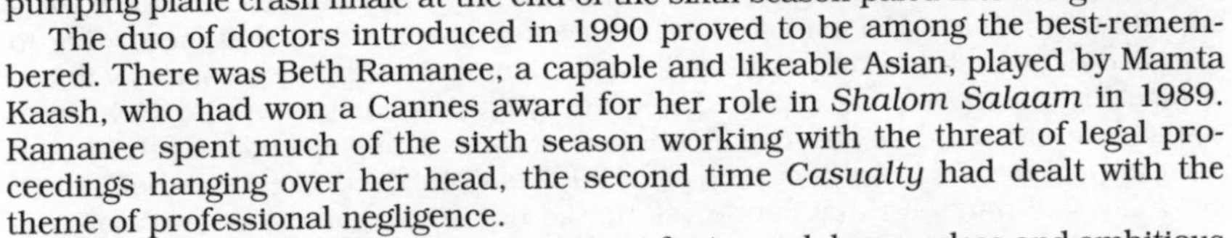

The duo of doctors introduced in 1990 proved to be among the best-remembered. There was Beth Ramanee, a capable and likeable Asian, played by Mamta Kaash, who had won a Cannes award for her role in *Shalom Salaam* in 1989. Ramanee spent much of the sixth season working with the threat of legal proceedings hanging over her head, the second time *Casualty* had dealt with the theme of professional negligence.

Nigel Le Vailant's Julian Chapman was at first a cool, humourless and ambitious doctor, but as time progressed even he began to thaw. Chapman's unpopularity with the staff perhaps began to wane when he spent the majority of one episode in combat gear, much to Jimmy's glee. Le Vailant commented that 'I understand Chapman because I had the same upbringing as he did.' His popularity with viewers, however, was never in doubt: a few years later the *Radio Times* said 'women the length and breadth of Britain would have happily undergone needless triple bypass surgery if the post-operative treatment included a quick probe with the business end of Dr Chapman's stethoscope'. Clive Mantle's introduction as cuddly Mike Barratt helped to reassure those traumatized by Julian's departure.

Political and medical criticism of *Casualty* began to decrease in the 1990s, although then-producer Geraint Morris argued that 'public and political attitudes have now caught up with us. The ward closures, cutbacks and lack of staff, funds and facilities that we reflected at first have now become accepted as reality by politicians and viewers alike.' Indeed, it is interesting to note that while the nursing profession used to be critical of *Casualty*, a Royal College of Nursing report in 1991 stated that *Casualty* is the only radio or television programme to portray nurses as being more than just 'exploited angels'.

One only has to glance at the range of themes that *Casualty* has covered to realize its radical heritage: domestic violence, a religious sect's objections to treatment, anorexia and bulimia, paedophilia, female circumcision and child prostitution. One episode dealt with a terrorist bomb blast, whilst another showed a deranged murderer roaming freely around the hospital. A nurse's boyfriend had AIDS, and the 1990 season dealt unflinchingly with incest. The important thing is not just that *Casualty* features such areas and problems, but that it features them well, with understanding and commitment.

It escaped few people's notice that Alan Yentob's first act on becoming Controller of the BBC was to schedule the final episode of the epic-length seventh season into a later slot. Whether this was due to real concern at the episode's graphic content or to the presence of ***Inspector Morse*** in the earlier slot on ITV, the result was the same: the show's biggest-ever audience. 'Boiling Point' was a masterpiece of topicality, featuring vigilantes, a petrol bomb attack against an ambulance, and the destruction of the entire A&E department by fire. The episode brought the force of meaningless, out-of-control violence into the living room at the exact moment when people were beginning to question what the amoral 80s had done to the British psyche. The resulting explosion of long-buried tension was both touching and true to life.

The public hated it. The *Radio Times* letters page came out at 2:1 against the episode, and Alan Yentob was forced to declare 'we got it wrong'. Interviewed prior to the launch of the next season, new producer Michael Ferguson stated that 'the programme shouldn't be about special effects, stunts and big scenarios. It should be personal' – despite the fact that the first episode of the eighth season involved a very messy train crash.

Such a timid response didn't immediately spell the end of *Casualty* as engaging drama, but Ferguson's season was perhaps the last to cling to the vision that made the programme so powerful back in 1986 at the start. Best remembered for the departure of Duffy, the episodes also saw the staff wrestling with the hospital's new status as a trust, contending with toxic waste and treating feuding cricketers. Topical issues such as smokers being treated on the NHS were dealt with in an entertaining but thought-provoking manner.

In 1994, Corinne Hollingworth, fresh from *Eldorado* and ***EastEnders***, was appointed producer. Her pedigree in 'traditional' soaps meant that, according to the *Radio Times*, 'The campaigning, left-wing elements of previous series will not appear in this series [sic], replaced instead by an emphasis on social and moral issues. And action.' The absence of 'politics' in the ensuing episodes was naive, at least in part because health care in the 1990s is politicized like never before. It's not a layer of narrative that can be 'skimmed off' and regarded as optional, and rarely had *Casualty* treated it as such. The 'social and moral issues' were still there (most notably the racist attack against Ash), but they were devoid of any context and marginalized by the increasing concentration on the relationships of the main characters. We had the return of an old flame (Baz), straight out of 'traditional' soap operas, and the seemingly desperate reintroduction of an 'Irish mother figure' in the form of Kate Wilson. *Casualty* had always dealt with the private lives of its lead characters, and the series had to evolve to remain popular in the face of *Medics*, *Chicago Hope*, *Peak Practice*, *E.R.* and (especially) the stunning polemic *Cardiac Arrest*. However, changing from a gripping on-going drama to a 24-week-per-year soap opera wasn't the way to do it.

Still, given that Conservative Party chairman Dr Brian Mawhinney tried to ban an episode in 1995, perhaps not all is lost.

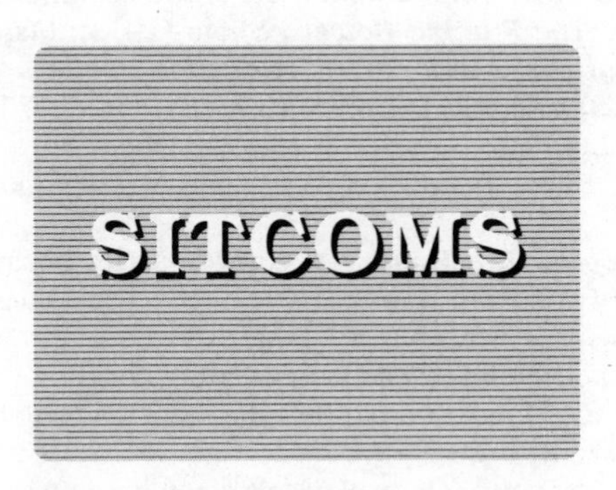

Sitcom is normally considered to be television's most reactionary genre: perversely, it is also one of TV's most popular dramatic styles, and certainly its most densely-populated.

At times the sitcom seems little more than a half-hour slab of padding, something to fit in between the more serious soaps or dramatic serials, presenting a changeless world of laugh-tracks, one-liners and mother-in-laws (often, all three at once). The British sitcom began in the 50s with *Family Affairs*, detailing the trials and tribulations of a middle-class family (the Conovers) who lived in Northwood. It had a live half-hour slot on Saturday nights, and was scripted by Eric Maschwitz. This seems to suggest that the sitcom has been conservative and middle class from the outset, but the genre is, in theory, no more constrained than any other. What has tended to happen is that a popular sitcom success will automatically produce imitation and thus, logically, stagnation.

During the 1950s the BBC imposed 'an absolute ban' on all 'jokes about lavatories, effeminacy in men ... suggestive references to honeymoon couples, chambermaids ... animal habits (e.g. rabbits), lodgers and commercial travellers', which is perhaps why situation comedies of the era found themselves so short of material. However, once these draconian limits had been broken (largely by early ITV sitcoms like ***The Army Game***), the genre became popular, and one that the BBC has dominated from the 60s to date.

The main reason for the BBC's eventual domination of the sitcom is a simple one: BBC programmes designed to fill half-hour slots are normally just short of 30 minutes in length, whereas on independent television adverts can cut the running time by three minutes. This often means that much characterization and subtlety is lost in ITV series. This is not to suggest that every BBC sitcom has been a superbly-executed masterpiece, or that there have been no great ITV sitcoms, but in general terms it does mean that most of those series that stay the distance and improve with age tend to come from the BBC.

In addition, the BBC's confidence was such that it made some brave decisions. When ***Steptoe and Son*** became a phenomenon in the early 60s the BBC saw a trend, and followed the Galton and Simpson example of allowing particular writers the freedom to create a series of pilot episodes. A process of 'natural selection' then determined which were relegated to the backwaters of history and which were turned into full series. *Comedy Playhouse*, which began in 1961, provided a launching pad for many influential series, including ***Till Death Us Do***

Part, The Liver Birds, Up Pompeii! and ***Last of the Summer Wine***. In addition there were gems like *The Frankie Howerd Show* (1963), Marty Feldman's *The Walrus and the Carpenter* (1965), *All Gas and Gaiters* and *Beggar My Neighbour* (both 1968), and Jilly Cooper's *It's Awfully Bad for Your Eyes Darling* (1971, with Joanna Lumley). However, it also launched *Terry and June* (which began life as *Happy Ever After* in 1974), so perhaps we shouldn't laud it too much.

If we class ***Hancock's Half Hour*** as a comedy series separate from sitcom, then the first great BBC sitcom was *Sykes*, which began in 1960. Starring Eric Sykes with Hattie Jacques as his sister, Richard Wattis as Mr Brown and Deryck Guyler as Corky the policeman, it was firmly set in suburbia, but the writing and performances were exceptional. It took the success of working-class sitcoms (***Till Death Us Do Part*** and ***The Likely Lads***) to remind the BBC that not all of its audience shared the taste and interests of television executives.

Not surprisingly, the mid-60s saw several archly bland and reactionary examples of what would later become know as the middle-class 'middle-everything' sitcom. Richard Waring's *Marriage Lines* was the progenitor of the sub-species. It featured Richard Briers and Prunella Scales as the newly-wed 'Darling, I'm home'-type couple, the Starlings. *The Good Life*, *Bless This House* (even Sid James wasn't immune), *Keep it in the Family*, *My Good Woman*, *Father Dear Father*, *Terry and June* and (raising the class structure a notch) *To the Manor Born* would all draw upon this style in later years. Waring continued the trend with *Not in Front of the Children*, *...And Mother Makes Three* and *...And Mother Makes Five*, starring Wendy Craig. Most of these series were 'one-joke' comedies, and often the joke itself wasn't very good: Johnny Mortimer and Brian Cooke's *Father Dear Father*, for example, had Patrick Cargill spending most of his time trying to keep his 'innocent' daughters (played by Ann Holloway and Natasha Pyne) away from boys whilst, in reality, they were a pair of 'ravers'.

Marriage Lines showed what could be achieved by putting blandness and safety before imagination. However, once the BBC had scored with ***Till Death Us Do Part***, and opened up a whole debate on what was and wasn't funny within a sitcom, ITV responded with venom. Johnny Speight's LWT series *Curry and Chips* had Eric Sykes as the foreman of a factory called Lillicrap Ltd, and featured Spike Milligan blacked-up as 'Paki'. It was offensively racist, although, somewhat inevitably, it drew more complaints about its language, a fate that also befell Jack Rosenthal's *The Dustbinmen*. The BBC, with the best writers in the field at its disposal (Galton and Simpson, Clement and La Frenais, Croft and Perry), could even afford to play with conventions and often created a new style out of this. Ronald Wolfe and Ronald Chesney's *The Rag Trade* seemed, initially, to be a move down market, but proved to be hugely popular during the 60s, and made its stars (Peter Jones, Miriam Karlin, Sheila Hancock and Barbara Windsor) into household names. The writers went on to *Meet the Wife* (a Thora Hird vehicle which is immortalized on the Beatles' *Sgt Pepper* album) and *The Bed-Sit Girl* before resurrecting *The Rag Trade* in a Victorian sweatshop setting for *Wild Wild Women*. When they moved to LWT in 1969 their major creation for ITV was *On the Buses*, independent TV's longest running and most self-consciously unfunny series.

If Reg Varney, Bob Grant, Stephen Lewis and their bus-driving chums resent this description, they can at least point to impressive ratings and foreign sales that still amaze. However, other ITV companies took similar routes and ended up with gross disasters on their hands. *Men of Affairs*, *Send in the Girls*, *Our House is a Nice House*, *The Many Wives of Patrick*, *That's My Boy*, *Bachelor Father*,

Me and My Girl – the names give away the plots as easily as any *TV Times* description. Most were about as funny as an afternoon at the dentist.

Yorkshire's *Queenie's Castle*, written by Keith Waterhouse and Willis Hall and starring Diana Dors, at least broke a few sexist moulds amid its depiction of a fire-breathing-dragon and her three sons. The company continued to try hard and finally came up with ***Rising Damp***, in which Eric Chappell managed to write a series that was good enough to have worked on the BBC. Chappell's other series, *The Squirrels*, *Only When I Laugh* and *Fiddlers Three*, were intermittently rewarding. Alan Plater's *Oh No! It's Selwyn Froggitt*, a kind of *Billy Liar* for nutters, is also fondly remembered. Granada failed miserably with most of its sitcoms, until Jack Rosenthal provided a spark of originality with *The Lovers*. ABC's *Never Mind the Quality, Feel the Width* featured an interesting premise of a culture clash between a Jewish tailor and his Irish partner (John Bluthal and Joe Lynch), but it ended up a ham-fisted mess. Writers Vince Powell and Harry Driver (who had previously written the legendary Harry Worth vehicle *Here's Harry*) went on to *Bless This House* and the disturbing *Love Thy Neighbour*, in which Jack Smethurst's racist Eddie Booth has to 'put up with' 'nig-nog' neighbour Rudolph Walker. It takes some believing that, even in the 70s, a TV executive somewhere actually agreed to this: even more shocking is the fact that the series was very popular and successful. Granada's *Yanks Go Home* had little in its favour apart from being just about the only thing other than *The Champions* to star Stuart Damon.

LWT had their share of nearly-great sitcoms. Humphrey Barclay's *Doctor in the House* had Cleese, Chapman, Oddie and Garden writing for it, and an impressive cast headed by Robin Nedwell, Geoffrey Davies, Barry Evans and George Layton. It ran for several years under a variety of different guises and even returned to the vastly different TV landscape of the 90s, as *Doctors in Charge*, proving that a good sitcom can, if handled with care, survive changes to the climate in which it was conceived. *Please Sir!*, the first John Esmonde and Bob Larbey series, was similarly long-lasting (most of the cast were close to their 30s by the time they left Fenn Street school and moved off to the unimpressive *Fenn Street Gang*). John Alderton's stuttering teacher was theoretically the star, but most viewers preferred Duffy, Dennis and (especially) Frankie Abbott.

Man About the House was curiously impressive in small doses too, thrusting Richard O'Sullivan into Paula Wilcox and Sally Thomsett's rented flat above dodgy landlords Yootha Joyce and Brian Murphy. Its spin-offs were *George and Mildred* and *Robin's Nest* and, when seen today, these series have a lot to say about sex (mostly about how frustrated O'Sullivan's Robin Tripp was in not getting any).

Newtonian logic of equal and opposite reactions can be easily observed in the world of sitcom. *Are You Being Served?*, Croft and Lloyd's ultimate presentation of innuendo-driven TV, was as nothing compared to *The Bottle Boys*, starring Robin Asquith as an amorous milkman. When *It Ain't Half Hot Mum* proved to be almost as popular (if not half as subtle) as ***Dad's Army***, ITV responded with *Get Some In* which, for once, proved that imitation is the sincerest form of flattery. Apart from giving Robert Lindsay his first starring role, the series also included, in Tony Selby's brutal corporal ('My name is Marsh – B.A.S.T.A.R.D., Marsh'), a classic comic creation. ITV notched up further successes with ***Shelley,*** *A Sharp Intake of Breath* and *Chance in a Million*.

The Good Life saw a return to suburbia, although at least Esmonde and Larbey had the sense to subvert the norm, as they would with the charming *Ever Decreasing Circles* and *A Fine Romance* in the 80s. *The Good Life* explored the

Craftily-subversive class-war message or everyday sitcom tosh? Margo, Tom, Jerry and Barbara from *The Good Life*

'alternative lifestyle' concept, very much in vogue, with safe middle-class couple Tom and Barbara Good (Richard Briers and Felicity Kendal) attempting to become self-sufficient, much to the chagrin of their pompous neighbours Margo and Jerry Leadbeater (Penelope Keith and Paul Eddington). Although its appeal might seem puzzling now, few can argue with its past popularity, its longevity perhaps best explained by gentle but occasionally insightful debunking of stereotypes. Its main ITV rival, *Keep it in the Family* (with Robert Gillespie and Pauline Yates), wasn't even that daring, and was about a tenth as funny.

The BBC took an alternative, but equally-popular direction, with *Some Mothers Do 'Ave 'Em*, the chaotic slapstick vehicle for the talents of Michael Crawford. Frank Spencer – complete with long mac and beret, or pyjamas and tasteless tanktop – delighted viewers with his child-like innocence and his unique ability to cause havoc. His relationship with long-suffering wife Betty (Michele Dotrice) gave the series a deep comic pathos, and the embarrassed eloquence of a mere shoulder twitch proved to be as hilarious as the wholesale destruction that he caused. Crawford did his own stunts, most famously running from a collapsing chimney stack, contending with traffic on roller skates, and hanging on to the rear bumper of his car while dangling over the edge of a cliff. Although his dialogue was ostensibly written by Raymond Allen, Crawford was a notorious ad libber (Allen once said to Crawford 'It was nice of you to use some of my words'), and he devised the storylines for the show's third season in 1978. Few will readily forget the sight of Frank dangling upside down over his neighbour's wife in bed, politely exclaiming in his mock-posh voice 'Good evening. I am not a peeping Thomas!'

In all sorts of ways since the mid-70s the sitcom has been coming to terms with its limitations. John Sullivan, once abused by critics for parodying them in ***Citizen Smith***, created three of the most important sitcoms of the 80s in ***Only Fools and Horses***, *Just Good Friends* and *Dear John*. *Just Good Friends* evolved out of Sullivan's awareness that his comedy lacked good, strong female roles (he called the female characters of ***Citizen Smith*** 'men in dresses'). Starring Paul Nicholas and Jan Francis, it was inspired by an item he read in the problem page in one of his wife's magazines. 'There was a letter from this woman who was in the same situation as Penny in *Just Good Friends* – five years after having been jilted, she'd come face to face with the sod who'd lost his bottle at the church steps. And she'd found that there was still something about him she liked ...'

By this time, Roy Clarke had already established himself as an elder statesman of sitcom, most obviously with ***Last of the Summer Wine***. He also wrote *Pygmalion Smith*, which starred Leonard Rossiter, for *Comedy Playhouse*, *Potter* (1979, with Arthur Lowe and, later, Robin Bailey), *The Clairvoyant* (1986, with Roy Kinnear), and the Police romp *Rosie* (1975–81, originally called *The Growing Pains of PC Penrose*), which saw Clarke writing from experience, as he was once a copper himself. *The Magnificent Evans* (1984), which starred Ronnie Barker, was, like *Pygmalion Smith*, concerned with the exploits of a photographer, although it was not to be Barker and Clarke's most satisfactory collaboration. This was *Open All Hours*, which Clarke wrote specifically for Barker. Like ***Porridge***, the pilot came as part of 1973's Ronnie Barker vehicle *Seven of One*. The first season did not begin until 1976 (on BBC2), and was not followed by a second until 1981. Despite this, Barker's splendid portrayal of the stuttering, penny-pinching shopkeeper, Arkwright, won great public acclaim, as he dominated poor Gr-Gr-Granville (David Jason) and pursued the buxom nurse Gladys Emmanuel (Lynda Baron). Were it not for Barker's retirement, *Open All Hours* would doubtless still be going today.

Clarke's more recent work has ranged from the remarkably modern *Pulaski*, *The Sharp End* and *Ain't Misbehavin'* to the vastly over-rated *Keeping Up Appearances*.

Most of the genre's other great writers continued to work successfully, although Carla Lane's standards have varied greatly over the years. Lane's work has become increasingly influenced by the conventions of the soap and the romantic drama. This would be fine if it weren't for the fact that, as former BBC producer Paul Jackson has pointed out, whole episodes of *Bread* seemed to go by without there being any jokes.

Much as before, in the 80s and 90s unusual formats – the Roman/Briton conflict of *Chelmsford 123*, the absurd adventures of the night-time security guards in *Nightingales* – have rubbed shoulders with comedies that merely disappoint (the unsatisfying girls-together antics of *Birds of a Feather*). There has been an emphasis on age – ***One Foot in the Grave***, *Waiting for God* and the engaging middle-aged romance of *As Time Goes By* – and on impossible dreams of youth (***Absolutely Fabulous***). If anything, the state of sitcom has rarely been healthier: it's easy to forget *Watching*, *Comrade Dad*, *Grace and Favour*, *You Rang M'Lord*, *So Haunt Me* and *All Night Long* when there are sitcoms of the quality of *2point4 Children*, *The Brittas Empire*, *Men Behaving Badly*, and *Chef!* What is interesting is how these 90s BBC sitcoms have such clear antecedents. Andrew Marshall's *2point4 Children* began in 1991 as a straight take on ***Butterflies***, with its mysterious leather-jacketed stranger promising some sort of extra-marital fling. Later seasons wisely concentrated on Bill and Ben Porter (Belinda Lang and Gary Olsen) and the children (played by Clare Woodgate/Clare Buckfield and John Pickard), balancing family drama with a sequence of surreal incidents not out of place in David Porter's beloved *X-Files*. And any show that mixes escaped cobras, *The Blues Brothers* (US 90) and dough used to simulate the effects of a Wonderbra can't be all bad.

1991 also saw the premiere of Richard Fegen and Andrew Norris's *The Brittas Empire*, starring Chris Barrie as the ubiquitous Gordon Brittas. Brittas is the manager of a sports centre (full marks for at least coming up with a different situation), a deluded Basil Fawlty-like character who is incompetent, patronizing and opinionated. The joke is that he really wants to serve the community and never intends to be rude, but his ability to turn a drama into a full-blown crisis would have Frank Spencer running for cover. Brittas's wife pops numerous pills and the receptionist keeps her children in drawers and cupboards at her desk. This was a sitcom where it often took a few episodes for the penny to drop, but it was worth making the effort, especially as each season seemed to end with a bigger and more literal bang than the previous.

Men Behaving Badly, a New Lad ***Likely Lads***, is the ultimate example of the BBC's pre-eminence in the field, having been 'poached' by the beeb from ITV in 1994. When Simon Nye's flat-sharing sitcom began in 1992 it featured Martin Clunes as Gary and Harry Enfield as Dermot. For the second season Enfield was replaced by Neil Morrissey as Tony, and when the third season was made a key part of the BBC's post-watershed timetabling, the child-adult characterizations really came to the fore. Tony's pathetic attempts to win the affection of Deborah (Leslie Ash) were as nothing compared to Gary's desperate, cynical relationship with Dorothy (Caroline Quentin). She was forced to wear a T-shirt emblazoned with the words 'Don't Even Think About It' after an appendectomy; he shooed her out of the house so he could try to chat up a Spanish au pair. All the expected jokes about booze, aerobic videos and the state of the flat were present and correct, and when Dorothy decided to 'chuck' Gary there was even a hint of pathos.

Chef! is a new ***Fawlty Towers*** only in as much as it features 'blow torch rhetorical brutality levelled against hapless inferiors', as *The Independent*'s Thomas Sutcliffe put it. Lenny Henry's Gareth Blackstock has an ego the size of a planet and the anger of a legion of Ian Paisleys, demolishing people with precise rants like 'Ah, Derek, let me explain the order of things for you. There's the aristocracy, the upper class, middle class, working class, dumb animals, waiters, creeping things, head lice, people who eat packet soup... And then you.' Peter Tilbury's scripts picked holes in pretentiousness in much the same ways as ***AbFab*** did, and the humour was of a similarly high standard.

The limitations of the sitcom are well known and, at times, the temptation of viewers and

Tony and Gary from *Men Behaving Badly*: new lads, and proud of it

critics alike is to turn their noses up at the thought of almost deliberate lowest-common-denominator television. But this obscures the fact that the great sitcoms of the sort that the rest of this chapter will discuss retain a lightness of touch and a power that can hit a nerve in their audience. The cleverness of *The Gaffer*, the weirdness of *Lame Ducks* and the farcical wit of *L for Lester* indicate that audience size is rarely a measure of quality. Having said that, many sitcoms represent TV hell: our list of sitcoms to avoid would include *That's My Boy*, *Me Mammy*, *French Fields*, *Come Back, Mrs Noah*, *Duty Free*, *No Place Like Home*, *The Other 'Alf* and *Never the Twain*. Still, if you have never laughed out loud at a finely-tuned comic moment in a sitcom (be it ***Steptoe and Son***, *Bless This House*, ***One Foot in the Grave*** or even a genuine 24-carat disaster like *Don't Wait Up*), then you are a lost cause. It is to be hoped that, in 20 years' time, a young writer involved in a project such as this will state that the writers of *Classic British TV* had got *Up the Elephant and Round the Castle* all wrong, and that it is an undiscovered classic. That really would be good for a laugh.

The Army Game

- **Granada Television** (ITV) ◆ B&W
- **152 episodes** (30 minutes) ◆ 1957–61
- **Creator:** Sid Colin
- **Writers include:** Sid Colin, Larry Stephens, Maurice Wiltshire, Lew Schwarz, David Climie, Barry Took, Marty Feldman, John Antrobus, Talbot Rothwell, David Cummings, Derek Collyer, Stanley Mars, Brad Ashton, Sid Nelson
- **Directors:** Milo Lewis, Max Morgan-Witts, Gordon Flemyng, Graeme McDonald
- **Producers:** Peter Eton, Eric Fawcett

Starring: Geoffrey Sumner (Major Upshot-Bagley) • William Hartnell (CSM Bullimore) • Bill Fraser (Sgt. Claude Snudge) • Michael Medwin (Cpl. Springer) • Norman Rossington (Pte. 'Cupcake' Cook) • Bernard Bresslaw (Pte. 'Popeye' Popplewell) • Charles Hawtrey (Pte. 'Professor' Hatchett) • Alfie Bass (Pte. 'Boots' Bisley) • Bernard Hunter (Capt. Pilsworthy) • C.B. Poultney (Major Geoffrey Gervaise Duckworth) • Ted Lune (Pte. Bone) • Frank Williams (Capt. Pocket) • Harry Fowler (Pte. 'Flogger' Hoskins) • Harry Towb (Pte. Dooley) • Mario Fabrizi (L/Cpl. Ernest 'Moosh' Merryweather) • Robert Desmond (Pte. Billy Baker) • Dick Emery (Pte. 'Chubby' Catchpole)

[Jack Allen, Keith Smith and Keith Banks appeared in several episodes during the second season, in the roles of Upshot-Bagley, 'Professor' and 'Cupcake' respectively.]

'There is nothing very special about the Nether Hopping transit camp and the surplus ordnance depot. It is a ramshackle, miserable-looking hutment camp, three miles from the nearest village. A camp forgotten by the War Office, where life follows the same lazy routine. The peace of Nether Hopping is, however, rudely shattered by the arrival of five newcomers ...'

In 1957, the Independent Television companies began to realize that there was life outside the 16th century. The BBC's comedy success of ***Hancock's Half Hour*** had caused ripples throughout the industry and whilst many early sitcoms on both channels display every excess that constitutes bad television, one towering achievement stood out from the mess of late-50s sitcoms.

The introductory quotation is how the embryonic *TV Times* chose to describe the debut of a new Granada comedy which slipped into the comfortable midweek slot, between the massively-popular *Criss-Cross Quiz* and Associated-Rediffusion's well-established *Play of the Week*. The series, based on the spectre of National Service, ran fortnightly, alternating on Wednesday nights with *The Carroll Levis Variety Show*. However, after 14 episodes, such was the popularity of *The Army Game* that it was switched to a weekly Friday night slot.

Scriptwriter Sid Colin had been in the RAF himself, and to make sure that technical facts were correct, Granada appointed a military adviser, Major John Foley, to the series. Producer Peter Eton and director Milo Lewis were then given the task of casting Colin's 'Everyman' army characters. Authority was represented by Geoffrey Sumner's seminal upper-class twit Upshot-Bagley, William Hartnell's brutally-funny Sergeant Major Bullimore and Bill Fraser's Sergeant Claude Snudge, whose 'I'll be leaving you now, sah!' quickly became a national catchphrase. It was, however, the cannon-fodder which made *The Army Game* so true to life and so popular.

The 'fly-boy' of the outfit was cockney Corporal Springer, who had decided that national service would be one long scrounge. The pessimist of the group was 'Bootsie' Bisley (who had been 'excused-boots' for most of his service life). Then there was 'Professor' Hatchett, the barrack-room lawyer whose hobbies included

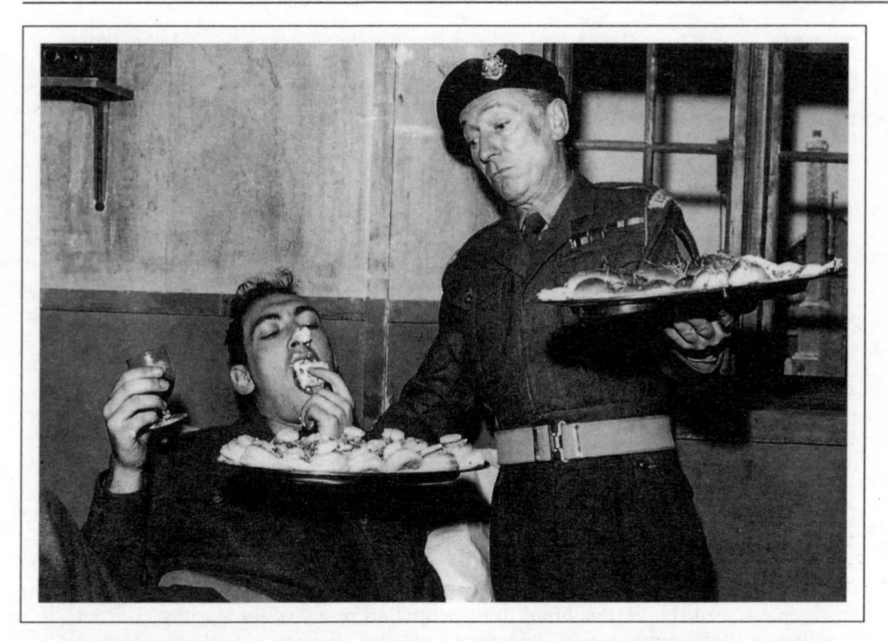

Role reversal. At the party to celebrate the 'promotion' of *The Army Game* to a weekly serial, William Hartnell waits on Bernard Bresslaw

knitting. 'Popeye' represented the brute strength of the quintet; his catchphrase – 'I only arsked' – whenever another stupid question was met with a series of disbelieving looks from his friends became the title of a spin-off film made in 1958. Bresslaw, like Hawtrey (and Hartnell), would graduate to the *Carry On* film series. Finally, there was the Scouse 'Cupcake', so called because of the food parcels he received from his mother.

By 1958, *The Army Game* was amongst the most popular series on British television. Its stars were somewhat protected from their growing popularity by the regular daily rehearsals and live performances of the 39-week turnaround series, and it was a surprised Michael Medwin and Norman Rossington who, on a publicity trip to London, found themselves mobbed in a department store. The series' comedy, though sometimes obvious, accurately reflected service life at a time when most of the male population of Britain over the age of 18 had some experience of it. In May 1958, the theme song, written by Pat Napper and sung by Leslie Fyson with Medwin, Bass and Bresslaw, reached number five in the British charts.

By the time the third season began, in late 1958, the original cast had begun to drift away. Charles Hawtrey was the first to go – his place as *The Army Game*'s zany element was taken by Lancastrian face-comedian Ted Lune as the cowardly Private Bone. Bernard Bresslaw followed Hawtrey soon afterwards. The pair would later star together in another Granada series, *Our House*, in 1961, before *Carry On* took them away from television altogether. Geoffrey Sumner was briefly replaced before Upshot-Bagley was also written out, and the camp was taken over by Major Duckworth. Then, William Hartnell, in his own words 'doomed to play sergeants and petty officers', went off to make *Carry on Sergeant* (GB 58) and 'Flogger' Hoskins, another cockney wide-boy, replaced Springer. In his first episode, 'Flogger' had to carry around a large kit-bag for most of the time, which had been weighted with lead by some practical joker. Of course, on live television, Harry Fowler simply had to carry on as best he could.

First season
(19 Jun–20 Dec 57)
Fourteen episodes

Second season
(10 Jan–13 Jun 58)
Twenty-three episodes

Third season
(19 Sep 58–12 Jun 59)
Thirty-nine episodes

Fourth season
(9 Oct 59–17 Jun 60)
Thirty-seven episodes
77 Enter a Dark Stranger
78 Snudge's Budgie
79 The Camera Never Lies
80 Where There's Smoke
82 The Take-Over Bid
83 Night Train to Itchwick
84 Officers and Gentlemen
85 Tiger Bisley

Fifth season
(27 Sep 60–20 Jun 61)
Thirty-nine episodes

The biggest blow to *The Army Game*, however, came during the summer break in 1960, when Peter Eton and Milo Lewis hit upon the idea of taking Alfie Bass and Bill Fraser from the army and putting them into civilian life as a comedy pair. *Bootsie and Snudge in Civvy Life* started in September 1960.

The Army itself had never been amused by *The Army Game*. Several commanding officers banned their men from watching the series which they considered a corrupting influence. Bill Fraser was constantly being stopped in the street by irate ex-NCOs demanding to know why Snudge let his ''orrible shower' get away with murder. New writers, including the team of Barry Took and Marty Feldman, were encouraged to be as irreverent as possible.

A fifth and final season saw the return of William Hartnell and Geoffrey Sumner, and the arrival of one major new character in 'Chubby' Catchpole, played by Dick Emery, whose catchphrase 'Hello honky-tonks' began as a line in an *Army Game* episode. However, by 1961, National Service was almost a thing of the past, and the series which had propelled many of its leading characters to stardom quietly ended with declining viewing figures despite a host of less impressive imitators (including another Granada series, *Colonel Thumper's Private War*).

The Army Game hasn't aged well, as the surviving telerecordings of the live episodes indicate. It is the product of an era shaped by war, where the army was an important part of everyday life. Historically speaking, the series took place at a crossroads and it is noticeable that, of the military comedy that has emerged since, almost all (***Dad's Army***, *It Ain't Half Hot Mum*) has been set during war-time. Only *Get Some In* attempted (with some success) to revive memories of enforced National Service and the young men who gave two of their best years in the service of the nation.

Steptoe and Son

- **BBC Television** (BBC1) ◆ **B&W (1962-65); Colour (1970-74)**
- **57 episodes** (standard length: 30 minutes)
- **Creators/writers:** Ray Galton, Alan Simpson
- **Producers:** Duncan Wood, John Howard Davies, David Croft, Graeme Muir, Douglas Argent

Starring: Wilfrid Brambell (Albert Steptoe) • Harry H. Corbett (Harold Steptoe)

Although it didn't seem that way at the time, the split between Tony Hancock and his writers Ray Galton and Alan Simpson in 1961 helped to push the sitcom in an entirely new direction. At the time, Galton and Simpson had been commissioned by Tom Sloan, Head of BBC Light Entertainment, to write ten plays under the title *Comedy Playhouse*. Freed from the difficulties of 'the lad himself', the pair came up with their finest creation, 'The Offer', the story of a father and son pair of rag and bone men, living in squalor and poverty in Shepherd's Bush, which began with Ron Grainer's instantly catchy signature tune.

The episode starred two fine, if relatively unknown, actors: Wilfrid Brambell as the mean, cantankerous 'dirty old man' Albert, and Harry H. Corbett (the 'H' standing for 'Hanything' to distinguish him from Sooty's creator) as his frustrated, social-climber of a son Harold (or 'Aaa-rold' as Brambell pronounced it). Sloan was so impressed with the episode that he begged Galton and Simpson to make a whole series, something the writers were reluctant to do because 'we think we've written a little piece of Pinter here and we can't repeat it!' After a great deal of persuasion, five further scripts were written and a series (which began with a repeat of 'The Offer') started in June 1962.

By the end of the first season, *Steptoe and Son* was being watched by audiences in excess of 20 million. Helped by the timeless comedy of episodes like 'The Piano', and the often gut-wrenching pathos of Harold's attempts to leave his grim lifestyle behind (most notably in 'The Holiday'), *Steptoe and Son* seemed to touch a raw nerve in the nation's psyche. The series exposed a number of home truths about the nature of blood ties, fuelled by the selfish possessiveness that Albert felt about his son (each of Harold's relationships with women being broken up by his father) and the extreme love-hate atmosphere that surrounded the pair.

Many psychologists probed the series, searching for hidden reasons as to why it was so successful, some feeling that *Steptoe* was a metaphor for the decline of Britain as an economic power, others that strong Freudian elements were the main factor. The real reason for the show's popularity, however, was the carefully constructed scripts and the outrageously funny situations in which the pair often found themselves. *Steptoe and Son* changed the whole pattern of sitcom

Comedy Playhouse
(5 Jan 62)
1 The Offer

First season
(14 Jun–12 Jul 62)
2 The Bird
3 The Piano
4 The Economist
5 The Diploma
6 The Holiday

Second season
(3 Jan–14 Feb 63)
7 Wallah Wallah Cat's Meat
8 The Bath
9 The Stepmother
10 Sixty-Five Today
11 A Musical Evening
12 Full House
13 Is that your Horse Outside?

Third season
(7 Jan–18 Feb 64)
14 Home Fit for Heroes
15 The Wooden Overcoats
16 The Lead Man Cometh
17 Steptoe à la Cart
18 Sunday for Seven Days
19 The Bonds that Bind Us
20 The Lodger

Fourth season
(4 Oct–15 Nov 65)
21 And Afterwards At …
22 Crossed Swords
23 Those Magnificent Men and their Heating Machines
24 The Siege of Steptoe Street
25 A Box in Town
26 My Old Man's a Tory
27 Pilgrim's Progress

and allowed working-class humour of the kind seen in ***The Likely Lads*** and ***Till Death Us Do Part*** to flourish.

A second season was just as successful. It included the memorable sight of Albert dunking his pickled onions into his bath water, and Harold's panic when the Steptoe's horse, Hercules, becomes ill in 'Wallah Wallah Cat's Meat'. (In this episode the pair con their friends and, against every principle of TV morality, get away with it.) A specially-written sketch was chosen as the main event on the 1963 Royal Variety Performance, where it was a huge hit, alongside the Beatles. (Themselves fans, the Fabs asked for Wilfrid Brambell for the role of Paul McCartney's 'clean' grandfather in *A Hard Day's Night* the following year.)

Further classics followed, drawing on the darker side of 60s London (notably the anti-war 'Home Fit for Heroes', 'The Bonds that Bind Us', and the anarcho-political 'My Old Man's a Tory'). Harold's discovery of a job lot of secondhand coffins in 'The Wooden Overcoats', his attempts to introduce his father to the cultural delights of Fellini in 'Sunday for Seven Days', and the epic frozen shenanigans of 'Those Magnificent Men and their Heating Machines', stand out as examples of *Steptoe and Son* at its peak. There is a unique subtlety in Galton and Simpson's portrayal of loneliness and inter-generational tension, while the sexual/class drama 'Is that your Horse Outside?' and the anti-establishment rant 'The Siege of Steptoe Street' are, literally, years ahead of their time for a comedy series.

The series transferred to radio in 1966, and, although Galton and Simpson would occasionally suggest a return, most of their energies were concentrated on *The Frankie Howerd Show*. Then, in 1969, Tom Sloan persuaded them to write a new series (according to Galton, they were in a Chinese restaurant in Kensington High Street when they finally gave in to Sloan).

The new colour season was an instant success, picking up the tragicomedy where it left off five years before. Harold, now in his forties, was absolutely desperate to break away from Oil Drum Lane and his father, but was always unable to do so.

The 1972 season was probably the pinnacle of the series. Highlights include the bitter family funeral in 'Oh, What a Beautiful Mourning' (a timeless example of observational comedy in a minimalist setting); the amateur dramatic rehearsals in 'A Star is Born'; Albert facing prison for fiddling his taxes in 'Live Now, PAYE Later'; the deep psychology of 'Loathe Story' (Joanna Lumley plays Harold's girlfriend); the absurd logistics of house sharing in 'Divided we Stand', and Leonard Rossiter as an escaped convict, choosing the one house in London not to use for a hideout, in 'The Desperate Hours'. These, along with those from the final season (especially 'Porn Yesterday', in which Albert's murky past comes back to haunt him, and the brilliant 'And so to Bed', where Harold's decision to buy a water bed has disastrous consequences), were amongst the first episodes of any series released by BBC video in the mid-80s. Later these formed the basis for one of the most successful repeat seasons of all time when, 14 years after the

Fifth season
(6 Mar–17 Apr 70)
28 A Death in the Family
29 A Winter's Tale
30 Any Old Iron?
31 Steptoe and Son and Son
32 The Colour Problem
33 TB or not TB
34 Men of Property

Sixth season
(2 Nov–21 Dec 70)
35 Robbery with Violence
36 Come Dancing
37 Two's Company
38 Tea for Two
39 Without Prejudice
40 Pot Black
41 The Three Feathers
42 Cuckoo in the Nest

Seventh season
(21 Feb–3 Apr 72)
43 Men of Letters
44 A Star is Born
45 Oh, What a Beautiful Mourning
46 Live Now, PAYE Later
47 Loathe Story
48 Divided we Stand
49 The Desperate Hours

Christmas special
(24 Dec 73, 45 minutes)

Eighth season
(4 Sep–10 Oct 74)
51 Back in Fashion
52 And so to Bed
53 Porn Yesterday
54 The Seven Steptoerai
55 Upstairs Downstairs, Upstairs Downstairs
56 Seance in a Wet Rag and Bone Yard

Christmas special
(26 Dec 74, 45 minutes)

last episode had been made, *Steptoe and Son* started breaking viewing records all over again with a new audience.

Sadly, neither Corbett nor Brambell lived to see it. They would undoubtedly have been satisfied that their legacy continues to influence comedy-makers and to entertain millions. For a long time it was thought that many of the monochrome gems had been lost because of the BBC's archive junking in the 70s, but after years of patient research by archivists, the BFI and Galton and Simpson themselves (who had their own collection of telerecordings), all have now been recovered, and most have been released on video.

Steptoe and Son is a monument to intelligent television – tense, claustrophobic, often dealing with deadly serious themes, yet as funny as anything that has ever been produced. The final scene of the Christmas special that ended the series sees Harold laying a fiendish plot and finally escaping his father. It might have been an anti-climax in lesser hands, but for Harold, and the audience, the relief is total.

A house divided as Harold discovers that 'My Old Man's a Tory'

The Likely Lads/Whatever Happened to the Likely Lads?

- **BBC Television** (BBC2 (1964-66), BBC1 (1973-74))
- B&W (1964-66); Colour (1973-74)
- **47 episodes** (standard length: 30 minutes)
- **Creators/writers:** Dick Clement, Ian La Frenais
- **Producers:** Dick Clement, James Gilbert, Bernard Thompson

Regular cast: James Bolam (Terry Collier) • Rodney Bewes (Bob Ferris)
With: Sheila Fern (Audrey) • Brigit Forsyth (Thelma)

In the words of Frank Muir, then Assistant Head of BBC Light Entertainment, Dick Clement and Ian La Frenais's *The Likely Lads* had 'a remarkable reception. Ratings on the audience reaction index soared up and up; the last episode reached the highest figure we have ever had apart from ***Steptoe and Son***.'

Clement, a newly-promoted radio producer, and his writing partner La Frenais (who sold insurance in Newcastle for a living), had the good fortune to have their TV debut discovered by BBC2's first controller, Michael Peacock, who saw the first *Likely Lads* episode in Bill Cotton's office, and promptly hijacked the series for the new channel.

The story centred on the eponymous heroes, Terry and Bob, two working-class lads employed by Ellisons' Electrical as apprentices. Uniquely for the time, they were not mods, rockers or any other 'types', but normal kids with a knack of getting themselves into funny situations. The actors who played them, James Bolam and Rodney Bewes, were already well-known, via *The Loneliness of the Long Distance Runner* (GB 62) and *Billy Liar* (GB 63) respectively. Together they established a rapport which, combined with well-observed scripts and superb comic timing, produced a series that pointed the way forward for sitcom, doubtless helped by the fact that it had a premise with which millions of 'lads' could identify. The series accurately focused on young men's obsessions: girls, football and transport (Bob buys a scooter in 'Rocker'). Bob was the often gullible drinking partner to Terry's chauvinistic Jack-the-lad. Whether for authenticity or simply because they liked it, the pair drank real brown ale during pub scenes. Bewes once estimated that on a particular episode, due to retakes, he drank nine pints.

The joy of *The Likely Lads* was that, for the first time, a comedy series was set realistically outside London, the first episode emphasizing the parochial nature of the humour, as the lads return from their first foreign holiday. 'Older Women are More Experienced' sent them out, unbeknown to each other, with a mother

THE LIKELY LADS
First season
(16 Dec 64–20 Jan 65)
1 Entente Cordiale
2 Double Date
3 Older Women are More Experienced
4 The Other Side of the Fence
5 Chance of a Lifetime
6 The Suitor

Second season
(16 Jun–21 Jul 65)
7 Baby, it's Cold Outside
8 A Star is Born
9 The Talk of the Town
10 The Last of the Big Spenders
11 Faraway Places
12 Where have all the Flowers Gone?

Third season
(4 Jun–23 Jul 66)
13 Outward Bound
14 Friends and Neighbours
15 Rocker
16 Brief Encounter
17 The Razor's Edge
18 Anchors Aweigh
19 Love and Marriage
20 Goodbye to All That

and daughter pair, whilst other episodes like 'Baby, it's Cold Outside' and 'The Razor's Edge' centred on the negative side of being young and less than affluent in 1960s Newcastle.

The lads made it on to the 1964 *Christmas Night with the Stars*, with a superbly-written segment in which they spend an entire Christmas Eve arguing over Bob's encyclopaedic knowledge of Rupert Bear annuals.

After three seasons and 20 episodes, *The Likely Lads* ended with 'Goodbye to All That', in which a depressed Bob joins the army. Terry follows, unable to face life without his friend, only to find that Bob had been discharged on the grounds of flat feet.

Six years later, they were back. Bewes, in particular, though successful in the Thames sitcom *Dear Mother, Love Albert* (which he created and co-produced), jumped at the chance to return to the role. *Whatever Happened to the Likely Lads?* is one of a select handful of television sequels that can be compared favourably with the original. Fans of the 60s predecessor were catered for, though thankfully an entirely new generation was equally charmed by the series.

The first episode begins with Bob, now a young executive with a pushy fiancée, Thelma, looking through holiday slides and coming across one of a drunken Terry Collier. Thelma feels it is an omen. Later, Bob, travelling back from a trip to London, bumps into a stranger in the dark of a train tunnel, who tells him he has just come out of the army. Bob tells the amusing story of a friend of his who was once suckered into joining up and, in one of TV's great comic moments, just before the train emerges into the light, a disembodied voice from the past says 'You bastard!'

'Moving On' is a beautiful piece of tragicomedy with Bob taking Terry around their old stamping grounds in Newcastle, most of which no longer exist or have changed beyond recognition. Terry describes Munchengladbach as 'the West Hartlepool of West Germany', and we learn that he married a German girl, the relationship failing largely because of the 1970 World Cup quarter-final (Terry spending most of extra-time 'sitting on the sideboard wrapped in a Union Jack singing "Rule Britannia"'). The series highlighted the constant battle Terry endured in trying to adjust to the change in attitudes that his friend had undergone. Terry, a throwback to the 60s, an optimistic era, finds Bob's pragmatic approach to what TV commentator Geoff Tibballs describes as 'the sober and soon-to-be-unemployed 70s' depressing. The series had many things to say on class (Bob considers himself middle-class and is keen to ignore his roots), the sex war and male bonding, one of the best episodes being 'The Old Magic' in which, in a pre-marriage fling, Bob allows Terry to drag him on a pub-crawl only for the pair to find themselves trying to chat-up Thelma's younger sister.

'No Hiding Place' is the series' masterpiece, Bob and Terry spend a day trying to avoid the result of a football match, being hounded by Flint (Brian Glover), who is determined to disclose the result and thus win a bet, also ruining their enjoyment of the highlights on TV. The scenes with the fugitives hiding in the home of Terry's sister, Audrey, a church and finally in Bob's new house, are priceless as a two-man exercise in comedic dialogue. (Terry is asked what he thinks of Koreans.

WHATEVER HAPPENED TO THE LIKELY LADS

First season
(9 Jan–3 Apr 73)
1 Strangers on a Train
2 Home is the Hero
3 Cold Feet
4 Moving On
5 I'll Never Forget Whatshername
6 Birthday Boy
7 No Hiding Place
8 Guess Who's Coming To Dinner?
9 Storm in a Tea Chest
10 The Old Magic
11 Count Down
12 Boys' Night In
13 End of an Era

Second season
(1 Jan–9 Apr 74)
14 Absent Friends
15 Heart to Heart
16 The Ant and the Grasshopper
17 One for the Road
18 The Great Race
19 Some Day We'll Laugh About This
20 In Harm's Way
21 Affairs and Relations
22 The Expert
23 Between Ourselves
24 The Go-Between
25 Conduct Unbecoming
26 The Shape of Things to Come

Christmas special
(24 Dec 74, 45 minutes)

'Cruel people,' he says, 'Much the same as all orientals.' 'That's a third of the world's population dismissed in a phrase,' notes Bob.) The season ended with Bob marrying Thelma in 'End of an Era', and deservedly won a BAFTA award for best situation comedy in 1974.

When Bob returns from his honeymoon he finds settling down to married life difficult with his cynical, worldly–wise friend as a constant reminder of his past. The pair, however, could still be relied upon to get themselves into ridiculous situations: a bicycle challenge in 'The Great Race', both arrested on the same night in 'One for the Road' and involved in the shady schemes of Bob's father-in-law (Bill Owen) in 'Affairs and Relations'. 'The Shape of Things to Come' saw Terry's favourite uncle dying and Bob being given an uncomfortable view of his potential future life by the old man's best friend. The final episode, a Christmas special, was made in 1974. The series could have continued but Clement and La Frenais were tied up with *Thick as Thieves* and ***Porridge*** and James Bolam with ***When the Boat Comes in***. 1976 saw a funny, if unrepresentative, film adaptation.

The ghosts of *The Likely Lads*, however, continue to haunt the work of its creators and stars. Clement and La Frenais's ***Auf Wiedersehen, Pet*** contains much of the *Whatever Happened to The Likely Lads?*' resigned Northern cynicism, whilst one of James Bolam's major post-*Likely Lads* creations, the hypochondriac, work–shy Royston Figgis in LWT's *Only When I Laugh*, is nothing more than Terry Collier on a very bad day. The series seems to have found a niche in the 90s too, both via successful repeats and the 'new laddism' of *Men Behaving Badly*, *Game On*, *You, Me and Him* and *Fantasy Football League*.

Clement and La Frenais have considered bringing back the series for the 90s, La Frenais noting that 'Bob would have probably lost his job and gone bankrupt. Terry, who'd gone though life without much ambition, would have no doubt received £200,000 for an unspecified injury received in a drunk-driving accident. And Bob would just keep saying "Terribly unfair, so terribly unfair."'

Till Death Us Do Part

- **BBC Television** (BBC1) ◆ **B&W** (1966-68); **Colour** (1972-75)
- **53 episodes** (standard length: *c.* 30 minutes)
- **Creator/writer:** Johnny Speight
- **Directors:** Douglas Argent, Colin Strong
- **Producers:** Dennis Main Wilson, David Croft
- **Executive producer** (*Comedy Playhouse*): Graeme Muir

Starring: Warren Mitchell (Alf Garnett) • Dandy Nichols (Else Garnett) • Una Stubbs (Rita) • Anthony Booth (Mike)

[Gretchen Franklin appeared as Else in the original *Comedy Playhouse* episode, and the family name was Ramsey.]

'*Speight is a racist. He's more of a racist than I'll ever be. He uses words like "Sambo" and "Jon-Jon" in conversation ... As for his scripts, his spelling is atrocious and half the time when you get a script from him you can't even read it. I contribute more than he does and he gets all the credit and all the money.*' (Alfred Garnett on writer Johnny Speight.)

Alf Ramsey's initial obsession was time, or, rather, Big Ben's inability to keep it accurately. It wouldn't matter to him if you told him that Big Ben was a bell or that surely his 30-year old watch was at fault. For Ramsey, declining standards above parliament were symptomatic of degeneration within and throughout his beloved England.

It is not for his attitude to time-keeping that Ramsey is now best known; nor even is he famous under that name. However, as Alf Garnett, misogynist ('It's all very well letting women have children, but they shouldn't be allowed to bring them up'), racist and bigoted West Ham supporter, he has entered the psyche of a nation. Things might have changed over the years (***EastEnders***' Gretchen Franklin originally played the 'silly moo'), but even into the 90s, Alf remained intransigent.

Any analysis of *Till Death Us Do Part* and its follow-ups must really begin with the character of Alf, for therein lies the humour, the notoriety and the success. Alf was created by Johnny Speight for the *Comedy Playhouse* series in 1965, probably based on the more extreme characters Speight met during his childhood in Canning Town – Speight's first joke was apparently 'The place I come from is so bad they're pulling it down to build a slum.' Briefly a member of the Communist party, Speight's political views have always informed the character 'in reverse': everything that Speight hates becomes delicious rant material for Garnett. Speight was an accomplished comedy writer, having written for Frankie Howerd's radio shows, and for Eric Sykes, Hattie Jacques and Arthur Haynes on TV. However, his political views are somewhat confused ('You can't teach a man socialism unless he's in a socialist society. Myself, I feel that Chairman Mao is the only one to have got it right. And I think China's the place of the future' – Speight, 1972), which arguably has led to a character who, rather than educating the viewers, merely encourages their prejudices. Because Garnett's beliefs never change (unlike, say, Huckleberry Finn's attitude to slavery), and because the opposing political point of view was expressed by Garnett's son-in-law, whom Speight called 'just as big an idiot' as Garnett, there is nothing constructive about *Till Death Us Do Part*, no 'solution' to Alf's racism or the problems that he moans about.

Of course, no one can deny that it's great comedy, but, in tackling difficult issues, Speight's writing encourages such scrutiny, and is consequently often found lacking. The *Radio Times* commented at the end of the second season that 'Everyone has known an Alf Garnett. Or met one. And, let's be honest, there's a bit of him in everyone of us. It hurts us to admit it, but it's there' – a typically 'liberal' response. The article claims that 'If you laugh with Alf Garnett you have

Comedy Playhouse
(22 Jul 65)

First season
(6 Jun–1 Aug 66)
2 Arguments, Arguments …
3 Hair Raising!
4 A House with Love in It
5 Intolerance
6 Two Toilets? … That's Posh
7 From Liverpool with Love
8 Claustrophobia

Second season
(26 Dec 66–27 Feb 67)
9 Peace and Goodwill
10 Sex Before Marriage
11 I Can Give It Up Any Time I Like
12 The Bulldog Breed
13 Caviar on the Dole
14 A Woman's Place is in the Home
15 A Wapping Mythology (The Workers' King)
16 In Sickness and in Health …
17 State Visit
18 Cleaning up TV

Special
(27 Mar 67, 40 minutes)
19 Till Closing Time Do Us Part

Third season
(5 Jan–16 Feb 68)
20 Monopoly
21 The Blood Donor
22 The Phone
23 The Funeral
24 Football
25 The Puppy
26 Aunt Maud

Fourth season
(13 Sep–25 Oct 72)
27 To Garnett a Grandson
28 The Bird Fancier
29 Women's Lib and Bournemouth
30 If We Want a Proper Democracy We've Got to Start Shooting a Few People
31 Up the 'Ammers
32 [untitled]

merely been entertained. If you laugh at him you have been entertained and informed – and that's a victory for Johnny Speight.' And yet, *Till Death* rarely encourages us to laugh at Garnett – although he is foolish and unsuccessful – but rather to laugh with him and his cheap jokes. And that's not just entertainment.

It is sad that when *Till Death Us Do Part* was criticized in the 60s and early 70s, attention focused not on its ideological contradictions but, rather, the swearing (most famously Mary Whitehouse counting 78 'bloody's in a single episode, which led to an episode ending with her book burning in the family fireplace). Whitehouse's reaction was a knee-jerk response to what was at least an attempt to do something important with a comedy programme. Speight commented that the 'BBC came out of the Reithian moral wilderness in the 60s. Lord Reith would have made a great Archbishop but he was bad for television. However, [Hugh] Carleton Greene was a brilliant Director General. He was an intelligent man with a contempt for politicians, and although he was under tremendous pressure from the Church and MPs to take *Till Death* off, he protected everyone on the show from a barrage of complaints. I didn't even know about some of them until I read his book!'

Till Death was saved by its obvious popularity, which, despite its failings, it richly deserved. By the end of its second season, *Till Death Us Do Part* had

Christmas at the Garnetts. Prepare for a miserable time

Christmas special
(26 Dec 72, 45 minutes)
33 Jesus Christ Superstar

Fifth season
(2 Jan–28 Feb 74)
34 TV Licence
35 The Royal Wedding
36 The Demon Drink
37 Strikes and Blackouts
38 Three Day Week [aka Else's Three Day Week]
39 Gran's Watch
40 [untitled]

Special
(31 Dec 74)
41 Outback Bound

Sixth season
(8 Jan–12 Feb 75)
Six episodes
43 Marital Bliss

Seventh season
(5 Nov–17 Dec 75)
Six episodes
52 A Hole in One

[The order of the third season's episodes is open to some debate (the *Radio Times* lists 'The Blood Donor' as the third episode; other sources list 'Monopoly', despite being an episode set on New Year's Eve), as are the titles and transmission order of the second, fourth and fifth seasons. ATV transmitted the special *The Thoughts of Chairman Alf* ('On Yer Actual Boxing Day') on 26 Dec 80, and a six-episode season entitled *Till Death* ... between 17 May and 21 Jun 81. The show was revived again by the BBC in 1985 as *In Sickness and in Health* (six seasons, forty-seven episodes).]

an audience of nearly 20 million; and when the programme was shown in Australia it was, at that time, the highest-rated programme ever.

The acting remained of a consistently high standard throughout the seven seasons (when Mitchell played Willy Loman to great acclaim in *Death of a Salesman* he was angered by one newspaper critic who praised his performance whilst saying that Mitchell was 'wasted' playing Garnett). The interaction between the characters was wonderful to behold: the stoic Else and giggling Rita looking on as Alf launched into a verbal attack on Mike, workshy Liverpudlian left-winger, variously called a 'scouse git' and 'Shirley Temple' (because of his hair). (The Monkees called their 1967 hit single 'Randy Scouse Git' in tribute to the series, which, with staggering hypocrisy, the BBC banned.)

Supporting actors were of a similarly high calibre, and included John Junkin, Roy Kinnear, Pat Coombs, Joan Sims and Bill Fraser. Sims virtually became a regular, as did Patricia Hayes and Alfie Bass, helping to disguise Dandy Nichols's absence from much of the sixth season. The final season claimed that Else had gone to Australia (which is about as far as you could reasonably get from Alf and still stay on this planet).

Unusual guest stars included Spike Milligan, footballers Ian St John and Willie Stevenson in the first season, Bobby Moore, Alan Ball and Martin Peters in the fourth season and George Best in 1975. (Upon seeing Best, playing a round of golf with Roy Castle, Alf shouts 'George, it's me. You remember me down at Upton Park shoutin' "Gerrof y'poncey, long-haired mick!"' This occurs in one of the series' most bizarre stories, 'A Hole in One', in which Alf and Burt discover that a local golf club has a tradition that anyone scoring a hole in one will buy a round in the club house. Because one of the greens is hidden from the tee, the pair are able to surreptitiously put balls into the hole and then sneak back to the club house, getting plastered as the episode progresses.)

The character of Alf Garnett would die without ammunition from the real world. The third season alone saw rants about Britain's entry into the Common Market, Liverpool bettering West Ham in the First Division, the devalued pound, the Beatles getting into transcendental meditation, defence cuts and, of course, the Labour party – and 'Darling Harold' – still being in power. If *Till Death Us Do Part* proved less successful when resurrected in the 80s as *In Sickness and in Health* then maybe that's as much to do with a shift in the political climate in Britain as with any change in Speight's approach to writing. Although Alf's verbal attacks on home help Winston (who was black and gay) showed that the format wasn't quite dead, and it was nice to see Else again, most who could remember the original would probably concede that its cutting edge as a social drama was becoming blunt. And when Dandy Nichols died in 1986 the series lost its second most famous and certainly most deeply-loved character.

So, over 30 years after its first showing, and two films and one lengthy and famous American adaptation (*All in the Family*) later, *Till Death Us Do Part*'s enigmatic appeal is no closer to be being solved. As T.C. Worsley wrote in the *Financial Times*, 'The more outrageous and extreme [Alf's] tirades grow, the more we adore him.'

Dad's Army

- **BBC Television** (BBC1) ◆ B&W (1968–69); Colour (1969–77)
- **80 episodes** (standard length: 30 minutes)
- **Creators/writers:** Jimmy Perry, David Croft
- **Directors include:** David Croft, Harold Snoad, Bob Spiers
- **Producer:** David Croft

Regular cast: Arthur Lowe (Capt. George Mainwaring) • John Le Mesurier (Sgt. Arthur Wilson) • Clive Dunn (L/Cpl. Jack Jones) • John Laurie (Pte. James Frazer) • James Beck (Pte. Joe Walker) • Arnold Ridley (Pte. Charles Godfrey) • Ian Lavender (Pte. Frank Pike)

With: Bill Pertwee (Chief ARP Warden William Hodges) • Frank Williams (Vicar) • Edward Sinclair (Verger) • Janet Davies (Mrs Pike) • Colin Bean (Pte. Sponge) • Talfryn Thomas (Cheeseman) • Robert Raglan (Colonel) • Harold Bennett (Mr Blewitt) • Pamela Cundell (Mrs Fox)

Writer Jimmy Perry was walking past Buckingham Palace one day, and nostalgically recalled the days when the Home Guard manned the sentry posts there during World War II. An actor, with experience in Joan Littlewood's Theatre Workshop, Perry had been in the Home Guard himself, in the Hertfordshire 1st Battalion, while he was too young to be conscripted. His instructor at the time had kept telling his men that the enemy 'didn't like it up 'em!' By the end of his walk, Jimmy had an idea for a comedy series.

He showed the idea to his friend, David Croft, then a BBC producer. Croft showed it to his boss, Michael Mills, the head of comedy. Mills said, 'This could run forever.'

Dad's Army is based, at heart, on a single class joke that Huw Weldon, when he first met the cast, failed to get. He assumed that John Le Mesurier was Captain

'Don't Panic!' The cast from the third season episode 'Battle School'

First season
(31 Jul–11 Sep 68)
1 The Man and the Hour
2 Museum Piece
3 Command Decision
4 The Enemy within the Gates
5 The Showing up of Corporal Jones
6 Shooting Pains

Second season
(1 Mar–5 Apr 69)
7 Operation Kilt
8 The Battle of Godfrey's Cottage
9 The Loneliness of the Long-Distance Walker
10 Sgt. Wilson's Little Secret
11 A Stripe for Frazer
12 Under Fire

Third season
(11 Sep–11 Dec 69)
13 The Armoured Might of Lance Corporal Jones
14 Battle School
15 The Lion has 'Phones
16 The Bullet is Not for Firing
17 Something Nasty in the Vault
18 Room at the Bottom
19 Big Guns
20 The Day the Balloon Went Up
21 War Dance
22 Menace from the Deep
23 Branded
24 Man Hunt
25 No Spring for Frazer
26 Sons of the Sea

Fourth season
(25 Sep–18 Dec 70)
27 The Big Parade
28 Don't Forget the Diver
29 Boots, Boots, Boots
30 Sergeant – Save My Boy!
31 Don't Fence Me In
32 Absent Friends
33 Put That Light Out!
34 The Two and a Half Feathers
35 Mum's Army
36 The Test
37 A. Wilson (Manager)?
38 Uninvited Guests
39 Fallen Idol

Christmas special
(27 Dec 71, 60 minutes)
40 Battle of the Giants!

Mainwaring and Arthur Lowe was Sergeant Wilson. In truth, that was how it was going to be, but Perry and Croft changed their minds. The central conflict in the show is that of a lower middle-class bank manager who finds himself commanding a man from the upper classes. Wilson is the voice of sanity, he always has the easier answer. If it wasn't for Wilson's unwillingness to get involved in anything, he'd make a much better officer.

The other central issue in the show is summed up by Mainwaring's exclamation in the first episode: 'Jerry's parachutists will be as dead as mutton from Stead and Simpson's to Timothy White's. We'd get a clear run down to the pier pavilion if that blasted woman would get out of the telephone box.' We laugh with the men of the Home Guard because of the contradictions between warfare and 'Little England'. However, in 1940, those contradictions were utterly real. As Alan Coren said in *The Times*, 'Clive Dunn might well ... have been the only thing standing between us and Dachau.' Mills had defended the fledgling series against internal claims of bad taste, and he was again correct. The viewers can't laugh at the Walmington-on-Sea platoon because not only is their situation truly desperate, but, in the best tradition of Fred Karno, Evelyn Waugh, and the lowly soldiers in *Henry V*, they're doing the best they can. Tom Hutchinson summed it up when he called the show 'a sweetly comic celebration of the British amateur'.

Mainwaring's platoon contained not only the laconic Wilson, but the hyper-loyal butcher, Lance Corporal Jack Jones. Jonesie had first seen service in the mid 1880s, 'trying to relieve General Gordon', and the 12 medals he occasionally wore were lovingly selected. They were exactly correct for the military career Perry and Croft had constructed for Jonesie, from Khartoum, through the Sudan, on to the North West Frontier, back under Kitchener for the battle of Omdurman, the Frontier again, then the Boer War and the Great War in France. Dunn himself had been made a POW on the night before he was due to be promoted to Lance Corporal, spending the rest of the war in a prison camp in Austria.

Tremendous accuracy was insisted upon, surely a factor in the series' popularity. The boots, watches, and Arthur Lowe's glasses were all originals, and similar attention was paid to newly-created items. Mainwaring's uniform, because of his wealth, was of a slightly better material than those of his men. The line 'I couldn't care less' was cut from one episode as being too modern, although it was used by Pike in the episode 'Brain Versus Brawn'. E.V.H. Emmett's voice was heard giving actual newsreel announcements in the first season, and period songs were played across scene breaks, Perry writing the lyrics to the authentic-sounding title music 'Who Do You Think You Are Kidding Mister Hitler?'. It was the last thing Bud Flanagan was to record before he died.

If the little butcher with the habit of asking for 'Permission to speak, sir' was a bit of a hero on the quiet, so was Godfrey, the medic who, more often than not, wanted to relieve his bladder when he spoke up. In 'Branded', Godfrey is revealed to have been a conscientious objector in the Great War. The other men consequently shun him, until he rescues Mainwaring from death in a smoke-filled

Fifth season
(6 Oct–29 Dec 72)
41 Asleep in the Deep
42 Keep Young and Beautiful
43 A Soldier's Farewell
44 Getting the Bird
45 The Desperate Drive of Corporal Jones
46 If the Cap Fits …
47 The King was in his Counting House
48 All is Safely Gathered In
49 When Did You Last See Your Money?
50 Brain Versus Brawn
51 A Brush with the Law
52 Round and Round went the Great Big Wheel
53 Time on my Hands

Sixth season
(31 Oct–12 Dec 73)
54 The Deadly Attachment
55 My British Buddy
56 The Royal Train
57 We Know our Onions
58 The Honourable Man
59 Things That Go Bump in the Night
60 The Recruit

Seventh season
(15 Nov–23 Dec 74)
61 Everybody's Trucking
62 A Man of Action
63 Gorilla Warfare
64 The Godiva Affair
65 The Captain's Car
66 Turkey Dinner

Eighth season
(5 Sep–10 Oct 75)
67 Ring Dem Bells
68 When you've Got to Go
69 Is There Honey Still for Tea?
70 Come in, your Time is Up
71 High Finance
72 The Face on the Poster

Christmas special
(26 Dec 75, 40 minutes)
73 My Brother and I

Christmas special
(26 Dec 76)
74 The Love of Three Oranges

Ninth season
(2 Oct–13 Nov 77)
75 Wake-Up Walmington
76 The Making of Private Pike
77 Knights of Madness
78 The Miser's Hoard
79 Number Engaged
80 Never Too Old *(40 mins)*

room. He reveals that he won the Military Medal for his courage as a medical orderly.

The rest of the platoon was made up of Walker, the spiv who avoided military service in the Army by developing an allergy to corned beef, Pike, too young for war but eager to join in because of all the gangster movies he watches, and Frazer, the Scottish undertaker whose 'We're doomed!' was the obvious answer to Jones's 'Don't panic!' Apart from a thorough knowledge of the characters' backgrounds (they were sure that Pike's 'Uncle Arthur' was secretly his Dad), Perry and Croft both had theatrical experience, and let the actors' personalities influence them. Croft commented to the *Radio Times* that John Laurie was like Frazer in some ways. 'He starts a show saying "I don't know if it will work" and ends it saying "Well, I thought it would be all right".'

Rounding out the cast were Hodges, the ARP man ('Wellington' to Mainwaring's 'Napoleon'), the somewhat critical vicar and his more forceful verger, all devoted to putting common sense (and thus, somehow, defeatism) in the way of the platoon's schemes. It wasn't all spite, though. Croft had been an air-raid warden himself.

Dad's Army caught on very quickly, achieving its greatest fame (books, a movie version, board games, a radio adaptation, even a stage musical) and highest ratings (18.5 million) in the early 70s. It was reported to be the Queen's favourite programme, won a Writers' Guild award in 1970, and the BAFTA award for Best Comedy in 1971. Len Brown and David Quantick, writing in the *NME*, have made some interesting assertions as to what made the series tick – notably that, like much great TV comedy, *Dad's Army* works because it centres on people trapped (in this case, a bunch of free spirits trapped in the bodies of old men, along with a 'stupid boy' and a lazy spiv).

In August 1973, James Beck died, and the show was thrown into crisis. No new character was to be created to replace the well-loved actor's performance as Walker, but occasional characters including the eccentric Welsh war correspondent Cheeseman and the podgy Private Sponge were given a little more to do. A sort of regular Perry and Croft repertory company, containing such people as Michael Knowles, Don Estelle, Felix Bowness and Jeffrey Holland, was already building up to provide walk-ons, but the show was never short of guest stars. Fred Trueman and Barbara Windsor graced the early seasons, with Perry himself making an appearance as comedian Charlie Cheeseman in the final show of the first season. Trueman appears in 'The Test', which involves a game of cricket between the Wardens and the Home Guard. The match is won by a six from, of all people, Godfrey. As the players leave the pitch, air-raid warnings sound. 'Here they come again,' says a resigned Mainwaring as the episode ends without laughter.

Typical moments included Mainwaring and Wilson finding themselves holding on to an unexploded bomb in their bank, Frazer and Godfrey disguising themselves as a panto cow (and, of course, meeting a bull) and Mainwaring holding the mooring line of a runaway barrage balloon and thus having to be pursued by Jones's converted butcher's van. The sequence gained a standing ovation from the studio audience who watched each episode. Mainwaring got to play through his own version of *Brief Encounter* (GB 45), presumably to the worry of his never-seen wife, Elizabeth, and the whole cast dressed up as Nazi sympathizers (including Pike in memorable gangster outfit). In 'A Soldier's Farewell', Mainwaring dreams the entire cast to Waterloo, after he takes the platoon to see the film *Napoleon* (and has a cheese supper with Wilson and Jonesie). Another dream sequence/flashback occurs in 'The Two and a Half Feathers', in which Jones is accused of cowardice. In 'Absent Friends' the men do not turn up for patrol in order to finish a darts game. Mainwaring orders them back and, after some hesitation, they comply, simply because they are unable to let the captain down, walking into an ambush of Irish fifth columnists. 'Don't Fence Me In' concerns the suspicion that Walker is aiding Italian POWs to escape. There was also pathos, in the form of Wilson's eventual promotion to bank manager: his branch is destroyed by a bomb a few minutes after he has taken up the position.

Most of the stars of *Dad's Army* are dead now, the only survivors of the main seven being the youngest, Ian Lavender (then aged 27, playing 17), and the 'oldest', Clive Dunn (then 48, playing early seventies). In their time, and in their incredible ratings revival in the 80s and 90s, they could, as Tom Stoppard said in *The Guardian*, 'bring a smile and a tear to every lover of England and Ealing'.

Perry and Croft went on to develop *It Ain't Half Hot Mum* and *Hi-De-Hi!* Both were very successful, but they hadn't quite the heart of their predecessor, featuring stereotyped foreigners and homosexuals in a way that never would have befitted the little Kent town of Walmington-on-Sea. The terrors of war may have threatened Bombardier Beaumont, but they actually arrived for Captain Mainwaring, most notably in the form of Philip Madoc's snarling U-boat captain. And, despite having the mickey taken out of them, they were as frightening as England had imagined them. 'Vat is your name?' the German captain asks after Pikey has sung an anti-Nazi version of 'Whistle While You Work'. 'Don't tell him, Pike,' replies Mainwaring with superb timing.

The last time the end theme, played by the Band of the Coldstream Guards, was heard was on Remembrance Sunday 1977. In the episode 'Never Too Old', Jonesie married the buxom widow, Mrs Fox. The series ended with a toast to the Home Guard, champagne in tin mugs.

The whole humour of the show was summed up by the platoon's attempt at a sea patrol. Having practised rowing in the church hall, when they go to sea they get lost in the fog. Hearing French voices, they think that they've drifted across the Channel, and, hitting land, sneak aboard a train. When they open the doors again, a man in a bowler hat is standing there. 'Quelle est la gare?' asks Mainwaring. The man replies that, actually, it's Eastbourne.

The Liver Birds

- **BBC Television** (BBC1) ◆ B&W (1969); Colour (1971-79)
- **79 episodes** (30 minutes)
- **Writers:** Carla Lane, Lew Schwarz, Myra Taylor, David Pursall, Jack Seddon
- **Directors include:** Douglas Argent, Ray Butt
- **Producers:** Sydney Lotterby, Douglas Argent, Roger Race

Regular cast: Pauline Collins (Dawn) (pilot and first season only) • Polly James (Beryl Hennessey) • Nerys Hughes (Sandra Hutchinson) • Elizabeth Estensen (Carol Boswell)

With: John Nettles (Paul) • Mollie Sugden (Mrs Hutchinson) • Eileen Kennally/Carmel McSharry (Mrs Boswell) • Michael Angelis (Lucian) • Tom Chadbon (Derek) • Jack Le White (Grandad) • Ray Dunbobbin (Mr Boswell) • Patrick McAlinney (Father O'Leary) • Ivan Beavis/William Moore (Mr Hutchinson) • Cyril Shaps (Mr Hennessey) • Sheila Fay (Mrs Hennessey) • Jonathan Lynn (Robert)

When Carla Lane was seven, one of her poems won a prize from the *Liverpool Echo*. She married at 17, and had two sons before her writing started to become more than a hobby. With co-author Myra Taylor, also a Liverpool housewife, and veteran comedy writer Lew Schwarz, assigned to develop the project by producer Sydney Lotterby, she was to create the archetypal flat-sharing sitcom.

The Liver Birds, with its theme song by the Scaffold (featuring Roger McGough and Polly James exchanging: 'You dancing?' 'You asking?' 'I'm asking.' 'I'm dancing.'), premiered as a one-off play in the series *Comedy Playhouse*. In the same season were Tessie O'Shea in *As Good Cooks Go*, and *Tooth and Claw* (Marty Feldman and Warren Mitchell as lawyers in a Feldman/Took script). The unknowns' effort seemed the least likely to succeed.

The pilot (and the first four episodes) featured Pauline Collins as the prissy Dawn, and Polly James as the ebullient Beryl. The two incompatible characters shared a bedsit in Huskisson Street, Liverpool, and the series was designed as a 'female ***Likely Lads***'. The show had local colour, taking advantage of location filming to place the series in the city – the title refering to the famous stone birds that stand atop the Liver Building. Guest appearances by such Liverpool icons as McGough (who performed his poetry in a club in the third season) emphasized the local flavour. It was all convincing enough to persuade a dubious *Daily Mail* journalist (quite rightly doubting Liverpool's stereotypical claim to all that's chirpy) that 'perhaps the place really is like that'.

Comedy Playhouse
(14 Apr 69)

First season
(25 Jul–15 Aug 69)
Four episodes

Second season
(7 Jan–25 Mar 71)
Twelve episodes
7 Look Before You Leap
10 The Good Samaritans
11 Three's a Crowd

Third season
(11 Feb–12 May 72)
Thirteen episodes

Fourth season
(2 Jan–3 Apr 74)
31 Anybody Here Seen Thingy?
32 Friends at First Sight
33 Life is Just a Bowl of Sugar
34 Where's Beryl?
35 Girl Saturday
36 Pack up your Troubles
37 Have Hen will Travel
38 Love Is
39 Anyone for Freedom
40 Follow that Ring
41 The Bride that Went Away
42 Let Sleeping Dogs Lie
43 And Then There Was One

Fifth season
(5 Sep–17 Oct 75)
44 It Takes All Kinds
45 Look After the Children …
46 You've Got to Laugh
47 Love is a Many Stupid Thing
48 Dinner for Three
49 The Lily and the Dandelion
50 Everybody is Beautiful

Christmas special
(23 Dec 75)
51 In Every Street

Sixth season
(13 Feb–12 Mar 76)
52 Facing up to Life
53 The Maypole
54 Honey
55 The Never-Ending End
56 Badgers and Otters

Carol Boswell's taste in groovy music isn't shared by Sandra

Collins left the show swiftly, never really finding a rapport with James, and the planned six episodes were cut to four. At the start of the second season, Nerys Hughes arrived, clutching her scouse accent nervously. Sandra was the perfect foil to Beryl's tomboyish energy. She had grand aspirations, whereas, as she said, 'You're so basic, Beryl.' If Beryl sounded like a cross between Jimmy Clitheroe and Gracie Fields, Sandra tried hard to pronounce her haitches, only dropping into real dialect in moments of anger. Beryl was a big Everton fan, but Sandra couldn't be bothered to follow football, until that is, she and Beryl put together a team of girls to take on their boyfriends. The boys gave them a ten goal lead, and then went on to beat them 43-10, Sandra trying to play in a crash helmet. 'Isn't there a move in this game where you have to kick the ball with your head?'

By the end of the second season tension was becoming visible in the writing team. Schwarz had left once it became clear that Lane and Taylor were more than capable on their own, though the BBC, in a typically cautious gesture, retained the services of Eric Idle as script editor. There is, however, little sign of the ***Python*** influence in the work, indicating that Idle recognized emerging talent when he saw it.

Seventh season
(17 Oct–5 Dec 76)
57 Friends and Lovers
58 She Dreams a Lot
59 A Mark on the World
60 Love 'Em – And Almost Leave 'Em
61 Oh the Shame of It
62 Cry Please
63 The 'Nearly' Hat
64 Yellow and Green Make Blue

Christmas special
(22 Dec 76)
65 It Insists on Coming Once a Year

Eighth season
(23 Sep–4 Nov 77)
66 Something Beginning
67 The Flower Picker
68 You've No Idea What I've Been Through
69 God Bless Us and Save Us
70 They Decide Up There What Goes On Down Here
71 The Edge
72 The Struggle

Christmas special
(23 Dec 77)
73 Open Your Eyes – And It Still Hasn't Gone

Ninth season
(24 Nov 78–5 Jan 79)
74 There's No Place Like Away from Home
75 The Sixth Day
76 Various Kinds of Old
77 Weeds
78 Somewhere to Live… Somewhere to Love
79 The Best Things in Life are Not Free

[Episode 57 was originally the final episode of the sixth season, but was postponed from its intended transmission on 19 Mar 76 by an unscheduled news broadcast. Episode 79 was scheduled for 29 Dec 78 but was postponed by a week.]

However, the two Liverpudlians' working relationship was becoming strained, which would culminate with Taylor leaving the project and Lane writing the later seasons on her own, earlier episodes having been given to other writers. The final parting, as Lane told the *Sun*, came on the way home from a meeting before work began on the third season. 'The BBC's head of comedy said he wanted something different, and suddenly, on the train, I realized what he wanted. I told Myra, and, there and then, we both knew the partnership was over.'

The difference in emphasis, as Lane said, was that, with Taylor, 'We used to think up funny situations and build dialogue around them.... Once I was on my own, I started thinking "wouldn't it be sad if ... " and making funny lines out of little tragedies.' Lane was developing an approach that would serve her for all her working life.

At the start of the third season, Beryl and Sandra moved to a smarter, three-bedroomed flat, giving Lane the chance to make her comedy more subtle. Sandra began going out with Paul, and had to cope with visits from Beryl's Dad, who complained about everything in a nasal whine. He had little reason to grumble, since the virginal lifestyle of his daughter and her friend continued, up to the point of heavy petting, right out of the swinging 60s and far into the 70s. 'Did you and Robert ever – ?' 'No, we did not!' 'Was it nice?'

Londoner Robert was Jonathan Lynn, later to write ***Yes, Minister***. His great claim to fame at this point in his life was that he got Beryl to the altar, filmed in a Catholic church in Liverpool on the same day as Princess Anne's wedding. The end of the fourth season was certainly the end of one phase of the series, a literal end of innocence. When the series returned, a year later, it was far darker, Carla Lane's talents as a tragedienne coming to the fore.

The focus of the tragedy was Carol Boswell, whose red afro, gaudy jump suits and ridiculous platform shoes made a raucous contrast with Sandra's nice dresses. Nerys Hughes had chosen her new partner herself, having seen Estensen in *John, Paul, George, Ringo ... and Bert* on stage. She dragged producer Sydney Lotterby along the following night.

Carol was much more liberated than her still-naïve (if maturing) flatmate, once keeping Sandra up all night 'counting her boyfriend's ribs'. She did, however, say a prayer every night: 'God bless me Ma, God bless me Da, wherever he is ... ', dialogue that points the way to Ria's obsessed monologues in ***Butterflies.*** At one point, Sandra, an agnostic, is pushed to follow her example: 'You don't know me, but my friend Carol talks to you quite often ...'

Carol had a large Catholic family, including Carmel McSharry as Mrs Boswell (a name Lane would later reuse). The Boswells would often clash with the very middle-class Hutchinsons (Mollie Sugden by this time delighting in the most meaty role of her career). But the big hero for the younger viewers was Carol's brother, Lucian – and his rabbits. 'It's me rabbits ... ' became a playground slogan, as Michael Angelis would shuffle out of the Boswell's yard to regale the girls with his latest tale of leporidary misfortune. It's typical of Lane that, just when we were getting used to him as a comic character, she put him on the edge of a tower block, threatening to jump. His rabbits had, of course, been stolen. Plans to give Lucien a series of his own adventures got as far as an untransmitted pilot episode but, sadly, no further.

Expanding the format, Sandra took to working at a kennels, resulting in many routines involving dealing with animals. Indeed, this led to near-separate series as the two women went their own way. Sandra met Derek, the vet whom she was to marry, in a mini-romance that predicted the introverted character studies of *Solo*. The couple were married at the end of the eighth season, and one more season followed, with Carol becoming their lodger. The Boswells had their house demolished and moved into a caravan, and the two mothers agreed a truce over a cup of gin. Sandra became pregnant, finally signalling the end of the series.

The Liver Birds was the place Carla Lane honed her talent, the first time she would write convincingly about emotional anguish. It became a far deeper programme than the initial format ever suggested, and it will be interesting to see if the programme can survive its contrived transition into the 90s.

Up Pompeii!

- **BBC Television** (BBC1), **ITV** (1991) ◆ **Colour**
- **16 episodes** (standard length: 30 minutes) ◆ **1969-70, 1975, 1991**
- **Creator:** Talbot Rothwell
- **Writers:** Talbot Rothwell, Sid Colin (LWT special: Brian Leveson, Paul Minett)
- **Producers:** Michael Mills, David Croft, Sydney Lotterby, Paul Lewis

And it came to pass that a former *Carry on* writer managed to interest the BBC in a series based on the recently uncovered eye-witness testimony of Lurcio, slave to senator Ludicrous Sextus in ancient Pompeii (before Vesuvius engulfed the city in molten lava), concerning the dodgy goings on with the vestal virgins. And lo, the BBC were twice tittered, nay, thrice even ...

The *Radio Times* announced the arrival of *Up Pompeii!* by describing the series as 'a sort of *Carry on up the Forum*'. As well as alluding to Howerd's stage success in *A Funny Thing Happened on the Way to the Forum*, the phrase hints at the influences, the double entendre and the seaside-postcard naughtiness (titter ye not, missus) that was to make it such a controversial delight in the early 70s. Seen for the first time today, *Up Pompeii!* doesn't seem much to get steamed up about, but to have watched it in 1970 is to understand how deliciously naughty it was then.

Before his death in 1992, Frankie Howerd had become a major star all over again, largely on the strength of the devoted following that *Up Pompeii!* gained during its too-brief run on TV (a later film adaptation helped to swell the number of disciples). *Up Pompeii!* also occupies a unique place in TV history as the first comedy series to openly use sexual innuendo (albeit in a very sniggering, schoolboy fashion) as one of its main selling points, opening up mainstream television to the sexual revolution of the 60s and 70s, something that had seemed about as likely as Lurcio finally getting to finish 'The Prologue'.

Howerd's charismatic, cheesed-off-about-everything performance – one step ahead of his stupid masters and about 14 behind everyone else, including the audience – was the main attraction. Howerd and Lurcio at times became interchangeable: indeed, it's fair to say that Howerd isn't even acting in the accepted sense, but simply playing a ridiculous extension of his stage persona. It's only a small step from the glorious stage ramblings ('No! No, missus. Yes, no – naughty! Naughty! Nay, nay, and thrice nay!') to Lurcio's unfinished self-aware banter. And yet, like all of Howerd's best work, even the spontaneity was rigorously rehearsed and thought-out: Lurcio's comments only seemed to be in response to the live audience's rumblings, although this explains why the obviously-recorded nature of the 1991 LWT special was so inhibiting. The tales of Howerd rehearsing in Somerset graveyards or to a field of cows ('better than some audiences I've had') have become legendary.

Howerd was invariably well-supported by the guest stars: George Baker as James Bondus, Bill Maynard as Percentus the money gatherer, and the memorable (and obvious) Nymphia, played by Barbara Windsor. However, what sets *Up Pompeii!* on a pedestal above its many varied and mostly awful imitators (which

Starring: Frankie Howerd (Lurcio) • Max Adrian/Wallis Eaton/Mark Dignam (Ludicrous) • Georgina Moon (Erotica) • Elizabeth Larner (Ammonia) • Kerry Gardner (Nausius) • Jeanne Mockford (Senna the soothsayer) • William Rushton (Plautus)

Comedy Playhouse
(17 Sep 69)

First season
(30 Mar–11 May 70)
2 Vestal Virgins
3 The Ides of March
4 The Senator and the Asp
5 Britaniccus
6 The Actors
7 Spartacus
8 The Love Potion

Second season
(14 Sep–26 Oct 70)
9 The Legacy
10 Roman Holiday
11 James Bondus
12 The Peace Treaty
13 Nymphia
14 Exodus

Special
(31 Mar 75, 45 minutes)
15 Further Up Pompeii!

LWT special
(14 Dec 91, 45 minutes)
16 Further Up Pompeii

[*Up Pompeii!* featured no on-screen titles, those listed come from BBC video releases.]

includes just about everything LWT attempted during the early 70s) is that, at heart, underneath the tit-jokes, belly-laughs and unabashed stupidity of the narrative, *Up Pompeii!* is actually a very clever, witty and unusual piece of television. Although its tone would, in the short term, give rise to the *On the Buses*-style of sitcom humour, its influence reached much further.

At the centre of *Up Pompeii!*'s invention is Lurcio's direct interplay with the audience – dialogue designed to keep the viewer (whom Lurcio alone seems to know is watching) in touch with events and provide Howerd with some of the most blisteringly funny puns about the nature of TV comedy ever uttered. 'What a funny man,' says Lurcio at one point, then answers some unheard reply with 'What do you mean, this show needs one?'. Later, Spurious the spy (Larry Martyn) informs Lurcio of an elaborate conspiracy. 'What a ghastly plot,' says Lurcio before adding, 'and this is the ghastliest plot we've had yet!' When Spurious is stabbed in the back he tells Lurcio that he is dying. 'You can't die here, this is the living room,' notes a deadpan Howerd before telling the audience 'You wouldn't get this from Harold Pinter!' This aspect would particularly influence the structure of ***'Allo 'Allo!***, amongst others.

Proceedings were further enlivened by the licence given to the rest of the cast to overact. The previously-mentioned stabbing of Spurious takes place early on, but he spends the rest of the episode wandering through scenes crying 'I'm going!' 'You should have gone twenty minutes ago,' notes Howerd. 'It's only supposed to be a small part.'

Up Pompeii!'s awareness of its fictional nature set the standard for other attempts to knock down the 'fourth wall' which would be taken to its logical extreme in the 80s by American series such as *Moonlighting* and *Parker Lewis can't Lose*, both of which depended for much of their success on the premise that the characters know they are in a television series and act accordingly. *Up Pompeii!*, of course, was doing this some 15 years earlier.

After just two seasons, *Up Pompeii!* ended, although the series spawned no less than three feature films (each with a different setting, rather like the various ***Blackadder*** incarnations), a one-off BBC revival in 1975 and an LWT special in 1991. 'Many things have changed since we last met,' says Lurcio at the beginning of the LWT show. 'It is now AD. No longer BC. Or even BBC!'

The BBC transferred the same format, complete with Howerd, to the kasbah for six 1973 episodes of *Whoops Baghdad*. Between the two *Up Pompeii!* specials came probably the most interesting Howerd rarity, *Then Churchill Said to Me*, in which he starred as Private Percy Potts, batman to Nicholas Courtney's Lt. Col. Robin Witherton in Churchill's bunker. Made in 1982, transmission was postponed because of the Falklands War and the imminent arrival of the very similar ***'Allo 'Allo!***. The UK Gold transmission of the series unfortunately showed that there was another reason it had remained unscreened: it wasn't very good.

However, the smutty, mocking and hugely important *Up Pompeii!* is one of the greatest assertions of Frankie Howerd's much-missed genius. Titter ye not.

Last of the Summer Wine

- **BBC Television** (BBC1) ◆ Colour
- **149 episodes** (standard length: *c.* 30 minutes) ◆ 1973-95
- **Creator/writer:** Roy Clarke
- **Producers:** James Gilbert, Bernard Thompson, Sydney Lotterby, Alan J.W. Bell

Regular cast: Bill Owen (Compo Semini) • Peter Sallis (Norman Clegg) • Michael Bates (Blamire) • Brian Wilde (Foggy Dewhurst) • Michael Aldridge (Seymour Utterthwaite)

With: John Comer (Sid) • Jane Freeman (Ivy) • Kathy Staff (Nora Batty) • Joe Gladwin (Wally Batty) • Jonathan Linsley (Crusher) • Gordon Wharmby (Wesley Pegden) • Robert Fyfe (Howard) • Juliette Kaplan (Pearl) • Jean Ferguson (Marina) • Thora Hird (Edie Pegden) • Jean Alexander (Auntie Wainwright) • Stephen Lewis (Smiler)

There are two pitfalls that await the television executive when deciding whether or not to axe a programme. One is to pay too much attention to ratings, especially in the early years of a programme. Often series take time to develop, to refine their style or to attract a dedicated audience. Verity Lambert has made a plea for a long-term attitude to television, citing her production ***Minder*** as an example of a successful show that was not initially a great success. The other pitfall is in allowing a programme to decline simply because no one has the strength of character to put it out of its misery.

Last of the Summer Wine, by avoiding the first trap back in the 70s, has now regrettably fallen into the latter.

Like ***Steptoe and Son*** and ***Till Death Do Us Part*** before it, *Last of the Summer Wine* began life as a one-off drama for *Comedy Playhouse*, in this case beginning the 1973 season. Unlike ***Steptoe*** and ***Till Death***, however, *Last of the Summer Wine* was not an immediate hit, although perhaps matters were not helped by the fact that the BBC screened the first season after the *Nine O'Clock News* on Monday nights. The humour itself was poles apart from the rabid ranting of Alf Garnett: it was slow and philosophical, and like a fine wine needed time to mature. The BBC stuck with it, 'lending' it slots

Comedy Playhouse
(4 Jan 73)
1 Of Funerals and Fish

First season
(12 Nov–17 Dec 73)
2 Short Back and Palais Glide
3 The Inventor of the Forty Foot Ferret
4 Pate and Chips
5 Spring Fever
6 The New Mobile Trio
7 Hail Smiling Morn or Thereabouts

Second season
(5 Mar–16 Apr 75)
8 Forked Lightning
9 Who's That Dancing With Nora Batty, Then?
10 The Changing Face of Rural Blamire
11 Some Enchanted Evening
12 A Quiet Drink
13 Ballad for Wind Instrument and Canoe
14 Northern Flying Circus

Third season
(27 Oct–8 Dec 76)
15 The Man from Oswestry
16 Mending Stuart's Leg
17 The Great Boarding-House Bathroom Caper
18 Cheering up Gordon
19 The Kink in Foggy's Niblick
20 Going to Gordon's Wedding
21 Isometrics and After

Fourth season
(9 Nov 77–4 Jan 78)
22 Ferret Come Home
23 Getting on Sydney's Wire
24 Jubilee
25 Flower Power Cut
26 Who Made a Bit of a Splash in Wales, Then?
27 Greenfingers
28 A Merry Heatwave
29 The Bandit from Stoke-on-Trent

Christmas special
(26 Dec 78)
30 Small Tune on a Penny Wassail

Fifth season
(18 Sep–30 Oct 79)
31 Full Steam Behind
32 The Flag and its Snag
33 The Flag and Further Snags
34 Deep in the Heart of Yorkshire
35 Earnshaw Strikes Again
36 Here We Go into the Wild Blue Yonder
37 Here We Go Again into the Wild Blue Yonder

Christmas special
(27 Dec 79)
38 And a Dewhurst Up a Fir Tree

recently vacated by ***Till Death*** and ***Reginald Perrin***, and was rewarded by seeing the programme develop from being narrow 'cult' viewing to a national success. It was granted the privilege of its first Christmas episode in 1978.

We can be grateful to the BBC for continuing to support *Summer Wine*, if only because its concentration on older people has provided an antidote to the middle-class joke-free sitcoms of the 70s and 80s. However, this has opened up the programme to some criticism. Dr Eric Midwinter, the director of the Centre for Policy on Ageing, has commented that the main thrust of *Summer Wine* is the 'libidinous pursuit by the outrageous Compo of the harridan Nora Batty, right down to the last exotic twist of her wrinkled stockings. Nonetheless, we should at least know what we are laughing at – the age-old images of the dirty old man and the ugly old woman, and the vulgarity implicit in their sexuality.' This is true but perhaps a little unfair. The major appeal of *Summer Wine* (and the reason children are amongst its biggest fans) is the warmth and fondness with which the characters are drawn: they are, despite their foolishness, charming and engaging. We laugh not at them but with them: they have the energy and spirit of children and are thus, somehow, commendable.

Compo's fascination for Mrs Batty (as she was initially known) is almost as old as the series itself, and the age-old themes have recurred almost every season. 'One of the Last Few Places Unexplored by Man' referred to Compo's burning desire to have his photograph taken in Nora's bedroom, and another episode ('The Mysterious Feet of Nora Batty') dealt with a fiendishly complicated plan to establish Nora's shoe size. 'Quick, Quick Slow' saw Compo utterly depressed as Smiler became Batty's lodger. (The joke is that Smiler, of course, feels utterly intimidated by the woman, and spends as little time there as possible.)

Although it does deal with larger-than-life characters and situations, *Summer Wine* has often sought to balance the comedy with a little pathos. A beautiful moment in 'Getting Sam Home' has Clegg, the weary, sensible foil to Compo's scruffy schoolboyishness, pondering the casualties of war. Although Roy Clarke has called his characters 'raging adolescents', and Peter Sallis has described the programme as being '*Just William* with pension books', it is hardly surprising that many fans' best-loved scenes are the introspective scenes that began a number of the earlier episodes. We hear the three men talking about their very real troubles and their deepest (albeit often most ludicrous) thoughts. Often they are invisible for a while, and then we finally see them, surveying the glorious Yorkshire countryside (the series is filmed in Holmfirth, just south of Huddersfield).

'Getting Sam Home', a feature-length special in 1983, also had the sort of convoluted plot that had previously only been hinted at in the half-hour episodes. Briefly, it

Christmas special
(25 Dec 81)
39 Whoops!

Sixth season
(4 Jan–15 Feb 82)
40 In the Service of Humanity
41 Car and Garter
42 The Odd Dog Men
43 A Bicycle Made for Three
44 One of the Last Few Places Unexplored by Man
45 Serenade for Tight Jeans and Metal Detector
46 From Wellies to Wet Suit

Christmas special
(25 Dec 82)
47 All Mod Conned

Seventh season
(30 Jan–6 Mar 83)
48 The Frozen Turkey Man
49 The White Man's Grave
50 The Waist Land
51 Cheering Up Ludovic
52 The Three Astaires
53 The Arts of Concealment

Christmas special
(27 Dec 83, 90 minutes)
54 Getting Sam Home

Christmas special
(30 Dec 84)
55 The Loxley Lozenge

Eighth season
(10 Feb–17 Mar 85)
56 The Mysterious Feet of Nora Batty
57 Keeping Britain Tidy
58 Enter the Phantom
59 Catching Digby's Donkey
60 The Woollen Mills of your Mind
61 Who's Looking After the Café, Then?

Special
(1 Jan 86, 85 minutes)
62 Uncle of the Bride

Christmas special
(28 Dec 86)
63 Merry Christmas Father Christmas

Ninth season
(4 Jan–22 Mar 87)
64 Why Does Norman Clegg Buy Ladies' Elastic Stockings?
65 The Heavily Reinforced Bottom
66 Dried Dates and Codfanglers
67 The Really Masculine Purse
68 Who's Feeling Ejected Then?
69 The Ice Cream Man Cometh
70 Set the People Free
71 Go with the Flow
72 Jaws
73 Edie and the Automobile
74 When You Take a Good Bite, Yorkshire Tastes Terrible
75 Wind Power

Christmas special
(25 Dec 87, 80 minutes)
76 Big Day at Dream Acres

Tenth season
(16 Oct–20 Nov 88)
77 The Experiment
78 The Treasure of the Deep
79 Dancing Feet
80 That Certain Smile
81 Downhill Racing
82 Day of the Welsh Ferret

Christmas special
(24 Dec 88, 60 minutes)
83 Crums

Eleventh season
(15 Oct–26 Nov 89)
84 Come Back, Jack Harry Teesdale
85 The Kiss and Mavis Poski
86 Oh Shut up and Eat Your Choc Ice
87 Who's that Bloke with Nora Batty, Then?
88 Happy Anniversary, Gough and Jessie
89 Getting Barry Higher in the World
90 Three Men and a Mangle

Christmas special
(23 Dec 89, 50 minutes)
91 What's Santa Bought for Nora, Then?

Twelfth season
(2 Sep–4 Nov 90)
92 Return of the Warrior
93 Come in Sunray Major
94 The Charity Balls
95 Walking Stiff Can Make You Famous
96 That's Not Captain Zero
97 Das (Welly) Boot
98 The Empire that Foggy Nearly Built
99 The Last Surviving Maurice Chevalier Impression
100 Roll On
101 A Landlady for Smiler

Christmas special
(27 Dec 90)
102 Barry's Christmas a.k.a. The Rescue of Father Christmas

Thirteenth season
(18 Oct–29 Nov 91)
103 Quick, Quick Slow
104 Give Us a Lift
105 Was That Nora Batty Singing?
106 Cashflow Problems
107 Passing the Earring
108 Pole Star

Christmas special
(22 Dec 91)
109 Situations Vacant

involved Compo, Clegg and Foggy sneaking their friend Sam out of his invalid bed for a final frolic with Lily-Bless-Her (Lynda Baron). Sam, of course, promptly died on them. A superb farce followed, and it was, in many ways, the pinnacle of the series.

It seems that since then the very nature of *Last of the Summer Wine* changed from the reflective to the downright silly. That is not to say that there had not been a rich element of the absurd in the 70s episodes: a bizarre encounter with horn-wearing Masonic types ('Who's a pretty bullock, then? Moo! Moo!') comes readily to mind. However, the plots of the individual episodes in the mid-80s began to get repetitive – there was almost always an encounter with Nora Batty, and for a while it seemed that every episode of *Summer Wine* involved testing out some fiendish mechanical contraption that would result in disaster. Sallis noted that the show had 'shifted from philosophical to physical. In the early days, the most we ever did was climb the occasional tree. Nowadays Compo's risking life and limb every week!'

In an attempt to revitalize the show, Clarke introduced a number of subplots of a more human nature – Thora Hird leading a suspicious group of local wives whose main topic of conversation was how to prevent old Howard from sneaking off from his spouse Pearl to see the younger Marina.

Despite the seeming lack of potential in a series that revolves around retired men, there have been some great stories: the fifth season saw

No wonder Compo looks glum: he's had to swap his beloved trousers for a uniform and the world's stupidest helmet ('Situations Vacant')

Fourteenth season
(25 Oct–26 Dec 92)
110 By the Magnificent Thighs of Ernie Burniston
111 Errol Flynn used to Have a Pair Like That
112 The Phantom of the Graveyard
113 The Self-Propelled Salad Strainer
114 Ordeal by Trousers
115 Happy Birthday Howard
116 Who's Got Rhythm?
117 Camera Shy
118 Wheelies
119 Stop that Castle!

Fifteenth season
(24 Oct–27 Dec 93)
120 How to Clear your Pipes
121 Where There's Smoke There's Barbecue
122 The Black Widow
123 Have You Got a Light Mate?
124 Stop that Bath
125 Springing Smiler
126 Concerto for Solo Bicycle
127 There are Gypsies at the Bottom of our Garden
128 Aladdin Gets on your Wick
129 Welcome to Earth

Special
(1 Jan 95, 60 minutes)
130 The Man Who Nearly Knew Pavarotti

Sixteenth season
(8 Jan–26 Feb 95)
131 The Glory Hole
132 Adopted by a Stray
133 The Defeat of the Stoneworm
134 Once in a Moonlit Junkyard
135 The Space Ace
136 The Most Powerful Eye-balls in West Yorkshire
137 The Dewhursts of Ogleby Hall
138 The Sweet Smell of Excess

Seventeenth season
(3 Sep–5 Nov 95)
139 Leaving Home Forever, or Till Teatime
140 Bicycle Bonanza
141 The Glamour of the Uniform
142 The First Human Being to Ride a Hill
143 Captain Clutterbuck's Treasure
144 Desperate for a Duffield
145 The Suit that Turned Left
146 Beware of the Elbow
147 The Thing in Wesley's Shed
148 Brushes at Dawn

Christmas special
(24 Dec 95, 60 minutes)
149 A Leg up for Christmas

[*First of the Summer Wine* was a 45-minute special transmitted on 3 Jan 88. It was followed by two seasons of six episodes, 4 Sep to 9 Oct 88 and 3 Sep to 8 Oct 89.]

an ambitious plan to 'complete' the British landscape by erecting a huge Union Jack (Corporal Signwriter Foggy's idea, of course: Clarke describes him as being 'spiritually in the 1940s'). In another two-episode romp, Compo ended up hang-gliding on a huge home-made construction, lovingly crafted by Wally Batty to look like one of his beloved pigeons.

When Foggy left the show in 1984 (Wilde and Owen have made no secret of their dislike for each other which, amongst other things, scuppered a stage adaptation in 1983), to be replaced by Michael Aldridge as Seymour, many people bemoaned the death of a classic line-up. In fact, those with longer memories were able to point out that this had happened before. Michael Bates left the series in 1976, original 'gang leader' Blamire departing in pursuit of a widow. The format was more than strong enough to take such knocks, although the deaths of John Comer and Joe Gladwin robbed the programme of two of its most-loved characters. (Wally's best line came in response to Nora's constant complaints about how tired she is. 'Why don't you sit down,' he says, without a trace of sympathy. 'You must be tired, you've been on your mouth all day.')

In 1990, Seymour left to be an assistant head teacher, and Foggy returned from six years of egg-decorating in Bridlington. Although the 'classic' line-up was in place once more, Clarke seemed unsure what to do with the format, with the cast of characters expanding all the time in a way that suggested soap more than sitcom. The public, still less the BBC, didn't seem to mind, Clarke monopolizing Sundays in the autumn schedules for 1995 with both *Last of the Summer Wine* and *Keeping Up Appearances*.

W. Stephen Gilbert, writing an ostensibly critical piece in *The Independent* in 1993, did much to sum up the paradoxical appeal of *Last of the Summer Wine*: 'It's always sunny even when they're well wrapped up against the wind. Nobody is hurt when they fall. And nobody dies, not Blamire, not John Comer's cantankerous proprietor of the tea shop (which remained mystifyingly empty until the budget was increased to allow for extras), not dear old Joe Gladwin's Wally: they just drop out between series. It's about an old age that never ages. No wonder we love it.'

Porridge

- **BBC Television** (BBC1) ◆ **Colour**
- **21 episodes** (standard length: 30 minutes) ◆ 1973-77
- **Creators/writers:** Dick Clement, Ian La Frenais
- **Producer/director:** Sydney Lotterby

Regular cast: Ronnie Barker (Fletcher) • Richard Beckinsale (Godber) • Fulton Mackay (Mr Mackay) • Brian Wilde (Mr Barrowclough)

With: Sam Kelly (Warren) • Tony Osoba (McLaren) • Christopher Biggins (Lukewarm) • Ken Jones (Ives) • Michael Barrington (Governor Venables) • Peter Vaughan (Harry Grout) • Brian Glover (Heslop) • Ronald Lacey (Harris) • David Jason (Blanco) • Maurice Denham (Rawley) • Patricia Brake (Ingrid) • Alun Armstrong (Spraggon) • David Daker (Jarvis)

Porridge may well be the finest sitcom ever created. A brilliant observation of prison life, it was the ideal vehicle for a group of comedy actors, led by Ronnie Barker, at the peak of their careers.

As with ***Steptoe and Son***, *Porridge* was created out of a comedy anthology, in this case *Seven of One*, a showcase for the talents of Barker in the hands of different writers. Dick Clement and Ian La Frenais, on a roll from their highly successful ***Whatever Happened to the Likely Lads?***, created 'Prisoner and Escort', which told the story of recidivist Norman Stanley Fletcher, about to begin a five-year prison sentence for theft, accompanied by two prison officers, Mackay and Barrowclough. The officers have wildly different approaches to the punishment of offenders and how much trust should be given to them. On the way, as a result of Fletcher relieving himself in the petrol tank, the van breaks down on the Cumberland Fells and, whilst Mackay goes for help, Fletcher and Barrowclough shelter in a lonely cottage.

Although the BBC clearly felt there was mileage in the characters, it was some time before a full series was commissioned. Clement and La Frenais turned instead to LWT, for whom they created *Thick as Thieves*, a sitcom starring Bob Hoskins and John Thaw which, with hindsight, is a clear stepping-stone from the working-class 'laddism' of ***Whatever Happened to the Likely Lads?*** to the proud honour-amongst-thieves style of *Porridge*. *Thick as Thieves*, significantly, ended after one season, just as the BBC decided to give *Porridge* the green light.

Confident that they had another classic on their hands, Ian La Frenais told the *Radio Times* that 'casting is the key. If the actors are right, all your troubles are over', whilst Clement commented that the series was 'about survival. It's about small victories, like little day-to-day triumphs people need in order to keep their self-respect.' The first season of *Porridge* was prefaced by a repeat of 'Prisoner and Escort'.

The series may seem, from a distance, to be glorifying crime, but the criminals in *Porridge* seldom seek to justify themselves or their activities. Unlike the Boswells in *Bread*, the inmates don't have a social message to ram home: or, if there is one, it is as understated as Galton and Simpson's subtle portraits of poverty and loneliness. Several of the series' heroes were outsider figures for their time. Fletcher was workshy (when the term still had some comic punch), Warren was illiterate, Lukewarm was gay and McLaren black. But whereas other comedy series would have used these traits to create crude one-joke characters, *Porridge* took social 'boxes' as a starting point and built real people from them. We were neither lectured by, nor encouraged to laugh at, the characters, because they were, simply, what they were. The code of honour-amongst-thieves held only

SEVEN OF ONE
(1 Apr 73)
1 Prisoner and Escort

First season
(5 Sep–10 Oct 74)
2 New Faces, Old Hands
3 The Hustler
4 A Night In
5 A Day Out
6 Ways and Means
7 Men Without Women

Second season
(24 Oct–28 Nov 75)
8 Just Deserts
9 Heartbreak Hotel
10 Disturbing the Peace
11 No Peace for the Wicked
12 Happy Release
13 The Harder they Fall

Christmas special
(24 Dec 75, 45 minutes)
14 No Way Out

Christmas special
(24 Dec 76, 45 minutes)
15 The Desperate Hours

Third season
(18 Feb–25 Mar 77)
16 A Storm in a Teacup
17 Poetic Justice
18 Rough Justice
19 Pardon Me
20 A Test of Character
21 Final Stretch

[*Going Straight* was transmitted between 24 Feb 78 and 7 Apr 78 (6 episodes).]

as far as the nearest 'tea leaf', and with gangsters like Harry Grout, or sneak-thieves like Harris, not to mention the ever hard-nosed and bossy Mackay around it was hard not to feel some sympathy for the men of Slade Prison. The gaol had only two rules: one – do not write on the walls; two – obey all the rules. (Mackay once explains to Fletcher's young cell-mate, Lennie Godber, that he is not victimizing him: he simply treats all prisoners with equal contempt.)

In retrospect, it was 'A Night In' – a ***Steptoe***-like 'two-men-in-one-room' play in which Fletcher senses that Godber is beginning to find the going tough, and helps him to cope with life inside – that really caught the freshness of approach in *Porridge*. 'A Day Out' has Fletcher and Godber in the prison work party (which includes Dylan, so called because of his similarity to the hippie rabbit in ***The Magic Roundabout***) and gave them a rare chance to have a look at the outside world. The season ended with 'Men Without Women', in which Fletcher hatches a devious plan to afford himself a weekend's compassionate leave.

Porridge's strength lay in its ability to work within a framework of basic characters, although the introduction of different elements like Blanco, a kindly father-figure (erroneously imprisoned for a murder he didn't commit, having gotten away with one that he did), and, later, Rawley, the judge responsible for sending Fletcher down, himself imprisoned on corruption charges, gave the series further scope. The 1975 Christmas episode – in which Fletcher plays a fine balancing act between Grout and Mackay and ends up getting himself into hospital for Christmas – has been rightly acclaimed as one of the finest pieces of television comedy ever.

The series ended on a high – both in terms of ratings and critical reception – after three seasons, with Godber being released. The final scene between Mackay and Fletcher has Fletcher stating that he has had enough and just wants to get out and 'go straight'.

In 1978, Clement, La Frenais, Lotterby, Barker, Beckinsale and Patricia Brake were involved in a sequel, *Going Straight*, which concentrated on Fletcher's immediate post-prison life. The first episode, in which Tony Osoba and Fulton Mackay also reprised their roles from *Porridge*, was a joy, but thereafter, deprived of the closeted anger that made *Porridge* so effective, *Going Straight* fell somewhat flat (although it did give Nicholas Lyndhurst early exposure as Fletcher's son, Raymond). The following year *Porridge* became a film, with genuine prison locations and a convoluted plot concerning a celebrity football match.

Porridge proved that sitcom can take place in almost any situation, provided it has quality scripts and cast. Repeats of the series in the late 80s achieved some of its highest-ever viewing figures, indicating that, while the format might have seemed limited, the changeless prison regime was in fact responsible for some timeless comedy.

Rising Damp

- **Yorkshire Television** (ITV) ◆ Colour
- **28 episodes** (30 minutes) ◆ 1974-78
- **Creator/writer:** Eric Chappell
- **Producers/directors:** Ian MacNaughton, Ronnie Baxter, Len Lurcuck, Vernon Lawrence

Starring: Leonard Rossiter (Rupert Rigsby) • Richard Beckinsale (Alan Moore) • Frances de la Tour (Ruth Jones) • Don Warrington (Philip Smith) • Derek Newark (Spooner) • Gay Rose (Brenda)

What is that thing above Alan's head?

The story of one man and his cat, a foul-tempered, smelly, moth-eaten thing. And then there was the cat.

Set in a nameless northern seaside town with its own university, *Rising Damp* was to ITV what ***Steptoe and Son*** had been to the BBC a decade earlier, proving that where there's a mean, cynical old git, there is also, usually, humour.

Eric Chappell, the creator of the ATV office sitcom *The Squirrels* (and, later, the disappointing *Fiddlers Three*), had originally invented the characters in a stage play entitled *The Banana Box* some years before – the Rigsby character then called Rooksby – and transferred them to television as one of a series of pilot episodes tested by Yorkshire, under the guidance of the station's new head of light entertainment, Duncan Wood. (The others included the pilot of Alan Plater's *Oh*

No! It's Selwyn Frogitt and Galton and Simpson's well-remembered, one-off football play *You'll Never Walk Alone*.) From the start, the *TV Times* noted that *Rising Damp* – produced by ***Monty Python***'s Ian MacNaughton – was the most obvious 'series material'.

The series was set in a seedy, tumbledown tenement owned by Rigsby, a character described by Leonard Rossiter as someone who 'makes Alf Garnett look like a tolerant chairman of the Race Relations Board'. His tenants include the sex-starved, excitable Ruth Jones (a brilliantly over-the-top performance by Shakespearian actress Frances de la Tour), the naive, skint, long-haired and equally sex-starved medical student Alan, and his room-mate, the bitingly sarcastic, son-of-a-tribal-chief, Philip.

Unlike other classic sitcoms, *Rising Damp*'s storylines are not, in themselves, instantly memorable. Sometimes there simply doesn't seem to be a central theme, while on other occasions the intrusive adverts puts paid to much intended subtlety and characterization. Also, ***Rising Damp***'s plotlines have an unfortunate air of familiarity about them. The similarities between certain episodes of *Rising Damp* and, for example, ***Fawlty Towers*** (the episode where Rigsby is swindled out of his savings by a con-man – Henry MacGee – posing as an old Etonian) or ***Steptoe and Son*** (the scene in which Rigsby raids the gas meter to pay for a night out) aren't plagiarism so much as an indication that the series relied for its popularity on the brilliance of its characters rather than any great originality of plot.

There are memorable episodes, of course: Rigsby, Alan and Philip taking Ruth to a local restaurant and making complete fools of themselves, or George Sewell posing as a detective to rob Rigsby. Any scene featuring Rigsby's legendary (if seldom seen) pussy, Vienna (so called because 'if he sees another pair of eyes out there it's goodnight Vienna'), was a joy. In one episode the cat was missing, presumed dead, and a mournful group gathered to sing 'Rock of Ages' in tribute, whilst Rigsby's constant frustrations at attempting to seduce Miss Jones would always be met firstly with refusal and secondly with a cat squeal off-camera as he took out his anger on the helpless beast.

Rising Damp's stab at politics was less successful. In one of the earliest episodes, Philip and Alan lend support to the local Labour candidate in a by-election whilst Rigsby, ever the social climber, becomes a member of the local Conservative association. Rigsby's description of the Labour candidate, Pendry, as homosexual and dishonest led to the series being sued by real-life Labour MP Tom Pendry who felt that the character had been used to defame him. He won his case and Yorkshire were left with a whopping damages bill.

Unlike Rigsby, Philip had the misfortune to be the object of Ruth's desires, which was a pity since he wasn't really interested in her, whilst Alan's few attempts at bringing girls back to the flat were ruined by Rigsby's interference. In short, three out of the four of *Rising Damp*'s central characters were

Pilot episode
(2 Sep 74)
1 Rising Damp [aka Rooksby]

First season
(13 Dec 74–17 Jan 75)
2 Black Magic
3 A Night Out
4 Charisma
5 All our Yesterdays
6 The Prowler
7 Stand up and be Counted

Second season
(7 Nov–19 Dec 75)
8 The Permissive Society
9 Food Glorious Food
10 A Body Like Mine
11 Moonlight and Roses
12 A Perfect Gentleman
13 The Last of the Big Spenders
14 Things that Go Bump in the Night

Christmas special
(26 Dec 75)
15 For the Man Who Has Everything

Third season
(12 Apr–24 May 77)
16 That's my Boy
17 Stage Struck
18 Clunk-Click
19 The Good Samaritans
20 Fawcett's Python
21 The Cocktail Hour
22 Suddenly at Home

Fourth season
(4 Apr–9 May 78)
23 Hello Young Lovers
24 Fire and Brimstone
25 Great Expectations
26 Pink Carnations
27 Under the Influence
28 Come on in the Water's Lovely

sexually-frustrated, and this provided a launching pad for plenty of subversion of traditional comedy situations, another of the reasons for *Rising Damp*'s huge popularity. Alison Pearson, writing in *The Independent*, notes that 'when Miss Jones ... says "I don't know if it's the light, Mr Rigsby, but you look strangely fascinating this evening", we crack up because the line carries the freight of the epic vanity that Leonard Rossiter gave the landlord. If his performance had even *winked* at the idea of Rigsby being a malodorous ferret, the joke would lose its root.'

Frances de la Tour left the series a star when Ruth ran off with her wimpish middle-aged boyfriend, Desmond, in 1975. There was no new season in 1976 as Rossiter was engaged in the debut of ***The Fall and Rise of Reginald Perrin***, but, after he had appeared in Yorkshire's *The Galton and Simpson Playhouse*, in the Ron Baxter-produced *I Tell You, It's Burt Reynolds*, alongside his wife Gillian Raine, and won the *TV Times* Funniest Man on TV award, he returned to *Rising Damp*, along with Frances de la Tour, for a third season in 1977.

The series was still witty and quick-fire, but the departure of Beckinsale before the fourth season left a huge void. It is a tribute to the quality of *Rising Damp*, however, that the late Richard Beckinsale is as much remembered for this as he is for ***Porridge*** or *The Lovers*. However, it is Leonard Rossiter, the insurance salesman who, like Reggie Perrin, suddenly decided as he entered middle-age that life held more for him than sitting behind a desk, that places *Rising Damp* amongst the greats.

With his hands-on-hips stance, quickly-nodding head, rolling-upwards eyes and cynical grin as a groan of 'My-y-y God' is uttered, Rigsby is an immortal comic creation.

Fawlty Towers

- **BBC Television** (BBC2) ◆ **Colour**
- **12 episodes** (30 minutes) ◆ **1975–79**
- **Creators/writers:** John Cleese, Connie Booth
- **Director:** Bob Spiers
- **Producers:** John Howard Davies, Douglas Argent

Starring: John Cleese (Basil Fawlty) • Prunella Scales (Sybil Fawlty) • Andrew Sachs (Manuel) • Connie Booth (Polly) • Ballard Berkeley (Major Gowen) • Gilly Flower (Miss Tibbs) • Renee Roberts (Miss Gatsby) • Brian Hall (Terry)

When the ***Monty Python*** team were filming near Torquay in 1972, they stayed in a hotel run by, in the words of John Cleese, 'the most wonderfully rude man I've ever met'. American Terry Gilliam's table manners were criticized for being too American; Eric Idle's briefcase was thrown into the street because it probably contained a bomb. 'He thought that guests were sent along to annoy him and to prevent him from running the hotel.'

Later, one of Cleese and Graham Chapman's scripts for LWT's *Doctor at Large* featured a rude hotel owner with a bossy wife, but it was when Cleese and then wife Connie Booth began writing *Fawlty Towers* that the mad hotel manager, to be played by Cleese himself, really took on a life of his own. *Fawlty Towers*, like perhaps no programme before it, stunned its audience with its non-stop humour, and it remains a high-water mark of finely-crafted British comedy that will probably never be bettered.

The concept of *Fawlty Towers* – the guest-hating owner, his dragon-like wife, and the incompetent Spanish disaster area foolishly employed as waiter – was only going to be as funny as the situations and scripts that evolved from the premise. Cleese and Booth worked tirelessly on the plots, which were created on long rolls of wallpaper, with each character or sub-plot having a different coloured felt-tip. Once they were happy with the course of events, each episode reportedly took four months to write and went through about ten drafts. And it showed – never before had 30 minutes been so packed with gags, visual and verbal (Cleese noted with distaste the amount of padding in most half-hour comedies); and rarely had plots been so delicately built, until they resembled huge towers of cards just waiting to crash down on Basil and his schemes. As Clive James noted of repeats of the second season, 'the fact that you knew roughly what was going to happen gave you time to appreciate how the comic structure had been assembled. Basil didn't just put his soot-covered hand on the Australian girl's breast. He went up a staircase, along a corridor, into a cupboard, out through a window, up a ladder, back through another window, in and out of the same cupboard again, and then put his hand on the Australian girl's breast, just in time for Mrs Fawlty to walk in and incinerate him with a look.'

The series began with 'A Touch of Class', an episode that illustrates well Basil's attitude to customers. He advertises in *Country Life*, hoping to attract a 'better class of person' – an approach almost guaranteed to

First season
(19 Sep–24 Oct 75)
1 A Touch of Class
2 The Builders
3 The Wedding Party
4 The Hotel Inspectors
5 Gourmet Night
6 The Germans

Second season
(19 Feb–26 Mar 79)
7 Communication Problems
8 The Psychiatrist
9 Waldorf Salad
10 The Kipper and the Corpse
11 The Anniversary
12 Basil the Rat

[Episode 12 was not broadcast until 25 Oct 79 owing to BBC industrial action (episode 11 was delayed by a week before being shown on 26 Mar 79).]

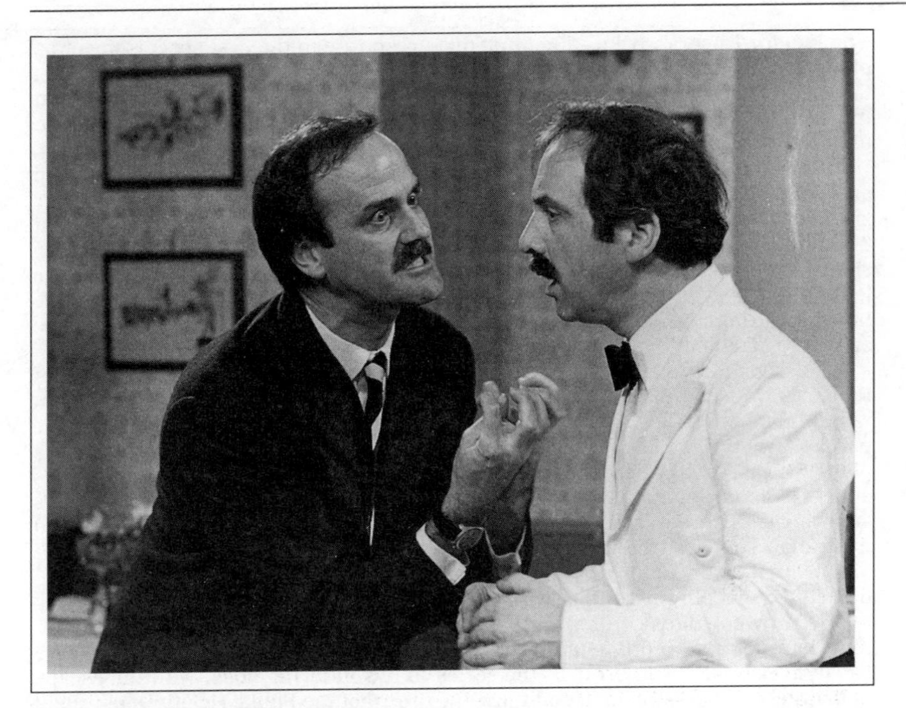

'Please try to understand before one of us dies ...'

anger pragmatic Sybil. Basil complains of losing 'tone': 'I mean, have you seen the people in room six? They've never even sat on chairs before.' It comes as no surprise to anyone – except Basil – that he soon gets taken in by a con-man impersonating a member of the aristocracy.

O'Reilly and his gang of incompetent builders graced Fawlty Towers with their presence in the second episode and botch a simple job so wonderfully that the episode ends with Basil charging into the distance with a plastic gnome ready for bodily insertion.

The modern sport of Manuel-abusing began in earnest in this episode, with a cranium-crunching slam into a newly doorless wall. Future attacks involved a frying pan (Cleese, attempting a glancing blow, hit Andrew Sachs so hard with it that the pan dented) and a spoon (which almost knocked Sach's teeth out). 'Be grateful,' Cleese commented, 'it's not a long run on stage. We only have to do it once.' Most worrying of all for Sachs was the sequence for the final episode of the first season where the kitchen (and Manuel) catch fire, which resulted in severely burnt shoulders and permanent scarring. 'In summer it's the bit that doesn't get brown. It looks as if my wings have fallen off.' The BBC paid Sachs £700 in compensation.

By the end of the season, Basil had accused a party of wedding guests of all manner of dubious sexual liaisons, assaulted a spoon-seller for not being a hotel inspector and, memorably, given his car 'a damn good thrashing' for its role in the abortive 'Gourmet Night'. The final episode, with its wonderful story of Sybil's ingrowing toe-nail, a cardigan-snagging moose head, an exploding fire extinguisher, and a clutch of German guests to whom Basil tries frantically not to mention the war, proved to be one of the very finest examples of British comedy. Cleese's long-legged impersonation of Hitler was probably the funniest visual gag on television since his Minister of Silly Walks in ***Monty Python***.

Although some people simply did not understand the joke of the series – complaining that Basil was the worst man on earth to run a hotel, which is precisely why *Fawlty Towers* works – the immediate response to the first six episodes was phenomenal. Even the hotel trade was positive, Cleese commenting that 'One of the nicest things about the programme is that a lot of people in the trade say that it is remarkably accurate about what goes on behind the scenes. One hotel chain uses the programme as a training film on what not to do.'

However, there was a long delay between seasons. Cleese and Booth split up and got involved in other projects, but they continued to labour away at another six scripts, which Cleese proudly claimed came in at about 120 pages each ('most 30-minute shows have about 65 pages' he noted in comparison). As well as being shown around the world (including in the States, where one channel showed the lot in a single evening), the first six episodes had already been transmitted three times in Britain. To say that expectation for the new episodes was high would be an understatement.

The second season begins with the epic encounter with the stoically deaf Mrs Richards, who complains about the view from her window ('... may I ask what you were hoping to see out of a Torquay hotel bedroom window? Sydney Opera House perhaps? The Hanging Gardens of Babylon?') and becomes embroiled in Basil's plan to have a secret bet on a horse. Manuel's English has improved, but not his ability to read situations. 'I know nah-thing,' he announces proudly, to Basil's annoyance. 'The Psychiatrist' featured the Doctors Abbott, the aforementioned Australian girl, and the hirsute medallion-covered Mr Johnson, who Basil calls 'the bravest orang-utan in Britain'. 'Waldorf Salad' (arguably the worst episode) depicts Basil's all-out conflict with America in the form of Mr Hamilton, and is followed by episodes dealing with a death in the hotel and Basil's aborted plan to celebrate his wedding anniversary (Polly is forced to impersonate Mrs Fawlty). 'Basil the Rat' brought the series to a wonderful close, with the escape of Manuel's 'Siberian hamster' at the same time that the Public Health Department are threatening to close the place down. An awesomely tacky pretend rat and an unconscious Basil were our last glimpses into the strange goings-on in *Fawlty Towers*.

For a while, there was talk of a film, probably involving Basil and co. going to Spain and encountering an even ruder hotel manager there, but Cleese has (rightly) resisted all attempts to persuade him to get involved in another series. The first episode of ***Not the Nine O'Clock News*** saw Cleese and Sachs briefly reprise their roles to make this point (Fawlty/Cleese, on the phone to a TV executive, refuses to do another series, suggesting a 'tacky revue' instead). Indeed, *Fawlty Towers* is well-remembered precisely because its distilled comedy marks it out as being so different from most other programmes where originality can often be beaten out of a series as it is milked for all that it's worth for years afterwards. Everything about *Fawlty Towers* was right, from the title music (and the rearranged 'Farty Towels' sign) to Ballard Berkeley's performance as the senile Major. As repeats (complete with *Radio Times* cover) in 1995 proved, as long as there is television, there will be eagerly-received episodes of *Fawlty Towers*.

The Fall and Rise of Reginald Perrin

- **BBC Television** (BBC1) ◆ Colour
- **22 episodes** (30 minutes) ◆ 1976–79
- **Creator/writer:** David Nobbs
- **Producers:** John Howard Davies, Gareth Gwenlan

'When Reginald Iolanthe Perrin set out for work on the Thursday morning, he had no intention of calling his mother-in-law a hippopotamus.'

But he does ... and so begins the great tale of a respectable man 'dropping out' of all that middle-class life has to offer (although, for some reason, the TV adaptation of David Nobbs's book *The Death of Reginald Perrin* begins on a Tuesday). As well as mirroring the faked death of Labour MP John Stonehouse, the literary echo is Somerset Maugham's *The Moon and Sixpence*. This featured Charles Strickland, a respectable stockbroker, husband, and father, abruptly leaving for Paris, although, as Rossiter pointed out, Strickland had his painting. Reggie didn't quite know what he wanted to do, be it working on a pig farm (the pigs loved him) or becoming a tycoon. Still, it couldn't have been easy for poor old Reggie; his initials are RIP, the train continually gets him into work 22½ minutes late, and whenever he goes in to see his obnoxious boss, CJ, he is forced to sit on a flatulent chair. (CJ's other annoying habits include his inability to accommodate people at times that are convenient to them, and his constant use of the phrase 'I didn't get where I am today by ... ' – most notably 'I didn't get where I am today by talking in clichés', and then proceeding to do so for an entire scene.)

Reggie's life is utterly repetitive – and the almost surreal monotony of the first episode in particular is reminiscent of the famous *déjà vu* sequence in ***Monty Python***, whilst the recurring dream sequences (notably Reggie and Joan making love in a field) gave the series a deep psychological edge.

As played by Leonard Rossiter, well-known for his award-winning performance in Brecht's *Arturo Ui* and his TV landlord, Rigsby, in ***Rising Damp***, Reginald Perrin struck a chord with 1970s Britain, and the show won many awards for TV comedy. *The Fall and Rise of Reginald Perrin* was a comedy unlike most others: it was a serial, not a series, with a very definite plot, involving Perrin's rebellion against his commuterized life, his fake death (walking into the sea during the series' title sequence), his outrageous alter egos, and his remarriage to his wife whilst disguised as his old friend Martin Welbourne. It made an important point, in that his quest for happiness seemed almost endless; he was not entirely happy as Welbourne, he was fired from Sunshine Deserts, and so was forced to start Grot, a shop selling useless and horrible things (his son-in-law's revolting wine, square-footballs, silent records) at vastly inflated prices. Grot was a wonderful attack on capitalism that ended up celebrating it, becoming a success, and making Perrin a tycoon. His victory was sealed when Sunshine Deserts went bust (the falling letters on the company building acting as a metaphor for its decline). But was he happy? He'd swapped his old routine for another (despite his occasional use of the bicycle), employed his old secretary, Joan, and some of his colleagues from Sunshine

Starring: Leonard Rossiter (Reginald Perrin) • Pauline Yates (Elizabeth Perrin) • John Barron (CJ) • Sue Nicholls (Joan Greengross) • Trevor Adams (Tony Webster) • Bruce Bould (David Harris-Jones) • John Horsley (Doc Morrissey) • Terence Conoley (Peter Cartwright) • Sally-Jane Spencer (Linda) • Geoffrey Palmer (Jimmy) • Tim Preece/Leslie Schofield (Tom) • Theresa Watson (Prue Harris-Jones) • Joseph Brady (McBlane)

First season
(8 Sep–20 Oct 76)
Seven episodes

Second season
(21 Sep–2 Nov 77)
Seven episodes

Third season
(29 Nov 78–24 Jan 79)
Eight episodes

Deserts (CJ, Tony 'Great' Webster, David 'Super' Harris-Jones) – and was horrifyingly turning into CJ, beginning to adopt his mannerisms and phrases. The second season ended much as the first, with Reggie, Elizabeth and CJ all faking suicide.

The lives of the characters had become very entangled. CJ and Elizabeth almost had an affair, as did Reggie and Joan: on their second near-discovery, Perrin remarks 'The drainpipe is in the usual place'. Reggie's family seemed to be composed of lunatics, including his brother-in-law Jimmy, with his ridiculous catchphrase ('Bit of a cock-up on the ... front') and his clipped-militaristic dialogue. A version of the character was given his own series in *Fairly Secret Army*.

Reggie had attempted to destroy Grot, the monster he had created, by employing idiots in key positions (Jimmy, Doc Morrissey and the Irish labourer Seamus – 'from the land o' the bogs and the little people' – whom Reggie makes Marketing Director and who turns out to be a business genius).

In the third season, Reggie begins a community, again using all of his old friends from Sunshine Deserts in the hope of at last finding the meaning of his 'worthless' existence. Less impressive than the first two seasons, the final season at least brought all the characters together under one roof, and introduced the memorable Scottish chef, McBlane, with the impenetrable accent ('Up yer clunge').

The Fall and Rise of Reginald Perrin seemed to have found its niche once again in the 90s, with a repeat season in 1991 gaining quite remarkable viewing figures. It had been successful enough to spawn a US equivalent (*Reggie*, starring *Soap*'s Richard Mulligan), but the BBC episodes remain classics in their own right.

We're never asked to accept the characters as real people, unlike in the majority of sitcoms, but as exaggerated ciphers, the swift to-and-fro of dialogue and scene-breaks suggesting stage farce rather than TV comedy. It took an actor of Rossiter's calibre to make Reggie into more than a symbol. He did this with a mocking delivery and, it seems, an element of spontaneity that indicated that he enjoyed the velocity of it all as much as the audience did.

As this book went to press, David Nobbs's sequel, *The Legacy of Reginald Perrin*, was being filmed. Perrin himself is dead – killed by a falling billboard advertising the very assurance company he was insured by – but most of the other characters return, called upon to do absurd things to meet the terms of Reggie's will. Let's hope it's a fitting tribute to a great character.

Citizen Smith

- **BBC Television** (BBC1) ◆ **Colour**
- **31 episodes** (30 minutes) ◆ **1977–80**
- **Creator/writer: John Sullivan**
- **Director: Ray Butt**
- **Producers: Peter Whitmore, Dennis Main Wilson, Ray Butt**

Wolfie Smith probably wouldn't approve of this book, celebrating as it does the 'Fascist' institution of television. Indeed, its authors would doubtless be under a death sentence 'come the glorious day' ('Last fag. Up against the wall. Bop! Bop!'). Of course, when the glorious day finally came, it wasn't like that at all: not, as Wolfie had promised (after eight pints), '40,000 marching over the Cotswolds', but four lunatics in a tank. So much for the revolution.

Citizen Smith came along just in time to save sitcom from the unstoppable advance of the middle-aged, middle-class blandness of *Happy Ever After*, *Keep it in the Family* and *The Good Life*. It became one of the most talked about series of its era – hated by reformed hippies (who, rightly, saw Wolfie as a wicked parody of themselves), real-life socialists (who couldn't understand what was so funny about someone who saw himself as the Che Guevara of Tooting) and the critics, and loved by almost everyone else. *Citizen Smith* stuck an irreverent two-fingers in the air at the convention that dictated that comedy and politics couldn't mix.

Citizen Smith was created by John Sullivan, who had grown up in Balham and Tooting where he remembered 'men selling *Soviet Weekly* and *The Morning Star* outside the Wimpy bar. Tooting is just outside the inner-city area which has been turned into one unlovely housing estate. Its streets, plain but solid, were not built for revolutionaries to live in.' Sullivan later recalled his first encounter with the original Wolfie Smith in a pub called the Nelson Arms. 'Suddenly from the depths of the bar came the strains of a geriatric guitar accompanied by a voice that sounded not unlike a cow in labour. The sound came from a gangling hippie. He was a Master-Dreamer in an age of fantasy and his outrageous claims became more colourful and absurd as each cadged pint was sunk.'

The problem was getting his idea across to the BBC. Thankfully, Sullivan had a job shifting scenery at Television Centre: as far as he was concerned, this was a palpable foot in the door. In contravention of unwritten rules, Sullivan used to go to the 'artistic' BBC bar, and one day spied veteran comedy producer Dennis Main Wilson there. 'I thought I'd introduce myself,' explained Sullivan, 'As we'll be working together soon.' 'Oh?' replied Wilson. 'On what?' 'On an idea I've had. It's about an urban guerrilla ...'

Wilson admired the stranger's cheek, and asked to see something. Sullivan took a two-week break to begin writing *Citizen Smith*.

For the central role of his would-be Trotsky, Sullivan recommended Robert Lindsay, best known for his cockney wide-boy, Jakey Smith, in Thames' National Service sitcom *Get Some In*. Jakey and Wolfie had a lot more in common than just Lindsay and the same surname ('Smifff, wif free 'f's', as Jakey's catchphrase

Starring: Robert Lindsay ('Wolfie' Smith) • Mike Grady (Ken) • Artro Morris/Peter Vaughan/Tony Steedman (Dad) • Hilda Braid (Mum) • Cheryl Hall (Shirley) • Tony Millan (Tucker) • Stephen Greif (Harry Fenning) • George Sweeney ('Speed') • Anna Nygh (Desiere) • Janine Duvitski (Phillipa) • David Garfield (Ronnie Lynch) • Susie Baker (Mandy Lynch)

had it): both were charismatic losers. Lindsay saw Wolfie as 'a con-man. He's a hangover from the 60s who hasn't progressed. His mates have careers but he's still busking.'

Wolfie was the guerrilla leader of the Tooting Popular Front, a six-man army of political terrorists more inept than the SDP. Wolfie's disciples included his best mate, Ken, an aspiring Buddhist monk, Tucker, a crushed victim of society with a wife and nine kids, Speed, a violent thug, and Wolfie's girlfriend, Shirley, played by Lindsay's wife, Cheryl Hall. Each episode was introduced by Sullivan's cunning reworking of 'The Red Flag' and Lindsay, in an afghan coat and Guevara-beret, emerging from Tooting Broadway tube station with his battle cry 'Power to the People!'

The opening sequence of the first episode showed Sullivan's eye for the absurd, as a graffiti-painting Wolfie runs out of wall midway through a slogan and blames the council for making the walls too small. His introduction to his girlfriend's parents proves even funnier. Neither calls him by his chosen name: Shirl's helplessly stupid mother christens him 'Foxy', whilst to her father he is forever 'the Yeti'. Wolfie's problems are not helped by the local gangster pub-owner, Harry Fenning, with whom his slate is never clean. Amongst the ludicrous plans Wolfie hatches to further his politics are the kidnap of the local MP in 'The Hostage' (the abduction is bungled and the Front grab Fenning by mistake), an alliance with a Basque terrorist in 'Spanish Fly', and an attempt to become a pop star in 'Rock Bottom'. Great comic moments – like the one in 'The Weekend' when Wolfie, Shirley, Ken and Desiree attempt a dirty weekend in a Bury St Edmunds hotel and Wolfie informs the receptionist that they require rooms under the name 'Mr and Mrs Smith ... Twice!' – pop up even in the most painfully corny episodes. A novel, adapted from the early episodes by Christopher Kenworthy, was published in 1978.

By the third season, Cheryl Hall had left the series, and the 'Dad' character passed to actor Tony Steedman. Sullivan was refining Wolfie's character, from the Beatles-loving, Fulham-supporting overgrown schoolboy of the first season to a power-starved megalomaniac. In 'Don't Look Down' Wolfie climbs on to a rooftop in a fake-suicide bid as a publicity- stunt for his (unpublished) autobiography. The policeman sent up to get him down, Harry Fenning's cousin, Tofkin, turns out to be a genuine basket-case. The character was to reappear in 'Tofkin's Revenge', where a plan to incriminate Fenning ends with his pub getting blown up, and again in 'Casablanca Was Never Like This'.

Sullivan's fascination with the differences between the idle rich and the idle poor (central to many of his later creations) crop up in 'The Party's Over', whilst

Pilot episode
Comedy special
(12 Apr 77)

First season
(3 Nov–22 Dec 77)
2 Crocodile Tears
3 Guess Who's Coming to Dinner
4 Abide with Me
5 The Weekend
6 The Hostage
7 The Path of True Love
8 But is it Art?
9 A Christmas Story

Second season
(1 Dec 78–5 Jan 79)
10 Speed's Return
11 Rebel Without a Pause
12 The Tooting Connection
13 Working Class Hero
14 Spanish Fly
15 Right to Work
16 Rock Bottom

Third season
(20 Sep–1 Nov 79)
17 Don't Look Down
18 Only Fools and Horses
19 The Big Job
20 Tofkin's Revenge
21 We Shall Not Be Moved
22 The Party's Over
23 The Glorious Day

Fourth season
(23 May–4 Jul 80)
24 Bigger than Guy Fawkes
25 Changes
26 The Final Try
27 The Letter of the Law
28 Prisoners
29 Casablanca Was Never Like This
30 Sweet Sorrow

1980 Christmas special
(31 Dec 80)
31 Buôn Natale

[Episodes 15 and 16 were not transmitted during the initial broadcast of the second season owing to strike action. They were eventually shown on 16 and 23 Aug 79.]

One of Ken's badges says 'Only Rotters Hunt Otters'. Right on

Wilfrid Brambell made one of his last TV appearances in 'Only Fools and Horses', a title Sullivan would put to good use a couple of years later. Probably the best-remembered episode of *Citizen Smith* is 'The Glorious Day', when, on outdoor manoeuvres, the Front finds an apparently abandoned tank and decide to invade the Houses of Parliament and begin the revolution.

Wolfie, Tucker, Ken and Speed emerge from prison a year later to a very much changed Tooting. Harry Fenning has mysteriously disappeared, his pub falling into the hands of rival gangster, Ronnie Lynch. 'The Final Try' is a subtle, hard-hitting episode concerning a tour by a multi-racial South African rugby side. At a reception, Wolfie is told by the manager that the black players are in another room because 'they find it difficult to break the habits of a lifetime'. 'Prisoners', on the other hand, was a basic rewrite of the ***Steptoe and Son*** episode 'The Desperate Hours', as Speed and a cell-mate escape from prison and hide at Wolfie's. A Christmas episode, filmed partly in Italy, brought the series to an end, with John Sullivan soon to move his south London tales a mile east to Peckham for ***Only Fools and Horses***.

Citizen Smith's legacy is that of the developing careers of Sullivan and Robert Lindsay, although both have expressed retrospective reservations about the series. Lindsay, as early as the second season, was telling the *Radio Times* that he was ill at ease with a character that 'lived in fantasy'. Sullivan said that the actors 'smiled too much. It lost its abrasive edge.' Others would argue that this is a case of selective judgement and that Wolfie Smith was one of the most original and brilliant comic creations of the 70s.

Butterflies

- **BBC Television** (BBC2) ◆ **Colour**
- **26 episodes** (30 minutes) ◆ **1978–83**
- **Creator/writer:** Carla Lane
- **Directors:** Gareth Gwenlen, John B. Hobbs, Mandie Fletcher, Sydney Lotterby
- **Producers:** Gareth Gwenlen, Sydney Lotterby

On the surface, *Butterflies* seemed to have little going for it. Written by someone who had previously contributed to the dull sitcom *Bless This House*, it featured a woman in the kind of mid-life crisis that only occurs in TV suburbia. It used stereotypes and included an insulting stab at youth culture that was five years behind the times when the series started.

Despite this, *Butterflies* is frequently brilliant and is fondly remembered by millions.

The passing of time and the affection with which it was held make *Butterflies*' faults seem all the more obvious now, although often they are in themselves cosmetic quibbles quite likely to provoke a wry smile, such as the helplessly banal attempt at 'hip' characters and dialogue (the tuned-in kid of 1978 would not have been caught dead wearing the hairstyles, the flares or uttering the 'groovy's and 'cool's that Adam and Russell did). Conceived by Carla Lane as a deliberate step away from normal sitcom concerns, the show's saving grace was always its sense of defeat and emptiness in the face of supposed romance. 'Making love on the edge of a pond is only beautiful if you happen to be a small rodent,' as Carla Lane told the *Radio Times*.

Butterflies depended for much of its appeal on the brilliant interplay between the various members of the Parkinson family. The Parkinsons are a typical middle-class family in the *Father Dear Father* mould, but with a certain 70s neurosis that set them apart from the Glovers and their contemporaries. The unappreciated Ria ('Who said anything about enjoying myself? I never enjoy myself'), after 19 years of marriage, sees her two teenage sons growing up and feels that life is slipping through her fingers. Her weary, manic-depressive husband, Ben ('I like singing. I don't do a lot of it because there isn't much to sing about'), a dentist who collects butterflies as a hobby, is desperate to keep his crumbling marriage together, and attempts to get his sons to conform to some sort of acceptable behaviour. (Geoffrey Palmer's magnificent performance was helped by the fact that he seemed to get most of the best lines.) Said offspring, the laconic Russell and the cynical Adam, find life one great 'gas' (an early episode has them incompetently busking), and simply want to avoid work and bed lots of women.

In the initial episode, Ria (Wendy Craig's most edgy and yet likeable role) meets 70s smoothy Leonard accidentally in a restaurant and begins the lengthy 'will-she-won't-she' near-affair which was to last for the entire series.

It was predictable stuff, but had many points in its favour, like the beautiful reworking of Dolly Parton's country hit 'Love is Like a Butterfly' as title music, the impressively large amount of location filming, and the tight construction of the series which, like ***The Fall and Rise of Reginald Perrin***, made it more

Starring: Wendy Craig (Ria) • Geoffrey Palmer (Ben) • Nicholas Lyndhurst (Adam) • Andrew Hall (Russell) • Bruce Montague (Leonard) • Michael Ripper (Thomas) • Joyce Windsor (Ruby)

of a serial-soap. Lane made good use of running plotlines and unresolved relationships, giving the show a philosophical edge, most obviously represented by Ria's 'conversations' with God ('Couldn't you think of something else besides death? Something less final, like a permanent dazed condition?').

The inter-family relationship is strained from the start. Ben and Russell won't talk to each other (they finally break the silence to compare notes on Ria's dreadful cooking), and this isn't helped in one of the series' most memorable stories as Russell chains himself to a statue as an artistic statement ('I used to think about chaining myself to things,' says an anguished Ben, 'but then I reminded myself that I am not a bicycle'). This episode started the running gag about Russell and Adam's 'amusing' T-shirt motifs, beginning with them wearing cross-over messages ('I'm a free spirit'/'So am I'). This trend reached a clever conclusion when Russell wore a shirt proclaiming 'He's a Sex Object', with a large arrow pointing towards his brother (in the midst of the following family discussion about money and jobs, Ben asks his son to stand further away from him in case anyone thinks that the logo applies to him).

Butterflies also contained several excellent supporting characters, such as the common-as-muck home help, Ruby ('Peein' down outside'), and Leonard's dry chauffeur, Thomas. This was heightened in the second season with the arrival of the nervous, put-upon neighbours, the Conrods (Milton Johns and Wendy Williams). Johns, in particular, has several side-splitting moments as a timid man trapped in his drive, unable to move for fear of the Grand Prix-style manoeuvrings from the other side of the road. The second season was a lot of fun (with one particularly socially-concerned episode in which Ria attempts to stop fox hunting), but the third, in 1980, seemed to see the series running on the spot.

There was a darker side to the series, as shown when Russell's girlfriend becomes pregnant and wants the baby but not Russell. *Butterflies* experimented with structure, using voice-over, surreal dream sequences and musical openings, but the stupid plot lines (which included Adam and Russell building a fall-out shelter and Adam taking a job as a long-distance lorry driver) killed any potential shift in focus. The season ended with Leonard, tired of waiting for Ria to make the break, leaving for America, apparently for good.

In the three years before the series returned, Nicholas Lyndhurst started his second bid for sitcom immortality in ***Only Fools and Horses***. Carla Lane had been busy with *Solo*, and was laying down areas of future development by pre-empting *Bread* in *Butterflies'* return (Adam and Russell, perhaps inevitably, given their history of celebrating idleness, turned their cynicism on the benefit system). There was a huge outcry when they were shown smoking marijuana in one episode (and especially when Ria joined them, with the line 'How long did you say it takes for one of these things to make the day go away?'). The fourth season became a lengthy tug-of-war between Ben and the returned Leonard, Ria spending the entire season very nearly telling Ben about her almost-affair. In the final episodes, she got fed up with being 'taken for granted' and left, but only to tell Leonard that she didn't wish to see him again and, at the climax, returned tearfully to her family.

Butterflies was loved in its day, easily gaining BBC2's biggest audience, and repeat seasons on the main BBC channel helped to swell the numbers who were charmed by the series' gentle exploration of modern family values. Perhaps it wasn't the most honest of works, given Carla Lane's usual *modus operandi*, but its sometimes bitter-sweet aftertaste has less to do with the ravages of time and small aesthetic points than the overall quality of the writing and performances. *Butterflies's* nihilistic core was also its salvation.

First season
(10 Nov–15 Dec 78)
Six episodes

Second season
(12 Nov–22 Dec 79)
Six episodes

Third season
(9 Sep–21 Oct 80)
Seven episodes

Fourth season
(7 Sep–19 Oct 83)
Seven episodes

Shelley

- **Thames** (ITV) ◆ **Colour**
- **71 episodes** (30 minutes) ◆ **1979-92**
- **Creator:** Peter Tilbury
- **Writers:** Peter Tilbury, Barry Pilton, Andy Hamilton, Guy Jenkin, Colin Bostock-Smith, Bernard McKenna
- **Producer/director:** Anthony Parker

Starring: Hywel Bennett (James Shelley) • Belinda Sinclair (Fran) • Josephine Hewson (Mrs Hawkins) • Kenneth Cope (Forsyth) • Warren Clarke (Paul) • Sylvia Kay (Isobel Shelley) • Rowena Cooper (Alice) • Frederick Jaeger (Gordon) • Garfield Morgan (Desmond) • Caroline Langrishe (Carol) • Andrew Castell (Graham) • Stephen Hoye (Phil) • David Ryall (Ted)

Peter Tilbury was an actor, who, together with Anthony Matheson, had a comedy play, *Sprout*, produced by Thames in 1974. He showed the producer of that play, Anthony Parker, the first two episodes of a comedy series he had planned. Parker was impressed, and took them to light entertainment chief Philip Jones. Parker was turned down, but continued to represent the show over the next three years. When the scripts were finally accepted, Thames went the whole hog and commissioned two entire seasons.

Shelley concerned the lifestyle of James Shelley, an unemployed 28-year-old with a PhD in geography. Parker described him as 'uncommitted, amoral, apolitical, selfish and randy'. He had a pregnant girlfriend, Fran, and a suspicious landlady, Mrs Hawkins (Mrs H, as he called her). He also had an unusual relationship with the DHSS, as personified by the various clerks he encountered there (one of whom was played by Kenneth Cope). At one point he asks if, since he's been unemployed for 69 weeks, he's entitled to holiday pay yet. As he says, 'It's us hard-core layabouts who are your bread and butter.'

Hywel Bennett, who'd just finished a memorable cameo in *Tinker, Tailor, Soldier, Spy*, played Shelley like an 80s Hancock, complete with petulant pout. He was quite a revelation, an intelligent man who found himself over-qualified for any job actually available. As a 'layabout' with a 'common-law wife' he was, even in 1980, an anti-establishment figure. With his theatrical background, Tilbury tended to shy away from involving Shelley in anything approaching a plot. One memorable episode involved only one set (around the kitchen table) and the three regular characters, Shelley trying to talk to Fran while she reads her Orwell. With hilarious consequences, as the *TV Times* might say.

And yet, it was hilarious. Tilbury had a gift for sarcastic one-liners that Bennett could fire off like nuclear missiles. Also, as Martin Jackson said in the *Daily Mail*, 'It expresses the state of the nation as accurately as any trade figures or change in the retail price index.' The first season gained huge public support, reaching the top ten programmes, only to be scheduled back to 10.30 p.m. halfway through the run. The late time slot was initially because of the show's supposedly 'adult' content, but, as one critic remarked, the only objectionable thing in the first episode was Fran kicking Shelley in the gonads to encourage him in his search for work.

The memorable Ron Grainer whistled theme tune was back in 1980. Margaret Forewood, then the *Sun*'s TV critic, was part of a campaign to encourage recognition of this wonderful little show, but there were signs that the format was wearing thin. On 18 June 1980, Shelley married Fran, and shortly afterwards, baby Emma arrived. Emma was to be the audience for some of her Dad's most

SHELLEY
First season
(12 Jul–2 Aug 79)
1 Moving In
2 The Nelson Touch
3 Gainfully Employed
4 The Distaff Side

Second season
(17 Apr–18 Jun 80)
5 Elders and Betters
6 May the Best Man Win
7 Nowt so Queer
8 Owner Occupiers
9 Expletive Deleted
10 Tea and Sympathy
11 Hearth and Home
12 Fully Furnished
13 Dearly Beloved

Third season
(22 Dec 80–9 Feb 81)
14 Christmas with Shelley
15 Of Mice and Men
16 Signing On
17 Nor Iron Bars a Cage
18 Foreign Affairs
19 Universal Trust
20 Dry Rot
21 You Have to Laugh

Fourth season
(18 Feb–1 Apr 82)
22 Unkindest Cuts
23 A Drop of the Pink Stuff
24 No News is Good ...
25 Credit where Credit's Due
26 Mortal Coils
27 Slaughterhouse Sling

Fifth season
(4 Nov–9 Dec 82)
28 On the Road to Damascus
29 Brave New World
30 Shelley vs Shelley
31 Noises Off
32 Tubes Help You Breed Less Easily
33 When the Chip Hits the Fan

Sixth season
(1 Dec 83–12 Jan 84)
34 Dry Dreams
35 It Nearly Always Happens to Somebody Else
36 Of Cabbages and Kings
37 The Party
38 Brief Encounter
39 [untitled]

THE RETURN OF SHELLEY
Seventh season
(11 Oct–15 Nov 88)
40 The Return of Shelley
41 In God we Trust
42 Emergency Ward 9
43 One of those Nights
44 Why Me?
45 The Big S

[The first two episodes of the second season were due to be broadcast during the first season but the 1979 ITV strike postponed their transmission.]

entertaining monologues, but her birth wasn't without problems. Fran, who had a subtle humour of her own that mainly revolved around bringing Shelley down, asked why a baby had to come out the same way it got in. Perhaps Dr Spock could answer her question. 'What does he know about it?' Shelley replied. 'He's a Vulcan.'

Shelley found work as a copywriter, and proceeded to write advertising slogans that won awards but didn't actually mention the product. He was becoming a little like Reggie Perrin, and his targets had grown more predictable. He was sacked, of course, in the third season and acquired a new, pacifist stance. 'Everybody sees nuclear war as an unavoidable forthcoming event, like the World Cup,' he said, memorably describing the Neutron Bomb as a 'sort of atomic bailiff'. The building societies were probably behind it, he reckoned. In the same sequence, when Fran said that four minutes would be more than enough time for Shelley to make love, he wonders if Reagan could be persuaded to extend the warning to 25 minutes, to 'allow for the female orgasm, plus two minutes to get your breath back'.

At the end of the third season, Tilbury gave his hero a job in the Foreign Office, and left the series. He was already developing a show, *It Takes a Worried Man*, where he played the title role, continually visiting his analyst for advice. If anything, it was better than his work on *Shelley*. In 1993 the writer found another splendid lead, creating and writing Lenny Henry's sarcastic *Chef!* The only previous sightings had been odd scripts for *Birds of a Feather* and a role in, of all things, an episode of *C.A.T.S. Eyes*.

The writers who took over from Tilbury instantly had Shelley lose the FO job, as well as, swiftly, Fran and Emma. He became involved in a series of dead-end scripts, moaning and alone. There was some thought given to the idea of low-format stories, so Shelley found himself trapped in a tube train for

SHELLEY
Eighth season
(17 Oct 89–9 Jan 90)
46 The Artful Lodger
47 Shelley Washes Whiter
48 A Happy Event
49 Born Freeish
50 Day of the Reptile
51 For Whom the Bell Tolls
52 The Gospel According to Shelley
53 Wages of Virtue
54 It's Only a Game
55 Killer Driller
56 Cold Turkey
57 A Problem Aired
58 Help!

Ninth season
(24 Sep–29 Oct 90)
59 A Trial Period
60 A Question of Attitude
61 Golden Oldies
62 The Bug
63 Second Best Man
64 Brainstrain

Special
(1 Jan 91)
65 Forward to the Past

Tenth season
(28 Jul–1 Sep 92)
66 The Deep End
67 Come Fly with Me
68 Love is ...
69 A Little Learning
70 Happy Birthday RIP
71 Accountants and Zulus

Fran gets a word in

one episode. Basically, with the separation, Shelley lost his sounding board, and the series became a sitcom again, with one major problem – it couldn't find a situation.

Shelley spent most of the season staying at the flat of a friend, his attempted reconciliation with Fran having proved a non-starter ('Has he got a problem in bed?' asks Mrs H. 'Yes,' replies the harassed wife, 'He can't get out of it.') The main comedy element of the season was the interplay between Shelley and the pompous doorman, Desmond, who saw the cynical layabout as synonymous with declining standards in the country at large.

During a five-year hiatus, Shelley went to the USA, and returned in a series that was a shadow of what it had been. He came back to England in the grip of yuppieness, hanging around with Carol and Graeme, who were 'something in the city'. The first thing he sees on British television prompts 'Is Benny Hill still doing that?' The series attacked the Americanization of Britain, but its politics had become too obvious, a watered-down version of a Ben Elton monologue. However, it proved as popular as the original, with ITV this time actively promoting its product. In the 1990 season Shelley moved in with a community of old folk, who made him feel older than ever, by recounting stories of what exciting and dangerous lives they'd had.

Shelley had become almost a caricature of himself, a man who had to answer everything with a sharp retort. Where once the character had a kind heart, he was trapped by public perceptions of the 'new Hancock'. Hywel Bennett's fine characterization continued to shine through, but the show changed from being an anarchic cult to, perhaps unfortunately, the popular show it always deserved to be.

Yes, Minister/Yes, Prime Minister

- **BBC Television** (BBC2) ◆ Colour
- **38 episodes** (standard length: 30 minutes) ◆ 1980-88
- **Creators/writers:** Antony Jay, Jonathan Lynn
- **Producers:** Stuart Allen, Sydney Lotterby, Peter Whitmore

Regular cast: Paul Eddington (Rt. Hon. James Hacker) • Nigel Hawthorne (Sir Humphrey Appleby) • Derek Fowlds (Bernard Wooley)

With: John Nettleton (Sir Arnold Robinson) • Diana Hoddinott (Annie Hacker)

'People laugh at what they recognize,' Jonathan Lynn told *The Guardian*. They recognized three figures in Lynn's new comedy instantly. One was the newly-promoted minister of administrative affairs, a man who was going to reform his department. They recognized a private secretary who had to do his best between him and a man who was determined that things should remain the same. The last figure was a British public nightmare, Sir Humphrey Appleby, the permanent under secretary, the man of the 66-word sentence who blocked every reform the minister wanted to make.

Lynn and Jay had met writing training films for John Cleese's Video Arts company. Lynn had been a contemporary of Cleese, Chapman, Oddie and Brooke-Taylor at Cambridge (appearing in ***The Liver Birds***, and writing for *Doctor in the House* and *On the Buses*). Jay had worked on ***TW3*** and *Tonight*. One single incident got both writers thinking about parliamentary hypocrisy. In the early 60s, Sir Frank Soskice signed a petition, while in opposition, to give wrongly-executed Timothy Evans a posthumous pardon. Once he became a minister, he was given the completed petition, and promptly rejected it.

Taking material from the Crossman diaries, and from several 'deep throat' sources in Whitehall, Lynn and Jay completed a pilot script for their new series in 1977, and managed to secure a sale to the BBC. However it was shelved until after the election. When it was made, the director of the pilot wanted to 'add jokes', something that the writers refused to allow. Lady Falkender, Harold Wilson's secretary, checked all the first-season scripts for political detail, and didn't find them wanting. As former MP Neil Carmichael said in the *Daily Mail*, 'It gives you an uneasy feeling that in 90 per cent of the cases this is just how it happened.'

The general plot was that Hacker would come up with some new scheme to shake up the Department, and Appleby would find some way to make him undo all his plans. The series introduced a new world to viewers: 'going native' was when a minister gave in and became like a civil servant, and a 'courageous' or 'controversial' decision was one with which the speaker didn't agree at all. The best thing a Department could do was to make a problem somebody else's (Hacker would exclaim 'We're talking about good and evil!', Humphrey would reply 'Ah, Church of England problem').

Apart from Bernard's occasional attacks of conscience, the only diversion from the power games was Hacker's wife, Annie, who voiced the appalled reaction of somebody unaware of parliamentary infighting.

Though no party was named as being in power, and the prime minister was male, Paul Eddington thought of Hacker as 'a Jim Prior type figure'. Robert McKenzie identified him as one of the new generation of Labour politicians, although Hacker was repeatedly shown carrying out Conservative party policies, and most Cabinet ministers were secretly convinced (and, amazingly, flattered) that he was based on them. Sixty advisors in the circles of power gave the writers

The private secretary, the civil servant from hell, and the poor, unsuspecting minister

their information, and the series was so loved by those in office that Eddington was allowed to be filmed walking into 10 Downing Street. Designers Valerie Warrender and Gloria Clayton were allowed to see the Cabinet rooms and the state drawing rooms. For security reasons, no outside views were ever shown, and the layout of the rooms was changed.

Yes, Minister always enjoyed unusual luck in the timing of episodes. 'The Economy Drive' briefly mentioned nuclear attack provisions, a subject covered by *Panorama* exactly an hour beforehand, and, once Hacker became PM, he fell out with his defence secretary on the same day that Michael Heseltine resigned. Six million viewers watched the first season, and Paul Channon, the minister then in charge of the Civil Service, joined the rest of Britain in finally having a name to attach to the face of bureaucracy. He started to call his permanent secretary 'Sir

YES, MINISTER
First season
(25 Feb–7 Apr 80)
1 Open Government
2 The Official Visit
3 The Economy Drive
4 Big Brother
5 The Writing on the Wall
6 The Right to Know
7 Jobs for the Boys

Second season
(23 Feb–6 Apr 81)
8 The Compassionate Society
9 Doing the Honours
10 The Death List
11 The Greasy Pole
12 The Devil You Know
13 The Quality of Life
14 A Question of Loyalty

Third season
(11 Nov–23 Dec 82)
15 Equal Opportunities
16 The Challenge
17 The Skeleton in the Cupboard
18 The Moral Dimension
19 The Bed of Nails
20 The Whisky Priest
21 The Middle-Class Rip-Off

Christmas Special
(17 Dec 84, 45 minutes)
22 Party Games

YES, PRIME MINISTER
Fourth season
(9 Jan–27 Feb 86)
23 The Grand Design
24 The Ministerial Broadcast
25 The Smoke Screen
26 The Key
27 A Real Partnership
28 A Victory for Democracy
29 The Bishop's Gambit
30 One of Us

Fifth season
(3 Dec–28 Jan 88)
31 Man Overboard
32 Official Secrets
33 A Diplomatic Incident
34 A Conflict of Interest
35 Power to the People
36 The Patron of the Arts
37 The National Education Service
38 The Tangled Web

Humphrey'. Apart from high audience figures (and 90+ percentage ratings on the BARB-compiled audience appreciation index), the show gained the BAFTA Best Comedy award, as it was to do for all three of its seasons. Other awards received included the TV and Radio Industry Club award, the Pye Colour TV Writer's award, and a Broadcasting Press Council award. Perhaps more tellingly, the series won a Freedom of Information award in 1986.

Politicians from all sides recognized the truth of *Yes, Minister* and loved it. Margaret Thatcher was recorded in the *Telegraph* as saying 'Its clearly-observed portrayal of what goes on in the corridors of power has given me hours of pure joy', and Roy Hattersley, in *The Listener*, commented that 'Like Anthony Trollope, they aspire to write fiction that is about politics, not just politicians. And like him, they achieve some remarkable successes.' Gerald Kaufman summed up the nature of the series when he described it as 'The Rt. Hon. Faust MP, constantly beset by the wiles of Sir Mephistopheles'.

In script meetings, Jay would play Humphrey and Lynn, Hacker. The resulting head-to-heads had a lot of Jeeves and Wooster about them, the only difference being that, instead of a mutual recognition of station, these two characters were actually battling for supremacy. *Yes, Minister* never talked down to the public, having, as Andrew Davies said in the *Times Educational Supplement*, 'Such confidence in itself and such high expectations of its audience.'

Thatcher had initially shared her love of the show with a group of children on a chat show, and went so far as to appear in a sketch with Eddington and Hawthorne in front of an audience of the National Viewers and Listeners Association in 1984. The sketch was written by her private secretary, Charles Powell, and her husband. As Antony Jay said afterwards, 'The Prime Minister has taken her rightful place in the field of comedy.'

Eddington, an SDP voter and pacifist Quaker, was amazed by the success of his character. The man who had commented in *The Times* that the series 'reached such depths of cynicism it actually gave me vertigo' found himself having breakfast with the Norwegian prime minister. As Jay said in the *Evening Standard*, 'More comic figures than [Hacker] have been elected.' The international appeal of a series that dealt with the universal issues of democracy and power had the programme translated into Urdu (as *Bajaa Irshad*, or 'Absolutely Correct, Sir') and Chinese by 1986. It was sold to 46 countries, and pirated in the eastern European states and South Africa.

At the end of 'Party Games', Hacker found himself, as the dull, moderate candidate between two extremists, elected as prime minister. Jay and Lynn began to reveal that Hacker was a Tory, and they must have been delighted by the obvious parallels between their script and the circumstances of John Major's rise to power.

In the 1986 New Year's Honours List, Eddington and Hawthorne received CBEs, and greater honour was to fall on Antony Jay's shoulders, as he was knighted the following year. Amongst the establishment, the only critics of the programme were, unsurprisingly, the civil servants, whose union report of 1986 attacked the representation of their members as 'parasitic, obstructive, and over-paid'. *Yes, Minister* and its sequel are remembered as series that portrayed politicians in exactly the way that the audience had always suspected they were. For once, a situation comedy aspired not just to topicality, but to answering deep questions about the way the whole system of western politics worked. As the best comedies do, it touched on truth continually, and transcended topicality to become truly iconic.

Jay and Lynn, with mixed success, have turned to writing movies in the USA. Nigel Hawthorne was nominated for an Oscar for his performance in *The Madness of King George* (GB 95), and Paul Eddington succumbed to illness in 1995, having continued acting to great acclaim while afflicted with skin cancer. He was as brave as his on-screen persona had always failed to be.

Only Fools and Horses

- **BBC Television** (BBC1) ◆ Colour
- **58 episodes** (standard length: *c*. 30 minutes) ◆ 1981-93
- **Creator and writer**: John Sullivan
- **Directors**: Martin Shardlow, Ray Butt, Susan Belbin, Mandie Fletcher, Tony Dow, Gareth Gwenlan
- **Producers**: Ray Butt, Gareth Gwenlan

After the success of ***Citizen Smith***, John Sullivan turned his eyes towards Peckham and created, in *Only Fools and Horses*, the ***Steptoe and Son*** of the 80s. Sullivan and director/producer Ray Butt had both worked in London markets, and whilst collaborating on ***Citizen Smith*** they agreed that this would be a good setting for comedy. However, Sullivan had to wait a while for the characters to form in his mind. 'I wanted three men of different generations, all without a woman in their lives... trying to organize themselves.' Sullivan's admiration of Roy Clarke and Galton and Simpson is very much in evidence when one considers the resulting characters: the wheeler-dealer in all things kitsch who wants to be a millionaire, his frequently dim-witted brother with but a CSE and a microscopic police record to his name, and their whinging grandfather who, despite everything, perhaps has more in common with the insane old men of ***Last of the Summer Wine*** than with Wilfrid Brambell's 'dirty old man'. Once the first season was completed – Sullivan admits that he never enjoys writing the first season of anything as 'you haven't had a chance to establish the characters in your mind' – he became more confident with his characters, until now 'I know everything about Del: I know where he went to school, I even know what desk he sat at.'

At first, the series seemed set to sink without trace. 'It had an audience of about 13,' noted Sullivan, 'all from my family.' However, by the second season the programme had attracted a dedicated following, the secret seeming to be the traditional sitcom values of strong characters, the humour rising from this and not being merely a series of jokes thrown into the dialogue. David Jason and Nicholas Lyndhurst approached their respective roles of Del and Rodney with immense comic confidence, and it is therefore not surprising that *Only Fools and Horses* continued into the 90s to ever-growing acclaim.

Del is the core character, older and more cynical than Rodney, and yet equally lacking at times in the simple virtues of common sense and clarity of thought. He continues to look for that elusive big break that will make his fortune. Until then, he is content to try to flog junk that no one else would dare touch (from revolving china cats that sing 'How much is that Doggy in the Window?' to woodworm-infested antiques), pulling off various scams because of his charm, wit and feeble pretensions. He'll sell anything to anybody, within reason – he sold a faulty computer to a vicar – and Jason notes that 'he's not honest, he's moral'.

It is Del's morality that endears him to the audience, the heart of gold behind his confident exterior, and his East End faith in the virtues of family solidarity

Regular cast: David Jason (Del Trotter) • Nicholas Lyndhurst (Rodney) • Lennard Pearce (Grandad) • Buster Merryfield (Uncle Albert)

With: Roger Lloyd Pack (Trigger) • John Challis (Boycie) • Patrick Murray (Mickey Pearce) • Kenneth MacDonald (Mike) • Sue Holderness (Marlene) • Paul Barber (Denzil) • Jim Broadbent (Roy Slater) • Denis Lill (Alan) • Gwyneth Strong (Cassandra) • Tessa Peake-Jones (Racquel)

First season
(8 Sep–13 Oct 81)
1 Big Brother
2 Go West Young Man
3 Cash and Curry
4 The Second Time Around
5 A Slow Bus to Chingford
6 The Russians are Coming

Christmas special
(28 Dec 81)
7 Christmas Crackers

Second season
(21 Oct–2 Dec 82)
8 The Long Legs of the Law
9 Ashes to Ashes
10 A Losing Streak
11 No Greater Love ...
12 The Yellow Peril
13 It Never Rains ...
14 A Touch of Glass

Christmas special
(30 Dec 82)
15 Diamonds are for Heather

Third season
(10 Nov–22 Dec 83)
16 Homesick
17 Healthy Competition
18 Friday the 14th
19 Yesterday Never Comes
20 May the Force Be with You
21 Wanted
22 Who's a Pretty Boy

Christmas special
(25 Dec 84)
23 Thicker than Water

Fourth season
(21 Feb–4 Apr 85)
24 Happy Returns
25 Strained Relations
26 Hole in One
27 It's Only Rock and Roll
28 Sleeping Dogs Lie
29 Watching the Girls Go By
30 As One Door Closes

Christmas special
(25 Dec 85, 90 minutes)
31 To Hull and Back

Fifth season
(31 Aug–5 Oct 86)
32 From Prussia with Love
33 The Miracle of Peckham
34 The Longest Night
35 Tea for Three
36 Video Nasty
37 Who Wants to be a Millionaire?

(a theme often handled better here than in ***EastEnders***). This side of Del's character was most severely tested in the bitter-sweet 1990 Christmas special, 'Rodney Come Home', when Rodney's marriage to Cassandra is on the rocks. Del even allows his relationship with girlfriend Racquel to be put under pressure in an abortive attempt to help Rodney and Cassandra get back together, his motivation being not only his touching love for his foolish (and more-than-slightly sexist) younger brother, but his commitment to Cassandra, whom he now sees as being 'family'. He is understandably hurt when Rodney suspects that he is motivated by business-based selfishness. For once, nothing could be further from the truth.

Rodney – the 'plonker' – can be the brains of the family (which isn't saying much). At other moments, he can be utterly stupid; indeed, when he brought a WPC back to their flat, stuffed with stolen goods, he simply couldn't comprehend Del's frustrated amazement. After being wound up by Del in one episode, he fears that he will be accused of being the 'Peckham Pouncer', and goes into hiding in the loft of Nelson Mandela House with enough tins for weeks (but forgets to take a tin-opener). His relationships with women are pretty futile, Lyndhurst describing him as being 'in a perpetual state of puberty'.

The third character was Lennard Pearce's Grandad, a sulking but hugely likeable old man, just as gullible as Rodney (Del manages to spook him with the help of an urn full of cremated remains in 'Ashes to Ashes'). When Pearce died in December 1983, Sullivan wanted to remain true to his vision of a three-generation group of men. However, no one wanted to replace Pearce with another actor, and so the character of Uncle Albert was born, a blustering, rambling old sea-dog, played with gusto by former bank manager Buster Merryfield. His introduction, after grandad's funeral, set up the character well. He could be annoying, silly and selfish, and yet, like the other Trotters,

Christmas special
(25 Dec 86, 75 minutes)
38 A Royal Flush

Christmas special
(25 Dec 87, 60 minutes)
39 The Frog's Legacy

Christmas special
(25 Dec 88, 80 minutes)
40 Dates

Sixth season
(8 Jan–12 Feb 89, 50-minute episodes)
41 Yuppy Love
42 Danger UXD
43 Chain Gang
44 The Unlucky Winner is ...
45 Sickness and Wealth
46 Little Problems

Christmas special
(25 Dec 89, 85 minutes)
47 The Jolly Boys' Outing

Christmas special
(25 Dec 90, 75 minutes)
48 Rodney Come Home

Seventh season
(30 Dec–3 Feb 91, 50-minute episodes)
49 The Sky's the Limit
50 The Chance of a Lunch Time
51 Stage Fright
52 The Class of '62
53 He Ain't Heavy, He's My Uncle
54 Three Men, a Woman and a Baby

Christmas specials:
Miami Twice
(24 Dec 91, 50 minutes)
55 The American Dream
(25 Dec 91, 90 minutes)
56 Oh to Be in England

Christmas special
(25 Dec 92, 65 minutes)
57 Mother Nature's Son

Christmas special
(25 Dec 93, 90 minutes)
58 Fatal Extraction

his heart was in the right place. Having learnt to fall without injuring himself during the war, he employed his old trick of falling down a pub cellar, hoping to get compensation from the brewery. However, his past soon catches up with him, and it is eventually revealed, after an embarrassing spectacle in court, that the only hole he hasn't fallen down is the black one in Calcutta. Del rounds on him, but eventually the truth comes out – he only did it to try to help Rodney and Del, and buy grandad a headstone.

As in ***Citizen Smith***, Sullivan populated his imaginary London with all manner of wonderful and bizarre characters, such as Del and Rodney's drinking partners from the Nags Head: the gangster Boycie, his desperate-for-a-child wife Marlene, the dry seen-it-all barman Mike and, one of the series' most loved characters, the gormless Trigger (who continually calls Rodney 'Dave'). Other occasional characters, including the nervous, put-upon lorry driver Denzil, the cat-burgler Jaffa (so called because he is sterile, and therefore seedless) and the outrageous bent copper Roy Slater, simply add to the fun.

The situations that the characters found themselves in were the icing on the cake, whether it be a brief genre-hop with the murderer-on-the-loose subplot of 'Friday the 14th', the search for Del's mum's buried treasure, or the classic 1985 Christmas special 'To Hull and Back', a diamond-smuggling caper which beat ***Minder*** in the Christmas Day Cockney ratings battle (a setback from which Arthur Daley perhaps never fully recovered). The legendary 'cleaning' of the Louis XIV chandelier deserves special mention as a masterstroke of TV comedy. David Jason commented that 'You knew all along that the chandelier would end up in a thousand bits, but when it did, it was just the best sort of visual humour.'

Whereas Sullivan initially perceived the programme (like, say, ***Steptoe*** and ***Porridge***) as being about men coping without women, by the 90s the unthinkable had happened: Rodney was married, and Del wasn't too far off popping the question either. Early 1991 saw the birth of his son and heir, Damian.

With just a hint of materialistic success, and women very much on their minds and in their lives, Del and Rodney lurched into the 90s, almost unchanged by over ten years of ups and downs and startling comedy.

'Allo 'Allo!

- **BBC Television** (BBC1) ◆ **Colour**
- **85 episodes** (standard length: *c.* 30 minutes) ◆ **1982-92**
- **Creators**: Jeremy Lloyd, David Croft
- **Writers:** Jeremy Lloyd, David Croft, John Chapman, Ian Davidson, Ronald Wolfe, Ronald Chesney, Paul Adam
- **Directors:** David Croft, Robin Carr, Martin Dennis, Susan Belbin, Richard Boden, Mike Stephens, Sue Longstaff, John B. Hobbs
- **Producers:** David Croft, Mike Stephens, John B. Hobbs

Starring: Gorden Kaye (René Artois) • Carmen Silvera (Edith) • Vicki Michelle (Yvette) • Francesca Gonshaw (Maria) • Jack Haig/Derek Royle/Robin Parkinson (M. Leclerc) • Kirsten Cooke (Michelle) • Guy Siner (Lt. Gruber) • Richard Marner (Col. von Strohm) • Kim Hartman (Helga Geerhart) • Richard Gibson/David Janson (Herr Flick) • Sam Kelly (Capt. Hans Geering) • John D. Collins (Flying Officer Fairfax) • Nicholas Frankau (Flying Officer Adamson/Carstairs) • Rose Hill (Fanny) • Hilary Minster (Gen. von Klinkerhoffen) • Kenneth Connor (M. Alfonse) • Arthur Bostrom (Crabtree) • John Louis Mansi (von Smallhausen) • Gavin Richards/Roger Kitter (Capt. Alberto Bertorelli) • Sue Hodge (Mimi La Bonc)

Despite everything, *'Allo 'Allo!* was both funny and popular. Its humour was no more sophisticated than that of *Terry and June*; its approach to comedy no less sexist than Benny Hill's. It used stereotypes and schoolboy jokes to achieve its effect; it was homophobic and xenophobic and every kind of '-ist' imaginable.

Regardless of this, *'Allo 'Allo!*'s longevity and the affection it inspired are fully justified. Its pedigree was certainly impeccable, Croft and Lloyd having already collaborated on *Are You Being Served?* (1973) and the less successful *Oh Happy Band!* with Harry Worth (1978). Although the idea for the series was Lloyd's, *'Allo 'Allo!* was initially written by Lloyd and Croft face-to-face across a table – playing the various parts in different voices. (Lloyd is also an actor, but Croft tends not to cast him.) In fact, as in most of Croft's series, the casting saw him homing in on character actors rather than those particularly known for their comic work. He'd worked with Gorden Kaye before, and Carmen Silvera was Mainwaring's 'little fling' in an early episode of ***Dad's Army***, although she was perhaps best-remembered for her role as Camilla in *Compact*.

The basic idea was to spoof ***Secret Army***, and *Are You Being Served?*'s famous use of the double entendre (especially Mrs Slocombe's pussy) should have prepared us for the innuendo-driven nature of the programme.

However, the mix of war-time cowardice and verbalized sex remained a controversial one (even for the actors – Sam Kelly refused to say 'Heil Hitler' and adopted 'Klomp!' himself). *'Allo 'Allo!* was, from the start, open to accusations of bad taste. Before the first season was screened, Croft commented that 'What we've set out to do is laugh at the dramatic attitudes of films and television series like ***Colditz*** and ***Secret Army*** – the mock-heroics and so on. What we're not doing is making fun of the Resistance or the reality of the last war.'

Of course, when it came down to it, *'Allo 'Allo!* was quite happy to make fun of anything or anyone. Whereas Croft and Perry's ***Dad's Army*** and *It Ain't Half Hot Mum* revolved around comparative backwaters of the war, *'Allo 'Allo!* plunged headlong into 'the front line', featuring the SS, the Gestapo, the Resistance and crashed British airmen. Later seasons had plots involving Churchill and an actual appearance by the Führer himself.

In part, *'Allo 'Allo!* got away with its subject matter because its tone was so obviously that of an exaggerated cartoon or caricature, whereas Croft's work with Perry has always had strong intimations of reality. *'Allo 'Allo!* looked not to *Chlochmerle* for inspiration, but to Whitehall – its farce was so extreme that it resembled pantomime. The disguises used by the characters were surreal (trees, Resistance girls – one memorable episode involved a pantomime cow), and the stereotyping of the various nationalities was at least fair in the sense that the English (the undercover gendarme who cannot speak French properly and the gormless airmen) often came out worst. Croft commented that 'We have a go at everyone equally. Our Germans are insensitive, nest-feathering and kinky; the French are devious, nest-feathering and immoral, and the British are real twits. No nation should feel it's been left out.' (Indeed, *'Allo 'Allo!* has now been sold to many European nations – it is especially popular in Scandinavia – as well as countries as diverse as Australia and Zambia.)

René addresses the audience directly (an idea derived from ***Up Pompeii!***, via *It Ain't Half Hot Mum*), which reassures the potentially worried viewer, as does the fact that none of the characters is ever killed (with the exception of René's 'twin brother' in the first season).

Mention of the death of René's brother brings us to one of *'Allo 'Allo!*'s strongest points – its gloriously convoluted plots. *'Allo 'Allo!*'s continuity was excellent, with the brother's death often mentioned (indeed, the appearance of René's brother's 'ghost' provided a superb end to one episode). Not since ***Reggie Perrin*** had a sitcom's plot been so crucial to its success, with *'Allo 'Allo!* going so far as to include cliffhangers.

Perhaps *'Allo 'Allo! was* in poor taste, but few would deny the consistency of its ribald humour. Whole seasons revolved around 'The Fallen Madonna

Rene has fooled Edith into thinking that he's dead and that he is instead his own twin brother. Trouble is, she wants a new husband to go with her new hat

Pilot episode
(30 Dec 82)

First season
(14 Sep–26 Oct 84)
Seven episodes

Second season
(21 Oct–3 Dec 85)
Seven episodes

Third season
(5 Dec 86–9 Jan 87)
Six episodes, including Christmas special
(26 Dec 86, 45 minutes)

Christmas special
(26 Dec 86, 45 minutes)

Fourth season
(7 Nov–12 Dec 87)
Six episodes

Fifth season
(3 Sep 88–25 Feb 89)
Twenty-six episodes

Sixth season
(2 Sep–21 Oct 89)
Eight episodes

Seventh season
(5 Jan–9 Mar 91)
Ten episodes

Christmas special
(24 Dec 91, 45 minutes)

Eighth season
(12 Jan–1 Mar 92)
Seven episodes

Ninth season
(9 Nov–14 Dec 92)
Six episodes

with the Big Boobies' by van Clomp, with chamber pots, Edith's search for a husband, and a duel between René and Alfonse (as a result of Crabtree parachuting into town) all featuring in some depth. Mimi appeared as a flying nun, and Fanny and Leclerc were finally married, although the celebration was somewhat marred by a cunning plan involving a barrage balloon, a wedding marquee and 24 cylinders of helium disguised as award-winning marrows.

Dynamite disguised as candlesticks always ended up in René's trousers, as did Swiss alarm clocks that chimed at inopportune moments. Alfonse contended with his 'dicky ticker' and his passion for Edith; René soldiered on via his cowardice, his long-suffering monologues, and his extra-marital romances.

Most popular of all, though, was the show's catchphrase, always delivered by Michelle of the Resistance, 'Leesten very carefully, I weel say zees only wance', and the poor 'French' of British agent-in-disguise, Crabtree. Crabtree's bizarre use of the language ('Good moaning'), and his Peter Sellers-like French accent, allowed lines of dialogue that would otherwise not have been tolerated on prime-time British television, 'He has pissed out!' being a typical exclamation. Arthur Bostrom can, apparently, speak fluent French.

Even René was not to be left out where catchphrases are concerned: a furtive embrace with one of the waitresses (or even, in one episode, an apparent kiss with Gruber) interrupted by Edith will be met by the stinging response 'You stupid woman!'

At times, *'Allo 'Allo!* was almost subtle, notably in Richard Gibson's effortless physical comedy and the famous 'rhyming' 1986 Christmas special ('the gateaux in the Chateau'). Later seasons saw the nationality-bashing moving up a gear with the introduction of the Italian Captain, Alberto Bertorelli (who sounded more than a little like Chico Marx), and the first of a number of changes of actor (prompted by Jack Haig's death before the 1989 season).

It is quite apt, considering its style of humour and the presence of Kenneth Connor in later seasons, that the first run of *'Allo 'Allo!* was immediately followed by a series of *Carry On* films.

One Foot in the Grave

- **BBC Television** (BBC1) ◆ Colour
- **34 episodes** (standard length: c. 30 minutes) ◆ 1990-95
- **Creator/writer:** David Renwick
- **Directors:** Susan Belbin, Sydney Lotterby
- **Producer:** Susan Belbin

Starring: Richard Wilson (Victor Meldrew) • Annette Crosbie (Margaret Meldrew) • Doreen Mantle (Jean Warboys) • Owen Brenman (Nick Swainey) • Angus Deayton (Patrick) • Janine Duvitski (Pippa)

David Renwick's *One Foot in the Grave* begins with 60-year-old Victor Meldrew getting the sack and being forced to contemplate an eternity with nothing to distract him except for the guillotining of family friend Mrs Warboys and his compilation of the *Observer's Book of Crap in Your Front Lawn*. Despite his concerns, life proves eventful enough: he's arrested for kerb-crawling (his car is playing up) and, although cleared of the charges, is fined £500 for throwing a Bible at the Magistrate. His long-suffering wife Margaret describes the retired Victor as being 'like a car stuck in the wrong gear', while he sees himself as simply the only sane person left in a world gone mad.

Victor is the sort of man who sets fire to *Reader's Digest* circulars and wonders why scientists can use a particle accelerator to explain the origins of the universe but still can't produce a toilet roll that tears properly. He is the people's champion, railing against the excesses and failures of the commercial world. When he stalks into a garage describing himself as 'Victor Meldrew, the crimson Avenger', the implication is that he's not just describing his car but setting himself up as a super-hero.

But it's tough being a Roger Cook for the denture generation. In 'Dramatic Fever' Victor gets a copper pipe twisted about his head and puts household refuse into the wrong car. But there are moments of convoluted triumph, like conning the computer systems salesman who cut him up on the road ('The Broken Reflection') and trapping an untrustworthy locksmith in his own porch ('The Affair of the Hollow Lady').

Victor's misfortunes make Frank Spencer seem positively blessed with luck. In 'Love and Death' he gets a glass of bitter superglued to his head while on holiday on the south coast. Only Victor would receive a phone call from the thieves who've stolen his video asking him if he has the manual to hand as they can't get the 14-day timer to work. And, while most of us are used to finding other people's rubbish in our hired skip, Victor finds an upturned 2CV in his. It's no wonder he could moan for England.

But David Renwick is too clever to make Victor just a whinging monster. The viewer is instead invited to sympathize, if not almost admire, the man. In a scene in 'The Worst Horror of All' that says an awful lot about snobbery, Victor is supposed to be a cringing doorman at a posh hotel but finds himself distracted by the plight of a disabled person further down the street. Eventually, after being humiliated by a vacuous yuppie and his simpering lady friend, he seems to apologize for his distracted behaviour before launching into an incredible rant: 'I'm very sorry, because I'm afraid I'm going to have to throw your toupee down the drain ... And do forgive me for not getting the fur coat out, because if you hadn't chopped all its legs off in the first place it could have climbed out on its own!'

It's moments such as this that allow us to forgive Victor's essential stupidity, like his Frankenstein-like operation to make a Christening present from various

First season
(4 Jan–8 Feb 90)
1 Alive and Buried
2 The Big Sleep
3 The Valley of Fear
4 I'll Retire to Bedlam
5 The Eternal Quadrangle
6 The Return of the Speckled Band

Second season
(4 Oct–15 Nov 90)
7 In Luton Airport No-One Can Hear You Scream
8 We Have Put Her Living in the Tomb
9 Dramatic Fever
10 Who Will Buy?
11 Love and Death
12 Timeless Time

Christmas special
(27 Dec 90, 60 minutes)
13 Who's Listening

Christmas special
(30 Dec 91, 50 minutes)
14 The Man in the Long Black Coat

Third season
(2 Feb–8 Mar 92)
15 Monday Morning will be Fine
16 Dreamland
17 The Broken Reflection
18 The Beast in the Cage
19 Beware the Trickster on the Roof
20 The Worst Horror of All

Fourth season
(31 Jan–7 Mar 93)
21 The Pit and the Pendulum
22 Descent into the Maelstrom
23 Hearts of Darkness
24 Warm Champagne
25 The Trial
26 Secret of the Seven Sorcerers

Christmas special
(26 Dec 93, 95 minutes)
27 One Foot in the Algarve

Christmas special
(25 Dec 94, 40 minutes)
28 The Man Who Blew Away

Fifth season
(1 Jan–29 Jan 95)
29 Only a Story
30 The Affair of the Hollow Lady
31 Rearranging the Dust
32 Hole in the Sky
33 The Exterminating Angel

Christmas special
(25 Dec 95, 60 minutes)
34 The Wisdom of the Witch

old toys (Margaret: 'I think I feel sick... That's not a teddy bear. That's the Abominable Dr Phibes in a fur coat.').

The first episode of *One Foot* also introduced Nick Swainey, the drippy and ineffectual bachelor with the heart of gold. The Meldrews moved next door to him during the second season, and with his unseen mother he became the Norman Bates of suburbia, the sort of man who reads Clive Barker for light relief. There was also barmy Mrs Warboys, not averse to driving around with a workman on the roof of her car, and visitors from Hell, Ronnie and Mildred (who are reputed not to strike during the hours of daylight).

The second season began with the Meldrews's return from their holiday to the news that their house has been demolished. Inspecting the site, Victor exclaims 'I don't believe it! ... The house has been razed to the ground and they're still delivering those bloody free newspapers!' He looks up his stars: 'Virgo. You will come back from holiday to receive an extremely unpleasant rectal examination from three men in peaked caps. Your luggage will go missing on the other side of the world. Your house will be completely consumed by a hideous fire ball. You will end up tonight freezing to death on a demolition site dressed as the Cisko Kid.'

After moving to a house where the previous occupant committed suicide in the bathroom, the episode ends with Victor and Margaret looking at the ruins of their old home: 'Twenty five years it took to grow that apple tree. I planted it in the spring of 1965. Feeding it, spraying it, mulching the soil, washing it through the droughts, giving it an annual dressing of potash and hydrogen every January. Not one sodding apple.'

Benighted neighbours Patrick and Pippa were introduced in 'Who will Buy?': by the end of the episode (through a series of misunderstandings) Pippa has shown Victor's ventriloquist's dummy how to urinate and Victor has virtually propositioned the pair of them. Margaret, meanwhile, has visited a blind man and, not wanting to hurt him, she pretends to read a letter from the man's family in Australia. The old man is later murdered, and it is revealed that he spent his savings on presents for his grandchildren because of the warmth of the made-up letter.

Such tragicomedy came to the fore with the first Christmas special later that year, which not surprisingly cast Victor in the role of attitude-changing Scrooge. He's forced to contend with a broken leg, Risk played over the phone, and a house full of 263 garden gnomes. Then we're introduced to Pippa's father, who is a vicar who no longer believes in God, and the devout woman whose husband has just been killed in a tragic accident.

Despite his cynicism Victor is given pause for thought by the woman's young son, who has written to Santa asking for his dad back. He resolves to help the

Reverend Crocker distribute food to the needy on Christmas day, only to end up in a ridiculous hostage situation with a machine gun-carrying man who can tell the time without a watch and thinks Armageddon is mere minutes away. Despite the high-quality humour, the emotional heart of the story remains of the plight of the boy, with tragic and heart-warming scenes almost impossible to endure. The episode ends with Patrick destroying the gnomes with the machine gun, Victor having filled a bottle of incredibly expensive wine with urine.

The next festive instalment, 'The Man in the Long Black Coat', furthers the Patrick/Victor conflict. Margaret has caught Victor trying to train Mrs Lacey's cat to vomit on Patrick's rockery, while Pippa (now pregnant) says of Patrick 'It's one thing to call someone a tosspot to their face, but when you go to the lengths of having it iced on the front of a Thornton's Easter egg ... ' Pippa is a bus-driver: she is involved in a crash and is over-the-limit because of a Christmas party. The serious point about drink-driving – she loses her baby – isn't diluted by an escapist, happy ending, although at least Patrick writes a 'Thank you' note for Victor's help during the incident. (The truce only lasts as long as Patrick's attempts to sell their house in the next season.)

Another key element of *One Foot in the Grave* is its allusiveness (how many sitcoms can claim Edgar Allen Poe as a major source of inspiration, or feature company names like Watson Mycroft Ltd?). This is also reflected in the programme's tone, with a deep surrealism seen as early as the second episode. In this Victor, dozing in the garden, awakes in fog with his radio playing 'Neptune' from *The Planets* suite. He thinks he's dead, then steps on a rake, and wakes up in hospital. He sees the bearded visage of a fellow patient but, thinking him to be God, Victor immediately attacks him, blaming him for losing his job, the rubbish that appears in his garden, and the difficulty he has in opening biscuit packets.

It's not surprising that Margaret needs the patience of a saint and the stamina of the Terminator just to cope. What is surprising – and wonderful – is that Renwick spends time portraying the true depths of their relationship. We're left in no doubt that their love is genuine, not just a comic artifice. In 'Warm Champagne' Margaret considers an affair with the charming Ben, who she met on holiday, but he's simply too shallow for her. Ben says that a sensitive woman such as Margaret shouldn't be saddled with an ogre like Victor, to which Margaret replies 'He's the most sensitive person I've ever met. And that's why I love him, and why I constantly want to ram his head through a television screen.' It's important that we remember that Victor isn't so much a tyrant as a hopeless idealist, and Richard Wilson's superb performance always encourages us to do just that.

The allusive symbolism and the tenderness of the Meldrews's love for each other are most obvious in 'Dreamland'. Margaret is suffering from weird recurring nightmares, in which she is locked in a prison cell, waiting to be hanged for battering to death a balding old man with white hair. She assumes the man to be Victor, but is puzzled by the dream's resolution: she receives a last-minute reprieve on the grounds of justifiable homicide, but she doesn't want to leave the prison and keeps clinging to the bars. The next day, Margaret disappears, and when her raincoat is found by the canal Victor fears the worst. He has barely had time to come to terms with his grief when Margaret suddenly turns up in bed. She explains that she wanted to escape for a few days, and impulsively took a coach to Margate, revisiting the funfair Dreamland, which she remembers from their honeymoon. (She says they got stuck in the Hall of Mirrors for an hour: 'The man had to come in and get us out. You said you didn't mind – you were happy to stay there and look at all the reflections of me.')

At the beach she began to understand her nightmares, remembering a time when she was young and released two budgies from their cage: one held on to the bars, while the other flew straight into the window and killed itself. Margaret's dream of murder isn't directed against Victor after all: 'The next day at school we were asked to write about something that had happened to us, and I wrote my story about the budgies. And the teacher, Mr Philips, made me read it out loud in front of the whole class. And everyone laughed. And I knew that he'd done it deliberately, just to be cruel to me, because, basically, he was a bastard. And he was bald, with white hair. And I remember thinking, even at that age, how much I wanted to batter him to death.'

This sudden and unannounced movement from comedy to drama – Annette Crosbie puts in one of the performances of her life – is typical of *One Foot in the Grave*. In 'The Pit and the Pendulum' Victor tries to comfort Margaret on the sudden death of her mother, despite being buried up to his neck. It's sitcom, as written by Pinter from a plot by Brecht.

'Descent into the Maelstrom' has Victor looking after Margaret, who's collapsed with nervous exhaustion ('I'd get more peace of mind being nursed by the Evil Dead'), while 'Hearts of Darkness' is an incredible and surreal version of *One Flew Over the Cuckoo's Nest* (US 75), with an abortive drive in the country giving way to Victor's overthrow of a corrupt geriatric care regime. There are homages to Conrad and *Apocalypse Now* (US 79), *Psycho* (US 60) and the work of Dennis Potter.

'The Trial' took a different tack, being the best example of *One Foot*'s various one-scene episodes. It's nothing more than Victor on his own, awaiting jury service, pondering yawning ('I wonder what makes you yawn, apart from anything starring Robert Mitchum?'), lockjaw, his misplanted yucca, crosswords ('Mad poet mugged by banjo player sees red when eating pickles'), Mrs Warboys's holiday to Cork, Jehovah's Witnesses and a toupee in a loaf of bread.

The 1994 Christmas episode and the ensuing season was a summary of all that went before. There was the usual pathos (the suicide of Mr Foskett, who left his collection of antique dentures to Victor, in 'The Man Who Blew Away'), and this time it was Victor's turn to almost have an affair ('The Affair of the Hollow Lady'). Margaret confronts the manipulative Millicent (Barbara Windsor) before smacking her with a boxing glove. Mrs Warboys was given room to develop ('This is nice. Not that I can taste it with my allergy, of course. Might be absolutely horrible'). 'Hole in the Sky' had Victor taking up seafood cookery ('... every meal's like ***The Quatermass Experiment*** – clams exploding in the microwave, God knows what') and featured another tragic twist of the emotions as Margaret (having microwaved the head of Victor's puppet) reveals that she's been made redundant and is consequently terrified of becoming like Victor.

With such an unusual husband, who can really blame her?

Television comedy in the 50s fell into two main types. There were the variety-based shows in the music-hall tradition (*Saturday Night at the London Palladium*, *The Ken Dodd Show*, *The Benny Hill Show*), and performance-based series that grew out of radio comedy. And it is in the latter that we find the first stirrings of greatness: *The Howerd Crowd* (1952), *Whack-O!* (1956), ***Hancock's Half Hour*** and *A Show Called Fred*, starring Spike Milligan and Peter Sellers. Michael Bentine's *It's a Square World* began in 1960, and was a pointer from the dour 50s to the near future. It was the first comedy show to be banned (a sketch showing a Chinese junk attacking and sinking the House of Commons was suspended until after the general election) and the first to feature surrealism on an epic scale (a 40-ft-long white whale squirting water outside the Natural History Museum). Biting satire began two years later with ***That Was the Week That Was***, and humour on television was never quite the same again.

TW3 spawned *Not So Much a Programme, More a Way of Life* and *BBC3*, and ITV responded with *On the Braden Beat* in 1962. The Goons made the transition to television in 1963 with the animated series *The Telegoons*, mainly based on the original radio soundtracks. The Goons – via Milligan's ground-breaking *The World of Beachcomber*, the various *Q* series and *There's a Lot of It About*, Sellers and Bentine's *Yes, It's the Cathode Ray Tube Show*, and Bentine's *Potty Time* - were a vital part of the quest for anarchic TV comedy.

One of the most important comic shows of the 60s was *The Frost Report*, at least in the sense that it brought together the Cleese, Chapman, Idle, Jones and Palin writing team for the first time. The programme, fronted by the unflappable Frost, was a return to the form of ***TW3***, and dealt with a different subject each week. Hardly surprising, then, that its anarchic writers felt increasingly constrained and soon moved on to create *At Last the 1948 Show* (Cleese and Chapman, plus Marty Feldman, Aimi MacDonald and Tim Brooke-Taylor) and *Do Not Adjust Your Set* (Palin, Jones, Gilliam and Idle, plus David Jason, Denise Coffey and the Bonzo Dog Doo-Dah Band). 1969 saw the start of Jones and Palin's *The Complete and Utter History of Britain* and something that was originally going to be called (amongst other things) *Vaseline Review* or *Gwen Dibley's Flying Circus*. Thanks to the impact of ***Monty Python***, and Peter Cook and Dudley Moore's ***Not Only ... But Also ...***, the 60s had a style of humour to suit its radical ethos. The influence continued into the 70s with Neil Innes's *The Innes Book of Records*, Innes and Idle's Beatles spoof *The Rutles: All You Need is Cash* and Michael Palin and Terry Jones's *Ripping Yarns*.

If the 60s was the era of mind-bending drugs and sex, the 70s was more about dour-faced introversion. Perhaps the man who best summed up the decade was Irish comic Dave Allen. 'In case you wonder what I do,' Allen has told theatre audiences on many occasions, 'I tend to stroll around and chat. I'd be grateful if you'd refrain from doing the same.'

Dave Allen at Large began in 1971, although Allen had gained his first solo show, *Tonight with Dave Allen*, in 1967. For years, Allen was a voice of sanity in a world suffocating under increasing layers of bureaucracy, a lone individual bellowing at institutional stupidity. 'I really do believe that humour is not so much about laughing at things that happen to other people as at what you do yourself and how you react,' Allen commented in 1990, after his long-awaited return to the small screen. 'I don't specifically go out of my way to make points, but somewhere along the line I make points because I'm annoyed. Authority irks me because it doesn't regard people as people, but as things or as percentages of something.'

The format of *Dave Allen at Large* was simplicity itself: monologues and rants from Allen perched atop a stool, cigarette in one hand, whisky in the other, interspersed with often lengthy filmed sketches. The humour of the inserts was often obvious, involving confession boxes, choir boys farting, or a spoof of *Tom Jones* (GB 63). One episode began with a lengthy spoof of *Tinker, Tailor, Soldier, Spy*, with Allen imprisoned and interrogated by shadowy figures. He eventually manages to escape, and grabs a car, driving through the night until he reaches a deserted warehouse in the middle of a field. Opening the door, he finds himself in the studio. 'How did they get you here tonight?' he asks the audience.

Allen and the writers kicked against standard definitions of 'comedy'. One memorable sequence saw nuclear war breaking out. Allen, alone and affected by radiation sickness, survives in a grim shelter, eating cold baked beans. He is desperate to hear good news on his small transistor radio. Weeks and months seem to pass before he emerges on to the surface. The vista is devastated, with acres of wrecked buildings. No one else moves through the rubble. Allen shouts wildly 'We've won!' - and the camera pulls back to show the figure lost amongst total devastation.

Allen's humour was cleverer than many gave him credit for: one entire five-minute sequence concerned anagrams of famous names (after revealing his own was 'Anal Delve'). Rev Ian Paisley memorably became 'Vile IRA Pansy'. Another episode featured an 'ethnic' version of the final scene from *Hamlet* (complete with Australian Horatio, Irish Hamlet, and Jewish Gertrude). Allen would usually introduce the sketches in some flippant manner (normally as an excuse for his glass to be refilled: it was, apparently, real whisky he was drinking). In one episode he gave a lengthy monologue on tax (deciding that the next thing the government would tax would be sex - 'A kind of PAYF ... I was thinking of 'Fornicate' myself ... '). He ended the sequence by stating that even his glass of whisky was only partly his. 'This much is mine,' he said, indicating a small amount at the bottom, 'and the rest belongs to the Chancellor. Unfortunately, to get down to my bit, I've got to go through his. Cheers!'

If Dave Allen was the mouthpiece of 70s concerns and neuroses, Dick Emery was always more interested in the ageing vulgarity of the music-hall. After appearances in ***The Army Game*** and 1958's *Educating Archie*, Emery was given his own programme, the imaginatively titled *The Dick Emery Show*, in 1963. It ran for almost 20 years. Emery's characters ranged from a toothy vicar to the immortal Mandy ('Ooh, you are awful - but I like you'). *NME*'s David Quantick has described Emery as 'the last of the ENSA [Entertainments National Service Association] comedians, always ready to dress up as a woman and tell rude jokes'. Somehow, the BBC 'allowed Emery to portray a skinhead whose main occupation was shaking piss down his trouser leg'.

The only man to come close to Emery's tastelessness was the irrepressible Kenny Everett, whose love-hate relationship with the BBC acquired epic proportions (the first episode of ***Not the Nine O'Clock News*** began with Everett compering a show saying 'The BBC and I have settled our old differences, and have allowed me back on as long as I don't say the word "pubes"' - he's then sent packing). *The Kenny Everett Video Show* began on ITV in 1978, but later transferred to the Beeb (as *The Kenny Everett Television Show*). The sexual content of the shows was huge - ranging from the writhing dance troupe Hot Gossip to frequent shots of Cleo Rocos's cleavage - but kids loved the ITV shows because of the cartoon version of Captain Kremmen. His most notable characters included Sid Snot, Gizzard Puke and the superb Cupid Stunt, continually telling tales of her latest movie, which always end with her clothes falling off ('But it's all done in the best possible taste').

Poles apart from the vulgarity of Everett or Emery stands the child-like innocence of Tommy Cooper. Cooper was a greatly-loved clown of the highest order, for everything about him was wrong: his magic tricks would fail, his suits seemed not to fit, he sweated under the studio lights, and laughed at his own terrible jokes. His contribution to TV spanned from 1957's *Cooper - Life with Tommy* to his final live performance in 1984. Cooper's masterpiece was his trick involving a wooden duck and a blindfold.

Benny Hill's contribution to TV covered even more years than Cooper's (*The Benny Hill Show* ran between 1955 and 1989). Hill's tone was that of the seaside postcard, but it was *The Two Ronnies* that showed best what could be done with old innuendoes and themes. Barker and Corbett first appeared together on *The Frost Report*, but always pursued separate careers. Indeed, it has to be said that Barker's most consistent work is undoubtedly to be found in ***Porridge***, as *The Two Ronnies* could sometimes be dull and overbearing, the musical items frequently proving tedious. However, despite the predictable opening and closing sequences ('In a packed programme tonight ...', 'On next week's show ...') and the hours given over to singers such as Elaine Paige and Barbara Dickson, there was more than a hint of greatness about *The Two Ronnies*. John Cleese, Graham Chapman, Michael Palin, Terry Jones and ***Reginald Perrin*** creator, David Nobbs, all wrote for the show, although the best scripting was invariably done by Barker himself, under his Gerald Wiley pseudonym. Barker's monologues displayed his great love of the English language, normally in the form of the chairman of some society who is unable to say certain words, letters or sounds, or mixes things up, or in some way subverts simple phrases to sound incredibly rude. Barker remained straight-faced and bank-manager-like throughout.

The ongoing sagas are also well remembered, covering the inept investigations of Charlie Farley and Piggy Malone, and 'The Worm that Turned', starring Diana Dors. An odd tale of women in authority and men wearing skirts, the resolution came in the form of the old fallacy that all women are afraid of mice. Best of all was Spike Milligan's thoroughly insane 'The Phantom Raspberry-Blower of Old London Town'. *The Two Ronnies* ended with Barker's retirement in 1988, some 17 years after it began.

The other great TV comedy duo - Morecambe and Wise - first appeared as an act on *Variety Parade* in 1953. The following year, perhaps too quickly, they got their own show, *Running Wild*, which was critically panned. 'How dare they put such mediocre talent on television?' railed one critic. The duo went back to the theatre to develop their act.

Glenda Jackson's finest hour: rehearsals for the 1971 Morecambe and Wise Christmas show

The Morecambe and Wise Show - initially known as *Two of a Kind* - began on ITV in 1961, producer Colin Clews supervising a variety show that on one occasion featured the Beatles dueting with Ernie on 'Moonlight Bay', while Eric had a go at 'Twist and Shout'. Eric and Ernie's writers at that time were Sid Green and Dick Hills, and many of the running jokes from this time are similar in tone, if not in detail, to what viewers later became used to. Eric would always be trying to finish the (probably rude) joke about two old men in deck chairs, and at the end of the show the comedians would attempt to leave the stage by a door, to find something different and surreal, such as a train or a custard pie, behind it each week. The theme song of the time was also different: Johnny Mercer's 'Two of a Kind'. In their time at ITV, Morecambe and Wise attempted (largely unsuccessfully) to break into movies, with *The Intelligence Men* and *That Riviera Touch* (both 1965), and *The Magnificent Two* (1967).

In 1968 the duo fell out with Lew Grade over money, and quit ATV. Bill Cotton, then head of light entertainment at the BBC, made them a vast cash offer. Changing channels introduced them to Eddie Braben, the writer with whom they developed their most famous routines, and the first BBC *Morecambe and Wise Show* was transmitted in September of that year. Unfortunately, Eric Morecambe suffered a heart attack two months later.

1968 to 1978 are generally recognized as the golden years of Morecambe and Wise (and, as a consequence, an older, golden age of TV comedy), their Christmas special becoming an annual institution. Braben shaped a partnership of child-like characters, with Wise always aspiring to be taken seriously (with the plays 'wot he wrote') and Morecambe always there to bring him back down to earth. One got the feeling that it was because if Wise ever got so elevated as to leave their comfy domesticity (the two were pictured, quite innocently, sharing a bed), Morecambe would feel very alone. (This theme was brought to the fore in the end sequences of their last years with Thames, where Eric would wander off home, with cloth cap and carrier bag, as Wise attempted to close the show.)

Through the BBC shows we learnt that 'you can't see the join', found that there's 'no answer to that', and watched as Morecambe caught an imaginary pebble in a paper bag, put his specs askew on his face, or strangled himself from behind the series' ever-present curtain. All these were attention-seeking devices, designed to lure the semi-mature Ern back into Eric's world, and the more ancient they were, the better. It was hardly surprising that Morecambe - a very thoughtful clown, though by no means a sad one - became an author in the later years of his life, producing the children's books *Mr Lonely* (1981), *The Reluctant Vampire* (1982), and *The Vampire's Revenge* (1983). Children could identify with the outsider figures that he created in his books, and in his stage persona.

Eric and Ernie would always leave the stage after a large woman (Janet Webb) had thanked the audience for watching 'her little show' or a little man (Arthur Tolcher) had played his mouth organ, doing a strange kind of hornpipe dance to the sound of 'Bring Me Sunshine'. Well-remembered sketches of these years include the masterly breakfast-time routine, where Eric and Ernie prepare their meal to the tune of 'The Stripper' on the radio.

The Christmas shows of this period featured an extraordinary range of guest stars, including Glenda Jackson (whose portrayal of Cleopatra she described as the highlight of her career) and Shirley Bassey (who managed to sing 'Smoke Gets in your Eyes' as Eric and Ern pulled her foot from a hole in the stage and replaced her shoe with an army boot). Other guests included Eric Porter, André Previn, Peter Cushing, Diana Rigg, John Mills, and Des O'Connor, whose career at this stage was almost entirely as the butt of Eric's jokes. The 1976 show featured ***The Sweeney*** as guests, a favour the pair repaid on the ITV show, as well as an ad libbing appearance from ex-premier Harold Wilson. This official recognition continued when the duo received OBEs and were made Freemen of the City of London. In 1977 the show was watched by a staggering 28 million people. There was a parade of familiar faces, including Barry Norman, jumping around to 'There is Nothing Like a Dame' in *South Pacific* sailor suits. The audience spent the entire show being told 'He is coming' from various hoardings, only to find at the end of the episode that 'He has gone'. Elton John tried, in vain, to play his latest single, and ended up doing so to the BBC cleaners.

In 1978 Eric and Ernie presided over something of an extravaganza, as Angela Rippon stepped out from behind her desk to high-kick her way through 'Let's Face the Music and Dance' and 'A You're Adorable'. Penelope Keith appeared on the show, initially mistaking Ernie for Kermit the Frog. However, there were strange stirrings on the other channel, Eric appearing on Christmas Eve on ITV's *World of Sport*, chatting to Dickie Davies. Morecambe and Wise were about to switch sides again, lured to Thames by another huge cash offer. The start of the first show on the other side saw Morecambe and Wise being thrown out of a BBC van at the gates of the Thames building.

However, Thames didn't get the vast Christmas special they anticipated. In 1979 Eric Morecambe went into hospital for heart surgery, and the 1979 Christmas show was a quiet interview with David Frost, intercut with archive footage from the duo's previous days at ITV. The Thames move was a troubled one at first, Eddie Braben remaining with the BBC. Various writers, including Barry Cryer, tried to get to grips with the Morecambe and Wise style and failed, despite the aid of guests such as Judi Dench and Donald Sinden. It took the arrival of Braben at Thames, in 1980, to get things moving again. At this point, the duo started to sing 'Bring Me Sunshine' again, something they had consciously dropped.

Memorable sketches from this era include two cartoon parodies, Eric and Ernie taking the places of the monkeys from the Disney movie *The Jungle Book* to perform 'I Wanna Be Like You', and performing as Tom and Jerry.

Eric Morecambe died in 1984, his heart problems having finally caught up with him. His work rate had decreased drastically in the 80s, Morecambe and Wise making very short seasons and Christmas shows at Thames. Ernie decided to make a career for himself, declining to take on another partner, a move he could easily have made, considering the skills and timing he'd acquired as television's best straight man. (Indeed, in the first days of the act, it had been Wise who dished out the insults, and Morecambe who took them.)

The memory of Eric Morecambe lives on today in repeats, and in the generation of new comedians who recognize the childish anarchy in his work. Never one to reinforce stereotypes (too sexless to be sexist, his reaction to a pretty girl being a very defensive 'Good evening, young sir!'), Morecambe's highly-refined body comedy can be seen in his post-modern successor, Vic Reeves.

Half a century after it started, the story of British television's greatest double act continues.

Hancock's Half Hour/Hancock

- **BBC Television** (1956-61), ATV (1963) ◆ B&W
- **76 episodes** (standard length: 30-minutes)
- **Creators/writers:** Ray Galton, Alan Simpson
- **ATV series writers:** Godfrey Harrison, Terry Nation, Richard Harris, Dennis Spooner
- **Producers:** Duncan Wood (BBC), Tony Hancock (ATV)
- **Director:** Alan Tarrant (ATV)

Regular cast: Tony Hancock (Anthony Aloysius Hancock) • Sid James (Sidney Balmoral James)

With: Irene Handl • Warren Mitchell • Kenneth Williams • Hattie Jacques • Hugh Lloyd • Arthur Mullard • John Le Mesurier • Mario Fabrizi • Johnny Vyvyan • Frank Thornton • Patricia Hayes • June Whitfield • Patrick Cargill • Pat Coombs • Terence Alexander • Dick Emery • John Vere • Alec Bregonzi • James Bulloch

The ironic fact that almost 30 years after his death Tony Hancock is influencing another generation of comedians wouldn't have been lost on the man himself. Remakes of some of Hancock's finest half-hours (starring Paul Merton, the latest in a long - and impressive - line of 'Hancocks for the 70s/80s/90s') are surprising only in as much as nobody thought of it sooner.

In terms of presentation, writing and performance, *Hancock's Half Hour* is without parallel. Although a proportion of the Hancock mystique comes from the very complex nature of 'the lad himself', it is to his performance as Britain's favourite loser that any critical analysis must address itself.

Tony Hancock began his career in radio comedy during the 40s. His initial fame was as Archie Andrews's teacher in *Educating Archie* and, once teamed with writers Ray Galton and Alan Simpson, he was given his own radio series in 1954. *Hancock's Half Hour* - radio version - was a surreal fantasy in which Hancock and his cohorts (Bill Kerr, Sid James, Kenneth Williams and Hattie Jacques) would enact outrageous scenarios each week (who could forget the episode with RAF pilot Hancock discovering Williams clinging to his wing at 25,000 feet?). Six seasons of the radio show were made, the final two broadcast in 1958-59, by which time the series had, with minimal adaptation, successfully transferred to television.

Whilst the BBC dithered over whether to turn their most famous radio asset into a TV star, ITV got in first, creating *The Tony Hancock Show*, produced by Jack Hylton. This was a sketch-based series, written by Eric Sykes (Galton and Simpson contributed some uncredited material), which ran for two brief seasons in 1956 and 1957.

Hancock's Half Hour - TV version - began with the same aesthetic quality as the radio series. Galton and Simpson were still learning to write for the new medium and many of the early episodes relied on verbal exchange. It was also decided that they could not carry the entire ménage from radio. Bill Kerr was dropped, Hattie Jacques made only a few appearances, and Kenneth Williams appeared in the second season only (none of the episodes from this era - bar the brilliant 'The Alpine Holiday' - exists in the archives). Sid James, on the other hand, was the ideal foil for Hancock, playing Tony's disreputable flatmate. James's ability with face-comedy (something he shared with Hancock) and positively obscene laugh made Sid an equal partner in the early days of *Hancock's Half Hour*.

Each episode was prefixed by a simple announcement, 'BBC television presents Tony Hancock in ...', at which point the breathless star would stammer the title. One of the most interesting early episodes was 'The Radio Show', which took many of the radio series' elements and debunked them.

The first two seasons, were, as with many comedies of the era, broadcast bi-weekly (every two weeks), alternating with variety programmes (the first season shared its slot with *Joyce Grenfell Requests the Pleasure*, whilst the second was paired with, of all things, *Victor Silvester's TV Dancing Club*). By the beginning of the third season, however, *Hancock's Half Hour* had become a weekly Monday-night fixture. This batch of stories included Hancock QC attempting to defend Sid from a charge of stealing jewellery. In a brilliant twist, Sid stitches up Hancock, who ends the episode in Dartmoor. As Roger Wilmut notes, the strain on everyone involved in these live performances was considerable since nothing could be done if anything went wrong. In 'There's an Airfield at the Bottom of my Garden', something did go wrong: several collapsible props collapsed long before they were supposed to. It was magical television, if unnerving for the actors, and the decision was made after this to pre-record all future episodes (something for which future generations should be eternally grateful).

The fourth season began with the epic 'Ericson the Viking'. Sid persuades Tony to make a historical drama series (much in vogue on ITV) and the resulting chaos (complete with Dick James-like theme song, portraying the hero 'nipping through the wood'), 'conceived, written, produced and directed' by Sidney Balmoral James, is taken off by the BBC and replaced with 'the 84th showing of the London to Brighton run in four minutes'. Subversion of other television genres also formed the basis for 'The Horror Serial'. Having been, along with most of the country, petrified by ***Quatermass and the Pit***, Tony and Sid discover a hole in their back garden and are convinced that the Martians have landed.

Other outstanding episodes include 'The Flight of the Red Shadow' (which includes one of the first television appearance of Rolf Harris), and the high jinks of the East Cheam repertory company in 'The Servants'. 'The Football Pools' includes one of Hancock's most brilliant rants, a five-minute description of his appearance in a schoolboy international (scoring an own goal having forgotten that the teams change ends at half-time).

Hancock's Half Hour extended the boundaries of comedy writing, Galton and Simpson creating an almost flawless character for Hancock: pompous, petty and argumentative, yet at the same time sympathetic. The man beneath the Homburg and greatcoat, and the blustering 'Stone me', was as complex as his real-life counterpart. In that respect, Galton and Simpson did their job almost too well. Hancock the man became Hancock the character and this may have helped to sow the seeds for his tragic demise.

HANCOCK'S HALF HOUR

First season
(6 Jul–14 Sep 56)
1 The First TV Show
2 The Artist
3 The Dancer
4 The Bequest
5 The Radio Show
6 The Chef that Died of Shame

Second season
(1 Apr–10 Jun 57)
7 The Alpine Holiday
8 Lady Chatterley's Revenge
9 The Russian Prince
10 The New Neighbour
11 The Pianist
12 The Auction

Third season
(30 Sep–23 Dec 57)
13 The Continental Holiday
14 The Great Detective
15 The Amusement Arcade
16 A Holiday in Scotland
17 Air Steward Hancock, the Last of the Many
18 The Regimental Reunion
19 The Adopted Family
20 The Elocution Teacher
21 The Lawyer (The Crown vs James, S. Hancock, QC, Defending)
22 How to Win Money and Influence People
23 There's an Airfield at the Bottom of my Garden
24 Hancock's Forty-Three Minutes [43 minutes]

Fourth season
(26 Dec 58–27 Mar 59)
25 Ericson the Viking
26 Underpaid! or Grandad's SOS
27 The Set that Failed
28 The New Nose
29 The Flight of the Red Shadow
30 The Horror Serial
31 The Italian Maid
32 Matrimony - Almost
33 The Beauty Contest
34 The Wrong Man
35 The Oak Tree
36 The Knighthood
37 The Servants

'It's red hot, mate ... As soon as I've finished this, I shall recommend they ban it!' ('The Missing Page')

Yet the quality of 'Twelve Angry Men' ('Does Magna Carta mean nothing to you? Did she die in vain? The Hungarian peasant girl who forced King John to sign the pledge at Runnymede and shut the pubs at half-past-ten?!') show clearly that when the writing and the timing of the star meshed perfectly, what emerged was genius. This continued in episodes like 'The Missing Page' (Hancock borrows a pulp novel, *Lady Don't Fall Backwards*, from the library, only to discover that the last page, revealing the denouement, has been torn out) and 'The Reunion Party' (which includes a remarkable silent segment of face-comedy as Hancock tries to remember the name of one of his former army colleagues).

During the broadcast of this sixth season, Hancock agreed to undergo the torture of an appearance on John Freeman's interview series *Face to Face*. Freeman grilled Tony on his personal life and, for the first time, cracks began to show through the public persona (Hancock and Freeman, however, became good friends).

Fifth season
(25 Sep–27 Nov 59)
38 The Economy Drive
39 The Two Murderers
40 Lord Byron Lived Here
41 Twelve Angry Men
42 The Train Journey
43 The Cruise
44 The Big Night
45 The Tycoon
46 Spanish Interlude
47 Football Pools

Sixth season
(4 Mar–6 May 60)
48 The Cold
49 The Missing Page
50 The Emigrant
51 The Reunion Party
52 Sid In Love
53 The Baby Sitters
54 The Ladies' Man
55 The Photographer
56 The East Cheam Centenary
57 The Poison Pen Letters

HANCOCK
Seventh season
(26 May–30 Jun 61, 25-minute episodes)
58 The Bedsitter [aka Hancock Alone]
59 The Bowmans
60 The Radio Ham
61 The Lift
62 The Blood Donor
63 The Succession - Son and Heir

Eighth season
(3 Jan–28 Mar 63, 25-minute episodes)
64 The Assistant
65 The Eye-Witness
66 Shooting Star
67 The Girl
68 The Man on the Corner
69 The Memory Test
70 The Early Call
71 The Craftsman
72 The Night Out
73 The Politician
74 The Reporter
75 The Writer
76 The Escort

By now Hancock had begun to think of moving from television - his film, *The Rebel* (a brilliant Galton and Simpson script) was released in 1960 - and a change of emphasis was attempted for the seventh season when Sid James's character was written out, and the episodes, shortened to 25 minutes became, simply, *Hancock*. The first episode, 'The Bedsitter', is classic TV writing: 25 minutes of sighs and occasional one-liners as Tony attempts to conquer his boredom. Then came 'The Radio Ham' ('Yes, I know it's raining in Tokyo') and 'The Blood Donor'. Hancock's performance in the latter episode is all the more remarkable for the fact that Hancock had been unable to learn his lines due to a car crash. Ray Galton once commented that 'if you look at 'The Blood Donor', you'll see Hancock's not looking at June Whitfield or anyone else - he's looking over their shoulder and he's reading it all.'

The split with Galton and Simpson came shortly afterwards, whilst Hancock was preparing his second film, *The Punch and Judy Man* (GB 63). Ray and Alan went on to create ***Steptoe and Son*** whilst Hancock, perhaps unwisely, attempted to recreate the BBC series on ATV. With the exception of a couple of episodes, the ATV episodes are a crushing disappointment.

The tragedy of Tony Hancock was that he was unable to escape from the mould which had grown around him thanks to *Hancock's Half Hour*. He returned to the theatre, but his material was still based on his old stage show; attempted to break into films in America; had a role in Peter Cook and Dudley Moore's *The Wrong Box*; and made another series for ITV (*Hancock's* in 1967). By the time of his suicide in Australia in 1968 Hancock was a broken man, tortured by his obsessional search for the core of his genius. Much of this conflict is captured in William Humble's 1991 *Screen One* play *Hancock*, in which Alfred Molina recreates the last seven years of Tony's life with breathtaking accuracy.

But despite the decline of the man (or perhaps because of it), Anthony Aloysius Hancock of 23 Railway Cuttings, East Cheam, the mythical creation of Galton and Simpson, will live forever.

That Was the Week That Was

- **BBC Television** ◆ **B&W**
- **38 episodes** (standard length: 50 minutes) ◆ 1962-63
- **Writers/the cast:** Keith Waterhouse, Willis Hall, Malcolm Bradbury, Christopher Booker, John Cleese, David Nobbs, Peter Dobreiner, Dennis Potter, David Nathan, Robert Gillespie, Antony Jay, Brian Glanville, Gerald Kaufman, Peter Cook, Jack Rosenthal, Peter Lewis, Charles Lewson, Peter Tinniswood, Brad Ashton, Bill Oddie, Peter Schaffer
- **Director/producer:** Ned Sherrin

Sir Cyril Osborne, the Conservative MP for Louth, called *That Was the Week That Was* 'a low sexy thing', adding that he felt that he 'would like to give the performers a good bath'. His complaint highlights two things: how different the world was when satire was first on television, and what an abundance of material there was for it to prey on.

Osborne had just been shouting at Bernard Levin, *TW3*'s resident interviewer and confrontationist, about the Denning Report. Each week, Levin would talk to a group of people about their profession, and generally abuse them in a populist way. He was quite successful in his encounters with scientists and PR executives, but was stopped in his tracks by a gang of angry farmers. 'We're used to handling dumb animals,' said an NFU spokesman, after Levin had begun the interview with the greeting 'Hello peasants'. Levin's most memorable encounter, however, was with Katina, an astrologer who squirted him with a plastic lemon, repeating 'the answer's a lemon'. (His most outrageous off-screen slagging came from a Cheshire vicar who called him a 'thick-lipped Jewboy'.)

Such moments were TV history, because *TW3* instantly caught the imagination of the viewing public. The *Daily Express* called it 'irreverent, tough, cynical, snobbish, leftish and witty', and it was indeed all these things. The press played a game of numerical switchboards, each week counting the numbers of angry calls that the show prompted. The record was 443, which, out of 13 million viewers, wasn't bad. Reginald Bevins, the Postmaster General, studied the scripts, and was asked by Tory MPs to ban all references to royalty and religion. He refused. The ITV answer to *TW3*, *What the Public Wants*, was dropped after four episodes because of a clause in the Television Act which stated that ITV programmes could not refer to living people. *TW3* only really escaped censorship because, being produced by Talks and Current Affairs, it wasn't subject to the light entertainment rulebook.

The host of the show was the young David Frost, discovered by Ned Sherrin (of *Tonight* fame) doing his improvised press conference as Harold Macmillan at the Blue Angel Club off Berkeley Square. Frost was a substitute for John Bird, who had dropped out, and took over the host duties completely when Brian Redhead declined to continue as co-host after an (unbroadcast) pilot.

The social and political backdrop to *TW3* was that of the early 60s, an era of changing attitudes to the power of television as a medium and humour's role in everyday life. In London, *Beyond the Fringe*, starring a number of Frost and Sherrin's contemporaries, was playing to packed houses, and at the

Starring: David Frost • Millicent Martin • Bernard Levin • Lance Percival • Roy Kinnear • William Rushton • Timothy Birdsall • John Wells • Kenneth Cope • David Kernan • Al Mancini • John Bird • Eleanor Bron • Roy Hudd

Establishment Club the satirists of a generation were creating new, and dangerous, targets for themselves.

TW3 was written in the week of, sometimes on the day of, broadcast, and contained much improvised material, setting new standards for the comedy of the time. Each week's edition would begin with Millicent Martin singing a new Caryl Brahms lyric to Ron Grainer's theme. In a similar vein, Lance Percival would provide topical (and often improvised) calypsos.

In the time before the Profumo scandal, *That Was the Week That Was* was the voice of an emergent young generation, appalled by the Macmillan government. Amongst the more biting attacks the team mounted were assaults on Norrie Paramour ('he takes all the messy unpredictability and excitement out of music'), Keith Joseph ('he has great experience of housing - he has three of his own') and Frost's astonishing personal attack on Sir Alec Douglas-Home. One of the most controversial items was Gerald Kaufman's list of silent MPs, those who hadn't spoken in the Commons for ten or fifteen years. It caused an outcry that reached the House itself, but hardly qualified as satire, being, as Kaufman pointed out, simply an easily-discovered truth. Also the subject of an uproar was 'A Consumer's Guide to Religions', ancestor to a thousand ***Monty Python*** and ***Not the Nine O'Clock News*** sketches. The sketch itself was quite harmless, comparing the benefits of various churches in what now seems a rather tame way. However, it was enough to get MPs talking of a ban once more.

The show took up the gauntlet on behalf of John Osborne after the playwright was accused of unpatriotism by the press, and featured many famous guests, such as Hattie Jacques and Peter Wyngarde. The atmosphere was that of an Oxbridge supper club, with music and debate at least as important a part of the mix as Satire. There was a capital S in those days, Satire, like Modern Jazz, being something new, a vital part of the movement against the establishment. As Sherrin said in *The Observer*, *TW3* 'took the relationship between audience and programme a step further', and, like Giles's cartoons, would be eagerly awaited for its verdict on whatever was happening that week.

Amongst the other memorable moments in the series were David Frost's listing of Britain's remaining dependencies ('and not forgetting Sweet Rockall') and the almost-laughless episode broadcast on the evening after the Kennedy assassination (Millicent Martin's astonishing and dignified performance of 'His Memory Lingers On' is the stuff of which TV legends are made). The series introduced to television, writers from beyond the normal range of gag-merchants. Playwrights, novelists and journalists (many later to become TV institutions) all contributed material that, although sometimes misplaced or silly, was frequently 'right on' in a way that TV comedy had never been before. It was as rough as the studio from where the show was broadcast, Sherrin allowing the audience to see cameras, microphones and everything that would normally have been hidden. It added to the impression of hard honesty.

A profile of home secretary Henry Brooke, describing him as 'the most hated man in Britain', ended 'If you're home secretary, you can get away with murder.' Frost would often follow such an attack with the line 'Seriously though, he's doing a grand job.'

A Keith Waterhouse and Willis Hall sketch had two 'viewers' (Kinnear and Martin) staring at a TV set in an obvious parody of the series' audience. 'Obscenity. It's all the go nowadays,' says Kinnear. 'You can say "bum", you can say "poo", you can say anything.'

TW3 was also pivotal in Frankie Howerd's nth revival: revered by Sherrin, Howerd mocked the

Special
(29 Sep 62, 150 minutes)

First season
(24 Nov 62–27 Apr 63)
Twenty-three episodes
7 That Was the Year That Was
24 Son of Juvenal

Second season
(28 Sep–21 Dec 63)
Thirteen episodes
37 Dick Whittington and his Fascist Hyena

Special
(28 Dec 63, 100 minutes)
38 That Was the Year That Was

Those famous people you're still too young to remember having seen in *TW3*

intelligence of the satire around him ('these days you need a degree to tell a joke about knickers'), but proved more than capable of attacking people in his own unique manner: 'Robin Day - strange man? Isn't he? Funny man ... Hasn't he got cruel glasses?'

TW3 ended at Christmas 1963, when the BBC got cold feet over the prospect of the programme being shown in an election year and possibly influencing the result. Most of the team went on to produce *Not So Much a Programme, More a Way of Life* in late 1964, and *BBC3* in 1965.

TW3 pitted itself against the establishment, although ironically (and perhaps inevitably) David Frost, 'the angry young man of 1963', having failed to successfully transfer *TW3* to American audiences, became a part of the establishment himself. Nevertheless, the wide-ranging influence that *TW3* had on both mainstream and alternative comedy can be seen in shows as diverse as *The Tube*, *A Stab in the Dark*, and *Have I Got News For You*. Allegedly.

Not Only... But Also...

- **BBC Television** (BBC2) ◆ **B&W** (1965-66); **Colour** (1970)
- **22 episodes** (standard length: *c.* 45 minutes)
- **Creators/writers:** Dudley Moore, Peter Cook
- **Additional material:** Robert Fuest, John Law
- **Producers:** Joe McGrath, Dick Clement, John Street, James Gilbert

Starring: Dudley Moore • Peter Cook • John Lennon • Barry Humphries • Peter Sellers • Una Stubbs • Eric Sykes • Henry Cooper • Cilla Black • Dusty Springfield • Spike Milligan • William Rushton • Frank Muir • Ronnie Barker

In 1964, the BBC asked Dudley Moore - son of a railway electrician who had won an organ scholarship to Oxford - to star in a one-off programme. He immediately roped in Peter Cook, a Cambridge graduate and his *Beyond the Fringe* partner, whose creation E.L. Wisty had already appeared in *On the Braden Beat*. Cook wrote two sketches: one about a man whose life's work was to teach ravens to fly underwater, and another about a pair of cloth-capped idiots, coincidentally called Pete and Dud. This latter pair was immediately popular; a full series with the same mix of humour and jazz was commissioned.

When *Not Only ... But Also ...* appeared in early 1965, it shared ***That Was the Week That Was***'s joyful absence of 'taste' within a vigorous sketch-based format largely free of satire and parochialism. The surreal humour was a perfect reflection of the time and included a song entitled 'L.S. Bumblebee' (not about drugs, of course), a sequence where Pete was captured by aliens, and a pseudo-American documentary on 'Swinging London'. In this, Hiram J. Pipesucker Jr interviewed 'destructive artist' Lionel Bloab, who's so far out he's barely in earshot, as well as the rector of Carnaby and All Trends and the manager of the world's most famous pop group, the Mothers.

The musical sections, which in mid-60s revue-style comedies were often 'the serious bit', were superbly tailored to both the insane style of humour and Moore's musical brilliance, ranging from the opening sequence (two plummy pianists who play underwater), through the repetitive 'Alan A'Dale' song and Moore's modern Beethoven (singing nothing but Tom Jones cover versions), to the closing 'Goodbye-ee', which made the top 20 in the first year of *Not Only ...*.

Funniest of all was Peter Cook's appearance as a suited, well-spoken interviewer/interpreter of Bo Dudley's R'n'B: '"Momma's got a brand new bag, yeah ... We're gonna groove it the whole night long, baby." Now this, presumably, is a reference to the fact that the mother having bought the bag decides to make some indentations on it ... .'

The programme also became known for its staggering introductions, the *Not Only ... But Also ...* logo being unfurled from Tower Bridge, or being carved by cavemen above a hillside white horse. A later episode would begin on the *Ark Royal*, with a lost cyclist attempting to rejoin the Birmingham-Mandalay cycle race ('No, this is the Samarkand by-pass!'). Sketches covered subjects as diverse as a one-legged man applying to play Tarzan in a film (later reused in Cook and Moore's under-rated film version of *The Hound of the Baskervilles*) and the bare-fist fight between Gentleman Jim and the Dagenham Dodger. The facts of life were discussed, with Peter Cook as the grave, slightly embarrassed father explaining to

First season
(9 Jan–3 Apr 65)
Seven episodes

Second season
(15 Jan–26 Feb 66)
Seven 30-minute episodes

Christmas special
(26 Dec 66, 50 minutes)

Third season
as *Show of the Week*
(18 Feb–13 May 70)
Seven episodes

young Dudley how he came to be: 'It was necessary for your mother to sit on a chair which I had recently vacated and was still warm from my body ... And sure enough four years later you were born.'

Not Only ... But Also ... parodied contemporary television - the superb Gerry Anderson pastiche 'Superthunderstingcar' - and etched out a unique line in Edward Lear-like nonsense verse. This included 'The Glidd of Glood' (an epic tale of staggering wealth and heartlessness), an adaptation of Lear's 'Uncle Arly', and John Lennon's 'Deaf Ted, Danootah (and Me)' (in which, Moore, Lennon and Norman Rossington indulged in some Richard Lester-style silliness). Lennon also appeared in the 1966 Christmas special as Dan, the commissionaire of a gents' toilet; other guests included Spike Milligan and Barry Humphries in an early equivalent of *Whose Line is it Anyway?* entitled 'Poets Cornered'.

Best of all, though, were Pete and Dud. They met for their brainless chats at the pub, in an art gallery, or at the zoo. At the latter location they discussed the gecko, which doesn't live very long because it hates eating flies, and the humming bird, which is able to kiss at immense distances thanks to its long, coiled-up tongue: 'That means that you could stand on the Chiswick flyover and kiss someone up the Staines by-pass.' To compensate for their lack of intelligence, their fantasy-lives were quite vigorous: 'Tap, tap, tap at the bloody window pane. I looked out - you know who it was? Bloody Greta Garbo.'

They also discussed passionate affairs with girls on buses ('She got off a stop before me, but I knew what she was after'), Moore commenting that 'I was really talking about the girls I adored when I was a nipper in Dagenham, where I always used to make sure I caught a particular bus to school because I knew certain girls would get on at different stops on the route.' These 'Dagenham dialogues' often evolved in this manner, with Moore and Cook deciding on a subject to talk about. They switched on a tape recorder and simply spoke to each other as Pete and Dud would. 'We listen to the playback, and go over and over it, taking things out and putting things in.' The end result was the approximate format for the ensuing dialogue, although spontaneity was the aim. Cook would often improvise cruelly; Moore would usually be on the verge of hysterics, stuffing his face with sandwiches to try to hide this from the audience. But they loved it: Pete and Dud's humour was all about fantasy and inclusion, anyway.

Not Only ... But Also ..., with its too-long sketches, absence of punchlines (an innovation sometimes wrongly credited to ***Python***), and rampant surrealism (a 'Good versus Evil' cricket match), established a benchmark which would only later be exceeded by changing the accepted face of comedy, almost beyond recognition. The Leaping Nuns of St Beryl and the gourmet guide to the North Circular were examples of the best of mid-60s comedy, and a tantalizing glimpse into the not-too-distant future.

Monty Python's Flying Circus/Monty Python

- **BBC Television** (BBC2) ◆ **Colour**
- **48 episodes** (1 unbroadcast in UK) (30 minutes) ◆ **1969-74**
- **Writers/performers:** Graham Chapman, John Cleese, Terry Gilliam, Eric Idle, Terry Jones, Michael Palin
- **Director:** Ian MacNaughton
- **Producer:** John Howard Davies

Comedy legends tend to come and go, but the legend that is *Monty Python's Flying Circus* seems set to live long in the memory of the viewers who were raised on its revolutionary and anarchic 'stream of consciousness' approach to humour. Whole sketches (the infamous dead parrot sketch), characters (John Cleese as the man from the Ministry of Silly Walks) and phrases ('And now for something completely different') have entered into the English language and psyche to such an extent that speech writers for an incumbent prime minister are able to pour scorn on an opposing party with the phrase 'It is an ex-parrot'.

Monty Python's Flying Circus was formed from the ashes of Cleese and Chapman's *At Last, the 1948 Show* and the Jones/Palin/Idle/Gilliam collaboration *Do Not Adjust Your Set*. The concept for *Python* was taken to the BBC by producer Barry Took in mid-1969, and was, in many ways, a continuation of ideas that its various creators had developed during the 60s as writers and performers on *The Frost Report*. Bored with seeing their submitted sketches rejected because 'they won't understand it in Bradford', the team knew that their future lay in a looser and more insane format.

From the beginning, the group was a diverse unit: Terry Jones's emotional free-form style, heavily influenced by Spike Milligan's *Q5*, clashed with Cleese's more traditional and logical sketch-orientated approach. However, from the script battles emerged early indications of the glorious and irreverent mix of the sublime and the ridiculous that was to be the programme's hallmark.

The first episode was transmitted in a late evening slot on a Sunday, a space previously filled by religious programmes (which gave rise to an early title suggestion of *Owl Stretching Time*). The audience was immediately subjected to the graphical burst of energy that formed the animated title sequence (prefaced by Michael Palin's obligatory 'It's Man'). To the strains of Sousa's 'Liberty Bell', cartoon surrealism ran rampant, until a giant foot (borrowed by Gilliam from Bronzino's 'Venus and Cupid') crushed everything beneath it with resounding finality.

MONTY PYTHON'S FLYING CIRCUS

First season
(5 Oct 69–11 Jan 70)

1 Whither Canada?
2 Sex and Violence
3 How to Recognise Different Types of Tree from Quite a Long Way Away
4 Owl-Stretching Time
5 Man's Crisis of Identity in the Latter Half of the Twentieth Century
6 The BBC Entry for the Zinc Stoat of Budapest (Current Affairs)
7 You're No Fun Any More
8 Episode 12B: Full Frontal Nudity
9 The Ant, an Introduction - Part 2, the Llama
10 'It's a Tree'
11 Episode Twos: The Royal Philharmonic Orchestra Goes to the Bathroom
12 Episode 17-26: The Naked Ant
13 'Intermission'

Second season
(15 Sep–22 Dec 70)

14 'Face the Press'
15 'Jarrow - New Year's Eve 1911'
16 'It's the Mind'
17 The Buzz Aldrin Show
18 'Blackmail'
19 'It's a Living'
20 'The Attila the Hun Show'
21 'Archaeology Today'
22 'How to Recognise Different Parts of the Body'
23 'Scott of the Sahara'
24 'HM Government Public Service Film No. 42 Para. 6: "How Not To Be Seen"'
25 'The Black Eagle'
26 'Royal Episode Thirteen'

Montreux special
(16 Apr 71)

This was television unlike anything that had gone before. Without any apparent reason, bizarre characters would flit from one scene (or episode) to another (the most famous example being the frequent appearances of Cardinals Ximanez, Fang and Biggles: 'No one expects the Spanish Inquisition!'). Many episodes had a running theme, perhaps mock-informative ('How to Recognise Different Types of Tree from Quite a Long Way Away') or anagrammatical (the series was retitled *Tony M. Nyphot's Flying Riscсu*). Sketches would terminate mid-sentence because they were 'silly', and often there would be no traditional punchline, the humour coming from the ridiculous situation rather than from the dialogue itself.

Thus we encountered deadly jokes that had a crucial military role in World War II, surviving Nazi leaders who take part in the Minehead by-election ('Mr Hitler, Hilter, he says that historically Taunton is part of Minehead already'), and Dennis Moore, a highwayman who steals lupins. The humour could be violent (musical mice that apparently squeaked at a certain pitch when hit by a large mallet) or simply strange (the Philosophy Department of the University of Woolamaloo in Australia seemed to be staffed entirely by Professors called Bruce). A classic instalment of 'World Forum' featured Mao Tse-tung, Lenin, Che Guevara and Karl Marx facing questions on previous winners of the FA Cup.

Subversion of expectation was always a standard *Monty Python* ploy. Often the title sequence would not appear at the beginning of the episode but half-way through, and the audience was never quite sure if the programme had ended or not. The BBC globe would be put to good use with fake announcements (usually by either Idle or Palin): 'Now on BBC television, a choice of viewing. On BBC2 - a discussion on censorship between Derek Hart, the Bishop of Woolwich, and a nude man. And on BBC1 - me telling you this.' Sketches frequently parodied other television shows. A classic example was the *Grandstand*-like 'Upperclass Twit of the Year': 'Ah there's Oliver, there's Oliver now, he's at the back ... He doesn't know when he's beaten, this boy, he doesn't know when he's winning either. He doesn't have any sort of sensory apparatus.'

Cleese was often to be found in a stock role as a po-faced BBC type brought out of mothballs to interview all manner of deformed madmen (including a man with three buttocks and someone who intends to jump across the English Channel). Palin became the anchorman on 'Blackmail', a vicious dig at 60s game shows: 'Three thousand pounds to stop us revealing your name, the name of the three other people involved, the youth organisation to which they belong, and the shop where you bought the equipment.'

Palin also played a number of hen-pecked little men who were experiencing marital problems or seemed to have all the problems of the world placed on their shoulders. Chapman invented the Colonel, the upright, no-nonsense British Army officer who was the show's barometer of silliness ('I've noticed a tendency for this programme to get rather silly ... Now, nobody likes a good laugh more than I do ... except perhaps my wife and some of her friends ... Oh

Third season
(19 Oct 72–18 Jan 73)
28 Whicker's World
29 'Mr and Mrs Brian Norris' Ford Popular'
30 'The Money Programme'
31 'Blood, Death, War, Horror'
32 The All-England Summarize Proust Competition
33 'Today in Parliament Has Now Become the Classic Serial'
34 'The Adventures of Biggles. Part One - Biggles Dictates a Letter'
35 The Cycling Tour [aka Mr Pither's Cycling Tour]
36 'And Now the Ten Seconds of Sex'
37 'The Life of Sir Philip Sidney'
38 'Boxing Tonight'
39 'A Party Political Broadcast on Behalf of the Conservative and Unionist Party'
40 Grandstand

German special
(not transmitted in the UK)
41 Monty Python in Deutschland

German special
(6 Oct 73)
42 Monty Python's Fliegendre Zirkus

MONTY PYTHON
Fourth season
(31 Oct–5 Dec 74)
43 The Golden Age of Ballooning
44 Michael Ellis
45 Light Entertainment War
46 Hamlet
47 Mr Neutron
48 Party Political Broadcast

[Episodes given in quotation marks are unofficial titles. The first German special was a co-production between BBC1 and WDR-TV; the second was produced by BBC2, GMBH and WDR.]

yes and Captain Johnston. Come to think of it, most people like a good laugh more than I do').

Eric Idle was the creative force behind Mr Nudge Nudge, the feeble semi-pervert and the sort of man one naturally tends to shy away from in pubs. In fact, Idle always seemed to end up playing the most obnoxious characters (notably night-club owners).

One of Terry Jones's oddest characters was the Bishop, an outrageous, scar-faced parody of contemporary American cop-shows. A mock title sequence featured every time his name was mentioned. However, Jones's forte seemed to be playing shrill women interviewed on the subject of French philosophers. These lower-class 'pepperpots', along with their male equivalents, the Gumbies (knotted handkerchiefs, clenched fists, and bellowed dialogue), formed one of the major human targets of *Monty Python's Flying Circus* (uniformly boring and spineless accountants seemed to be the other).

If *Python*'s class system was rigid, its depiction of women was almost non-existent. Although sometimes parodied, one standard female character was the sexually-available woman (Carol Cleveland enticing milkmen to her lair) or the fawning girl (Connie Booth during the 'Lumberjack Song'). Alternatively, women would be shown as gossiping housewives (played by various members of the team, and often given names like 'Mrs Niggerbaiter').

Outrageous names were another crucial facet of Python's humour, ranging from the moderately silly (Raymond Luxury Yacht, pronounced Throatwobbler Mangrove) to the remarkable (Johann Gambolputty de von Ausfern-schplenden-schlitter-crasscrenbon-fried-digger-dingle-dangle-dongle-dungle-burstein-von-knacker-thrasher-apple-banger-horowitz-ticolensic-grander-knotty-spelltinkle-grandlich-grumblemeyer-spelterwasser-kurstlich-himbleeisen-bahnwagen-gutenabend-bitte-ein-nürnburger-bratwustle-gerspurten-mitz-weimache-luber-hundsfut-gumberaber-shönendanker-kalbsfleisch-mittler-aucher-von Hautkopft of Ulm).

After the first season concluded that 'God exists, by two falls to a submission', the second and third seasons saw more of the same. Pasolini's new film *The Third Testmatch* was criticized by a number of disgruntled cricketers ('And in t'film, we get Fred Titmus ... the symbol of man's regeneration through radical Marxism ... Fair enough ... But we never once get a chance to see him turn his off-breaks on that Brisbane sticky'). One episode ('The Cycling Tour') even included a (bizarre) plot with Palin as a knotted handkerchief-wearing Little Englander in a travelogue nightmare that predicted the actor's later, real-life travels in *Around the World in 80 Days* and *Pole to Pole*.

However, tensions within the group were becoming intrusive. John Cleese, in particular, found the success of the series inhibiting and, although still a member of the writing team, he did not appear in the final, vestigial season. *Monty Python*'s future as a creative team lay in films: *Monty Python and the Holy Grail* (1975), *Monty Python's Life of Brian* (1979), and *Monty Python's The Meaning of Life* (1983), whilst individual members went on to produce challenging and often brilliant television: Cleese with ***Fawlty Towers***, Idle with *Rutland Weekend Television*, and Palin and Jones with *Ripping Yarns*.

Monty Python's Flying Circus had a profound influence on the next generation of televisual comedy. It took the stylistic risks that other shows have copied, paving the way for much of the 'new wave' of comedy in the late 70s and 80s.

The Goodies

- **BBC Television** (BBC2) (1970-80), **LWT** (ITV) (1981-82)
- **Colour**
- **75 episodes** (standard length: 30 minutes)
- **Creators:** Tim Brooke-Taylor, Graeme Garden, Bill Oddie
- **Producers/directors:** John Howard Davies, Jim Franklin, Bob Spiers
- **Executive producer:** Alan Bell (LWT series only)

Starring: Tim Brooke-Taylor • Graeme Garden • Bill Oddie

In 1963 the Footlights sent out another review that was to have a profound effect on British comedy. Humphrey Barclay's *Cambridge Circus* included David Hatch, later head of BBC radio comedy, Jo Kendall and Jonathan Lynn, along with writing partners John Cleese and Graham Chapman, and Bill Oddie and Tim Brooke-Taylor. When exams forced Chapman's withdrawal, his replacement was another young medical student, Graeme Garden.

It was largely the same team that Trevor Nunn assembled to create the cult BBC radio series *I'm Sorry, I'll Read That Again* soon afterwards. This was the gestation, not only for ***Monty Python's Flying Circus***, but also for one of the great cult series of the 70s, *The Goodies*.

As Garden and Oddie developed their TV writing skills on episodes of *Doctor in the House*, Brooke-Taylor worked on *At Last the 1948 Show*. As a building block in the comedy of both ***Monty Python*** and *The Goodies*, *At Last* was vital. It also allowed Brooke-Taylor (who co-produced the series) room to experiment with slapstick, something that was to become a key *Goodies* style. Tim followed this by spending 1968 as Marty Feldman's straight-man in *Marty*.

The roots of *The Goodies* also include the BBC's *Twice a Fortnight* (1967), a late-night sketch-based show featuring Jones, Palin, Oddie and Garden with Dilys Watling and Jonathan Lynn, and BBC2's *Broaden Your Mind*, a star vehicle for Garden and Brooke-Taylor in 1968.

Initially known as *Super-Chaps Three*, *The Goodies* had Tim, Graeme and Bill playing exaggerated versions of themselves. Brooke-Taylor was the patriotic coward, Garden was the over-the-top SF 'Mad Scientist', and Oddie was the scruffy cynic. The *Radio Times* announced that 'The Goodies - as opposed to 'The Baddies' - are a firm of three who lay themselves open to some very strange commissions.' Tim, Bill and Graeme - their theme song stated - would do 'anything, anyplace, anytime'. In their first adventure they are hired by the royal family to protect the crown jewels, but mess it up.

Certain elements became standard: ridiculously speeded-up action sequences, slapstick violence and Garden's talent for mimicry. Oddie's musical ability became, with the help of musical arrangers Michael Gibbs and Dave McRae, a vital element (chase sequences were accompanied by Oddie's songs such as 'Come Back' or 'Dumb Animals'). It also became a source of external income, as a string of singles sold extremely well. And whilst they weren't the Monkees by any stretch of the imagination, the Goodies on *Top of the Pops* doing 'The In-Betweenies' or 'Funky Gibbon' does have a nostalgic kitsch about it.

An early plot device was Bill achieving 'total awareness' via the effects of mind-expanding sherbet. The team used scene breaks to parody ITV adverts, and 'Radio Goodies' saw Graeme flipping and becoming an eye-rolling Nazi.

The second season featured the boys tracking the Loch Ness Monster, saving the country's art treasures, meeting evil android replicas of themselves and, most famously, battling a giant white kitten, Twinkle, in a brilliant parody of *King Kong*. The season featured guest appearances by Stanley Baxter, Bernard Bresslaw, Roy

Kinnear, June Whitfield, Patrick Troughton and Michael Aspel (whose contribution to the Montreux special ended when the kitten stood on him). Although there was no new season in 1972, the team was active, performing in sketches on *Engelburt with the Younger Generation*, and at Christmas they appeared on that bastion of BBC1 respectability *Christmas Night with the Stars*, alongside Mike Yarwood and the Two Ronnies.

'Ideally, *The Goodies* will be great in 70 years time,' said Tim Brooke-Taylor. 'We are trying to produce the greatest half-hour of comedy anyone has ever seen, each week!' *The Goodies* benefited from manic scripting, which was well-suited to the excesses of the era. In many ways, *The Goodies* are as much a part of the 70s as flared trousers and progressive rock, and their three-seater bicycle became one of television's most recognizable symbols.

The series targeted the establishment, especially royalty (despite the fact that Prince Charles cited the series as one of his favourites, and even offered to play himself in the episode 'Scatty Safari'), and became something of a Sunday evening institution, with a large (mostly young) following.

The Goodies was more than happy to experiment with unusual subject matter, parodying film musicals in 'The Lost Island of Munga' and science fiction in 'Invasion of the Moon Creatures' (a story that ripped-off ***Doctor Who*** to such an extent that even the TARDIS puts in an appearance). 'Hospital for Hire' dealt with inequality, and featured Harry H. Corbett and a memorably understated sight gag featuring Sooty. 'Superstar' took the team one step closer to the pop-music adulation they craved, with DJ John Peel introducing Bill (renamed 'Randy Pandy') on *Top of the Pops*. Later, after Peel had given one of their singles a slagging, he was beaten up by the group in the Marquee Club, and for the next few years Peel suffered as many and as frequent attacks through the series (he 'bored for Britain' in one episode) as more obvious showbiz targets like Max Bygraves, Tony Blackburn and, the series' particular favourite, Nicholas Parsons.

The memorable 1973 Christmas special 'The Goodies and the Bean Stalk' featured a plethora of guest stars, including Alfie Bass, John Cleese, Eddie Waring and Arthur Ellis. 'Kung-Fu Capers', shown in the fifth season in 1975, is a classic example of the team at work: taking a topical theme, cleverly subverting it, getting one of the group (in this case Bill) involved in a 'flip' variant of the main theme, and ending the episode with a collection of chases and high-jinks, overplayed with Oddie's music.

The Goodies took over the British film industry and, having sacked all of the directors (even Ken Russell, despite the fact that they liked him for having Oliver Reed burnt at the stake), fought over the kind of films they should make. They travelled to take part in a religious rugby competition with Jon Pertwee's druids, spent an entire episode alone on a lighthouse that turned into a spaceship, and squirted each other to death with tomato sauce in 'Bun-Fight at the OK Tea-

First season
(8 Nov–20 Dec 70)
1 The Tower of London
2 Snooze
3 Love the Police
4 Caught in the Act
5 The Greenies
6 Cecily
7 Radio Goodies

Second season
(1 Oct 71–14 Jan 72)
8 The Loch Ness Monster
9 Sporting Goodies
10 Pollution
11 The Lost Tribe of the Orinoco
12 The Stolen Musicians
13 Culture for the Masses
14 Kitten Kong
15 Wicked Waltzing
16 Fresh Farm Food
17 Women's Lib
18 Sex and Violence
19 Charity Bounce
20 The Baddies

Montreux special
(9 Apr 72)

Third season
(4 Feb–11 Mar 73)
22 The New Office
23 A-Hunting we will Go
24 Winter Olympics
25 Black Magic
26 The Lost Island of Munga
27 Way Outward Bound

Summer special
(7 Jul 73)
28 Superstar

Fourth season
(1–15 Dec 73)
29 Camelot
30 Invasion of the Moon Creatures
31 Hospital for Hire

Christmas special
(24 Dec 73, 45 minutes)
32 The Goodies and the Bean Stalk

Fourth season (continued)
(29 Dec 73–12 Jan 74)
33 The Stone Age
34 Goodies in the Nick
35 The Race

Fifth season
(10 Feb–5 May 75)
36 Movies
37 Clown Virus
38 Radio 2
39 Wacky Wales
40 Frankenfido
41 Scatty Safari
42 Kung-Fu Capers
43 The Lighthouse
44 Rome Antics

Rooms'. The season ended with Tim chanting 'I'm a tea-pot!' and the trio considering cannibalism when their pad is encased in concrete.

'Goodies Rule - OK?', the 1975 Christmas special, saw the Goodies playing 'Wild Thing' to an audience of spliff-smoking policemen at Wembley stadium and television puppets taking over the government. The following year, the Goodies got involved in the cod war by breeding the world's largest fish, started a 50s revival, became advertising men and sold the world string and, in another genre-hop, saw their sons revive cricket and the MCC in '2001 and a Bit'. The season ended with an 'almost live' performance of the group's best-known musical numbers.

However, Brooke-Taylor, Garden and Oddie were known to be upset by their treatment at the BBC, who had always regarded the series as a children's show. Whilst the next season saw an erratic mix of brilliance and ineptitude (notably the trio's blinkered view of New Wave), there were problems getting script approval, notably with the episode 'Royal Command', another attack on royalty which was scheduled for the day that Princess Anne was due to give birth. In the event, the BBC stopped the broadcast of the episode, holding it back until the end of the season. Despite these problems the 1977 Christmas special was one of the finest half-hours of TV comedy ever made, climaxing with the end of the world.

Maybe they should have left it there. The final BBC season, after a two-year hiatus, began by detailing the Rice and Lloyd-Webber-style rise of Timita ('Don't cry for me, Marge and Tina'). 'Saturday Night Grease', apart from being 18 months too late in terms of musical fashion, also landed the series in hot water with Mary Whitehouse. The opening sequence caused Mary to blow her top, stating 'Tim Brooke-Taylor was seen undressing, to mock John Travolta in an exceedingly tight pair of underpants with a distinctive carrot motif on the front.' She went on to describe *The Goodies* as 'too sexually orientated', which proved that she had been watching a different programme from the rest of us for the previous decade. However, the Corporation's non-committal reaction to such criticism convinced the team that their future lay elsewhere and they quit the BBC to join LWT.

Although the LWT series was not a patch on their BBC work, it did at least include one classic, 'Football Crazy'. *The Goodies* ended that same year, leaving behind a devoted following. Brooke-Taylor drifted into hopeless sitcoms (*You Must Be the Husband*), while Garden and Oddie continued as writing partners on the best-forgotten *Astronauts*. Oddie later found success as a children's TV host (*The Saturday Banana*), as presenter of the BBC's *Festival*, and as a serious actor. His commitment to environmental matters and wildlife, once mocked in 'Dodonuts', now seems sane and valid in the 90s.

UK Gold's repeat of the entire BBC *Goodies* reminds us that the 70s did have a ridiculous edge, far removed from the bitterness of the era. The Goodies may have worn star jumpers and Hai-Karate aftershave, but television was a better place for having known them.

45 Cunning Stunts
46 South Africa
47 Bun-Fight at the OK Tea-Rooms
48 The End

Christmas special
(21 Dec 75, 45 minutes)
49 Goodies Rule - OK?

Sixth season
(21 Sep–2 Nov 76)
50 Lips or Almighty Cod
51 Hype Pressure
52 Daylight Robbery on the Orient Express
53 Black and White Beauty
54 It Might As Well Be String
55 2001 and a Bit
56 The Goodies - Almost Live

Seventh season
(1 Nov–6 Dec 77)
57 Alternative Roots
58 Dodonuts
59 Scoutrageous
60 Punky Business
61 Royal Command

Christmas special
(22 Dec 77)
62 Earthanasia

Eighth season
(14 Jan–18 Feb 80)
63 Goodies and Politics
64 Saturday Night Grease
65 A Kick in the Arts
66 U-Friend or UFO
67 Animals
68 War Babies

Christmas special
(27 Dec 81)
69 Snow White 2

Ninth season
(9 Jan–13 Feb 82)
70 Robot
71 Football Crazy
72 Big Foot
73 Change of Life
74 Holidays
75 Animals

[The Montreux special is a remake of episode 14 for the Golden Rose of Montreux (for which it won a Silver Rose). Episode titles - still the subject of some debate - are derived from the BBC archives and *Laugh* magazine.]

Not the Nine O'Clock News

- **BBC Television** (BBC1) ◆ Colour
- **26 episodes** (30 minutes) ◆ 1979-82
- **Writers include:** Guy Jenkin, Andy Hamilton, Richard Curtis, Rowan Atkinson, Peter Brewis, Laurie Rowley, Colin Bostock-Smith, Howard Goodall, Colin Gilbert, David Renwick, Arnold Brown, Mel Smith, Griff Rhys Jones, Chris Judge Smith, Alastair Beaton, Andrew Marshall, Tony Hilton, Nigel Planer, Peter Richardson, Barry Bowes, Nat Clare, John Lloyd, Mike Radford, Philip Pope, Paul Smith, Terry Kyan
- **Producers:** Sean Hardie, John Lloyd

Starring: Rowan Atkinson • Pamela Stephenson • Mel Smith • Chris Langham (first season only) • Griff Rhys Jones

The spirit of punk arrived on BBC2 with *Not the Nine O'Clock News*, an inspired mix of satire, caustic observation and re-dubbed news footage (which, as Richard Ingrams noted in *The Spectator*, had the effect of making the real news seem ridiculous). The reaction of the critics alone was enough to justify its existence: 'You don't have to love animals to the point of eccentricity to feel that squashing hedgehogs is an unnecessary artifice,' said Patrick Stoddart in the *Evening News*. He'd totally missed the point. It wasn't the eccentric animal lover that the satire was aimed at, but the hedgehogs themselves. Or maybe it was people who use the word 'artifice'.

Initial attention focused almost exclusively on Pamela Stephenson and Rowan Atkinson (who had met Mel Smith while studying at university). Both were talented impersonators, and their spot-on parodies were refreshing at a time when Mike Yarwood was in serious decline. Atkinson's exaggerated physical mannerisms lent themselves well to nerds and aliens, while Stephenson's Janet Street-Porter and Esther Rantzen became notorious, perhaps persuading Rantzen to go for her highly-publicized dental surgery. Stephenson's Angela Rippon, with its incredibly mannered pronunciations of words like 'Mugabe', was also a joy.

The good thing about these characters, as far as the young audience was concerned, was that they weren't fond homages, but vicious personal attacks. Not only wasn't this the *Nine O'Clock News*, it wasn't Eric and Ernie either. Sir Keith Joseph was labelled as an alien 'mole', and Michael Parkinson was savaged by Atkinson's putting 'grovel grovel' between each sentence. The team took the mickey out of ***Monty Python's Flying Circus***, a very necessary killing for British comedy at the time, with a sketch that detailed the General Synod's blasphemous film *Life of Christ*.

First season
(16 Oct–20 Nov 79)
Six episodes

A season of six episodes starring Rowan Atkinson, Chris Emmett, Christopher Godwin, John Gorman and Jonathan Hyde was planned for transmission in Apr 79. The first two episodes were recorded but never shown

The difference between the two shows was obvious - Pamela Stephenson. The Pythons had never given their female characters much to do, claiming that they found writing for women impossible. Stephenson, on the other hand, took up the punk ethic of outraging the audience with directness, beginning with the adverts of the day ('American Express? That'll do nicely, sir, and would you like to rub my tits?') and the Miss World contest ('Come on, big boy, show us your willy!'). Despite this, some targets seemed familiar: *Not the Nine O'Clock News*, like ***Python*** before it, satirized the television of the day, covering *University Challenge*, *Question Time*, *Points of View* ('Mr Mulligan of Roehampton called to say, "I think the BBC is a load of old crap"') and an interview with Gerald the Gorilla ('Wild? I was absolutely livid!'). The team's regard for television was summed up with their composite programme *Donald Sinden Looks at English Churches*.

'Part dross and part delight' was Séan Day-Lewis's reaction in the *Telegraph*, and most critics were united in their praise of Atkinson and Stephenson (who, with her soundbite witticisms and habit of calling up critics and threatening to spank them, had become something of a media darling) and their lukewarm response to Mel Smith and Chris Langham. Langham left during the first season, to appear infrequently on television, write for *The Muppet Show*, and become Clive Anderson's occasional sparring-partner on Channel 4. His replacement was a 20-year-old radio producer, Griff Rhys Jones.

Smith and Jones began a successful series of finger-puppet interludes that were the prelude to the 'head to heads' of their own series. Anne and Mark were fingers in tiny wellies. Stephenson moved with the times, giving her Jan Leeming a pair of vast earrings. Roy Hudd wrote a letter to the *Standard*'s Peter McKay, saying that it was time for some comedy with 'a bit of balls'. Certainly, *Not the Nine O'Clock News* could be as offensive (or as wonderful) as anything previously seen on television: '*Death of a Princess* - an Apology' and 'I think I've learned a valuable lesson from Chappaquiddick' being two topical examples. The *Not the Nine O'Clock News* solution to soccer hooliganism was to 'cut off their goolies', and they claimed that the Italian entry in the Eurovision Song Contest, 'I Can't Get No Contraception', was withdrawn after the Pope advised them to pull it out at the last minute.

However, it was around this time that critical reaction ceased to be outraged and began to enshrine the series as a national institution. This wasn't good news for something so determinedly anarchic. Neither was winning, in 1980, the Silver Rose for innovation at the Montreux Festival.

Many of the sketches from this era are still fondly remembered and recited, the *Not* team becoming exactly the Pythonesque programme it set out to replace. 'Stout Life', 'Gay Christian' and 'Constable Savage' are all, in their own way, about as funny as that sketch concerning a deceased bird. 'The Trucking Song', with its references to hedgehog sandwiches, started off a whole vein of British humour (e.g. hedgehog crisps) that seems so ingrained now that it is hard to imagine that it started with a single sketch. Stephenson's 'Ayatollah Song', her Reggie Bosanquet lament and her parody of Kate Bush were melodic enough to stick in the memory, but best of all was the exaggerated punk of 'Gob on You' ('Sex is boring/Pain is fun/I wanna cut my fingers off one by one'). Griff's petulant John McEnroe helped to create a new national catchphrase in 'You cannot be serious!' We were reminded of the companies that had 'failed in Wales', and experienced a precise dissection of the New Romantic era that *Not* was so much a part of in 'Nice Video, Shame About the Song'.

It was said after the third season that the team was splitting up. Certainly, nobody seemed eager to continue the experience. Atkinson was talking with John Lloyd about a historical project, and Smith and Jones, as the emergent stars of the third season, had enjoyed the experience of working together. Still, after a year's break, a final season was decided upon, to critical anticipation.

If this was the most-watched series, with audiences up to nine million, it was also the most controversial. Ronald Reagan had commissioned a tasteless television spectacular called *Let Poland Be Poland* at the height of the Solidarity crisis, and, though British television had

Second season
(31 Mar–5 May 80)
Six episodes
11 Don't Get Your Vicars in a Twist
13 Drama Today
14 Mae'n Naw O'r Gloch!

Third season
(27 Oct–15 Dec 80)
Eight episodes

Fourth season
(1 Feb–12 Mar 82)
Six episodes

wisely elected not to screen it, the *Not* team called it fair game. The sketch where robbers broke into a Polish bank and emerged with a chicken drumstick jammed the switchboards, as did the newsreel where Princess Diana appeared to be suing Durex over the birth of her child.

The show spun off into books such as *Not the Royal Wedding*, and the calendar *Not 1982*, which included *Hitch-Hiker's Guide to the Galaxy* material from Douglas Adams and the incredible 'Skinhead Hamlet'. LPs and a stage show, *Not In Front of the Audience*, followed, the cast members variously going on to ***Blackadder,*** *Alas Smith and Jones* and marriage with Billy Connolly. Compilations of *Not the Nine O'Clock News* were shown in late 1995, and proved that the series still has the power to shock.

Lest it be thought that *Not* was incapable of subtlety, an extract from the *Radio Times* (where one week's blurb in 1982 was written completely in Gaelic) is worth repeating. Under the title and credits, it read: 'My Dear Posy, I hope you are well. I'm sorry that I wasn't able to write to you, but I had a lot of work to do here in the *Radio Times* - in my role of sub-editing. A thousand thanks for the socks. Give my love to Sinead on my behalf. Yours affectionately, John.'

'There is no alternative and non-alternative comedy. There is only good and bad comedy. I have a particular favourite comedy double act, in which the partners used to slap each other about the face and then get into bed and spend the night together, which sounds like a very alternative act indeed. The people involved were, of course, Morecambe and Wise.'

Ben Elton's comments help to smash the myth that the TV comedy of the 80s was intent on destroying all that had gone before and spitting on the grave of showbiz. Although often loudly displaying studiously right-on, politically-correct tendencies, the new generation of writers and performers were usually still a part of the development of mainstream comedy. So, for example, Frank Skinner's championing of (and the subsequent regeneration of the careers of) Bob Monkhouse and Jimmy Tarbuck is an indication that the 'new wave' are, perhaps, not that different from what has gone before. Political divisions were often raised, and the fact that Jim Davidson and co. were so proudly Conservative meant that they were seen as an easy target. But the era's comedy was as much a reaction to Russ Abbot's Cooperman as to Benny Hill and Thatcher. You're either part of the solution, or you're part of the problem.

The great freedom that comedy enjoyed in the 80s proved to be one of style rather than content, encouraging experimentation with sitcom (***The Young Ones***, *Girls on Top*, ***Red Dwarf***), the topical revue (***Spitting Image***, *Saturday Live*, *Friday Night Live*) and the stand-up/sketch show. There were the expected accusations of 'bad taste' (often from a previous generation of performers, alarmed as much by their own dwindling popularity as anything - and hadn't 60s comedians suffered the same brickbats from the music-hall crowd of two decades earlier?). Despite this, much 80s comedy was a development of themes first seen in ***That Was the Week That Was*** or the sitcoms of Croft, Perry and Lloyd. Hancock, Howerd, *Carry On* and *Round the Horne* were beloved by most of the new generation too, something conveniently forgotten by those who saw ***The Young Ones*** as 'dangerous, violent rubbish'.

Not the Nine O'Clock News was an effective bridge between the decades, being a mixture of punk controversy and 80s liberalism, although the sketch-based shows that followed are perhaps as well remembered for the acts they launched as for the quality of the comedy. *A Kick up the 80s* (a patchy series made memorable by Rik Mayall's Kevin Turvey), *Three of a Kind*, *Laugh? I Nearly Paid My Licence Fee* (which wasn't very funny apart from Robbie Coltrane), *KYTV*, and

BBC Scotland's *Naked Video* (the birthplace of Rab C. Nesbitt) are examples. Coltrane was also in Granada's *Alfresco* (1987), which helped establish the careers of Fry and Laurie, Emma Thompson, Ben Elton and Siobhan Redmond. This was a huge improvement on 1982's *OTT*, billed as the 'adult *Tiswas*', which starred Chris Tarrant, Helen Atkinson-Wood, Lenny Henry and Alexei Sayle. It was only notable for the subsequent success of Sayle and Henry. *Alexei Sayle's Stuff* (and, later, *The All-New Alexei Sayle Show*) was thoughtful and absurd, forming, with *A Bit of Fry and Laurie* and *French and Saunders*, a trio of dangerously experimental BBC2 comedy shows. *The Lenny Henry Show* proved to be one of the great chameleons of TV comedy, its style changing from season to season, from stand-up to neo-sitcom. It's only a short hop from here to *Murder Most Horrid* and ***Absolutely Fabulous***.

Who Dares Wins (1983) will, we hope, be seen as one of the most important comic programmes of the era. Starring Rory McGrath, Philip Pope, Jimmy Mulville, Tony Robinson and Julia Hills, it was less tied to topicality than ***Not the Nine O'Clock News***, and its sketches (Robinson as a gardening expert dealing with McGrath's 'problem plants' which have been set alight or attacked with an axe) deserved a wider audience than they gained on Channel 4. Its most popular moments detailed the aspirations of two pandas in London Zoo, plotting their escape as Belgian dentists or bragging about their sexual exploits. From these beginnings, Hat Trick Productions has steadily grown in importance, until it now appears that it owns 90s comedy, with productions such as *Chelmsford 123*, *Whose Line is it Anyway?*, *This is David Lander*, ***Drop the Dead Donkey***, *Have I Got News For You*, ***Harry Enfield's Television Programme***, *Paul Merton - The Series*, *S & M*, *Room 101*, *An Evening With Gary Lineker*, *Eleven Men Against Eleven* and *Game On*. If it's funny, and 90s, it's probably Hat Trick!

From the ashes of ***Not the Nine O'Clock News*** emerged *Alas Smith and Jones*, which began in 1984, asked some difficult questions in the name of comedy, including 'How did James Burke get away with it for so long?'. The fourth division football results and Chas and Dave-style 'cockney knees-up' LPs got a deserved slagging. Pamela Stephenson's ex-husband Nicholas Ball appeared in a sketch that effortlessly lampooned ridiculous ***Sweeney***-esque rhyming slang. Smith and Jones quickly became known for their 'head-to-head' discussions, many of which were written by barrister-turned-media-guru Clive Anderson. Mel Smith later starred in two seasons of Terry Kyan and Paul Smith's *Colin's Sandwich*, a sitcom concerning an unfortunate BR worker and part-time writer. Mel Smith thought of it as a ***Hancock*** for the 80s.

In 1980 the Comedy Store, a new comic club in Leicester Square, was becoming successful. With money supplied by theatre producer Michael White, Peter Richardson decided to set up a club of his own for the new acts appearing at the Comedy Store, establishing the Comic Strip in premises above the Raymond Revuebar in Soho. The new club featured the Outer Limits (Richardson and Nigel Planer), 20th Century Coyote (Rik Mayall and Adrian Edmondson) and the first stage appearance of French and Saunders. Mayall, Edmondson, Planer, Richardson, Alexei Sayle, Andy de la Tour and Keith Allen next appeared in Paul Jackson's two groundbreaking shows from BBC Manchester, *Boom Boom Out Go the Lights*, in 1981. Because this group, plus Pauline Melville and Arnold Brown, all worked with each other, a 'new wave' was instantly born.

Michael White was impressed with the atmosphere and audiences at the Comic Strip. Here was a comedy without the inbuilt sexist attitudes that marked all before it. White managed to secure a slot on the first night of the embryonic Channel 4 for Richardson and friends. 'Five Go Mad in Dorset' had Richardson,

French, Saunders, Edmondson and Timmy the dog enjoying an adventure with 'lashings of ginger beer' that owed as much to the 70s *Famous Five* TV series as to Enid Blyton's books. Nosher Powell played one of two 'suspicious characters' who wandered past at intervals chanting their fiendish plot ('Blah, blah, blah. Secret plans!'). Ronald Allen played Uncle Quentin, overacting gloriously. 'I'm a screaming homosexual, you little prigs!' he shouts as he is arrested by Raymond Francis, Inspector Lockhart of *No Hiding Place*.

Richardson's intention, when *The Comic Strip Presents...* began, was to produce films that had the same kind of humour, and had vaguely the same people in them, but employed a huge range of visual styles. 'War' was a story about the American invasion of Britain. In 'The Beat Generation', Michael White made an appearance as himself in 1960, with Keith Allen as Brian Epstein. The initial appearance of Eddie Monsoon - a TV presenter similar to Edmondson's *Saturday Live* character Sir Adrian Dangerous - was vetoed by Channel 4 on the basis of general bad taste. The tabloids, already aggressive towards Channel 4, had a field day. (The character finally appeared in a second-season story, a pseudo-documentary introduced by Tony Bilbow.)

The highlight of the first season, and the episode that tied *The Comic Strip Presents...* most closely to pop culture, was 'Bad News Tour', Edmondson's parody of an incompetent heavy metal band out on the road. 'I could play 'Stairway to Heaven' when I was 13. Jimmy Page didn't write it until he was 23. I think that says a lot,' says Edmondson's 'Vim'. It was a grittier, low-budget version of *This is Spinal Tap*, although, to be fair, the targets were different. The band appeared on *The Tube*, and, after their second play, made records and were bottled off stage at the Castle Donnington Festival. Stardom!

'A Fistful of Travellers Cheques' took two of the characters from 'War' off to a Sergio Leone movie to great effect. 'Slags' also adapted a popular film genre, science fiction, mixing elements from *Blade Runner* and *Psycho* with a Thomas Dolby soundtrack. *The Bullshitters: Roll Out the Gun-Barrel* was *The Comic Strip* in everything but name, produced by White, written by and starring Keith Allen and Peter Richardson, and featuring Robbie Coltrane. The lead characters were Bonehead and Foyle, two ultra-macho agents in an incredibly accurate camp parody of ***The Professionals*** (they had previously been in Allen's *Whatever You Want* and would reappear in the 1993 BBC *Comic Strip* play 'Detectives on the Verge of a Nervous Breakdown').

'Consuela' was a dry run for the forthcoming *French and Saunders*, giving Dawn French the chance to portray a sinister Spanish maid, whilst 'Private Enterprise' was another satire on the music business. However, it was the last season on Channel 4 that established *The Comic Strip Presents ...*, with many of the regulars now having shows of their own. 'Strike' was the first in a line of Hollywood socialist epics, a canny look at the way the American media remodel British life. Peter Richardson was Al Pacino playing Arthur Scargill, Jennifer Saunders was Meryl Streep playing Mrs Scargill. Alexei Sayle is the young writer who sees his work turned into standard Hollywood crap, but the final production wins a sackful of awards (as, ironically, did 'Strike'). 'Mr Jolly Lives Next Door' featured Peter Cook as an axe-wielding killer in Mayall and Edmondson's most extreme comedy of violence, a direct ancestor of *Bottom*. 'Didn't You Kill My Brother?' was a rehearsal for Alexei Sayle's series, *Stuff*.

The switch to the BBC came in 1989 with a series which seemed to be playing on the team's past glories, Richardson and his partner Peter Richens writing every episode. 'GLC' was a fun return to the concept of 'Strike': Robbie Coltrane was Charles Bronson playing Ken Livingstone, Saunders was Brigette Nielsen playing Thatcher, and Richardson was Lee van Cleef as Tony Benn. It even featured a line at the expense of the comedians themselves as they desert Livingstone before a final shoot-out, having lots of 'right on' things to do. Asking if an unseen Scargill is going to desert him too, the reply is 'Just gimme a gun!' This example of self-mockery would have been unthinkable just half a decade earlier.

Both the BBC and Channel 4 attempted to provide an outlet for potential series in the spirit of *Comedy Playhouse* in the 60s. BBC2's *Comic Asides* launched Norman Lovett in the pithy, dreamlike *I, Lovett*, whilst more recently Nick Revell's *N7* and the *Absolutely* spin-off *Mac* show great promise. Channel 4's similar *A Bunch of Fives* included equally rewarding shorts by Frank Skinner and Reeves and Mortimer. *Dead at Thirty* by Paul Whitehouse and Charlie Higson, later collaborators with Harry Enfield, and creators of the 'brilliant' *The Fast Show*, deserved a series of its own too, but, unlike Skinner's *Blue Heaven*, didn't get one.

The BBC's equivalent of *Saturday Live* was *Paramount City*: whereas the ITV show always managed to attract the cream of new British and American talent (Steven Wright for example), the BBC had to put up with performers of a far wider quality. However, the show gave early exposure to Nick Revell and comic-poet John Hegley; Curtis and Ishmael were given regular slots in the later shows (often a guide to Jive). Subsequent seasons of *The Real McCoy* showed off the talents of the duo and other prominent young black comics, and included a superb spoof of Breakfast TV and the exploits of Y'Damn Fool Man. However, the BBC seemed to do their best to ensure that the show stayed firmly in the ghetto.

There were some interesting cul-de-sacs along the way. Ben Elton's follow-up to ***The Young Ones***, *Filthy, Rich and Catflap*, was at times a brilliant comment on the nature of fame and a development of Rik Mayall and Adrian Edmondson's Dangerous Brothers characterizations. The critics seemed blind to the classic physical comedy, and common consensus was that it was a poor follow-up to *The Young Ones*, which of course they had loved all the time. Elton's subsequent TV credits included his 'labour of love' *Happy Families* (with Jennifer Saunders), during which a piano, rather than piano-wire, was strung across the road, and *The Man from Auntie*, a reasonable attempt to meld his increasingly assured stand-up routines to a 90s format.

'Old timers' Dave Allen, Billy Connolly and Jasper Carrott proved that there is no need for such embellishments. Through his association with *The Secret Policeman's Ball*, Connolly was more than aware of the advance of the young upstarts. In the mid-80s, his career seemed listless, his reputation rooted in the headcase gigs of a decade ago. *An Audience with Billy Connolly* changed all that, producing the funniest 50 minutes in Channel 4's history. The highlights of a live performance before a celebrity audience - and one of a series that included fine performances by Bob Monkhouse and Kenneth Williams and several rubbish Dame Edna Everage 'specials' - the humour leapt from the stage. Connolly, impersonating the Queen joining in with his proposed new national anthem (*The Archers* theme), or singing a Third World standard ('We come from Gebrovia, and we don't give a shit!'), proved that there was life in the old dog yet.

This was also true of Dave Allen. When God's comic returned to TV in 1990, he wisely - and bravely - dispensed with the sketches of *Dave Allen at Large*. Instead, we glimpsed a man obsessed by his age and the march of time, although the one monologue that contained an f-word prompted a vitriolic response from the tabloids that implied that the show was a stream of blasphemies. The reaction was particularly sad because it obscured the great comedy that was evident: the epic tale of communication problems with his son and his friends

('Isseddinn?') was one of the funniest things on television that year. Allen's hate affair with the tabloids continued in 1993 when his Carlton series drew criticism along with huge viewing figures.

Jasper Carrott was, along with Connolly and Mike Harding, an example of the 70s wave of 'alternative comedians'. Popular with a student audience, they emerged from the folk-club circuit with a mixture of songs and stories that proved to be just the shot in the arm that comedy needed in the wake of *The Comedians* and its ilk. In 1982, the BBC poached Carrott from LWT to fill the Saturday night, post-*Match of the Day* slot vacated by the end of *Parkinson*. The material in *Carrott's Lib* came from writers like Ian Hislop and Duncan Campbell and managed to juggle topicality with Carrott's previous man-in-the-street persona: 'Tony Benn is responsible for all of the evil in the world. He was in Denmark last week leading the English soccer hooligans. Bobby Robson is an anagram of Tony Benn. In code.'

When one episode went out late due to an overrun of the *Horse of the Year Show*, Carrott used this to mock people who had pre-set their video recorders, and the series proudly broke the Official Secrets Act by reading a ridiculous government Nuclear Aftermath report on air. The series, however, got into trouble over some of Carrott's insults, most notably when MP Michael Meacher sued the BBC for slander. *The Sun* became involved in a lengthy slanging match with Carrott after the comedian suggested that Irish jokes should be replaced with '*Sun* reader jokes'. The Christmas 1983 episode featured Carrott's by-now familiar eye-popping rants against kebabs, cagoule wearers with dandruff, Reliant Robin cars, and pseudo-intellectuals. After the disappointing *Carrott's Confidential* (1987-89), *Canned Carrott* (1990-92) refined the best elements of previous series. Most of the sketches were left to Steve Punt and Hugh Dennis: their 'video shop' sketch was a classic piece of TV comedy. Jasper himself was a guru figure, issuing pearls of wisdom from his high stool: 'And to everyone who's bought a BSB Satellite dish: Hello, Mr Johnson!' Additionally, the Chaplinesque 'Wiggy' sequences and *The Detectives* (with Carrott and Robert Powell as a pair of indescribably stupid policemen) were inventive and very funny. (The latter proved so popular that it became a series in its own right in 1993, followed by three further seasons.)

Laurence Marks and Maurice Gran, creators of such sitcoms as *Shine on Harvey Moon*, *Roll Over Beethoven*, *Relative Strangers* (and, later, *Birds of a Feather*), found an unusual ally in Rik Mayall when they embarked on *The New Statesman* in 1987. This concerned the exploits of MP Alan B'Stard, a ruthless, scheming example of Thatcherism made flesh. Casual viewers were surprised that Mayall could play the handsome devil when he wanted, and B'Stard's callous disdain prompted as much humour as the slapstick comedy of ***The Young Ones***. It also provoked outrage - the first episode revolved around the murder of a taxi driver - and scorn in the political world. When they won a BAFTA some years later, Marks and Gran acknowledged what a risk the series had been for Yorkshire. With top-notch direction by Graeme Harper, and superb performances by Mayall, Michael Troughton (as the put-upon Piers Fletcher-Dervish) and Marsha Fitzalan the comedy remained strong over four seasons (although the next Marks/ Gran/Harper collaboration, the 'recession comedy' *Get Back*, was very disappointing).

TV comedy in the 80s seemed to go in two different directions: on the one hand, the back-to-basics style of the stand-up comic, and, on the other, an increasingly sophisticated use of the comic drama. A particularly clever and well-remembered example was the 1981's *Private Schultz*. Written by Jack

Pulman (the adapter of *War and Peace*, *Crime and Punishment* and ***I, Claudius***), and produced by Philip Hinchcliffe, *Schultz* starred a pre-*Boon* Michael Elphick, previously best known for several 'third thug from the left'-type roles, along with Billie Whitelaw and Ian Richardson. A witty tale of a cowardly thief in wartime Germany who is conscripted into the SS and hatches a plan to flood England with forged fivers, the series showed, as Pulman noted, 'the hollowness of materialism'.

The following year Channel 4 produced *Whoops! Apocalypse*, a tale of insane politics and global Armageddon dominated by Peter Jones's Superman-obsessed PM and John Cleese's terrorist. Authors Andrew Marshall and David Renwick went on to write *Hot Metal* (starring Robert Hardy) and *Alexei Sayle's Stuff*, before branching out as solo sitcom writers with *2point4 Children* and ***One Foot in the Grave*** respectively. Channel 4 also scored with 1984's *Fairly Secret Army* and Malcolm Bradbury's adaptation of Tom Sharpe's *Porterhouse Blue* (1987), complete with the best performance of David Jason's career and the legendary condom scene.

ITV did its bit to rub the BBC's corporate nose into its own lack of vitality. 1983's *Brass* managed to spoof just about every historical drama ever, and the 1985 adaptation of Sue Townsend's *The Secret Diary of Adrian Mole, Aged 13¾* was a cheerful slice of early-teen angst. In 1990, Fry and Laurie embarked upon a definitive adaptation of P. G. Wodehouse's *Jeeves and Wooster*. Central's attempts at the anarchic end of 80s comedy, *Hardwick House* (a straight cross between ***Grange Hill*** and ***The Young Ones***), proved a disaster, however, being abandoned after two episodes (broadcast on consecutive nights), following tabloid outrage.

As the 90s began it seemed that for every *Victoria Wood - As Seen on TV*, ITV had a *Hale and Pace* waiting in the wings. Better than that, Channel 4 had Vic Reeves and Bob Mortimer, timeless comedians whose subtlety and exact sampling of other cultural texts in *Vic Reeves' Big Night Out* was uniquely post-modern. They were head-hunted by the BBC and their *The Smell of Reeves and Mortimer*, and the spoof celebrity-quiz *Shooting Stars*, continue to delight. BBC2 was also the home to two of the most under-rated comedy shows of the 90s, Craig Ferguson's stream-of-conscience rant *The Ferguson Theory* and the surreal *Inside Victor Lewis Smith*.

Whilst Channel 4 were notching up further successes with the sketch-based anarchy of *Absolutely* (and its spin-off *Mr Don and Mr George*), the mock-bedsit sitcom of Sean Hughes's *Sean's Show* and the droll stand-up comedy of *The Jack Dee Show*, the BBC's next major success came via a very unusual route: Radio One. With *The Mary Whitehouse Experience*, and the strange combination of Steve Punt, Hugh Dennis, Rob Newman and David Baddiel, 'comedy as the new rock and roll' as a cliché was born. It was never going to last long, with Rob and Dave's student comedy, hip music references and new-laddism clashing with the more conventional showbiz targets of Steve and Hugh. The team split after two astonishing seasons to produce *Newman and Baddiel in Pieces* and *The Imaginatively-Titled Punt and Dennis Show* (neither of which was anywhere near as good as *Mary*). These days Newman has left comedy behind for a writing career, whilst Baddiel and his flatmate Frank Skinner (star of Channel 4's *Packet of Three*) have created the ultimate new-lad comedy show, *Fantasy Football League*, a breathless mix of chat show, sport critique, and sketch-based comedy.

Another Channel 4 star who found a home at the BBC was Steve Coogan whose inserts into Jonathan Ross's *The Saturday Zoo* as student-hating northern hard-man Paul Calf ('Bag o' shite!') made him a national treasure. In addition to two outrageous Calf 'video diary' spoofs, Coogan also starred in *The Day Today*, perhaps the most adventurous new comedy of the 90s. An adaptation of the BBC radio series *On the Hour*, it took ideas first used in ***Not the Nine O'Clock News*** to the absolute limit, featuring cannibalistic train-crash victims and Sinn Fein spokesmen inhaling helium. Chris Morris played the anchorman-from-hell, who could eat Jeremy Paxman for breakfast and never failed to give Brian O'Hanra'h'ahanrahan (Patrick Marber) a hard time, while Coogan excelled as feeble sports broadcaster Alan Partridge ('Goal! Eat my goal'). The same general group of actors and writers have also been involved in *Glam Metal Detectives*, *The Fast Show*, *Fist of Fun*, Armando Iannucci's *The Saturday Armistice*, and the evolution of Partridge into a chat-show host in *Knowing Me, Knowing You ... With Alan Partridge*. Cleverly, at around the time that Caroline Hook was interviewing real celebs on *The Mrs Merton Show*, Coogan began to turn his back on Partridge, proving his versatility with *Coogan's Run*.

The future of stand-up comedy continues with the BBC's *Stand-Up Show* (highlight so far, John Thompson's 'Bernard Right-On') and Channel 4's *Just For Laughs* (1987), which helped to launch the career of Eddie Izzard, amongst others.

Just as in the 60s the Oxbridge mafia of the ***Pythons***, ***Goodies*** and *Beyond the Fringe*rs became icons of their generation, so we confidently predict that the faces of 90s comedy - Angus Deayton, Paul Merton, Harry Enfield and Paul Whitehouse, Frank Skinner and David Baddiel, Nick Hancock, Reeves and Mortimer - will carry on a tradition that stretches back to Tony Hancock, Frankie Howerd and Morecambe and Wise.

The Young Ones

- **BBC Television** (BBC2) ◆ **Colour**
- **12 episodes** (30 minutes) ◆ **1982-84**
- **Creators/writers:** Ben Elton, Rik Mayall, Lise Mayer
- **Additional material:** Alexei Sayle
- **Producer:** Paul Jackson

Regular cast: Adrian Edmondson (Vyvyan) • Rik Mayall (Rick) • Nigel Planer (Neil) • Christopher Ryan (Mike) • Alexei Sayle (the Balowski family)

With: Ben Elton • Andy de la Tour • Patrick Newell • Robbie Coltrane • Roger Sloman • Dave Rappaport • Pauline Melville • Mark Arden • Steve Frost • Dawn French • Jennifer Saunders • Keith Allen • Arnold Brown • Gareth Hale • Norman Pace • Paul Merton • Griff Rhys Jones • Mel Smith • Tony Robinson • Emma Thompson • Stephen Fry • Hugh Laurie • Alan Freeman • Lee Cornes • Terry Jones • Christopher Barrie • Daniel Peacock • Helen Atkinson Wood • Jonathan Caplan • Helen Lederer • Lenny Henry • Norman Lovett

The Young Ones, seen today, is a television programme caught in time, a glorious rant against everything that was Britain in the early 80s. On first transmission, however, it seemed like the revolution 'the kids' had all been waiting for, or dangerously naive and childish rubbish, depending on your viewpoint. That's to be expected: *The Young Ones* exhibited a deliberately infantile style of humour, one of the writers' proudest boasts. Despite the plethora of bottom-jokes, the under-five politics and the general air of craziness that attached itself to the series, *The Young Ones* was important, because it created a stir, within the country and the television industry itself, unlike almost anything before.

The series' origins lay in Michael White's Soho club, The Comic Strip, and the Paul Jackson-produced specials *Boom Boom Out Go the Lights*. In 1982, armed with scripts by Mayall, Elton and Lise Mayer about a group of students, Jackson was given the go-ahead to develop a series. The original idea was to pair Mayall and Edmondson (playing variations of their '20th Century Coyote' characters, the Dangerous brothers) with Planer and Richardson. As the scripts developed, it became clear that Richardson's character - Mike-the-Cool-Person - was going nowhere fast and so he quit to concentrate on setting up a project with Channel 4 for the entire Michael White stable (which eventually became *The Comic Strip Presents ...*).

In Richardson's place came diminutive Canadian actor Christopher Ryan. He joined Planer's mournful hippie, Mayall's silly radical, and Edmondson's dangerously violent punk. Also included was Alexei Sayle who was given his own (self-penned) five-minute segment of each episode, usually with only the most tenuous link to the plot, which was basically an extended rant from his stage show. Sayle normally appeared as a member of the Balowski family, including Jerzy, their Russian landlord, whose knowledge of Merseybeat was flawless.

From the outset, the series exhibited a brutally funny self-loathing and all of the hostility that characterized 'alternative comedy'. Rick and Vyvyan hated each other and everybody hated Neil. A regular feature was the mocking of standard television formats, including the debunking of 'yoof-TV' (as represented by *Something Else* or *The Oxford Road Show*). 'Nozin' Aroun'' has Ben Elton's Peter Powell-style presenter, Baz ('It's our world, too!'), giving his generation sound advice on unemployment.

We were soon introduced to Vyvyan's psychotic hamster, SPG, the first of several furry creatures and inanimate objects brought to life by the scripts' eye for the absurd. Examples from later episodes included a talking banister, an 'irrelevant' matchbox, and a tomato singing 'I've just got to ketchup with my life'. Another popular staple element was the pop group in each episode. Some of the bands who appeared worked within the context of the story (Motorhead in 'Bambi' and the Damned in 'Nasty', for example), whilst others, such as Madness (who appeared twice), fitted the comic-strip nature of *The Young Ones*. However, this is one of the most dated aspects of the series today (who remembers Nine Below Zero or Amazulu now?).

Aside from containing just about the only good line given to Ryan in the entire first season ('When I eat a meal worth £4.50, I'm not payin' for it'), the first episode concerned the council's efforts to knock the house down. It was all completely bonkers of course, and within days had, effectively, divided the entire country into those who saw the series as the only thing on television remotely in touch with the real world ('the kids'), and those who saw it as obscene, violent, rubbish ('horrid old people'). The BBC, to their credit, defended the series from the start and, despite a suspiciously concerted and vicious campaign by several national newspapers, refused to remove it or to criticize the strong language. Gradually, after the series had won a few awards, the critics relented with a grudging praise for its 'wacky', 'madcap' humour: hell hath no fury like a British tabloid forced to change its opinion.

'Oil' had Vyvyan discovering oil in the cellar and, whilst Neil and Rick had a lengthy discussion about their TV's 'little white dot', Mike declared himself 'El Presidente'. Alexei Sayle's Radical Posture performed 'Doctor Martin's Boots', to which Rick responded 'Don't you hasbeens ever read the *NME*? You'd think "Devil Woman" had never been written.'

The next episode concerned an atom bomb that landed in the students' front room. Rick wanted to blackmail Thatcher with it, Mike wanted to sell it to Colonel Gaddafi and Vyvyan wanted to set it off. The TV-detector man arrived and Rick, in a panic at discovering they had no licence, wrote a poem of his innocence. Vyvyan simply ate the telly.

The series' eagerness to parody other TV genres was emphasized in 'Boring' with 'Oh Crikey', a *Terry and June*-style sitcom complete with the vicar calling for tea and someone's trousers falling down. A siege interrupts the Young Ones' evening (the TV reporter noting 'at least we got the mad coon with the gun'), and Vyvyan's mum (Pauline Melville) proved to be even more obnoxious than her son. Meanwhile, in hell (you knew it was hell because there was a Duran Duran poster on the wall), the demon Futoomch (Dave Rappaport) was desperately awaiting a summons to earth. *The Young Ones*' savage portrayal of the police as dim-witted clowns or racist bigots (Rick's 'People's Poet' dream sequence began with 'Another typical day, the pigs are harassing the kids') was also much criticised by the popular press.

'Interesting' centred on the sort of house party familiar to most students, ending with a huge fight. Dawn French and Jennifer Saunders made their TV debuts in this episode, whilst the Four Horsemen of the Apocalypse sequence also featured Keith Allen, proving a fine example of the links between apparently unconnected scenes. A sandwich, casually discarded by one of the horsemen, crashes through the roof of the party some moments later. The ***Monty Python***-style mock-caption was also used to great effect when viewers were solemnly informed that 'the BBC would like to warn all small children that pushing people into old fridges is a bloody stupid thing to do.'

'Flood' opened with Arnold Brown as a prisoner accused of 'being Scottish and Jewish - two racial stereotypes for the price of one!' Rick and Vyvyan argue over

First season *(9 Nov–14 Dec 82)*	**Second season** *(8 May–19 Jun 84)*
1 Demolition	7 Bambi
2 Oil	8 Cash
3 Bomb	9 Nasty
4 Boring	10 Time
5 Interesting	11 Sick
6 Flood	12 Summer Holiday

the differences between 'love' and 'being poofy' (which has to do with touching bottoms, apparently). Meanwhile, Balowski is turned into an 'axe-wielding homicidal maniac' and finds himself in a scene drawn from *The Lion, the Witch and the Wardrobe*. Later, the episode plagiarized *The Shining*, and the season ended with SPG swimming through the flood waters like the biblical dove (holding not an olive branch but a Coca-Cola can).

The second season had an increased budget, the series having become almost respectable, although certain aspects, like the subliminal message experiment, still attracted notoriety. 'Bambi' had the students appearing, along with their mascot, the pig-ferret Bacon Sandwich, on *University Challenge* in which they faced the rich and stupid Footlights College Oxbridge and discussed a Disney nasty with its star Bamber Gascoigne (Griff Rhys Jones).

The students were so skint in 'Cash' (especially after Vyvyan announces that he is pregnant) that Neil was forced to join the Pigs, where he met Mussolini and found that the only requirement to be a policeman was to be able to make a daft noise into your radio. 'Nasty', filmed in 'horrorscope, the ultimate in thingy', is the series' masterpiece. Mike hires a video from 'Arry the Bastard (Sayle), who then pretends to be a vampire in order to make sure that they are unable to return it before noon and made to forfeit their deposit. (Old Lady: Do you dig graves? Neil: Yeah, they're all right ...)

The final episode was full of clever sight gags (Elephant Head), student jokes (Neil's birthday party) and TV satire (Ben Elton in an outrageous parody of lager adverts). The plot involves the boys failing their exams and becoming bank robbers instead. The episode, and the series, ended with them driving their 'getaway bus' over the edge of a cliff.

The Young Ones were, briefly, resurrected in 1986 along with the 'the total and utter king of rock-and-roll' Cliff Richard, for a comedy version of 'Living Doll' in aid of Comic Relief. The single went to number one.

Helped by constant exposure with *The Comic Strip Presents ...*, and various related projects, the Young Ones remained visible, though as the 80s wore on their reputation waned somewhat. Mayall, Planer and Edmondson's post-*Young Ones* series, the Ben Elton-scripted *Filthy, Rich and Catflap*, was criticized for being '*The Young Ones*: The Next Generation', although the series had many points in its favour, including a return to the original Comic Strip ethic of subverting 'showbiz'. More recently *Bottom*, despite being a violently amusing piece, reminded us that Mayall and Edmondson have not come an awfully long way, humour wise, in the ten years since *The Young Ones*.

Sayle meanwhile, via *Alexei Sayle's Stuff* and *The All New Alexei Sayle Show*, emerged as the shining star from the wreckage of *The Young Ones*, even outstripping Ben Elton who concentrated increasingly on writing at the expense of stand-up.

Perhaps *The Young Ones*' legacy isn't so great, despite a decade of imitators. After all, Thatcher outlasted them.

Blackadder

- **BBC Television** (BBC1) ◆ **Colour**
- **25 episodes** (standard length: *c.* 30 minutes) ◆ **1983-89**
- **Creators:** Richard Curtis, Rowan Atkinson
- **Writers:** Richard Curtis, Rowan Atkinson, Ben Elton
- **Directors:** Martin Shardlow, Mandie Fletcher, Richard Boden
- **Producer:** John Lloyd

Regular cast: Rowan Atkinson (Blackadder) • Tony Robinson (Baldrick)
With: (***The Black Adder***) Tim McInnerny (Lord Percy) • Brian Blessed (Richard IV) • Elspet Gray (Queen) • Robert East (Harry, Prince of Wales) • Peter Cook (Richard III) • Peter Benson (Henry VII) • Alex Norton (McAngus) • Miriam Margolyes (Princess Maria) • Jim Broadbent (Interpreter) • Frank Finlay (Pursuivant) • Patrick Allen (The Moorhen) • Rik Mayall (Mad Gerald) • Stephen Fry (Guard); (***Blackadder II***) Tim McInnerny (Lord Percy) • Miranda Richardson (Elizabeth I) • Stephen Fry (Lord Melchett) • Patsy Byrne (Nursie) • Gabrielle Glaister (Bob/Kate) • Rik Mayall (Lord Flashheart) • Tom Baker (Captain Rum) • Simon Jones (Sir Walter Raleigh) • Miriam Margolyes (Lady Whiteadder) • Hugh Laurie (Simon Partridge/Prince Ludwig); (***Blackadder the Third***) Hugh Laurie (The Prince Regent) • Helen Atkinson-Wood (Mrs Miggins) • Denis Lil (Sir Talbot Buxomly MP) • Robbie Coltrane (Dr Samuel Johnson) • Tim McInnerny (Lord Topper) • Nigel Planer (Lord Smedley) • Hugh Paddick (Keanrick) • Kenneth Connor (Mossop) • Ben Elton (Anarchist) • Miranda Richardson (Amy Hardwood) • Stephen Fry (Duke of Wellington) • Gertan Klauber (King George III); (***Blackadder's Christmas Carol***) Robbie Coltrane (Spirit of Christmas) • Miranda Richardson (Elizabeth I) • Stephen Fry (Lord Melchett) • Hugh Laurie (The Prince Regent) • Miriam Margolyes (Queen Victoria) • Patsy Byrne (King Bernard); (***Blackadder Goes Forth***) Tim McInnerny (Capt. Kevin Darling) • Stephen Fry (General Sir Anthony Cecil Hogmanay Melchett) • Hugh Laurie (Lt. The Honourable George Colthurst St Barleigh) • Gabrielle Glaister (Driver Parkhurst) • Rik Mayall (Sqn. Cdr Lord Flashheart) • Adrian Edmondson (Baron von Richtoven) • Miranda Richardson (Nurse Mary) • Geoffrey Palmer (Field Marshall Haig)

From out of the swirling mists of the Dark Ages comes a lone horseman, cursed from youth by a deformed haircut and sporting a particularly evil pair of tights ...

The Black Adder is but a footnote to history's index, but no less loathsome for that. The son of Richard IV (one of the so-called Princes in the Tower), whom history has no trace of - thanks to Henry Tudor's skilful rewriting of events - Edmund Duke of Edinburgh was a devious, oily little weed with ideas above his intellect. The nickname the Black Vegetable would have been more apt.

The hideous Blackadder genes re-emerge throughout history, becoming more intelligent and cunning as the centuries pass. At his side are the various members of the dung-eating Baldrick family, living proof that evolution sometimes works in reverse.

The myth of Blackadder was dreamt up by Rowan Atkinson and long-term collaborator Richard Curtis as an attempt to do something different from the topical comedy of ***Not the Nine O'Clock News***. Producer John Lloyd explained that they were bored of making jokes about minor Labour MPs and people piddling in telephone boxes. 'People in the late 15th century lived with violent death as a matter of course. When a plague arrived up to a third of the population could be wiped out in a few months. This is a comedy dealing with matters of enormous seriousness.'

Although a sitcom of sorts, *The Black Adder* required a budget far beyond the suburban cardboard living rooms of most BBC comedies. Huge sets were constructed; exterior filming was extensive, and the BBC even had use of a fresh horse or two. It was felt that this backdrop would intensify the comedy, Atkinson commenting that 'We've found that if you set jokes in a very hard and nasty background, the jokes actually become funnier.'

Despite all this - the location filming around Alnwick Castle in Northumberland, the 65 extras and a dozen horses - *The Black Adder* still managed to look cheap, with victorious armies reduced to a handful of stout men in plastic armour. The whole thing had the look of a noble folly, and perhaps that is one of the reasons it worked. The first episode set up the characters, and the complicated alternative history backdrop, with great aplomb, Edmund, Baldrick and Percy being sketched in with broad comic strokes. Peter Cook made a cameo appearance as Richard III ('Baa!'), viciously and accidentally murdered by Blackadder. (If the Shakespearean allusions - 'Now is the summer of our mild content!' - sailed over some viewers' heads, one could always enjoy the clever slapstick: the head of Richard III was placed back on the corpse and the arms pumped vigorously in a futile attempt to breathe life into the royal frame.)

Having survived Bosworth Field, his appointment as Archbishop of Canterbury, and the advances of an enthusiastic dog, Edmund felt his luck was beginning to turn when his father began contemplating using him as a diplomatic pawn, establishing by marriage alliances across Europe. To his horror, Edmund nearly married the huge Spanish Princess Maria (complete with interpreter), and had to feign homosexuality in an attempt to defuse her explosive lust (and instead accelerated it, his camp costume being taken as an attempt to dress up in the manner of a Spanish noble). He survived and lived to fight another day, only to marry a princess so young that five o'clock bedtime stories were in order.

The final episode of *The Black Adder* saw a futile alliance between Edmund and the six most evil men in the kingdom: Friar Bellows, Sean the Irish Bastard, Sir Wilfred Death, Guy of Glastonbury, Three-Fingered Pete, and Jack Large ('the bull-buggering beast-killer of no fixed abode'). It all ended in tears, of course, and not a little bloodshed.

That was very nearly the end of *Blackadder.* Although popular, the programme had proved hugely expensive, and Atkinson felt the 'action got in the way of the humour'. A radical change was proposed for the second *Blackadder:* Ben Elton was brought in as Curtis's co-writer, and it would be filmed in front of a studio audience, utilizing a limited number of (consequently cheaper) sets. The second season was about to go ahead when Michael Grade, who had just been brought in as BBC1 Controller, cancelled the show. Atkinson was quoted in the *Mirror* as saying that Grade 'took one look at the cost of the first series, weighed it up against the ratings and dismissed it as a ridiculous extravagance. "Not enough

THE BLACK ADDER
(15 Jun–20 Jul 83)
1 The Foretelling
2 Born to be King
3 The Archbishop
4 The Queen of Spain's Beard
5 Witchsmeller Pursuivant
6 The Black Seal

BLACKADDER II
(9 Jan–20 Feb 86)
7 Bells
8 Head
9 Potato
10 Money
11 Beer
12 Chains

BLACKADDER THE THIRD
(17 Sep–22 Oct 87)
13 Dish and Dishonesty
14 Ink and Incapability
15 Nob and Nobility
16 Sense and Senility
17 Amy and Amiability [aka Cape and Capability]
18 Duel and Duality

BLACKADDER'S CHRISTMAS CAROL
(23 Dec 88, 45-minute special)

BLACKADDER GOES FORTH
(28 Sep–2 Nov 89)
20 Plan A: Captain Cook
21 Plan B: Corporal Punishment
22 Plan C: Major Star
23 Plan D: Private Plane
24 Plan E: General Hospital
25 Plan F: Goodbyeee

[An untransmitted pilot episode - a version of episode 2 - starred Atkinson, McInnerny, Gray, Philip Fox as Baldrick, Robert Bathurst as Prince Henry, and John Savident as the king. Episode 8 is the first episode of Blackadder II, but it has never been transmitted in this position.]

Edmund Blackadder, the end of the family line, and Baldrick, about to hatch another cunning plan

laughs to the pound" was the phrase used at the time and I suppose it was quite a reasonable attitude.'

However, no one told Grade that *Blackadder II* was to be much cheaper than its predecessor: 'It was a classic BBC cock-up. The light entertainment department failed catastrophically to represent our interests and it could have spelt the death of *Blackadder* there and then. Fortunately, after he was put in the picture, he changed his mind.'

When Atkinson appeared on *Wogan* on the evening of the first episode of *Blackadder II*, claiming that the second *Blackadder* was even funnier than the first, few might have believed him. But he was right. The crucial change of emphasis was in Blackadder himself: he turned from a cringing imbecile to an icy, cynical, almost-20th-century man in an age of fools, with Atkinson's beard helping to transform his 'elastic' features. Set in the early 1560s, *Blackadder II* featured the exploits of the great-great-grandson of the pathetic original, his companions being more stupid versions of Baldrick and Percy. The tradition of Baldrick-baiting began in earnest.

The scripts of Curtis and Elton were excellent, a pinnacle of 80s comedy. 'Bells' featured Blackadder's brief love affair with Bob, ruined by the sudden appearance of his old friend Lord Flashheart ('Am I glad to see you, or have I got a canoe in my pocket?!'). 'Potato' saw an attempt to emulate the achievements of Sir Walter Raleigh, which resulted in a futile expedition to the New World with mad Captain Redbeard Rum at the helm. The baby-eating Bishop of Bath and Wells was the star of 'Money': Blackadder is in arrears and, unless he finds some cash, will end up being hot-pokered to death. After an abortive attempt at encouraging Baldrick into dockyard prostitution ('How much do you charge for a good hard shag?' enquiries one interested punter), Blackadder is forced to sell his house ('Baldrick - go forth into the street and let it be known that Lord Blackadder wishes to sell his house. Percy - just go forth into the street'). Blackadder eventually gets himself out of trouble by engineering the 16th-century equivalent of an incriminating photograph (involving a none-too-willing Percy and a genius painter).

The final two episodes had Blackadder trying to simultaneously entertain the puritanical Whiteadders and host a debauched party, only to be finally captured by the odious master of disguise, Prince Ludwig. Although he escapes, and saves the life of childish-but-deadly Queen Elizabeth, it all ends very unpleasantly again.

The third instalment of the *Blackadder* chronicles saw Edmund as the scheming and sock-stealing Georgian Butler to the Prince Regent. Percy had gone (McInnerny - an actor otherwise known for his strong Shakespearean roles - was worried about typecasting, although he did return for a cameo in one episode), but Baldrick's desire to own a turnip knew no bounds. Mrs Miggins - whose 'pie shoppe' had been referred to in *Blackadder II* - made a belated appearance. Blackadder also encountered the Pitt family of increasingly young politicians, Dr Samuel Johnson (managing to destroy his dictionary in the process), and the dashing highwaywoman, Amy Hardwood. The scripts were more literary than before, befitting the era portrayed, and the series won a BAFTA award for Best Light Entertainment series in 1988 (a feat that *Blackadder Goes Forth* would equal two years later).

1988 also saw two special episodes, beginning with a 15-minute interlude (*Blackadder: The Cavalier Years*, featuring Stephen Fry as a suspiciously contemporary-sounding King Charles I) filmed for the first Comic Relief Red Nose Day. In December *Blackadder's Christmas Carol* brought together most of the characters and actors of the previous seasons. The end result was, unfortunately, less than the sum of its parts, but the strength of the cast paved the way for the final *Blackadder* set in World War I.

In *Blackadder Goes Forth* Tim McInnerny returned (as Captain Darling), Fry and Laurie both had regular roles, Flashheart reappeared (with Adrian Edmondson, as Baron von Richtoven, in hot pursuit), Miranda Richardson played Nurse Mary, and the 'Bob' episode from *Blackadder II* was rehashed, with Gabrielle Glaister this time playing Driver Parkhurst. Whereas ***Red Dwarf*** repeating its own plots smacked of desperation, here the intention seemed playfully confident.

As a summary of all that went before, *Blackadder Goes Forth* is at least as good as anything else transmitted under the *Blackadder* banner, and for its gutsy treatment of war it deserves special praise. The most deadly scenario of all prompted some of the strongest humour, with each episode revolving around a different escape plan (cookery, revues, aircraft, hospitalization, artistry and madness). Stephen Fry commented that *Blackadder Goes Forth* 'shows the resilience of the people in those appalling conditions. What it mocks is the recalcitrance of the generals. Melchett represents the high command, and mad is not too strong a word for him.'

The last episode, transmitted a few days before Remembrance Sunday, was almost too painful to watch. It emphasized the tragi-comic feel of the series perfectly ('Permission to wobble bottom lip, Sir'), with the cowardly Darling finally pushed into the front line. (Knowing that he faces certain death, he records his heartfelt thoughts in his diary: 'Bugger'.) Even Edmund has run out of ideas, and the fateful order to go over the top is received. Blackadder, Baldrick, George and Darling charge across no man's land, explosions and gunshots splattering about them; the silent action becomes hideous slow motion, replaced by an image of a field of poppies in the breeze. No music, no hyperbole - just an image of death and wasted life. 'Comedy' has never been stronger than that.

Auf Wiedersehen, Pet

- **Witzend/Central Television** (ITV) ◆ Colour
- **26 episodes** (60 minutes) ◆ 1983-86
- **Creators:** Dick Clement, Ian La Frenais, based on an idea by Franc Roddam
- **Writers:** Dick Clement, Ian La Frenais, Stan Hey, Bernie Cooper, Francis Megahy
- **Directors:** Roger Bamford, Baz Taylor, Anthony Garner
- **Producers:** Martin McKean, Alan McKeown

Regular cast: Tim Healy (Denis) • Kevin Whately (Neville) • Gary Holton (Wayne) • Jimmy Nail (Oz) • Pat Roach (Bomber) • Timothy Spall (Barry) • Christopher Fairbank (Moxey)

With: Michael Sheard (Grunwald) • Julia Tobin (Brenda) • Heinz Bernard (Pfister) • Caroline Hutchinson (Vera) • Peter Birch (Ulrich) • Brigitte Khan (Dagmar) • Su Elliott (Marjorie) • Michael Elphick (Magowan) • Bill Paterson (Ally Fraser) • Val McLane (Norma) • Lesley Saint-John (Vicki) • Melanie Hill (Hazel) • James Bate (Hallwood) • Ying-Tong-John (Big Baz) • Bryan Pringle (Arthur Pringle) • John Bowler (Ratcliffe) • James Booth (Kenny Ames) • Madelaine Newton (Christine) • Kevin Lloyd (Harry) • Barry Hollinshead (Rod) • Stephen Greif (Stephano)

Auf Wiedersehen, Pet was *the* television success story of 1983; one of those surprise hits that occasionally finds its way into the schedules. The original idea for the series came from *Quadrophenia* director Franc Roddam about a group of itinerant workers, living in squalor. This would have made a fine sitcom, but Clement and La Frenais had other, bolder ideas.

The main strength of *Auf Wiedersehen, Pet* was its characters, the self-styled 'Magnificent Seven'. The leader of this motley bunch was Denis, an older, more world-wise version of Terry Collier from *The Likely Lads*. He had grown up amid the relative affluence of the late 50s and 60s, then survived through hard times in the 70s, only to find himself, at the beginning of the 80s, a classic symbol of the early days of Thatcher's Britain; a northerner, out of work, representing an industry and a class from another age.

Neville was Bob to Healy's Terry. Recently married, Neville wants to provide for his wife, whom he misses desperately. He sees Denis as his only link with the world he left behind and worries about everything. During an early episode Neville discovers an unexploded wartime bomb and becomes a hero to the indigenous workmen, whilst other first season plots include Neville working in an Indian restaurant, and gaining an embarrassing tattoo during a drunken night out.

Oz was as bigoted and generally unpleasant a slob as you could wish to meet. Played superbly by the hard-faced Newcastle club singer Jimmy Nail (who had screen-tested for a minor part and ended up becoming a major star), Oz was a symbol for everything that was wrong about the Englishman abroad. Nail became a regional symbol too, offered cans of lager wherever he went on Tyneside. However, in his interviews about the series, Nail (a thoughtful man, many miles from his on-screen persona) tried to play down the character's bad qualities and stressed the learning process that Oz undergoes as the series progresses. It did no good: on one occasion, when Newcastle United met Liverpool in an FA Cup tie, the Geordie fans taunted the Kop with the chant 'Oz is harder than Yosser'. Shortly before the Berlin Wall came down it was noted that amongst the graffiti on the wall was written 'built by Germans, demolished by Oz'.

Also on hand were Wayne, a girl-mad cockney carpenter; Bomber, an ex-wrestler from Bristol who was the series' most down-to-earth character; Barry, the terminally boring Brummie electrician, and Moxey, an enigmatic scouser (and arsonist!). The seven arrive at a Dusseldorf building site and share a hut, living each other's dreams, frustrations and hopes. 'Suspicion' centres on the possibility of a thief in their midst, Neville is charged with rape in 'The Accused', Oz is accidentally taken back to England with football fans in 'The Girls They Left Behind', whilst another memorable, semi-regular character, the criminally-deranged Irish labourer Magowan, disrupts the near-harmony of the hut in 'The Alien'.

Another interloper, an army deserter (Ray Winstone), provides some pathos in 'The Fugitive', whilst the best episode - 'Last Rites' - has Oz, Barry and Moxey buying German porn videos and trying to ship them back to England in the coffin of an expatriate. Needless to say, Oz hadn't thought about the possibility of cremation.

The 'Magnificent Seven', about to do some damage to Ally Frazer's country house

First season
(11 Nov 83–10 Feb 84)
1 If I were a Carpenter
2 Who Won the War Anyway?
3 The Girls They Left Behind
4 Suspicion
5 Home Thoughts from Abroad
6 The Accused
7 Private Lives
8 The Fugitive
9 The Alien
10 Last Rites
11 The Lovers
12 Love and Other Four Letter Words
13 When the Boat Goes Out

Second season
(21 Feb–16 May 86)
14 The Return of the Seven (part one)
15 The Return of the Seven (part two)
16 A Law for the Rich
17 Another Country
18 A Home from Home
19 Cowboys
20 No Sex Please, We're Brickies
21 Marjorie Doesn't Live Here Anymore
22 Hasta la Vista
23 Scoop
24 Law and Disorder
25 For Better or Worse
26 Quo Vadis, Pet

The series also detailed developing relationships, notably of the unhappily-married Denis with Dagmar, and Wayne with the beautiful secretary Christa (Lysette Anthony). The series ended as most of the lads return home (Wayne elects to stay behind and get married). Oz is badly injured in a pub brawl with Magowan and the hut is destroyed in a shower of pyrotechnics.

The sections of the series filmed in Germany - the building site scenes were shot at Borehamwood - proved to be a colourful experience. The producers hired a coachload of vice girls from Hamburg's red light district to appear in one episode only to find that many were transvestites. They also hired a number of squaddies from a nearby army camp to play extras in the bar scenes: the soldiers quickly got into the mood by drinking more than 600 bottles of beer between them and were so legless when filming started that the scene had to be scrapped. One actor was chased by gun-toting police, whilst Pat Roach broke his foot during a stunt that went wrong. The incident was written into the scripts (Oz dropping a heavy weight on to Bomber's foot whilst trying to persuade him to invest in his porn video racket). Despite these problems, a classic was created.

Quite why *Auf Wiedersehen, Pet* became such a huge success during the winter of 1983 is debatable. Certainly, the series exposed a weakness in British society, with its opening shots of job centres and petty crime. The comedy was of a high calibre, and the performances - down to the fringe characters like the German authority figures - were excellent. The other writers quickly grasped the dichotomous nature of a series that included equal doses of social comment and wild humour. For whatever reason, *Auf Wiedersehen, Pet* catapulted its actors to celebrity status. Even the series' theme song, a cheerfully awful pub-singalong, 'That's Livin' Alright', co-written by La Frenais and sung by Joe Fagin, became a surprise top ten hit.

All of this, however, had a disastrous effect on Gary Holton, whose drink and drugs problems eventually led to his untimely death at the age of 33 during the filming of a second season in 1985. With some rewriting, Wayne put in an appearance in each of the episodes, all of the location filming having been done before he died.

The second season switched locale, beginning back in England (after a couple of hilarious scenes of Barry and Oz in the Falklands), before travelling, for the last five episodes, to Marbella. In the two years since Germany, Denis has lost a fortune gambling and now works for Tyneside gangster Ally Fraser (a superb performance by Bill Paterson), Neville has become a father and is again unemployed, Oz has disappeared to America, much to the chagrin of his wife, left to bring up young Rod on her own. Bomber has returned to wrestling, Moxey to crime and Wayne to his old womanizing ways. Only Barry, soon to be married and with his own building business, seems to have his life in some sort of order. Typically, Barry misses the 'good old days' of Germany and invites the others to help him complete his dream home. Back on Tyneside, Ally Fraser asks Denis to put together a team to renovate a Victorian mansion in Derbyshire that he has (illegally) bought.

'A Law for the Rich' begins with the group (minus Barry) in a motorway cafe discussing which members of the real Magnificent Seven they consider themselves to be. It is a magical scene which illustrates perfectly the interplay between the various characters. Later, they book into a hotel, run by an ex-RAF-type who makes the following episodes a joy with his angry dialogue. They are initially thrown out after Wayne seduces the man's daughter but, later, discover an incriminating video and blackmail their way back in. Neville spends a Saturday afternoon at home, in bed with his wife, listening to radio commentary on Newcastle United's latest match (in a memorable out-take, shown on *It'll Be Alright on the Night*, Whately loses his concentration when United score). The group go on strike as Ally Fraser's corner-cutting plans for the house become apparent. 'Cowboys' ends with a huge fist-fight against Fraser's men.

Fraser relents and offers the boys a job in Marbella. Returning to Newcastle, Oz attempts to patch up his disastrous marriage, only to discover that his wife and son are about to leave for a new life in Italy. 'Hasta la Vista' ends with a beautiful scene filmed beneath the Tyne Bridge in which Oz shows a sensitive, emotional side to his character, saying goodbye to the son he has lost through his own neglect. Whilst in Spain, they become involved with 'Costa del Crime' exiles and are chased by press men who think they are a gang of armed bank-robbers. The season ends with them on a cruiser, pursued by coast-guards, heading for Morocco.

A third season - which La Frenais suggested could be set in Moscow with the group rebuilding the British Embassy - was planned but proved too expensive, whilst the remaining members of the cast were unwilling to carry on without Gary Holton, a significant testament to the bond that had formed between them. In addition to Spall and Nail's appearance together in the 1987 film *Dream Demons*, the surviving six members of *Auf Wiedersehen, Pet* are all regularly seen on television. Nail, as the co-creator (with La Frenais), writer and star of *Spender*, and later, *Crocodile Shoes*, and Whately, as John Thaw's co-star in ***Inspector Morse*** and the lead in *Peak Practice*, have even managed to distance themselves from the series in which they made their name. Spall too has become a star again with *Frank Stubbs Promotes* and *Outside Edge*. Fairbank and Healy continue to turn up in the most unlikely places (Fairbank with a small role in the first *Batman* film, for example, or Healy's BBC series *The Boys from the Bush*).

The legacy of *Auf Wiedersehen, Pet* is that of a series that crossed genre boundaries. A sitcom in construction, the series proved too ambitious to be fitted into 30-minute slices of quick laughs and so it, along with *Boys from the Blackstuff*, was seen as a standard-bearer for a new form of socially-relevant comedy-drama. But, although *Blackstuff* had its humorous moments amid the depiction of life in a northern city in the early 80s, it can hardly be described as a bundle of laughs. *Auf Wiedersehen, Pet*, with its wry commentary on England's perception of itself and its humane treatment of the working class, remains one of television's finest comic creations.

Spitting Image

- **Central/Spitting Image Productions/ABC** (ITV) ◆ **Colour**
- **142 episodes** (standard length: *c*.30 minutes) ◆ **1984-96**
- **Creators:** Peter Fluck, Roger Law, based on original lunch with Martin Lambie Nairn
- **Writers include:** Ian Hislop, Nick Newman, Geoff Atkinson, Rob Grant, Doug Naylor, Moray Hunter, John Docherty, James Hendrie, Steve Punt
- **Directors include:** Peter Harris, Bob Cousins, John Stroud, Sean Hardie, Graham C. Williams, Geoffrey Sax, John Henderson, Steve Bandelack, Richard Bradley, Steve Connelly, Andy de Emmony, Beryl Richards
- **Producers:** Jon Blair, John Lloyd, Geoffrey Perkins, David Tyler, Bill Dare, Giles Pilbrow
- **Executive producer** ('Down and Out in the Whitehouse'): David Frost

Voices: Chris Barrie • Adrian Edmondson • Steve Nallon • Enn Reitel • Harry Enfield • Pamela Stephenson • Jon Glover • Jan Ravens • Jessica Martin • Rory Bremner • Kate Robbins • Hugh Dennis • Steve Coogan • Alistair McGowan • Roger Blake

'*Weekending* with puppets', its critics have called it; Norma Major commented, 'They've got a puppet of John that's completely grey, haven't they? I haven't seen it, but I've heard about it. I think they've gone too far to be funny.' It has featured attacks on royalty, God, and Gazza, and has portrayed Norman Tebbit as a skinhead thug and Margaret Thatcher as a sneering, deformed (and masculine) beast. When *Spitting Image* was at its height, the name Roy Hattersley summoned up an image not of the real Labour MP but of the gobbing caricature. In its time, it really was that evocative.

The latex creations of Peter Fluck and Roger Law (or Luck and Flaw, as they were thankfully known) were sometimes the best things about a show in which the scripts were initially patchy. Fluck and Law had met at art college in Cambridge, and in 1975 they became partners, making caricatures of the famous in plasticine. In 1981 a programme using puppets based on these models was mooted; it finally went ahead in 1984, the puppets being made in a workshop at Limehouse Studios, in London's Docklands.

The programme nearly vanished without trace during its first season as, although it began with an audience of 7.9 million, its viewers dwindled rapidly. Within three weeks it was facing cancellation, as even the puppets were static and unimpressive. However, problems were ironed out by the second season, by which time *Spitting Image*'s popularity was assured. Topicality kept it fresh - some 'sketches' were only filmed or edited hours before transmission - and the caustic scripting made it compelling, if sometimes uncomfortable, viewing.

The targets were the famous, and the caricatures were often harsh or surreal (Kenneth Baker as slug, for instance). At its best, the vitriolic humour was an elegant form of personal abuse. Very occasionally the famous claimed not to mind: Paul Daniels and Michael Heseltine initially wanted to buy their puppets; Denis Healey appeared on the programme, the first non-puppet to do so; Jeffrey Archer sent a tape to the team to improve the quality of his voice; and Stephen Hendry said that his zit-covered puppet was quite good-looking. However, even defenders of the programme would probably admit that *Spitting Image* was, on occasions, crass and tasteless. Its creators, however, maintained that it did have some standards: in the run-up to the Gulf War,

Rabid Royal Corgi Alert

First season
(26 Feb–17 Jun 84)
Twelve episodes

Second season
(6 Jan–24 Mar 85)
Eleven episodes

Montreux special
(27 Apr 85)

Third season
(12 Jan–9 Feb 86)
Five episodes

Fourth season
(30 Mar–4 May 86)
Six episodes

'Down and Out in the Whitehouse'
(14 Sep 86, 45 minutes)

Fifth season
(28 Sep–2 Nov 86)
Six episodes

The Spitting Image 1987 Movie Awards
(4 Apr 87)

Election special
(11 Jun 87, 50 minutes)

Sixth season
(1 Nov–6 Dec 87)
Six episodes

Christmas special
(27 Dec 87)

'The Ronnie and Nancy Show'
(17 Apr 88)

'Bumbledown'
(29 Oct 88, 45 minutes)

Seventh season
(6 Nov–11 Dec 88)
Six episodes

'The Sound of Maggie!'
(6 May 89, 45 minutes)

Eighth season
(11 Jun–9 Jul 89)
Five episodes

Roger Law said that they'd 'do' Saddam Hussein, but 'if people are dying in the Gulf, we won't be making a joke of it'.

There were attempts to turn its attacks away from politics and royalty: the milk-bottle-sniffing, sinus-crippled Melvyn Bragg, the Jive-talkin' dude-Pope, Barry Norman ('And why not? That, in a sense, is what I'm here for'), the big-drinking, woman-shattering Oliver Reed, Steve 'Interesting' Davis, Leonard Nimoy, desperate to be taken for a serious actor ('To be or not to be, that is illogical, Captain'), and so on. But these were always the exception rather than the rule.

Accentuating the tabloid approach to the royal family (Charles as a hippie; the Queen Mum as a 'woman of the people'), the Prince of Wales was cursed with huge ears, a desire to talk to plants, and a doubtful intelligence. Hype and outrage surrounded the appearance of the Queen Mother puppet, the gutter press blustering and raging hypocritically. In the end, she appeared right at the end of the show, trotting on and laughing, doubtless, at the millions who tuned in expecting to be shocked.

Eventually they were: the Queen Mum was a dumb horse-racing fan and, what was worse, she was common. Princess Michael had a Hitler moustache; Princess Margaret was perpetually drunk. Concern about Andrew and Fergie's 'laziness' and ignorance of their own children became a running gag, leading to the legendary 'What's your name?' sequence. Royalists were disgusted, Paul Daniels commenting that the royal family are 'shown as complete idiots, when we all know they do a magnificent job'.

If royalty is an easy target - critics claim that they can't answer back - politics is where *Spitting Image* should have been able to bare its teeth. However, the show was studiously neutral, with each party getting its fair share of mud-slinging. Norman Fowler ('Fowlpest'), in his time, was an NHS vampire; John Prescott was a lager-lout; Paddy Ashdown a senseless liberal ('I am not on one side, nor on the other, but somewhere in between'). There were perceptive moments, which helped counter-balance the impotence: during the 1987 election the David Steel puppet orgasmically exclaimed to Dr Owen 'Oh, David, I feel a late surge coming on ... ' Years later, jubilation at Labour HQ at finally being points ahead of the Tories in the polls was followed by Kinnock's shock announcement that, in order to stay ahead, for the next few months they must do and say absolutely nothing. Prophetic stuff.

The 'political' humour was if anything even more basic when it came to Ronald Reagan. Weeks went by when the President's brain was missing, and he was often seen being beaten at chess by his dog, Lucky. 'Bumbledown' was an epic-length exposé of the actor-president, producer Geoffrey Perkins commenting that 'Our aim was to tell the story of Ronald Reagan from the first moment he opened his eyes as a baby to the moment he shut them again when he became President ... We wanted to get inside Reagan's head, which proved to be easy but not very informative.'

Ninth season
(12 Nov–17 Dec 89)
Six episodes

Tenth season
(13 May–24 Jun 90)
Six episodes

Eleventh season
(11 Nov–16 Dec 90)
Six episodes

Twelfth season
(14 Apr–19 May 91)
Six episodes

Thirteenth season
(10 Nov–15 Dec 91)
Six episodes

Election special
(8 Apr 92)

Fourteenth season
(12 Apr–17 May 92)
Six episodes

Fifteenth season
(4 Oct–8 Nov 92)
Six episodes

Sixteenth season
(16 May–20 Jun 93)
Six episodes

Seventeenth season
(7 Nov–12 Dec 93)
Six episodes

Spitting Image Pantomime
[aka 'Cinderella Goose and the Seven Beanstalks in Boots in the Wood']
(26 Dec 93)

Eighteenth season
(1 May–12 Jun 94)
Seven episodes

Nineteenth season
(6 Nov–18 Dec 94)
Seven episodes

Ye Olde Spitting Image
(1 Jan 95)

Twentieth season
(14 Jan-18 Feb 96)
Six episodes

Spitting Image was at its best when it was angry. An early episode featured a marvellously caustic attack on South African white rule via the Philip Pope song 'I've Never Met a Nice South African'. The anger reached a finely-honed summit with the post-Thatcher-special 'The Sound of Maggie!', where Falklands echoes gave the whole programme a poignant edge.

The songs were a vital part of *Spitting Image*'s popular appeal. The infamous 'Chicken Song', a spoof of the preposterous stupidity of 'Agadoo' by Black Lace, proved that satire is often too subtle for its intended audience as it got to number one in the charts. One of the most touching musical moments in a later season came as Sting re-sang the Police's 'Every Breath You Take' as 'Every Bomb You Make' over monochrome pictures of various puppets. The whole sequence became something of a heartfelt plea, and the series perhaps should have ended there.

It didn't, and soon became long in the tooth, although there were always nuggets amongst the dross: '101 Things to do with a Björk', or Arnold Schwarzenegger extolling his virtues and strength in a song with the sad chorus 'Ya, my villy ist tiny'.

Late 1995 saw *Crapston Villas*, an animated soap for Channel 4, and the wonderful *The Strip Show*, a pilot episode of unconnected cartoon and 'claymation' sketches. The *Spitting Image* team have abandoned topicality but seem to have found a new vein of humour.

Red Dwarf

- **Paul Jackson Productions/BBC North West/Grant Naylor** (BBC2)
- Colour
- **36 episodes** (30 minutes) ◆ **1988–93**
- **Creators/writers:** Rob Grant, Doug Naylor
- **Directors:** Ed Bye, Juliet May
- **Producers:** Ed Bye, Hilary Bevan Jones

Starring: Craig Charles (Dave Lister) • Christopher Barrie (Arnold J. Rimmer) • Danny John-Jules (Cat) • Norman Lovett/Hattie Hayridge (Holly) • Robert Llewellyn (Kryten)

Once described by Clive Anderson as '***Doctor Who*** with jokes', *Red Dwarf* is undoubtedly *the* cult series of the late 80s, an informed, hip and extremely funny extension of many of the best elements of traditional sitcom and, perhaps ironically, its ideological opposite, telefantasy.

The story is a simple one (for science fiction if not for sitcom): a 24th-century earth mining ship, the *Red Dwarf*, has its entire crew wiped out, save for one survivor who must (along with the ship's computer, a hologram of his bunk-mate, an over-evolved cat and an android) attempt to find his way back to Earth.

Red Dwarf was the brainchild of Rob Grant and Doug Naylor, chief writers on ***Spitting Image***. Their concept was developed for TV by Paul Jackson and producer/director Ed Bye, and made under a co-production deal with the BBC which allowed Jackson and his team complete control over casting and script selection. The first series went into production in 1987 with a talented cast assembled for the lead roles.

Originally, Grant, Naylor and Jackson had the idea of using 'proper' actors for the main roles rather than comedians: Alfred Molina and Alan Rickman were the first choices for Lister and Rimmer, respectively. However, the production team finally decided that this would have been too much of a risk. Craig Charles, Liverpudlian poet and comedian, best known for his appearances on *The Tube* and *Saturday Live*, was cast as Dave Lister, 'the last human alive'. The hologram of his dead bunk-mate, Arnold Judas Rimmer, was played by Chris Barrie, a superb impressionist who had provided many of the voices for the ***Spitting Image*** puppets and was also a familiar TV face from several Paul Jackson shows, including a stint as co-presenter of *Carrott's Lib*. Norman Lovett, who provided the face and voice of the ship's computer, Holly, was also a veteran of the Jackson stable. Lovett's deadpan comic timing was initially one of the show's main attractions, his 'Captain's Log'-style opening being an important feature of the first two seasons.

The main cast was completed by Danny John-Jules, a dancer with much theatrical experience who was chosen to play television's first feline sapien, Cat, a descendant of Lister's pregnant pussy, Frankenstein, with a wicked dress sense. C.J. (Clare) Grogan, former singer with Altered Images, also appeared in several episodes in the role of Christine Kochanski, Lister's ideal female companion. Contrary to common belief, the rousing Howard Goodall song that closes the show is sung not by Grogan but by a sound-alike session singer.

Craig Charles has insisted that *Red Dwarf* is, in essence, closer in spirit to ***Porridge*** or ***Steptoe and Son*** than *Hitch-Hikers Guide to the Galaxy* since it 'deals with people in a confined space who don't get on with each other. The space is the situation, not the comedy.' It is true that, for the most part, the first season did steer well clear of using anything other than traditional SF clichés,

RED DWARF
(15 Feb–21 Mar 88)
1 The End
2 Future Echoes
3 Balance of Power
4 Waiting for God
5 Confidence and Paranoia
6 ME^2

RED DWARF II
(6 Sep–11 Oct 88)
7 Kryten
8 Better Than Life
9 Thanks for the Memory
10 Stasis Leak
11 Queeg
12 Parallel Universe

RED DWARF III:
The Saga Continuums
(14 Nov–19 Dec 89)
13 Backwards
14 Marooned
15 Polymorph
16 Bodyswap
17 Timeslides
18 The Last Day

[*Red Dwarf III* is also prefixed *The Same Generation (Nearly)*.]

RED DWARF IV
(14 Feb–21 Mar 91)
19 Camille
20 DNA
21 Justice
22 White Hole
23 Dimension Jump
24 Meltdown

RED DWARF V
(20 Feb–26 Mar 92)
25 Holoship
26 The Inquisitor
27 Terrorform
28 Quarantine
29 Demons and Angels
30 Back to Reality

RED DWARF VI
(7 Oct–11 Nov 93)
31 Psirens
32 Legion
33 Gunmen of the Apocalypse
34 Emohawk: Polymorph II
35 Rimmerworld
36 Out of Time

the first episode in particular proving disappointing, and probably losing the series a lot of viewers with its coy opening scenes. However, the series' strength lay in its writers' understanding of their subject and the superb comic timing of the main characters.

The main problem with the first season was that the central characters were a touch too stereotyped, allowing little room for development. Thankfully, this was rectified by the second season and Lister and Rimmer have grown over the years into characters very different from the bickering counterparts in the first episode. Indeed, the BBC were initially so concerned that they insisted on some form of control. Rob Grant notes that 'Gareth Gwenlan at the BBC was worried because there were no French windows in it. He suggested we start on a sofa, pull away to French windows, then pull back further to reveal a space ship, so that people would know what to expect.'

Although the first season was the weakest, concentrating as it did on the clash between the characters rather than big concepts, it did include several fascinating story ideas. 'Future Echoes' hinged on the premise of the ship breaking the time barrier and Rimmer seeing Lister 'die'. 'Confidence and Paranoia' (which included one of the first TV appearances of comedian Craig Ferguson) featured Lister catching a mutated form of space-pneumonia which turns hallucinations into reality, and the series ended with the splendid 'ME^2' in which a duplicate Rimmer was created and Arnold decided to move in with himself. The first season also introduced the word 'smeg' (as in 'smeghead' or 'smeg off') to the English language.

The next season, with an increased budget, has many champions who acclaim it as the best yet produced. In 'Kryten' the crew receive a distress call from another vessel and arrive to find that 'the first intelligent life form we meet for three million and two years' is the 'android version of Norman Bates'. The role of the robot Kryten, here played by David Ross, would later be incorporated as a returning character. 'Better Than Life' concerned Total Immersion Video Games, which were plugged into the player's brain and allowed them to create their own fantasy world. This episode showed a very underrated side to the series, where the writers were able to deal with quite deep emotional subjects (e.g. Rimmer received a letter informing him that his father had died) and yet remain brutally funny at the same time. 'Queeg', on the other hand, was one great practical joke played by Holly, with a moral at the end of the story ('Don't underestimate what you've got because, basically, I'm fantastic'). The final episode, which began with the opening titles replaced by a sub-Motown song-and-dance number, 'Tongue-Tied', choreographed by Charles Augins, takes place in a ludicrously obvious parallel universe in which sexual mores are reversed and Lister finds himself pregnant by a female version of himself (played with slob-like charm by Angela Bruce).

Perhaps the best episode of the programme's history, 'Thanks for the Memory', begins with the crew discovering that a number of strange events have occurred about which they have no memory. Gradually, they realize that the broken leg, half-finished jigsaw puzzle and erased computer files are not the result of alien communication ('I'd hate to be around when one of these guys is giving a speech,' notes Cat), but of Lister's misplaced attempt to give Rimmer some of his memories as a present. The end, when Rimmer realizes that a grand love affair wasn't his, is very touching.

By the third season, changes were afoot. Norman Lovett decided to leave the series, his place being taken by Hattie Hayridge, who had played the parallel Hilly in the last episode of the second season. Kryten returned, now played with a soft Canadian accent by Robert Llewellyn. Changes in costume were also apparent (notably Chris Barrie's *Captain Scarlet*-type uniform) and the sets became darker (based on *Aliens*, according to Paul Jackson). The scripts, for a while at least, seemed to lose some of their vibrancy. However, 'Marooned', a basic one-set, one-act play between Lister and Rimmer in a crashed shuttle-craft that cannily expanded on the black and white of the characters, and 'Polymorph', an outrageous rip-off of every ***Doctor Who*** story never made (complete with an 'armour-plated killing machine' space-monster), are both excellent examples of how the series allowed for experimentation.

Another aspect of *Red Dwarf* that provides much amusement is its constant debunking of traditional science-fiction attitudes. In 'The Last Day' Kryten is to be switched off so that he can be replaced by a later model. Upon being told that the rest of the crew will not allow this, he launches into an impassioned speech about the nature of 'this human emotion, friendship'. Lister's reply was 'Knock-off the *Star Trek* crap, Kryten, it's too early in the morning'. A similar moment occurs at the end of 'Justice' when Lister, in the middle of a rant about the nature of blind human acceptance of suffering and death, falls down a manhole.

By the fourth season the show was regularly achieving viewing figures in excess of five million, and was being referred to as 'the award-winning cult series *Red Dwarf*' by the BBC, a sure sign that it was beginning to be taken seriously. Again the series reached the quality of the second season, especially with the episodes 'White Hole', in which Lister plays pool with planets, 'Dimension Jump', and 'DNA', a sequel to 'Polymorph' with plagiarized dialogue from *Die Hard II* ('How can the same smeg happen to the same guy two years running?'). To some extent, the laughs got fewer on the ground as the special effects increased: rather than a two-men-in-a-small-space show, the programme had become 'concept of the week'. (This is especially noticeable in the fifth season in which Grant and Naylor moved the series even further away from its comic roots, with jokes being spaced out to give more room for characterization and the science fiction elements.) It seems as though the writers took a close look at what makes the series tick and decided to make *Red Dwarf* into a telefantasy series with jokes rather than a sitcom about space. This upset some early fans but was welcomed by others who saw it as a logical step in *Red Dwarf*'s development.

'Dimension Jump' illustrates this approach perfectly, concerning as it does yet another parallel universe. In this one, 'Ace' Rimmer is a pilot in the space corps, instead of our own sad git. Ace travels through a dimension gap and we were given an insight into the way in which our Rimmer may have turned out had he 'been given the breaks', the punchline being, of course, that our Rimmer *was* the one who got the breaks, whereas 'Ace' had to fight for everything since he was a small boy. Fine comedy and thought-provoking drama in one 30-minute episode: a true example of how remarkable a series *Red Dwarf* can be.

The fifth season saw Rimmer finally getting (and losing) a girlfriend, and 'concepts of the week' that included computer viruses, time anomalies and Rimmer's disturbed psyche. 'Demons and Angels' saw the apparent destruction of the ship whilst 'Back to Reality' suggested that the first five seasons had all been a video-game-induced dream.

If the show had undoubtedly become less of a comedy and more of a science-fiction series, the unsatisfactory sixth season tended to fail in both departments. The crew were now adrift, trying to return to their ship, thus leaving Holly out of the picture. Popular characters such as Dwayne Dibley and Ace Rimmer were roughly levered back into the show, shallow if glamorous effects were spread on thick, and the whole thing had the feel of being rehashed. Rimmer, especially, became somewhat more charismatic and less of a straightman, a sure sign that the format was starting to creak. A long break was in order, with the BBC initially failing to confirm that there was going to be another season at all. That did seem rather unfair as the season ended on a ***Blake's 7***-inspired cliffhanger, with Rimmer, in what was, for once, a heroic move, striving to stop the imminent destruction of his friends. It looked like he didn't succeed.

Still, after a hiatus - that included Craig Charles's lengthy trial-by-jury-and-media - a mammoth new series is in production. It's rumoured to feature new writers, and such a breath of fresh air will be welcome. On balance, it will be good to have *Red Dwarf* back, since it means that the BBC will continue to take science fiction seriously ... when it's in the form of comedy.

Harry Enfield

Norbert Smith - A Life

- **Hat Trick Productions** (C4) ◆ Colour
- 3 Nov 1989, 50 minutes
- **Writers:** Harry Enfield, Geoffrey Perkins
- **Director:** Geoff Posner
- **Producer:** Geoffrey Perkins
- **Executive producer:** Denise O'Donoghue

Starring: Harry Enfield • Melvyn Bragg • Renee Asherson

Harry Enfield's Television Programme

- **BBC Television/Hat Trick** (BBC2) ◆ Colour
- **13 episodes** (30 minutes) ◆ 1990-92
- **Writers:** Harry Enfield, Charlie Higson, Geoffrey Perkins, Paul Whitehouse Additional material: Ian Hislop, Nick Newman, Richard Preddy, Gary Howe
- **Directors:** Geoffrey Perkins, John Berkin, Geoff Posner, Metin Hüseyin
- **Producers:** Mary Bell, Geoffrey Perkins, Geoff Posner
- **Executive producers:** Denise O'Donoghue, Mary Bell (*Harry Enfield's Festive Television Programme*)

Starring: Harry Enfield • Paul Whitehouse • Jon Glover, Kathy Burke • Caroline John • Rupert Holliday-Evans • David Barber • Joe McGann • Garry Bleasdale • Caroline Quentin • Martin Clunes • Neil Pearson • Doon McKichan • Sean Pertwee • Jon Glover • Kate Robbins • Sara Crow • Brian Regan • Paul Usher • Alan Freeman

Harry Enfield has always been bothered by success. His first big breakthrough was on *Saturday Live* with his characters Stavros and Loadsamoney. The Greek kebab shop owner with the Arsenal fetish and the peculiar speech habits ('Up the Arse!') and the plasterer with too much money were instant hits, the latter especially evolving into a troubling capitalist hero-figure, an albatross around Enfield's neck in the same way that Alf Garnett had been to Warren Mitchell. Beset by tabloid attention, he talked of turning Loadsamoney gay, and finally killed him off in a car crash on a BBC Comic Relief telethon. For many comedians, such a 'death' would be a triviality to be ignored next time the character was called for. Not for Enfield. Loadsamoney stayed dead.

For a while, it looked as if (figuratively speaking) Enfield was, too. He was largely ignored as Martin Clunes's initial partner in the first ITV season of *Men Behaving Badly*. With his most well-known characters consigned to the scrap heap, Enfield's celebrity was on the wane.

HARRY ENFIELD'S TELEVISION PROGRAMME

First season
(8 Nov–13 Dec 90)
Six episodes

Second season
(2 Apr–7 May 92)
Six episodes

That's one reason why *Norbert Smith - A Life* was such a surprise. The fake biography of a minor British actor, the programme showcased Enfield's ability for acute parody, mimicking many different film styles, as well as the arts documentary itself. From somebody who was publicly known at the time for a couple of

Smashey and Nicey - The End of an Era

- **BBC Television** (BBC1) ◆ **Colour**
- 4 Apr 1994, 45 minutes
- **Writers:** Harry Enfield, Paul Whitehouse
- **Director:** Daniel Kleinman
- **Producer:** Alison Owen
- **Executive producer:** Peter Bennett-Jones

Starring: Harry Enfield • Paul Whitehouse • Alan Freeman • David Jensen • John Peel • Bob Geldof • Tony Blackburn • Angus Deayton

Harry Enfield and Chums

- **BBC Television** (BBC1) ◆ **Colour**
- **6 episodes** (30 minutes) ◆ 1994
- **Writers:** Harry Enfield, Paul Whitehouse
- **Additional material:** Ian Hislop, Nick Newman, Harry Thompson, Simon Greenall, Kay Stonham, Geoffrey Perkins, Barry Fantoni
- **Director:** John Stroud
- **Producer:** Harry Thompson
- **Executive producers:** Peter Bennett-Jones, Maureen McMunn

Starring: Harry Enfield • Paul Whitehouse • Kathy Burke • David Barber • Garry Bleasdale • Ben Elton • Martin Clunes • Jimmy Hill • Des Lynam • Jon Glover • John Stalker • Louisa Rix • Leslie Ash

stupid catchphrases, it was a revelation, an obvious attempt to demonstrate Enfield's huge range.

Enfield, together with regular writing partners Charlie Higson (ex of the band the Higsons) and Paul Whitehouse, found a new home at the BBC. He put together *Harry Enfield's Television Programme*, a show that would feature many different recurring characters in sketches, a format exactly like that of *The Dick Emery Show* in the 70s. Here were born the annoying golf-capped 'Only me!', Tim Nice-But-Dim, the Slobs, Lee and Lance ('Is that what you want? 'Cos that's what'll happen!'), the Old Gits, and, most memorably, arch DJs Smashey and Nicey. These two medallioned, farm-owning, Bachman Turner Overdrive fans wrought a change in the social fabric of Britain by providing a satirical weapon against bloated DJs everywhere. It's not too fanciful to attribute the fall of the old guard at Radio One over the next few years to the truth and accuracy of this parody. Smashey and Nicey had vocal tics that might have been Simon Bates's, Tony Blackburn's or DLT's, but their biggest figure of fun was Alan Freeman.

Harry Enfield's Festive Television Programme
(23 Dec 92)

HARRY ENFIELD AND CHUMS
First season
(4 Nov–16 Dec 94)

As Dick Emery had done, Enfield would combine his characters in complex long sketches, including a wonderful parody of Michael Apted in '28 Up', where Wayne Slob and Tim Nice-But-Dim are interviewed and are surprised to discover that they're exactly the same age.

Catchphrases from this era, like 'You don't want to do that', and, most incredibly, 'tree!' (used only once in the aliens sketch), still infest British culture, evidence of the impact Enfield's very recognizable characters had. It was at this point that he started to become an important figure in advertising, lending his characters to such products as Hula Hoops, Dime Bars ('Armadillo!') and Worthington bitter. For somebody who seemed to want to be every British icon at once, this was strangely apt.

With his cartoon approach to characters and vocal talents, Enfield was a natural to link up with adult comic *Viz* to voice *Billy the Fish*. The *Viz* connection continued in the pages of the comic itself, an influence on the anti-Loadsamoney character, Buggerallmoney.

It became apparent that Enfield wasn't going to make the same mistake again. Characters past their sell by date, even very popular ones, were deleted from view when they got too big to handle. Certainly, this was the case with Smashey and Nicey, on the verge of becoming real celebrities when they hosted *Top of the Pops*, and laid to rest in the extraordinary special *The End of an Era*. One character would never hold Enfield's versatility to ransom again.

It was becoming apparent that Enfield's co-stars Paul Whitehouse and Kathy Burke were important parts of the show in their own right, especially with the critical success garnered by Whitehouse and Higson's excellent and well-observed *The Fast Show* on BBC2 ('Suits you, sir'). This is possibly why Enfield's next project - the make-or-break transition to BBC1 - was called *Harry Enfield and Chums*. New characters included the archetypal Moody Teenager (complete with wonderfully breaking voice), who had been Little Brother on BBC2, the Self-Righteous Brothers, with their litany of impotent rage ('Oi, Armstrong, no!'), and the Lovely Wobbly Randy Old Ladies ('Young man!').

With his own talent, such useful partners, and change enshrined as part of his repertoire, there seems no reason why Harry Enfield should not continue to be one of the best-known performers on British TV.

Drop the Dead Donkey

- **Hat Trick Productions** (C4) ◆ Colour
- **46 episodes** (30 minutes) ◆ 1990-94
- **Creators/writers/producers:** Andy Hamilton, Guy Jenkin
- **Additional material:** Rory McGrath, Nick Revell, Malcolm Williamson, Elly Brewer
- **Director:** Liddy Oldroyd
- **Executive producer:** Denise O'Donoghue

Starring: Robert Duncan (Gus Hedges) • Haydn Gwynne (Alex Pates) • Neil Pearson (Dave Charnley) • Jeff Rawle (George Dent) • David Swift (Henry Davenport) • Stephen Tompkinson (Damien Day) • Victoria Wicks (Sally Smedley) • Sara Stewart (Jenny) • Susannah Doyle (Joy Merryweather) • Ingrid Lacey (Helen Cooper)

There are two ways of classifying Channel 4's *Drop the Dead Donkey*. One is as a worthy successor to topical satire of ***That Was the Week That Was***, *The Frost Report* and ***Not the Nine O'Clock News***. The other is as a sitcom - but no sitcom was ever as provocatively in-your-face as *Drop the Dead Donkey*.

The series was devised, written and produced by Andy Hamilton and Guy Jenkin, whose backgrounds as gag-writers on *Not the Nine O'Clock News* should have hinted at its hard-hitting quality. *Donkey* was one of a handful of Hat Trick Productions which, along with its stablemates *Whose Line is It Anyway?*, *Paul Merton – The Series* and BBC2's *Have I Got News for You*, swept the board at the 1991 British Comedy Awards.

The series is set in the newsroom of Globelink News, a media circus which in the first episode is bought by unseen mogul Sir Roysten Merchant, much to the dismay of the staff. These include George Dent, the ineffectual, permanently put-upon editor and his assistant, Alex Pate, who spends most of her time (when she's not being pestered on the phone by her senile mother) swapping brilliant one-liners with the series' real stars: the cynical, gambling, office-charmer Dave Charnley, and the suave, ruthless, near-psychotic news reporter Damien Day.

First season
(9 Aug–11 Oct 90)
1 A New Dawn
2 Sally's Arrival
3 A Clash of Interests
4 A Blast from the Past
5 Old Father Time
6 Sex, Lies and Audiotape
7 [untitled]
8 The Root of All Evil
9 [untitled]
10 The Big Day

Second season
(26 Sep–19 Dec 91)
11 The Gulf Report
12 The Trevorman Cometh [aka Budget Troubles]
13 Henry and Dido [aka When Newsreaders Collide]
14 Baseball [aka Sibling Rivalry]
15 Drunk Minister [aka What Shall We Do with the Drunken Cabinet Minister?]
16 Alex and the Interpreter
17 Hoax
18 Don't Mention the Arabs
19 Damien Down and Out [aka No News Like Bad News]
20 The Evangelist [aka Divorce Blues]
21 George's Daughter
22 Dave's Day
23 The Christmas Party

Third season
(7 Jan–18 Mar 93)
24 In Place of Alex
25 Sally's Accountant
26 Henry's Lost Love
27 Helen'll Fix It
28 Sally's Libel
29 Lady Merchant [aka Sir Roysten's Wife]
30 The New Newsreader
31 Joy
32 Paintball
33 George and his Daughter
34 Awards

Fourth season
(29 Sep–15 Dec 94)
35 The Undiscovered Country
36 Quality Time
37 The Day of the Mum
38 Births and Deaths
39 Helen's Parents
40 Sally in *TV Times*
41 Crime Time
42 No More Mr Nice Guy
43 Henry's Autobiography
44 The Strike
45 The Wedding
46 Damien and the Weather Girl

[Episode titles are not given on-screen. Our titles derive from video releases, Hat Trick production information, and from listings in the *TV Times, Radio Times and The Independent.*]

Damien uses 'creative props' in his reports (George says that his teddy-bear, Dimbles, has 'visited more major disasters than Margaret Thatcher').

Sir Roysten puts in place his own bullshit-speak executive, Gus Hedges (he of the 'I'm not here' catchphrase), and simpering airhead newsreader Sally Smedley. She is to work alongside the experienced, seen it/drank it/shagged it-all anchorman Henry Davenport. The fine cast found themselves well served by the effortless quality of their scripts, adopting a dry delivery that underplayed the sometimes near-the-knuckle nature of the comedy.

The hook of the series was that, although the basic plots of episodes were written in advance, spaces were left for up-to-date news gags to be inserted, whilst the episodes themselves were filmed days before transmission (and edited on the day itself) to keep the humour as fresh as possible. When the first episodes were broadcast, many journalists and newsmen were reported to be astonished by the accuracy with which the series had captured the average newsroom.

The first season crept into Channel 4's schedules with little pre-publicity in the summer of 1990. What audience it had, mainly stumbled across the series by accident. Some viewers were doubtless put off by the somewhat obscure title (supposed to refer to a last-minute decision to drop a story, but actually a meaningless phrase: the original proposal was *Dead Belgians Don't Count*). Nevertheless, helped by word-of-mouth, the series gained a dedicated following which led to an almost immediate repeat run, the episodes prefixed by caption slides and a voice-over to explain some of the, by now non-topical, references.

Great moments included the office sweepstake on what Henry's first words would be to Sally on her arrival (on learning that Henry is having a drink in his dressing-room Dave declares 'Fancy a shag is down to ten to one'), the running jokes about George's nightmare home life (in a dream-sequence Henry reads a news report of the collapse of George's house), Gus employing a 'stress expert' who causes more harm than good, and Dave recording Sally making love to a technician.

Although mostly studio-bound, the series did occasionally record filmed inserts, mostly Damien's news items, which included the famous firing squad scene and one in which Damien thinks that an African child looks 'too happy' to do a Michael Buerk-style 'seething tide of humanity' report and so beats her up. The final episode had a proposed visit to the station by the prime minister scuppered due to faulty lighting.

By the time the second season began, with an episode in which the team reviewed their coverage of the Gulf War, the audience had grown. The season covered such unusual subjects as Sally's conversion to Christianity, George's sadistic teenage daughter, the office softball team's first (and last) game, and the long-running saga of the office photocopier (with Trevor Cooper as the long-suffering repair man). Damien finds that there is a reporter even more ruthless than himself, the office faces the threat of 40 per cent redundancies, a Russian diplomat falls in love with Alex and, after the Christmas party, Dave and Alex end up in bed together.

It would be unfair to think of *Drop the Dead Donkey* as a series that merely exploits topicality. For a comedy series that depends for much of its punch on immediacy, the early episodes still seem fresh and (most importantly) funny six years later, whilst the charm of the series is surprisingly subtle, especially considering the time restrictions of commercial television. The series attacked political hypocrisy, media cynicism and new-manism in a most refreshing way. The characterization of the Globelink employees - even semi-regular characters like the cheerless PA Joy - was never less than brilliant. Sometimes the humour was built around serious themes, such as Dave's money problems or Damien's undercover story living as a down-and-out for a week. Little pieces of information about characters' backgrounds between the jokes help to give the series a fullness not normally associated with the areas in which *Drop the Dead Donkey* moves.

After winning many awards for comedy, including a 1992 Emmy for Best Popular Arts Programme, the 1993 season took the series to an even wider audience. Alex had gone, replaced by Helen, a proud lesbian whom Dave and George

The annual Globelink 'Togetherness Minute' gets underway

adore. Henry and Sally lose all of their money to a crooked financier, and a new sports presenter, Pat 'The Panther' Pringle, suffers a virtual breakdown when the howling error that ended his goalkeeping career is replayed during his newsreading debut. ('I had ninety quid riding on that semi-final,' notes Dave. 'That was a lot of money for a twelve year old.') Real-life politicians Teddy Taylor, Ken Livingstone and Neil Kinnock turned up to join in the fun.

The fourth season went on to achieve the series' highest viewing figures, although there was a feeling that some of the targets had become a little obvious. However, a wonderful sense of introspection continued to balance the biting humour: Damien is forced to confront his overbearing mother who is at the root of his psychoses, while Henry seems to regret his decline from committed journalist to sozzled old hack. The series ended in farcical style with Damien's liaisons with a weather girl who's addicted to sex in dangerous places.

Many of *Drop the Dead Donkey*'s stars (especially Pearson and Tompkinson) have graduated successfully to other series. Although a proposed 1995 feature-length episode was abandoned during production, *Drop the Dead Donkey* – the series that discovered 'Virginia Bottomley' is an anagram of 'I'm an evil Tory bigot' – is set to return in the autumn of 1996.

Absolutely Fabulous

- **BBC Television** (BBC2 (1992-94), BBC1 (1995)) ◆ **Colour**
- **18 episodes** (30 minutes)
- **Based on:** an original idea by Jennifer Saunders, Dawn French
- **Writer:** Jennifer Saunders
- **Director:** Bob Spiers
- **Producer:** Jon Plowman

Regular cast: Jennifer Saunders (Edina Monsoon) • Joanna Lumley (Patsy Stone) • June Whitfield (June Monsoon) • Julia Sawalha (Saffron Monsoon)

With: Jane Horrocks (Bubble) • Christopher Malcolm (Justin) • Christopher Ryan (Marshall) • Eleanor Bron (Patsy's Mother) • Kathy Burke (Magda) • Helen Lederer (Catriona Kirk) • Harriet Thorpe (Fleur Capabianca) • Naoko Mori (Sarah) • Adrian Edmondson (Hamish) • Gary Beadle (Oliver) • Lulu (Herself)

It's ok to behave badly, it's ok to be only human. That's the breakthrough message, the first thought of the 90s, that informs two of the finest comedy series of that decade: *Men Behaving Badly* for one gender, *Absolutely Fabulous* for the other.

AbFab, as it's become abbreviated, concerns Jennifer Saunders's Edina Monsoon (a name familiar to viewers of *The Comic Strip Presents*...), a neurotic PR executive, and her relationship with prim daughter Saffron (Julia Sawalha) and nice mother (June Whitfield). The confusing factor in all this is Edie's friend Patsy (Joanna Lumley), an ultra-domineering, ultra-bitchy, yet hugely vulnerable and stupid best mate from hell. At work, Edie is hindered by Bubble (Jane Horrocks), an acutely-observed caricature of a PA.

There are no regular male characters, and, indeed, some straight men might find the series acutely uncomfortable, letting them see, as it does, a complete world that they don't feature in. Gay men, on the other hand, grasped the show to their bosom instantly, resulting in such cultural grabs as the 1994 Sydney Gay and Lesbian Mardi Gras which became virtually an *AbFab* theme party.

Like all good comedy, *AbFab* is true: this generation is irritatingly more conservative than their parents, our best friend always gets up to more than we do, and, yes, we've met PAs just like that, darling. This truth is supposed to be the stuff of satire, but, if so, it's satire between mates, because, monstrous though she is, a lot of people would be proud to be compared to Patsy. This neat trick, inviting us to both ridicule and empathize with characters at the same time, is pure ***Dad's Army***, the highest form of sitcom. The novelty of *AbFab* is that this is the first time we'd been invited to see like this into the lives of women. You can hear the release of it in the audience laughter of the first season: waves of it, each joke breaking into the next in a continual roar of 'Oh my God, that's you and me!' It's not just the character comedy, but script editor Ruby Wax's collection of sharp put-downs that achieves that effect.

The first season is, basically, a cartoon, with characters who are just a bunch of reactions, and all the funnier for that: Edie is selfish, shallow and insecure, Patsy is selfish, shallow and proud of it. Saffy is their protector and frustrated conscience, and Mother has a mean line in innocent (or are they?) *bons mots*. While John Thaw was making a go of *A Year In Province*, Patsy and Edina utterly fail to spend a week there. Edina buys an isolation tank, but is afraid to go in it alone (and can't leave her mobile phone behind). Patsy gets herself an appearance as a fashion advisor on breakfast TV but is unable to remember the word 'accessories'. (Dawn French, who played a proto-Saffy in the *French and*

Saunders sketch that the show is based on, reprised her perky breakfast TV anchorwoman role.)

Instantly, the series became a cultural icon, with catchphrases ('sweetie, darling' and 'surfaces!') and characters and lines ('the last mosquito that bit me had to book into the Betty Ford clinic') that became part of everyday life. The Pet Shop Boys released an *Absolutely Fabulous* single, with sampled dialogue. *Marie Claire*, the fashion magazine, who like most of the series' supposed satirical targets thoroughly loved the parody, allowed Patsy and Edina to 'edit' a supplement in their January 1995 issue. Unfortunately, they then found themselves pinned down by a curt Channel 4 documentary *Absolutely Marie Claire*, obviously made by people who didn't get the point. The cultural fragments of *AbFab* - Bollie Stolly, Harvey Nicks, etc. - will be around long after the series, and the tiny world it described, have gone.

This critical reception (a vital subset of the female viewers the show targeted was female TV executives), including two BAFTAs and a career resurrection for Joanna Lumley, had a terrible effect on the series. In the second season the show became gorged on its own success and thought itself invulnerable. Perhaps it was because the catchphrases were now heard everywhere, and their repetition on TV ceased to be funny. Perhaps it was because every guest star who expressed an interest was invited aboard: Mandy Rice-Davies, Helena Bonham-Carter, Richard E. Grant, Suzi Quatro, Germaine Greer and the voice of Sylvia Anderson featured in the same episode. From being an invitation to laugh at the foibles of the chattering classes the series had verged toward being an invitation for the chattering classes to have a party, one to which the viewer wasn't necessarily invited.

There are some good second season moments, though. This year's foreign adventure was to Morocco, with Saffy sold to slave traders, and the revelation that Patsy had spent some time as a man. 'Death' is a surprisingly deep dark comedy, and 'Birth' sees the house burnt down, Patsy found unscathed, if messed-up, in the ruins.

Interest was, if one can say such a thing about continuing awards and a move to BBC1, dying down. The series was so over-exposed that it seemed to have been around forever. For the third, and declared last, series, Saunders did some brave things, perhaps influenced by the knowledge that American TV was interested in the show. The characters were fleshed out, an initially shocking move that led to less cartoon-style stereotype comedy but allowed deeper issues to be addressed and might have even allowed a continuation. Patsy's motivations, and even a chink of sympathy, were revealed by the arrival of Kate O'Mara as her sister Jackie. In a moment unthinkable in the first series, Edina smacks a man who's been toying with Saffy's affections, her first and only noble gesture. Of course, amongst all this, the waves of laughter had long departed (with the exception of the glorious farce of 'Sex', almost a gesture to show that Saunders could still write a cartoon), but the series ended as a solid and complete statement, rather than sadly wandering off, and the bravery of all those involved in not trying to milk the concept has to be admired.

Avenues not explored by *AbFab* include Jonny, Nikolas Grace's character in the first episode, who was going to be a regular. Rumour had it before every season that Edie's missing son, Serge, was going to come back, played by Dexter Fletcher. (This being another product of the *Comic Strip*/***Press Gang*** mafia, as linked by Bob Spiers.)

It is just as well that the proposed Roseanne Barr version of *Absolutely Fabulous* never made it to the screen. It's doubtful that American TV would have agreed that it's ok to behave badly and be human.

First season
(12 Nov–17 Dec 92)
1 Fashion
2 Fat
3 France
4 Iso-Tank
5 Magazine
6 Birthday

Second season
(27 Jan–10 Mar 94)
7 Hospital
8 Death
9 Morocco
10 New Best Friend
11 Poor
12 Birth

Third season
(30 Mar–11 May 95)
13 Door Handle
14 Happy New Year
15 Sex
16 Jealous
17 Fear
18 The End

The dichotomy of British children's television can be summed up in one line from Hilary Kingsley and Geoff Tibballs's *Box of Delights*, which suggests that while *Blue Peter*'s John Noakes would invariably be 'haring around the Isle of Man TT course, the Magpie team would be in the studio playing with their Scalextric'. The contrast between *Blue Peter* and *Magpie* not only shows clear class and cultural divisions but highlights the nature of the BBC and ITV approaches to children's entertainment.

Blue Peter began in 1958, and, by the time that the classic 60s line-up of Val Singleton, John Noakes and Peter Purves was in place (along with Petra, Patch, Jason and, later, Shep), the programme represented a perfect image of what most parents wanted their children to watch. They could learn about foreign culture on the many special assignments, develop a social conscience via the numerous appeals, and discover the joys of cookery. All manner of gifts could be made from simple throwaway articles, such as washing-up liquid bottles and sticky-back plastic (although few outside the Home Counties could ever find any of the stuff). Occasional pop bands appeared, and there were the memorable moments involving defecating animals (namely Lulu the elephant).

But, for the most part, producer Biddy Baxter and her crew presented a show that was dominated by middle-class notions of what children wanted to see. *Blue Peter*, along with ITV's *How*, saw children as little chartered accountants, the kind of young people that Robert Robinson spent a decade patronizing on *Ask the Family*. It took *Magpie* to shake some pop-star glam into the world of kid's TV. After Jenny Hanley replaced Susan Stranks to join Tony Bastable and Marc Bolan lookalike Mick Robertson, *Magpie*'s trendy attitude provided a welcome - and novel - alternative to *Blue Peter*'s more conservative approach.

Children's TV has tended not only towards the middle classes but towards the Home Counties, being shy of regionalization in terms of accent or content. There are exceptions - *Chorlton and the Wheelies*, *The Flumps*, *Why Don't You (Just Switch Off your Television Set and Go and Do Something Less Boring Instead)?* - but only *Byker Grove* can consistently claim to have expanded regional horizons. The BBC was always stuck - however unfairly - with the reputation of producing children's series that appealed greatly to the sons and daughters of the bourgeoisie, but did little on the inner-city housing estates. From the ground-breaking ***Watch with Mother*** in the 50s, BBC children's TV was safe and cheerful. While ITV's early attempts at challenging the supremacy of Bill and Ben and Spotty Dog centred largely around *Small Time* (with Pussy Cat Willum), by the mid 60s they were offering homes to BBC defectors including Sooty and Pinky and Perky.

John Ryan's *Captain Pugwash* was something of an institution at the beeb. It took the form of a continuous narrative, often stretching over 20 episodes, concerning the crew of the *Black Pig* - Pugwash, the crusty old sea-dog, his first mate, the able seamen (Willy and Barnabas) and the cabin-boy Tom (who seemed to have more brains than the rest of the crew put together) - and their battles with the evil, black-hearted rapscallion, Cut-Throat Jake. Episodes consisted of the most basic animation imaginable: painted backdrops in front of which cardboard cut-out characters made spasmodic, jerky movements. *Captain Pugwash* was so popular that John Ryan was able to sell the BBC another series, *The Adventures of Sir Prancelot*, about a crusading knight and his many and varied battles. Following the example of many of the BBC's historical drama sagas, it had the characters swing from one cliffhanging finale to the next (which is much harder to do in a five-minute animated series than it sounds). The imported *Tales of the Riverbank*, voiced by Johnny Morris, is held with similar affection by a generation.

If real animals were cute, puppets were even cuter. While working as Oliver Postgate's partner in Smallfilms, Peter Firmin had created ITV's *Musical Box*, with Rolf Harris and then Wally Whyton. He also made an owl puppet, Ollie Beak, for Whyton who divided his time between operating Ollie and talking to the puppet Pussy Cat Willum, who was animated by Janet Nichols. Muriel Young provided Wally with some memorable moments of pure comedy as they ad libbed between programmes if there weren't sufficient commercials. One New Year's Day, Wally remembers Ollie Beak coming in with a balloon and announcing 'I've been to the Chelsea Owls' Ball'. 'I didn't know owls had balls,' replied Muriel. 'I don't know how we carried on,' said Whyton later.

Firmin's next ITV project, making the two puppets for *The Three Scampis*, led to one of the BBC's most successful children's character, Basil Brush. The fox with the Terry Thomas voice (supplied by Ivan Owen) moved to the BBC and became a regular feature on *The David Nixon Show*. Most commentators stated that he was the best reason for watching the magician's programme, and sure enough Basil got his own series in 1968. This ran for over ten years as the classic bridge on early Saturday evenings between *Grandstand* and ***Doctor Who***. Brush, with his human partners Rodney Bewes, Derek Fowlds, Roy North, Howard Williams and Billy Boyle, fast-talked his way into the affections of every child in the country. It was impossible not to love Basil, although the wise-cracking fox could be a handful for his co-presenter. 'He liked to surprise me,' Roy North once said, with something approaching understatement. Ivan Owen reportedly became a millionaire through the character. Not a bad way to make money, sticking your hand up a fox's bottom (Boom! Boom!).

Back in the real world, we had *Play School*, which attempted to turn dungarees into fashionable clothing, made Brian Cant into an omnipotent surrogate parent for a generation, and formed television's first exercise in how to patronize your audience. If Humpty and Big Ted playfully guided the young audience through the Round Window towards the joys of *Blue Peter* (they cooked, too), then ITV's pre-school offerings - *Pipkins* and, especially, *Rainbow* - did little to anticipate the comparative anarchy of *Magpie*.

While imported action adventure series like *White Horses* (with its exquisite Michael Carr and Ben Nisbet theme song), *The Flashing Blade* and the enchanting *The Singing Ringing Tree* made their mark in the late 60s, the home-produced variant, like *Freewheelers* or ***The Tomorrow People***, tend to be better remembered these days as telefantasy series for the young rather than children's series *per se*. *The Double Deckers*, on the other hand, was one of the TV institutions of the early 70s, concentrating on a bunch of free-spirited kids who, in the best traditions of Cliff Richard, spent their time in a double-decker bus. Of the cast, Peter Firth's career continued ever upwards, whilst Brinsley Forde gave up acting and became a member of Aswad, but whatever happened to Melvyn Hayes?

Former pop star Freddie Garrity's *Little Big Time* (1971) provided some memorably scary moments, notably in Mike Hazlewood's serial *Oliver in the Overworld*. *Tottering Towers* (1972) featured William Mervyn as the duke of a haunted castle, and Stacey Gregg and Tom Owen as his ghost-hunting grandchildren.

For older children, escapist fantasy came to the BBC in 1966 in the 'swingin'' form of *Quick, Before They Catch Us*, starring Pamela Franklin. In the early 70s, the BBC created a new trend with Kenneth Cope's teenage football saga *Striker* and Sid Waddell's *Jossy's Giants*. This attractive format climaxed in ITV's *Murphy's Mob*, a long-running and popular series starring Ken Hutchison as the manager of a struggling second-division club, trying to stave off relegation as well as a bunch of meddling kids (Kevin Keegan never had these problems). The series also featured Milton Johns, Janet Fielding, Lynda Bellingham and the diminutive Keith Jayne, who was still playing a 15-year-old after six seasons. Other children's drama series of note include the spooky *Carrie's War*, the popular *Follyfoot* and the anarchic *Kids from 47A*. Traditional 'classics' (1968's memorable adaptation of *The Railway Children* is a great example) were a staple diet of the BBC's children's output. Something that, via *Tom's Midnight Garden*, *Five Children and It* and *The Return of the Psammead*, remains to this day.

For the most part, however, it was the animated series that kept children glued to the box. Elisabeth Beresford's *The Wombles*, narrated by Bernard Cribbins, was 20 years ahead of its time, stressing environmental conservation (although Mike Batt's string of songs for the creatures were something of an acquired taste). Psychedelia came to television in the form of Hilary Hayton's *Crystal Tipps and Alistair*, a fable surrounding a girl with a severely swollen haircut and her psychotic dog. *Roobarb* (voiced by Richard Briers) was a surreal mixture of half-completed animation and silly voices.

Michael Cole's *Bod* was a bizarre five-minute epic, narrated by John Le Mesurier, which featured droll stories concerning the deformed eponymous hero (whose body was a triangle), together with Aunt Flo, Frank the Postman, Farmer Barleymow and PC Copper. *The Mr Men*, voiced by Arthur Lowe, was patchy, depending for much of its charm on the identity of the lead character: the stories involving Mr Tickle, Mr Silly or Mr Small were pretty good for a laugh.

The late 70s provided a further contrast between the BBC's and ITV's styles of live action children's TV. Saturday morning, normally a slot given over to cartoons, adventure serials and linking features such as the BBC's *Zokko!*, received an umbrella-look when the BBC began *The Multi-Coloured Swap Shop*, with main presenters Noel Edmonds and Keith Chegwin. ITV's response to the BBC's slightly bland concept was the wild anarchy of *Tiswas*. *Tiswas*, with its custard pies, Spit the Dog, Sally James's 'almost legendary' pop interviews and a mix of studio slapstick and cartoons, blew the BBC show out of the water. Introduced by Chris Tarrant, with the help of Lenny Henry, Bob Carolgees, John Gorman and Clive Webb, *Tiswas* led to an adult version (the diabolical *OTT*) and is still remembered with a smile by millions of (mainly adult) viewers. And remember, the Phantom Phlan Phlinger is still out there somewhere.

When children's television works well, the influence carries on towards adulthood, **Grange Hill** and **Press Gang** covering adult themes in the context of the teenage rites-of-passage serial. When true adulthood comes, we don't so much put away childish things, as bring them into our new world: thus we have Basil Brush and Parker from *Thunderbirds* as guest managers on *Fantasy Football League* and Danny Baker's celebrations of icons such as Johnny Morris, Pinky and Perky and Peter Purves on *TV Heroes*. Even *Rolf on Saturday - OK?* is probably nostalgically remembered by someone.

Children's television often seems to be dying on the vine at ITV, and flourishing at the BBC, but there continue to be signs of life on the commercial station. *Children's Ward* (latterly *The Ward*) deals with modern issues at least as well, if not so boldly, as the BBC's *Byker Grove*. The latter series, based in a Geordie youth club, can claim to be central to a great many children's lives, a ***Grange Hill*** for the 90s which reflects the needs of its audience. A poll of its viewers concluded that they wanted more of issues such as teenage pregnancy, drug use and death, as long as that last one didn't touch heart-throb PJ.

Both these series are far more energetic than the BBC's static *Chronicles of Narnia* and their current fetish for nostalgia trips like *Just William*. Having said that, ITV have mysteriously long-running rubbish like *Woof!* to their credit. The corporation have decided to reoccupy the high ground of adaptations with quality productions like *Elidor* and the enormously welcome return of Richard Carpenter with his adaptation of *The Borrowers*. *The Animals of Farthing Wood* was animation at its heart-warming best.

ITV remain mired in co-productions and lacklustre original series, though Cosgrove Hall continue to impress with *Avenger Penguins*, and series like *Reboot* and Terry Pratchett's *Johnny and the Dead* can't help but stand out.

Of course, the depth and range of children's television in many ways prevents detailed analysis of the genre as a whole. ***Clangers*** has little in common with *Animal Magic*, which has little in common with *Vision On*, which has little in common with *Mary, Mungo and Midge*. The programmes are not immune to evolution and change: ***Danger Mouse*** grew from being a continuous five-minute serial cartoon into a self-contained weekly series.

Ultimately, children's TV represents a building block in preparing the child to face the outside world. The naiveté which still exists around the very young gives way to phases of questioning, discovery, the development of humour and, finally, the loss of innocence. To today's youngsters, with a children's TV diet that is becoming increasingly (and depressingly) Americanized, we offer our sympathy, but to them, we are probably boring old has-beens anyway. After all, we would sooner watch ***Clangers*** than *Mighty Morphin Power Rangers*. We may be wrong in believing that the former is better (and more adult) television, but we have yet to be convinced.

Watch with Mother

- **BBC Television** (BBC1)
- **Originally B&W**
- 1953-80

It is probably difficult for a generation of youngsters who have grown up on an undiluted diet of *Neighbours*, Nobby the Sheep and WWF Wrestling to comprehend a time when the extent of TV output for the very young was a pre-school version of *Jackanory* and four elementary puppet series. These featured the adventures of a boy and his bear, two strange dudes who lived in flowerpots, three shy woodland creatures, and a family of wooden dolls and their dog who had failed the audition for the Ministry of Silly Walks. Today's kids would doubtless regard these primitive offerings - from a period when, as Geoff Tibballs notes, 'television was still in nappies' - as tacky (and monochrome). However, an earlier generation - who spent their formative years learning to speak by imitating Peter Hawkins's *Bill and Ben* voices - would probably regard the five individual series, transmitted under the collective *Watch with Mother* banner during the late 50s and early 60s, as little short of legendary.

Television was learning to toddle in 1950. The main children's series that the fledgling BBC produced was *For the Children*, starring Annette Mills, which had been running, in one form or another, since 1946 and featured puppeteer Ann Hogarth's creations Louise the lamb, Sally the sea-lion, Prudence and Primrose kitten and television's first immortal symbol, Muffin the Mule. In 1951 the corporation's children's output increased from one to three days a week, being broadcast at 3.45 p.m. on Tuesdays, Wednesdays and Thursdays. The idea was to create a collective bond between mother and child through the shared experience of watching television together, although how successful such a strategy can be is always open to debate.

In 1950 less than one family in twenty owned a television set. However, within three years there would be a dramatic increase in the sale of sets following the Queen's Coronation, and it was against this backdrop of optimism that *Watch with Mother* was launched.

Andy Pandy was with *Watch with Mother* from the beginning. Created by Lingstrom and Mary Adams, Head of Television Talks, the scripts were written by Maria Bird, who also narrated the piece. Andy was a doll who lived, along with his friends Teddy Bear and Looby Loo, in a large basket and came out to play each Tuesday. Audrey Atterbury and Molly Gibson 'pulled the strings' and opera singer Gladys Whitred sang the songs, including the closing epic ('Time to stop play, just for today'). Only 26 episodes were made, but they, along with all the other early-50s *Watch with Mother* classics, were still being repeated as late as 1968. Thirteen new episodes were made in colour in 1970.

The same team came up with another masterpiece two years later when Andy was joined on *Watch with Mother* by *The Flowerpot Men*, perhaps the most well-loved television series of all time. Although the episodes were only made for a little under two years, they too were repeated, to an entirely new audience of tots, for the next two decades.

Voiced by Peter Hawkins, a sound-artist who would write himself into television history as the man behind the voices of *The Woodentops*, *Captain Pugwash* and the Daleks, Bill and Ben's legendary 'falobadobs' became some of the most imitated of all television's catchphrases, leading to worried complaints from some parents that *Watch with Mother* was destroying the English language. Television as the great corrupter: some things, it seems, never change.

Bill and Ben lived in a pair of flowerpots at the bottom of the garden, separated by a little weed ('Weeeeee-d'), in utter dread of the sinister, unseen, figure of the gardener. Each episode centred on some unanswered question of guilt: 'Was it Bill or was it Ben?' Only Weed ever seemed to know the answer.

A year later, the charming *Rag, Tag and Bobtail* was added to the growing roster of talent. A delightful series concerning the adventures of a hedgehog, a mouse and a rabbit, told by Charles E. Stidwill and written by Louise Cochrane, *Rag, Tag and Bobtail* became the regular Thursday addition to *Watch with Mother*. By 1955, the weekday line-up had been completed with the addition of two further series.

Picture Book, as the title suggests, was a kind of early version of *Jackanory*. The principal storyteller was Patricia Driscoll, who was later to play Maid Marian in *The Adventures of Robin Hood*. After Driscoll left for pastures Lincoln-greener, her place was taken by Vera McKechnie. *The Woodentops*, on the other hand, was another product from the *Andy Pandy/Flowerpot Men* stable. Again written by Maria Bird, jerked about by Audrey Atterbury and Molly Gibson, and voiced by Peter Hawkins (along with Eileen Browne and Josefina Ray), *The Woodentops* concerned a family of wooden dolls who lived on a farm. There was Mr and Mrs Woodentop, the twins Willy and Jenny, baby Woodentop, Mrs Scrubbit, Sam the farmhand, Buttercup the cow and, of course, 'the biggest Spotty dog you ever did see'.

This line-up remained unchanged for over ten years, although by the mid-60s the perennial favourites tended to alternate on a specific day (normally Monday) whilst the rest of the week was given over to newer delights such as the ***Camberwick Green/Trumpton/Chigley*** trilogy, *Bizzy Lizzy* and *The Herbs*. By the 70s, when *Andy Pandy*, *The Flowerpot Men* and *The Woodentops* were all shown for the final time, *Watch with Mother* had diversified into escapist fantasy (*Mr Benn*), high-rise angst (*Mary, Mungo and Midge*) and the surreal adventures of *Bod*.

In 1980, nearly 30 years after it began, the title *Watch with Mother* was changed to *See-Saw* (the old phrase being considered 'too old fashioned' by the BBC, who explained that these days mothers were often not around to watch and that most children saw their daytime TV with a child-minder or at a play-group). The priorities may change, but *Watch with Mother* retains its emotive grip on the audience that grew up with it and when, in 1988, the BBC released a video containing extracts from the 50s episodes - the 'golden age' of the show - the tape became one of the biggest selling in the corporation's history.

The little people for whom *Watch with Mother* was made all those years ago may have grown up and acquired little people of their own who are much more concerned with *Biker Mice from Mars* than with tales of flowerpot men, but what's the point of being grown up if you can't act like a child every now and then?

The Magic Roundabout

- **BBC Television** (BBC1), **C4** ◆ **B&W/Colour**
- **Episode length:** 5 minutes
- 1965–71, 1974–77, 1992–94
- **Creator:** Serge Danot
- **Writers/narrators** (English version): Eric Thompson (1965-77), Nigel Planer (1992-94)

It is hard to be objective about *The Magic Roundabout*. Children loved it because it was funny: that much was obvious. However, when you read about Oxford dons petitioning the BBC to get the series moved to a later time slot so that they wouldn't miss it and a mother in Macclesfield calling her child Zebedee, you know you are dealing with something to which the normal rules of a popular television series do not apply.

The Magic Roundabout almost defies description, but here goes: there is a roundabout owned by the 100-year-old Mr Rusty. One of the children who plays on the roundabout, Florence, is able to travel to another dimension (a magical garden) with the aid of a jack-in-the-box called Zebedee. In the garden lives a Hancock-like egoist dog, Dougal, a resigned-but-cheerful snail, Brian, a flower-chewing pink-spotted cow, Ermintrude, and a spaced-out hippie rabbit, Dylan, together with Mr MacHenry and his magic bicycle, a talking train and all kinds of other weirdos.

The Magic Roundabout became one of the most talked about television programmes of the 60s, being seen by many as some kind of definitive statement on the era. All this fuss about a five-minute animated series which, in its native France, had been running for nearly ten years.

The Magic Roundabout was created by Serge Danot as a series for the very young. The original version's scripts are similar in tone to *Play School* but were rewritten (complete with adult allusions) by the dry-voiced Eric Thompson when the BBC bought the show in 1965. Thompson, father of actress Emma, chose to make *The Magic Roundabout* into a vague satire on 60s pop-culture, especially evident with Dylan who, many people suspected, was living on something considerably harder than grass (although maybe that's exactly what he was on...).

These tiny pieces of kitsch were first broadcast by the BBC in the unusual slot of 5.40 p.m., just before the main evening news, in a gap created by the decision to broadcast regional news programmes after the 5.45 news rather than before. Within a couple of months the series had gained a huge following amongst children and, at this stage, a mostly undetected audience of adults. All of that changed in 1967 when the BBC decided to pull *The Magic Roundabout* back an hour in a restructuring of their late afternoon schedules. There are still tales told within the BBC of the deluge of letters and phone calls that accompanied this announcement. *The Magic Roundabout* stayed at 5.40 p.m. and its place in TV history was assured.

First season
(18 Oct–22 Dec 65)
Thirty-nine episodes

Second season
(b. 3 Oct 66)

Third season
(b. 2 Oct 67)

1970 season
(b. 5 Oct 70)

[The initial BBC run ended in Feb 71. The second BBC run extended from Feb 74 to Jan 77. More exact details of the BBC's transmission are currently unavailable.]

First Channel 4 season
(2 Jan–13 Mar 92)
Fifty-two episodes

Second Channel 4 season
(20 Apr–9 Sep 93, 1 Jan–12 Feb 94)
Fifty episodes

The episodes themselves were wonderfully tongue-in-cheek, concentrating on Dougal and Brian's brilliant interplay and Florence's wide-eyed innocence (acting as the voice of the children watching). Many a hip reference (Ken Russell, Jack Scott, Edward Heath, the Beatles) was made, and Dylan, so cool he was in danger of freezing, would casually dismiss every exasperated moan from Dougal with a languid 'Hey, mannnnn!'. Zebedee arrived at the climax of each episode like a *deus ex machina* to end the action with a thoughtful 'time for bed'. With the advent of colour the episodes could at last be appreciated in the outrageously psychedelic shades that they became famous for. It is not hard to understand why, like Disney's *Fantasia*, *The Magic Roundabout* became a buzzword for the counter-culture audience. It looked amazing, it was said, when the viewer was on drugs. Even Dougal's sugar-cube fetish was said to be a subtle reference to LSD abuse.

In 1968 the BBC made a second error when they took the series off and replaced it with another French import, George Croses's *Hector's House*. There was another outcry against what one student paper described as a 'Fascist conspiracy'. In the end, *The Magic Roundabout* returned six months later, and it and *Hector's House* alternated a few months at a time, both series getting viewing figures that approached eight million. The series' fans included the Goodies, whose 1975 Christmas special included giant-sized 'monster' versions of Dougal and Zebedee, and Jasper Carrott, who recorded a risqué take-off of the series' scripts as the b-side of his single 'Funky Moped'. There was even a full-length feature version of the series - the brilliant *Dougal and the Blue Cat* - but by 1977 the series was felt to be anachronistic and it was cancelled.

Still the series wouldn't die. The video boom of the 80s persuaded the BBC to release a batch of episodes which sold ridiculously well. Channel 4 went one better, acquiring the rights to a number of Danot episodes that had never been shown on British television. Due to the death of Eric Thompson, the task of recreating the magical world was given to Nigel Planer.

The Planer *Magic Roundabouts* have proved to be popular and have pleased the old fans whilst introducing the series to a whole new generation of viewers. Some of the jokes may seem a little too modern for Dougal, Brian or Mr Rusty, but one zonked 'groovy' from Dylan can put a smile on millions of faces across Britain.

And when Zebedee suggested that Dougal's proposed autobiography should be called *My Sugar-cube Hell*, doubtless many reformed hippies had a sudden flashback to afternoons in the late 60s, waiting for the most important five minutes of the day.

Camberwick Green/Trumpton/Chigley

- **BBC Television** (BBC1) ◆ Colour
- **39 episodes** (15 minutes) ◆ 1966-69
- **Creator/producer:** Gordon Murray
- **Writers:** Gordon Murray, Alison Prince (co-author of *Trumpton* only)

Narrator: Brian Cant

Generations of children (and their equally addicted parents) sat enthralled by a soap opera populated by puppets whose mundane trials and tribulations were on a par with anything on 'real' television. *Camberwick Green*'s animation was simple, the roads traversed by bike or fire engine were repetitive, and the greatest mystery it ever alluded to was the strange absence of Mr Honeyman (doubtless gossiped to death). Feminists might accuse it of perpetuating contemporary stereotypes, but it was also innocence personified, the 'drama' involving nothing more than races between Windy Miller's penny-farthing bicycle and farmer

Gordon Murray tells Windy that if he gets drunk on scrumpy again PC McGarry will have to arrest him – a scene from *Camberwick Green*

Jonathan Bell's tractor (which ran out of petrol, of course, thus vindicating old rural values). Trumpton and its environs lacked murderers, BSE and vandalism; all was sweetness and light.

Camberwick Green and its sequels formed a benchmark for children's programmes that has rarely been surpassed. Its appeal to adults is legendary (special mention must be made of scouse pop group Half Man Half Biscuit's infamous 'The Trumpton Riots' and their wicked parody of 'Time Flies By ... '). With only a handful of episodes made for each series, Gordon Murray's mini-soaps must be some of the most repeated programmes in the history of television (the very first transmission of *Camberwick Green* was immediately followed by a repeat of most of the episodes).

Camberwick Green began on the first Monday of 1966 in the hugely popular ***Watch with Mother*** slot, cleverly utilizing a music box to introduce the lead character for each episode. 'Here is a box, a musical box, wound up and ready to play ... '

The usual location was the village itself, although events often involved local farms, and the second episode introduced the show's most famous character, Windy Miller (how he missed that windmill sail every week was a never-ending source of amazement). The expertise of Captain Snort and the lads at Pippin Fort was often called upon, although they proved to be about as likely to yomp into battle as Captain Flack's cat-rescuing firemen in *Trumpton* were to meet a real fire, much to the chagrin of both commanders. (One feels that if Flack and his faithful men - 'Pugh, Pugh, Barney McGrew, Cuthbert, Dibble, Grubb' - were ever called upon to douse a towering inferno they would probably pass out in the excitement.)

Murray's gift for hearty characterization was clear from the outset. He made the simple puppets, which were animated by Bob Bura and John Hardwick, and Brian Cant's tone was perfect for the series. However, not all *Camberwick Green* characters proved as popular as Dr Mopp, Mickey Murphy, Mrs Honeyman (plus baby), Roger Varley the sweep or PC McGarry (number 452) - the latter two being examples of a select number of characters who were not confined to one series, also being seen in *Chigley*. Who remembers Mrs Dingle the postmistress, Packet the Post Office puppy, or Mr Dagenham the salesman, who even had an episode to himself?

Murray's follow-up was set in the nearby town of Trumpton, the county capital. More formulaic than *Camberwick Green*, as each episode featured the firemen, *Trumpton* was no less popular than its predecessor. The first episode featured Captain Flack and the lads using their fire engine to stick up posters which, if not actually illegal, was certainly threatening to put the bill poster out of a job. Still, they soon redeemed themselves, rescuing the mayor's hat and, at the end of the series, saving the impressive Trumpton greenhouse from a crumbling chimney.

CAMBERWICK GREEN
(3 Jan–28 Mar 66)
1 Peter the Postman
2 Windy Miller
3 Mr Crockett, the Garage Man
4 Dr Mopp
5 Farmer Jonathan Bell
6 Captain Snort
7 Paddy Murphy
8 Roger Varley, the Sweep
9 PC McGarry
10 Mr Dagenham, the Salesman
11 Mr Carraway, the Fishmonger
12 Mickey Murphy, the Baker
13 Mrs Honeyman and her Baby

TRUMPTON
(3 Jan–28 Mar 67)
1 The Bill Poster
2 Miss Lovelace and the Mayor's Hat
3 Mrs Cobbit and the Ice-Cream Man
4 Miss Lovelace and the Statue
5 Mr Platt and the Painter
6 The Mayor's Birthday
7 Telephone
8 The Rag and Bone Man
9 The Window Cleaner
10 Cuthbert's Morning Off
11 The Plumber
12 Pigeons
13 The Greenhouse

CHIGLEY
(6 Oct–29 Dec 69)
1 Lord Belborough's Secret
2 Bessie to the Rescue
3 The Balloon
4 The Fountain
5 The Garden Wall
6 Binnie and Bessie
7 Lord Belborough's Lucky Day
8 The Broken Bridge
9 Clay for Mr Farthing
10 Trouble with the Crane
11 Apples Galore
12 Willie Munn
13 A Present for Lord Belborough

(The most memorable feature of the Trumpton skyline, however, was the clock which began each episode. 'This is the clock, the Trumpton clock, telling the time, never too quickly, never too slowly: telling the time for Trumpton.')

The other major *Trumpton* characters were the Mayor and the Town Clerk, Mr Troop, and the brain-crushingly annoying Miss Lovelace, who made Mrs Honeyman seem like a paragon of virtue by comparison. How we wished those horrible yappy dogs would end up under the wheels of a car ...

Murray's creations staggered into the 20th century with *Chigley*, an unspecified area of the Trumptonshire countryside partly given over to light industry and dominated by the biscuit factory run by Mr Creswell (employees held a dance at the end of every episode). *Chigley* also featured the pottery and the stately home of Lord Belborough and his impressive butler, Mr Brackett. They ran a vintage steam railway for charitable purposes, the locomotive Bessie often coming to the rescue. Best of all, though, was the wharf with attendant barges and cranes, under the watchful eye of Mr Rumpling. It was from here that Belborough received dubious packages and, in one episode, frogmen were called in to aid in the rescue of a submerged crate. This was edge-of-the-seat stuff.

By the end of 1969 it was all over, bar decades of repeats. Under 40 episodes were made, but each one was a gem. There is a mythical part of Britain that is, for ever, Trumptonshire.

Clangers

- **BBC Television/Smallfilms** (BBC1) ◆ **Colour**
- **27 episodes** (10 minutes) ◆ **1969-74**
- **Creators/writers/producers:** Oliver Postgate, Peter Firmin

Oliver Postgate, together with designer Peter Firmin and their associates at Smallfilms, are responsible for some of the most charming and powerful children's television ever made. *Clangers* is perhaps the pinnacle, though their first puppet characters were *Pingwings*, small woollen penguins who lived in a barn at Berrydown Farm. The duo lived on their wits by the films they sold, working in the barn of Firmin's 18th-century farmhouse near Canterbury.

Pingwings and *Ivor the Engine* were both sold to ITV, *Ivor* being transmitted at lunchtime (though when the series was remade for the BBC he went into the ***Magic Roundabout*** slot just before the news), meaning that board members of Associated Rediffusion had to interrupt their meetings to watch it.

Ivor the Engine was a little green steam engine who talked to his driver, Jones the Steam, in hoots from his organ-pipe whistle. They both worked for the Merioneth and Llantisilly Rail Traction Company Ltd, Jones's immediate boss being Dai Station. Ivor's fire-box provided a home for Idris, a tiny Welsh dragon with a high-pitched voice, after the beast's volcano home became uninhabitable. The stories, quaint and safe, were narrated by Postgate himself.

Next came *Noggin the Nog*, a Scandinavian epic which, as *Ivor* had done, used its episodes to construct much longer narratives. Its title sequence - with Vernon Elliott's icy, evocative music - is still the subject of nostalgic reverie ('In the Lands of the North ... the men of the Northlands sit by their great log fires and they tell a tale ... ') Noggin was a Viking prince, married to the Eskimo Nooka, and a good mate of the mighty Thor Nogson, Olaf the Lofty, Prince Knut (his son), and a very strange bird called Graculus. His arch enemy, and uncle, was the sneeringly bad Nogbad the Bad. Smallfilms sold their new series to the BBC.

The Pogles followed and were ranged against a nasty witch in the first series but she was not seen in the next two seasons of *Pogles' Wood*. The Pogles were a family of small people who lived with Tog, a ginger/pink soft toy brought to life when he helped defeat the witch, and their magic talking plant in a real woodland setting. There was nothing the Pogle family liked more than 'Bread and Butter and Honey', as they sang in a memorable song.

The height of Postgate and Firmin's contribution to popular culture, however, came in 1969 when the BBC screened *Clangers* for the first time. The Clangers live on a small planet (they can walk around it in a few minutes) that looks a bit like the moon, except that it is dotted with metal lids, which they use as protec-

First season
(16 Nov–22 Feb 70)
1 Flying
2 The Visitor
3 Chicken
4 Music
5 The Intruder
6 Visiting Friends
7 Fishing
8 Top Hat
9 The Egg
10 The Hoot
11 Meeting
12 Treasure
13 Goods

Second season
(18 Apr–13 Jun 71)
14 The Table Cloth
15 The Rock Collector
16 Glow-Honey
17 The Teapot
18 The Cloud
19 The Egg
20 The Noise Machine
21 The Seed
22 Pride

Third season
(13 Oct–10 Nov 72)
23 Bags
24 Blow-Fruit
25 Pipe Organ
26 The Music of the Spheres

Election special
(10 Oct 74)
27 Vote for Froglet

tion against things that fall from the sky. Clangers themselves are soft pink creatures, with ears that droop when they are sad or frightened. They live inside the planet, sharing the world with the Soup Dragon who lives in the soup wells (and provides the Clangers with one of their two main food groups), and new arrivals the Froglets, inexplicable orange things who travel in a top hat and live in a vertical pond at the centre of the planet. Major Clanger and Mother Clanger live with Small, Tiny and Grandmother Clangers. Their simple lifestyle of eating Blue String Pudding, communicating with the Iron Chicken (who lives in an iron nest a little way off in space) and finding notes from the Music Trees to power Major Clanger's Music Boat hurts nobody.

Only visitors cause trouble, though the Clangers always do their best to make them feel at home. The Cloud hangs around the planet, providing a spot of rain, and the Skymoos will arrive to eat any vegetable menace. Human astronauts plant a Stars and Stripes on the planet (which Mother Clanger uses as a tablecloth), and return to be scared by the Soup Dragon and covered in Blue String Pudding.

The episodes 'The Visitor' and 'Treasure' reveal most about Postgate's ideas for the series. In the former, a television lands, and the Clangers are fascinated. They like the sweet music the thing provides (though only the Soup Dragon grooves to heavy rock), but when a Napoleonic figure (Postgate himself) comes on the screen, they're upset by his calls to follow him. (The Clangers speak in whistles, and all human speech in the series is muttered gibberish, so we don't know exactly what he says.) They feed the box some soup, which only seems to make it angrier, and finally decide to eject it back into space. In the latter episode, a supply of gold coins lands, and the Clangers all become very selfish, hoarding them up and ignoring each other. Only when Tiny discovers that you can eat them (it's chocolate money) does everyone make friends again. These two parables about greed and brainwashing say a lot about the exemplary life of the Clangers, and Postgate's narration would often attain a poetic quality as it contemplated the differences between life in their world and ours. Like all good children's television the series managed to be moral in the most homespun (or home-knitted) way, and the Clangers continue to be rediscovered by new generations.

Smallfilms's last big production was *Bagpuss*, the saggy old cloth cat created by Peter Firmin. Bagpuss was owned by a little Victorian girl called Emily. Emily owned a rather special kind of shop, a place where she would leave things she had found in the window for the original owners to see and collect. The job of Bagpuss and his friends when brought to life (and from sepia to colour) by the rhyme 'Bagpuss, oh Bagpuss, oh fat furry cat-puss, wake up and look at this thing that I bring. Wake up, be light, be golden and bright, Bagpuss oh hear what I sing', was to find out what the objects were and repair them.

This task fell on the capable shoulders of Professor Yaffle, the old wooden woodpecker bookend, Madeleine the rag doll, and Gabriel the toad, together with the Mice of the Marvellous Mechanical Mouse Organ. (Their leader, Charlie Mouse, would exhort his workers to 'Heave! Heave!', though if they weren't allowed to sing he would threaten that 'Mice strike!') The team would construct stories and songs around the object, leaving the Mice to sing 'We will mend it, we will bend it, we will fix it with glue, glue, glue ...' Memorable scenes from the series included the story of the Hamish, a bizarre Tartan thing, the Mice sailing a slipper down the stairs singing 'Row Row Row the Boat', and the Professor's rather shameful discovery that the mice's chocolate-biscuit-making machine required the continual recycling of just one chocolate biscuit.

Postgate and Firmin have made several films since then, including *Tottie* and *Pinny's House*, the latter based on Firmin's books, but *Clangers*, *Ivor*, *Bagpuss* and *Noggin* remain their best-loved programmes.

Grange Hill

- **BBC Television** (BBC1) ◆ **Colour**
- **361 episodes** (*c*. 30 minutes) ◆ **1978-96**
- **Creator:** Phil Redmond
- **Writers include:** Phil Redmond, Alan Janes, Margaret Simpson, Jane Hollowood, Barry Purchese, David Angus, Frances Galleymore, John Godber, Chris Ellis, Kevin Hood, Sarah Daniels
- **Directors include:** Colin Cant, Roger Singleton-Turner, Christine Secombe, Edward Pugh, David Bell, Margie Barbour, John Smith, Robert Gabriel, Richard Kelly, Andrew Whitman, Riitta-Leena Lynn, Nigel Douglas
- **Producers:** Colin Cant, Susi Hush, Kenny McBain, Ben Rea, Ronald Smedley, Albert Barber, Christine Secombe
- **Executive producers:** Anna Home, Richard Callanan

The longevity of *Grange Hill*, and its status as a 'predecessor' to ***EastEnders***, gives us a hint of the programme's importance. Since its inception in 1978 it has remained robustly popular with its intended audience, defining its genre for over 15 years. Only recently have programmes such as *Byker Grove* come close to challenging Phil Redmond's creation.

The fact that *Grange Hill* is a children's programme, and that its chosen genre is soap opera, makes it all the more unusual. Few series can claim to renew their audience with the regularity of *Grange Hill*, teenagers (and younger children) tending to watch the programme during their years at school before being replaced by the next generation. Adults might watch *Grange Hill* with their children - and remain its most vociferous critics - but few can appreciate the cathartic and liberating thrill that it offers to those who can directly identify with the hopes and fears of the pupils. Its strange escapism - reflecting school life in such a way that comfort can be drawn from the fictional events - ensures that its viewers do not labour under the misapprehension that, say, bullying or the pressure of exams are unique to them. (Only the cynical might ponder why school children - who, almost without fail, loathe school - have so consistently voted *Grange Hill* their favourite programme.)

As well as mirroring the perceived reality of the comprehensive system, like all true soaps *Grange Hill* has had an effect on the strata of society that it represents. It featured a student-written school magazine and abolished the school uniform at a time when most real schools seemed draconian by comparison, and later introduced a radio station and the continental idea of flexitime. It is impossible to say whether students actually pushed for reforms as a direct result of such fiction, but when one sees north-eastern schools making the news because of their low vandalism rate and high student involvement in the running of the school, one is reminded of *Grange Hill* plots some years previously.

The almost immediate success of *Grange Hill* also lay in the obvious reality of its location (filming took place at Kingsbury High School in north-west London) and the depth of former comedy writer Redmond's scripts. Indeed, the best of *Grange Hill*'s characters down the years have been at least as interesting as those in the 'proper' soaps - from Todd Carty's loveable rogue Tucker Jenkins, given his own series when school life terminated, to Michael Sheard's authoritarian, toupee-wearing Mr Bronson.

The criticism that *Grange Hill* has received has been wide-ranging, and often unjustified. Mary Whitehouse said that the series encouraged bad behaviour, ignoring the fact that troublemakers are, invariably, punished; in 1980 an NUT official complained that teachers were treated as buffoons; and, a year earlier, the Women's Institute of Castle Cary, Somerset, passed a motion demanding an instant end to *Grange Hill*. (The previous year, the programme had received a BAFTA award for being the best children's programme.) Phil Redmond commented after one sustained attack: 'I find it rather silly that teachers should write complaining, say, that the headmaster, Mr Llewellyn's, handling of a minor riot in the dining room, with the kids defying the teachers, was some kind of leftish Marxist conspiracy. What they obviously wanted was Llewellyn striding into the scene with a big stick to put the little rebels in their place' - whereas, instead of confrontation, Redmond opted for a more humane, conciliatory approach.

Grange Hill's 'sin' was to actually dare to show the reality of school life, or, at least, a version of it. Somewhat surprisingly, the programme was continually criticized for bad language, although the feeble expletives used by the pupils was the most unrealistic aspect of the entire programme. As noted in ***The Young Ones***, 'We're the only kids in England who don't say f–.' The subject matter was wide: the ubiquitous school bully, shoplifting, a dare craze, truancy, vandalism, smoking, bicycle thieves, racism, crushes on teachers. As the pupils grew older, rivalry with other schools, especially Brookdale and Rodney Bennett (with whom Grange Hill eventually merged), faded in comparison to worries about sex and the prospect of unemployment.

In 1991, after a period comparatively free of criticism when the show seemed content to concentrate on environmental concerns, *Grange Hill* finally tackled the issue that had made it most wary: pupil pregnancy. As one might expect, Mary Whitehouse's National Viewers and Listeners Association condemned the programme, claiming that abortion should not be discussed at so early an hour, doubtless assuming that teenagers can be educated through ignorance. (Indeed, by waiting for so long before tackling the issue, *Grange Hill*'s realism was at stake. The school must have the lowest pregnancy rate in the country!) Chrissy, aged 15, became a mother in the 1992 season, Polly Toynbee defending the programme's bravery in the *Radio Times*.

Subsequent years concentrated on the prejudice against the Irish traveller Mary (played by real traveller Helen McDonagh), an American teacher's controversial version of *Romeo and Juliet*, AIDS and drugs. Rachel Burns, who suffers

Starring: Robert Craig-Morgan (Justin Bennett) • George Armstrong (Alan Hargreaves/Humphries) • Terry Sue Patt (Benny Green) • Todd Carty (Peter 'Tucker' Jenkins) • Michelle Herbert (Trisha Yates) • Vincent Hall (Michael Doyle) • Lyndy Brill (Cathy Hargreaves) • Linda Slater (Susi McMahon) • Ruth Davies (Penny Lewis) • Sean Arnold (Mr Llewellyn) • Mark Chapman/Eadie (Andrew Stanton) • Michael Cronin (Mr Baxter) • Robert Hartley (Mr Keating) • James Wynn (Mr Graham Sutcliffe) • Paula-Ann Bland (Claire Scott) • Mark Burdis ('Stewpot' Stewart) • Peter Moran/Emmett (Pogo Patterson) • Mark Savage ('Gripper' Stebson) • Mark Baxter (Duane Orpington) • Rene Alperstein (Pamela Cartwright) • Gwyneth Powell (Mrs Bridget McClusky) • Brian Capron (Mr Hopwood) • Lee MacDonald (Samuel 'Zammo' McGuire) • Erkan Mustafa (Roland Browning) • Alison Bettles (Fay Lucas) • Nadia Chambers (Annette Firman) • Susan Tully (Suzanne Ross) • Fraser Cairns ('Scruffy' McGuffy) • Jenny Twigge (Mrs McGuire) • John Drummond (Trevor Cleaver) • Simone Hyams (Caroline 'Calley' Donnington) • John Alford (Robbie Wright) • Tina Mahon (Veronica 'Ronnie' Birtles) • Nicholas Donnolly (Mr Mackenzie) • Karen Ford (Ms Booth) • Michael Sheard (Mr Maurice Bronson) • Samantha Lewis (Georgina Hayes) • George Wilson/Christopher (Eric 'Ziggy' Greaves) • Ricky Simmonds (Ant Jones) • Rachel Victora Roberts (Justine Dean) • Sonya Kearns (Chrissy Mainwaring) • Paul Adams (Matthew Pearson) • Michelle Gayle (Fiona Wilson) • Stuart Organ (Mr Peter Robson) • Sean Maguire ('Tegs' Ratcliffe) • Lee Cornes (Mr Geoff Hankin) • Anna Quayle (Mrs Monroe) • Julie Buckfield (Natalie Stevens) • Clare Buckfield (Natasha Stevens) • Adam Ray (Mr Tom Brisley) • Martino Lazzeri (Joe Williams) • Francesca Martinez (Rachel Burns)

First season
(8 Feb–5 Apr 78)
Nine episodes

Second season
(2 Feb–2 Mar 79)
Eighteen episodes

Third season
(8 Jan–29 Feb 80)
Sixteen episodes

Fourth season
(30 Dec 80–27 Feb 81)
Eighteen episodes

Christmas special
(28 Dec 81)

Fifth season
(5 Jan–5 Mar 82)
Eighteen episodes

Sixth season
(4 Jan–4 Mar 83)
Eighteen episodes

Seventh season
(3 Jan–2 Mar 84)
Eighteen episodes

Eighth season
(18 Feb–22 Apr 85)
Sixteen episodes

Christmas special
(27 Dec 85)

Ninth season
(7 Jan–1 Apr 86)
Twenty-four episodes

Tenth season
(6 Jan–27 Mar 87)
Twenty-four episodes

Eleventh season
(5 Jan–11 Mar 88)
Twenty episodes

Twelfth season
(3 Jan–10 Mar 89)
Twenty episodes

Thirteenth season
(2 Jan–9 Mar 90)
Twenty episodes

Fourteenth season
(8 Jan–15 Mar 91)
Twenty episodes

Fifteenth season
(7 Jan–13 Mar 92)
Twenty episodes

Sixteenth season
(5 Jan–12 Mar 93)
Twenty episodes

Seventeenth season
(4 Jan–11 Mar 94)
Twenty episodes

Eighteenth season
(3 Jan–10 Mar 95)
Twenty episodes

Nineteenth season
(23 Jan–28 Mar 96)
Twenty episodes

[*Grange Hill* has, on occasion, been transmitted on BBC2 to make way for the Budget.]

from cerebral palsy, showed considerable bravery when one of the first-year pupils took LSD.

This wasn't the first time *Grange Hill* had handled big issues like drugs, as it had always tried to inform and educate as well as expose (an early plotline advocated judo for girls as a means of self-defence). The final episode of the 1986 season was followed by the 25-minute special *It's Not Just Zammo*, produced by *Newsround* and Drugswatch and presented by John Craven and Nick Ross. The plight of drug-addicted Zammo - and the 'Just Say No' single - were sensible responses to a problem that cannot be ignored.

By concentrating on controversies, one is likely to be blinded to many factors in *Grange Hill*'s favour: the learning and freedom espoused by the various trips (France, the Grand Union Canal, the Isle of Wight, Germany), and the charm of incidental stories, such as the fate of Harriet the donkey. After all, when we hear *Grange Hill* terming the GCSE the 'General Collapse of Secondary Education', we know its heart must be in the right place.

Danger Mouse

- **Cosgrove Hall/Thames** (ITV) ◆ Colour
- **160 episodes** (standard length: 10 minutes) ◆ 1981-92
- **Creators:** Mike Harding, Brian Trueman
- **Writers:** Brian Trueman, Angus Allen
- **Director:** Brian Cosgrove
- **Producers:** Brian Cosgrove, Mark Hall
- **Executive producer:** John Hambley

Voices: David Jason ◆ Terry Scott ◆ Brian Trueman ◆ Edward Kelsey

It has frequently been said that there is no such thing as children's literature, in the sense that while there are novels aimed at adults, all good children's stories will have an adult appeal. *Alice in Wonderland*, *The House at Pooh Corner*, and *The Wind in the Willows* prove the point admirably.

The same can, of course, be said for television. *Bagpuss*, ***Trumpton***, ***The Magic Roundabout***: all had an appeal that transcended age. However, in most of these programmes, adult concepts, in the broadest sense of the term, were largely absent. There was no hidden agenda, no layer of humour marked 'For adults only'.

From the start, *Danger Mouse* was different. It was not adult in the sense of being laden with innuendo, but it was multi-layered to directly appeal to 'children of all ages'. Indeed, Brian Trueman's scripts, with their allusions and self-reference, often seemed to be in danger of leaving children behind. How many ten-year-olds are familiar with Shakespeare and Kipling?

A broad spoof of James Bond and comic-strip superheroes, white-clad, eye-patched Danger Mouse and trusty but cowardly assistant Penfold would speed to the rescue of the world from their post-box secret base, in almost-constant com-

First season
(28 Sep–28 Oct 81)
1 Rogue Robots
2 Who Stole the Bagpipes?
3 Trouble with Ghosts
4 The Chicken Run
5 The Martian Misfit
6 The Dream Machine
7 Lord of the Bungle
8 Die Laughing
9 The World of Machines
10 Ice Station Camel

Second season
(4 Jan-12 Feb 82)
Five 5-min episodes per story
11 Custard
12 Close Encounters of the Absurd Kind
13 The Duel
14 The Day of the Suds
15 The Bad Luck Eye of the Little Yellow God
16 The Four Tasks of Danger Mouse

First season (continued)
(25 Oct–1 Nov 82)
17 The Strange Case of the Ghost Bus
18 Trip to America

Third season
(3–21 Jan 83)
Five 5-min episodes per story
19 Wild Wild Goose Chase
20 The Return of Count Duckula
21 Demons aren't Dull
22 The Invasion of Colonel K
23 Danger Mouse Saves the World Again!
24 The Odd Ball Run-a-Round

Fourth season
(11 Apr–27 May 83)
Five 5-min episodes per story
25 150 Million Years Lost
26 Planet of the Cats
27 Four Heads are Better Than Two
28 The Planet of Terror
29 The Great Bone Idol
30 Public Enemy No. One

Fifth season
(20 Feb–10 Apr 84)
31 Long Lost Crown Affair
32 By George it's a Dragon
33 Tiptoe through the Penfolds
34 Project Moon
35 The Next Ice Age Begins at Midnight
36 The Aliens are Coming
37 Remote-Controlled Chaos
38 The Man from Gadget
39 Tampering with Time Tickles
40 Nero Power

Fifth season (continued)
(25 Dec 84)
41 Once Upon a Time Slip

Sixth season
(3 Jan–28 Mar 85)
42 Viva Danger Mouse
43 Play it Again, Wolfgang
44 Hear, Hear
45 Multiplication Fable
46 The Spy who Stayed in with a Cold
46 It's All White, White Wonder
47 The Hickory Dickory Dock Dilemma
48 What a Three-Point Turn-Up for the Book
49 Quark! Quark!
50 Alping is Snow Easy Matter
51 Aaargh! Spiders!
52 One of our Stately Homes is Missing
53 Afternoon Off - with the Fangboner

The Great White Wonder and Penfold, off to save the world

munication with the authoritarian Colonel K. Danger Mouse (voiced by David Jason - 'Good grief!') was an epic creation, cool and unflappable, but Penfold (Terry Scott - 'Oo 'eck!') got all the best lines.

Their enemy was the toad Baron Greenback, who continually wanted to either enslave the world or destroy it, and his weird caterpillar pet, Nero. Greenback's minions were crow-like Italian gangsters, with Stiletto Mafioso in the unfortunate role of spokesman and scapegoat. (When the American cable station Nickleodeon bought the series it was felt that too many Italian Americans would object to Stiletto's ethnicity, so he became a cockney, some of these re-dubbed episodes later being inadvertently transmitted by ITV.) The Baron escaped from Danger Mouse every time, and the repetition of the chief villain was one of the few flaws in the early seasons. Still, the cast of characters

Seventh season
(4 Apr–27 Jun 85)
54 Beware of Mexicans Delivering Milk
55 Cat-astrophe
56 The Good, the Bad and the Motionless
57 Statues
58 The Clock Strikes Back!
59 'Ee! Tea!
60 Bandits, Beans and Ballyhoo!
61 Have you Fled from any Good Books Lately?
62 Tut Tut it's not Pharaoh
63 Lost, Found and Spellbound
64 Penfold, BF
65 Mechanised Mayhem

Fifth season (continued)
(25 Dec 85)
66 Journey to the Earth's ... Cor!

Eighth season
(13 Nov–18 Dec 86)
(25-minute episodes)
67 Danger Mouse on the Orient Express
68 The Ultra-Secret Secret
69 Duckula meets Frankenstoat
70 Where There's a Well There's a Way
71 All Fall Down
72 Turn of the Tide

Fifth season (continued)
(20–27 Feb 87)
73 Gremlin Alert
74 Cor! What a Picture

Ninth season
(3–10 Jan 91)
(25-minute episodes)
75 I Spy with my Little Eye
76 Bigfoot Falls

Ninth season (continued)
(9 Jan–2 Apr 92)
(25-minute episodes)
77 Statue of Liberty Caper
78 Penfold Transformed
79 Dune with a View
80 Don Coyote and Sancho Penfold
81 Crumhorn Strikes Back
82 Ants Trees and Whoops-a-Daisy
83 There's a Penfold in My Suit
84 Rhyme and Punishment
85 Pillow Fright
86 Heavy Duty
87 The Intergalactic 147

[Stories were often initially transmitted some years after the rest of the season to which they (theoretically) belonged, often forming part of a 'repeats season'. *Count Duckula* (65 episodes) was first transmitted on 6 Sep 88.]

and enemies became increasingly daft: vegan vampire Count Duckula, Professor Squarkencluck, the awesome Frankenstoat, Mac the Fork (a snake) and Dudley Poison (an owl). The plots were wonderfully silly: episodes involved armies of giant chickens or malignant washing machines. Greenback managed to drive Danger Mouse's car by remote control, and fill the Albert Hall with cloned Penfolds, but perhaps the best early story was the epic 'Close Encounters of the Absurd Kind', which made Spielberg's romp look like the kid's stuff it was.

The early five-minute, cliff-hanging format suited the themes well, with the *Dick Barton*-like breathless narration becoming more hysterical and aware of its own fictional nature as the seasons progressed. In one episode the narrator became bored with a wonderfully surreal adventure featuring penguins, and decided, simply by talking about it, to throw Danger Mouse and co. back to the time of Robin Hood. Another ends: 'Next week, join Danger Mouse for an exciting adventure involving the plague of exploding microphones that has been terrorizing announcers all over - BANG!' Danger Mouse also benefited from Brian Cosgrove and Mark Hall's crystal-clear cartoon animation and Mike Harding's hummably simple theme music.

Danger Mouse careered into the 90s, ejecting en route an epic gothic spin-off, *Count Duckula*. By mining another genre, *Duckula* had access to a whole new range of allusions and a different, more localized style of humour. The horror story plots, the creepy castle locations and daft menaces (the Hunchbudgie of Nôtre Dame being an obvious example) provided the programme with much high-quality comedy. ('The Pharaoh Uptshe will only be awoken by an invocation to the god Ra.' 'You mean ...?' 'Yes. Hey Ra, and Uptshe rises!') Its 'steals' were more obvious, and perhaps children found them easier to spot - Dr Jekyll and Mr Hyde, Jack and the Beanstalk - reaching epic proportions in 'Return of the Curse of the Secret of the Mummy's Tomb meets Franken Duckula's Monster'. However, like *Danger Mouse* before it, *Duckula* never neglected its older viewers: how many kids' programmes would, tongue-in-cheek, call episodes 'Restoration Comedy' or 'Transylvanian Homesick Blues'? Duckula himself had certainly come a long way from his initial guest appearance on the mouse's show as the duck that pulled hats out of rabbits.

Real life only threatened *Danger Mouse* once. In 1991 the ninth season was curtailed after only two episodes, the time being needed for extended news coverage of the Gulf War. Wonder what the White Wonder would have made of that?

Press Gang

- **Richmond Films/Central** (ITV) ◆ **Colour**
- **43 episodes** (30 minutes) ◆ **1989-93**
- **Writer:** Steven Moffat (from an idea by Bill Moffat)
- **Directors include:** Bob Spiers, John Hall, Lorne Magory, Gerry O'Hara, Bren Simson, Bill Ward, James Devis
- **Producer:** Sandra C. Hastie

Regular cast: Julia Sawalha (Lynda Day) • Dexter Fletcher (Spike Thomson) • Lee Ross (Kenny Phillips) • Paul Reynolds (Colin Mathews) • Kelda Holmes (Sarah Jackson) • Mmoloki Chrystie (Frazz Davis) • Lucy Benjamin (Julie Craig) • Gabrielle Anwar (Sam Black)

With: Clive Wood (Matt Kerr) • Nick Stringer (Mr Sullivan) • Joanna Dukes (Tiddler) • Rosie Marcel (Sophie) • Claire Hearnden (Laura) • Andy Crowe (Billy Homer) • Penelope Nice (Mrs Day) • Toni Barry (Zoe) • Claire Forlani (Judy Wellman) • Aisling Flitton (Kelly) • David Collings (Mr Winters)

It is hard to imagine life before *Press Gang*, but life there must have been.

Bill Moffat was a Paisley headmaster with an idea for a series. He showed it to Sandra Hastie, a producer for Richmond Films. Bill said that his son (a 24-year-old teacher) should write it. Hastie was dubious until she saw his work. It was 'the best ever first script'. She took it to Lewis Rudd, head of youth programming at Central. The idea was this: an adult newspaper (run by Matt Kerr) funds a junior version, produced at Norbridge High. The paper fosters talent, but also provides a training scheme for non-teachable elements at the school.

The editor of the *Junior Gazette* is Lynda Day, a young girl who 'needs an industrial laser to pierce her ears'. Lynda is tyrannical over her newsroom, and devoted to the paper. Lynda makes jokes about her own ruthlessness, but we sympathize with her because she's repressed a lot of her human qualities. Social occasions make her break out in hiccups, and she has to say 'I love you' in anagrams.

Spike Thomson is the son of an American father and a British mother. He's a witty troublemaker, capable of sudden violence, and named after the dog in Tom and Jerry. Spike was played so well by the British Dexter Fletcher that most people seem to think Fletcher comes from California. Spike is more in love with Lynda than she with him, and, try as he might, he is drawn back to her.

Lynda's best friend, and assistant editor, is Kenny. Kenny has been Lynda's conscience and protector since childhood. He's the shoulder that everybody in the newsroom cries on. Kenny is terminally unlucky in love, twice missing his chance with an Irish girl who he doesn't even realize he's met. The Kenny/Lynda relationship is one of the best depictions of male/female friendship on TV.

Colin Matthews is the second Thatcherite at the *Junior Gazette*. He's someone who could sell anything to anybody. An absurd character at the best of times, Colin is often the one to inject a note of horrid truth into the series, delivering a lecture on child abuse in 'Something Terrible'.

Typically, the school setting is only the start for *Press Gang*. Unlike ***Grange Hill***, the inhabitants of Norbridge High live in a hormonally-charged, vaguely Americanized world of dates and disguises. It could be appalling, but Moffat's sharp dialogue, and his occasional nod to the horrors awaiting outside childhood, save it, and convince us that this is what it felt like for us too.

Press Gang matured in the second season, introducing Sam, head of the graphics department, who was interested in everything Lynda wasn't (boys as a career, fashion, music) and proved equally bitchy. Moffat delights in fantasy, at one point fast-forwarding to the future, when Lynda owns a national paper (and has had Spike's girlfriend arrested as a drug smuggler), and at another doing *It's a Wonderful Life* (as *Moonlighting* had done). 'At Last a Dragon' has Spike taking Lynda out to a dinner of press luminaries, a place where she can make contacts for the future. She's terrified, hiccuping constantly, and Spike makes apologies for her as she prepares to leave early. Then he encounters Colin, trying to sell fake oil wells. Angry at being exposed, Colin gives Spike a lecture on economic reality, saying that the future Lynda won't be interested in a drifter like Spike. On the way out, Lynda thanks Spike for saving her: he grabs her and pulls her back inside. By the end of the evening, she's on her way up the career ladder. At Lynda's gate, the couple stop, and prepare for a goodnight kiss.

'I think you're getting the wrong idea about this kiss' says Lynda. 'No ... this is just a thank you kiss between friends, right?' 'I knew you were getting the wrong idea.'

Snogged senseless, Spike wanders home, and notices a street lamp that hasn't ignited. With a little tap that recalls Jimmy Cagney and Bruce Willis, he zaps it alight. Then he leaps into the air in a joyous freeze-frame.

Bob Spiers, the man responsible for most of *Press Gang's* visual style, cut his teeth on ***The Goodies*** and *The Comic Strip Presents....* The typical *Junior Gazette* shot is a travelling argument between two characters, the punchline of which transfers to another argument going in the opposite direction.

The third season was different, Hastie allowing the characters to mature. Spike has gone back to the USA, Lynda's first line, on discovering that her office paper-skewer is full, being 'I need a new spike!' Asleep one night, an aircraft swishes overhead and, in a magical moment, she hiccups. The degree of audience attention required for that joke to work is enormous, one of the numerous ways

'But we're her friends!' Sarah, Frazz, Kenny, Spike, Lynda and Colin

First season
(16 Jan–10 Apr 89)
1 Page One
2 Photo Finish
3 One Easy Lesson
4 Deadline
5 A Night in
6 Interface
7 How to Make a Killing (part one)
8 How to Make a Killing (part two)
9 Both Sides of the Paper
10 Money, Love and Birdseed
11 Monday-Tuesday
12 Shouldn't I be Taller?

Second season
(18 Jan–12 Apr 90)
13 Breakfast at Czar's
14 Picking up the Pieces
15 Going Back to Jasper Street
16 The Week and Pizza
17 Love and the Junior Gazette
18 At Last a Dragon
19 Something Terrible (part one)
20 Something Terrible (part two)
21 Friends Like These
22 The Rest of my Life
23 Yesterday's News
24 Rock Solid
25 The Big Finish?

Third season
(7 May–11 Jun 91)
26 The Big Hello
27 Killer on the Line
28 Chance is a Fine Thing
29 The Last Word (part one)
30 The Last Word (part two)
31 Holding On

Fourth season
(7 Jan–11 Feb 92)
32 Bad News
33 Un-X-pected
34 She's Got It Taped
35 Love and War
36 In the Picture
37 Day Dreams

Fifth season
(16 Apr–21 May 93)
38 Head and Heart
39 Friendly Fire
40 A Quarter to Midnight
41 Food, Love and Insecurity
42 Windfall
43 There are Crocodiles

in which the series respects the intelligence of its viewers. The continuity in all respects is phenomenal. Not only were the same actresses hired for years-apart appearances as Kenny and Colin's would-be girlfriends, but when, in 'The Big Hello', a corrupt town councillor is trapped through a gimmick involving an answerphone, the list of his crimes includes not only the bad planning that once trapped Spike underground, but the dodgy extension to the sports centre that the team was reporting on in the first episode of season two. (This is also one of the episodes that shows the effect of Moffat's other major influence, *The Front Page*, and the whole genre that followed it.)

'The Last Word' is one of the best examples of British television series scripting. It begins with Kenny finding out that Lynda has 'flirting time with Spike' written into her daily schedule, and ends with a death. A man in a clown mask walks into the office with a gun, and scenes switch back and forth to a funeral. Moffat carefully pares down the survivors, until it becomes clear that one of the main characters is to be the victim. Lynda's efforts to beat the gunman on a mental level, Spike's sudden attempt at violence, and Lee Ross's incredible performance as Kenny is pushed to the edge and shows himself to be willing to die for his friends, make these the best *Press Gang* episodes.

The fourth season was a strange beast, with a tired acceptance of growing up. Kenny had gone, for one thing, and the show was becoming more self-referential. The central theme of the season was parenthood: Spike's father dies, causing him to erupt and destroy the newsroom; his mother seems to be an older version of Lynda, which makes Lynda wonder about the nature of their relationship. Finally, in 'Day Dreams', Lynda's old teacher returns as her guardian angel, and shows her the future.

Steven Moffat wrote the complex and adult *Joking Apart* for BBC2, but returned to *Press Gang* for one last season, which proved to be the whole series in miniature. Two stories that deal with adult issues with the series' own brand of ethics, two incredibly complex farces, a tense thriller, and 'Friendly Fire', which demonstrated the continuity and nostalgia that infuse this series about youth. The finale of the whole series, 'There are Crocodiles', has Lynda facing the boy who killed himself in 'Monday-Tuesday', her own personal demon, as it seems she's caused another death. The newsroom burns around her. Edited down from a 35-minute original, the final episode is nothing short of inspirational, as Lynda denies she's the product of history, guilt or anything but her own hard liberalism, and escapes, philosophically and spatially.

Press Gang was a series that could transport you back to how you felt as a teenager, sharper than the world but with as much angst as acute wit. More than any other series in this book it has to be seen to be appreciated.

Press Gang, the best series in the world.

In Bill Eagles's 1993 BBC documentary *Barlow, Regan, Pyall and Fancy*, Troy Kennedy Martin dismisses the police series for giving the viewer easy answers. 'They superimpose over the anarchy of life a superficial order.'

That's certainly true of ***Dixon of Dock Green***. British television's obsession with crime and the police begins (and in many ways ends) with George Dixon, one of television's first icons. Dixon represented everything that was England in the 50s. He did not take bribes, arrest innocent Irishmen or abuse prisoners because of race or class (he did, in one celebrated episode, conclude that wife-battering was moderately acceptable, but then so did the first episode of ***Z Cars***). George Dixon and his Dock Green colleagues represented a safe image of Britain's protectors from the influence of 'outside evil', as represented by the cosh boys and gangsters who threatened the security of the middle-class television-owning population of Britain.

Dixon of Dock Green wasn't the first British crime series. The pre-war years had produced *Telecrime*, an irregular series of whodunits, along with oddities like Frank Vosper's *Love From a Stranger* (1938). *The Inch Man* (1951) and *Fabian of the Yard* (1954, with Bruce Seton as detective Robert Fabian) continued the trend, but ***Dixon of Dock Green*** was a towering presence over the genre that it shaped for 21 years. Although much of its legacy was negative, and many series were a reaction against it, Ted Willis's creation and its influence should not be underestimated.

In the years that followed the arrival of George Dixon, other programmes trod the ***Dixon*** beat. *Shadow Squad*, produced by Associated Rediffusion in 1957, was a vehicle for Rex Garner, George Moon and Peter Williams. The series, which gave early writing experience to Tony Warren and Harry Kershaw, had viewing figures of over 12 million, but ended just as it was getting interesting (the final episode became TV's first self-reflecting entity by revealing the production crew on air).

Murder Bag (1957), created by Glyn Davies, featured Raymond Francis as Inspector Tom Lockhart. Written by Barry Baker (who had also worked on *Shadow Squad*) and Peter Ling, *Murder Bag* (and *Crime Sheet* which followed it) honed the popular image of the police as protectors of liberty and justice, interested only in keeping the streets safe. *Crime Sheet* became *No Hiding Place* in 1959, with Lockhart (now teamed with Eric Lander as Harry Baxter) becoming the first direct challenge to Dixon's throne. *No Hiding Place* was a touch less stuffy than the BBC series. It didn't contain homilies on the basic goodness of society: it showed that an underworld did exist. 236 episodes were made between 1959 and 1967, Lander leaving after 140 to be replaced by Johnny Briggs as Sgt. Russell. Terence Feely, Leon Griffiths, Terry Nation, Roger Marshall and Dennis Spooner all cut their teeth on tales of Lockhart and his patch. (Lander had a spin-off himself with *Echo Two-Four* in 1963.) Add in the Danziger Brothers filmed series for ITV (*Saber of London*, *The Man from Interpol*), and the climate was right for George Dixon's uptight qualities to be laughed at.

Dixon of Dock Green, however, saw off the pretenders, and grew in strength during the early 60s, closeted in its own twilight world of early Saturday evenings (sandwiched between ***Doctor Who*** and *The Black and White Minstrel Show*) as a national institution. When George gave teenage runaway Jill Adams a smacked bottom in 1963, he wasn't suspended for it but was applauded by most sections of society for bringing some sanity to the problems of 'youth'.

The independent companies tried to be adventurous in response. The film series *Dial 999* brought Robert Beatty to London as a Mountie on detachment, and presented the city in flashy travelogue visuals, whilst claiming to be authentic and made in co-operation with Scotland Yard. They even admitted organized crime existed (in the first episode William Hartnell was seen as the city's Mr Big, pursued by Beatty and his English partner Duncan Lamont). For the most part, however, it wasn't until television discovered intercontinental crime (with *Maigret* in 1960) and socio-realism (***Z Cars*** in 1962) that the first cracks in the public perception of what a crime drama could encompass began to surface.

Maigret was a series of excellent adaptations of Georges Simenon's whodunits, Rupert Davies achieving fame late in his career, as Jack Warner had done. By choosing Davies to play Maigret the BBC managed to avoid silly accents and patronizing images of Frenchness (when Davies met Georges Simenon in Lausanne he was presented with a book in which the author had written 'At last I have found the perfect Maigret'). The character of Lucas - a mere feed to le Patron's brilliance in the novels - was, thanks to Ewen Solon's performance, also popular with the viewers. In the episode 'The Winning Ticket' Solon suggested jumping from a ten-foot wall to make the sequence look more realistic, and broke his leg in three places.

There were twists on the usual detective story: 'Maigret and the Madman' has the lead character shot and confined to bed for the entire episode, although his relentless investigations continued unhindered. 'High Politics' has Maigret dabbling in the political world he so despises, whereas 'Love From Felicie' examines the man's own ethical standards as he reads a personal diary. The usual themes were Gallic jealousy and the extreme passions within a family, and Maigret's inability to take a peaceful holiday (doubtless to the great consternation of the long-suffering Madame Maigret). The BBC's confidence in the series even extended to filming some exteriors in Paris, a most expensive venture in the 60s.

Z Cars, however, was the mould-breaker, portraying a world of poverty and dog-eat-dog that was familiar to most television owners (the cod working-class of Dock Green didn't exist in the real world, but the head-bangers of Newtown probably did). Future *Law and Order* and ***Between the Lines*** producer Tony Garnett appeared in both series playing similar 'angry-young-working-class-male' roles. In ***Dixon of Dock Green*** there was no doubt that he was the villain, but in ***Z Cars*** things weren't so clear cut: '***Z Cars*** was much edgier and more complex,' said Garnett. 'That was the difference in the two shows. ***Dixon*** was family entertainment for a Saturday evening. The quality of reassurance.' Aside from its own notable achievements, ***Z Cars*** also led directly to the spin-offs

Softly Softly and *Barlow at Large* and, indirectly, to ***The Sweeney*** and its BBC clone *Target*.

Crime drama also covers the world of espionage, the domain of secret agents and beautiful girls. The early 60s saw the beginnings of the James Bond films and countless television variations on the theme (Bernard Archard in *Spy-Catcher* is one example), but the most important development in the world of spying came with *Danger Man*, which was about as far away from 007 as the Z Victor boys were from George Dixon.

Danger Man, devised by Ralph Smart for ITC in 1960, made its star, Patrick McGoohan, the highest-paid actor on TV. John Drake, 'The spy with no gun and no girl', worked for NATO, and had adventures in European capitals that looked suspiciously like re-dressed Borehamwood backlots. Writers included Brian Clemens and Ian Stuart Black. The series laid the foundations for later excursions in the field by ITC: *The Baron*, *Man in a Suitcase*, ***Randall and Hopkirk (Deceased)***, *The Champions*, ***Department S***, ***Jason King***, and *The Adventurer*. The BBC's *Paul Temple* (with Francis Matthews) was a competent variant.

John Creasey's *The Baron* concerned art dealer Steve Forrest, who was seconded to British Intelligence. What it lacked in common sense (Monty Berman and Terry Nation were never television's most down-to-earth writers), *Man in a Suitcase* (Dennis Spooner and Richard Harris's most satisfying blend of the outrageous) more than made up for. It made a star out of the cool, laconic Richard Bradford, whose tremendous ex-CIA bounty-hunter, McGill, managed to fight thugs every episode without once dropping the cigarette from the corner of his mouth or losing his shades.

The dark side of espionage was represented by ***Callan***, the BBC's *The Mask of Janus* and Roger Marshall and Anthony Marriott's grim private-detective saga *Public Eye* (in which Alfred Burke's seedy anti-hero Frank Marker spent a decade walking a knife edge between the law and anarchy). *Public Eye* lacked the exotic trappings of the ITC series. It had weird episode titles, off-beat plots, sleazy criminals, and even sent its hero to prison after being convicted of possession.

When Edward Boyd created *The Odd Man* for Granada in 1962, it was seen at the time as simply another step away from the formulaic nature of the police series. In retrospect, it was much more. Critic Dave Rogers described it as 'a dark, weird and wonderful series of Hitchcockian overtones ... relating how five recurring characters interacted when faced with crimes of murder, vengeance and international intrigue'. Aside from having two episodes written by Jack Rosenthal and Harry Driver, the series, whose nominal star was theatrical agent Edward Richfield, mainly focused on Keith Barron's Sergeant Swift and William Mervyn's Inspector Rose. *The Odd Man* was so popular that, after two seasons, Granada took Swift and Rose into another series, *It's Dark Outside*. This was described by its producer, Derek Bennett, as a 'weird, edgy, neurotic, high-powered and sometimes frightening picture of the modern world'. The series also starred John Carson, Anthony Ainley, and Oliver Reed as the main villain. It had a number one hit theme song ('Where are You Now?' by Jackie Trent) and led to a third series, *Mr Rose*, featuring the, now-retired, Rose in 1967. This latter series was devised by Philip Mackie, and used writers such as David Whitaker, Robert Holmes, Roy Clarke and Martin Worth. The chain continued when Boyd took some of his plot elements into ***The XYY Man*** and ***Strangers***.

Television's fascination with historical crime drama began partly out of necessity (TV's dependency on literary adaptations) and partly because the crime story is archetypal and, therefore, timeless. If ***Dixon of Dock Green*** represented conformity and familiarity, then how much more so did the works of Agatha Christie and Sir Arthur Conan Doyle? The BBC led the way with regular Sherlock Holmes adaptations, while the market for this type of story opened even further with the huge success of Ian Carmichael's portrayal as Dorothy L. Sayers's Lord Peter Wimsey (a role later played with greater depth and more attention to source material by Edward Petherbridge), and with charming Victorian melodrama like *Raffles* (featuring Anthony Valentine) and the underrated *Cribb* (starring Alan Dobie).

But the standard-bearer of the genre was still the modern police series and the 60s and 70s saw dozens of them. Some tried to mimic ***Dixon*** and present gentle tales of toned-down criminality that could all be sorted out with a kind word. *Hunter's Walk* was created by Ted Willis after he had left ***Dock Green*** behind, and was set in the peaceful surroundings of Northamptonshire, whilst *Cluff* was a kind of north-country *Maigret* featuring Leslie Sands. The later *Sutherland's Law*, with Iain Cuthbertson and Gareth Thomas, also belongs in this category.

Other series tried to out-grit ***Z Cars***, including ATV's *Gideon's Way*, with John Gregson. These days the series is best remembered for featuring one of John Hurt's first TV appearances, escaping from prison with fellow inmate Derren Nesbitt. Nesbitt would later star in the hard-hitting *Special Branch*, the first of Euston's new breed of police series. This was a landmark in being the first series to present a 'policeman hero' as a trendy ladies-man in the Steed/Jason King mould. When Nesbitt left the series after three years, he was replaced by a pair of wise-cracking CID head-cases played by Patrick Mower and George Sewell. Another mould was about to be broken.

Meanwhile more traditional moulds were being glued back together as *The Strange Report* (in which Anthony Quayle's criminologist Adam Strange solved cases that baffled even Scotland Yard) and *The Expert* (with Marius Goring) updated the themes of the amateur sleuth. Ivor Jay's *Fraud Squad* brought crime into the financial world, and *Van Der Valk* (a splendidly viewer-friendly series starring Barry Foster, Nigel Stock and Susan Travers) resurrected the spirit of *Maigret*. Other ITV crime series of the era include *Crane*, a hugely popular detective series starring Patrick Allen (which spawned a spin-off series, *Orlando*), *The Main Chance*, a star vehicle for John Stride, and *Big Breadwinner Hog*, a memorably nasty look at the seamier side of London's underworld starring Peter Egan (the first episode climaxed with a character having corrosive liquid thrown in his face). *The Persuaders!*, on the other hand, was the garish 70s personified, with Roger Moore and Tony Curtis as a pair of playboy adventurers blackmailed into fighting injustice. The shirts were louder than the gunfire as Moore and Curtis bickered their way across the Continent with a swagger and wit that saves the series from the outright parody it probably deserves.

New Scotland Yard was television's first (of many) 'new ***Z Cars***'. If the Newtown boys were the first policemen who looked and talked in realistic terms, then John Woodvine, John Carlisle, Clive Francis (the son of the actor who played Inspector Lockhart) and their Scotland Yard colleagues sounded like they really knew the streets. The series had writers including Philip Martin, Don Houghton, Victor Pemberton and Richard Harris (who named two of his characters Clemens and Fennell after ***The Avengers***' producers), and ran for three years, ending just as its obvious successor, ***The Sweeney***, began.

If perception of the police force was changing, so was the medium's attitude to criminals. In 1971, Verity Lambert decided it was time that some of the criminals had their say. She and Rex Firkin (who would later produce *New Scotland Yard*) brought Keith Waterhouse and Willis Hall's *Budgie* to LWT, and broke the back of the police drama series, opening the way for later series like *Big Deal*. After a few episodes spent with Budgie Bird in Soho, 'running' for Iain Cuthbertson's mesmeric Glasgow gangster Charlie Endell ('There are two thing ah hate in life, Budgie, an' you're both of them!'), it was impossible for audiences to see criminals in the same light. Budgie's life was a mess, his wife (Georgina Hale) having an affair with his best mate, 'Wossname' (James Bolam), whilst Budgie was banged up with psychotic Dutchie Holland (Bill Dean). If Adam Faith was the face of the early 70s, it was because his character touched something in all of us. Even George Dixon would have been spat at had he tried to arrest Budgie. In 1976, Dixon left our screens for the last time. In the same year, the Sex Pistols were singing about 'Anarchy in the UK', and in ***The Sweeney*** Regan and Carter were trying hard to stop it.

By the late 70s there were more questions being asked about the 'whys' of crime than the simple 'whos'. The traditional police series diversified and became much less black-and-white in its scope and intent. There was the comedy-drama of ***Minder*** and *Lovejoy*, tough inner city detective series like *Hazell*, ***Shoestring*** and *The Hanged Man*, community policing in *Juliet Bravo*, ethnic tension in *Gangsters* and *The Chinese Detective*, feminism in *The Gentle Touch*, escapist fantasy with ***The Professionals***, *Dempsey and Makepeace*, and *C.A.T.S. Eyes*, location travelogue in ***Bergerac*** and ***Strangers***, and spy-realism in *The Sandbaggers*. All of these have something worthwhile about them (yes, even *Demspey and Makepeace* on a good day, though Roy Clarke's *Pulaski*, with the brilliant pairing of David Andrews and Caroline Langrishe, parodied it wonderfully).

Hazell, the creation of Gordon Williams and Terry Venables, sizzled under Richard Harris's assured hand and made Nicholas Ball's cynical cockney private eye into a cult figure. Ian Kennedy Martin created both *The Chinese Detective* (starring David Yip as the loner Johnny Ho), which ripped into the police's (and society's) racism with gay abandon, and *Juliet Bravo* (with Stephanie Turner and David Hargreaves in roles, and a setting that predicted *Heartbeat*). Even *C.A.T.S. Eyes*, a one time byword for everything that is arrogant about TV's underestimation of the public intelligence, managed one cracking episode (Don Houghton's 'Frightmare', in which Lesley Ash, spiked with drugs, spends half the episode suffering disturbing hallucinations).

Gangsters, which began as a Philip Martin script for *Play for Today*, was better. The play was a hard-hitting tale of drug-trafficking, illegal immigration and multi-racial extortion. Directed with considerable flair by Philip Saville, it won rave reviews, notably for the performance of Maurice Colbourne as the anti-hero Jack Kline. The series that followed, featured British television's first ethnic leading man, Khan (Ahmed Khalil). He was an undercover security service agent, a much more sympathetic character than the lethal Kline whom Khan gets off a manslaughter charge to help him penetrate the white underworld. Although all of the loose ends were buried in a concrete slab by the end of the six episodes, a second season followed, adding Chinese triads to the plot. In the final episode, Kline is killed by a triad executioner, and the series ended, to much baffled scratching of heads. Martin, who appeared at various moments in India dictating his script to a local typist, completed the final page and threw it out of the window at a crowd of boys below. It was all very strange.

Not all crime shows of the 70s exhibited the care lavished on *Gangsters*. Indeed, as a whole, the 'police drama' just got nasty. ***The Sweeney*** did it with some style, updating ***Z Cars*** for a younger, tougher, audience with more stomach than their parents. G.F. Newman's *Law and Order* did it brutally, but with one foot firmly in the real world. ('It shows the police, to a man, to be prepared to bend the rules. I don't want the police to do that in my name', noted Newman. Top policeman Paul Condon has called the series 'a sickening travesty'. Others may disagree.) *Target*, a mistaken venture from day one, did it with comic-strip brutality that left even TV drama's strongest defenders in the same corner as Mary Whitehouse. *Target*, too, produced one great episode, 'Big Elephant', directed by Douglas Camfield who must have thought he was doing ***Shoestring*** that week, with Ken Hutchison as a tramp who accidentally finds himself with two million quid's worth of heroin and Katy Manning as a pathetic smack addict.

The BBC's production of John le Carré's *Tinker Tailor Soldier Spy*, directed by John Irvin and produced by Jonathan Powell, probably killed off the popular image of the spy as James Bond. Alec Guinness's superb performance as Smiley was matched by the incredible supporting cast, which included Bernard Hepton, Terence Rigby, Ian Richardson, George Sewell, Nigel Stock, Hywel Bennett, Beryl Reid, Joss Ackland, Sian Phillips, Michael Jayston and Ian Holm. Three years later, Smiley was back in *Smiley's People*, which reflected the 80s perception that law and order was becoming a less simple equation than before.

The historical series was revived effectively by Granada in ***The Adventures of Sherlock Holmes***, and then refined by the BBC's *Miss Marple* and LWT's *Agatha Christie's Poirot*, and continues to draw huge audiences to *Campion*, *Cadfael*, and the Michael Gambon remake of *Maigret*. Gerald Seymour's sympathetic and realistic thrillers *Harry's Game* and *The Glory Boys* undermined notions of good and evil in political terrorism.

The Bill, on the other hand, began as a simple exercise in producing a ***Z Cars*** for the 80s. Thames' most successful series since ***Minder*** got a fully fledged soap format in 1988, going twice weekly (as ***Z Cars*** had once done). ***The Bill***, as might have been expected, received criticism for daring to show some policemen as 'liars, cheats and bullies'. However, it still represents the acceptable face of police drama. It is not unreasonable to suggest that *The Fear*, ***Between the Lines***, ***Cracker***, *Back-Up* and *Thief Takers* all owe much of their success to the groundwork laid by ***The Bill***.

The development of the genre became the focus of huge debate when, following the success of adaptations of P.D. James's Inspector Dalgleish stories in the early 80s (starring former *Sandbagger* Roy Marsden), ***The Ruth Rendell Mysteries*** and Colin Dexter's ***Inspector Morse*** became ITV's two biggest commercial success stories of the era. Using a mixture of traditional crime elements, but set against idyllic backdrops, with large doses of new-manism, philosophical deduction and intelligence, crime drama was back in the province of its spiritual heirs, Holmes and Poirot. The casting of John Thaw (as Jack Regan the classic example of 70s intolerance at its height) in the role of the opera-loving, crossword puzzle-solving, real-ale drinking, depressive Morse was a stroke of genius, not only providing Thaw with a great part, but also putting the new trend into historical perspective. From here, it's only a short jump to *Resnick*, *Wycliffe*, *A Touch of Frost*, *The Inspector Alleyn Mysteries*, *The Chief*, *99-1*, *Pie in the Sky* and many other 90s productions. Tom Wilkinson, Jack Shepherd, David Jason, Patrick Malahide, Tim Pigott-Smith, Martin Shaw, Leslie Grantham, Richard Griffiths and millions of viewers have a lot to thank Thaw and Dexter for.

The trend even extended to Glasgow with *Taggart*, where, before his recent death, Mark McManus's performance was at the centre of a serial covering similar themes against a harsh industrial backdrop, streaked with creator Glenn Chandler's wry humour. If crime drama of the 80s had one significant image, it was that of Taggart and Jardine (James MacPherson) standing amid the carnage of 'Rogues Gallery', discussing, in philosophical terms, the existence of God. It is magical, and has no respect for George Dixon.

The BBC's major offering of the era, *Rockcliffe's Babies*, was a great series, which made Joe McGann a star and led Ian Hogg as the eponymous Rockcliffe into a spin-off after two hugely successful seasons. *Rockcliffe's Babies*, with its trainee detectives (the stunning Susannah Shelling and Alphonsia Emmanuel, street-kid Brett Fancy, West Country boy John Blakey), went into tenement shanty-towns unlike anywhere that the average viewer had ever been. It didn't matter, because the stories felt right. The BBC made a serious mistake in assuming that Rockcliffe himself was the reason for the series' success, and the following *Rockcliffe's Folly* was aptly named.

Meanwhile, strange things were happening to suspense fiction. Playwright Howard Brenton created the complex narrative of *Dead Head*, a surreal, multi-layered story concerning a serial killer. The thriller included some graphic, sadistic violence and (apparently of vital importance to the *Daily Express*) a scene in which hero Eddie Cass (Denis Lawson) is tied to a bed and raped by a welly-wearing yuppie (Tacy Kneale). The rest of the cast included Lindsay Duncan, George Baker, Simon Callow and James Warwick. In a similar vein, Desmond Lowden's tense thriller *Chain* saw computer whizz-kid Peter Capaldi and lawyer Robert Pugh investigating fraud and murder. *Bird of Prey* (starring Richard Griffiths) also dealt plausibly with computer-crime, whilst *Thin Air* (with Kate Hardie and Nicky Henson), *Muck and Brass* (starring Mel Smith), and *GBH* tackled corruption.

In 1989, to celebrate the fortieth anniversary of the 'death' of George Dixon in *The Blue Lamp*, Arthur Ellis's *The Black and Blue Lamp* was broadcast. This borderline telefantasy play focused on Dixon's killer, Tom Riley, and Constable 'Taffy' Hughes, walking out of *The Blue Lamp* and into a quasi-80s crime drama series *The Filth*, full of coppers on the take and hip street-talk. The sight of cosh-boy Riley whimpering as he is beaten up in his cell for simply asking what a 'blag' is was a disturbing highlight of British crime drama. The police, represented by John Woodvine and Kenneth Cranham, were the villains of the piece, and Riley's world no longer has any meaning. *The Black and Blue Lamp* was an attempt to show how attitudes to the police in the media (and in life itself) have changed over the past 40 years.

An interesting aspect of crime drama in the 90s has been television's willingness to subvert themes done to death by the film industry. Serial-killers are ten-a-penny in Hollywood, but Lynda La Plante's BAFTA-winning *Prime Suspect*, in which Helen Mirren and her murder-squad detectives track a sadistic killer, was compelling and had much to say on sexism in the force. *Virtual Murder* was a British *Moonlighting*, starring Nicholas Clay and Kim Thomson as a criminal psychologist and his partner.

Jimmy Nail and Ian La Frenais's *Spender* had Nail as an outcast returning to his roots amongst the vast and changing landscape of the north-east. There was room for broad comedy (notably in the character of Stick (Sammy Johnson), Spender's building society-robbing leg man), social themes and police corruption (the involvement of Ian Cullen's detective in drug trafficking to pay for his daughter's university education). Other episodes dealt with politics (Amanda Redman's Tory candidate answering questions on the health service with theoretical Thatcherism) and the pressures of tabloid fame (a Gazza-like footballer disappearing after being hounded to the point of breakdown). The series took the 'rock soundtrack' nihilism of American series like *Miami Vice* to a new and unusual extreme. 'Street' and dangerous, the 1991 season ended with a story about 'ram-raiding', the 90s phenomenon that mixes car crime and burglary - a television first. The series had a weird poetry of its own, although it, along with ***Jason King***, ***The Sweeney***, ***The Professionals*** and ***The Bill***, were beautifully satirized by the *Comic Strip* episode 'Detectives on the Verge of a Nervous Breakdown'. Similarly, *The Detectives* possibly says more about the public's perception of the crime drama genre than a hundred books might.

As Ben Elton noted in *Gridlock*, a generation raised on George Dixon's comforting and philosophical monologues 'on the nature of the villainy he encountered' did not for a long time see the police force as being anything other than hearty public servants. However, the succession of miscarriages of justice that came to light in the late 80s and early 90s has shattered much of the public's confidence in the boys in blue. In part, the history of TV crime is that of the evolution of public perception of the police.

Former Devon and Cornwall Chief Constable John Alderson states in *Barlow, Regan, Pyall and Fancy* that 'It is important for fictional drama to portray the worst side of the police.' The public always get the type of police series that they think they deserve.

Dixon of Dock Green

- **BBC Television** (BBC1) ◆ B&W (1955-69); Colour (1969-76)
- **430 episodes** (standard length: *c.* 45 minutes)
- **Creator:** Ted Willis
- **Writers include:** Ted Willis, Rex Edwards, Eric Paice, David Ellis, Gerald Kelsey, N.J. Crisp, Arthur Swinson, Jack Trevor Story, Derek Benfield, Bill Craig, John Wiles, Ivor Jay, Cyril Abraham, David Fisher, Ludovic Peters, Derek Ingrey, Robert Holmes, Luanshya Greer, P. J. Hammond, Mike Watts, Tony Williamson, Ben Bassett
- **Directors include:** Michael Goodwin, Robin Nash, David Askey, Austen Spriggs, Vere Lorrimer, Douglas Argent, Mary Ridge, Ian Wyatt, Michael E. Briant
- **Producers:** Douglas Moodie, G.B. Lupino, Ronald Marsh, Philip Barker, Eric Fawcett, Robin Nash, Joe Waters

Regular cast: Jack Warner (George Dixon) • Peter Byrne (Andy Crawford)

With: Billie Whitelaw/Jeanette Hutchinson/Anna Dawson (Mary Crawford) • Arthur Rigby (Sgt. Flint) • Robert Cawdron (Insp./DI Bob Cherry) • Geoffrey Adams (PC/DC Lauderdale) • Harold Scott (Duffy Clayton) • Nicholas Donnelly (PC/Sgt. Johnny Wills) • Neil Wilson (PC Tubb Barrell) • Moira Mannion (Sgt./WPI Grace Millard) • Graham Ashley (PC/DS Tommy Hughes) • David Webster (PC Jamie MacPherson) • Max Latimer (PC 'Tiny' Bush) • Anne Ridler (WP Sgt. Chris Freeman) • Anthony Parker (PC Bob Penney) • Hilda Fenemore (Jennie Wren) • Jan Miller (WPC Alex Johns) • John Hughes (PC John Jones) • Jocelyn Rhodes (WPC Kay Shaw/Lauderdale) • Janet Moss (WPC 'Barney' Barnes) • Michael Nightingale (DC Jack Cotton) • Paul Elliott (Cadet Michael Bonnet) • Christopher Gilmore (PC Clyde), Duncan Lamont (Sgt. Bob Cooper) • Ronald Bridges (PC Ted Bryant) • Robert Arnold (PC/DC Swain) • Zeph Gladstone (WPC Liz Harris) • Anne Carroll (WPC Shirley Palmer) • Jean Dallas (WPC Betty Williams) • Peter Thornton (PC Burton) • Geoffrey Kenion (PC Roberts) • Pamela Buchner (WDC Ann Foster) • Andrew Bradford (PC Brian Turner) • Joe Dunlop (DC Pearson), Scott Fredericks (PC Forbes) • Michael Osborne (PC Newton) • Gregory de Polnay (DS Brewer) • Richard Heffer (DS Alan Burton) • Ben Howard (DC Len Clayton)

'Evenin' all ... '. One of the most emotive and nostalgic of television images for older viewers is of flickering monochrome shots from outside a police station, the chimes of Big Ben and a whistled 'Maybe It's Because I'm a Londoner' as a shadowy figure comes into the spotlight, revealing a kindly-faced policeman.

Dixon of Dock Green, possibly because it was so important in its day, has of late become an object of ridicule. When some of the surviving episodes from the 50s were repeated by the BBC, mere days after the release of the Birmingham Six, younger viewers could be excused for asking themselves just what it was about this safe and self-congratulatory exercise that could still be talked about in reverential terms by their parents and grandparents. In its day it was television's most important and influential show. It's not without coincidence that the first episode of ***Doctor Who*** begins as an apparent tribute to *Dixon*, featuring a policeman plodding his lonely beat through the fog-covered London streets. Yet, by its demise, *Dixon* was an anachronism, and a dangerously naive one at that.

George Dixon, the 'ordinary copper' of Jeff Darnell's later, and more famous, signature tune, first appeared in the 1949 Ealing film, *The Blue Lamp*, in which he was shot dead after 23 minutes by Tom Riley (Dirk Bogarde). Dixon was played with period bravery and honesty by Jack Warner, best known for his cockney private on the wartime radio series *Garrison Theatre*. He was simply one of many examples of the British bobby in films of the era but, thanks to his heroic death, he stuck in the minds of cinema audiences.

Six years later, the BBC needed a police drama to replace *Fabian of the Yard*. Series head, Ronnie Waldman, hit upon the idea of resurrecting Dixon and, after acquiring the rights to the character from Sir Michael Balcon, asked *The Blue Lamp*'s writer Ted Willis to provide him with six scripts. Willis hadn't the faintest idea where he would get six police stories from, so he spent some weeks at Paddington Green station researching his subject. He decided that the series would be non-violent, and employed many of his contacts to feed him incidents which could be turned into scripts. Willis estimated that, at one time, he had more than 250 policemen 'on the payroll'.

Jack Warner was delighted to recreate the role. 'He's a solid, dependable sort of bloke,' said Warner, 'people have seen so much of these phoney American-type detectives that Dixon makes a nice change. He's got no fancy ideas on detection ... He's just trying to do his job.' Each episode would begin with George addressing the audience directly, giving them some aspect of life or policing to think about, after which the plot was used to illustrate the point. A closing coda wrapped up the tale, usually in a cautionary way. As Geoff Tibballs notes, 'these would be more along the line of "And little Johnny's promised to remember to cross the road safely from now on" rather than "And little Johnny's now serving life for topping the lollipop lady"'.

Dixon projected the perfect image of the force - an honest, cheerful man who would never stoop to planting evidence or beating up suspects. In the first episode, 'PC Crawford's First Pinch', Dixon shows a young constable, Andy Crawford, around 'his patch'. Crawford would soon become a CID officer and marry George's daughter, Mary. Other popular characters included icy Desk Sergeant Flint ('alibis are like pie crusts, made to be broken'), the chirpy Tubb Barrell, the brash Constable Lauderdale and the dependable Sergeant Grace Millard. Episodes tended to concentrate on one crime at a time, all of which would be solved satisfactorily. Sean Connery appeared as a minor villain in the first episode of the second season, whilst character actors like Kevin Stoney regularly appeared. Rex Edwards acted as co-scripter on the second and third seasons, helping to ease the burden on Willis. By 1957 *Dixon* was being watched by a staggering audience of ten million.

Episodes at this stage were 30 minutes long, although several seasons ended with extended 45-minute sagas. In 1961 the format changed to longer episodes, helping to flesh out parts like Harold Scott's local 'character' Duffy or the young David Hemmings, who made several impressive appearances as the disturbed youth Billy McGee. In 1960 the entire cast went to Paris for an episode ('The Hot Seat', 15 Oct 60), whilst some variety was added to the normal plots by featuring episodes of the Crawfords on holiday or George fishing.

Despite being the BBC's most popular programme during the late 50s, *Dixon* always fared badly with regard to episodes being recorded and retained in the archives: of the 430 made, today only 30 or so remain. Only five examples of Dixon at its peak, in the 50s, are left (all from the 1956 season), although, luckily, they illustrate perfectly some of the series' many strengths and flaws.

One of these episodes, 'The Rotten Apple' (11 Aug 56), was a television first, showing Paul Eddington as a 'bent copper', Tom Carr. George's patience is broken when Carr suggests that he is also 'on the take', although the extent of this anger is to call Carr 'a dirty, cheap swindler'. Indeed the series' 'street-talk', which became the accepted norm for the genre, would, as the years progressed, become more and more anachronistic and clichéd (compared to ***The Sweeney***'s 'You're nicked', gentle *Dixon* dialogue like 'Give it up, son' carried all the menace of a ballet troupe in a rugby club). 'The Rotten Apple' also had a stereotyped Jewish 'bookie', Maurie (Harry Ross), an example of the unconscious racism in the series which was further highlighted in another episode in which a woman stated that she believed she could trust George because she once saw him 'help out a Negro'.

Although often corny and stilted by sophisticated modern standards, the dialogue in *Dixon* was actually one of its strengths. In 'The Roaring Boy' (18 Aug 56) Kenneth Cope played 'an angry young man with a gun', an army deserter who holds his girlfriend and George hostage. His initial lines like 'All right, copper, move and I'll plug ya' may sound ridiculous, but some of his views on life have the potency of kitchen-sink drama. When George tells him that his daughter is marrying another policeman, Cope replies 'You lot stick together closer than ants'. The tension of the one-room drama increases as George becomes irritated with the self-pitying nature of Cope's anger, and the episode ends when Dixon drops his helmet to the floor and, stooping to pick it up, pulls the carpet from under the gunman.

Other episodes centred on retrospectively more controversial subjects. In 'Pound of Flesh' (25 Aug 56) - in which George vented his anger on crooked money-lenders - the opening monologue included his memorable acceptance of wife-battering: 'Part of a copper's job is to know when not to interfere. If I arrested every bloke in Dock Green who clipped his wife, I'd be working overtime.' At the episode's climax, George was happy to note that 'It was all sorted out in the end, with no bones broken.' What would happen if ***The Bill*** ventured similar opinions today hardly bears thinking about.

The marriage of Andy and Mary in 'Father in Law' (1 Sep 56) included location filming for the first time, and presented a beautiful picture of a 50s family wedding, complete with stolen wallet (to add drama). It gave Jack Warner the chance to sing a couple of funny songs, show some emotion when talking about his deceased wife, and, of course, appear out of uniform for once.

Dixon of Dock Green became a Saturday evening institution, occupying a regular early evening slot following *Juke Box Jury* (and later, ***Doctor Who***) for six months of every year. By 1963, when Ted Willis left the series in the hands of writers like David Ellis, Eric Paice, Gerald Kelsey and Norman Crisp, it was established as the definitive crime drama; but things were changing. When Willis left he told the *Radio Times* the accusations that *Dixon* presented a 'cosy picture of police work' were in some ways true, 'just as it is true that other programmes on the police emphasize the tougher and more violent aspects of crime prevention. I think we were right to stick to an approach which, within its limits, is a true one.' Willis was, of course, referring to ***Z Cars***, the brash newcomer which, in 1962, arrived to challenge everything for which *Dixon of Dock Green* stood.

First season
(9 Jul–13 Aug 55)
Six 30-minute episodes

Second season
(9 Jun–1 Sep 56)
Thirteen 30-minute episodes

Third season
(12 Jan–30 Mar 57)
Eleven 30-minute episodes

Fourth season
(7 Sep 57–29 Mar 58)
One 45-minute, twenty-eight 30-minuteepisodes

Fifth season
(27 Sep 58–28 Mar 59)
One 45-minute,twenty-six 30-minute episodes

Sixth season
(12 Sep 59–2 Apr 60)
One 45-minute, twenty-nine 30-minute episodes

Seventh season
(1 Oct 60–22 Apr 61)
One 45-minute, twenty-eight 30-minute episodes

Eighth season
(9 Sep 61–3 Mar 62)
One 30-minute, twenty-five 45-minute episodes

Ninth season
(15 Sep 62–23 Mar 63)
Twenty-eight episodes

Tenth season
(5 Oct 63–28 Mar 64)
Twenty-six episodes

Eleventh season
(19 Sep 64–13 Mar 65)
Twenty-six episodes

Twelfth season
(2 Oct 65–30 Apr 66)
Thirty-one episodes

Thirteenth season
(1 Oct–24 Dec 66)
Thirteen episodes

Fourteenth season
(30 Sep 67–10 Feb 68)
Twenty episodes

Fifteenth season
(7 Sep–21 Dec 68)
Sixteen episodes

Sixteenth season
(6 Sep–27 Dec 69)
Seventeen episodes

Seventeenth season
(14 Nov 70–6 Mar 71)
Seventeen episodes

Eighteenth season
(20 Nov 71–12 Feb 72)
Thirteen episodes

Nineteenth season
(23 Sep–30 Dec 72)
Fourteen episodes

Twentieth season
(29 Dec 73–20 Apr 74)
Seventeen episodes

Twenty-first season
(15 Feb–10 May 75)
Thirteen episodes

Twenty-second season
(13 Mar–1 May 76)
Eight episodes

Jack Warner was not impressed. 'When **Z Cars** has worn out as many tyres as I have worn out boots pounding the beat then they'll have something to crow about,' he said, adding 'Rough stuff? We've had our moments. I have been coshed and a boy has been murdered.' Willis himself was more concerned. At first he believed that the challenge of **Z Cars** could be overcome, but he was upset that so many people seemed to be comparing his series unfavourably with the Merseyside show. Irritated, he took a scene from a **Z Cars** episode in which Charlie Barlow interrogated a young offender and inserted it, word for word, into a *Dixon* script. It was only then that Willis realized the differences between the series. 'Whereas Stratford Johns kept saying "Come on!", Jack would say "Now, come on", and it came out as cosy as if I had written it,' said Willis in frustration. 'I realized then that there was no way you could change Jack.'

With the new writers, *Dixon* subtly changed. George, close to 60, was promoted to desk sergeant when Flint retired. Crawford and Lauderdale came more to the fore as writers as diverse as Peter Ling, Dick Sharples and *Marriage Lines'* creator Richard Waring all scripted episodes (Sharples's 'Jigsaw' (7 Nov 64) was one of the best of the eleventh season). But *Dixon* was still safe and comfortable, a regular staple of *Christmas Night with the Stars*. Warner, a lovely man who was genuinely touched by his honorary membership of several police forces, acknowledged that his portrayal could be viewed as old-fashioned, with characteristics of integrity and honesty, but didn't see anything wrong with that. Maybe he was right.

Of course, the series was still popular and there were some good episodes like 'The Late Customer' (4 Dec 65) focusing on the possibility of an innocent man convicted. The 1965 Christmas Day story, 'Georgina', saw Warner in a virtual one-man performance as he tended to an injured woman whilst waiting for the arrival of an ambulance. It was far removed from the cosiness of much of the series. For the most part, however, as John Russell Taylor noted in *The Listener* in 1964, its tone was a sickening 'patronising paternalism'.

Dixon also began to experiment with its format (Norman Crisp's episode 'The Heister' (5 Feb 66) featured flashback sequences and Jo Rowbottom playing two roles). Writers attempted to get tough when villain Anthony Booth shot Dixon in 'Touch and Go' (19 Feb 66), and 'Mr "X"' (23 Apr 66) centred on the crime of blackmail. For the most part, however, *Dixon* was an establishment piece, continuing to support hanging some years after capital punishment had been abolished. Future stars, such as Patrick Mower, Malcolm McDowell, Richard O'Sullivan, Tessa Wyatt and James Beck, appeared.

With the switch to colour, in 1969, producer Joe Waters tried to inject some realism into the twilight *Dixon* world by getting writers to tackle current areas of public concern, as **Z Cars** had been successfully doing. For a while it worked, several subsequent episodes centring on the theme of 'couldn't-care-less' parents. 'Two Children' (9 Jan 71) had a pair of youngsters - one a pre-teen Pauline Quirke - truanting, shoplifting and hiding around derelict houses in grim documentary-style scenes, reminiscent of *Cathy Come Home*. Another, Robert Holmes's 'The Unwanted' (26 Jan 74), had Trudy Jane Hughes sparking off a chain of events that led to a murder hunt when she bunked off school (at least by now George had been persuaded away from the 'whip 'em hard' school of thought, most of the episode's criticism centring on the girl's mother, played by Jill Gascoine).

By 1975 the series had become a virtual parody, although with ***The Sweeney*** busting heads on what were supposed to be the same London streets, it would have been impossible for *Dixon* to be perceived as anything else. The episodes were memorable for all the wrong reasons: 'Baubles, Bangles and Beads' (15 Mar 75) for its unbelievably clichéd portrayal of hippie culture (and hideous racism, having a Sikh guru exposed as a white con-man, blacked up). 'It's a Gift' (1 Mar 75) will always be remembered for an out-take that became legendary in BBC circles, as petty thief Victor Maddern proves unable to say the line 'Dock Green nick' (turning it into something much less wholesome) and the filming dissolves into pantomime.

'It's a Gift', with its cockney 'wide-boy' gangsters, could have been made in the 50s. Certainly there seems little difference, scriptwise, between this and an episode from 20 years before. The final season featured a retired Dixon. Jack Warner was 80 when the last episodes were made, and he died in 1981. His coffin was borne by constables from the Paddington Green Police station where Ted Willis had got many of his ideas. A spokesman from the Metropolitan Police said George was 'a charming character who served the Met and the public so well. His warmth and understanding of the problems of London PCs will long be remembered with affection.'

Rumours of a possible remake continue. It will be interesting to see if the adventures of Dixon could work in today's more cynical world, where the police are often seen as breakers rather than upholders of the law. It would, however, be the continuation of a television legacy that stretches back almost to the dawn of the broadcasting era, and a tribute to a character who, despite the ravages of time, could never have his innate goodness taken away.

Z Cars

- **BBC Television** (BBC1) ◆ B&W (1962-70); Colour (1970-78)
- **799 episodes** (including 1 unbroadcast) (standard length: 50 minutes)
- **Creator:** Troy Kennedy Martin
- **Writers include:** Troy Kennedy Martin, Allan Prior, Robert Barr, John Hopkins, James Doran, Leslie Sands, Keith Dewhurst, Elwyn Jones, Alan Plater, Joan Clark, Brian Hayles, Bill Barron, Eric Coltart, William Emms, Ray Jenkins, John Elliot, Donald Bull, Cyril Abraham, Tony Williamson, David Ellis, Adele Rose, Brian Finch, Ben Bassett, Peter Grimwade, Leslie Duxbury, Peter J. Hammond, Philip Martin, Len Rush, John Drew, Jack Gerson, Bill Lyons, Tony Holland, John Foster, Nick McCarty, Tony Perrin, Bob Baker, Dave Martin, Jack Ronder, Ted Lewis, Ian Curteis, Anthony Read, Roger Parkes
- **Directors include:** John McGrath, Morris Barry, Shaun Sutton, Eric Hills, Herbert Wise, Michael Leeston-Smith, James MacTaggart, Robin Midgley, Rudolph Cartier, Michael Hayes, Ken Loach, Ian MacNaughton, Moira Armstrong, Douglas Camfield, Vere Lorrimer, Michael Ferguson, Barry Letts, Gerald Blake, Tristan de Vere Cole, Julia Smith, Hugh David, Christopher Barry, Paddy Russell, David Maloney, Derek Martinus, Tim Combe, Joan Craft, Paul Ciappessoni, Mary Ridge, Eric Davidson, Matthew Robinson, Derrick Goodwin, George Spenton-Foster
- **Producers:** David Rose, Colin Morris, Ronald Travers, Richard Beynon, Ron Craddock, Roderick Graham

In 1978, as the final season of *Z Cars* began, the *Radio Times* announced that some weeks before a man had walked into a national TV archive with a videotape of one of the earliest *Z Cars* episodes. He was a BBC engineer and had liked the programme so much when originally broadcast that he stole the tape and kept it for 16 years in a wardrobe, believing that one day it would mean something.

He was, decided the *Radio Times*, correct, declaring that in socio-historical terms *Z Cars* ran parallel to the plays of John Osborne and Arnold Wesker, the films of Tony Richardson and the novels of Alan Sillitoe. Writer Keith Dewhurst stated that 'we believed that although the Empire was dead there was some energy, some unmined wisdom of experience of ordinary people that could take its place. We believed the booming medium of television was perfectly suited to our ideas, because it was popular and profound. A police thriller could also be a moving work of art.'

Troy Kennedy Martin created *Z Cars* out of a 60s icon: the patrol car. Confined to bed with mumps, he passed the time listening to police messages on his radio. 'I got a vastly different impression of the police than that given by ***Dixon of Dock Green***,' he said. Having taken inspiration from *Jacks and Knaves*, Elywn Jones's police series based around the exploits of infamous Liverpool CID officer Bill Prendergast, Kennedy Martin wrote a script concerning the death of a policeman and the creation, in the wake of this, of a new crime division. This took 'the hardest, brightest lads' off the beat and put them into cars. It was called 'Four of a Kind' and was one of the greatest 50 minutes of TV drama ever created.

Producer David Rose then had to find another six scripts in something like ten days to create a series. Whilst Kennedy Martin worked on further stories, script editor John Hopkins sought out other writers with the same kind of quickfire dramatic ability. He found Allan Prior and *Spy-Catcher* creator Robert Barr. With Hopkins donning his script-writing mantle (he would eventually write over 50 episodes), enough material was produced to guarantee production. The directors, including John McGrath, Morris Barry and future head of BBC drama Shaun Sutton, were of a similarly experimental mould, McGrath noting 'we wanted to break-up those long boring moralistic scenes that television was full of'. The effect of this, according to Dr Stuart Laing in *Banging in Reality*, was 'a new TV form. There were six or seven cameras, back projection ... The people at home had never seen the like of it.'

Police drama in 1962 was safe and predictable (***Dixon of Dock Green*** had been running for seven years, *No Hiding Place* for five), and the genre's lines had long been drawn. The police were the standard bearers for justice, they were to be respected and feared. If 'realism' ever intruded upon events (as in the 'Rotten Apple' episode of ***Dixon***), it was stressed that this was a unique occurrence. *Z Cars* changed that. In the opening scene, Detective Chief Inspector Barlow and DS Watt stand by the grave of their fallen colleague, smoking cigarettes and talking in cynical terms about the chances of the murderer hanging for his crime (Watt contemptuously calls the police psychiatrist 'the trick cyclist'). In the car on the way to the station, they discuss Newtown (based on Kirby, which had a 'wild west reputation' according to Kennedy Martin) and its housing estates, full of 'thieves, tearaways and villains'. Barlow tells Watt that it has been decided to set up a new crime division with mobile police officers. They are to pick the cream of the force for it.

Meanwhile, one of this elite, Bob Steele, is at home, having lunch with his friend, Bert Lynch. There is a nasty stain on the wall where the previous night's hot-pot has been flung by Janey Steele (Dorothy White) during an argument. Janey sports a black eye, and Lynch berates (but does nothing about) his colleague for the way he treats his wife. Lynch's next scene has him discussing a bet on a horse race (he agrees to join the new crime patrol for the sole reason that it will get him out of the rain). The next constable on Barlow and Watt's list, Fancy Smith, is described by his inspector as 'a Ted in a copper's uniform'. Brian Blessed based much of Fancy's characterization on the chief constable of Lancashire, a man called Poulfrey. 'He knew villains, he could smell them. He

Starring: Stratford Johns (Charlie Barlow) • Frank Windsor (John Watt) • James Ellis (Bert Lynch) • Brian Blessed (William 'Fancy' Smith) • Joseph Brady (Jack 'Jock' Weir) • Jeremy Kemp (Bob Steele) • Leonard Williams (Percy Twentyman) • Terence Edmond (Ian Sweet) • Virginia Stride (BD Girl Katy Hoskins) • Dudley Foster (DI/Det. Supt Dunn) • Michael Forrest (DC Hicks) • Colin Welland (PC David Graham) • Robert Keegan (Sgt. Blackitt) • Diane Aubrey (Sally Clarkson) • James Cossins (Sgt. Michaelson) • Leonard Rossiter (DI Bamber) • John Philips (DCS/Chief Supt./Asst Chief Constable/Chief Constable Robins) • Leslie Sands (DS Miller) • Geoffrey Whitehead (PC Ken Baker) • Edward Kelsey (PC Arthur Boyle) • Donald Webster (PC Foster) • Michael Gover (Chief Supt. Boland) • Donald Gee (PC Ray Walker) • John Barrie (DI Sam Hudson) • John Slater (DS Tom Stone) • Sebastian Breaks (PC Steve Tate) • Stephen Yardley (PC Alec May) • David Daker (PC Owen Culshaw) • Luanshya Greer (WPC Jane Shepherd) • George Sewell (DI Brogan) • Pauline Taylor (WPC Parkin) • Bernard Holley (PC Bill Newcombe) • Christopher Coll (DC Kane) • Joss Ackland (DI Todd) • John Wreford (PC Jackson) • John Woodvine (DI Alan Witty) • Ron Davies (PC Doug Roach) • Paul Angelis (PC Bruce Bannerman) • Derek Waring (DI Goss) • Ian Cullen (PC/DC Joe Skinner) • Douglas Fielding (PC/Sgt. Mick Quilley) • John Challis (Sgt. Culshaw) • Ray Lonnen (DI Moffat) • Stephanie Turner (WPC Jill Howarth) • Geoffrey Whitehead (DS Miller) • Jack Carr (PC Covill) • James Walsh (PC Lindsay) • Barry Lowe (PC Horrocks) • Jennie Goossens (BD Girl) • John Swindells (Sgt. Bowman) • Geoffrey Hayes (DC Scatliff) • Allan O'Keefe (PC Render) • Kenton Moore (CI Logie) • John Collin (DS Hagger) • June Watson/Sharon Duce (WPC Cameron) • Gary Watson (DI Connor) • Nicholas Smith (PC Jeff Yates) • Alison Steadman (WPC Bayliss) • David Jackson (DC Braithwaite) • Paul Stewart (Sgt. Chubb) • Brian Grellis (DC Bowker) • Tommy Boyle (DI Madden) • Victoria Plucknett (WPC Jane Beck)

could have been a borstal boy, a poacher, but he'd decided to become a gamekeeper instead.'

Barlow and Watt rounded up their team, completed by rugby-playing Scot Jock Weir, much to the annoyance of the police establishment, as represented by desk-sergeant Twentyman and to the envy of the young constables like Ian Sweet. The 'Z Victor' team, 'two young constables in every car, ready to deal with your troubles as they happen', as the *Radio Times* announced, had arrived (their Ford Zephyrs could do 0 to 60 in 20 seconds!). The elders of the police service were, to say the least, shocked. In an article some years later, Bill Roberts, the former head of Lancashire CID and one of the programme's advisers, described the horror with which the series was greeted by senior officers. 'This was not the way,' the elders said, 'in which the image of the police should be presented.'

Perhaps the best example of this was the character of Barlow. Stratford Johns played him like a psychopath. 'I was annoyed that the police had always been portrayed as pipe-smoking bunglers,' said Johns. His Barlow was a snarling, bad-tempered brute. 'Why are you doing it like that?' David Rose asked on the first episode. 'Barlow went home last night, had a row with his wife, got out of bed, went downstairs and drank half a bottle of Scotch, sitting on his own. He went back to bed and got up with a hangover,' replied Johns. The prototype for a generation of bad-tempered policemen was born.

Within weeks the series had an audience of 15 million. *Z Cars*, with its catchy theme tune (an adaptation of the folk song 'Johnny Todd'), became a national obsession. As with ***Coronation Street***, the injection of some earthy northern realism into the formulaic world of TV drama was a breath of fresh air.

If the on-screen drama was extraordinary, it was largely down to the writing. Kennedy Martin, Hopkins, Prior and Barr, together with newer writers like James Doran and Keith Dewhurst, were presenting realism as a new toy to play with. In Prior's 'Threats and Menace' (6 Mar 62) Janey and Bob Steele have problems with an unruly family living next door. Kennedy Martin's 'Teamwork' (3 Jul 62) has crime levels rising and pressure increasing on every team member to get results, whilst Hopkins' 'Affray' (19 Jun 62) shows violence in the city reaching riot proportions, climaxing in the death of an officer. Nevertheless, as Bill Roberts noted, *Z Cars* 'never glamorized crime. It tended to show crime in its true form - dirty and ugly.'

New characters appeared, like the quick-witted, sarcastic Inspector Dunn, initially as a short-term replacement for Stratford Johns who was ill. Major changes occurred during the second season, Leonard Williams having died of a heart attack. Bob Keegan, playing the sour-faced Sergeant Blackitt, made a fine replacement, whilst Jeremy Kemp left the series to be replaced by a young Colin Welland. Leslie Sands (who also wrote several episodes) made a number of impressive appearances as Barlow's boss, Superintendent Miller. In 'Hide – and Go Seek' (16 Oct 63) John Thaw appeared as a constable.

'Enquiry' (27 Mar 63) saw the possibility of a thief amongst the constables and an investigation conducted with bitter recriminations by Leonard Rossiter's Chief Inspector Bamber. Keith Dewhurst's 'Come on the Lads' (19 Jun 63) had another topical theme, football hooliganism. Dewhurst, a former newspaper man who lived in Salford and had spent two years reporting on Manchester United, had already written one of the second season's most well-remembered episodes, 'Johnny Sailor' (7 Nov 62). Alan Plater also began writing for the series. Two years later, in a *Radio Times* article entitled 'My Favourite Series', he described *Z Cars* as a programme which has 'no grand conception, it is not a series about crime, punishment, power, or even pigeon-fancying. It is about people living in present -day society, and what happens when the pressures and conflicts explode - maybe quietly - into law-breaking.'

John Hopkins's 'Police Work' (3 Jul 63) was a remarkable season closer, as Weir and Smith, sent by the coroner to fetch a witness from an isolated cottage, found themselves in a deadly situation. Hopkins's ear for naturalistic dialogue

Another new-fangled piece of technology for the Z Victor boys as Jock and Fancy phone for help

and keen sense of pace was emphasized in 'Made for Each Other' (11 Sep 63), in which Fancy became emotionally involved with a teenage girl (Judi Dench) found hiding in an empty house. Hopkins also wrote 'A Place of Safety' (24 Jun 64), which was one of the first episodes on British television to tackle racism in a non-patronizing way, with the Newtown boys confronted by a black man attacking his white landlord with an axe. The immigrant's wife (a stunning performance by Alaknanda Samarth) touches the lives of both Barlow and Fancy, telling the former that 'you like to think that you're different from all the others, but really you are the same'. The final scene, of Fancy sitting alone in his patrol car, showed, in Hopkins's words, 'a man on the verge of a huge philosophical discovery'. Fancy is relieved to be disturbed by a radio message. 'Thank God for that,' he says, ending the episode. Doubtless, thousands of viewers felt the same way.

Such work was a stepping-stone for Hopkins towards his later *Fable*, a parody that proved so controversial that the BBC postponed it in case it influenced a by-election. Hopkins saw one of *Z Cars*' major achievements as taking 'the crime story out of the safe vacuum of unreality and setting it where an action causes reaction and, as the circle widens out from the initial explosion, has its consequences'. This took its toll on the author, however, as 'the stories I told took me down dark roads into areas that were not good for me'. One of these, 'Centre of Disturbance' (13 May 64), had the terrifying premise of a shooting in Newtown Shopping Centre, and was directed by future ***Doomwatch*** producer Terence Dudley. Ken Loach, a year before *Up the Junction*, also directed several episodes during this period, as did Rudolph Cartier. The season's most dramatic storyline involved the death of PC Sweet, drowned whilst trying to save a young boy, which prompted a tremendous wave of sympathy for policemen.

Not every new writer on the project followed the plot. G.F. Newman attended a script conference and, upon being asked for ideas, said 'Sergeant Watt is offered a bribe for £500, which he accepts' - at which point he was told that perhaps this wasn't the series for him.

Despite the quality of the product, Z Cars was one of the first series to really suffer from the BBC's purge of its back catalogue. Many early live episodes were either not recorded at all or were later junked. Steve Bryant in *The Television Heritage* notes that in terms of what was saved and what wasn't 'cultural attitudes were as important a factor as economic or technical considerations. A *Wednesday Play* is more likely to have survived than an episode of Z Cars, although it is in the latter that many of the stalwarts of TV drama began their careers.'

A clash between generations was the central theme in 'Finders Keepers' (23 Sep 64), with Gordon Gostelow in an acclaimed performance as a tramp. Novelist Stan Barstow contributed a script ('The Luck of the Game', 13 Jan 65), although the established writers could still be relied upon. Plater's 'Partners' (17 Mar 65, in which a doctor is accused of indecent assault) and Elwyn Jones's 'The Long Spoon' (17 Feb 65, which poses the question 'Is Barlow corrupt?') were highlights. 'The Fanatics' (24 Mar 65) saw an invasion of Newtown by Scottish football fans, while 'Error of Judgement' (9 Jun 65) questioned unnecessary violence. Eric Colbart's 'Contrary to Regulations' (23 Nov 65) was one of the first TV episodes to discuss drug addiction (with Mike Pratt as an addict), and 'Inspection' (2 Nov 65, in which Bernard Archard played the inspector of constabulary) was deliberately set within the confines of the station, having characters the country had grown to know and love being discussed by an outsider.

After 170 episodes, *Z Cars* ended just before Christmas 1965 with Alan Plater's episode 'That's the Way It Is'. Barlow and Watt (together with the now retired Blackitt) leave to set up a new crime force in Bristol. The resulting *Softly Softly* (later *Softly Softly: Task Force*) reunited David Rose and writers such as Jones, Plater, Prior and Barr. Johns and Windsor starred alongside Norman Bowler, David Lloyd Meredith, Alexis Kanner and Terence Rigby (as PC Snow). The series, with much higher production values than *Z Cars*, included contributions from Kingsley Amis and even had spin-offs of its own. *Barlow at Large* and *Barlow* took the character into the home office, while *Jack the Ripper* (1973) and *Second Verdict* (1976) had fictional coppers Barlow and Watt trying to solve real-life mysteries such as the fate of the princes in the tower.

Despite the success of *Softly Softly* the BBC decided that there was still life in *Z Cars*. In 1967 the series was resurrected in a twice-weekly format, produced by Colin Morris. Only James Ellis and Joseph Brady were left from the classic line-up. Barlow and Watt's shoes were filled by John Barrie and John Slater, whilst the new constables included David Daker and Stephen Yardley. Some continuity with the original series was maintained, however, through occasional references to the current whereabouts of Fancy, Barlow or Watt, and, after the introduction of new writers (including soap-veterans like Cyril Abraham and Donald Bull), by the return of Keith Dewhurst and Allan Prior. The first storyline, 'I Don't Want Evidence' (6-7 Mar 67), involved a case of arson. It was as if *Z Cars* had never been away.

The turnover of the cast became more rapid, George Sewell, Bernard Holley, Joss Ackland and John Woodvine becoming regulars. Some memorable episodes of the late-60s include 'The Great Art Robbery' (21-22 Aug 67, featuring Kenneth Cope and Iain Gregory as 'the notorious Hancock brothers'), 'The Saint of Concrete Canyon' (1-2 Apr 68, a multi-character piece set in a high-rise block), Brian Finch's 'The Battleground' (29-30 Apr 68, a story of childhood arson), and 'The Guilty Ones' (13-14 May 68, the first of several stories concerning child abuse and teenage runaways). Allan Prior's 'Attack' (2-3 Sep 69) concerned an armed robbery on a post office and Peter Grimwade's 'Spare the Rod' (16-17 Jun 69) debated the rights and wrongs of corporal punishment in a local comprehensive. 'Score to Settle' (29-30 Dec 69) introduced the series' new heart-throb, Ian Cullen's Geordie constable Joe Skinner, who became the new partner for Douglas Fielding's Alec Quilley.

Although the focus of the series had changed, with characters often more important than crimes, episodes such as 'It's Only a Game' (27 Apr 70), in which the local football team's relegation problems caused an outbreak of violence, could be seen as accurately reflecting new areas of concern in 70s society. The growing disrespect for the police amongst the youth was highlighted in 'All Coppers are Nanas' (16-17 Feb 70), and the problems of isolation and loneliness came to the fore in Bill Brown's lyrical 'Eleanor Rigby Slept Here' (16-17 Mar 70). Allan Prior told *Radio Times* that he didn't consider *Z Cars* to be 'police stories'. 'I prefer it to a prestige single play because it's topical and about the working class. Nowadays TV is bigger and safer, and too conservative.'

In 1971, after a run of almost four years, producer Ron Craddock and script editor P.J. Hammond decided to change the format once again. 'I should think we have more screen time than every other BBC programme,' Craddock noted, adding that the strain of running a continuous series was inhibiting. 'There's no margin for error, and if anything goes wrong we're really up the creek.' The first story of 1972, 'Last Bus to Newtown', marked the tenth anniversary of the series, and returned to the self-contained 50-minute episode format. 'Although some people clearly look back on *Z Cars* with a nostalgic eye,' said John Slater, 'it's not the same programme. The force has changed, crime has changed as well and we've had to change with them. We tell stories of our time. We've had programmes on race relations, student demos ... We're telling the truth, as near as dammit.'

The return to longer episodes suited the inclusion of extra characters, and in episodes such as 'Women at Work' (1 Feb 73, which featured Barbara Shelley and a teenage Rosalyn Landor) *Z Cars* seemed to be back to its very best. Julia Smith was mainly responsible for the significant increase in location filming on the series (she also worked with her future ***EastEnders*** co-creator Tony Holland, who had replaced Hammond as script editor). Other regular cast members of the era included Alison Steadman, Ray Lonnen, John Collin and future *Juliet Bravo* Stephanie Turner. Guest actors included Paul Darrow (as a thief), Patrick Troughton (as a local councillor) and a young Patsy Kensit.

By the mid-70s, however, with ***The Sweeney*** appealing to an entirely different audience, *Z Cars* was being seen in much the same light as ***Dixon of Dock Green*** had been over a decade before. As an attempt to update the concept in the face of such competition, Bill Lyons's 'Eviction' (3 Mar 75) dragged the series into a topical area of public concern, whilst P.J. Hammond's three-parter ('Distance'/'Ritual'/'Legacy', 21 Apr-5 May 75) had Joe Skinner shot dead by villain Ralph Bates in a shocking episode climax. The loss of one of their most popular characters was a brave move for *Z Cars* and one which,

First season
(2 Jan–31 Jul 62)
Thirty-one episodes

Second season
(19 Sep 62–3 Jul 63)
Forty-two episodes

Third season
(4 Sep 63–24 Jun 64)
Forty-two episodes

Fourth season
(9 Sep 64–30 Jun 65)
Forty-three episodes

Fifth season
(5 Oct–21 Dec 65)
Twelve episodes

Sixth season
(6 Mar 67–24 Jun 71)
Four hundred and seven 25-minute episodes, nine 50-minute episodes

Seventh season
(2 Aug 71–22 Aug 72)
Fifty-five 5-minute, twenty 50-minute episodes

Eighth season
(11 Sep 72–2 Jul 73)
Forty episodes, one unbroadcast

Ninth season
(22 Oct 73–3 Jun 74)
Twenty-eight episodes

Tenth season
(9 Sep 74–12 May 75)
Thirty-one episodes

Eleventh season
(5 Jan–29 Mar 76)
Thirteen episodes

Twelfth season
(5 Apr–5 Jul 77)
Thirteen episodes

Thirteenth season
(28 Jun–20 Sep 78)
Thirteen episodes

['Cadet' was billed in the *Radio Times* for transmission on 12 Nov 73, but it has never been broadcast. *Softly Softly* and *Softly Softly: Task Force* ran for 12 seasons (269 50-minute episodes) between 5 Jan 66 and 15 Dec 76. *Barlow at Large* and *Barlow* ran for four seasons (29 episodes) between 15 Sep 71 and 26 Feb 75.]

with hindsight, probably helped to keep the series going for another year or two.

There were some fine episodes, Allan Prior's 'Guns' (5 Jan 76) and Ian Curteis's 'Contact' (2 Feb 76) for example, but the attempts to make *Z Cars* conform with perceived contemporary police ethics was unworkable. Whilst Regan and company could swap witty one-liners between the shoot-outs, or go tearing around in their TR7s, Lynch, Moffat, Quilley, Hagger and Render had neither the hardware, nor the budget, to take part in an action series. *Z Cars* was, arguably, still as realistic as it had always been, but realism had become boring.

Script editor Graham Williams prepared for *Z Cars* by trailing the New York Police Department, and used the experience to create a show of his own: *Target*. Originally an intelligent vehicle for Colin Blakely and scripted by Roger Marshall, this went radically out of control after Williams left to produce ***Doctor Who***. His replacement, Philip Hinchcliffe, attempted to make *Target* into another ***Sweeney***. The BBC now had their own Regan clone, in Patrick Mower's Hackett, and, despite the fact that many writers refused to have their names associated with *Target*, the BBC seemed happier producing a series such as this rather than *Z Cars* or *Softly Softly*.

The final season of *Z Cars* was a near self-parody, although Paula Milne's 'A Woman's Place' (26 Jul 78) tackled crime drama's sexism very effectively. The last episode (written by creator Troy Kennedy Martin, and directed by John McGrath) brought *Z Cars* full circle, featuring the return of the now Detective Chief Superintendent Watt, together with cameo appearances by Brian Blessed, Joseph Brady, Colin Welland and Jeremy Kemp going in to the Newtown station. It was self-reflective, of course, and ultimately a disappointing end to 16 years of television history.

The Saint

- **ATV/New World/Granada/ITC/Bamore** (ITV)
- B&W (1962-65); Colour (1966-69)
- **118 episodes** (50 minutes)
- **Based on:** characters created by Leslie Charteris
- **Writers include:** Jack Sanders, Gerald Kelsey, Dick Sharples, Richard Harris, Julian Bond, John Gilling, Harry W. Junkin, John Kruse, Bill Strutton, Robert Stewart, Paddy Manning O'Brine, Ian Kennedy Martin, Michael Cramoy, Ian Stuart Black, Terry Nation, Paul Erickson, Brian Degas, Alfred Shaghnessy, Michael Pertwee, Michael Winder, Philip Broadley, Donald James, Robert Holmes
- **Directors include:** Michael Truman, John Gilling, Jeremy Summers, John Paddy Carstairs, Robert S. Baker, Anthony Bushell, Roy Ward Baker, John Moxey, Peter Yates, James Hill, Roger Moore, Leslie Norman, Pat Jackson, Robert Tronson, Gordon Flemyng, Freddie Francis, Ray Austin
- **Producers:** Robert S. Baker, Monty Berman

Starring: Roger Moore (Simon Templar) • Ivor Dean (Chief Inspector Teal) • Arnold Diamond (Inspector Fernack)

[Campbell Singer, Wensley Pithey and Norman Pitt all played Teal in one episode each during the early seasons. Allan Gifford played Fernack on one occasion.]

Simon Templar, a man of private means, fought crime under the title of his initials, ST, and, rather alarmingly, talked to the camera before he did it. The character came from books by Leslie Charteris, the technique came from theatrical history, and the result was enduring television.

Templar had already appeared in a very successful film series in the 40s and 50s, and the early TV episodes were imbued with the paternalistic conservatism of the Macmillan era, with Simon standing for good manners, private philanthropy, and both corporal and capital punishment. The series supported the establishment, usually in the form of the aristocracy. Industrial disputes were the work of troublemakers; socialism and taxation were twin evils, and those who acquired, rather than inherited, wealth were portrayed as *nouveau riche* vulgarians.

First season
(4 Oct–20 Dec 62)
1 The Talented Husband
2 The Latin Touch
3 The Careful Terrorist
4 The Covetous Headsman
5 The Loaded Tourist
6 The Pearls of Peace
7 The Arrow of God
8 The Element of Doubt
9 The Effete Angler
10 The Golden Journey
11 The Man who was Lucky
12 The Charitable Countess

Second season
(19 Sep 63–19 Mar 64)
13 The Fellow Traveller
14 Starring the Saint
15 Judith
16 Theresa
17 The Elusive Ellshaw
18 Marcia
19 The Work of Art
20 Iris
21 The King of the Beggars
22 The Rough Diamonds
23 The Saint Plays with Fire
24 The Well-Meaning Mayor
25 The Sporting Chance
26 The Bunco Artists
27 The Benevolent Burglary
28 The Wonderful War
29 The Noble Sportsman
30 The Romantic Matron
31 Luella
32 The Lawless Lady
33 The Good Medicine
34 The Invisible Millionaire
35 The High Fence
36 Sophia
37 The Gentle Ladies
38 The Ever-Loving Spouse
39 The Saint Sees It Through

Third season
(8 Oct 64–11 Mar 65)
40 The Miracle Tea Party
41 Lida
42 Jeannine
43 The Scorpion
44 The Revolution Racket
45 The Saint Steps In
46 The Loving Brothers
47 The Man Who Liked Toys
48 The Death Penalty
49 The Imprudent Politician
50 The Hi-jackers
51 The Unkind Philanthropist
52 The Damsel in Distress
53 The Contract
54 The Set-up
55 The Rhine Maiden
56 The Inescapable Word
57 The Sign of the Claw
58 The Golden Frog
59 The Frightened Inn-Keeper
60 Sibao
61 The Crime of the Century
62 The Happy Suicide

Fourth season
(1 Jul–26 Aug 65)
63 The Chequered Flag
64 The Abductors
65 The Crooked Ring
66 The Smart Detective
67 The Persistent Parasite
68 The Man Who Could Not Die
69 The Saint Bids Diamonds
70 The Spanish Cow
71 The Old Treasure Story

The element that set *The Saint* in its period was the moment where Templar would first announce his name, and, as he cast his eyes despairingly to the ceiling, a halo would appear. The overall effect was swinging in the extreme, and Templar became a man moving against the background of 60s London. Witty dialogue and characters drawn from the modern scene (DJs, hip artists, even Anna Carteret as a pop singer), plus Templar's edgy status with the law, helped make the series popular with younger folk. With this in mind, the character wasn't allowed to maim, kill, disfigure or pick locks, and, even though he carried a gun, he wasn't likely to shoot anybody with it, for reasons of budget as much as ethics. All of the black-and-white episodes adapted the Charteris novels faithfully, but most of the colour stories were originals, the television character evolving into a less brutal man than that of the books, much as Moore's James Bond was to change from a sixth-form bully into a gentle figure of fun.

Patrick McGoohan had turned down the role because of Templar's aggressive bachelorhood, and so Roger Moore found himself in a part that was to shape his future career. Templar drove a Swedish Volvo P-1800, Jaguar having refused the series the loan of an E-Type. Typically for an ITC production, when he wasn't driving it in Hertfordshire, he was driving it against a filmed background, or on a studio set. The series ranged all over Europe, into Australia (for 'The Loving Brothers', which had an all-Aussie cast and director), and even into the South-East Asian jungle as Simon went on anti-terrorist patrol in 'The Sign of the Claw'. Automobile action included Simon showing off his prowess as a racing driver in 'The Chequered Flag' and driving a Rolls-Royce backwards down a mountain faster than the pursuing Mercedes.

As the show went on, the plots got wilder, particularly, it seemed, when the series went to Scotland. There it encountered a bizarre radiation weapon, and, of course, the Loch Ness Monster.

Guest stars on the series included Honor Blackman, Warren Mitchell, Oliver Reed, Patrick Troughton, Nanette Newman, Julian Glover, Ronnie Barker and Edward Woodward. Donald Sutherland, Peter Wyngarde and Lois Maxwell appeared twice, as did Nosher Powell, an ex-boxer with an eye on an acting career. He first faced off against Moore in a boxing match in 'The Crooked Ring'.

Actresses queued up for the chance to appear as 'this week's *Saint* girl'. As was ITC policy, many appeared in several stories, Annette Andre clocking up five appearances, beaten only by Justine Lord with eight.

Moore took a greater part in the series as it went on, directing eight episodes himself (one of which, 'The House on Dragon's Rock', carried an 'unsuitable for children and people of a nervous disposition' warning in some areas and was

Fifth season
(30 Sep 66–2 Jun 67)
72 Queen's Ransom
73 Interlude in Venice
74 The Russian Prisoner
75 The Reluctant Revolution
76 The Helpful Pirate
77 The Convenient Monster
78 The Angel's Eye
79 The Man who Liked Lions
80 The Better Mousetrap
81 Little Girl Lost
82 Paper Chase
83 Locate and Destroy
84 Flight Plan
85 Escape Route
86 The Persistent Patriots
87 The Fast Women
88 The Death Game
89 The Art Collectors
90 To Kill a Saint
91 The Counterfeit Countess
92 Simon and Delilah
93 Island of Chance
94 The Gadget Lovers
95 Double in Diamonds
96 The Power Artists
97 When Spring is Sprung

Sixth season
(22 Sep 68–9 Feb 69)
98 The Gadic Collection
99 The Best Laid Schemes
100 Invitation to Danger
101 Legacy for the Saint
102 The Desperate Diplomat
103 The Organisation Man
104 The Double Take
105 The Time to Die
106 The Master Plan
107 The House on Dragon's Rock
108 The Scales of Justice
109 The Fiction Makers (part one)
110 The Fiction Makers (part two)
111 The People Importers
112 Where the Money is
113 Vendetta for the Saint (part one)
114 Vendetta for the Saint (part two)
115 The Ex-King of Diamonds
116 The Man who Gambled with Life
117 The Portrait of Brenda
118 The World Beater

[The first two seasons were not networked; the dates derive from ATV (Midlands). Episode 58 was intended for transmission on 4 Feb 65 but was replaced by episode 57. Episode 107 was scheduled as the second story from the fifth season (7 Oct 66) but was replaced by episode 73. *Return of the Saint* ran for 24 episodes between 10 Sep 78 and 11 Mar 79. LWT's *The Saint* ran for six episodes between 2 Sep 89 and 4 Aug 90.]

shown at a much later time). The actor bought up the rights to the series as 'TV's first millionaire', and, with partner Robert S. Baker, continues looking for new uses for his investment. *The Return of the Saint* fitted neatly into ***The New Avengers'*** timeslot in 1979, and had some of its nostalgic appeal, but was a very straightforward, humourless action series. Ian Ogilvy performed well, but without the natural wit that Moore had brought to the part. Many original *Saint* personnel were retained, but perhaps the show was never designed to work against genuine foreign settings. In 1987, a pilot for a mooted American series, entitled *The Saint in Manhatten*, starring Andrew Clarke, was premiered. It was lacklustre, but the worst was yet to come. Simon Dutton was wooden in the relaunched role to say the least, but he was competing against plots and scripts that would have made Moore wince. The 1989 version of the series earned a unique place in television history - it was cancelled after two episodes, the remainder of the season being shown at a later date.

Undeterred, Moore is currently talking about a Hollywood movie version. One of television's most enduring characters is far from dead.

Callan

- **ABC/Thames/ATV** (ITV) ◆ **B&W** (1967-69); **Colour** (1970-72, 1981)
- **45 episodes** (standard length: 60 minutes)
- **Creator:** James Mitchell
- **Writers include:** James Mitchell, Robert Banks Stewart, Ray Jenkins, Trevor Preston, Michael Winder, Bill Craig, George Markstein
- **Directors include:** Reginald Collin, Bill Bain, Robert Tronson, Piers Haggard, Peter Duguid, Peter Sasdy, Mike Vardy, James Goddard
- **Producers:** Leonard Lewis, Terence Feely, Reginald Collin, Shaun O'Riordan ('Wet Job')

Regular cast: Edward Woodward (Callan) • Russell Hunter (Lonely)

With: Anthony Valentine (Toby Meres) • Ronald Radd/Michael Goodliffe/Derek Bond/William Squire (Hunter) • Patrick Mower (Cross) • Geoffrey Chater (Bishop) • Lisa Langdon (Liz) • Clifford Rose (Snell) • T.P. McKenna (Richmond)

Callan was to ***The Avengers*** what *The Spy Who Came in from the Cold* was to James Bond. Set in the intelligence community, it featured David Callan, an unglamorous hit man whose job was to eliminate those his superiors considered dangerous. In its time, the series was massively popular, Edward Woodward winning the *TV Times* Best Actor award three years running.

Callan was created by Tyneside author James Mitchell, who had worked on ***The Avengers*** and ***The Troubleshooters***, as a deliberate attempt to do something removed from the jet-set plots of those series. Callan first appeared in the *Armchair Theatre* play 'A Magnum for Schneider'. Having challenged the authority of his section head (we later discover that they go under the codename Hunter) Callan is given an opportunity to redeem himself. His mission is to kill a gun-runner called Schneider, although this is, in part, a departmental trap, the sinister Meres (Peter Bowles) having been ordered to frame Callan for Schneider's murder. Callan realizes he is being manipulated and turns the tables on his superiors. Looking for a series to replace *Redcap*, Terence Feely proposed that *Callan* might fit the bill, and during the filming of the play, Lloyd Shirley gave the go-ahead for a further six episodes, which Mitchell provided with the aid of fellow ***Avengers*** writer Robert Banks Stewart.

Callan had an extraordinary title sequence, beginning with a swinging light bulb exploding in slow motion at the sound of a gunshot. It had excellent characters, including Russell Hunter as Callan's 'stooge' Lonely, a cowardly sneak-thief who had acquired his nickname because when nervous he 'stunk like a skunk'. Initially, Lonely believed Callan to be a gangster. Although often treating Lonely with contempt, Callan looked after his safety, later recruiting Lonely to the section as a driver. Anthony Valentine took over the role of Meres and developed a smooth, deadly character (he is said to have received much fan-mail from masochistic women). Central to the series was the paradoxical morality of Callan; a ruthless killer, but also someone with a fixed ethical code.

Although a freelance operative in the first season, Callan is brought into the section at the start of the second season, a new Hunter involving him in a deadly game. The various Hunters had contrasting relationships with Callan: Derek Bond's Hunter was a professional espionage man and a friend of Callan's (they are on first-name terms), whereas Michael Goodliffe's character was a civil service bureaucrat, out of touch with the cruel realities of the job.

'Let's Kill Everybody' saw a rogue agent killing Callan's colleagues. The first Hunter (Ronald Radd) turned up in two episodes under his real name, Colonel Leslie, now looking after aspects of Britain's relationships with Arab countries.

Armchair Theatre
(4 Feb 67)
1 A Magnum for Schneider

First season
(8 Jul–12 Aug 67)
2 The Good Ones are All Dead
3 Goodbye Nobby Clarke
4 The Death of Robert E. Lee
5 Goodness Burns Too Bright
6 But He's a Lord, Mr Callan
7 You Should Have Got Here Sooner

Second season
(8 Jan–16 Apr 69)
8 Red Knight, White Knight
9 The Most Promising Girl of her Year
10 You're under Starter's Orders
11 The Little Bits and Pieces of Love
12 Let's Kill Everybody
13 Heir Apparent
14 Land of Light and Peace
15 Blackmailers should be Discouraged
16 Death of a Friend
17 Jack-on-Top
18 Once a Big Man, Always a Big Man
19 The Running Dog
20 The Worst Soldier I Ever Saw
21 Nice People Die at Home
22 Death of a Hunter

Third season
(8 Apr–24 Jun 70)
23 Where Else Could I Go?
24 Summoned to Appear
25 The Same Trick Twice
26 A Village Called "G"
27 Suddenly - At Home
28 Act of Kindness
29 God Help your Friends
30 Breakout
31 Amos Green Must Live

Fourth season
(1 Mar–24 May 72)
32 That'll be the Day
33 Call me Sir!
34 First Refusal
35 Rules of the Game
36 If He Can, So Could I
37 None of your Business
38 Charlie Says It's Goodbye
39 I Never Wanted the Job
40 The Carrier
41 The Contract
42 The Richmond File: Call Me Enemy
43 The Richmond File: Do you Recognise the Woman?
44 The Richmond File: A Man Like Me

1981 Special
(2 Sep 81, 90 minutes)
45 Wet Job

[Due to events including a late Peter Osgood equalizer in the 1970 Cup Final replay and the General Election, the last six episodes of the third season were subject to numerous changes of broadcast date. The intended order was episodes 28, 27, 26, 31, 29, 30.]

Callan was shot and wounded by Meres in 'Death of a Hunter', a story designed as the series' finale. When rumours about the intention to kill Callan leaked, the audience was outraged (there was even a 'Callan Lives!' graffiti campaign). Perhaps aided by the fact that *Callan* was Harold Wilson's favourite programme, its new producer, Thames, wisely brought the character back, with the ramifications of his return to duty occupying the early episodes of the new, colour season. This featured a new partner to replace the departed Meres (due to Valentine securing a role in the BBC's *Codename*) in Patrick Mower's trigger-happy Cross, and a new Hunter (the dour-faced William Squire). In 'Summoned to Appear', whilst chasing an assassin at a railway station, Cross accidentally pushes a bystander in front of an oncoming train. Callan is detained as a witness and, having stated that the man committed suicide, is again struck by his conscience. 'God Help your Friends' saw Callan ordered to kill the romance between a departmental secretary (Stephanie Beacham) and a suspected spy (Michael Jayston).

For the fourth season, Callan was promoted to be the new Hunter, although the dramatic death of Cross, killed in 'If He Can, So Could I', causes the return of his predecessor, Patrick Mower leaving for a star-making role in *Special Branch*. 'Rules of the Game' featured Mike Pratt as a (wrongly) assumed Russian spy, whilst 'I Never Wanted the Job' had Lonely witnessing a murder and finding himself on the run from the killers. The final three episodes concentrated on the agent Richmond, whom Callan kills at the climax of 'A Man Like Me', directly disobeying Hunter's orders. Knowing that his career with the section is at an end, the satisfied Callan walks away.

In 1974 a film adaptation saw Woodward and Russell Hunter reprise their roles. For a long time it seemed as though that was the end of the *Callan* story, with Mitchell busy on ***When the Boat Comes in*** and resuming his novelist career that stretched back to 1964 when he wrote under the pen name James Munro. However, in 1981 ATV commissioned a play from Mitchell in which the now-retired Callan (living under the name Tucker and selling militaria) is recalled to the service for a final mission. 'Wet Job' also saw the return of Lonely, who had gone straight and was now running a plumbing company. It wasn't as good as the old series, but it was nice to see the characters again.

After this, the lure of America took Woodward to New York to create *The Equalizer*, the opposite extreme of the spy genre with its almost superhuman central figure. The Americans loved it, apparently, but to those who saw Woodward's harrowed, world-weary figure of two decades before it was a staggering disappointment.

Department S/Jason King

- **ITC/Scoton** (ITV) ◆ **Colour**
- **54 episodes** (50 minutes) ◆ **1969-72**
- **Creators:** Monty Berman, Dennis Spooner
- **Writers:** Gerald Kelsey, Philip Broadley, Terry Nation, Donald James, Tony Williamson, Leslie Darbon, Harry H. Junkin, Dennis Spooner, Robert Banks Stewart
- **Directors:** Cyril Frankel, Ray Austin, John Gilling, Roy Ward Baker, Paul Dickson, Gill Taylor, Leslie Norman, Jeremy Summers
- **Producer:** Monty Berman

Department S was a branch of Interpol concerned with the investigation of insoluble mysteries, a sort of provisional wing of *Arthur C. Clarke's Mysterious World*. As veteran scriptwriter Dennis Spooner envisaged them, they were the people who'd investigate the *Marie Celeste* if she was found abandoned in the 60s. Each episode would start with a date and place caption, an index to the general level of realism that the show attempted to maintain.

This was the heyday of ITC, Lew Grade's production company. It had already had hits with ***The Saint***, *The Champions* and *Man in a Suitcase*, and was expert at producing international settings on a backlot at Borehamwood. There was a kind of repertory company of actors and writers who gave an ITC flavour to whatever was being produced. Unfortunately, this flavour was, with some exceptions (such as ***The Prisoner***), the taste of inoffensive blandness. This was mainly because, forever trying to crack the American market, there was a transatlantic air to most of their work.

On two grounds, then, *Department S* was different. First, it certainly wasn't bland, the style of mysteries being deliberately outrageous. Second, it might have officially starred a straightforward American character, Stewart Sullivan, but he was continually upstaged by the very British Jason King. King was a product of the times, a slightly too-old Carnaby Street playboy who had money of his own, and was basically part of the Department because he enjoyed it. He wore incredible facial hair ('Get your hair cut!' a workman shouts after him in 'The Trojan Tanker') and the most outrageous shirts on television. He was a crime novelist, whose Mark Caine books gave him a continual champagne fund, and the ability to look at a mystery with an author's eye. No wonder the writers gave him all the best lines. King once kept a bottle of champagne from Sullivan, saying, 'I would offer you a glass, but it is bad for you in small doses.'

The third member of the team was Annabelle Hurst, who formed the other half of an ***Avengers***-ish team with Jason, both quipping in frilled shirts while Sullivan slugged it out in his crumpled suit. Annabelle, with her scientific expertise and dress sense, was ITC's first cool chick. Sir Curtis Seretse, the team's chief, was an Oxbridge black, a quietly wonderful gesture to how youthfully liberal the series was trying to be. The mysteries to be solved were actually quite clever, including the death of a man roaming London in a spacesuit, who finally collapses from exposure, and all the passengers in a tube train dying. There was

Starring: Joel Fabiani (Stewart Sullivan) • Rosemary Nicols (Annabelle Hurst) • Peter Wyngarde (Jason King) • Dennis Alaba Peters (Sir Curtis Seretse) • Dennis Price (Sir Brian) • Ronald Lacey (Ryland) • Ann Sharp (Nicola Harvester)

subtlety in the tale of a whole shift at a chemical factory taking the day off, and a wonderful variation on the 'locked room' mystery, with a dead woman and a gibbering man found inside a perfectly furnished room in a disused factory. One story that seemed strangely plausible was that of the airliner that casually arrived six days late. Many of these mysteries originated from ITC staff writer Philip Broadley, and others were set as posers in Spooner's original format. One of the most memorable images of the series was the pre-title sequence to 'The Man Who Got a New Face', in which a sleeping man has a clown's mask stuck to his face and wakes to find himself unable to remove it, suffering a fatal heart-attack in the process.

There were guest stars aplenty, including Anthony Hopkins as the scientist Halliday, who had created a new nerve gas and had an attack of conscience ('A Small War of Nerves'). Frank Forsyth, Anthony Valentine, Iain Cuthbertson and Tony Selby also enlivened proceedings.

After the series finished, to no great critical response, ITC realized that a younger audience had been watching for one reason only: Jason King. Rather than commission a new season of *Department S*, the novelist was given a show of his own, and thus entered the realm of several TV characters of the time (Adam Adamant, Pertwee's *Doctor Who,* John Steed) who were not only dandies, but whose bizarre fashions indicated their distance from the 'square' establishment. All of these characters disdained money, either because they had lots of it, or didn't need it, and all had a complex relationship with officialdom. In Jason's case, he was continually hounded to work for the intelligence services once more by Sir Brian, but insisted that he'd given up on all that (it was a wonder he didn't show up in the Village). What persuaded him to do so was the threat of back taxes, and Sir Brian's assistant, Ryland, who was seemingly looking forward to the decadent adventurer's demise. But quite often Jason would find trouble enough on his own. He was equally loathe to respond to the pleadings of his publisher, Nicola Harvester, preferring instead to get involved, Saint-like, with foreign intrigue and foreign women, writing the occasional book when it suited him.

The series, according to Spooner, was not entirely to Lew Grade's taste, parodying the style of other ITC shows as it did, and playing with tongue firmly in cheek. Comedy was a bit of an alien strain to ITC, with productions rarely straying from the earnest tone of *Man in a Suitcase* and *The Champions*. Each episode was also filmed on 16 mm colour film, unlike contemporary playboy adventure *The*

DEPARTMENT S
First season
(9 Mar–27 Apr 69)
1 Six Days
2 The Trojan Tanker
3 A Cellar Full of Silence
4 The Pied Piper of Hambledown
5 One of our Aircraft is Empty
6 The Man in the Elegant Room
7 Handicap Dead
8 A Ticket to Nowhere

Second season
(17 Sep 69–4 Mar 70)
9 Black Out
10 The Double Death of Charlie Crippen
11 Who Plays the Dummy?
12 The Treasure of the Costa del Sol
13 The Man Who Got a New Face
14 Les Fleurs du Mal
15 The Shift that Never Was
16 The Man from 'X'
17 Dead Men Die Twice
18 The Perfect Operation
19 The Duplicated Man
20 The Mysterious Man in the Flying Machine
21 Death on Reflection
22 The Last Train to Redbridge
23 A Small War of Nerves
24 The Bones of Byrom Blaine
25 Spenser Bodily is Sixty Years Old
26 The Ghost of Mary Burnham
27 A Fish out of Water
28 The Soup of the Day

JASON KING
(15 Sep 71–28 Apr 72)
1 Wanna Buy a Television Series?
2 A Page Before Dying
3 Buried in the Cold, Cold Ground
4 A Deadly Line in Digits
5 Variations on a Theme
6 As Easy as A,B,C
7 To Russia with ... Panache
8 A Red Red Rose Forever
9 All That Glisters (part one)
10 All That Glisters (part two)
11 Flamingos Only Fly on Tuesdays
12 Toki
13 The Constance Missal
14 Uneasy Lies the Head
15 Nadine
16 A Kiss for a Beautiful Killer
17 If It's Got to Go – It's Got to Go
18 A Thin Band of Air
19 It's Too Bad About Auntie
20 The Stones of Venice
21 A Royal Flush
22 Every Picture Tells a Story
23 Chapter One: The Company I Keep
24 Zenia
25 An Author in Search of Two Characters
26 That Isn't Me, It's Somebody Else

[*Department S* and *Jason King* were not syndicated. The above dates are those of the ATV (Midlands) region.]

Persuaders!, which was on 35 mm, suggesting that ITC didn't think that such an obviously British series could break the American market. Indeed it didn't, never having been shown in the States. Still, guest stars such as Nicholas Courtney, Michele Dotrice, Philip Madoc, Felicity Kendal (who played the title role in 'Toki') and Julian Glover were always worth watching.

The plots involved Jason being transported across the Berlin Wall in a safe and to Moscow in a wooden crate. In Robert Banks Stewart's 'Every Picture Tells a Story' he finds that a Mark Caine comic strip contains strange messages when translated into Chinese. Indeed, the writers seemed delighted to be scripting a series about an author. At one stage everything that Jason writes seems to come true, and in another episode a gang of villains decide to follow his plots for their crimes, pinning the blame on him. In 'An Author in Search of Two Characters', Dennis Spooner even has King discussing two television hacks named Philip Broadley and Tony Williamson with someone from the Writer's Guild. While Jason wandered the world, making money and winning awards, the real writers behind him were the last generation of the ITC script factory, largely anonymous and hardly rich. No wonder the series didn't take itself seriously.

The Sweeney

- **Thames/Euston Films** (ITV) ◆ **Colour**
- **54 episodes** (standard length: 60 minutes) ◆ **1974-78**
- **Creator:** Ian Kennedy Martin
- **Writers:** Ian Kennedy Martin, Murray Smith, Ranald Graham, Roger Marshall, Robert Banks Stewart, Troy Kennedy Martin, P.J. Hammond, Donald Churchill, Tudor Gates, Martin Hall, Allan Prior, Richard Harris, Tony Hoare, Andrew Wilson, Ray Jenkins, Tony Marsh, Trevor Preston, Ted Childs, Robert Wales, Peter Hill
- **Directors:** Douglas Camfield, Chris Burt, James Goddard, Viktor Ritelis, Chris Menaul, Graham Baker, Peter Smith, Ben Bolt, Bill Brayne, David Wickes, Tom Clegg, James Goddard, Terry Green, Sid Roberson, Mike Vardy, Ted Childs
- **Producer:** Ted Childs

In June 1974, Ian Kennedy Martin's play 'Regan' was premiered on the ITV network in an *Armchair Cinema* special. It was about an inspector in the Flying Squad ('Sweeney Todd', as the papers kept reminding their readers) called Jack Regan. He was worried about all the specialist squads that the Met was developing, angry with bureaucracy in a way that transcended the usual clichés about rebel policemen, and far too casual for his own good. Regan grew up in Manchester, and already had a divorce and a daughter (Alison) behind him. His partner, and safety valve, was George Carter, a family man from Notting Hill, but with enough spring in his step to suggest that if it hadn't been for the boxing trophies he'd be on the other side of the law.

Ian Kennedy Martin had gone into the business of the Flying Squad (a group of motorized coppers with specialist drivers) and created the first modern police procedural show. What ***Z Cars*** had once been, *The Sweeney* became. The BBC show was still being screened when its successor arrived, and was swiftly made to look genteel by comparison. Jack Quarrie, a former Flying Squad officer, advised on detail, and if Ernest Bond, the chief of detective operations, called the show 'a load of rubbish', the officers that the cast drank with said different.

The series dealt well with the boredom and tension of the job. In one episode Regan uses his detective skills to search his boss's desk for his own fitness report. In another, a young constable, out in the countryside watching a farmhouse, is totally forgotten, and falls ill from exposure.

The programme swiftly acquired a reputation for violence, Regan having no scruples about hurting suspects. 'We do not accept that police officers as a matter of course are foul-mouthed, sadistically violent and promiscuous,' said Mary Whitehouse. The action was integral to the format, because, as the original guidelines said, 'In general terms, we can cope with action more readily than we can with multi-handed dialogue. Also, we cannot enjoy the luxury of extensive rehearsal.' The Euston Films team (who would later develop ***Minder***, ***Reilly - Ace of Spies***, *Out*, *Widows* and numerous other successful ventures) was a subsidiary of Thames, and had an approach that paralleled that of the Flying Squad itself: multiple film units, going on location with small budgets. An exciting

Starring: John Thaw (DI Jack Regan) • Dennis Waterman (DS George Carter) • Garfield Morgan (Chief Insp. Frank Haskins)

'We're the Sweeney, son, and we ain't had our dinner yet!'

pre-titles sequence led into each episode, and the all-film production led to one of the more obvious features of the show: the sound. Knuckles cracked and gun-shots blasted.

That said, the programme developed a subtlety and grammar of its own. As Troy Kennedy Martin said in the book *Crimewriters*, this was 'a world of vanity and self-mockery', a breeding ground for clipped poetry. 'What are you going to be when you grow up?' asks a newly-out prisoner of his daughter. 'A social worker,' she replies. Listening to police jargon, a housewife remarks that 'It's just like joining the masons all over again'. Carter describes his relationship with his girlfriend (his wife, played by Stephanie Turner, having been killed in the episode 'Hit and Run') as 'purely heterosexual'.

All the characters in ***The Sweeney*** had lives beyond the job. Haskins, Regan's nervy but sympathetic boss, had continual problems with his wife, Doreen. Before she died, Alison kept urging Carter to abandon Regan to his fate and start climbing the promotional ladder. These pressures added to the atmosphere of unglamorous policemen, who made mistakes. In the first episode Regan forgot to lock his car, and had vital evidence stolen. Indeed, his weary expression was the result of the writers' joy at getting him into grindingly downbeat situations. In Troy Kennedy Martin's 'Night Out', Regan, supposedly watching a bank, found himself spending the night in a room above a pub with an old flame. The villains staged an attack and he had to shin down a ladder. In no other police series would he have actually fallen off and landed in a puddle.

In the sensational 'Thou Shalt Not Kill!', a pair of armed bank robbers take the manager and a female customer hostage during a siege, and Regan and Haskins are presented with the dilemma of whether to use their marksmen and kill the criminals or 'sweat it out'. Regan favours the former but Haskins chooses the latter and the scenario goes disastrously wrong, ending in the death of the manager and the disfigurement of the girl. Regan blasted his superior with the memorable line 'The chances of villains taking hostages again would be a lot less than they're gonna be now.' Other memorable episodes include the kidnap of Regan's daughter in Trevor Preston's 'Abduction', the repercussions of an internal investigation after Regan is accused of using unreasonable force on a prisoner in 'Big Brother', and the surreal dream sequences of 'Nightmare'.

The series certainly had a strong sense of humour. Regan was continually looking for his fantasy, a girl in a German helmet, and had a habit of referring to the World Cup Squad of 1966: 'Where are you now, Nobby, when we need you?' Warren Mitchell appeared in drag, and Patrick Mower and George Layton made two memorable appearances in Roger Marshall's scripts as Colin and Ray, the Australian villains who hijacked a bus to steal a Goya, knocking out the driver with his bag of change. Diana Dors proved a dangerous mother-in-law to one of Regan's suspects, and finished the show by squashing his wedding cake. Other guest stars included Brian Blessed, Julian Glover, Patrick Troughton, Lesley-Anne Down, Roy Kinnear, John Hurt, George Cole, Hywel Bennett and Michael Elphick.

There was a writers' competition to include a line that almost became a catchphrase, 'Get yer trousers on, you're nicked.' Indeed, with hindsight, the dialogue often seems laden with slang and expressions that would have seemed false back in the late 60s: a black character exclaiming 'What are you staring at, you stupid honky bitch?', a minor thief moaning 'And there's no way without that lawyer breathing down my Gregory.'

One of the most memorable comic sequences from the show is when Carter kicks down a door, walks into a room where a family is having dinner, and reads a speech from a piece of paper in dodgy Italian. The family explain that they are English. Carter checks the number on the door, apologizes, and leaves. A moment later, another crash and another translated speech is heard from upstairs.

Real comedians eventually got in on the act in 1978. Morecambe and Wise, at their own request, had a script written around them for an episode ('Hearts and Minds') in which they appeared as themselves, threatened by Arab villains. Chase sequences and comedy set pieces merged easily with the regular grammar of the show, one of the best scenes being when Eric desperately threw boxes of pilchards into the path of the pursuing Arabs. This was all a pay-back for Thaw and Waterman's appearance in the previous Christmas' *Morecambe and Wise Show*.

There was much of the ambiguity of real life about *The Sweeney*. Real villains went free, while patsies took the blame. Regan was grateful if he just about managed to break even. If Haskins was trying to be an Olympian copper like Barlow

Armchair Cinema
(4 Jun 74, 90 minutes)
1 Regan

First season
(2 Jan–27 Mar 75)
2 Ringer
3 Jackpot
4 Thin Ice
5 Queen's Pawn
6 Jigsaw
7 Night Out
8 The Placer
9 Cover Story
10 Golden Boy
11 Stoppo Driver
12 Big Spender
13 Contact Breaker
14 Abduction

Second season
(1 Sep–24 Nov 75)
15 Chalk and Cheese
16 Faces
17 Supersnout
18 Big Brother
19 Hit and Run
20 Trap
21 Golden Fleece
22 Poppy
23 Stay Lucky, Eh?
24 Trojan Bus
25 I Want the Man
26 Country Boy
27 Thou Shalt Not Kill!

Third season
(6 Sep–20 Dec 76)
28 Selected Target
29 In from the Cold
30 Visiting Fireman
31 Tomorrow Man
32 Taste of Fear
33 Bad Apple
34 May
35 Sweet Smell of Succession
36 Down to you, Brother
37 Pay Off
38 Loving Arms
39 Lady Luck
40 On the Run

Fourth season
(7 Sep–28 Dec 78)
41 Messenger of the Gods
42 Hard Men
43 Drag Act
44 Trust Red
45 Nightmare
46 Money, Money, Money
47 Bait
48 The Bigger they Are
49 Feet of Clay
50 One of your Own
51 Hearts and Minds
52 Latin Lady
53 Victims
54 Jack or Knave

[Episode 27 was scheduled for transmission in the slot occupied by episode 24, but was delayed until the end of the season.]

on the other side, then he had the Kray twins under his command. In P.J. Hammond's 'Pay Off', Carter's new girlfriend was cynically used by Regan as a decoy, and was nearly killed in a gunfight. Carter could only protest that he didn't know. With both men loners, the show became a very male story of loneliness and drink.

In the final story, 'Jack or Knave', Regan was arrested on suspicion of corruption, and found himself in a cell. He was eventually cleared, but the experience finally pushed him over the edge. He left the force. Thaw, having already been a morose copper in *Redcap*, was destined to play another, if a more intellectual, one in ***Inspector Morse***. Waterman was to continue with almost the same character in Euston Films' ***Minder***.

In many ways, *The Sweeney* can be summed up by its signature tune. Bold and strident at the start, promising action and violence, but with a melancholy poetry inside that showed itself in the soulful jazz version that played over the end credits. Two movies were made, neither of which really got the point, being brutal for brutality's sake. Despite the protests of Mary Whitehouse, *The Sweeney* was only ever as violent as the real world required it to be.

The XYY Man/Strangers/Bulman

- **Granada** (ITV) ◆ Colour
- **65 episodes** (50 minutes) ◆ 1976-82, 1985-87
- **Writers include:** Ivor Marshall, Tim Aspinall, Eddie Boyd, Murray Smith. Bruce Crowther, Leslie Duxbury, Brian Finch, C.P. Taylor, Henry Livings, Paul Wheeler
- **Directors include:** Ken Grieve, Carol Wilks, Ben Bolt, William Brayne, John Bruce, Tristan de Vere Cole, Philip Draycott, William Gilmour, Quentin Lawrence, Jonathan Wright-Miller, Brian Mills, Lawrence Moody, Baz Taylor, Roger Tucker, Sarah Harding, Christopher King, Gareth Morgan
- **Producers:** Richard Everitt, Steve Hawes, Sita Williams

Regular cast: Don Henderson (George Bulman)

With: Stephen Yardley (Spider Scott) • Vivienne McKee (Maggie Parsons) • Mark Dignam (Fairfax) • Dennis Blanch (Derek Willis) • John Ronane (Singer) • Frances Tomelty (Linda Doran) • Fiona Mollison (Vanessa Bennett) • Mark McManus (DCI Lambie) • Siobhan Redmond (Lucy McGinty) • Thorley Walters (William Dugdale) • David Hargreaves (DI Rainbow) • Troy Foster (DC Charlie Baker) • George Pravda (Pushkin) • Lol Coxhill (Sonny Boy Saltz)

The origins of the Bulman saga lie in three series that Granada producer Richard Everitt worked on in the 60s. *The Odd Man*, *It's Dark Outside* and *Mr Rose* featured characters created by Edward Boyd, and focused on the bizarre adventures of detective Rose (William Mervyn). In 1975, Everitt picked up a novel by Kenneth Royce. The book was *The XYY Man*, the title referring to cat burglar Spider Scott, a man with an extra Y chromosome. This made him both tall and more likely to get involved in anti-social behaviour.

Everitt cast the 6ft 4in Stephen Yardley as Scott, and created a series that was hard-hitting and realistic. The initial mini-series was a success, and Granada commissioned three further stories. The second of these was an adaptation of a Royce story by ex-policeman Murray Smith, the last was an original script from Boyd.

If Scott stayed on the right side of the law, it was because the police could never prove anything, a trait that Smith especially delighted in, treating the criminals and police as rival gangs, with internal troubles of their own. The third gang in *The XYY Man* were the 'spooks' of MI5, as represented by Fairfax, who had uses of his own for Scott. Smith took a liking to a certain character that Royce had described as 'A little, dapper man of military bearing.'

Viewers can be thankful that director Ken Grieve chose to cast against type. Don Henderson was chosen to play Detective Sergeant George Kitchener Bulman. The bulky actor was an ex-policeman himself, but had retired from the force because he'd started to feel sorry for some of the criminals. The actor wore woollen gloves to hide his wedding ring, and used a nasal inhaler onscreen to clear a (real) head cold. Bulman was seen as a bit of a hard case. He was assisted by DC Derek Willis, who wasn't in the books. Willis would often be outshone by his boss, but was a bit more suited to physical action. The characters ran parallel to Regan and Carter of ***The Sweeney***, but Bulman was always more intellectual, and stranger, than his Flying Squad counterpart.

And he didn't get away with as much. As a result of nine disciplinary hearings in a row, Bulman was sent 'up north' to join C23, called the 'strangers' because the local mobs didn't know them. Willis went with his old boss. This was the premise of the new series that Smith and Everitt created.

In Manchester, Bulman found that his boss was the useless DI Rainbow. The squad now included David Singer, a pleasant local man, and self-defence expert

Linda Doran. By now the Bulman gimmicks were firmly in place. George carried a Key Market Kops plastic bag and wore his 'Will Power' Shakespeare T-Shirt (with collared shirt underneath) when off-duty. The scarf he habitually wore concealed the actor's problems with throat cancer. Bulman owned a hamster, was studying for an Open University degree (the exams for which he had to miss in the first season of *Bulman*) and was a pacifist (as was Henderson). He had changed so much from his original 'Bullhead' character that when Royce wrote three new *XYY* novels he added a line to the effect that Bulman had 'always been misunderstood'.

Highlights of the second season of *Strangers* included the arrival of DC Vanessa Bennett. Initially a driving specialist, she managed to personify Smith's emerging weirdness. Her first comment to Bulman, on getting into her car, was 'Brmmm, brmmm!' She was tough, unclichéd, gorgeous and ordinary. As a TV character, she was a decade ahead of her time.

The final episode of the second season, the wonderful 'Marriages, Deaths and Births', began at the wedding of the son of the Carmos family of Greek gangsters. Bulman walks up the aisle and arrests the groom. Young buck Nick Carmos kidnaps Bulman, who is only rescued when Nick's father kills his son. (Smith seems fascinated by public ceremonies, depicting in detail a Caribbean wake in the fifth season, and another criminal wedding in one of his (far too good) episodes of *Dempsey and Makepeace*.)

The format changed for the third season. Mike Moran's jazz theme remained, but the titles became more sinister, featuring a prowling black cat and a snapping mousetrap. C23 returned to London to become the Inter-City Squad, and the season had a bigger budget (episodes set all over the country, all on film, adding an unusual travelogue atmosphere). The squad was under DCI Jack Lambie (Mark McManus playing an early Taggart-like character). Lambie was harder than Bulman, with a reputation for torturing suspects. The squad was more involved in the intelligence community, frequently running into the plummy spook Dugdale.

'The Moscow Subway Murders' opened the fourth season with Inspector Pushkin of the Moscow police (George Pravda) journeying to Britain to solve said crime. The squad called each other by their Christian names: even Bulman, promoted to Chief Inspector after being shot in the apocalyptic 'No Orchids for Missing Blandisch', was just George. They were getting involved with each other too, Bennett and Willis having an on-off relationship that was seen in glimpses, arguments and sulking. 'Soldiers of Misfortune' featured the problem of a series of people being shot in the leg, the natural result of which was a gang of three sten-gun-carrying assassins, their legs in plaster casts.

The gem of the season was Edward Boyd's complex 'The Flowers of Edinburgh', in which Bennett got involved with the mysterious Ludo, who took

THE XYYMAN
First season
(3–17 Jul 76)
1 The Proposition
2 The Execution
3 The Resolution

Second season
(27 Jun–29 Aug 77)
4 Friends and Enemies (part one)
5 The Missing Civil Servant (part two)
6 The Big Bang (part three)
7 At the Bottom of the River (part four)
8 When we were Very Greedy (part one)
9 Now we are Dead (part two)
10 Whisper who Dares (part three)
11 Law and Order (part one)
12 The Detrimental Robot (part two)
13 A View to a Death (part three)

STRANGERS
First season
(5 Jun–17 Jul 78)
1 The Paradise Set
2 Duty Roster
3 Silver Lining
4 Accidental Death
5 Briscoe
6 Right and Wrong
7 Paying Guests

Second season
(9 Jan–6 Feb 79)
8 The Wheeler Dealers
9 Call of the Wild
10 Clever Dick
11 Friends in High Places
12 Marriages, Deaths and Births

Third season
(14 Oct–25 Nov 80)
13 Retribution
14 You Can't Win Them All
15 Armed and Dangerous
16 Racing Certainty
17 Clowns don't Cry
18 Tom Thumb and other Stories
19 No Orchids for Missing Blandisch

her to visit an ancient brothel, while the squad pursued a transvestite hitman. Shot in elegant Edinburgh locations, the episode brought together all the influences that made *Strangers* such a vintage brew.

The final season also produced some classics. 'The Lost Chord' was a perfect example of Smith's *Strangers*. The squad investigate the activities of Cambridge professor of humanities Ogden Whittingham (Michael Gough), who seemed to be killing those Fascists that barrister Nigel Cruikshank (Graeme Garden) kept getting off the hook. 'I can't argue with your taste in victims,' says Bulman, to press disapproval. He is finally arrested when, all avenues of investigation closed, Bulman settles down to play boogie-woogie at the professor's piano only to find that one key doesn't work. A fatal length of piano wire is missing. However, Dugdale insists that Whittingham should not be found guilty and puts Cruikshank on the case. The professor walks free from court and shakes his defence counsel by the hand. The solicitor gets into his car, which promptly explodes.

The final two episodes seemed to make an effort to touch on all the themes for which the show was famous. In the first part we saw a criminal escape from jail using an explosive volume of Oscar Wilde, and Bulman and Willis going undercover in a jazz band. Willis was shot in the face by a shotgun full of salt, and Bennett's new boyfriend was killed on the eve of a family celebration. In the final episode the doom-laden atmosphere continued, Bulman attending the funeral and wake, and Inspector Pushkin returning. The final showdown was the gunfight to end all gunfights, a gang of arms dealers holed up with their stock. Bulman and Pushkin arrive on a motorcycle combination and the soundtrack swells with 'The Ride of the Valkyries'.

In the end, Bulman reveals that he is going to marry Lambie's ex, and he sees this as a good excuse to leave the force. He leaves his gloves behind. There were already plans for his own series.

Things didn't work out, it seems, with Lambie's ex, and George bought an old shop in Shanghai Road, south-west London, intending to mend clocks for a living. However, two things happen at once. The ex-owner of the shop is found dead, and Lucy McGinty, the daughter of an old friend in the CID, arrives. Lucy abandons her course in medieval studies at St Andrews in order to study practical criminology with George. She exhorts him to become a PI, but he initially refuses, saying that he's 'decided to go straight, pay my debt to society'. In the end, of course, she succeeds.

Everitt then took a back seat as executive producer on *Bulman*, and the change was apparent. Too much media attention was centred on George, and what had been a cult had its kinks ironed out to become a popular series.

Bulman was becoming self-consciously eccentric and positively cuddly. Lambie, Willis, and Dugdale made appearances in the first season, but something wasn't quite right. We met Bulman's ex-wife, Rosalind, and his son, Tom, and there were entertaining guest stars, including Maggie Smith and Peter Wyngarde, but everything was too twee. Without the police to react against, Bulman was getting tired.

Fourth season
(25 Sep–30 Oct 81)
20 The Moscow Subway Murders
21 The Loneliness of the Long-Distance Copper
22 A Dear Green Place
23 Stand and Deliver
24 The Flowers of Edinburgh
25 Soldiers of Misfortune

Fifth season
(8 Sep–20 Oct 82)
26 A Much Under-Estimated Man
27 A Swift and Evil Rozzer
28 The Tender Trap
29 The Lost Chord
30 A Free Weekend in the Country
31 Charlie's Brother's Birthday
32 With these Gloves you can Pass through Mirrors

BULMAN
First season
(5 Jun–28 Aug 85)
1 Winds of Change
2 The Daughter was a Dancer
3 Pandora's Many Boxes
4 Death of a Hit Man
5 The Name of the Game
6 One of our Pigeons is Missing
7 Sins of Omission
8 Another Part of the Jungle
9 Born into the Purple
10 A Cup for the Winner
11 I Met a Man who wasn't There
12 A Movable Feast
13 A Man of Conviction

Second season
(20 Jun–8 Aug 87)
14 Chinese Whispers
15 Death by Misadventure
16 White Lies
17 Chicken of the Baskervilles
18 Thin Ice
19 W.C. Fields was Right
20 Ministry of Accidents

[The above order is taken from *625* magazine and *British Television Drama Research Guide 1950-1995*. Granada have an alternative order (reflecting production?) with episode 13 as the last in season two, and season four comprising episodes 20, 22, 21, 24, 23 and 28. Episode 17 was scheduled for 11 Jul 87 but was delayed by a week.]

The 'Strangers'

It was perhaps in the realization of this that Murray Smith began to inject some genuinely disturbing material into the series. In 'A Man of Conviction' Bulman goes to prison to finger ganglord Joe Revell (Alfred Lynch) and has a contract put out on him. George and Lucy flee to Shanghai at the end of the season and join a commune. It would have been a fitting end.

However, plans were well-advanced for another 13-episode season. The ratings had been good, but internal politics at Granada were turning against *Bulman*. The proposed season was chopped down to seven episodes, and scheduled inconveniently. Bulman cut off his ponytail and returned to Britain to start a gang war which made life safe for him once again, but things were always perilous. The final three episodes were very grim indeed. In 'Thin Ice' Dugdale returned, apparently dying at the hands of his own people. Bulman and Lucy had become part of a jazz band, and it became clear that they were involved in a spook conspiracy. In the final episode they were mown down in a hail of machine-gun fire. The 'deaths' were as real as Dugdale's turned out to be, and the series ended with the two friends going underground once again.

There were rumours about a third season but Granada remained tight-lipped. Finally, Murray Smith went to the BBC, taking Henderson with him for *The Paradise Club*. Two seasons of the gangland thriller were made, mixing police lore, whimsy and a new gang, the Church of England, in a highly enjoyable format. Tiny details of continuity, like references to the 'Taxicab wars' remained intact too, as did the character names of the spooks that haunted Henderson's ex-priest Frank Kane.

It seems that we've seen the last of Bulman, but somebody like him is likely to resurface at any time. Murray Smith, even with his new career as a thriller writer, isn't about to abandon a televisual lineage that stretches across two channels and three decades.

The Professionals

- **An Avengers Mark 1 Production/LWT** (ITV) ◆ Colour
- **57 episodes** (1 unbroadcast in UK) (60 minutes) ◆ 1977-83
- **Creator:** Brian Clemens
- **Writers include:** Brian Clemens, Anthony Read, Dennis Spooner, Gerry O'Hara, Don Houghton, Ranald Graham, Christopher Wicking, Roger Marshall, Tony Barwick
- **Directors include:** Douglas Camfield, William Brayne, Ray Austin, Charles Crichton, Pat Jackson, Martin Campbell, Denis Lewiston
- **Producers:** Sidney Hayers, Raymond Menmuir
- **Executive producers:** Albert Fennell, Brian Clemens

Starring: Gordon Jackson (George Cowley) • Lewis Collins (Bodie) • Martin Shaw (Ray Doyle)

History has not been kind to *The Professionals*: constantly derided as a moronic example of the violent trend of television in the early 80s, brilliantly parodied in the Comic Strip production *The Bullshitters*, and doomed, were it not for the power of Martin Shaw's veto, to walk the graveyard of the mid-afternoon repeat slots on the ITV regions. It's difficult to find anyone with a good word to say about *The Professionals*. However, although it was an attempt to muscle in on the success of Euston's ***The Sweeney***, its roots lay in a much older and more innovative sub-genre.

The Professionals was a production from the creative team that had produced two seasons of ***The New Avengers*** between 1976 and 1977, and was created by Brian Clemens almost directly out of a number of ideas that had been explored in some later episodes of that series. Martin Shaw and Lewis Collins had appeared in the story 'Obsession', playing very similar characters to Doyle and Bodie, while an early version of the George Cowley character was present in 'Medium Rare'. When ***The New Avengers*** ended, Clemens decided to create a new branch of the British Secret Service - CI5 - that would lead to a contemporary action adventure series along the lines of the Euston productions, while still maintaining the traditional ***Avengers*** quirky atmosphere. Somewhere along the line, the quirkiness was lost, and, once in production, *The Professionals* became an even more macho vehicle, albeit one with higher production values than many of its peers. Allegedly, the original choices for the roles of Bodie and Doyle were Anthony Andrews and Jon Finch. Finch turned down the part of Doyle, and screen tests showed that Andrews and Martin Shaw looked too similar, leading to the casting of Lewis Collins. However, this story seems unlikely, the actors' pairing in 'Obsession' very clearly suggesting that this was the setting up of a future partnership.

Early *Professionals* highlights included 'Killer with a Long Arm', which concerned an assassin with a high-velocity rifle, capable of hitting targets over two miles away, and 'Heroes', where a newspaper published the names and addresses of a number of witnesses to a terrorist killing. The excellent 'Long Shot' saw Bodie trapped with the staff of the American Embassy by terrorists, unable to alert his colleagues. (Fact, however, often proves stranger than fiction. LWT exported the show around the world, and it seems to have been taken a little too seriously by some people as, during the Libyan People's Bureau incident in 1984, the British embassy in Tripoli was besieged by hordes chanting 'Down with CI5'.)

The problem with the series - one that Martin Shaw, trapped in a four-year contract, was well aware of - was that it was so consistently moronic. Female characters were ciphers (the 'explosions before characterization' policy of the show meant that they didn't even get to be 'love interest' very often), and the closest Shaw got to softening his ex-policeman character was the revelation that he occasionally liked to cook a bit of pasta. Bodie, on the other hand, was very much a continuation of the sporty thug that Collins had played in *The Cuckoo Waltz*. The series was geared to appeal to ten-year-old boys everywhere, complete with the prejudices of the man on the street. In the potentially liberal episode 'In the Public Interest', where a police force has taken over a city, the sympathetic, roughed-up owner of a gay bookshop turns out not to be gay himself, but 'just had friends who were'. Whenever an interfering, left-wing reporter-type appeared, they would be either killed, seduced, or converted to the cause.

'Klansman', a Clemens script that concerned inner-city racism, was deemed too violent for British transmission and has never been shown in this country. The second season was, if anything, even more violent, with plots concerning such themes as the death of a suspect ('The Rack') and bribery and corruption in government ('Not a Very Civil, Civil Servant'), ending with Bodie framed for murder in 'Fall Girl'.

By the third season the formula was wearing thin, and few writers seemed to be able to resist the temptation to churn out clichéd and tired rehashes of old plots. (Hammer veteran Don Houghton managed to, as did Christopher Wicking, another horror film regular.) Wicking's first script for the programme, 'The Madness of Mickey Hamilton', was probably the highlight of the third season. Most of the rest of the scripts utilized one of three backgrounds: political intrigue, drug trafficking, or international terrorism. Critics loathed the series, Philip Purser stating 'of all the rotten new breed of thuggish cops and secret agents... this little gang is the least attractive.' He went on to describe Martin Shaw thus: 'The curly-headed one reminds me fatally of Harpo Marx.'

Clemens's involvement had drastically declined by the fourth season, and the formula nature of the plots (which were always enlivened by the detail and strangeness of Clemens's approach) was making the show boring. Clemens returned to write 'Need to Know', which could almost have been called 'thoughtful', as Bodie and Doyle philosophically waited for the attack of two similar killers from the other side. Ranald Graham provided an unusual plotline with 'Wild Justice', which posed the question 'Is Bodie cracking up?'

The final season was an improvement, although it did include a couple of examples of the series at its comical or violent worst ('The Untouchables' and

First season
(30 Dec 77–17 Mar 78)
1 Private Madness, Public Danger
2 The Female Factor
3 Old Dog with New Tricks
4 Killer with a Long Arm
5 Heroes
6 Where the Jungle Ends
7 Close Quarters
8 Everest was Also Conquered
9 When the Heat Cools Off
10 Long Shot
11 Stake Out
12 Look After Annie
13 Klansmen [unbroadcast]

Second season
(7 Oct–9 Dec 78)
14 Hunter/Hunted
15 The Rack
16 First Night
17 Man without a Past
18 In the Public Interest
19 Rogue
20 Not a Very Civil, Civil Servant
21 A Stirring of Dust
22 Blind Run
23 Fall Girl

Third season
(27 Oct–15 Dec 79)
24 The Purging of CI5
25 Backtrack
26 Stopover
27 Dead Reckoning
28 The Madness of Mickey Hamilton
29 A Hiding to Nothing
30 Runner
31 Servant of Two Masters

Fourth season
(7 Sep–27 Dec 80)
32 The Acorn Syndrome
33 Wild Justice
34 Fugitive
35 Involvement
36 Need to Know
37 Take Away
38 Black Out
39 Blood Sports
40 Slush Fund
41 The Gun
42 Hijack
43 Mixed Doubles
44 Weekend in the Country
45 Kickback
46 It's Only a Beautiful Picture...

Fifth season
(7 Nov 82–6 Feb 83)
47 Foxhole on the Roof
48 Operation Susie
49 You'll Be All Right
50 Lawson's Last Stand
51 Discovered in a Graveyard
52 Spy Probe
53 Cry Wolf
54 The Untouchables
55 The Ojuka Situation
56 A Man called Quinn
57 No Stone

[Episodes 25, 28 and 31 were filmed for the second season but transmitted during the third. Similarly, episodes 47, 48, 49, 51, 54 and 55 were filmed for the fourth season but shown during the fifth.]

'Lawson's Last Stand', respectively). Chris Wicking's 'Discovered in a Graveyard' came as close as the series ever got to a crossover into telefantasy: Doyle is shot early in the episode, and spends the rest of his time in a strange, dream-like netherworld, debating with his colleagues as to whether he really wanted to live or not. This is not as surprising as it sounds; Shaw (a vegetarian non-drinker) loathed every moment of his role ('That godawful haircut ... Lewis used to call me the Bionic Gollywog!') and fought the team on almost every conceivable issue. Doubtless he was keen to exploit this move away from traditional crime serial motifs.

By the end of its run *The Professionals* had outstayed its welcome. *The Bullshitters* (and its *Comic Strip Presents* sequel 'Detectives on the Verge of a Nervous Breakdown') wonderfully satirised many of the programme's most well-remembered elements, poking fun at the often comic strip nature of the supposedly 'graphic and realistic' violence that was once one of the series' proudest boasts. Certainly, by its demise, the public had grown intolerant of this type of action.

Considered by its critics a five-season joke that didn't have an effective punch-line, *The Professionals* was one of LWT's biggest ever exports. Its effects on the genre might not have been significant, but it remains a well-remembered example of the crime genre. It's just a shame that it couldn't be anything else.

Shoestring

- **BBC Television** (BBC1) ◆ Colour
- **21 episodes** (50 minutes) ◆ 1979-80
- **Creator:** Robert Banks Stewart
- **Writers include:** Robert Banks Stewart, Bob Baker, Dave Humphries, Robert Bennett, Terence Feely, Philip Martin, Peter Miller, William Hood, Bill Craig, Chris Boucher
- **Directors include:** Douglas Camfield, Marek Kanievska, Mike Vardy, Martyn Friend, Paul Ciappessoni, Henry Herbert, Ben Bolt, Lawrence Moody
- **Producers:** Robert Banks Stewart, Richard Harris

Starring: Trevor Eve (Eddie Shoestring) • Michael Medwin (Don Stachley) • Doran Godwin (Erica Bayliss) • Liz Crowther (Sonia)

Shoestring was set in and around Bristol, the series making much use of the photogenic Avon and Wiltshire countryside (indeed, the action would frequently switch from Bristol to Swindon in the blink of an eye). This helped to give the series a look unlike many of its London counterparts, which were limited to the same shots of inner-city, graffiti-covered streets. Later exercises in provincial crime drama - such as ***Strangers***, *Spender*, ***Cracker*** and *Wycliffe* - would also benefit from this freedom. The 'hook' of ***Shoestring*** was that rather than being a policeman, the detective in question was a scruffy, nosy ex-computer operator and former mental patient who, in the first episode, takes on a case for Radio West, and, after solving it, becomes the station's on-air detective, the 'private ear'. This meant that Shoestring, as a member of the media, was regarded with open suspicion by the police. An interesting blend of punk and hippie, he was a return to the 'nice' detective. He always had time for everybody, even if they didn't have time for him, although his relationship with authority was further complicated by the fact that Eddie's landlady (and occasional lover), Erica, was a legal advisor working for the establishment.

Trevor Eve was a newcomer to television, but his theatre work had included the role of Paul McCartney in Willy Russell's *John, Paul, George, Ringo… and Bert*. Eddie's boss was played by Michael Medwin, the first of a series of nostalgia figures that Robert Banks Stewart would cast in his shows.

The first episode set the tone for the multi-layered nature of many of the scripts as a popular Radio West DJ (William Russell) is somehow involved in the death of a local prostitute. This introduces Eddie to various aspects of the West Country underworld, as represented by official gangsters such as Len Tilley (Tony Haygarth) and, more sinisterly, by the 'shirt-and-tie' thugs led by Sean Arnold, who beat Eddie senseless in a deserted railway carriage as he returns home with a Chinese takeaway. The episode was fast-paced and witty, directed with flair by veteran Douglas Camfield, but was more deep and complex than many of its contemporaries. The use of filmed, as opposed to video-taped, exteriors and, especially, the large use of night filming, helped to give the series a sense of darkness. Added to this, having *Shoestring* set in a radio station gave plenty of opportunity for the use of then-current pop music as a backdrop and this, along with Trevor Eve's fashionably casual dress-sense (notably the 'skinny tie', then very much in vogue) gave the series a large youth following.

The first season included several notable episodes which relied heavily on dense pacing and plot, best exemplified by 'An Uncertain Circle' and 'Listen to

Me', the first involving a supposedly dead deep-sea diver and the second a wife's desperate attempts to clear her husband of a murder he didn't commit. 'Nine Tenths of the Law' was another fine episode, one of many in the series to question the exact nature of right and wrong as a child is kidnapped by her natural father in a 'tug-of-love' case similar to several real-life cases of the time. The episode saw one of the final TV appearances of Harry H. Corbett as the child's sinister grandfather.

Philip Martin's 'Find the Lady' was the highlight of the season, largely for its use of Toyah Wilcox and her band (some eight months before their first hit) in a mystery story which also included fine performances by Gary Holton and Christopher Biggins. The image of the band playing their single 'Danced' over the final credits was another of the techniques used to paint the series with New Wave icons. For its understanding and treatment of youth, *Shoestring* has a large claim to being British television's first post-punk creation.

Classic images from the first season included Eddie, force-fed whisky and staggering down the fast lane of the M4 in 'Stamp Duty', and the edge-of-the-seat fight between Eddie and a serial rapist (Patrick Malahide) in 'Listen to Me'. Such was the impact of the first series of *Shoestring* (with regular viewing figures around the 20 million mark) that when a second season was scheduled for late 1980 the ITV regions responded by pulling forward several episodes from the fourth season of ***The Professionals*** into direct competition.

Shoestring won the ratings war with stories that continued to be rich in drama and excitement. 'Mocking Bird' had a jealous DJ (David Sibley) working for Radio West as a security guard, attacking women and then phoning into the station with clues as to where he would strike next, leading to an extraordinary climax as Eddie almost suffers another nervous breakdown. 'The Mayfly Dance', one of the series' best-remembered episodes, saw Eddie asked to find a pop star who had disappeared at the height of his fame 20 years previously, uncovering along the way a complex murder mystery with a most unexpected conclusion. 'The Farmer had a Wife', which included a tiny role for the then-unknown Daniel Day Lewis, was a further example of the way in which Shoestring's involvement in cases, whilst providing his radio station with good 'copy', was often fatally unwanted for those unfortunate enough to be involved.

Perhaps the most memorable episode of the series was the final one, Chris Boucher's Christmas story 'The Dangerous Game' which, aside from having a future TV star turning up every few minutes (Michael Elphick, Celia Imrie, Maurice Colbourne and ***The Bill***'s Eric Richard, to name but four), featured an unbearably tense final 15 minutes. Having spoilt his own festivities finding a number of potentially-lethal 'Lunar Race 2000' toys, Eddie discovers that the last one is over the Severn Bridge in Wales. On Christmas morning he manages to get to the house in question, only to discover that the children had already plugged in the toy and had been saved by a power cut. 'The Dangerous Game' showed off the character of Eddie, a direct contrast to the macho heroes of ***The Professionals***. Vulnerable, neurotic, and prone to drinking, Shoestring was never keen to get into a fight, probably because he'd often lose

First season
(30 Sep–16 Dec 79)
1 Private Ear
2 Knock for Knock
3 Higher Ground
4 An Uncertain Circle
5 Listen to Me
6 Nine Tenths of the Law
7 The Link-Up
8 Stamp Duty
9 Find the Lady
10 The Partnership
11 I'm a Believer

Second season
(5 Oct–21 Dec 80)
12 Room with a View
13 The Teddy Bears' Nightmare
14 Mocking Bird
15 The Mayfly Dance
16 The Farmer had a Wife
17 Utmost Good Faith
18 Looking for Mr Wright
19 Another Man's Castle
20 Where Was I?
21 The Dangerous Game

(as exemplified when he tried to take on Diana Dors's fairground workers in 'Looking for Mr Wright'), and his car wasn't exactly flashy.

Another season was planned, but Trevor Eve was wary of being typecast as his alter-ego and opted to move back into the theatre, where his performance in Mark Medoff's *Children of a Lesser God* won much critical acclaim. Robert Banks Stewart turned his attention instead to Jersey, and created ***Bergerac***, an entirely different form of anti-establishment lawman, but in many ways a much more conventional one.

Five years later, Banks Stewart attempted to recreate *Shoestring*'s success with *Call Me Mister*, a brave, if not altogether successful, mix of some of the elements that had made both *Shoestring* and ***Bergerac*** so popular. It was generally badly-received, its level of violence, amongst other things, being cited as a reason for cancellation. A similar fate befell Banks Stewart's 1992 crime series *Moon and Son*, which was scrapped because of low ratings while a second season was in preparation.

Minder

- **Thames/Euston Films/Central** (ITV) ◆ Colour
- **108 episodes** (standard length: 60 minutes) ◆ 1979-94
- **Creator:** Leon Griffiths
- **Writers include:** Leon Griffiths, Paul Wheeler, Murray Smith, Bernie Cooper, Tony Hoare, Andrew Payne, Jeremy Burnham, Willis Hall, Trevor Preston, David Yallop, Tony Jordan, Kevin Clarke
- **Directors include:** Peter Sasdy, Roy Ward Baker, Frances Megahy, Ian Toynton, Christopher King, James Gatward, Robert Young, Tom Clegg, Terry Green, Mike Vardy, Diarmuid Lawrence, Roger Bamford
- **Producers:** Lloyd Shirley, George Taylor, Ian Toynton
- **Executive Producers:** Verity Lambert, Johnny Goodman

Starring: George Cole (Arthur Daley) • Dennis Waterman (Terry McCann) • Glynn Edwards (Dave) • George Layton (Des) • Patrick Malahide (DS Chisholm) • Peter Childs (Sgt. Rycott) • Anthony Valentine (Maurice) • Michael Troughton (DI Melsip) • Gary Webster (Ray Daley) • Nicholas Day (DS Morley) • Stephen Tompkinson (DC Park)

Leon Griffiths didn't know it, but he was on to a 'nice little earner' when, in the mid-70s, he wrote a film script entitled *Minder* (cockney slang for bodyguard). His agent liked it but told Griffiths that he'd never be able to sell it, so the writer filed the script away and went back to writing TV plays (1978's *Dinner at the Sporting Club*, for example). Then his agent suggested that two of the characters in *Minder*, a used car salesman (with a lock-up crammed full of merchandise that had fallen off the back of several lorries) and his tough but stupid minder, would be perfect for a television series. Griffiths wrote a 15-page proposal for a series and took it to Euston films. By a happy coincidence, they had recently completed work on ***The Sweeney*** and were looking for a vehicle for Dennis Waterman.

Euston executive Verity Lambert accepted Griffiths's idea, suggesting that the part of the roguish entrepreneur would be perfectly suited to George Cole. Griffiths admitted that the audience might initially have been very confused by *Minder*: 'They weren't quite sure what to do. Should they laugh? It's very unusual in this country to have a drama series where you can actually laugh out loud ... It took about six weeks before the audience thought "Yeah, this is pretty good".' Additionally, there was a problem with the fact that the *TV Times* was on strike. 'I'm sure,' said Griffiths, 'the audience had no idea what they were seeing. They probably thought it was ***The Sweeney***; that any minute they were going to see John Thaw come crashing in. But the critics were ahead of the audience, and the third season suddenly became a kind of cult, though I've no idea why and I'm pretty sure nobody at Thames knows either.'

The central characters were probably the reason why. Cole's Arfur Daley, the man with the trilby, expensive overcoat and cigar, with a Captain Mainwaring-style never-seen wife ("er indoors') and a sensational line in dodgy schemes, became a hero. The hapless Terry McCann, his ex-boxer and jailbird 'hard lad', had to be content to feed Daley most of the best lines and get involved in a punch-up once every episode.

Still, *Minder* managed to be different. In the opening episode, Terry, doing his weekly washing, was taken hostage by three militant rastas in the launderette. As the siege progresses Arthur seizes the opportunity to sell Terry's story to every national newspaper he can. The police, as represented by

Patrick Malahide's droll Sergeant Chisholm, assume that Terry is part of the gang. It was bold, witty and utterly strange stuff, bringing the off-centre world of 'the new exotica of London' (described by Hillary Kingsley and Geoff Tibballs as 'the cul-de-sacs, breakers' yards and railway arches in places like Fulham and Camden') to an audience more used to shots of Tower Bridge and the Post Office Tower.

The first season included episodes like 'Bury My Half at Waltham Green', in which Terry and ex-con Nicky Henson were pursued across London by the other members of Henson's gang, including Tony Selby and Kenneth Cope, in search of the buried loot. Although the series had good press, the ratings were far from spectacular, and when the second season failed to pick up significantly, *Minder* should have finished there and then. However, it had an ally in Bryan Cowgill, the managing director of Thames, who doggedly stuck with the show and was to be rewarded when, as Griffiths noted, from the third season the word about *Minder* began to spread. But Griffiths himself almost wasn't around to see it.

Having written most of the early episodes, Griffiths suffered a stroke, and it seemed at the time that he would never work again. The second season was taken over by the other writers. Paul Wheeler's 'Don't Tell Them Willie Boy was Here' had Terry 'minding' a John Conteh-type boxing champion making a comeback, whilst Willis Hall's 'All About Scoring, Innit?' cast Karl Howman as Terry's footballer idol who couldn't stop drinking, gambling and womanizing. The series introduced further memorable characters such as the mechanic Des, Arthur's dodgy business contacts Yorkie (Brian Glover) and Whaley (Roy Kinnear), and Toyah Wilcox as a teenage landlady, renting out a family flat to young couples and then having them evicted as squatters. The season ended with the memorable sight of Arthur falling into a cow pat whilst Terry minded a fearsome bull.

The face of authority was represented by Chisholm or Sergeant Rycott, who would get alternate episodes, whilst the other major character was Dave, the landlord of the Winchester, Arthur and Terry's own form of gentlemen's club. Leon Griffiths stated 'In the first season, we still weren't sure where we were going… what part Dave and the club were going to play, or Arthur's lock-up, and

First season
(29 Oct 79–21 Jan 80)
1 Gunfight at the OK Launderette
2 Bury My Half at Waltham Green
3 The Smaller They Are…
4 A Tethered Goat
5 The Bounty Hunter
6 Aces High - and Sometimes Very Low
7 The Bengali Tiger
8 Come in T-64, Your Time is Ticking Away
9 Monday Night Fever
10 The Dessert Song
11 You Gotta Have Friends

Second season
(11 Sep–18 Dec 80)
12 National Pelmet
13 Whose Wife is it Anyway?
14 You Lose Some, You Win Some
15 Don't Tell Them Willie Boy was Here
16 Not a Bad Lad, Dad
17 The Beer Hunter
18 A Nice Little Wine
19 All Mod Cons
20 Diamonds are a Girl's Worst Enemy
21 The Old School Tie
22 All About Scoring, Innit?
23 Caught in the Act, Fact
24 A Lot of Bull and a Pat on the Back

Third season
(13 Jan–7 Apr 82)
25 Dead Men Do Tell Tales
26 You Need Hands
27 Rembrandt Doesn't Live Here Anymore
28 Looking for Mickey
29 Dreamhouse
30 Another Bride, Another Groom
31 The Birdman of Wormwood Scrubs
32 The Son Also Rises
33 Why Pay Tax?
34 Broken Arrow
35 Poetic Justice, Innit?
36 Back in Good Old England
37 In

Christmas special
(26 Dec 83)
38 Minder's Christmas Bonus

Fourth season
(11 Jan–21 Mar 84)
39 Rocky Eight and a Half
40 Senior Citizen Caine
41 High Drains Pilferer
42 Sorry Pal, Wrong Number
43 The Car Lot Baggers
44 If Money be the Food of Love, Play On
45 A Star is Gorn
46 Willesden Suite
47 Windows
48 Get Daley!
49 A Well Fashioned Fit-Up

Fifth season
(5 Sep–31 Oct 84)
50 Goodbye Sailor
51 What Makes Shamy Run?
52 A Number of Old Wives' Tales
53 The Second Time Around
54 Second Hand Pose
55 The Long Ride Back to Scratchwood
56 Hypnotising Rita
57 The Balance of Power

Christmas special
(26 Dec 84)
58 Around the Corner

Sixth season
(4 Sep–9 Oct 85)
59 Give us this Day Arthur Daley's Bread
60 Life in the Fast Food Lane
61 The Return of the Invincible Man
62 Arthur is Dead, Long Live Arthur
63 From Fulham with Love
64 Waiting for Goddard

Christmas special
(25 Dec 85, 120 minutes)
65 Minder on the Orient Express

how important they were going to be. So in a sense it's a finding-out period. A character like Dave is always good to have. He's like the parish priest in a way. Terry can tell him what's happening or Arthur can tell him his problems.'

In 1980, after the second season, *Minder* won a Writers Guild award which was presented to Leon Griffiths even though he'd had nothing to do with the season. Doubtless inspired by this, Griffiths began responding steadily to a course of intensive therapy, and by the end of the third season the man who was formerly almost incapable of conversation and expression had courageously forced his way back into the scripting chair. This run of 13 episodes was probably the pinnacle of *Minder*, including Terry minding a pop star's mansion and trying to cope with his dangerous brother in 'Dreamhouse', scores to be settled for the newly released Ernie Dodds (Max Wall) in 'The Birdman of Wormwood Scrubs' (the episode on which Waterman met his partner Rula Lenska), and Griffith's superb 'In', where Arthur was picked up by the police in a case of mistaken identity. They even got to play out their own version of *Twelve Angry Men*, with Arthur as a jury foreman in 'Poetic Justice, Innit?'

A sure sign that *Minder* had progressed from a cult to genuine popularity came when the theme song 'I Could Be So Good for You' (sung by Waterman) became a top five hit in 1980. This was followed in 1983 by the novelty Christmas hit 'What Are We Gonna Get 'Er Indoors' by Cole and Waterman. In between, a London band called the Firm produced a cheerfully awful single entitled 'Arthur Daley (E's Alright)', which was also a minor hit.

By 1984, *Minder* was one of the most popular programmes on television with its stars reportedly the highest-paid actors in Britain. However, the 1984 season itself was something of a disappointment, with the emphasis on characterization rather than plot, although 'Windows' (which guest starred Patrick Troughton), in which Arthur opened a health club, and 'The Car Lot Baggers' (where Jimmy Nail proved that playing anything other than Geordies wasn't really his forte) were well up to standard.

With each season came an announcement from either Cole or Waterman that it would be their last, and the end seemed to have been reached in 1985 when the Christmas special 'Minder on the Orient Express' carried most of the regular cast

Christmas special
(26 Dec 88, 90 minutes)
66 An Officer and a Car Salesman

Seventh season
(2 Jan–6 Feb 89)
67 It's a Sorry Lorry, Morrie
68 Days of Fines and Closures
69 Fatal Impression
70 The Last Video Show
71 Fiddler on the Hoof
72 The Wrong Goodbye

Eighth season
(5 Sep–21 Nov 91)
73 The Loneliness of the Long Distance Entrepreneur
74 A Bouquet of Barbed Wire
75 Whatever Happened to Her Indoors?
76 Three Cons Make a Mountain
77 Guess Who's Coming to Pinner?
78 The Last Temptation of Daley
79 A Bird in the Hand is Worth Two in Shepherd's Bush
80 Him Indoors
81 The Greatest Show in Willesden
82 Too Many Crooks
83 The Odds Couple
84 The Coach that Came in from the Cold

Christmas special
(25 Dec 91)
85 The Cruel Canal

Ninth season
(7 Jan–1 Apr 93)
86 I'll Never Forget Whats'ername
87 No Way to Treat a Daley
88 Uneasy Rider
89 Looking for Mr Goodtime
90 Opportunity Knocks and Bruises
91 Gone with the Winchester
92 How to Succeed in Business Without Really Retiring
93 The Roof of All Evil
94 Last Orders at the Winchester
95 Cars and Pints and Pains
96 The Great Trilby
97 A Taste of Money
98 For a Few Dollars More

Tenth season
(6 Jan–10 Mar 94)
99 A Fridge Too Far
100 Another Case of Van Blank
101 All Things Brighton Beautiful
102 One Flew over the Parents' Nest
103 The Immaculate Contraption
104 All Quiet on the West End Front
105 The Great Depression of 1994
106 On the Autofront
107 Bring me the Head of Arthur Daley
108 The Long Good Thursday

['Minder's Christmas Bonus' is a 'clips show', linked together with new material. An ITV strike in 1984 affected the transmission of the last three episodes of the fifth season (the *intended* dates are given above). It is believed that episode 55 was aired in the London region only; the subsequent episodes were replaced by repeats in all areas. Episode 58 was shown in its intended slot, the strike having finished. Episode 56 was shown in all regions on 1 Jan 85; it is still not clear when episode 57 was first transmitted.]

(including Chisholm and Rycott, together for the first time) into an Agatha Christie whodunit. But they did return - in 1988 - for another Christmas special and a seventh season.

By now, Waterman had discovered life away from the action series, having acted in 1986's *The Life and Loves of a She-Devil* and a couple of sitcoms. His partnership with Cole was finally broken in 1991 when Waterman refused to do another season of *Minder*. So the unthinkable happened: the series carried on without him.

The introduction of Arthur's new conned and underpaid employee, his nephew, Ray, was a great risk for Euston, but thanks to the inspired casting of 26-year-old Gary Webster, it worked brilliantly. The complete opposite of lager-drinking, street-wise Terry, Ray was a well-fleshed-out 'new man', drinking orange juice and mineral water and armed with 'O'-levels in French and woodwork. He rather looked up to Arthur, who, aware that Terry had left to move to Australia with a woman, never encouraged Ray's romances. The 1991 season was the best for several years, with the opening episode (revolving around a Daley family wedding and drug-smuggling car importers) one of the sharpest and wittiest in the series' history. Kevin Jackson, writing in *The Independent*, summed up the critical reaction: 'There may be a few die-hard Terry nostalgists here and there who dissent from the proposition, but most paid-up Friends of Winchester seem to agree that *Minder* is not merely as funny as it ever was, but funnier... Gary Webster has acted like a shot of monkey glands on the show's central relationship.' His inclusion took 'the show still further away from its notional origins in thick-ear exploits and made it even more frankly a sitcom'.

Although *Minder* seemed indestructible, a series of strokes and a brain tumour finally got the better of Leon Griffiths in 1992. Griffiths achieved immortality via Arthur, whose malapropisms have passed into the English language ('The world is your lobster, my son' being the most-quoted example). And, though the series is now officially over, you get the impression that somewhere in London there will always be a Daley, beavering away, dodging the law, pulling strokes and trying to get on a nice little earner ...

Bergerac

- **BBC Television/The Seven Network, Australia** (BBC1) ◆ Colour
- **87 episodes** (standard length: 55 minutes) ◆ 1981-91
- **Creator:** Robert Banks Stewart
- **Writers include:** Robert Banks Stewart, Bob Baker, Alistair Bell, Dennis Spooner, Terence Feely, Robert Holmes, Brian Clemens, Rod Beacham, Nick McCarty, Bill Craig, Brian Finch, John Fletcher, Chris Boucher, John Collee, David Crane, John Milne, Ian Kennedy Martin
- **Directors include:** Ian Toynton, Martyn Friend, Lawrence Moody, Ben Bolt, Paul Ciappessoni, Robert Tronson, Robert Young, Graeme Harper, Baz Taylor, Tristan de Vere Cole, Geoffrey Sax, Matthew Robinson
- **Producers:** Robert Banks Stewart, Jonathan Alwyn, George Gallaccio, Juliet Grimm

Sun, boats, women - and still Jim looks miserable

Regular cast: John Nettles (Jim Bergerac) • Terence Alexander (Charlie Hungerford) • Sean Arnold (Barney Crozier)

With: Cecile Paoli (Francine) • Deborah Grant (Deborah Bergerac) • Tony Melody (Chief) • Mela White (Diamante Lil) • Annette Badland (Charlotte) • Lindsay Heath (Kim Bergerac) • Kevin Stoney (Horatio Nelson) • Geoffrey Leesley (Terry Wilson) • Jonathan Adams (Dr Lejeune) • Celia Imrie (Marianne Bellshade) • Lee Montague (Dupont) • Liza Goddard (Philippa Vale) • Louise Jameson (Susan Young) • Nancy Mansfield (Peggy Masters) • Jolyon Baker (Barry Goddard) • John Telfer (Willy Pettit) • David Kershaw (Ben Lomas) • Sue Lloyd (Eva Southurst) • Jack Watling (Frank Blakemore) • Therese Liotard (Danielle Aubry) • Michael Mellinger (Albert Leufroid) • Roger Sloman (Deffand)

First season
(18 Oct–20 Dec 81)
1 Picking it Up
2 Nice People Die in Bed
3 Unlucky Dip
4 Campaign for Silence
5 See you in Moscow
6 Portrait of Yesterday
7 Last Chance for a Loser
8 Late for a Funeral
9 Relative Values
10 The Hood and the Harlequin

Second season
(9 Jan–6 Mar 83)
11 A Message for the Rich
12 Always Leave Them Laughing
13 Clap Hands, Here Comes Charlie
14 Prime Target
15 Almost Like a Holiday
16 Fall of a Birdman
17 A Miracle Every Week
18 A Perfect Recapture
19 The Moonlight Girls

Third season
(3 Dec 83–4 Feb 84)
20 Ninety Per Cent Proof
21 A Hole in the Bucket
22 Holiday Snaps
23 Ice Maiden
24 Come Out Fighting
25 A Touch of Eastern Promise
26 A Cry in the Night
27 The Company you Keep
28 Tug of War
29 House Guests

Fourth season
(11 Oct–20 Dec 85)
30 The Last Interview
31 Off Shore Trades
32 What Dreams May Come?
33 Low Profile
34 Return of the Ice Maiden
35 Chrissie
36 The Tennis Racket
37 Sins of the Fathers
38 Avenge O Lord

Christmas special
(26 Dec 86, 90 minutes)
39 Fires in the Fall

Fifth season
(3 Jan–21 Feb 87)
40 The Memory Man
41 Winner Takes All
42 Root and Branch
43 A Desirable Little Residence
44 The Deadly Virus
45 SPARTA
46 Thanks for Everything
47 Poison

Difficult as it is to believe, if Trevor Eve had agreed to do another season of ***Shoestring*** in 1981 it's possible that one of the BBC's most popular series may never have appeared. And John Nettles would still be remembered as Nerys Hughes's boyfriend in ***The Liver Birds***.

Despite some visual links, the differences between the two series were as great as those between Eddie's Ford Cortina dragging itself around Bristol and Swindon and Jim Bergerac's 1947 Triumph TR1 charging through the backroads of Jersey.

Created as a stop-gap, *Bergerac* would eventually become a BBC perennial. At its height, in the late 80s, *Bergerac* regularly pulled in ratings pushing 15 million. Yet when the series began it was viewed cynically by critics who accused the series of treading old ground.

The hero, like Eddie Shoestring, was recovering from a large dose of misfortune: in Bergerac's case, a gammy leg and a drink problem, not unconnected to the break-up of his marriage, and his shady father-in-law, Charlie Hungerford, who seemed to have his fingers in just about every case with which Bergerac came into contact. Bergerac worked for the Jersey Bureau des Etrangers, whose case-load involved crimes committed by or against non-islanders. His by-the-book partner, Barney Crozier, would eventually rise to chief inspector, whilst Jim remained a sergeant. John Nettles was to say of his character, 'He's stiff-necked, inarticulate and hopeless with women, but he's a good cop and has a certain doggedness which I like.'

What set the series apart from similar productions was the quality scriptwriting that managed to find a new crime to plague the island every week. Bergerac's weekly adventures neatly balanced his cases and his new-found happiness with the first of several girlfriends, Francine. *Bergerac*'s soap opera feel was enhanced by a number of recurring minor characters, including secretary Charlotte, the 'three-lines-per-episode' pathologist Dr Lejeune, and Diamante Lil, the owner of the local boozer.

Between the first and second seasons, John Nettles broke his right leg in a motorcycle accident. When the series returned, several eagle-eyed viewers wondered why Jim was now limping on a different leg. It was with the second season that *Bergerac* began to click, with Francine replaced by a lawyer, Marianne, as the woman in the sergeant's life. Guest stars included Joanne Whalley, Anthony Valentine, and Norman Wisdom as a safe-cracker in 'Almost Like a Holiday'. 'Fall of a Birdman' saw Richard Griffiths as a mountaineer stealing rare birds eggs, while 'A Miracle Every Week' concerned the arrival on Jersey of Art Malik's Buddhist guru who discovers that his church is being manipulated by a group of unscrupulous businessmen (Nicholas Ball, Derek Thompson and Denis Lawson).

Bergerac spent the third season without a regular female companion (this hiatus being used to develop Deborah Bergerac's character). A highlight was Nick

Christmas special
(26 Dec 87, 90 minutes)
48 Treasure Hunt

Sixth season
(2 Jan–13 Feb 88)
49 Whatever Lola Wants
50 Crossed Swords
51 A Horse of a Different Colour
52 Burnt
53 The Sin of Forgiveness
54 A Man of Sorrows
55 Private Fight

Christmas special
(27 Dec 88, 90 minutes)
56 Retirement Plan

Seventh season
(28 Jan–18 Mar 89)
57 Sea Changes
58 Natural Enemies
59 Tangos in the Night
60 The Other Woman
61 Weekend Off
62 When Did You Last See Your Father?
63 Old Acquaintance
64 Trenchard's Last Case

Christmas special
(26 Dec 89, 100 minutes)
65 Second Time Around

Eighth season
(14 Jan–18 Mar 90)
66 A True Detective
67 My Name's Sergeant Bergerac
68 The Dig
69 Roots of Evil
70 Entente Cordiale
71 In Love and War
72 Under Wraps
73 All the Sad Songs
74 The Messenger Boy
75 Diplomatic Incident

Christmas special
(26 Dec 90, 100 minutes)
76 There for the Picking

Ninth season
(5 Jan–9 Mar 91)
77 Something to Hide
78 The Dark Horse
79 Snow in Provence
80 The Evil that Men Do
81 My Friend Charlie
82 On the Rocks
83 The Waiting Game
84 Warriors
85 The Assassin
86 The Lohans

Christmas special
(26 Dec 91, 110 minutes)
87 All For Love

McCarty's complex whodunit 'Holiday Snaps', whilst 'Ice Maiden' introduced one of the series' most popular characters, Philippa Vale, a brilliant jewel thief with a heart of gold.

Major changes took place in 1985. Charlotte, Bergerac's secretary, was replaced by Peggy, Crozier was promoted to become Bergerac's boss, and, in the process of moving into a new apartment, Bergerac met estate agent Susan Young. All of these issues were dealt with in the first ten minutes of Banks Stewart's impressive season opener 'The Last Interview', starring Barry Foster as a TV journalist haunted by his past and pursued by the Mafia.

This fourth season is possibly the most consistent and well-produced of all *Bergerac*. It included Ian McCulloch's chilling portrayal of an emotionless murderer ('Off Shore Trades'), a second, even more impressive Phillipa Vale story ('Return of the Ice Maiden'), and Warren Clarke as 'Hollywood's favourite Nazi', making a film on the island and bringing old wartime grievances to the surface ('Sins of the Fathers', superbly directed by Graeme Harper). 'Avenge O Lord' saw a hitman (Ian Redford) searching for an arms dealer (Bernard Hepton) responsible for the death of his men, but best of all was Brian Finch's experimental 'What Dreams May Come?', a near-telefantasy tale concerning a coven led by Charles Gray. This was the first of what became an annual journey into surreal territory.

1986 saw the first of the feature-length specials that were to make *Bergerac* into traditional Christmas fare during the late 80s. 'Fires in the Fall' was also just about the series' best ever episode: a strange, vivid, near-horror story about attempts by Amanda Redman and spiritualist conman Barrie Ingham to swindle Margaretta Scott out of her fortune with a hidden family secret. Chilling scenes involving a sinister hooded figure bumping off several characters ensured that the episode wouldn't quickly be forgotten by any of the 18 million viewers who saw it.

In the fifth season, 'Winner Takes All' - the last episode written by the late Robert Holmes - centred on a computer genius (Michael Gambon) convinced that a threat on his life is an elaborate hoax. 'Root and Branch' was another frightening psychology play as Sterrat (Christopher Fairbank), a man who Jim convicted years before, sets out to frighten Deborah to death. 'SPARTA' tied the activities of a neo-Nazi organization into a ledger-book stolen by Philippa Vale, and the season ended with 'Poison', in which Bergerac's old headmaster (Alfred Burke) is involved in masonic skulduggery, killing his victims with hemlock.

Whether it was a change in production style (George Gallacio took over from Jonathan Alwyn), or simply the culmination of a mostly silent campaign, 1988 saw the first voices of dissent raised against *Bergerac*. This sixth season included several fine episodes, notably John Collee's 'The Sin of Forgiveness' which pitted John Bennett's Israeli Nazi-hunter against a retired Auschwitz guard. It was an experimental episode, however, which caused the most fuss. John Fletcher's 'A Man of Sorrows' drew gasps of displeasure from critics who professed a dislike for the episode's 'obscure' narrative (ignoring Jack Galloway's superb performance as a policeman destroyed by the capital's dehumanization). George Baker and William Simons also appeared in this episode, which has stood the test of time better than most. This period also saw the introduction of two new young detective constables, the laddish Willy Pettit and the introverted Ben Lomas.

The seventh season seemed to spend most of its time chronicling the disintegrating relationship between Bergerac and Susan, although the series was still able to attract big name guest stars (Susan Penhaligon, Kenneth Cope, Stephen McGann, David Troughton), and two episodes, John Collee's scary 'The Other Woman' and John Milne's 'Weekend Off' (which featured a return to the series of Deborah Grant), are worthy of note.

The announcement that Louise Jameson was leaving the series came as little surprise to *Bergerac* viewers since Jim and Susan had barely been on speaking terms for more than a year, although the manner of her departure at the beginning of the eighth season in 'A True Detective' was a brave one, killing the character off within the first ten minutes. This was then followed by outrageous comedy ('My Name's Sergeant Bergerac' with Tony Robinson and Ronald Allen) and one of the most extreme examples of surrealism in John Collee's 'The Dig' (with Trevor Cooper and George Sweeney: 'sub-Hammer rubbish' according to one reviewer). 'Entente Cordiale' pointed the way forward, taking Jim to France, where he meets Danielle Aubry. As the season progresses, Bergerac shows more and more dissatisfaction with the job he is doing, especially in 'Roots of Evil' where the past of an industrialist (Geoffrey Palmer) catches up with him. At the end of the season, Bergerac leaves the Force.

That should have been the end, but then every season as far back as 1985 was usually announced as such. Instead a change of format was attempted, with Bergerac working as a private investigator mainly based in France. The changed format opened with a Christmas episode, 'There for the Picking', a clever tale spoiled only by a rather weak ending. But, sadly, the following season was not a great success, either critically or in terms of ratings. It seemed to many that the once vibrant and energetic production had finally run out of steam. A 1991 Christmas special marked the end of the series, although in 1993, an episode of Jasper Carrott and Robert Powell's spoof series *The Detectives* ('Studs') was set on Jersey and included Nettles and Alexander reprising their *Bergerac* roles. A tiny but fascinating footnote to one of the BBC's most important and successful crime series.

The Bill

- **Thames/Yorkshire/Carlton** (ITV) ◆ Colour
- **Standard episode length:** 30 minutes ◆ 1983 to date
- **Creator:** Geoff McQueen
- **Writers include:** Geoff McQueen, Barry Appleton, John Kershaw, Ginnie Hole, Chris Russell, Tim Aspinall, Peter J. Hammond, Graeme Curry, Julian Jones, Kevin Clarke, Roger Parkes, Edwin Pearce, David Halliwell, Kieran Prendiville, Brendan J. Cassin, Shirley Cooklin, Al Hunter, John Milne, J.C. Wilsher, Brian Finch, Simon Moss, Gary Lyons, Arthur McKenzie, Philip Martin, Steve Trafford, Jonathan Rich, Pat Dunlop, Robin Mukherjee, Dick Sharples, Chris Penfold, Chris Boucher, Ian Briggs, Susan Shattock, Martyn Wade, Carolyn Sally Jones, Eric Deacon, Matthew Wingett, Anthony Valentine, Victoria Taylor, Duncan Gould, Julian Jones, Tony Etchells, Edward Canfor-Dumas, Joanne Maguire, Candy Denman, Elizabeth-Anne Wheal
- **Producers:** Michael Chapman, Peter Cregeen, Richard Bramall, Brenda Ennis, Michael Ferguson, Geraint Morris, Pat Sandys, Tony Virgo, Peter Wolfes, Richard Handford, Mike Dormer, Graham Theakston, Chris Clough, Michael Simpson
- **Executive Producers:** Lloyd Shirley, Peter Creegan, Michael Chapman

From obscure acorns...

Geoff McQueen's first script for TV, *Till His Eyes Watered*, was a 'whodunit' with one of the most mind-blowing murder weapons ever devised (a piece of toilet paper smeared with botulism). Nasty. The play remains, tragically, unproduced! Nevertheless, it brought the writer to the attention of Michael Verney-Elliot, the producer of LWT's *The Gentle Touch*, for whom McQueen began writing episodes soon afterwards. McQueen also created the BBC snooker drama *Give Us a Break* (starring Robert Lindsay and Paul McGann) and the series *Big Deal* (with Ray Brooks and Sharon Duce).

In 1983, he contributed a single play to the Thames anthology drama format *Storyboard*. 'Woodentop' was the story of a young police constable, Jim Carver, on his first day on the beat. Carver, and his WPC partner June Ackland, have remained with the series to this day. Making much use of hand-held cameras, and naturalistic lighting and dialogue, 'Woodentop' gave the public an authentic police procedural show. In other words, a ***Z Cars*** for the 80s. Thames, recognizing a potential winner, commissioned a 12-episode series based on the characters at Sun Hill police station.

The Bill followed the ***Z Cars*** format by having multi-stranded stories, reflecting as accurately as possible the diversity of police work. It was decided that every scene in the series should be experienced from the viewpoint of the police, meaning that the crimes that each episode focused upon were never actually witnessed being perpetrated (unless an officer happened to be passing). What would be seen were the effects, the investigations and sometimes (though by no means always) the outcomes. From the start there was a division between the roles of the maverick CID men, with their jargon and hard-drinking machismo, and the young uniform constables, watched over by the parental sergeants Bob Cryer and Alec Peters who occupied the first scene in the opening episode. As Tony Lynch notes in his book on *The Bill*, 'the acting had an earthy, improvised feel about it; while the camera-work, mostly hand-held and certainly very mobile and free-wheeling, was exciting and documentary-like'.

Starring: Mark Wingett (PC/DC Jim Carver) • Trudie Goodwin (WPC June Ackland) • Colin Blumenau (PC Taffy Edwards) • Gary Olsen (PC Dave Litten) • Robert Pugh/John Salthouse (DI Roy Galloway) • Eric Richard (Sgt. Bob Cryer) • Tony Scannell (DS Ted Roach) • Nula Cornwell (WPC Viv Martella) • Jeffrey Stewart (PC Reg Hollis) • Robert Hudson (PC Yorkie Smith) • Graham Cole (PC Tony Stamp) • Peter Ellis (Chief Supt. Charles Brownlow) • Larry Dean (Sgt. Alec Peters) • Roger Leach (Sgt. Tom Penny) • Ronny Cush (PC Abe Lyttleton) • Ralph Brown (PC Pete Muswell) • Simon Slater (Insp. Kite) • Chris Walker (PC Nick Shaw) • Mark Powley (PC Ken Melvin) • Sonesh Sira (PC Patel) • Barbara Thorn (Insp. Christine Frazer) • Kelly Lawrence (WPC Claire Brind) • Ashley Gunstock (PC Robin Frank) • Lynne Miller (WPC Cathy Marshall) • Nick Reding (PC Pete Ramsey) • Clive Wood (DCI Gordon Wray) • Ben Roberts (Chief Insp. Derek Conway) • Jon Iles (DC Mike Dashwood) • Christopher Ellison (Sgt./DI Frank Burnside) • Seeta Indrani (WPC Norika Datta) • Vikki Gee-Dare (WPC Suzanne Ford) • Natasha Williams (WPC Delia French) • Huw Higginson (PC George Garfield) • Andrew MacKintosh (DS Alistair Greig) • Kevin Lloyd (DC Alfred 'Tosh' Lines) • Tom Butcher (PC Steve Loxton) • Sam Miller (Sgt. John Maitland) • Colin Tarrant (Insp. Andrew Monroe) • Andrew Paul (PC Dave Quinnan) • Carolyn Pickles (DCI Kim Reid) • Nick Stringer (PC Ron Smollett) • Jonathan Dow (PC Barry Stringer) • Colin Alldridge (PC Phil Young) • Tony O'Callaghan (Sgt. Matthew Boyden) • Simon Rouse (DCI Jack Meadows) • Louise Harrison (WPC Donna Harris) • Mary Jo Randle (WDC/WDS Jo Morgan) • Liz Crowther (Sgt. Kendall) • Tom Cotcher (DC Alan Woods) • Stephen Beckett (PC Jarivs) • Philip Whitchurch (Chief Insp. Philip Cato) • Gary Whelan (DS/DI Harry Haines) • Martin Marquez (DS Danny Pearce) • Clive Wedderburn (PC Gary McCann) • Lisa Geoghan (WPC Polly Page) • Kerry Pears (WPC Suzi Croft) • Jaye Griffiths (DI Sally Johnson) • Robert Perkins (Sgt. Ray Steele) • Shaun Scott (DS/DI Chris Deakin) • Ian Fletcher (DC Rod Skase) • Billy Murray (DS Don Beech) • Alan Westaway (PC Nick Slater) • Andrea Mason (WPC Debbie Keane) • Mark Spalding (Chief Insp. Paul Stritch) • Russell Boulter (DS John Boulton)

The first episode, 'Funny Ol' Business - Cops and Robbers', featured a look at the underbelly of the police force, very much in the 70s ***Sweeney*/*Law and Order*-style**, with an allegedly corrupt CID inspector from another station getting up the noses of the Sun Hill boys who have 'busted' his 'snout'. Ironically, the character was one 'Tommy' Burnside, and the actor playing him Christopher Ellison: four years later, with a slight change of name, Burnside became a regular. There were already some great characters in evidence, the hot-headed, womanizing Irish detective Ted Roach, and his ice-cool partner Mike Dashwood, and, amongst the uniform branch, the steady Tony Stamp, the hard-as-nails Dave Litten, and the pain-in-the-neck Police Federation representative Reg Hollis. There was also Viv Martella (the closest the series ever got to a uniformed sex symbol) who spent one episode memorably pissed out of her brain during an undercover operation at a hotel. We got occasional looks at the officers out of uniform, in the pub, and at home, but the focus of the series was always 'The Job'.

Storyboard
(16 Aug 83)
1 Woodentop

First season
(16 Oct 84–22 Jan 85)
Eleven 60-minute episodes

Three seasons of hour-long episodes followed. The series was popular, and very well done, presenting the full range of police work - not just the exciting murder and rape inquiries and topical issues like drugs, but also the more mundane matters of petty vandalism, mugging, burglary and car theft – the realities of 80s crime – and all of the paperwork that went with it. *The Bill* presented its coppers not as righteous, vicious crusaders, like ***The Sweeney***, or as namby-pamby social-workers in uniform, like ***Dixon of Dock Green***, but somewhere in between. In that sense it really was the logical successor to ***Z Cars***.

Thames was so pleased with the series that it decided in 1987 to change *The Bill*'s format into a twice-weekly series of half-hour episodes. On 19 July 1988 *The Bill* followed ***Z Cars*** into the world of the soap opera. Here begins the series' greatness, because, unlike the 60s series which had always seemed a little uneasy with its shortened format, *The Bill* blossomed magnificently.

Second season
(11 Nov 85–10 Feb 86)
Twelve 60-minute episodes

Third season
(21 Sep–7 Dec 87)
Twelve 60-minute episodes

Fourth season
(19 Jul 88 to date)
standard episode length: 30 minutes

The format, self-contained episodes concentrating on perhaps just three or four of the 20-or-so regular characters, plus guest villains and victims, suited *The Bill* as if it had been designed that way all along. The addition of more great characters, the prickly Christine Frazer, chubby disaster-area Tosh Lines and (best of all) the renamed Frank Burnside taking over the running of the CID section, was a further boost. Burnside was dangerous and mean, a willing bender of the rules. A Jack Regan for the 80s, rather than a Charlie Barlow. Christopher Ellison, who had appeared in an early ***Sweeney*** episode, played Burnside with a sly dose of Michael Caine-cockney wit (Tony Lynch quotes an example from 'Cry Havoc' (23 Apr 91), in which Burnside suggests a particularly noisy woman should be charged with 'possession of an offensive mouth'). Burnside, with his plain-clothes team of Roach, Lines, Dashwood, Greig, Carver (and, later, Martella) was the exciting, all-action, blood and thunder end of *The Bill*. The CID episodes involving terrorism, murder investigations or drug busts proved to be particularly effective, although there is sometimes an element of the ridiculous in the way Sun Hill seems to have the biggest clear-up rate of any police station in Great Britain.

Sometimes the episodes will be so minimalist as to defy logic (one memorable episode consisted of a suspected terrorist interrogated by Burnside and Meadows for all bar about five minutes of screen time). On the other hand, there were the huge, sweeping, experimental multi-character episodes for which *The Bill* became, rightly, praised. 'Duplicates' (22 Nov 88) showed the reconstruction of a murdered girl's last known movements for a *Crimewatch*-style TV show with a clearly stressed-out Claire Brind in the girl's clothes suffering the indignity of her male colleagues' jibes. 'The Silent Gun' (1 Dec 88) portrayed a siege, firearms procedure and the ethics of who shoots first (the gunman turns out to be a deaf man who hasn't heard Cryer and Conway's warnings). 'Digging Up the Past' (27 Dec 88) concentrated on a forensics investigation after a skeleton is found. 'Steamers' (26 Jan 89) had Malcolm Haynes undercover and infiltrating a yardie gang; the episode focused on the racism, both intentional and abstract, that every black policeman must face from all sides.

'A Good Result' (2 Mar 89) was the memorable episode where Yorkie Smith also went undercover with a group of organized northern football hooligans. Death came to Sun Hill, Ken Melvin killed by a bomb in 'Victims' (8 May 90) and Martella shot in 'The Short Straw' (26 Mar 93). The poetic beauty of the aftermath of both incidents (particularly the Melvin funeral episode) is far removed from most viewers' expectations. The series tackled sexual harassment, the inequalities of the promotion system, corruption, violence against prisoners, and the rights of the individual to varying degrees of success; it has been claimed that by showing some policemen as 'liars, cheats and bullies', this cheapens the series' many favourable points. This doesn't seem to be a view shared by the police, however, John Stalker once famously commenting that *The Bill* 'is in a class of its own [giving] an accurate view on what modern policemen do'.

It could be argued that by showing a multi-faceted wide-boy character like Dave Quinnan (and, before him, Pete Ramsey - and before him, Dave Litton), *The Bill* presents a truer and fairer reflection of the type of young man attracted to life in the force than more two-dimensional series. The series prides itself on employing police advisors - ex-coppers like Wilf Knight and Brian Hart - who read each script for obvious lack of technical insight. The writers on *The Bill* range from experienced TV pros like Peter Hammond, Chris Boucher and Barry Appleton, to many writers new to television, *The Bill* being frequently cited as one of the few places where someone trying to break into the industry can get a script accepted. Two of the best and most prolific of the series' writers are J.C. Wilsher, who used many of the themes and ideas he had explored in *The Bill* in ***Between the Lines***, and Arthur Mckenzie, the genial ex-detective inspector from Tyneside who, perhaps more than anyone, has managed to inject a sense of brutal reality into the series.

For the most part *The Bill* has avoided running storylines. Occasionally an episode may have had a sequel or two, usually weeks or even months later, when a particular plot (or set of characters) was returned to. That was until 1995 when a three-part story about a maniac trying to kill June Ackland gained some of the series' highest-ever viewing figures. From recent publicity it seems that the production team are keen to develop this. If *The Bill* follows ***Casualty*** into the world of the continuous narrative then, as with the hospital series, it may have to be prepared to lose some of its power for the sake of maintaining a regular audience. *The Bill* can probably afford to do this, but whether it should is a different and more complex question.

The series remains popular because it is also something of a generic patchwork. It contains elements from just about every previous influential police drama. It is not just a ***Z Cars*** for the 80s/90s, it's a *Fabian of the Yard* or a *Dial 999* too. One of the myths that its production company seem happy to perpetuate, for example, is that *The Bill* is a reaction to the 70s police series. It isn't anything of the kind; in fact, it's a direct descendant of ***The Sweeney*** and co.

The Bill has come a long way since Geoff McQueen was given a blank canvas upon which to create the ultimate police series. The change of format turned it from a rattling-good drama series into a series of elegant, pointed, and accurate playlets that define a moment. It has passed ***Z Cars*** in terms of the number of individual episodes (having gone thrice weekly in 1993), and will probably continue to be a major part of the ITV networks for many years to come. Some of those who made it great have left (Tony Scannell, in controversy, Nula Conwell dramatically, Christopher Ellison in a sadly underplayed manner), whilst other characters come and go, adding to the timeless, on-going feel of the series. Sadly, Geoff McQueen died days after completing his script for the futuristic police thriller *Rules of Engagement* (1995), but the popularity of his most famous creation seems only to grow as the years pass.

Not bad for a series with the worst end-title sequence in television history.

Sherlock Holmes

- **Granada** (ITV) ◆ **Colour**
- **41 episodes** (standard length: 60 minutes) ◆ 1984-94
- **Based on:** stories by Sir Arthur Conan Doyle
- **Writers include:** Anthony Skene, Alan Plater, Alfred Shaughnessy, Jeremy Paul, Bill Craig, Richard Harris, Derek Marlowe, John Hawkesworth
- **Directors include:** Paul Annett, Alan Grint, John Bruce, Peter Hammond, John Gorrie, June Howson
- **Producers:** Michael Cox, June Wyndham Davies

Starring: Jeremy Brett (Sherlock Holmes) • David Burke/Edward Hardwicke (Dr Watson) • Colin Jeavons (Insp. Lestrade) • Rosalie Williams (Mrs Hudson) • Charles Gray (Mycroft Holmes)

For over 90 years, actors across the world have struggled to perfect the 'definitive' version of Arthur Conan Doyle's immortal detective. Basil Rathbone got close with a Hollywood film series in the 40s, but his performances were soured by the anachronistic jingoism of the movies and by Nigel Bruce's bumbling Dr Watson.

Television had tried Holmes on several occasions before the 80s. As early as 1951 the BBC produced a series of six adaptations featuring the future Sheriff of Nottingham, Alan Wheatley, as Holmes (with a pre-Inspector Lockhart Raymond Francis as Watson and Bill Owen as Lestrade). It was, as Geoff Tibballs notes, 'an unlikely trio'.

In 1965 the BBC staged a well-mounted series of 12 stories with Douglas Wilmer as Holmes and Nigel Stock as a Nigel Bruce-style Watson. Three years later, the series was continued, again featuring Stock, but with Peter Cushing in the role of the great detective. Cushing, of course, had already played Holmes in Hammer's superior 1959 adaptation of *The Hound of the Baskervilles*, and this thoughtful, passionate actor brought much of his own accumulated 'Holmesology' to the role. He stressed that Watson is not a fool - 'There's no way that Holmes would suffer him if he were' - and the 15 episodes were the first truly authoritative television production. Unfortunately, future treatments of the Holmes legend tended towards Rathbonisms for their inspiration, notably the BBC's 1982 serialization of *The Hound of the Baskervilles*, starring Tom Baker as Holmes and Terence Rigby as Watson.

In 1984, Granada producer Michael Cox decided it was time to create the definitive article, going back to the original source of the Conan Doyle stories, the *Strand* magazine, and Sidney Paget's illustrations, to recreate the look and tone of the series. Cox determined to do something that virtually no adapter of Holmes to that point had ever successfully achieved: in the producer's own words, 'get Watson right'. The casting of David Burke as a young, fit and lively Watson was a brave move.

Nevertheless, most of the attention was focused on the man chosen to follow Rathbone, Cushing *et al.*, Shakespearian actor Jeremy Brett. Brett brought a sense of dark drama to the role, his Holmes seeming to be a heartbeat away from manic depression. All of the vices (the cocaine addiction, mood swings, misogyny and anger at stupidity) were brought to the fore as the latest incumbent of 221B Baker Street thrilled audiences. The critics loved it and so did the viewers.

The first two seasons rested largely on straightforward adaptations, beautifully capturing, with historical accuracy as well as gothic fancy, Victorian London. These were as close as anyone had ever got to perfecting Conan Doyle's creation on television. The deerstalker made only one appearance, in 'The Solitary Cyclist', an episode where Holmes had a fist fight in a pub, one of the many scenes designed directly from the Paget illustrations.

To substantiate the reputation of Moriarty as Holmes's great enemy (he only actually appeared in one Conan Doyle story), he is introduced as the villain behind 'The Red-Headed League', a story which highlighted the series' technique of complementing the less televisual of Conan Doyle's plots by drawing attention to other aspects of the story. Emphasis was placed on the visuals and the subtle characterization of Holmes. This did, however, result in some slow television. For example, the Christmas episode (broadcast in June) had Holmes and Watson finding a missing gem inside a goose. The episode is filled out with colourful visits to various street vendors and an accurate portrait of the Victorian festivities.

The theatricality of Brett's Holmes is what distinguishes him from his predecessors. At the moment of solving a case, he displays a childish glee in unveiling the solution like a magic trick, an approach that owes more to Noël Coward than to Rathbone.

The second season ended with what Conan Doyle had always intended to be the grand finale for Holmes, 'The Final Problem', in which the hero apparently plunges to his death during an epic struggle with Moriarty at the Reichenbach Falls.

However, there were problems. Jeremy Brett found that 'Holmes was threatening me. He became the dark side of the moon because he is moody and solitary and I am sociable and gregarious. It got dangerous for me.' Anxiety about the part, coming soon after the death of his wife, resulted in Brett suffering a nervous breakdown in 1986. After a two-month convalescence, however, he was back playing Holmes at his very best.

The return of Holmes was never really in doubt, but changes had been made due to David Burke's refusal to continue to play Watson. Edward Hardwicke was cast as a slightly older (although no less intelligent and subtle) Watson in 'The Empty House', set some years after Holmes's apparent death. The two actors who played Watson are so similar in performance that most viewers didn't notice the difference. Lestrade also returned, ably played as a vain, though intelligent, career policeman by Colin Jeavons.

THE ADVENTURES OF SHERLOCK HOLMES
First season
(24 Apr–5 Jun 84)
1 A Scandal in Bohemia
2 The Dancing Men
3 The Naval Treaty
4 The Solitary Cyclist
5 The Crooked Man
6 The Speckled Band
7 The Blue Carbuncle

Second season
(25 Aug–29 Sep 85)
8 The Copper Beeches
9 The Greek Interpreter
10 The Norwood Builder
11 The Resident Patient
12 The Red-Headed League
13 The Final Problem

THE RETURN OF SHERLOCK HOLMES
Third season
(9 Jul–20 Aug 86)
14 The Empty House
15 The Abbey Grange
16 The Second Stain
17 The Musgrave Ritual
18 The Man with the Twisted Lip
19 The Priory School
20 The Six Napoleons

SHERLOCK HOLMES
(29 Dec 87, 120 minutes)
21 The Sign of Four

THE RETURN OF SHERLOCK HOLMES
Fourth season
(6–27 Apr 87)
22 The Devil's Foot
23 Silver Blaze
24 Wisteria Lodge
25 The Bruce Partington Plans

SHERLOCK HOLMES
(31 Aug 88, 120 minutes)
26 The Hound of the Baskervilles

THE CASEBOOK OF SHERLOCK HOLMES
Fifth season
(21 Feb–28 Mar 91)
27 The Disappearance of Lady Frances Carfax
28 The Problem of Thor Bridge
29 Shoscombe Old Place
30 The Boscombe Valley Mystery
31 The Illustrious Client
32 The Creeping Man

SHERLOCK HOLMES
(2 Jan 92, 120 minutes)
33 The Master Blackmailer
(27 Jan 93, 120 minutes)
34 The Last Vampyre
(3 Feb 93, 120 minutes)
35 The Eligible Bachelor

THE MEMOIRS OF SHERLOCK HOLMES
Sixth season
(7 Mar–11 Apr 94)
36 The Three Gables
37 The Dying Detective
38 The Golden Pince-Nez
39 The Red Circle
40 The Mazarin Stone
41 The Cardboard Box

[An alternative (production?) order for the third season exists as follows: episodes 14, 19, 16, 17, 15, 18, 20.]

There was a real friendship between Holmes and Watson. In 'The Devil's Foot', Holmes even called Watson 'John', a character trait unique to Brett. 'The Devil's Foot' was the episode where Holmes gave up his drug habit, burying his needle in the sand, and ironically falling victim to a narcotic dust, producing one of the best hallucinatory sequences on television.

The seven episodes of the 1986 season were, perhaps, the pinnacle of the show. Alan Plater's adaptation of 'The Man with the Twisted Lip' took an apparently unfilmable story and turned it into an hour's gripping television. Although work on an immediate follow-up had to be halted due to Brett's continuing health problems, the feature-length adaptation of 'The Sign of Four', which starred John Thaw and Jenny Seagrove, at Christmas 1987, seemed like the ultimate performance of the Holmes mythos. All of the elements which had made the Granada series so popular were evoked to produce, perhaps once and for all, the definitive Holmes.

After that it seemed as though enthusiasm for the series dried up somewhat. Another extended episode, the inevitable 'The Hound of the Baskervilles', where Brett visibly relaxed, allowing his Holmes to become jocular and, indeed, chubby in his few appearances, was a huge ratings success. But the lack of challenging material from then on proved that only 20 or so of Conan Doyle's adventures have the necessary mouldability to be successfully adapted. 'The Master Blackmailer', with its existential ending (virtually the only way to conclude a story where Holmes is only an observer), proved that there were still Holmes stories to tell and innovative ways of telling them, but the other two '*Morse* format' specials lacked something - 'The Last Vampyre' and 'The Eligible Bachelor'. They both had a touch of the stereotypical Holmes about them, distant from their original sources, and, in the case of 'Vampyre', swerved dangerously close to the pea souper gothic of bad American versions.

Audience reaction wasn't good, and the production company put some effort into returning the show to its former glory. Granada, even though the series was one of its most popular franchises (Baker Street forming part of their studio tour), would only commit to three episodes, but the makers gambled by producing six, and, to its credit, the channel bought them all. The *Memoirs*, while showing the same invention and interpretative skill as the early shows, suffers greatly from the ill-health of Jeremy Brett. 'The Dying Detective', with horrid irony, was virtually filmed around him. With Edward Hardwicke being absent for 'The Golden Pince-Nez', filming *Shadowlands* (Watson's role was taken by Mycroft), the series sometimes felt like an exercise in damage limitation. Of note is Peter Wyngarde's marvellous turn in 'The Three Gables'.

Jeremy Brett finally lost his battle with illness in 1995, with 19 of Conan Doyle's tales left untold. It's a shame that this most thoughtful and sweet actor, who made his Holmes the definitive interpretation, didn't get to finish the canon.

Edge of Darkness

- **BBC Television/Lionheart** (BBC2) ◆ Colour
- **6 episodes** (50 minutes) ◆ 1985
- **Writer:** Troy Kennedy Martin
- **Director:** Martin Campbell
- **Producer:** Michael Wearing

Starring: Bob Peck (Ronald Craven) • Joe Don Baker (Darius Jedburgh) • Joanne Whalley (Emma Craven) • Charles Kay (Pendelton) • Ian McNeice (Harcourt) • Zoe Wanamaker (Clementine) • John Woodvine (Ross) • Jack Watson (Godbolt) • Tim McInnerny (Terry) • Kenneth Nelson (Grogan)

On a Welsh hillside, which doubles for a Scottish one, at the end of shooting on Troy Kennedy Martin's ground-breaking nuclear thriller, *Edge of Darkness*, actor Bob Peck was faced with the idea of falling to a sniper's bullet, and mutating, over hundreds of years, into a radiation-ravaged tree. The idea didn't appeal to him. Instead, he opted for a final shout, his daughter's name, the initial subject of the serial: 'Emma!'

Troy Kennedy Martin is one of Britain's most respected screenwriters, having created ***Z Cars*** with John McGrath, and having written *Reilly - Ace of Spies* and several episodes of ***The Sweeney***. Apart from an adaptation of *The Old Men at the Zoo* (1983) and the final episode of ***Z Cars***, Kennedy Martin had done little work for the BBC since 1964, blaming his left-wing politics and anti-naturalistic crusade for his departure to the USA to write movies (including *The Italian Job* (GB 69)).

Around 1978, he was mourning the loss of his mother, and had been separated from his daughter through divorce. He began to consider a work about the grey areas of policing. By 1981, he had completed a first draft for a pilot episode of a script he called *Magnox*, which was going to be about union problems in the nuclear industry. Kennedy Martin talked to Walter Patterson, then energy advisor for Friends of the Earth, who told him of several fears concerning plutonium missing off the international register of the nuclear material. In 1982, having been turned down by another producer ('leave out the politics, the man's relationship with his daughter and the nuclear side of it, then it might be a really good story' was the conversation that *Time Out* reported), Kennedy Martin took his scripts to Jonathan Powell, newly-appointed head of series and serials at the BBC.

Powell was looking to move the station away from classic adaptations, and asked producer Michael Wearing to read the scripts. Wearing was impressed enough to take on *Magnox* rather than *Blott on the Landscape*. Things looked all set, but two things happened to complicate matters.

On 23 March 1983 US President Ronald Reagan made his 'Star Wars' speech. Kennedy Martin was appalled by the notion of spaceborne defence systems, and adjusted his scripts to accommodate the ideas. Then, Martin Campbell, a director with a track record on ***Shoestring***, ***Minder*** and *Muck and Brass*, as well as 2nd Unit status on *Reilly*, was appointed to the project. Kennedy Martin and Campbell clashed almost immediately, Campbell asking for major rewrites that went against all Kennedy Martin's instincts. The writer, known for his longhand manuscripts and visually-orientated sense of action, basically objected to supplying much more explanatory dialogue. It was a question of mythological storytelling versus careful plotting, with the writer on one end, the director on the other, and Wearing carefully compromising in the middle.

The *Magnox* title was dropped in favour of *Dark Forces*, and then *Edge of Darkness*. The serial concerned Ronald Craven, a detective inspector from

Yorkshire. His radical scientist daughter, Emma, is murdered by McCroon, whom Craven had betrayed when he worked with informants in Northern Ireland. The question of whether McCroon was after him or Emma bothers Craven, and he begins an investigation, together with a grief-symptom vision of Emma. (Actually, ghost is nearer the mark: she tells him information he doesn't know, particularly of a list of underground stations - which actually turn out to be a map of how to get into the Northmoor nuclear facility - hidden in a cookery book.) After her death, Craven wanders around her room, gun in hand, finding a vibrator, a Geiger counter, a sackful of radioactive clothes and a gun. As Pendleton says, 'She was some sort of terrorist, wasn't she?' Craven weighs up the gun against Emma's teddy bear, and decides to find out who killed off the only survivor from the environmentalist Gaia group's incursion into Northmoor nuclear waste plant.

After another memorable encounter with McCroon, Craven interrogating the assassin while on the wrong end of his gun, Craven is hospitalized. He is only saved from madness by the intervention of large Texan CIA spook Darius Jedburgh, and Buchanite British cabinet-office spies Pendleton and Harcourt, who put Craven on to the track of the real killers. Craven finds himself pursued from a computing lab into the Barbican Centre, where the police lose him. Finally, Craven and Jedburgh go down into Northmoor itself, aided by union boss James Godbolt, and having found an escape bunker containing a luxurious supply of food and wine, gain access to the 'hot cell' where the plutonium was found by the Gaians. Jedburgh takes some away in a Harrods bag, slaughtering several CIA men in the process, and Craven is left to call Pendleton for help on a long-disused phone line, the other end picked up by a curious Civil Service employee in a deserted store-room.

The motivator behind all this mayhem is Jerry Grogan, boss of the Fusion Corporation, a modern-day Templar with a wish to take mankind to the stars. In what *The Independent* in the week of the Rio Earth Summit called 'The Jedburgh Address', Jedburgh makes a speech to a packed conference hall at St Andrews, and fuses two bars of plutonium in front of Grogan's face. Finally, Craven finds Jedburgh, who has made the plutonium into a bomb-shape to be set off by a nuclear bullet. They discuss the future of the planet, and how Craven has finally found peace within himself. He's on the side of the planet, and in any confrontation between the planet and man, the planet will win. Jedburgh is killed by soldiers who inform Craven that he's with them, to which Craven can only reply 'I am not on your side.'

In the end, he's left on that hillside, watching as the plutonium is recovered. The government knew of the whole plot, and is keen that Northmoor remains a secret nuclear waste processing plant, but Harcourt is vainly trying to get his report through to the DPP. Craven's report, on the other hand, has gone underground to Gaia.

The central problem between Kennedy Martin and Campbell was how much did Craven know. Had he been aware of Emma's descent into Northmoor, or hadn't he? Peck (who had been Campbell's choice for the role, Kennedy Martin opting for John Thaw) thus made a virtue of the confused direction, playing Craven with stony-faced enigmatic glances. He spent two days with Bradford police, researching the part, although the police took their name off the script once they saw the line about the vibrator. Peck and Kennedy Martin gave Craven a very close, physical relationship with his daughter, which a hyper-sensitive BBC saw as vaguely incestuous. To stave off internal problems, Wearing simply admitted that there was an element of that present, double-bluffing in much the same way as he'd used the initial format 'policeman seeks revenge for murder of daughter' to allow the strangeness of what followed to pass unmentioned.

(4 Nov–9 Dec 85)

1 Compassionate Leave
2 Into the Shadows
3 Burden of Proof
4 Breakthrough
5 Northmoor
6 Fusion

Edge offered many memorable scenes to a viewing public unfamiliar with plutonium, such as policemen retreating quickly from a body that buzzes on a Geiger detector, and the blackened and tired faces of Craven and Jedburgh in the last stages of radiation sickness. (The lead coffins that their assassins brought with them were particularly chilling.) It also proved very prophetic, predicting a Gulf War and a Conservative green strategy based on the idea that nuclear power stations were ozone-friendly, a stance too astonishing to even contemplate in 1985. Sue Cook, Michael Meacher MP and weatherman Bill Giles all appeared as themselves, giving credibility to a depiction of a frightening nuclear state. The serial depicted the Establishment as a series of warring cliques, and Pendleton and Harcourt get some of the best lines in suitably macabre style: 'We're funded by the GLC as a Lesbian Co-operative', and the wonderful exchange, when Jedburgh had vanished: 'He said something about meeting Moriarty at the Falls.' 'If there's an Irish element to this, I shall retire.'

Four-and-a-half million viewers tuned in on BBC2, pushing the appreciation index up to 86, and Michael Grade, then controller of BBC1, was so taken by the series that he wanted to clear the airwaves the following Saturday and repeat it. As it was, the BBC1 repeat, a few weeks later, claimed eight million viewers, and ranked as one of the fastest repeats in BBC history. In 1986, BAFTA gave the series Best Drama and Peck the Best Actor awards, with nominations for Whalley and Baker, as well as Best Original TV Music.

The music for *Edge* was composed by Michael Kamen, who went on to score movies like *Lethal Weapon* (US 87), and played by Eric Clapton, who improvised some of the passages direct to a video playback. It contributed to the atmosphere of the series, as did the extremely noisy sound and the very dark lighting.

Kennedy Martin envisioned the Grogan/Jedburgh confrontation as the end result of a battle between two separate strains of thought. Grogan is a Knight Templar, a man who believes in the use of science as a mystery religion, for the profit of the elite, and the greater profit of the Nuclear State. Jedburgh is a Knight of the Marches, a people's man who is mainly interested in how people will live in this 'New Jerusalem in the Milky Way'. Craven is somewhere between the two, a 'green man' who leaves vengeance to the black flowers which Gaia (the planetary self-regulating system as proposed by J.E. Lovelock) has spread to halt the tyranny of mankind. As Kennedy Martin said in his Australian BHP Television Lecture, it was Craven's destiny to 'confront and possibly destroy in the name of the planet the free market forces of entrepreneurial capitalism as represented by Jerry Grogan'.

Ultimately, *Edge of Darkness* belongs in the same category of nervous mid-80s BBC drama as *Frankie and Johnny* (another Campbell), *The Russian Soldier*, *Dead Head* (the same lighting team), *The Detective* and ***The Singing Detective*** (also starring Joanne Whalley, the 'red rave from the grave' as *City Limits* called her). All of these dramas are about the tyranny of the State, the nature of humanity, and what the future holds. All of them have a schizoid, post-modern edge, and all of them deal with storytelling in some way. The lighting and sound techniques, dark and booming, give all the texts a visual coherency that will doubtless suggest to future generations what life under Thatcher and the Bomb felt like. Martin Campbell, in a move which would doubtless appeal to Kennedy Martin's sense of irony, is now a director of James Bond movies.

Edge of Darkness was not only the first genuine myth of the nuclear era, but also the definitive text of 80s television.

Inspector Morse

- **Zenith/Central** (ITV) ◆ Colour
- **29 episodes** (120 minutes) ◆ 1987-95
- **Based on:** characters and situations created by Colin Dexter
- **Writers:** Anthony Minghella, Julian Mitchell, Thomas Ellice, Charles Wood, Michael Wilcox, Peter Buckman, Alma Cullen, Jeremy Burnham, Daniel Boyle, Geoffrey Case, Peter Nichols, John Brown, Russell Lewis
- **Directors:** Alistair Reid, Brian Parker, Peter Hammond, Edward Bennett, Peter Duffell, Herbert Wise, James Scott, Anthony Simmons, Jim Goddard, John Madden, Sandy Johnson, Danny Boyle, Adrian Shergold, Roy Battersby, Colin Gregg, Antonia Bird, Stuart Orme
- **Producers:** Kenny McBain, Chris Burt, David Lascelles, Deirdre Keir
- **Executive Producer:** Ted Childs

Starring: John Thaw (Chief Insp. Morse) • Kevin Whately (DS Lewis) • Peter Woodthorpe (Max) • Amanda Hilwood (Dr Grayling Russell) • Norman Jones (Chief Supt. Bell) • James Grout (Chief Supt. Strange) • Alun Armstrong (Chief Supt. Holdsby)

Not all crimes are solved by extravagant car chases and the kicking-in of heads. Indeed, some detectives' aversion to the physical world is such that the crime is played out, and normally solved, solely in the mind, suspects being interviewed away from the claustrophobia of the police cell in an attempt to elucidate honest confession and revelation of character. These cerebral sleuths, whose theories are sometimes so complex that they lead to the wrong person, are accompanied by minions who are realists, and the drama is usually played out against the beautiful backdrop of a renaissance city.

The fact that this description fits *Maigret* about as closely as *Inspector Morse* shows us the cyclical nature of the fictional detective, and hints at one reason for *Morse*'s huge success. John Thaw notes of Morse that he is 'in lots of ways ... very old-fashioned, a classic British fictional detective of the type who has been around for 50 years or more'.

As a programme, *Morse*'s success has rarely been matched, with a global audience of 75 million people in over 50 countries. All the more surprising for a show where each episode (including UK-length adverts) lasts two hours, where the plots are convoluted and the pace pedestrian, and the on-going musical motifs are classical opera.

Morse (hated first name not yet known) first appeared in Colin Dexter's 1975 novel *Last Bus to Woodstock*. Dexter was a teacher and crossword-compiler, and bought to the genre a renewed appreciation of its potential layers of meaning and twists of plot. Morse himself, from the outset, had 'an aura of loneliness about him', as Thaw later commented. Dexter described him as liking 'ladies, poetry and music, and he is very fond of booze, especially real ale. He's terribly mean about money, and can be very unfair to people of slightly lesser intellect, such as Sergeant Lewis, who is a man of monumental stupidity in some ways.' Indeed, Morse is very similar to Dexter (except for the bit about money, he will almost invariably point out), his range of reference and allusion reflecting Dexter's former role as a GCE examiner in Latin, Greek, Ancient History and English. Dexter's other great passion led him to be *The Observer* crossword-writing champion for three years, Morse's name and all the other character names from the

First season
(6 Jan–20 Jan 87)
1 The Dead of Jericho
2 The Silent World of Nicholas Quinn
3 Service of All the Dead

Special
(25 Dec 87)
4 The Wolvercote Tongue

Second season
(8 Mar–22 Mar 88)
5 Last Seen Wearing
6 The Setting of the Sun
7 Last Bus to Woodstock

Third season
(4–25 Jan 89)
8 Ghost in the Machine
9 The Last Enemy
10 Deceived by Flight
11 The Secret of Bay 5B

Fourth season
(3–24 Jan 90)
12 The Infernal Serpent
13 The Sins of the Fathers
14 Driven to Distraction
15 Masonic Mysteries

Fifth season
(20 Feb–27 Mar 91)
16 Second Time Around
17 Fat Chance
18 Who Killed Harry Field?
19 Greeks Bearing Gifts
20 Promised Land

Sixth season
(26 Feb–15 Apr 92)
21 Dead on Time
22 Happy Families
23 The Death of the Self
24 Absolute Conviction
25 Cherubim and Seraphim

Seventh season
(6–20 Jan 93)
26 Deadly Slumber
27 The Day of the Devil
28 Twilight of the Gods

Special
(29 Nov 95)
29 The Way through the Woods

first novel, with the exception of the murderer, coming from other *Observer* prizewinners.

Such audacious construction and near-invisible trickery is reflected in the programme's formal structure, with its mannered direction and recurring symbols reflecting the many layers of the scripts. Even the music has its particular role to play, being a mixture of specially-recorded classical pieces and Barrington Pheloung's expansive incidental music. (Pheloung's theme, not surprisingly, is based around the Morse Code equivalent of the letters M, O, R, S, and E.) The first two seasons concentrated on adapting Dexter's novels (in the wrong order), but original scripts followed, often derived from a Dexter plot. Dexter, Hitchcock-like, can be seen somewhere in the background of most episodes.

Morse's inception dates back to the time when Ted Childs, Central Television's controller of drama, felt that Independent Television should attempt something in the vein of the BBC's *Miss Marple*, a quality whodunit that had managed to attract writers of the calibre of Alan Plater. Kenny McBain, at that point producing the first series of *Boon*, mentioned that he had been reading Dexter's novels, and, once the general concept got the green light, they struggled to get the idea of a series of two-hour mini-plays accepted by TV executives. 'A lot of people were reluctant to endorse this innovation. The belief was that an ITV audience would not sit and watch a rather convoluted piece of fairly intense detection for two hours,' said Childs.

Crucial to the show's success was to be the time and care laboured over each episode, seen as a separate play and not part of a series treadmill, and the casting. Childs knew John Thaw from his days producing ***The Sweeney***, and felt that the actor had the ability to play Morse. The problem might have come from Thaw himself, who stopped playing Regan after saying that he'd had enough of cops and robbers. Thaw was doing his usual eclectic mix of stage/TV comedy/drama - specifically a Ray Cooney farce in Toronto - when he was approached to play Morse. Thaw's reading of Dexter excited him, and he didn't feel that he had recanted his previous comments. 'After ***The Sweeney***, I didn't say I would never play another policeman. I said I would never play another Regan. Morse is not like him in any way.'

As played by Thaw, Morse proved to be one of those great television contradictions: a character who shouldn't be likeable (he is by turns grumpy, morose, self-obsessed, critical, insensitive, mean), but who dominates the screen to such an extent that the viewers love him. Even when calling Lewis an idiot ('You'll never get on if you can't master your subjunctives, Lewis') or showing an utter lack of respect to bereaved relatives, you can't help but like Morse. And, as we learned more about him (his Oxford fiancée turned up in 'Dead on Time', and tragedy reached his family in 'Cherubim and Seraphim'), we were invited to consider why he ended up such a sad figure.

A character like Morse needed a well-balanced foil, and so Lewis was changed into a younger family man (in the novels he is a contemporary of Morse), with just the right amount of common sense to keep Morse at least vaguely in the bounds of reality. Indeed, Lewis often provides the key to the solving of a mystery, whether it be a chance remark ('You reckon she'll stay with him when the money runs out?') or literally coming to the rescue and holding the baby in 'Greeks Bearing Gifts'. In 'Dead on Time', Morse is unable to see past his own relationship-prompted biases, and Lewis has to bypass Morse in an attempt to solve the mystery. At other times, it's Morse's triumphant book-reading that provides the key ('Happy Families'), which comes as a welcome relief to the man whose reputation has just been dragged through the gutter by the press ('Clever Dick' is one memorable headline).

Kevin Whately, who was also in a Cooney farce when the part was offered to him, strengthened his portrayal of Lewis as the seasons passed. Lewis proved to be more than a one-dimensional feed, his relationship with Morse developing through such subtle scenes as doing the washing up together in 'Second Time Around' and going to see *The Magic Flute* in 'Masonic Mysteries'. Lewis's home life has been consistently and quietly expanded, playing cricket with his son in

'The Way through the Woods'... leads to murder, incriminating photographs and a gun-wielding maniac

'Deceived by Flight', and hoping desperately to get home for school sports day in 'The Death of the Self'. In both this episode and 'Fat Chance', the almost-'Her indoors'-like figure of Mrs Lewis helps Lewis's investigation, whilst his daughter in 'Cherubim and Seraphim' is listening to the same House music that has feverishly undercut a spate of recent suicides. Indeed, he manages to get the better of Morse by explaining what fractals are, and dons a red cap so as not to seem so out of place at a rave at the episode's conclusion. Morse is so intent on remembering his teenage depressions that, not for the first time, he is blind to the eventual solution: not depression, but ecstasy in all its forms.

Morse has always oozed visual extravagance, each shot so well-composed it could be a painting, revelling in its Oxford locations and the enclosed claustrophobia of its cloisters, churches and colleges. Although critics have described the show as being a detective travelogue, we do get to see working-class Oxford as well. In 'Promised Land' the location switched completely, events having moved to Australia, which allowed Lewis to unwind but prompted increased agitation in Morse, and 'The Death of the Self' dwelt lovingly on the Italian countryside, Puccini blaring. Morse's involvement with opera singer Nicole Burgess (Frances Barber) was one of a handful of romantic interludes guaranteed to put a spring into the miserable copper's step. It never quite ends in fireworks for Morse, blaming either his job or his hesitant character for his various failed relationships. Although he'd never admit it, at times he almost seems to envy Lewis's straightforward family life.

Morse himself remains the perfect image of the detective in the modern age, and a fallible throw-back to a previous era. The programme sums up a sense of optimism that swept British television in the late 80s, and if the planned one-off episodes remain as engrossing as 1995's 'The Way through the Woods' there is no reason why it shouldn't have an ongoing role to play as well.

The Ruth Rendell Mysteries

- **TVS/Meridian/Blue Heaven Productions** (ITV) ◆ Colour
- **65 episodes** (standard length: 60 minutes) ◆ 1987-96
- **Based on:** novels by Ruth Rendell
- Devised for television by John Davies
- **Writers include:** Clive Exton, Paula Milne, Roger Marshall, Trevor Preston, Matthew Jacobs, George Baker, Julian Bond, Alan Plater
- **Directors include:** Mary McMurray, Don Leaver, Herbert Wise, Sandy Johnson, John Gorrie, Marc Evans, Alan Grint, Jim Goddard
- **Producers:** John Davies, Neil Zeiger
- **Executive producer:** Graham Benson

The 80s trend of the 'thinking policeman' began with the successful adaptations of stories featuring P.D. James's poet and idealist Adam Dalgleish in 1984. At around the same time TVS producer John Davies purchased the rights to the Inspector Wexford novels of Ruth Rendell. From the publication of her first novel, *From Doon with Death* in 1964, Rendell's reputation and readership had grown steadily with each book. The Wexford novels had a Home Counties soap quality about them (sub-plots often spill from one book to the next) which made the stories naturals for television. Unfortunately, Davies chose to film the stories out of order, taking two at random, *Wolf to the Slaughter* and *A Guilty Thing Surprised*, as his initial offerings. This made continuity in later stories something of a problem when such storylines as the death of Inspector Burden's wife needed to be fitted into place.

The casting of George Baker in the role of Wexford was a masterstroke. Ruth Rendell freely admits that the image she carries of Wexford and many of his character traits (notably his penchant for literary quotation) were taken from her own father. Baker, with his dignified manner and well-developed ability with humour, brought Wexford to life in a way that Rendell found enchanting. Her post-TV series novels were written, she said, with Baker in mind.

Wexford's assistant, the frail, aptly-named Inspector Burden, proved to be a significant challenge for Christopher Ravencroft. A dour and often irritating character who has been dealt a tragic hand by life, Burden is missing altogether from some novels (notably *Murder Being Once Done*) and appears only briefly in others. On television the trials and tribulations of the Burden family (Mike's difficult relationship with his children, his wife's death from cancer,

Regular cast (except for stories listed under 'Starring'): George Baker (DCI Reg Wexford) • Christopher Ravenscroft (DI Mike Burden)

With (except for stories listed under 'Starring'): Louie Ramsay (Dora Wexford) • Ann Penfold (Jean Burden) • Ken Kitson (Sgt. Martin) • John Burgess (Dr Crocker) • Deborah Poplett (Shiela Wexford) • Dave Hill (Det. Chief Constable Freeborn) • Emma Smith (Pat Burden) • Diane Keen (Jenny Burden) • Sean Pertwee/Robin Kermode (Sgt. Barry Vine)

Starring (stories): **21** John Duttine • Mel Martin • Trevor Cooper • Abigail McKern; **22** Colin Firth • Robert Urquhart • George Costigan • Emma Croft; **23** Eleanor David • Mark Frankel • Peter Egan • Jane Gurnett; **24** Lisa Harrow • Simon Ward • Karen Archer • David Collings • Honeysuckle Weeks • Pascal Hunt • Cordelia Bugeja • Eleanor Bron • Tom Chadbon; **26** Amanda Redman • Owen Teale • Sarak Parks • Adam Welsh; **27** Keith Barron • Ronald Pickup • Michael Fitzgerald • Don Henderson

1 Wolf to the Slaughter
(2–23 Aug 87)
Four episodes

2 A Guilty Thing Surprised
(19 Jun–3 Jul 88)
Three episodes)

3 Shake Hands Forever
(23 Sep–7 Oct 88)
Three episodes

4 No Crying He Makes
(23 Dec 88, 90 minutes)

5 No More Dying Then
(22 Oct–5 Nov 89)
Three episodes

6 A Sleeping Life
(12–26 Nov 89)
Three episodes

7 The Veiled One
(17 Dec 89, 120 minutes)

8 Some Lie and Some Die
(30 Sep–14 Oct 90)
Three episodes

9 The Best Man to Die
(21 Oct–4 Nov 90)
Three episodes

10 An Unkindness of Ravens
(11–18 Nov 90)
Two episodes

11 Put on by Cunning
(24 Dec 90, 120 minutes)

12 A New Lease of Death
(29 Sep–13 Oct 91)
Three episodes

13 Murder Being Once Done
(20 Oct–3 Nov 91)
Three episodes

14 From Doon with Death
(10–17 Nov 91)
Two episodes

15 Means of Evil
(24 Nov–1 Dec 91)
Two episodes

16 Achilles Heel
(26 Dec 91, 120 minutes)

and, later, his remarriage) were used to give *The Ruth Rendell Mysteries* its soap-opera appeal.

Filmed in and around Romsey in Hampshire (doubling for Rendell's fictional Kingsmarkham), the beautiful countryside and peaceful splendour of the area is ruined by a murder rate that dwarfs that of New York (or Oxford). The on-going feel of the series was further enhanced, as the later stories showed, by elements of Wexford's home life intruding into his cases (his daughter's political activities are central to 'The Veiled One'). Through it all, Wexford's wife, Dora, proves to be the pillar upon which Wexford is built (although as the 80s progressed, Dora moved away from the 'little woman at home' stereotype of the early stories and became more independent and assertive).

The series really clicked in the third story, 'Shake Hands Forever', in which Wexford was convinced that a businessman, Hathall (Tom Wilkinson), had murdered his wife, despite the man having a cast-iron alibi. Wexford's pursuit of Hathall covered two years and turned into an obsession that almost cost Reg his job but, in the best *Colombo* tradition, he emerged triumphant and was proved to have been right all along.

The first of the extended episodes, 'No Crying He Makes' (based on one of Rendell's short stories), was followed the next year by a wild and surreal adaptation of 'The Veiled One' which, as with several episodes of ***Bergerac*** from the same period, tried to push back the boundaries of crime drama TV and were consequently criticized for the lack of a cohesive plot. One is left feeling that many TV critics are under the impression that crime drama is the one genre on television where subversion is to be actively discouraged. Certainly, their anger that *The Ruth Rendell Mysteries* should experiment in such a way was frighteningly unjust.

The four stories transmitted in 1990 marked the pinnacle of Ruth Rendell on television. 'Some Lie and Some Die', a story written in the early 70s about rock festivals, became a perfect vehicle for the series to spread its popularity

17 The Speaker of Mandarin
(27 Sep–11 Oct 92)
Three episodes

18 The Mouse in the Corner
(18–25 Oct 92)
Two episodes

19 An Unwanted Woman
(1–8 Nov 92)
Two episodes

20 Kissing the Gunner's Daughter
(15 Nov–6 Dec 92)
Four episodes

21 Talking to Strange Men
(27 Dec 92, 120 minutes)

22 Master of the Moor
(2–16 Sep 94)
Three episodes

23 Vanity Dies Hard
(24 Mar 95–7 Apr 95)
Three episodes

24 The Strawberry Tree
(21–28 Apr 95)
Two episodes

25 Simisola
(26 Jan–9 Feb 96)
Three episodes

26 The Secret House of Death
(8–15 Mar 96)
Two episodes

27 A Case of Coincidence
(22–29 Mar 96)
Two episodes

base by filming at Glastonbury. The story of pop star Zeno (a superb performance by Peter Capaldi), and his relationship with a local girl who was murdered, twisted and turned over three complex and intense episodes. Rendell's poem in the novel, 'Let Me Believe', was adapted into a song for Capaldi by the series' musical advisor, former Shadows drummer Brian Bennett. 'The Best Man to Die', a more straightforward detective story with a clever plot and a stunning twist in the tail, achieved equal appreciation. 'Put on by Cunning', featuring a fine guest-performance by Cherie Lunghi, took the series to America, and achieved the series' best-ever viewing figures.

Although the 1991 season saw George Baker's writing debut, it was a problematic time not only for Baker, suffering the trauma of his wife's death, but also for the entire production team due to the loss of TVS's franchise which seemed to spell the end for Wexford. However, thanks in no small part to its significant popularity overseas, the series continued, firstly as a 15-minute segment on ITV's 1992 Telethon (a light-hearted romp that was linked to similar sequences of ***Sherlock Holmes***, *Van Der Valk* and *Taggart*), and then as a full season. It adapted the remaining Wexford novels and included 'The Speaker of Mandarin', with filming in Hong Kong doubling for China, and 'The Mouse in the Corner', which reached the small screen before the novel was published.

1996's 'Simisola' was the first Wexford *Ruth Rendell Mystery* in three years. Although Kingsmarkham tales are now the exception rather than the rule, viewers can be grateful for producer Neil Zeiger's continuing attempts to bring the Wexford stories to life.

Between the Lines

- **BBC Television/World Productions** (formerly Island World) (BBC1)
- Colour
- **35 episodes** (*c*. 50 minutes) ◆ 1992-94
- **Creator:** J. C. Wilsher
- **Writers:** J. C. Wilsher, Russell Lewis, Steve Trafford, Michael Russell, Rob Heyland, Ray Brennan, Ron Rose, Nicholas Martin, Julian Jones, Steve Griffiths, Simon Andrew Stirling, Gordon Hann, Dusty Hughes
- **Directors:** Charles McDougall, Alan Dossor, Roy Battersby, Tom Clegg, Jenny Killick, Robert Bierman, Peter Smith, Richard Standeven, Ian Knox, Ross Devenish
- **Producers:** Peter Norris, Joy Lale
- **Executive producer:** Tony Garnett

Starring: Neil Pearson (Tony Clark) • Tom Georgeson (Harry Naylor) • Siobhan Redmond (Maureen Connell) • Tony Doyle (John Deakin) • Lynda Steadman (Sue Clark) • Lesley Vickerage (WPC Jenny Dean) • David Lyon (Commander Brian Huxtable) • John Shrapnel (DAC Trevor Dunning) • Jaye Griffiths (Molly Cope) • Jerome Flynn (DS Eddie Hargreaves) • Robin Lermitte (Det. Supt./Chief Supt. David Graves) • Elaine Donnelly (Joyce Naylor) • Hugh Ross (Commander Graham Sullivan) • Francesca Annis (Angela Berridge) • Barbara Wilshere (Kate Roberts) • Sylvestre le Touzel (Sarah Teale) • Eve Bland (Ellie Hughes)

Few programmes have been as morally grey as *Between the Lines*. Whereas a large amount of supposedly adult drama works by referring to child-like conceptions of good and evil, by the 90s anyone with even a passing knowledge of current affairs would have expected something more adventurous from a police-based drama. Questions such as 'Are there any bent coppers?' and 'Are some policemen racist?' are questions for another, more innocent age.

The idea for the series came from J.C. Wilsher, a regular contributor to ***The Bill***. Researching the Police Complaints Investigation Bureau - that part of the force dedicated to investigating other officers - he uncovered a vast amount of intriguing material. The potential themes were enormous. To what extent do the police decide in advance who is guilty? Should one 'unsafe' aspect of a conviction allow criminals to go free? Can the police be allowed to investigate themselves? If an officer is found guilty of, say, perverting the course of justice, are stronger actions than feeble cautions, 'words of advice' and 'damage limitation' required? ***The Bill*** had featured its fair share of bent coppers and 'fitted-up' suspects over the years, but to do CIB justice required more than a cameo in a 25-minute drama.

The lead character in *Between the Lines* was Tony Clark, recently promoted to superintendent. In the first episode, CIB asks him to investigate his old nick, where a senior officer is suspected of doing 'a bit of private enterprise'. If that weren't bad enough, his personal life is discussed unflinchingly by his superior officer, the darkly-charismatic John Deakin. Is Clark above reproach? 'Well, nobody's fireproof, are they sir?' Deakin's threat to Clark is redolent with menace: 'If we find you're having us over backwards, Tony, we'll do your legs like a steamroller.' (Small wonder Deakin is seen hitting a dog with a book about St Francis of Assisi in the later episode 'Blooded'.)

Clark is certainly no George Dixon. His charm and his ability to get results is only matched by his cynicism, womanizing and mental instability. Neil Pearson refuted suggestions that his character was sexually powerful. 'He is emotionally immature and sexually unstable... Clark isn't a loner - he's lonely.'

Married to Sue, a long-suffering nurse, Clark has been having a 'casual' affair with WPC Jenny Dean, merely the latest of many. Tony and Sue appear to have little in common (she reads *The Guardian*, he *The Telegraph*), and he manipulates his wife in social situations to aid his investigations. Sue knows of Tony's past infidelities, but wants to make a new start: when it proves obvious in later episodes that he's still seeing another woman, Sue accuses Clark's colleague Maureen Connell of having a fling with him. 'You couldn't be more wrong,' Mo says, prefiguring developments made explicit in the second season.

Clark - along with Connell and seen-it-all chain-smoking DI Harry Naylor - gets the results Deakin is looking for, despite the officers they investigate holding them in complete contempt. (In 'The Only Good Copper', Clark and the others have to investigate claims made against a dead policeman, which leads to the slashing of Naylor's car tyres and a dead rat on Clark's desk.) To his disgust, Tony's stay with CIB is made a permanent one.

Even Hal Lindes's theme music gives a hint of the show's ambiguity, moving from haunting acoustic simplicity à la ***Inspector Morse*** to something epic, powerful but almost overbearing. Not surprisingly, critical praise was swift in coming, *The Independent* stating that 'This looks set to be a brave series. The dialogue has that right tang of realism about it [and] it is not afraid to look at dirty tactics, among even the best coppers. What one hopes for in the following episodes is some new debate about the old chestnut: should the police be allowed to police themselves?'

Such discussion was not long in coming. Roman satirist Juvenal's well-known query 'Quis custodiet ipso Custodes?' (Who is to guard the guards themselves?) - quoted in the episode 'The Fifth Estate' - formed the backbone to the huge arcs of storyline that were soon to develop. The subject matter in episodes such as 'Out of the Game' (the shooting of an unarmed young man), 'Lest Ye Be Judged' (the 'fitting-up' of a suspect), 'Breaking Point' (police 'bully-boy' tactics at a demonstration) and 'Nothing Personal' (the suicide of a black man in police custody) lent the series a real-life impact: the very stories one read in the press would have their dramatic equivalent in a *Between the Lines* plot. The episodes dealt with the increasing politicization of the police force and had the knack of seeming credible, concentrating on mountains of paperwork to the virtual exclusion of car chases and fights.

The visceral content of the series - the dirty walkways, dingy flats and unflinching explosions of violence - became clear with the second episode. Clark and the others watch the graphic death of a suspected gunman, captured by a camcorder. The footage comes in the middle of a sequence taken at a family birthday party. As Harry comments, 'Won't be sending this to Jeremy Beadle, then.' The episode concentrated on the mental stability of the chief superintendent and the trauma suffered by the marksmen who took the youth 'out of the game'. A policeman incapable of dealing with the terrifying situation he was in is juxtaposed with the commanding officer, driving around the estate like some tinpot dictator and casually beating rioters. Mad is not too strong a word for him. Along the way, Clark uncovers a murder, but Deakin prevents him from investigating further as it's entirely beyond his brief. Such frustration was an intrinsic element of *Between the Lines*, many episodes ending with the real villain going free. The events of 'Lies and Damned Lies', for example, are entirely precipitated by the machinations of an ambitious Tory MP, but by the conclusion the key witness has died of an (accidental) heart attack, ensuring that the accused CID officers get off. The Sergeant who 'grassed' is urged to 'think about retirement', and finds himself ostracized by his former colleagues. His car is covered with paint. The episode ends - without music - as the distraught policeman locks himself in his garage and starts up his car.

'Words of Advice' has Clark renewing his relationship with Jenny Dean, and thus proving possibly the worst person in the world to investigate a married black officer who sexually assaulted a white WPC. It also featured one of the sex scenes that gave the programme its tabloid nickname *Between the Loins*. Pearson expressed his unease at Clark's womanizing and the sexual content, leading to some changes of emphasis in the second season. However, from this episode onwards it was obvious that Tony Clark was on a downward spiral, the betrayal of his wife ('Are you at it, Tony?') and increasingly angry denials of infidelity

First season
(4 Sep–4 Dec 92)
1 Private Enterprise
2 Out of the Game
3 Words of Advice
4 Lies and Damned Lies
5 A Watch and Chain of Course
6 Lest Ye Be Judged
7 Breaking Point
8 The Only Good Copper
9 Watching the Detectives
10 Nothing to Declare
11 Nothing Personal
12 Nobody's Fireproof
13 The Chill Factor

Second season
(5 Oct–21 Dec 93)
14 New Order
15 Manslaughter
16 Crack Up
17 Honourable Man
18 "Some Must Watch ..."
19 Manoeuvre 11
20 The Fifth Estate
21 The Great Detective
22 Jumping the Lights
23 What's the Strength of This?
24 Big Boys' Rules (part one)
25 Big Boys' Rules (part two)

Third season
(19 Oct–21 Dec 94)
26 Foxtrot Oscar
27 A Safe Pair of Hands
28 A Face in the Crowd
29 Shoot to Kill
30 Close Protection
31 Blooded
32 Unknown Soldier
33 Free Trade
34 The End User (part one)
35 The End User (part two)

mirroring the breech of public trust caused by the actions of the officers (and the system) he was investigating.

'Lest Ye Be Judged' had Clark and the team investigating Teddy Dicks, a 'stitched-up' suspect in Liverpool. Clark's attempts to finish with Jenny only lead to a relationship with Molly Cope, cynical local reporter ('"Police Stop White Man in Car." Now, that is a scoop!'). Clark and the others uncover enough evidence to believe that at least one of Teddy Dicks's convictions are unsafe. The arresting officer, however, is sure of himself: 'Did you deny him access to a solicitor, beat him, deny him food? I think you did most or all of these things.' 'Prove it.' We see the officer's family and are invited to consider the great love he has for his children. By comparison, we're left in little doubt that Dicks (Edward Tudor-Pole) is unstable, and almost certainly guilty of at least some of the crimes of which he was accused. Harry is angry at how the investigation is progressing, approaching matters pragmatically: 'That little shit's lethal. All right, so they slapped him around a bit, but they got a confession. So he was scared for an hour or so, and they bent the rules, but how scared were the little old ladies he waved guns in front of, eh? How scared were the little kids he forced to lie down on the floor? How many nightmares, how many wet beds?' Harry was always the pragmatist, the voice of common sense and police loyalty (even going as far as to indicate how an interviewee should respond in 'The Only Good Copper').

In 'Breaking Point' (the title referring to Clark's marriage as much to the poorly-handled riot) a constable is badly burnt by a Molotov cocktail. Seeking revenge, a 'rioter' (actually innocent of any violence) is beaten into a coma by a colleague of the first policeman. The series seemed to say that such actions - though never commendable - are almost understandable, given the 'them and us' attitude that permeates modern policing. Although for once the investigation goes well, Sue Clark sees Tony with Jenny Dean, and she leaves him. As Deakin says in the next episode, 'Your home life's in ruins over some bit of skirt, you're drinking too much, brawling in pubs, getting slapped by grieving widows. You're a wreck.'

'A Watch and Chain of Course' began the involved plot that insinuated itself into most of the remaining episodes. Michael Carswell, a bouncer, had been imprisoned for murder on the basis of an alleged confession in the back of a Panda car. The driver - and uniquely in a position to incriminate the arresting officers - was Jenny Dean. She is advised by Clark to tell the truth - his relationship with her removing him from the investigation - and is pressurized by her boyfriend, Eddie Hargreaves, not to implicate *him*. When a senior police officer is arrested for kerb-crawling in 'Nobody's Fireproof' towards the end of the season it seems that an intimidated prostitute might shed some light on the Carswell case. A pornographer/pimp seems to have been paying DAC Dunning to keep him safe. As Deakin observes, 'Be aware, there's a message in all this. Nobody's fireproof.' The episode ends with another suicide - Jenny Dean throwing herself into the propellers of a pleasure cruiser on the Thames - and with a grim-faced Naylor breaking the news to Clark behind closed doors.

The spider's web plot was unravelled in the final episode. Clark discovers that Dunning is in fact innocent: he has, instead, been 'fitted up' by Deakin. Clark decides to move against Deakin, who played a part in Jenny's suicide, despite that fact that he doesn't like Dunning and considers Deakin his 'best guvnor'. There is a tense climax onboard HMS *Belfast* - the closest the first season came to using standard crime show conventions - and Deakin is arrested. There is no triumph for Tony, though. On his own, he glimpses Sue through the pouring rain.

If the critics isolated a single flaw during the otherwise-acclaimed first season of *Between the Lines* it tended to be the dialogue, only just the right side of the clichés established by ***The Sweeney*** and lampooned by *The Comic Strip* (and never more obvious than in the casual use of the ubiquitous 'guv'). Still, according to the 1993 BBC documentary *Barlow, Regan, Pyall and Fancy*, there had always been a two-way transmission of vernacular between the police and the fictional equivalents on the small screen. If nothing else, *Between the Lines* was very aware of this kind of symbiosis: 'It's the word on the street.' 'You watch too many films.'

The glories of the vernacular enlivened many a routine questioning session (how few police dramas have relied on the twin tape recorder and bare walls to produce such moments of high drama). Given the grim subject matter there was also a strong vein of humour: 'Old African saying, Harry: "The higher up the monkey climbs, the more he shows his bottom."' Rural police are known as 'Turnip Tops', and a suspect is said to have 'more form than Desert Orchid'. In 'Breaking Point' a senior police officer rubs over incriminating video footage with clips of Edd the Duck. An interview with Jenny Dean in 'Nobody's Fireproof' revealed a great deal about the force's sexism: 'The officer I later learned to be DS Hargreaves got out, came over to me, and said his vehicle was immobilized, and could I offer assistance?' 'What, in those words?' 'No. He said "My big end's playing up, gorgeous. Have you got the capacity?"'

The interaction between the characters was also satisfying. Deakin is shown as liking Clark because he recognizes something of himself. On the other hand, he thinks Clark's peer Graves is career-minded and shallow: 'The extent to which Clark frequently pisses me off pales into insignificance beside my intense and permanent dislike of you.'

Graves was not alone in being in a very different position when the second series began a year later. Deakin has avoided prison but has left the force, and the expected promotion went to Graves instead of Clark. Graves is now Tony's boss, and he often calls him 'Anthony' on a point of principle. The first story dealt with neo-fascists and a Holocaust-denying American author, but the second was a revelation.

'Manslaughter' could almost have been an episode of ***Inspector Morse*** as it deals with a 'simple' murder. The complicating factor is that the killer is a CID officer who claims to have had an argument with his wife and simply lost control. Mo is infuriated by what she sees as the sexism of the legal system: 'A man's strength is his murder weapon. A woman would have to go into the kitchen, pick up a knife, and come back to the row. Those few seconds can mean the difference between diminished responsibility and murder. She could go down for 15 years, but because he just got on with it and strangled her, he could walk.'

Clark and the others only investigate matters fully because they're desperate to avoid the mountains of paperwork involved in an account-fiddling case, and they discover that the policeman was having an affair with his wife's younger sister, embellishing his own story with phrases taken from previous 'domestic' cases he's investigated. They conclude that the killing was premeditated, but they run out of time and can't charge him. As *The Independent* review pointed out, this episode fully embodies the programme's ambiguous attitude to the nature of law and justice.

Subsequent episodes dealt with the shooting of (another) black youth and the terrifying world of crack addiction, and the sexual peccadilloes of a politician, exposed by the very officers supposed to protect him from the tabloid's glare. The first proper dabble into the muddy waters of the friction between the police force and the secret service came in '"Some Must Watch..."', where a break-in at a TA building is dealt with by armed police officers. After shooting one man ('armed' only with a cordless drill), the other intruders are arrested, and claim to be working for MI5. The investigation - variously involving the Army, Special Branch, CIB, the Home Office and MI5 - begins to uncover the conflict between MI5 and Special Branch which was to overshadow many subsequent episodes. In the post-Cold War world, 'Five' have already been given anti-terrorism and they're desperate to muscle in on other areas of Special Branch's business ('They want to be the FBI,' remarks a senior police officer). The trouble is, they're even less accountable than Branch (a bumbling MI5 spook turns up and tries to sweep everything under the carpet). Clark is eventually blackmailed into silence: they have been bugging his phone, and know that he passed information to his friend Molly Cope. The new love of Clark's life, however, was Angela Berridge, who worked for the Home Office. Although married, Berridge began an on-off fling with Clark in 'The Fifth Estate', having liaised with him during the TA break-in case.

The private lives of Harry and Mo were no more straightforward. Joyce Naylor is diagnosed as having motor neurone disease, leading to Harry doing civilian security work on top of his police investigations in order to fund private treatment. Meanwhile, Mo loses her partner, Richard, and begins a relationship with Kate Roberts, who is being portrayed by the papers as a 'disgraced' senior woman police officer's lesbian lover. Reflecting real-life cases, the female officer is continually denied promotion until she is forced to take the police authority to an industrial tribunal. Other story strands seemed suspiciously familiar, too, most notably the use of horses against a demonstration/riot when it was unsafe to do so ('Manoeuvre 11') and a tape of a royal phone call ('The Fifth Estate').

If the clash between MI5 and Special Branch wasn't complex enough, 'Jumping the Lights' sketched the conflict between Traffic (who have 'ended more careers than CIB') and the Vice Squad. While investigating a hit-and-run, Clark discovers for himself that it's not good to get on the wrong side of the traffic police. At the episode's conclusion the team discover that a police officer *was* at the wheel of the car, but, because he also inspected the vehicle in his professional capacity, this will be impossible to prove.

J.C. Wilsher's 'What's the Strength of This?' had Harry's 'extra-curricular' activities exposed and investigated, leading to him being demoted and returned to CID. The final two episodes brought the season to a shattering climax, from which, arguably, the series could never recover.

'Big Boys' Rules' begins with the execution of a Catholic man in Epping Forest. He had recently visited a civil rights lawyer, claiming that Special Branch put pressure on him to become a police informer in Northern Ireland, and years later to commit various criminal actions on their behalf. Harry is working on a seemingly unconnected burglary and murder case, but Clark and Connell uncover a trail that leads right to John Deakin's door. Clark says that this time 'We're going to dump so much on Deakin he'll think he's standing under Nellie the Elephant.' Little does Tony know that Angela Berridge has contacted him not for a meeting to discuss their relationship but to give Deakin an opportunity to talk to Clark.

Deakin has photos and audio/video footage of Clark's liaisons with Berridge, and threatens to distribute them to the press and police. If that isn't enough, Deakin reminds Clark that Berridge might become a target for the IRA: both Deakin and Berridge, it seems, are working for Five. Clark is left trying to tie up some loose ends for Deakin, with Harry and Mo as 'backup'. He is attacked by the thug that Deakin used to steal some highly confidential defence documents, but Harry comes to the rescue, shooting the man three times. Clark tells Naylor to go: he cannot move, and he'll have to carry the can himself. Arrested for murder, Clark signs a statement, prepared by Berridge and Deakin, that seems to fit the facts. In an excellent conclusion that echoes numerous previous stories, only this time with the roles reversed, the investigating officer is less than impressed. 'That's the biggest load of old bollocks I've ever heard in my life.' Clark calmly signs his statement. 'Prove it.'

It could have ended there. Perhaps it should have done. At a stroke J.C. Wilsher had ensured that *Between the Lines* would never become tired or dull,

'I think there's a line ...' 'But no one knows where to draw it.' Harry, Tony and Mo, from the second season

ploughing on for season after season and diluting the strength of the original concept. Simply put, there are only so many ways you can investigate bent coppers. And for Clark, there was no way back now.

But executive producer Tony Garnett and his team was keen to push on, make one last throw of the dice. The third season was unlike anything that went before, with a wider scope balanced by a more traditional cop/spy adventure show emphasis. There was more humour, beginning with Clark resigning from the police and then being 'nicked' by Harry and Mo masquerading as traffic police. The ensuing scene is both tender and depressing, as Harry and Mo take Tony to a leaving party where there are no other guests. The first episode also saw Joyce's suicide via an overdose, dying in Harry's arms, and Naylor's resignation from the police. Mo lasted longer, until, in 'A Face in the Crowd', she is accused of passing police information to Clark and is kicked out of the force. Not surprisingly, there was a deep bitterness at the hand fate had played all three throughout the ensuing episodes.

Clark eventually set up his own security company, although almost inevitably the work comes via Deakin. In 'Foxtrot Oscar', Tony and Harry travel to Tunis to try to track down a man who went to the papers, claiming to have had an underage gay relationship with a junior minister who opposes lowering the age of consent. Harry grumbles about the heat, and Tony falls into the water when trying to catch the man windsurfing, but the conclusion is chilling enough: the man withdraws his story because he's been bribed by Special Branch. Similarly, 'A Safe Pair of Hands' juxtaposed a comedy chase through the kitchens and a running gag about an escaped dove from a magic act with Harry's desire to commit suicide and his dangerously unstable violence. As usual this season, Deakin didn't tell Clark half the story: ostensibly doing private security work for a hotel, Clark and Naylor were actually doing MI5's dirty work, trying to recover a nuclear device after a murder committed by Mossad.

'Shoot to Kill', as well as introducing Tony's new love, TV documentary producer Sarah Teale, dealt with a Gibraltar-like SAS shooting of unarmed terrorists. The episode showed *Between the Lines*' ever-cynical take on party politics (the incident ranks with the sinking of the *Belgrano*, it is said, as good PR), and again exposed the conflict between MI5 (and Six) and Special Branch, with MI5 not averse to leaking information to the IRA to ensure that its shadier dealings remain unnoticed. In this instance, Deakin was working for Branch, passing on information to Sarah Teale.

Between the Lines had clearly moved beyond bent coppers and police cover-ups and was now fully immersed in the world of intelligence. This season perhaps suffered in comparison with the previous two simply because it was so different. But the tone, the commitment - the powerful writing and acting - all remained undiminished. It was therefore well-equipped to deal with foreign politics ('Close Protection', where a Chilean general is almost killed by his own people in an attempt to implicate the Left), the deadly rivalry that exists between pharmaceutical companies ('Blooded'), and the terrifying world of the defence industry ('Unknown Soldier'). If the episodes had more explosions and shootings than before - the sequence with Harry as a hostage in 'Blooded' is incredibly tense - it was still in no danger of becoming ***The Professionals***. In 'Unknown Soldier', Clark is kidnapped and told to let the case go. No cardboard hero, he is clearly terrified, and does so.

As before, the season concluded with an episode that leads into an overt two-parter. Although 'Free Trade' is ostensibly about vigilantes (posing as police) shooting a group of yardies, the background story is all-important: Mo is offered her job back if she spies on Deakin for MI5, while one of Deakin's MI5 contacts is shown to be running guns with tacit approval. Clark's 'inheritance' of a container full of arms and explosives showed how deeply he was getting involved, and the world in which he operated was getting even more complex than before. Not only are the various intelligence and police units battling for supremacy, but even within MI5 there are factions striving for dominance.

The two-part 'The End User' was a fitting finale to the programme, its labyrinthine plot involving the Czech secret service, a murder in a Jewish cemetery, a neo-Nazi meeting in Antwerp, and guns that might or might not be going to the IRA or the Loyalists. In scenes involving Tony and Sarah, Harry and his new love Ellie, and Mo and Kate, the tension is almost unbearable. They are all genuinely terrified at what might happen and by the dangerous game they are playing. As Harry says, 'All I know is that when we were in CIB we used to shed light on things, and now we're just digging holes in the back garden.'

Clark and the others come to believe that they have been used to arm an anti-Catholic 'ethnic cleansing' process in Northern Ireland. Mo has to contend with both Kate's departure from her life and Deakin's statement that she's betrayed her friends for 30 pieces of silver. Although her return to the Met is assured, the lives of Harry and Tony are in danger as they have gone to try to prevent the weaponry 'disappearing' at the docks. When the container doesn't come off the ship as planned, Clark and Naylor are blamed by the Loyalists. Armed police move into position, and Harry flicks a cigarette towards a fuel dump. There is a massive explosion. We see Mo's tear-stained face, mute with grief, blinking against the blinding light.

Between the Lines, then, ended as it began, unflinching in its portrayal of the terrible uncertainties of the modern world. Although never as popular with the public as ***Cracker***, both series have established a high-water mark for episodic drama, with J.C. Wilsher's creation proving to be one of the most consistently engaging serials ever transmitted on British television.

Cracker

- **Granada** (ITV) ◆ **Colour**
- **23 episodes** (standard length: 60 minutes) ◆ **1993-95**
- **Creator:** Jimmy McGovern
- **Writers:** Jimmy McGovern, Ted Whitehead, Paul Abbott
- **Directors:** Michael Winterbottom, Andy Wilson, Simon Cellan Jones, Tim Fywell, Julian Jarrold, Jean Stewart, Roy Battersby, Charles McDougal
- **Producers:** Gub Neal, Paul Abbott, Hilary Bevan Jones

Starring: Robbie Coltrane (Dr Edward Fitzgerald) • Barbara Flynn (Judith Fitzgerald) • Christopher Eccleston (DCI Billborough) • Lorcan Cranitch (DS Jimmy Beck) • Geraldine Sommerville (DS Jane Penhaligon) • Kieran O'Brien (Mark Fitzgerald) • Ian Mercer (DS Giggs) • Beryl Reid (Mrs Fitzgerald) • Ricky Tomlinson (DCI Wise) • Robert Cavanah (Temple)

Dr Edward Fitzgerald, or Fitz, works as a freelance criminal psychologist, regularly employed by DI Billborough on his team's murder investigations. He fancies DS Penhaligon and faces constant irritation from the sarky DS Jimmy Beck. His main task is to interview suspects until they crack, hence the title. That's how they must have sold this series to the network, anyway. The truth is rather more complex.

That Fitz should be a fat, adulterous, compulsive gambler with an acidic wit is one surprising thing. That he should be part of a series where the immediacy of issues-based drama (the kind of thing that ***Casualty*** deals in) is smashed against big filmic melodrama and a relentless gothic atmosphere is another. The cosy format the show might have adopted was always being shattered, two of the above named supporting characters dying, the other being raped. The thing that grabbed audiences was the harshness of the show, the way it took an issue like race and ignored all of the pussyfooting care that a show like ***Casualty*** would have brought to it. This resulted in protests and incredulity, but also in an audience who agreed: yes, the real world did get as bad as this sometimes. That could have been a terrible thing to do, but McGovern brought to the series both a hard underlying morality, a willingness to deal with every character as an individual rather than a type, and a wry, macabre, working man's sense of humour.

The episode title 'The Mad Woman in the Attic' refers to memory, or in this case the lack of it, as one of Fitz's students is murdered on a train. The suspected killer, thrown from the train, claims not to remember what happened. In the process of solving the mystery, Fitz finds himself employed by Billborough.

Critical response was swift and complimentary. Many welcomed Coltrane's performance - the *Telegraph* noting that the role confirmed him 'as one of our

First season
(27 Sep–8 Nov 93)
1 The Mad Woman in the Attic (Two episodes)
2 To Say I Love You (Three episodes)
3 One Day a Lemming Will Fly (Two episodes)

Second season
(10 Oct–5 Dec 94)
4 To Be a Somebody (Two episodes)
5 The Big Crunch (Three episodes)
6 Men Should Weep (Three episodes)

Third Season
(22 Oct–27 Nov 95)
7 Brotherly Love (Three episodes, first episode 75 minutes)
8 Best Boys (Two episodes)
9 True Romance (Two episodes)

['Brotherly Love' (part one) was scheduled for transmission on 16 Oct 95 but was replaced by a repeat of 'Men Should Weep' (part three).]

most excitingly versatile performers' - but Jimmy McGovern's fine script garnered its fair share of plaudits, too. Former comprehensive teacher McGovern had written 80 scripts for ***Brookside*** (and prefigured later themes by suggesting the rape of Sheila Grant) and two TV plays, *Traitors* (1990) and *Needle* (1992). He was well-versed at bringing strong characters to the screen, but Fitz was a revelation. 'I initially envisaged Fitz as a small, wiry, tough figure like John Cassavetes,' McGovern revealed in an interview with *The Guardian* a couple of years later. But the first draft script impressed Robbie Coltrane, and everything changed. 'My daughters said it was a brilliant choice, because what I'd written was an out-and-out bastard. Robbie comes in with this massive legacy of affection.'

The second story, 'To Say I Love You', saw the audience creeping up to ten million. It took the myth of Bonnie and Clyde and turned it on its head, with the dangerous couple on the rampage being, respectively, a girl with a grudge against her blind sister and her too nice family, and a stuttering boy who could only express himself through song. We felt for them, despite the terrible things they did, because they seemed so different from the society they hated, but amongst all the adrenaline rush of love and murder we were also encouraged to see their victims as people. As a dissection of rage and a circle of abuse, it's far better than *Natural Born Killers* (US 94), being at the same time a celebration and a condemnation of designer violence. The two sides of *Cracker* demonstrated: the glamour of filmic melodrama, the truth and horror underneath.

The season ended with 'One Day a Lemming Will Fly', a story that allowed Jimmy Beck - then both a hate figure and a dark hero to put-upon white, middle-aged males everywhere - to express his bile about homosexuality, and showed a gay teacher caught up in the hunt for a serial killer. Almost as a gesture to demonstrate the difference of the series, the season ended with Fitz standing-up Penhaligon on an invitation to a dirty weekend, and, more wonderfully, a total lack of closure, as the real killer remained out there, uncaught, realistically uncatchable.

Whereas at the start the ITV bosses had refused to commission another series, the viewing figures at the end of the season were such that they changed their minds and asked McGovern to write a new season of 17 episodes. McGovern refused, and a compromise was reached: nine new episodes, of which McGovern would write six.

'To Be a Somebody' was the serial that really fixed *Cracker* in the public consciousness. Like the best of McGovern's work, the script was 'a dark, sulphurous monologue that comes off the page like a head-butt', as *The Independent on Sunday*'s Robert Butler put it. The story concerned the left-wing Albie cracking under the death of his father, shaving his head to become a skinhead, and setting off on a crusade to revenge the Hillsborough football stadium disaster. With scenes filmed at Hillsborough itself, and a startling performance from Robert Carlyle, this was the serial that caught the moment best, the disintegration of self and society in the last days of late capitalism. Albie kills the decent, Gary Lineker-like family man Billborough after Jimmy Beck fails in his chance to catch him. The epitome of 90s decency calls in all the evidence he can about his own murder before dying on an empty street, with no one in what had once been society around to help him. Jimmy Beck, like a latterday Judas, is shattered. The unit's new boss is DCI Wise, a bit rougher at the edges, but just as decent.

After that, 'The Big Crunch' was a tremendous disappointment. Written by Ted Whitehead (best known for his adaptation of *The Life and Loves of a She-Devil*), this was the first serial from somebody other than McGovern, and it showed. There was a sudden return to ordinariness, the crime thriller that only *tried* to be strange. The confused and contradictory plot attempted both sympathy and horror in its tale of the hushing-up of an affair between an

Cracker: *n.* 1. a person or thing that cracks. 2. *Brit. slang* a thing or person of notable qualities and abilities

authoritarian priest and a girl in his congregation by murderous blue-rinse supporters. The whole thing had something to do with the work of Stephen Hawking, but that seemed almost like an afterthought. Whitehead ought to have gone for the dramatic and not tried to walk the same thin edge of complexity that McGovern does.

McGovern closed the second season with 'Men Should Weep', the story that caused the most uproar, and the one that effectively changed the format of the show forever. A black serial rapist is at large, the fulfilment of many stereotypes, enough to get Granada picketed. But the rapist turns out to have been scarred by racism itself, consciously enacting the stereotype. The central horror of the story, the rape of Jane Penhaligon (of which we're only shown the aftermath), isn't by him, but is the crime of Jimmy Beck. Perhaps it was in poor taste to hang suspense on the identity of the rapist. Certainly the cliffhanger ending, with Penhaligon holding a gun in Beck's mouth, was the stuff of Hollywood rather than socially-aware drama. But many of these concerns were offset by the intensity and honesty of Geraldine Somerville's performance. Penhaligon remained a real person after the rape, expressing, in the months that followed, a gradually resurgent sense of humour, and even a returning sexuality. In short, she wasn't just a victim to be the subject of a revenge fantasy.

By the time of 'Brotherly Love', the series was clearly ITV's biggest drama, a ratings windfall. Originally, the first episode was going to be broadcast on Monday night, but since it was an hour and a quarter long (sheer indulgence, since the script didn't seem to merit it), the IBA objected, and the episode was hastily rescheduled for the following Sunday. (McGovern's Screen Two film *Priest* was similarly ill-treated, its length meaning a clash with *Newsnight*, which controller Michael Jackson would not tolerate. 'It says so much about their priorities,' complained McGovern. 'It's OK for sport to move the news but not drama.')

The central plot of 'Brotherly Love' was rather ordinary, following a Catholic man, his brother a priest, who regularly employed prostitutes and was charged with the murder of one. The secondary story, however, was the final fall of Jimmy Beck. With his guilt in the matter of Penhaligon's rape still uncertain, and the two of them working together, he'd begun to disintegrate. Finally, he managed to extract a confession of his own from both a suspect (handcuffed to him on the roof of a building) and himself, as he told Penhaligon that he'd raped her. He then dragged the man to both their deaths. It was, at the same time, a take on a Hollywood melodrama (*Lethal Weapon*), a scene of mythic significance (a redeeming fall) and something that seemed real and true.

After that, everything was bound to be an anti-climax, with Paul Abbott, the producer of the second season, taking over the scripting chores. 'Best Boys' was a shallow and shy version of 'To Say I Love You', with two gay men (so coy as to leave you wondering whether or not they were just mates) being drawn into murder. Finally, 'True Romance' saw a woman, obsessed by Fitz, killing in his name. In a disappointing finale, she badly injured the psychologist's once shiftless, now working, son, and concern for him united Fitz with his wife, once tempted by Fitz's better-behaved brother, and their new-born child. Penhaligon left the police force, bitter at the bile directed at her by Judith. Everything rather petered out.

Jimmy McGovern went on to write *Hearts and Minds*, a vehicle for Christopher Eccleston as a teacher in a hard school, and the excellent and controversial *Priest*. The latest news of *Cracker* is that there is to be one more episode, a special set in, astonishingly, Hong Kong. It's hard to tell whether one should hope for closure, for realism, melodrama or social comment. One can only say for certain that all will be present in some measure.

The television medium is uniquely suited to expanding viewers' imaginations: suspend your disbelief and the universe is at your fingertips. Thus from almost the dawn of the television era producers have turned to styles like horror, science fiction, the supernatural and surrealism for inspiration. The BBC's early interest in fantasy was perhaps inevitable given that most of the definitive written works in this field were British: the gothic novelists of the 1820s, the Victorian penny dreadfuls, the ghost stories of M. R. James, and the scientific romances of H.G. Wells. As early as 1937 the BBC produced a live performance of Arnold Ridley's *The Ghost Train*, though the real birth of telefantasy as a genre occurred on 11 February 1938 with a live 25-minute performance from Alexandra Palace of Czech writer Karel Capek's *R.U.R.*, which had introduced the word 'robot' to the English language. The birth of TV horror followed soon afterwards, in 1939, with a production of Edgar Allen Poe's *The Tell-Tale Heart*.

The immediate post-war years brought literary adaptations of Wells's *The Time Machine* and J.B. Priestley's *Summer Day's Dream* in 1949, and *The Strange Case of Dr Jekyll and Mr Hyde* and *A Christmas Carol* in 1950. A 1952 version of Wells's *The Wonderful Visit* starred a young Kenneth Williams, while 1954 saw a powerful adaptation of *The Monkey's Paw*. The same era also saw the first experiments in episodic science-fiction sagas. 1951's *Stranger from Space* was an 11-episode fortnightly insert into the children's programme *Whirligig*. Written by Hazel Adair and Ronald Marriott, the series concerned a Martian (Michael Newell) who crashes his 'space boat' and is found by a young boy (Brian Smith). Telefantasy legend Peter Hawkins had a role, as did Valentine Dyall in 1952's sequel. Similar serials from the period include 1954's *The Lost Planet* and 1956's *Space School*, all produced by Kevin Sheldon.

An August 1952 production of Stanley Young's *Mystery Story* saw the telefantasy debut of a writer who was to shape the genre for the next two decades – Nigel Kneale. Kneale was also involved in the adaptation of Charles Irving's paranoid nuclear chiller *Number Three*, but it was with his own ***The Quatermass Experiment*** (1953) that he changed the face of TV drama. Kneale's development of the art through the three ***Quatermass*** serials and ground-breaking productions of Orwell's *Nineteen Eighty-Four* and his own *The Creature* would continue throughout the next decade, when plays like *The Road*, *The Year of the Sex Olympics*, *Bam! Pow! Zap!* and *The Stone Tape* would pull telefantasy into areas never dreamed of in the 50s. Compared to the revisionist work of the Kneale/Rudolph Cartier stable, contemporary plays like Charles Main's *TimeSlip*

(1953) or *The Offshore Island* (a 1958 post-nuclear tale) seem dull, if worthy, by comparison. The era was also notable for George Kerr's alien-invasion classic *The Voices* (1955), Evelyn Fraser's cryogenic murder mystery *The Critical Point* starring Leo McKern (1957), and *Hands Across the Sky*, a 1960 opera concerning aliens and featuring the memorable libretto 'I chased him through the uranium deposit/ Now he's locked himself in the heavy water closet!'

The cause of serious science fiction received a boost in 1961 with *A for Andromeda*. Written by John Elliot, from a story by controversial astronomer Fred Hoyle, this starred Esmond Knight, Mary Morris, Peter Halliday and Julie Christie as the eponymous heroine. A combination of boardroom politics (a predecessor of Elliot's ***The Troubleshooters***) and science-fiction speculation, *A for Andromeda* was highly popular and led to a sequel, *The Andromeda Breakthrough*, the following year, with Susan Hampshire in the title role. The BBC tried to repeat the *Andromeda* formula with Tom Clarke's intelligent serial *The Escape of RD7* and plays like *The Test* and *The Big Pull*. 1964's series *R3* starring Jon Rollason falls into the same category.

The Monsters, a four-part 1962 series about a Loch Ness-type Monster, may have failed to excite the viewers but, with an eye on the success of the ABC *Pathfinder* family science-fiction serials, the BBC confirmed its commitment to the genre in 1963 with Sydney Newman's creation of British telefantasy's flagship, ***Doctor Who***.

During 1962 the BBC provincial anthology series *Suspense* began and featured plays with telefantasy content. These included *Virus X*, *Project Survival*, the eerie *The Tourelle Skull*, and the space-mission drama *The Edge of Discovery*. The success of such experiments and of another one-off production, *The Caves of Steel*, in BBC2's *Story Parade*, as well as the popularity of ATV's *Out of this World*, encouraged the BBC to use time on the new minority channel to attempt an anthology series of its own. *Out of the Unknown* began in 1965; during its first two seasons it largely concentrated on adapting classic science-fiction stories, dramatized by writers like Terry Nation, Leon Griffiths, Troy Kennedy Martin and Bruce Stewart. It starred Mike Pratt, David Hemmings, Milo O'Shea and Warren Mitchell, and was produced by Irene Shubik. The series was made on 625-line videotape (a technological marvel in 1965) and featured then state-of-the-art visual effects. Plays like *The Dead Past* and *Time in Advance* won critical praise whilst the opening story of the second season, an adaptation of E.M. Forster's 'The Machine Stops' starring Michael Gothard and Yvonne Mitchell, is particularly well remembered.

The series returned in colour in 1969, produced by Alan Bromly. By now plays were often original stories by writers like Donald Bull and Brian Hayles. The two most successful episodes, however, were adaptations of John Wyndham's alternative-dimension love story 'Random Quest' (starring Keith Barron) and David Climie's extremely weird version of Peter Philip's 'Get Off My Cloud' (in which a science-fiction writer is trapped in his own imaginary world). This latter drama starred Peter Barkworth and Peter Jeffrey and featured cameo appearances by the Daleks and the TARDIS. A fourth season in 1971 had the emphasis on outright horror, notably in Nigel Kneale's *The Chopper*, in which Patrick Troughton is haunted by the ghost of a dead motorcyclist.

The 60s also saw a number of telefantasy dramas in the *Wednesday Play* slot, including *Campaign for One* (starring Barry Foster and Jeremy Kemp), *The Girl Who Loved Robots* and John Hopkins's *Horror of Darkness*. (Other telefantasy plays of the era include *Fable*, *The House*, Dennis Potter's *Alice* and *Where the Buffalo Roam*, and David Mercer's psychedelic *In Two Minds*.) The 1965

Gaslight Theatre version of *Sweeney Todd* and Ken Taylor's 1966 *Play of the Month* adaptation of Wells's *Days to Come* (starring Judi Dench and Dinsdale Landen) are also worthy of note.

1966 was also the year when, as critic Kim Newman notes, 'period quaintness and modernist absurdity were combined in *Adam Adamant Lives!*, which featured a defrosted Edwardian detective (Gerald Harper) and his mini-skirted, dolly-bird sidekick (Juliet Harmer), a teaming obviously intended to echo those of Patrick Macnee and his karate-kicking girlfriends in ***The Avengers***.' Trapped in a block of ice to 'die forever' by his arch foe, the Face, in 1902, Adam Llewelyn de Vere Adamant ('so clever, but oh so vulnerable!') thawed out to find himself in swinging London 64 years later in this witty series created by Richard Harris, Sydney Newman and Donald Tosh, produced by Verity Lambert and script-edited by Tony Williamson. The series also starred Jack May as Adam's butler, and featured stories by Robert Banks Stewart, Brian Clemens, Vince Powell and Harry Driver. It is fondly remembered for episodes like 'Allah is Not Always With You', 'The League of Uncharitable Ladies' and the downright bizarre 'To Set a Deadly Fashion', and for its kitsch swinging-London visuals. However, a second season was largely a travesty, with the series' wit replaced by slapstick comedy. Nevertheless, *Adam Adamant Lives!* provided a stepping stone to Hollywood for Ridley Scott, who directed three episodes. Kathy Kirby's theme song was released as a single in 1966.

Between 1966 and 1973, BBC2's major outlet for new writing talent was *Thirty Minute Theatre* where writers as diverse as Dawn Pavitt and Terry Wale (*The Isle is Full of Noise*), Anthony Bloomfield (*Turn Off! I Know the Ending*), Tom Stoppard (*Another Moon Called Earth*), John Wiles (*Come Death*) and Derrick Sherwin (*The Metal Martyr* and *The Time Keepers*) created telefantasy on a tiny budget. Other memorable fantasy plays from the series include Desmond Lowden's *The News Benders* (a newsroom satire directed by Rudolph Cartier), *The Tape Recorder*, the first colour drama production broadcast on British television, and Susan Pleat's torrid *I Wouldn't Tell on you Miss*.

Classic adaptations continued to appear, often star-studded affairs such as Jonathan Miller's controversial version of *Alice in Wonderland* (1966). Miller's 1968 *Omnibus* adaptation of M.R. James's *Whistle and I'll Come to You* was the beginning a long BBC fascination with the English ghost story. The trend of anthology science fiction/horror continued in 1968 with the colour *Late Night Horror*, produced by Harry Moore, which contained adaptations of Arthur Conan Doyle and Roald Dahl amongst others.

Perhaps the strangest telefantasy moment of the 60s came on Boxing Day 1967 when the Beatles' semi-incoherent home movie, *The Magical Mystery Tour*, was first shown. Although made in colour, the first transmission was in monochrome which somewhat spoiled the party. A mixture of production numbers and psychedelia (with the hint of a plot thrown in), *The Magical Mystery Tour* was a ham-fisted mess, albeit one perfectly in keeping with the excesses of the era. And, as Paul McCartney has noted, there aren't many programmes where you can watch John Lennon singing 'I Am the Walrus' backed by a troupe of dancing policemen. Goo Goo Goo Joob!

An intellectual snobbery against 'sci-fi' remained, meaning that valid telefantasy plays like *Theatre 625*'s *Home Sweet Honeycomb* or *Thirty Minute Theatre*'s *A Nice Cool Pad in the Sky* received plaudits for their imagination but were criticized for pandering to lowest common denominator tastes. Telefantasy often remained in the TV ghetto of late-night scheduling, where little masterpieces like 1967's *The Five-Nineteen* (a horror story with Francesca Annis) or the BBC2 serial

Witch-Hunt would be missed or forgotten. The success of occasional high-profile *Wednesday Plays* like Edward Boyd's *A Black Candle for Mrs Gogarty* (1967), or the brooding sexual madness of Leon Whiteson's *Blood of the Lamb* (1969), made this attitude all the more puzzling, especially when Sean McCarthy and Johnny Byrne's 1970 'trip-movie-as-social-comment' *Season of the Witch* (starring Robert Powell, Julie Driscoll and Paul Nicholas) helped to extend the boundaries of the genre still further.

Tony Williamson's 1969 series *Counterstrike* concerned an alien (played by Jon Finch) sent to defend Earth from invasion. A tense psychological thriller which has been likened to a low-budget version of US series *The Invaders*, *Counterstrike*'s writers included Anthony Skene (whose episode was a rewrite of his ***Prisoner*** script 'A, B and C'), Cyril Abraham and Dick Sharples. Ten episodes were made, though one, 'Out of Mind', was cancelled due to programme overrun and has never been shown (it was subsequently junked, a tragic loss). Williamson, meanwhile, went to ITC and ***Randall and Hopkirk (Deceased)***.

After ***Doomwatch***'s successful debut, a pair of hugely popular anthology horror series helped to cement the genre's new 70s 'grown up' image. 1972's *Dead of Night*, produced by Innes Lloyd and script-edited by Louis Marks for BBC2, consisted of seven supernatural tales. Robert Holmes's *Return Flight* (starring Peter Barkworth), about a plane on a collision course with something that doesn't seem to exist, and Don Taylor's *The Exorcism* were particularly effective. Nigel Kneale's *The Stone Tape*, made by the same production team and broadcast on Christmas Day 1972, remains one of the most frightening pieces of television ever made. A similar production was Terry Nation's *The Incredible Robert Baldick*, starring Robert Hardy, in 1972. There was also the long-running *A Ghost Story for Christmas* which began in 1971 with Lawrence Gordon Clare's adaptation of *The Stalls of Barchester* and continued in later years with *A Warning to the Curious* (1972), David Rudkin's *The Ash Tree* (1975, with Edward Petherbridge and Lalla Ward), Andrew Davies's dramatization of Dickens's *The Signalman* (1976, starring Denholm Elliott), and Clive Exton's *Stigma* (1977), all produced by Rosemary Hill. The BBC's love of the classic English ghost story remains to this day via *White Lady* (1987), *The Green Man* (1990) and, latterly, *The Blue Boy* and *Ghosts* (both 1995).

Another anthology series was *Menace* produced by Jordan Lawrence. Several of the episodes contained supernatural themes, including *Killing Time* (with George Cole), Hugh Whitemore's *Deliver us from Evil* (with John Gielgud), and James MacTaggert's *Boys and Girls Come Out to Play*, a surreal horror story in which a schoolgirl (Sarah Sutton) under the influence of pep-pills and a haunting musical box tune commits arson and murder.

Children's telefantasy was very important in the early 70s, with series like *The Witch's Daughter* (1971), the popular *Lizzie Dripping* (1973), 1974's spooky *Carrie's War* (with Juliet Waley), and *The Phoenix and the Carpet* (1976), along with two Anna Home series written by Peter Dickinson, *ManDog* (1972) and *The Changes* (1975). The latter concerned a girl (Vicky Williams) in a future where an unknown force possesses adults to destroy machinery and revert to superstition, and featured several memorable episodes (including 'The Bad Wires' - a nightmare of television iconography gone evil - and the finale which linked the story to Arthurian legend). Another charming children's series was *Tom's Midnight Garden*, adapted by John Tully from Phillippa Pierce's novel. First produced in 1968, the story was remade in colour in 1974, and again in 1989.

The cause of adult science fiction took a dent in 1973 when Barry Letts and Terrance Dicks (then producer and script editor on ***Doctor Who***) created

Moonbase 3, a 'realistic' (and therefore very dull) series about a moon colony of the 21st century. Starring Donald Houston and Ralph Bates, the series limped through six episodes, although the last, 'View from a Dead Planet', in which all life on Earth appears to have ended, was grim and effective. Equally apocalyptic were David Rudkin's *Play for Today, Penda's Fen* (1975, starring Spencer Banks), chilling *Playhouse* productions like *The Breakthrough* (1975) and docudrama series like *Leap in the Dark* and *The Mind Beyond*. The trend reached its inevitable conclusion with Terry Nation's superb post-apocalypse saga ***Survivors***.

Telefantasy series of the 70s included Philip Martin's perplexing *Gangsters* and Philip Mackie's alternative universe drama *An Englishman's Castle*. The utterly strange *The Aphrodite Inheritance* (with Brian Blessed) was created by Michael J. Bird and continued many of the themes of his earlier and equally beautiful Cretian drama *The Lotus Eaters*. *Scotch on the Rocks* (1974), a five-part adaptation by James MacTaggert of a novel by future Foreign Secretary Douglas Hurd and *Private Eye* co-founder Andrew Osmond, concerned a Scottish revolution, and starred Bill Simpson, Maria Aitken, Iain Cuthbertson, Maurice Roeves and Cyril Luckham. It also involved the BBC in civil action by the Scottish National Party which objected to the series' depiction of SNP-inspired violence. And, of course, there was ***Blake's 7***, a piece of space opera that far exceeded its humble origins to become one of the BBC's most popular dramas.

Supernatural gave the horror anthology a timely boost in 1977. Described as 'eight stories from the Victorian Club of the Damned', the series was written by Robert Müller and Sue Lake in a format similar to *A Ghost Story for Christmas* and featured actors of the calibre of Robert Hardy, Gordon Jackson and Ian Hendry. This was a good time for the genre, with the classic adaptation of *Count Dracula* (1977, starring Louis Jordan) and *Omnibus*'s *Schalkan the Painter* gaining huge viewing figures.

Wilfred Greatorex's paranoid middle-class nightmare *1990* starred Edward Woodward as a journalist and Barbara Kellerman as his girlfriend, in a nightmarish *Nineteen Eighty-Four*-style scenario about a future police-state government. Two seasons were made, the second also featuring Lisa Harrow and Yvonne Mitchell.

A co-production with a West German company (Sudfunk-Stuttgart) created an extremely beautiful and very strange children's serial called *The Moon Stallion*, written by Brian Hayles, produced by Anna Home and starring Sarah Sutton as a blind girl with a telepathic link to ancient forces conducted through a chalk horse in Wiltshire. Jack Gerson's *The Omega Factor* was made for BBC Scotland in 1979. The series, a proto-*X-Files*, produced by George Gallaccio, concerned a psychic, Tom Crane (James Hazeldine), working for a government department to investigate the paranormal after the death of his wife at the hands of an evil psychic from the sinister Omega organization. The series also starred Louise Jameson and John Carlisle. Several of the episodes, notably 'The Undiscovered Country', 'Visitations' and 'St Anthony's Fire' are memorable, particularly an early sequence where Crane is 'pursued' by a force that extinguishes the street lights as he walks past them.

Also of note was *The Flipside of Dominick Hyde*, a clever and touching *Play for Today* written by Jeremy Paul and Alan Gibson in 1980. This concerned a time traveller from the future (Peter Firth) who came back to London in the 80s to try and find his mysterious great-grandfather. Whilst there he meets and falls in love with Jane (Caroline Langrishe), whom he makes pregnant, despite the fact that he has a wife (Pippa Guard) and son in the future. In a somewhat inevitable paradox, Dominick turns out to be his own ancestor and, to fulfil his role in history, has to return to the future. Rick James's beautifully distinctive song 'You'd Better Believe it, Babe' was the final touch to this masterpiece. In 1982, a sequel, *Another Flip for Dominick*, returned Firth to the 80s.

Another *Play for Today* from the same period was *Psy Warriors* by David Leland, directed by Alan Clarke, concerning psychological interrogation training carried out on soldiers. In this climate, challenging plays like *Red Shift*, *A Strange Smell*, Philip Martin's *The Unborn* (starring Jack Shepherd) and *The Remainder Man*, Michael Hunt's *Honourable Discharge*, and the brilliant *Orion*, also appeared.

Douglas Adams's phenomenally popular comic science-fiction radio serial *The Hitch-Hiker's Guide to the Galaxy* began in 1978, and by the time it reached television in 1981 it had already evolved into two books. Arguably this television adaptation, starring Peter Jones, Simon Jones, David Dixon, Mark Wing-Davey, Sandra Dickinson and Stephen Moore, set the seal on Adams's success, turning a cult into an institution. The serial brought the 'narration' of the book to life, and, in doing so, created an entirely new televisual language of information-imparting computer graphics, supplemented by dramatic illustrations and trivia scrolling unheeded along the screen. Everything from pop programmes and *Daily Telegraph* adverts to *The Terminator* (US 84) have subsequently used similar formats.

The early 80s saw a positive glut of BBC telefantasy, with literary science-fiction adaptations including Douglas Livingstone's version of *The Day of the Triffids* starring John Duttine, Maurice Colbourne and Emma Relph in 1981, and a period adaptation of *The Invisible Man* in 1984, produced by Barry Letts, with Pip Donaghy, Frank Middlemass and David Gwillim. There were also high-brow dramas such as David Rudkin's bizarre three-hour epic *Artemis 81*, with Hywel Bennett, Sting and Dan O'Herlihy, Anthony Garner's *Z for Zachariah* (1984), a grim, after-the-bomb story featuring Anthony Andrews and Pippa Hinchley, and *The Queen of Annagh*, Terence Hodgkinson's 1982 'during World War III' play starring Diane Fletcher.

Play for Tomorrow, a Neil Zeiger-produced series of six futuristic plays, also evolved in 1982. Michael Wilcox's *Cricket*, with Malcolm Terris, Jeremy Childs and Simon Rouse, was one of the most distinctive, a black comedy which saw a computer selecting a cricket team whilst the players acted as a guerrilla army. Perhaps the best of the bunch was Stephen Lowe's *Shades*, a pessimistic pro-CND piece with an excellent young cast led by Tracey Childs, Stuart McKenzie, Emily Moore and Neil Pearson and featuring novel usage of contemporary pop music (notably the Jam's 'Burning Sky').

Post-nuclear tales were popular and topical in the early 80s, the trend best exemplified by the horrifyingly realistic two-hour drama-documentary *Threads*, written by Barry Hines and produced by Mike Jackson, which centred on the lead-up to and long-term effects of a nuclear strike on Britain. Filmed in Sheffield with Karen Meagher, Reece Dinsdale and about 400 local people as extras, and mixing in footage of bomb-blasted shop fronts to simulate a nuclear firestorm, *Threads* remains, alongside Peter Watkins's notorious 1965 film *The War Game* (itself finally shown after a two-decade ban in the mid-80s to a terrific response), as powerful and provocative as anything that television has ever produced. Troy Kennedy Martin's adaptation of Angus Wilson's *The Old Men at the Zoo* (1983) covered similar themes.

The Nightmare Man was pretty scary too, albeit in a much more traditional 'monster on the loose' vein. It was adapted by Robert Holmes from David Wiltshire's novel *Child of the Vodyanoi* and directed with atmospheric brilliance by Douglas Camfield, and dealt with an unknown killer on an isolated and mist-covered Scottish island. Starring James Warwick, Maurice Roeves and Celia Imrie, the serial was well received. The same, unfortunately, cannot be said of *The Tripods*, a two-season adaptation of the first two books of John Christopher's trilogy.

The Tripods could have been one of the most impressive of all telefantasy productions. Sadly, due to a mixture of lacklustre scripts, the inexperience of several of the young cast, and a plodding snail's pace, it fell flat on its face. On a brighter note, the performances of John Shackley, Roderick Horn, John Woodvine and Pamela Salem were, at least, watchable. One of the saddest aspects of *The Tripods* was that Charlotte Long, the young female lead, died in a motoring tragedy shortly before the series' debut.

In the area of children's telefantasy Paul Stone's charming version of *The Box of Delights* in 1984, with a superb cast headed by Patrick Troughton (one of his final performances) and Robert Stephens, and the adaptations of C.S. Lewis's *The Chronicles of Narnia* beginning in 1988, proved tremendously popular. The sub-genre could also produce little oddities like 1987's pseudo-documentary schools series *Welcome to My World* (with Robert Powell), two seasons of *West Country Tales*, and the spooky *Mystery of the Disappearing Schoolgirls*. The trend continues into the 90s with series as diverse as *Moondial*, *Dark Season*, *Century Falls*, *Return of the Psammead* and *The Demon Headmaster*.

Whilst such 'straight' drama series as ***The Singing Detective***, ***Edge of Darkness***, *Dead Head* and even certain episodes of ***Bergerac*** have dabbled in areas of surrealism, dreams and the supernatural, the 80s saw only occasional steps into the telefantasy arena, notably David Pirie's *Rainy Day Women* (1984) starring Charles Dance, Lindsay Duncan, Ian Hogg, Cyril Cusack and Gwyneth Strong, and Michael Hastings's *Stars of the Roller State Disco*, directed by Alan Clarke.

When Michael Grade announced his decision to postpone the 23rd season of ***Doctor Who*** in 1985, several newspapers quoted a BBC source stating that a replacement series had been found. It was to be called *Star Cops*. Over two years later a series bearing that title finally appeared on BBC2 for a nine-episode run. *Star Cops* should have been a great success but, due to a combination of factors - particularly its transmission time - the series was shelved after its first season.

Star Cops, the brainchild of Chris Boucher, was an effort to merge telefantasy with crime drama. If that makes the series sound like a forerunner to the childish *Space Precinct* then it's worth noting that the BBC itself did not consider it to be science fiction at all, preferring to describe the series in press releases as 'a futuristic police series' and using Boucher's work on ***Bergerac***, ***Shoestring*** and *Juliet Bravo* as justification. The other major writer on the series was *The Observer*'s resident doctor John Collee.

David Calder played Nathan Spring, a career policeman who had become disenchanted with the system on Earth. His companions were Box, an electronic 'intelligent listening device' (in other words, a Dictaphone that could answer back), also voiced by Calder, and his assistant, David Theroux, played by American actor Erick Ray Evans. The opening episode was a disappointment, although with the murder of Spring's girlfriend early in the second episode the series showed itself to be a lot harder and more cynical than it at first appeared. Two more important characters were soon introduced: Pal Kenzy (Linda Newton), an abrasive and, initially, corrupt official who, through a devious publicity stunt, got herself tied to the Star Cops after Spring had given her the boot; and the series' main comedy element, Colin Devis (Trevor Cooper), an overweight chauvinist (his 'Fancy a quick game of Hide The Sausage?' is one of the series best-remembered lines).

Star Cops contained some marvellous visual effects by Mike Kelt and Malcolm James, and strong performances from guest actors, including Roy Holder and Geoffrey Bayldon. The episodes directed by Graeme Harper were especially inventive, whilst the scripts (despite an unfortunate habit of stereotyping ethnic groups) were intelligent and witty. The crimes that the characters were called on to investigate included computer sabotage in 'Intelligent Listening For Beginners', a conspiracy surrounding a missing scientist in 'Trivial Games and Paranoid Pursuits', Mafia drug trafficking in 'This Case to Be Opened in a Million Years' and media-hoaxes in 'Little Green Men and other Martians'. A tenth episode, Philip Martin's 'Death on the Moon', was due to be recorded, but a technicians' strike at the BBC forced its postponement. The release of the series on video in 1993 proved that it was more popular than its meagre ratings suggested.

Nick Dunning's *The Lorelei* with Amanda Redman and Trevor Preston's *Children Crossing* starring Peter Firth, both for *Screen Two*, took the BBC's telefantasy legacy into the 90s. There were other important pieces, like Benjamin Zepheniah's spirited and surreal *Dread Poets Society* (in which Byron, Keats and the Shelleys appear on an inter-city train taking the author to a job interview), *Kingdom Come*, and Ben Elton's ecologically sound *Stark*. *Black Easter* (1995), with Trevor Eve, was a macabre tale set in a futuristic Europe.

Although the BBC's commitment to telefantasy seemed to wane during the early 90s, reaction to Stephen Volk's 1992 *Screen One*, *Ghostwatch*, must have made those who question the size and commitment of the telefantasy audience sit up and take notice. A pseudo-documentary about a haunted house, broadcast on Halloween, it starred Michael Parkinson, Craig Charles and Sarah Greene, and was proof positive of television's ability to provoke and question. 1995 at last saw the BBC returning telefantasy to prime-time with *Bugs*, starring Jesse Birdsall, Jaye Griffiths and Craig McLachlan. Despite its sometimes paint-by-numbers plots, and the potentially fatal tag of 'an ***Avengers*** for the 90s' (if anything, it's a ***Department S*** for the 90s!), *Bugs* is highly enjoyable, if lightweight, adventure drama. Its success, like those of imported American telefantasy series such as *Star Trek: The Next Generation*, *Quantum Leap* and, especially, *The X-Files*, seems to have made the BBC aware of just how large the potential audience for well-made telefantasy is. As a search for a 'British *X-Files*' reportedly continues, it is ironic that should such a series be made, it would merely be the latest torch bearer in a line that stretches back to ***Quatermass*** and beyond.

Quatermass

- **BBC Television/Euston Films** (ITV) (*Quatermass*)
- B&W (1953, 1955, 1958-59); Colour (1979)
- **22 episodes**
- **Writer:** Nigel Kneale
- **Directors:** Rudolph Cartier; Piers Haggard (*Quatermass*)
- **Producers:** Rudolph Cartier; Ted Childs (*Quatermass*)
- **Executive producer:** Verity Lambert (*Quatermass*)

Starring: ***(The Quatermass Experiment)*** – Reginald Tate (Professor Bernard Quatermass) • Isabel Dean (Judith Carroon) • Hugh Kelly (John Paterson) • Duncan Lamont (Victor Carroon) • Paul Whitsun-Jones (James Fullalove); ***(Quatermass II)*** – John Robinson (Quatermass) • Monica Grey (Paula Quatermass) • Hugh Griffiths (Dr Leo Pugh) • John Stone (Captain John Dillon) • Rupert Davies (Vincent Broadhead) • Austin Trevor (Fowler); ***(Quatermass and the Pit)*** – Andre Morrell (Quatermass) • Cec Linder (Dr Matthew Roney) • Christine Finn (Barbara Judd) • Anthony Bushell (Col. Breen) • John Stratton (Capt. Potter) • Michael Ripper (Sergeant) • Harold Goodwin (Cpl. Gibson) • John Walker (Private West) • Brian Worth (James Fullalove) • Richard Shaw (Sladden); ***(Quatermass)*** – John Mills (Quatermass) • Simon MacCorkindale (Joe Kapp) • Barbara Kellerman (Clare Kapp) • Ralph Arliss (Kickalong) • Paul Rosebury (Caraway) • Jane Bertish (Bee) • Rebecca Saire (Hettie) • Tony Sibbald (Marshall) • Toyah Wilcox (Sal) • Brewster Mason (Guror) • Margaret Tyzack (Annie Morgan)

For someone who claimed to have read virtually no science fiction before writing *The Quatermass Experiment*, and who has 'no great respect for horror films ... Some of the so-called old classics are pitiful pieces of trash', Nigel Kneale managed to imaginatively articulate public neurosis like no one before and few since. Kneale, who gripped a nation with his tale of a spaceship returning to earth, infected with an alien organism, stopped his children watching ***Doctor Who*** because he felt it was too frightening. *The Quatermass Experiment*, on the other hand, 'wasn't really horrific at all. The horror element was about one per cent of the total running time. In fact a lot of it was meant to be very funny.'

In 1953, 31-year-old Kneale was a staff writer at the BBC. Previously he had worked for the BBC script unit, sifting through submissions, 'catching the potential disasters and trying to render them just a little more like TV'. The head of drama, Michael Barry, was so impressed by Kneale that he spent his entire budget allocated for new scripts on him. When it came to his first script, Kneale embarked upon an ambitious serial of a type not seen before on televi-

THE QUATERMASS EXPERIMENT
(18 Jul–22 Aug 53, 30-minute episodes)
1 Contact has been Established
2 Persons Reported Missing
3 Very Special Knowledge
4 Believed to be Suffering
5 An Unidentified Species
6 State of Emergency

QUATERMASS II
(22 Oct–26 Nov 55, c. 30-minute episodes)
1 The Bolts
2 The Mark
3 The Food
4 The Coming
5 The Frenzy
6 The Destroyers

QUATERMASS AND THE PIT
(22 Dec 58–26 Jan 59, 35-minute episodes)
1 The Halfmen
2 The Ghosts
3 Imps and Demons
4 The Enchanted
5 The Wild Hunt
6 Hob

QUATERMASS
(24 Oct–14 Nov 79, 60-minute episodes)
1 Ringstone Round
2 Lovely Lightning
3 What Lies Beneath
4 An Endangered Species

sion, and, in the process, established the medium's potential for high-quality, popular drama.

Kneale gave the old man-turned-monster theme a new edge, much of the serial being a hunt for the infected astronaut, concluding with Bernard Quatermass confronting the growing monster in Westminster Abbey, appealing to the once-human part of the monster to destroy itself. The monster in this final sequence was actually a pair of rubber gloves covered with painted vegetation, 'played' by Kneale through holes in a cut-out of Westminster Abbey.

The Quatermass Experiment was cheap, of course, the budget being just over £3500, and entirely live, but Kneale and director Rudolph Cartier concentrated on the characters and the dialogue to produce gripping television. Quatermass himself (the surname was chosen from a phone directory) was the voice of reason, in a world ruled by obsessives, whether they were from the military, the media or religious groups. Kneale very much had the feeling that thousands would be gripped by his tale. 'You could stagger out afterwards and look down on all the TV aerials and get a real feeling that people had seen it.'

The sequel, *Quatermass II*, featured aliens attempting to invade earth by possessing human beings. The Quatermass character was the only link with the first serial (his stalled plans for a new moon rocket provided a comparatively realistic sub-plot), as the nature of the unearthly menace, and the feel of the programme itself, was very different from Kneale's first serial. Reginald Tate died weeks before filming began, and so John Robinson took on the role of the professor.

Landing in meteors, the aliens build a replica of Quatermass's moonbase as a factory, where they manufacture their foodstuffs. A man is contaminated by the food, and dies from burns. The location filming at Shellhaven refinery in Essex formed an impressively grim backdrop to many of the ensuing events.

Quatermass II set itself far more firmly in an obvious science-fiction niche, which perhaps upset those looking for something more 'sophisticated', although it was, not surprisingly, a popular success. Kneale still had points that he wanted

Quatermass and Dr Roney and what they found in the pit

to raise: his has never been a mindless science fiction. 'There were references there to mysterious Government establishments like Porton Down, which were believed to kill you if you got too close. The base was filled with creatures from outer space but they were "explained away". Really it was about semantics, about verbal cheating. The workforce were told that this was "a perfectly normal occurrence" and that "it was all to be expected". Finally they broke in and in what I suppose [was] the nearest I got to a political scene, they hesitated when they were met with soothing music, offers of conciliation and free meals.'

Quatermass was back three years later (this time a definitive performance by Andre Morell) in the pinnacle of the series, that moved the emphasis from alien invasion to a science-fiction explanation of archetypal and supernatural images and fears. *Quatermass and the Pit* begins with parts of London being rebuilt after the Blitz. At Hobbs Lane, a five-million-year-old skull is dug up, soon followed by an alien projectile. An imp-like ghost is seen, and then the husks of three insect creatures are found. Quatermass begins to draw the various and increasingly haunting phenomena together: the Martians visited Earth millions of years ago, and bequeathed to the ancestors of the human race various deep fears and images, including 'The Wild Hunt', when the Martian hives were purged. The serial ends with chaos breaking out as the people of London are driven to a new racial purge, to which even Quatermass is not immune.

Each *Quatermass* serial explored a particular contemporary public fear, their popularity stemming from the fact that Kneale appeared to be voicing through drama the latest suspicions of the population. Kneale's subsequent work continued many of the themes he had first explored in the *Quatermass* serials, and in 1979 the final *Quatermass* reached the screen. *Quatermass* (retitled *The Quatermass Conclusion* for the American market) was a spawling and depressing tale on an epic scale. The budget was well over one million pounds, although Kneale described it as being 'the most human *Quatermass* of all'. It was not hugely popular: perhaps the visions of the fatalistic future earth, the anarchic antics of the hippie-like Planet People, and formless alien attack, were not quite what people expected of Nigel Kneale. The original script had been written in the late 60s, and elements like an oil crisis and the rise of street gangs were rather out of date. Having said that, it shared a nihilism with plays like ***Edge of Darkness*** and *Made in Britain*. *Quatermass* was a bleakly enjoyable drama, as thought-provoking as any Nigel Kneale had crafted during his influential decades of work for television.

Doctor Who

- **BBC Television** (BBC1)
- B&W (1963–69); Colour (1970–89, 1996)
- **703 episodes** (1 episode not shown during the initial run and 6 [incomplete] episodes unbroadcast) (standard length: c. 25 minutes)
- **Devised by:** Sydney Newman
- **Writers include:** Anthony Coburn, Terry Nation, David Whitaker, John Lucarotti, Dennis Spooner, Louis Marks, Brian Hayles, Ian Stuart Black, Kit Pedler, Gerry Davis, Malcolm Hulke, Mervyn Haisman, Henry Lincoln, Peter Ling, Robert Holmes, Terrance Dicks, Don Houghton, Bob Baker, Dave Martin, Robert Sloman, Robert Banks Stewart, Chris Boucher, Anthony Read, Douglas Adams, David Fisher, Stephen Gallagher, Johnny Byrne, Christopher H. Bidmead, Terence Dudley, Eric Saward, Philip Martin, Stephen Wyatt, Ian Briggs, Ben Aaronovitch
- **Directors include:** Waris Hussein, Christopher Barry, Richard Martin, Douglas Camfield, Derek Martinus, Michael Leeston-Smith, Paddy Russell, Bill Sellars, Michael Ferguson, Julia Smith, Morris Barry, Tristan de Vere Cole, David Maloney, Michael E. Briant, Paul Bernard, Lennie Mayne, George Spenton-Foster, Michael Hayes, Peter Grimwade, Peter Moffatt, Fiona Cumming, Matthew Robinson, Graeme Harper, Chris Clough, Alan Wareing
- **Producers:** Verity Lambert, Mervyn Pinfield, John Wiles, Innes Lloyd, Peter Bryant, Derrick Sherwin, Barry Letts, Philip Hinchcliffe, Graham Williams, John Nathan-Turner, Alex Beaton, Philip Seagal, Jo Wright

'*The Doctor believes in good and fights evil. Though often caught up in violent situations, he is a man of peace. He is never cruel or cowardly. In fact, to put it simply, the Doctor is a hero. That, at least, hasn't changed - and it never will.*' Terrance Dicks, *Doctor Who* script editor (1968–74).

Doctor Who was conceived in 1963 as an 'educational' family programme that would use the conventions of science fiction to explore Earth history and Orwellian futures. Had it been produced by Don Taylor and written by Dennis Potter - if it had remained faithful to Sydney Newman's vision - it would doubtless be well-remembered. It is, however, unlikely to have lasted for a quarter of a century and have shaped the popular psyche in the way that it has.

The success of *Doctor Who* is due to its evolution, constantly synthesizing new ideas as the production team changed. But certain concepts were immutable.

The lead character began as a mysterious, grumpy but ultimately likeable grandfather figure, an alien scientist with a huge time machine that (thanks to his race's ingenuity in temporal physics and the BBC's limited budget) appeared to fit perfectly into the small, everyday shape of a police box. The craft was the TARDIS (which originally stood for Time And Relative Dimension In Space); the alien explorer was known only as the Doctor.

To help the younger viewers identify with what was going on (and to ask 'What's that mean, Doctor?' at regular intervals), the Doctor was given three companions: his granddaughter, and the two teachers who rather foolishly wanted to investigate their most mysterious and unearthly pupil. Although at times William Russell's square-jawed Ian Chesterton was the main focus of the series, it was the enigmatic Doctor, played by William Hartnell, who really caught the public's imagination.

Of course, being science fiction, noble educational sentiments didn't last long. After a superbly mysterious opening episode (transmitted the day after President Kennedy's assassination, and repeated a week later), and a three-part adventure set at the dawn of history, the second serial, written by Terry Nation, took the Doctor and his friends to the planet Skaro to meet the Daleks. ('The Daleks' has overshadowed the first story to such an extent that many people still believe that Terry Nation created not only the pepperpots but also *Doctor Who* itself, an error that was included in the UK edition of Trivial Pursuit.)

Designer Ray Cusick gave life to the nightmarish creatures of Nation's dystopian adventure, and 'Dalekmania' soon swept the country. Over the next three years the public eagerly bought Dalek models, Dalek costumes, Dalek guns, even a novelty record ('I'm Gonna Spend My Christmas with a Dalek'). There were two film adaptations (*Dr Who and the Daleks* (1965) and *Daleks - Invasion Earth 2150AD* (1966)), which starred Peter Cushing as the Doctor, a very human scientist, thus making the H.G. Wells derivations clearer than ever. The contemporary importance of the Daleks can best be exemplified by the footage of the Beatles performing 'Ticket to Ride' that appears in the third Dalek story, 'The Chase'.

In taking the Doctor to alien worlds, however, producer Verity Lambert and script editor David Whitaker clashed violently with Sydney Newman, who objected to the programme becoming a 'bug-eyed-monster' series. Nevertheless, the early space adventures - and Whitaker's 'The Edge of Destruction', a strange, claustrophobic story set entirely aboard the TARDIS - are usually better remembered than the historical stories. Lambert had the courage of her convictions and managed to weld together disparate elements - Whitaker's romanticism and the other writers' experimentation with structure, Newman's thrust for realism - to create a format that was still running 26 years later.

The historical stories, so important to Newman's concept, were lavish and elegant, and John Lucarotti's mock-Shakespearean 'The Aztecs' and David Whitaker's 'The Crusade' showed what could be done by injecting a little pace and excitement into the formula. The second season ended with Dennis Spooner's 'The Time Meddler', which mixed humour, history and science fiction in broadly equal measures, the plot concerning a renegade member of the Doctor's race who wanted to alter history by helping Harold to victory at Hastings with atomic bazookas. Subsequent pseudo-historicals would tend to be done with greater finesse, but Spooner's story did at least pave the way for such merging of genres.

The other major style of story - space opera, for want of a better description - was exemplified by 'The Web Planet', a reasonably successful attempt at bringing man-sized insect aliens to life. For a long time, though, it was much easier to bring back the Daleks, giving them a 13-episode slice of the third season. The one-part prologue 'Mission to the Unknown' didn't even feature the Doctor and his companions.

Starring: The Doctor – William Hartnell (1963–66) • Patrick Troughton (1966–69) • Jon Pertwee (1970–74) • Tom Baker (1974–81) • Peter Davison (1982–84) • Colin Baker (1984–86) • Sylvester McCoy (1987–89, 1996) • Paul McGann (1996–)

Also starring: Carole Ann Ford (Susan) • William Russell (Ian Chesterton) • Jacqueline Hill (Barbara Wright) • Maureen O'Brien (Vicki) • Peter Purves (Steven Taylor) • Adrienne Hill (Katarina) • Jean Marsh (Sara Kingdom) • Jackie Lane (Dodo Chaplet) • Anneke Wills (Polly) • Michael Craze (Ben Jackson) • Frazer Hines (Jamie McCrimmon) • Deborah Watling (Victoria Waterfield) • Nicholas Courtney (The Brigadier) • Wendy Padbury (Zoë Herriot) • John Levene (Benton) • Caroline John (Liz Shaw) • Katy Manning (Jo Grant) • Richard Franklin (Mike Yates) • Elisabeth Sladen (Sarah Jane Smith) • Ian Marter (Harry Sullivan) • Louise Jameson (Leela) • John Leeson/David Brierley (voice of K-9) • Mary Tamm/Lalla Ward (Romana) • Matthew Waterhouse (Adric) • Sarah Sutton (Nyssa) • Janet Fielding (Tegan Jovanka) • Mark Strickson (Vislor Turlough) • Gerald Flood (voice of Kamelion) • Nicola Bryant (Peri Brown) • Bonnie Langford (Melanie Bush) • Sophie Aldred (Ace) • Daphne Ashbrook (Grace Holloway)

New styles were always being tried. Brian Hayles's 'The Celestial Toymaker' was the show's first stab at surrealism, with the Doctor and his companions trapped in a bizarre Lewis Carroll-like world populated by characters such as the King and Queen of Hearts and the terrifying schoolboy Cyril. At the opposite end of the spectrum, Ian Stuart Black's 'The War Machines' - which had more in common with ***The Avengers*** than educational drama - saw a sinister threat appearing on contemporary Earth for the first time. In the recently-constructed Post Office Tower, super-computer WOTAN planned world domination, instructing its tank-like robots to smash their way through mid-60s London. (This juxtaposition paved the way for a famous sequence in 'The Invasion', where Cybermen emerge from the sewers near St Paul's Cathedral.)

By the beginning of the fourth season the most important decision concerning the show's future had already been taken: the Doctor would change. William Hartnell had become ill, and a younger actor was needed for the role. It was decided that the Doctor should regenerate and become literally a new man. And so, at the end of the Doctor's first encounter with the Cybermen (Kit Pedler and Gerry Davis's 'The Tenth Planet'), William Hartnell fell to the floor of the TARDIS, his face fading away as the next era of ***Doctor Who*** was born.

Patrick Troughton was the man chosen to take Hartnell's place. As there was no point in trying to copy Hartnell's characterization Troughton was given the task of creating a completely new persona for the Doctor. He quickly stamped his mark on the role. There were changes behind the scenes, too. Producer Innes Lloyd phased out the straight historical stories (Troughton's second adventure 'The Highlanders' was the last until 1982) and concentrated instead on the Cybermen and the climactic destruction of the Daleks - or so it seemed - in the memorable 'The Evil of the Daleks'. Terry Nation planned a series based entirely around the Daleks, but this idea never came to pass. However, the absence of the seemingly ubiquitous Daleks allowed other monsters to grow in stature, notably the Cybermen and the Yeti (both of whom had two stories in the fifth season) and the whispering reptilian Ice Warriors.

Two of the most impressive and well-remembered serials of the era, however, were not monster stories in the traditional sense. Victor Pemberton's 'Fury from the Deep' (fifth season) was a thrilling quasi-***Quatermass*** tale of mutant seaweed taking over a refinery, whilst Peter Ling's bizarre 'The Mind Robber' (sixth season) took the Doctor into a world of fictional characters. However, Patrick Troughton's final season lacked the all-round quality of previous years, a number of stories falling through and having to be replaced with the ten-part 'The War Games'. As a finale to the 60s, 'The War Games' depressingly sums up the sense of tiredness that pervaded the series, with most of the cast and crew keen to move on. The programme's popularity had fallen, and the Doctor was on trial before his own people, the Time Lords. He was found guilty of interference in other cultures, and was sentenced to exile and forced regeneration. With Troughton's body spinning into the distance one could have been excused for thinking that this was the end of *Doctor Who*.

Despite rumours of a new Nigel Kneale series to replace it, *Doctor Who* did continue, albeit with a radical change in format. In Troughton's final season 'The Invasion' had introduced the United Nations Intelligence Taskforce (UNIT), a military force dedicated to protecting the Earth from alien attack. UNIT's British leader was Brigadier Lethbridge-Stewart, who had been introduced in the second Yeti story, 'The Web of Fear'. It was proposed that the Doctor, forced to stay on Earth, should act as UNIT's adviser. The icing on the cake was that, for the first time, *Doctor Who* was to be made in colour.

The new Doctor was Jon Pertwee, previously best known for radio comedy. He seemed, on paper, a logical progression from Patrick Troughton, and yet Pertwee played it (largely) straight, although his character showed subtle depths in Don Houghton's complex political allegory 'Inferno'. Another strong (but also controversial) story was Pertwee's debut, Robert Holmes's 'Spearhead from Space', which, as well as dealing with the problems of the Doctor's regeneration and his reintroduction to UNIT, told the story of the planned infiltration of earth by the Nestene Consciousness, a creature with an ability to manipulate plastic. It created an army of killer mannequins known as Autons. One memorable sequence had a group of shop window dummies smashing their way through the glass and on to the street, calmly shooting shoppers.

The ensuing controversy was typical of that which dogged *Doctor Who* from the beginning, accelerated perhaps by the common but erroneous assumption that it was a children's show. Although the Daleks, by and large, escaped much criticism, the Cybermen were lambasted, notably after the violent 1967 serial 'The Tomb of the Cybermen'. In stories yet to come, *Doctor Who* would be criticized for showing deadly plastic toys and replica policemen ('Terror of the Autons', the sequel to 'Spearhead'), a horrifying Nazi/World War I scenario ('Genesis of the Daleks', from the first Tom Baker season), a malevolent brain ('The Brain of Morbius'), a nightmare world where the Doctor is almost killed by having his head held under water ('The Deadly Assassin'), and so on. For the majority of Jon Pertwee's tenure, however, horror was dropped in favour of alien invasions of earth, all-action militaristic romps and ever-growing viewing figures. The show almost became respectable in 1974 when the scriptwriters - Robert Holmes, Malcolm Hulke, Terry Nation, Brian Hayles and Robert Sloman - won a BAFTA award, a suitable acknowledgement of the popularity that producer Barry Letts and script editor Terrance Dicks had achieved with the programme.

After a season or two it seemed sensible to allow the Doctor to go wandering through time and space once more, and so later Pertwee seasons alternated the UNIT stories with tales set on exotic alien planets. The Daleks returned (three times), the Doctor met his previous two incarnations in an anniversary special, the troll-like Sontarans made their debut, and dinosaurs invaded London. The Doctor's 'Moriarty', the Master (Roger Delgado), had already been introduced. The entire eighth season was a 25-week struggle between the protagonists that concluded with 'The Dæmons', a Dennis Wheatley-inspired story shot mostly on location in Wiltshire and featuring a Devil-like alien, Azal. In many ways this story sums up the Pertwee era perfectly.

Pertwee was the 'green' Doctor, his stories often dealing with shady scientific institutions that angered our co-inhabitants on earth ('Doctor Who and the Silurians', 'The Sea Devils') or filled Welsh mines with toxic sludge ('The Green Death', normally remembered as 'that *Doctor Who* story with the maggots'). The third Doctor was forced to regenerate after battling giant spiders in a story redolent with Buddhist images of rebirth ('Planet of the Spiders').

Tom Baker - then virtually unknown on television - was the chosen replacement. Baker was working on a building site at the time he was cast (interestingly, one of his few TV appearances before then had been playing the part of a site manager in an episode of *Softly Softly: Task Force* in 1970). Elisabeth Sladen's companion Sarah Jane Smith bridged the Pertwee and Baker eras, although she was rarely the radical feminist departure that was intended, proving to be as much of a 'screamer' as those that came before. (Indeed, despite several attempts at strong female companions - notably the savage Leela - it was not until the introduction of Sophie Aldred as Ace in the 80s that this aspect of the show truly caught up with the real world.)

New producer Philip Hinchcliffe and script editor Robert Holmes began to steer the programme away from what they saw as comfortable science-fiction 'Cowboys and Indians' and towards gothic, psychological horror. Influenced by Hammer, classic science fiction ('The Seeds of Doom' ripped-off *The Thing from Another World* quite shamelessly) and ideas of possession and bodily mutation, the programme frightened viewers like never before. With neo-historicals like the nerve-tingling 'Planet of Evil' (which pre-empted *Alien*) and Louis Marks's 'The Masque of Mandragora' gaining critical interest, viewing figures peaked at 14 million. Holmes contributed two vital stories: the Doctor's return to his home planet Gallifrey ('The Deadly Assassin', a surreal homage to *The Manchurian*

Candidate) and a *Phantom of the Opera* variant set in Victorian London ('The Talons of Weng-Chiang').

Ultimately, the success of Hinchcliffe and Holmes proved to be their undoing. The nightmarish drowning sequence in 'The Deadly Assassin' was harshly attacked, particularly by Mary Whitehouse, and Philip Hinchcliffe was moved on to the trashy police series *Target*. His successor, Graham Williams, was told to tone down the programme's horror content. Realizing that this would leave a vacuum at *Doctor Who*'s centre, Williams began to harness Tom Baker's natural energy and introduced a strong humorous slant to proceedings, later accelerated by Douglas Adams as script editor. The stories produced by Williams are often well-remembered, particularly the Hammeresque 'Image of the Fendahl', the cynically political 'The Sun Makers', and the Parisian 'City of Death'. However, production values declined, and the introduction of the cute robot-dog-computer companion, K-9, takes some defending. The seventeenth season, in particular, was a chaotic mix of the brilliant and the tacky.

The producer of the final Tom Baker season, and the man entrusted with taking the show into the 80s, was John Nathan-Turner, who went on to oversee the show for the next nine years. Under his leadership, the Doctor would change three times, and the show's popularity would build and then decline once more. The comedy was replaced with gripping pseudo-science and stories like Steve Gallagher's 'Warriors' Gate' - set in a gateway between universes - are among the most perplexing in the programme's history. Visually influenced by the films of Cocteau, 'Warriors' Gate' showed what could be achieved by taking the concept seriously again. Script editor Christopher H. Bidmead, a science journalist and computer pundit, wrote Tom Baker's finale 'Logopolis', a story that managed to point the way forward and echo the past. It introduced a new incarnation of the Master, now played by Anthony Ainley, Roger Delgado having died in a tragic car accident in 1973.

Original pilot episode
(26 Aug 91, BBC2)
1 'An Unearthly Child'

First season
(23 Nov 63–12 Sep 64)
2 'An Unearthly Child' (Four episodes)
3 'The Daleks' (Seven episodes)
4 'The Edge of Destruction' (Two episodes)
5 'Marco Polo' (Seven episodes)
6 'The Keys of Marinus' (Six episodes)
7 'The Aztecs' (Four episodes)
8 'The Sensorites' (Six episodes)
9 'The Reign of Terror' (Six episodes)

Second season
(31 Oct 64–24 July 65)
10 'Planet of Giants' (Three episodes)
11 'The Dalek Invasion of Earth' (Six episodes)
12 'The Rescue' (Two episodes)
13 'The Romans' (Four episodes)
14 'The Web Planet' (Six episodes)
15 'The Crusade' (Four episodes)
16 'The Space Museum' (Four episodes)
17 'The Chase' (Six episodes)
18 'The Time Meddler' (Four episodes)

Third season
(11 Sep 65–16 Jul 66)
19 'Galaxy 4' (Four episodes)
20 'Mission to the Unknown' (One episode)
21 'The Myth Makers' (Four episodes)
22 'The Daleks' Master Plan' (Twelve episodes)
23 'The Massacre' (Four episodes)
24 'The Ark' (Four episodes)
25 'The Celestial Toymaker' (Four episodes)
26 'The Gunfighters' (Four episodes)
27 The Savages (Four episodes)
28 The War Machines (Four episodes)

Fourth season
(10 Sep 66–1 Jul 67)
29 The Smugglers (Four episodes)
30 The Tenth Planet (Four episodes)
31 The Power of the Daleks (Six episodes)
32 The Highlanders (Four episodes)
33 The Underwater Menace (Four episodes)
34 The Moonbase (Four episodes)
35 The Macra Terror (Four episodes)
36 The Faceless Ones (Six episodes)
37 The Evil of the Daleks (Seven episodes)

Fifth season
(2 Sep 67–1 Jun 68)
38 The Tomb of the Cybermen (Four episodes)
39 The Abominable Snowmen (Six episodes)
40 The Ice Warriors (Six episodes)
41 The Enemy of the World (Six episodes)
42 The Web of Fear (Six episodes)
43 Fury from the Deep Six episodes)
44 The Wheel in Space (Six episodes)

Sixth season
(10 Aug 68–21 Jun 69)
45 The Dominators (Five episodes)
46 The Mind Robber (Five episodes)
47 The Invasion (Eight episodes)
48 The Krotons (Four episodes)
49 The Seeds of Death (Six episodes)
50 The Space Pirates (Six episodes)
51 The War Games (Ten episodes)

Seventh season
(3 Jan–20 Jun 70)
52 Spearhead from Space (Four episodes)
53 Doctor Who and the Silurians (Seven episodes)
54 The Ambassadors of Death (Seven episodes)
55 Inferno (Seven episodes)

Eighth season
(2 Jan–19 Jun 71)
56 Terror of the Autons
(Four episodes)
57 The Mind of Evil
(Six episodes)
58 The Claws of Axos
(Four episodes)
59 Colony in Space
(Six episodes)
60 The Dæmons
(Five episodes)

Ninth season
(1 Jan–24 Jun 72)
61 Day of the Daleks
(Four episodes)
62 The Curse of Peladon
(Four episodes)
63 The Sea Devils
(Six episodes)
64 The Mutants
(Six episodes)
65 The Time Monster
(Six episodes)

Tenth season
(30 Dec 72–23 Jun 73)
66 The Three Doctors
(Four episodes)
67 Carnival of Monsters
(Four episodes)
68 Frontier in Space
(Six episodes)
69 Planet of the Daleks
(Six episodes)
70 The Green Death
(Six episodes)

Eleventh season
(15 Dec 73–8 Jun 74)
71 The Time Warrior
(Four episodes)
72 Invasion of the Dinosaurs
(Six episodes)
73 Death to the Daleks
(Four episodes)
74 The Monster of Peladon
(Six episodes)
75 Planet of the Spiders
(Six episodes)

Twelfth season
(28 Dec 74–10 May 75)
76 Robot
(Four episodes)
77 The Ark in Space
(Four episodes)
78 The Sontaran Experiment
(Two episodes)
79 Genesis of the Daleks
(Six episodes)
80 Revenge of the Cybermen
(Four episodes)

Thirteenth season
(30 Aug 75–6 Mar 76)
81 Terror of the Zygons
(Four episodes)
82 Planet of Evil
(Four episodes)
83 Pyramids of Mars
(Four episodes)
84 The Android Invasion
(Four episodes)
85 The Brain of Morbius
(Four episodes)
86 The Seeds of Doom
(Six episodes)

Fourteenth season
(4 Sep 76–2 Apr 77)
87 The Masque of Mandragora
(Four episodes)
88 The Hand of Fear
(Four episodes)
89 The Deadly Assassin
(Four episodes)
90 The Face of Evil
(Four episodes)
91 The Robots of Death
(Four episodes)
92 The Talons of Weng-Chiang
(Six episodes)

Fifteenth season
(3 Sep 77–11 Mar 78)
93 Horror of Fang Rock
(Four episodes)
94 The Invisible Enemy
(Four episodes)
95 Image of the Fendahl
(Four episodes)
96 The Sun Makers
(Four episodes)
97 Underworld
(Four episodes)
98 The Invasion of Time
(Four episodes)

Sixteenth season
(2 Sep 78–24 Feb 79)
99 The Ribos Operation
(Four episodes)
100 The Pirate Planet
(Four episodes)
101 The Stones of Blood
(Four episodes)
102 The Androids of Tara
(Four episodes)
103 The Power of Kroll
(Four episodes)
104 The Armageddon Factor
(Six episodes)

Seventeenth season
(1 Sep 79–12 Jan 80)
105 Destiny of the Daleks
(Four episodes)
106 City of Death
(Four episodes)
107 The Creature from the Pit
(Four episodes)
108 Nightmare of Eden
(Four episodes)
109 The Horns of Nimon
(Four episodes)
110 Shada
(Six episodes, not completed, unbroadcast)

Eighteenth season
(30 Aug 80–21 Mar 81)
111 The Leisure Hive
(Four episodes)
112 Meglos
(Four episodes)
113 Full Circle
(Four episodes)
114 State of Decay
(Four episodes)
115 Warriors' Gate
(Four episodes)
116 The Keeper of Traken
(Four episodes)
117 Logopolis
(Four episodes)

Nineteenth season
(4 Jan–30 Mar 82)
118 Castrovalva
(Four episodes)
119 Four to Doomsday
(Four episodes)
120 Kinda
(Four episodes)
121 The Visitation
(Four episodes)
122 Black Orchid
(Two episodes)
123 Earthshock
(Four episodes)
124 Time-Flight
(Four episodes)

Twentieth season
(3 Jan–16 Mar 83)
125 Arc of Infinity
(Four episodes)
126 Snakedance
(Four episodes)
127 Mawdryn Undead
(Four episodes)
128 Terminus
(Four episodes)
129 Enlightenment
(Four episodes)
130 The King's Demons
(Two episodes)

20th anniversary special
(25 Nov 83, 90 minutes)
131 The Five Doctors

Twenty-first season
(5 Jan–30 Mar 84)
132 Warriors of the Deep
(Four episodes)
133 The Awakening
(Two episodes)
134 Frontios
(Four episodes)
135 Resurrection of the Daleks
(Two 45-minute episodes)
136 Planet of Fire
(Four episodes)
137 The Caves of Androzani
(Four episodes)
138 The Twin Dilemma
(Four episodes)

Twenty-second season
(5 Jan–30 Mar 85, 45-minute episodes)
139 Attack of the Cybermen
(Two episodes)
140 Vengeance on Varos
(Two episodes)
141 The Mark of the Rani
(Two episodes)
142 The Two Doctors
(Three episodes)
143 Timelash
(Two episodes)
144 Revelation of the Daleks
(Two episodes)

Twenty-third season
(6 Sep–6 Dec 86)
145 The Trial of a Time Lord
(Fourteen episodes)

Twenty-fourth season
(7 Sep–7 Dec 87)
146 Time and the Rani
(Four episodes)
147 Paradise Towers
(Four episodes)
148 Delta and the Bannermen
(Three episodes)
149 Dragonfire
(Three episodes)

Twenty-fifth season
(5 Oct 88–4 Jan 89)
150 Remembrance of the Daleks
(Four episodes)
151 The Happiness Patrol
(Three episodes)
152 Silver Nemesis
(Three episodes)
153 The Greatest Show in the Galaxy
(Four episodes)

Twenty-sixth season
(6 Sep–6 Dec 89)
154 Battlefield
(Four episodes)
155 Ghost Light
(Three episodes)
156 The Curse of Fenric
(Four episodes)
157 Survival
(Three episodes)

Special
(27 May 96, 85 minutes)
158 'Enemy Within' [unofficial title]

[For the first 25 stories, each episode had an individual title and therefore story titles in quotation marks often did not appear on-screen. The original pilot episode was shown as part of a celebration of Lime Grove studios. Work on episode 110 was halted by industrial action: although incomplete, the story has been released on BBC video. A 50-minute spin-off programme *K-9 and Company* (episode title: 'A Girl's Best Friend') was transmitted on 28 Dec 81.]

Whilst many of the concepts and approaches associated with the 18th season were dropped once Bidmead had moved on, the next three years were something of a renaissance, with dramatic and clever plots the order of the day. Indeed, 'Kinda', written by Christopher Bailey, is probably the most complex and allegorical story transmitted under the *Doctor Who* banner, dealing with madness, colonialism, race memory and Buddhism. 'Castrovalva', written by Bidmead and inspired by the paintings of Escher, was challenging, intelligent television, and showed a maturity far removed from most viewers' perception of the series.

Best of all, though, was the new Doctor, played by Peter Davison. Witty yet subtly vulnerable, he was an innocent in a complex universe where he fought the usual array of space monsters but found himself questioning his lifestyle and the nature of the evil that he encountered. When the Cybermen returned for a gung-ho adventure ('Earthshock'), the story ended with the death of the Doctor's companion Adric.

The show progressed effortlessly towards its 20th anniversary, celebrated by the feature-length tale 'The Five Doctors'. Although Tom Baker did not want to appear in the story (a decision he later seemed to regret), footage from the unfinished story 'Shada' was used. Richard Hurndall played the role of the first Doctor, William Hartnell having died in 1975.

Peter Davison's excellent characterization battled valiantly after seven years of Tom Baker's domination of the public imagination, but he left in 1984, worried about being typecast. Things then seemed to go badly wrong, with Colin Baker (best known for *The Brothers*) stepping into the role. The stories suddenly lacked sparkle - indeed, they were often downright nasty, with even stalwart writer Robert Holmes churning out ill-advised scripts - and Colin Baker's portrayal was impossible to like, being smug and sometimes sadistically violent. The Doctor and his companion, Peri, had no time for each other and continually squabbled. Script editor Eric Saward, despite having worked on previous seasons, presided over a collection of stories in which the central concepts of the show were all-but abandoned. Viewing figures dropped dramatically, and Michael Grade put the show on hold. The Doctor eventually returned in 'The Trial of a Time Lord': just as Troughton had done, he was pleading for his life before his own people. The stories were a little better than before, but the wholesale improvement clearly had not been achieved. It was time for another regeneration.

Sylvester McCoy was announced as the new Doctor, and most people expected a madman at the helm of the TARDIS. Instead they ended up with by far the most interesting portrayal of the Doctor: the Time Lord as a cosmic chess player, studiously weighing the odds and, although dedicated to the overthrow of evil, sometimes cynical in his manipulation of human beings, particularly those close to him. After a juddery first season the scripts began to get to grips with the ideas that script editor Andrew Cartmel was pushing. The Daleks returned with a bang, and the pseudo-historical adventure ('Ghost Light') and the stock style of horror ('The Curse of Fenric') were revamped with particular effectiveness.

Despite being dramatic and well-acted, and garnering some critical interest, the Sylvester McCoy seasons were not popular with the viewers, losing out to scheduling (being placed opposite ***Coronation Street***) and public ignorance. This stands in stark contrast to the acclaim the programme has received over the years. The series has been critically praised by Alan Coren and Clive James, while *Doctor Who*'s public supporters have included Barry Norman, Michael Parkinson and Melvyn Bragg (who fronted a 1977 *Lively Arts* documentary on the programme). *Doctor Who*'s influence continues to be reflected not only in the Cyberpunk movement and American series such as *Quantum Leap*, but also in films like *Back to the Future* (US 85) and *Bill and Ted's Excellent Adventure* (US 89). Few other TV programmes can claim a place in the *Oxford English Dictionary* (just look up 'Dalek').

The announcement of Paul McGann as the new Doctor in January 1996 went some way to placating fans dismayed by the BBC's decision to bring back *Doctor Who* as an American co-production. Despite the seven-year wait there might be life in the concept yet.

Doomwatch

- **BBC Television** (BBC1) ◆ Colour
- **38 episodes** (1 unbroadcast) (50 minutes) ◆ 1970-72
- **Creators:** Kit Pedler, Gerry Davis
- **Writers include:** Kit Pedler, Gerry Davis, Dennis Spooner, Terence Dudley, Don Shaw, Martin Worth, Louis Marks, Brian Hayles
- **Directors include:** Paul Ciappessoni, Jonathan Alwyn, Terence Dudley, David Proudfoot, Eric Hills, Darrol Blake, Lennie Mayne
- **Producer:** Terence Dudley

Regular cast: John Paul (Dr Spencer Quist) • Simon Oates (Dr John Ridge) • Robert Powell (Toby Wren) • John Nolan (Geoff Hardcastle) • Jean Trend (Dr Fay Chantry) • John Barron (The Minister) • Elizabeth Weaver (Dr Anne Tarrant) • John Brown (Commander Stafford)

With: Joby Blanchard (Colin Bradley) • Vivien Sherrard (Barbara Mason) • Wendy Hall (Pat Hunnisett)

The reason that *Doomwatch* had a lasting and prophetic appeal can be attributed to the fact that it was not just a work of fiction. A 'green' programme years before the term was fashionable, it was created by a scientist, Dr Kit Pedler, and a scriptwriter, Gerry Davis, who had first worked together when Davis was script editor on ***Doctor Who***, creating the Cybermen. Pedler was working at the University of London, and had created quite a stir as an apocalyptic science pundit. They took their format to BBC producer Terence Dudley.

Dudley was immediately excited by the concept. Doomwatch was the codename of the Department of Measurement of Scientific Work, a vote-catching quango that was supposed to be all bark and no bite. It would come into conflict

Doomwatch - the Department of Fashion Victims. Quist, Bradley and Ridge, from the first season

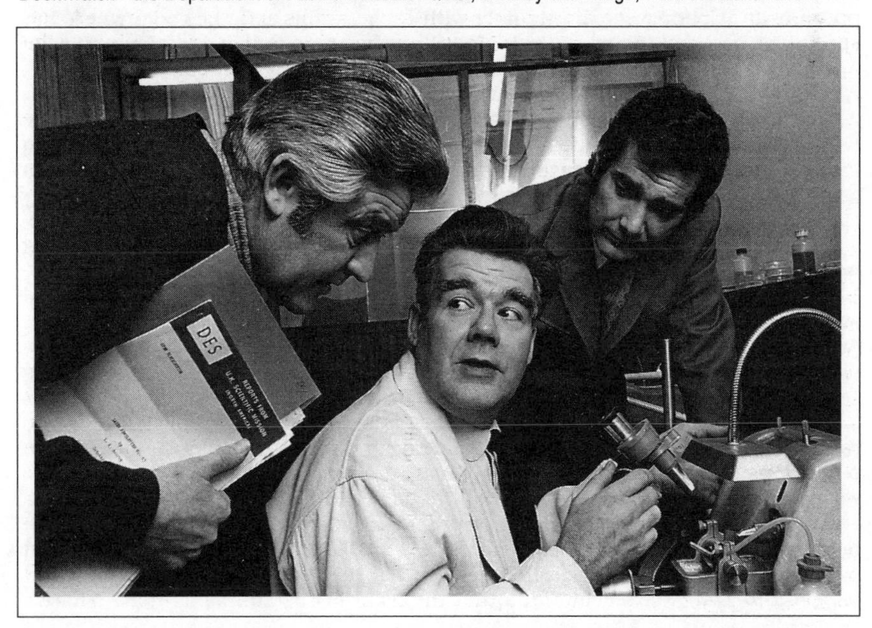

with its masters when the personalities of the staff bit the hands that fed them. Initially, the head of serials felt that the title was too downbeat, but Dudley held out, and *Doomwatch*, as a programme and a word, went on to catch the public imagination in the same way that ***Quatermass*** had done over a decade earlier.

The leader of the department was Dr Spencer Quist, a dedicated, thoughtful character who had assisted in the development of the H-bomb, losing his wife to radiation sickness in the process. His assistant was John Ridge, that familiar figure from 70s drama, the macho dandy-about-town, an espionage agent who sweet-talked secretaries and had a quip for every oil spillage. Completing the central trio was Toby Wren, a gentle, dedicated researcher, played by the then-unknown Robert Powell. Wren was to become the series' heart-throb. The characters relied on the dour Yorkshireman Colin Bradley for laboratory work, and had a cipher of a secretary in Wendy Hall.

The first episode, 'The Plastic Eaters', set the tone for what was to come. The *Radio Times* cover launching the show featured a melted plastic aircraft in a briefcase, and the image was as memorable as the episode. Quist was looking into the causes of an aircraft crash in Brazil, and sent the newly-arrived Wren to the scene while Ridge infiltrated a government bio-warfare lab. It turned out that the plastic of the aircraft had been dissolved by a newly-developed virus designed to dispose of waste (as the audience had seen in a striking pre-credit sequence where the luggage rack and joystick of the plane melted away). It was too late to warn Wren not to take the plastic sample from his case on the flight home, but he managed to save the day, the aircraft crash-landing in Cornwall. Thanks to Doomwatch, the project was halted.

Audiences were captivated by the blend of ecological comment and high drama, but the reaction was nothing compared to that for some of the episodes that followed. Dennis Spooner's 'Burial at Sea' had a yachtful of pop stars affected by a buried canister of toxic gas, neatly anticipating the plan to dump American nerve gas in the Atlantic. However, it was the fourth episode, Dudley's own 'Tomorrow, the Rat', that gained the show its notoriety. A species of intelligent rat has been developed in the lab, animals that can wedge open traps with cutlery and keep mice as cattle. In a chilling pre-title sequence the creatures attack a baby in its push-chair. Later, the female scientist who developed the beasts, possibly anticipating her dinner-date with Ridge, walks into the room where her specimens are kept, dripping with blood from wounds inflicted by the mother of an attacked child. The episode ends with Ridge finding her half-eaten corpse. Questions were raised in Parliament.

Other first-season episodes featured drug-aided subliminal advertising ('The Devil's Sweets'), the mental anguish caused by sonic booms ('The Red Sky'), and hormonal change in Welsh factory workers ('The Battery People'). The blend was what Pedler called 'sci-fact', dramatic situations staged around real contemporary fears. A priest was quoted as saying that the series 'strips down pretensions, arrogance and pride of sophisticated society and shows what Christian men should be concerned with'.

The last story of the season, 'Survival Code', was going to cause more of a storm than anything that had preceded it; 12 million viewers tuned in to see it. An aircraft carrying nuclear weapons crashes in the sea, and Doomwatch are forbidden to interfere as the RAF recovers the bombs. However, one warhead has gone missing, and ends up at the pier in Byfield Regis. The arcade owner decides to dismantle it, thinking that it is a satellite. Scared when his family fall victim to radiation sickness, and unknowingly starting and halting the bomb's countdown process, he finally elects to dispose of it by dumping it in the sea. However, the weapon becomes stuck in the slats of the pier, and his daughter calls in Quist's squad. Quist himself begins to remove the detonators from the bomb, but when he breaks his wrist the impetuous Toby steps in. He thinks that he has succeeded when the RAF arrives, but, as remembered at the start of the next season and on a *Radio Times* cover, he finds that things aren't as simple as that. 'There's

First season
(9 Feb–11 May 70)
1 The Plastic Eaters
2 Friday's Child
3 Burial at Sea
4 Tomorrow, the Rat
5 Project Sahara
6 Re-entry Forbidden
7 The Devil's Sweets
8 The Red Sky
9 Spectre at the Feast
10 Train and De-Train
11 The Battery People
12 Hear No Evil
13 Survival Code

Second season
(14 Dec 70–22 Mar 71)
14 You Killed Toby Wren
15 Invasion
16 The Islanders
17 No Room for Error
18 By the Pricking of My Thumbs...
19 The Iron Doctor
20 Flight into Yesterday
21 The Web of Fear
22 In the Dark
23 The Human Time Bomb
24 The Inquest
25 The Logicians
26 Public Enemy

Third season
(5 Jun–14 Aug 72)
27 Fire and Brimstone
28 High Mountain
29 Say Knife, Fat Man
30 Waiting for a Knighthood
31 Without the Bomb
32 Hair Trigger
33 Deadly Dangerous Tomorrow
34 Enquiry
35 Flood
36 Cause of Death
37 The Killer Dolphins
38 Sex and Violence (unbroadcast)

another wire!' 'Don't pull it. Follow it back to the terminal,' exclaims the RAF expert. Quist and Ridge shelter as a conventional explosion lights up the pier.

Killing off the show's most popular character generated a storm of publicity, and a high-profile launch for the second season. 'You Killed Toby Wren' played on the show's strengths, Ridge walking out after a row with Quist, who is taking psychiatric advice on whether to continue his work. Ridge finds himself involved with a female scientist who is engaged in gruesome genetic experiments, including a chick with a human head. He is told that he had narrowly avoided becoming the father of one of these hybrids, and is welcomed back to the fold by a recovered Quist.

The second season introduced the unmemorable scientist Geoff Hardcastle, and Dr Fay Chantry, who was supposed to head off feminist criticism of the series, and was as under-used as might be expected. The series seemed tired, many of the issues having been explored earlier, and standard anti-pollution stories appeared more and more. John Goulds's 'In the Dark' was an exception, Patrick Troughton putting in a memorable performance as a man whose body was being kept alive by machines. Also worthwhile was Robert Holmes's 'The Inquest', which dealt with a rabies outbreak in England. However, the series that had scored so many bull's-eyes was missing the mark, with episodes on the 'dire consequences' of culture shock, high-rise living, and jet lag.

During the second season, Pedler and Davis departed, claiming that producer Dudley had 'made a total travesty of the programme'. Certainly the opening episode of the third season, in which Ridge stole a flask of anthrax and threatened to destroy humanity for its crimes, seemed like a desperate attempt to drag the whole series back on course. Ridge appeared from time to time as a rather manic protester, his behaviour later being attributed to the lead paint he had stored in his garage. Apart from excusing silly scripting, this episode, 'Waiting for a Knighthood', was one of the last season's notable ones. A minister had been covering up the truth about lead pollution because he wanted his knighthood. Researching the episode, Dudley was told by then Deputy Secretary of State, Eldon Griffiths, that there was no danger from lead whatsoever.

Martin Worth's 'Say Knife, Fat Man' showed a group of students building an atomic bomb, while 'Flood' explored the possibility of London being submerged. One of the most memorable images of this era was the Indian family camping in St James's Park in Worth's 'Deadly Dangerous Tomorrow'.

The series had become wordy, directionless and dull, the cast varying with every episode. When *Doomwatch* was made into a film in 1972, Quist, Ridge and Bradley only made cameo appearances.

When Quist survived his plunge into the pool of 'The Killer Dolphins', the series ended with a tiny echo of its greatest moment, the death of Toby Wren. Wolf Rilla's 'The Devil's Demolition' - also known as 'I Never Promised You a Rose Garden' - was scrapped during production. However, the controversy wasn't over. Stewart Douglass's 'Sex and Violence', concerning a campaign for 'decency' in the media, was, ironically, pulled from the schedules by Paul Fox, controller of BBC1. Proof that *Doomwatch* - a series that could, at its best, illuminate the deepest fears of the British public - never quite lost its power to shock.

Survivors

- **BBC Television** (BBC1) ◆ **Colour**
- **38 episodes** (50 minutes) ◆ **1975-77**
- **Creator:** Terry Nation
- **Writers include:** Terry Nation, Jack Ronder, Clive Exton, Don Shaw, Ian McCulloch, Martin Worth, Roger Parkes, Roger Marshall
- **Directors include:** Pennant Roberts, Gerald Blake, Terence Williams, Eric Hills, George Spenton-Foster, Tristan de Vere Cole, Peter Jefferies
- **Producer:** Terence Dudley

Regular cast: Carolyn Seymour (Abby Grant) • Ian McCulloch (Greg Preston) • Lucy Fleming (Jenny Richards) • Talfryn Thomas (Tom Price) • Denis Lill (Charles Vaughan) • Celia Gregory (Ruth) • John Abineri (Hubert)

With: Stephen Dudley (John) • Tanya Ronder/Angie Stevens (Lizzie) • Julie Neubert (Wendy) • Hana-Maria Pravda (Mrs Cohen) • Christopher Tranchell (Paul Pitman) • John Hallett (Barney) • Michael Gover (Russell) • Terry Scully (Vic Thatcher) • Eileen Helsby (Charmian Watworth) • Lorna Lewis (Pet) • Gordon Salkild (Jack) • Peter Duncan (Dave) • Anna Pitt/Sally Osborn (Agnes) • Gigi Gratti (Daniella) • Heather Wright (Melanie) • June Page (Sally) • Roger Monk (Pete) • Stephen Tate (Alan) • Dan Meaden (Seth) • Edward Underdown (Frank) • William Dysart (Alec) • Brian Peck (Dave Long)

The title-sequence of a TV series can often tell the viewer far more than simply the name of what they are watching. If done properly, it can reveal style and content, set a particular mood, and even tell a story in its own right.

In a laboratory an oriental scientist drops a flask in slow motion on to a hard surface. As the glass explodes, spilling a green liquid, Anthony Isaac's powerful music begins. Now we are in various airports around the world as a variety of oriental diplomats and businessmen, each unknowingly infected by a deadly plague, become the carriers of death. Passport stamps indicate that the virus has spread to Moscow, New York, Paris, London. A lone church bell tolls as the screen fades to red.

If the opening of Terry Nation's *Survivors* was designed to freak out its audience then it certainly succeeded. *Survivors* was a story of post-apocalyptic life. Taking the premise that 95 per cent of the world's population could be wiped out within a matter of weeks, Nation was fascinated by the means through which the remaining five per cent could live when deprived of simple things 20th-century man takes for granted – electricity, medical care, transport. In other words, could modern-day man survive a change that would mean reverting to a much more basic lifestyle, without resorting to barbarism? Nation said that he was of the generation that placed a man on the Moon, but as an individual he didn't know how to make an axe.

Terence Dudley, former producer on ***Doomwatch***, was given the task of shaping Nation's four-part outline into an on-going series (the producer and writer fell out soon afterwards and Nation contributed only to the first season). Like ***Doomwatch***, *Survivors* was to spend much of its time lambasting the wasteful nature of modern technology and stressing the need for environmental ecology - in both cases giving dire warnings about the future.

In the first episode, Nation painted a picture of a comfortable middle-class society suddenly tumbling down around his first two survivors: company secretary Jenny Richards and housewife Abby Grant, who watches her husband (Peter Bowles) die and then sets out on a quest to find her son, Peter. They were joined in the second episode by the series' nominal 'hero' figure, Greg Preston. The fourth

First season
(16 Apr–16 Jul 75)
1 The Fourth Horseman
2 Genesis
3 Gone Away
4 Corn Dolly
5 Gone to the Angels
6 Garland's War
7 Starvation
8 Spoil of War
9 Law and Order
10 The Future Hour
11 Revenge
12 Something of Value
13 A Beginning

Second season
(31 Mar–23 Jun 76)
14 Birth of a Hope
15 Greater Love
16 Lights of London (part one)
17 Lights of London (part two)
18 The Face of the Tiger
19 The Witch
20 A Friend in Need
21 By Bread Alone
22 The Chosen
23 Parasites
24 New Arrivals
25 Over the Hills
26 New World

Third season
(16 Mar–8 Jun 77)
27 Manhunt
28 A Little Learning
29 Law of the Jungle
30 Mad Dog
31 Bridgehead
32 Reunion
33 The Peacemaker
34 Sparks
35 The Enemy
36 The Last Laugh
37 Long Live the King
38 Power

character on whom the first season concentrated was the itinerant Welsh labourer Tom Price, whose cowardly and scheming nature seemed to view the breakdown of society as a positive liberation.

A criticism often levelled at *Survivors* is that with such stringent class codes maintained, even in the aftermath of a catastrophe, it could be viewed as little more than a serious version of *The Good Life*. This is a little unfair, although one working-class character who wasn't a thief, a power-crazed megalomaniac, or a degenerate savage might have come in handy. Additionally, the 'wine tasting' sequence in 'Birth of a Hope' clearly highlights the series' bourgeois trappings.

Jack Ronder's 'Corn Dolly' was a particularly effective early episode, introducing Charles Vaughan, the leader of an agricultural community who believes that the key to survival is through childbirth and advocates impregnating as many women as possible. 'Spoil of War', written by Clive Exton under the pseudonym M.K. Jeeves, introduced a plethora of new characters, and 'Law and Order' gave the community a moral dilemma when a murder is committed (and the wrong man - a retard - is executed for it, having been unable to defend himself). The season ended with Nation's 'A Beginning', which saw the departure of Abby Grant with the charismatic country squire Jimmy Garland, still searching for her son.

The next season began with a fire destroying much of the community. Those who are left join Charles Vaughan's nearby village. In Don Shaw's 'Greater Love' Paul Pitman dies having risked his life to acquire medicine for Jenny who has given birth to Greg's son. After catching an infection himself, Paul is exiled from the village to minimize the risk of contagion. Other memorable episodes included 'The Face of the Tiger', where the community makes the chilling discovery of a child murderer in their midst, Roger Marshall's 'Parasites', guest starring Patrick Troughton, Martin Worth's 'Over the Hills', in which the women of the village rebel against their role as baby-making machines, and Ian McCulloch's writing debut 'A Friend in Need'. A two-part adventure took Greg, Charles and Ruth (the commune's likeable doctor) to rat-infested London, and the season concluded with the departure of Greg in a balloon bound for Norway. McCulloch only appeared in two episodes in the third and final season, both of which he wrote himself.

The third season was more disjointed - less a continuous narrative, more a series of snapshots of the grim nature of life - although the standard of scripts and acting was as high as ever. 'Mad Dog', in which Charles is saved from a pack of rabid dogs and has to face the possibility that he has contracted rabies himself, was a startling episode which achieved notoriety at the time for its graphic depiction of the disease. There were, however, problems with the episode, which overran, causing the cancellation of the season's planned final episode, a Roger Parkes story called 'Bleak Start'.

Other memorable episodes include 'Law of the Jungle', which saw a guest appearance by Brian Blessed as the hunter Brod. McCulloch reappeared in 'A Little Learning', but wasn't seen again until 'The Last Laugh', an evocative and well-remembered finale for his character in which, having been beaten up by a group of bandits, he finds the man he has been looking for, Dr Adams (Clifton Jones), only to discover that Adams has smallpox. For two days, the incubation period, Greg is isolated with the doctor and when, on the morning of the third day, he emerges apparently fit and well, the audience breathes a huge sigh of relief. However, as he mounts his horse, Greg suddenly vomits, the first sign that he too has the disease. Later, he tricks the bandits who have captured his Norwegian girlfriend, Agnes, and rides off with them to almost certain death at the episode's climax.

Still Greg's presence hung over the series. In 'Long Live the King', his death is only a minor hiccup in the efforts to create a new state with him as its figurehead, as a growing band of survivors, based at an old army camp in Yorkshire, find a new source of wealth in petrol and begin to print bank notes stating 'I, Greg Preston, promise to pay the bearer one hundred gallons of petrol'. The episode ends with a Union Jack, displaying the initials GP, flying over the camp.

In many ways it's a pity that *Survivors* didn't end on this optimistic note. One further episode, 'Power', was made, concerning Charles and Jenny's attempts to create a hydroelectric plant in Scotland. Despite a strong performance by Iain Cuthbertson, it was something of an anti-climax after the impressive beauty of the previous two episodes.

Survivors clearly became far less grim and obsessive as the series progressed. Despite the loss of Preston, the thriving survivors seemed, by the end of the series, to be creating a future for the human race, something that seemed unlikely in the dark days of the first season. Perhaps *Survivors* carried a little too much human spirit and hope with it to be as authentic as Terry Nation wanted, but this paradoxical optimism was undoubtedly a key factor in its appeal.

A *Survivors* repeat on UK Gold in 1993 brought the series to a new, enthusiastic audience. Sadly, a recent proposed revival of the series by BBC Scotland didn't get beyond the planning stages.

An everyday story of post-apocalyptic survival and nasty beards

Blake's 7

- **BBC Television** (BBC1) ◆ Colour
- **52 episodes** (50 minutes) ◆ 1978-81
- **Creator:** Terry Nation
- **Writers:** Terry Nation, Chris Boucher, Robert Holmes, Roger Parkes, Allan Prior, Ben Steed, Rod Beacham, James Follett, Tanith Lee, Trevor Hoyle, Bill Lyons, Colin Davis, Simon Masters
- **Directors include:** Michael E. Briant, Vere Lorrimer, Mary Ridge, Pennant Roberts, George Spenton-Foster, David Sullivan Proudfoot
- **Producers:** David Maloney, Vere Lorrimer

Regular cast: Paul Darrow (Avon) • Gareth Thomas (Blake) • Michael Keating (Vila) • Sally Knyvette (Jenna) • Jan Chappell (Cally) • David Jackson (Gan) • Steven Pacey (Tarrant) • Josette Simon (Dayna) • Glynis Barber (Soolin) • Peter Tuddenham (voices of Zen, Orac and Slave)

With: Jacqueline Pearce (Servalan) • Stephen Greif/Brian Croucher (Travis)

Blake's 7 began as a spontaneous idea from Terry Nation: at the end of a BBC script conference, realizing that no progress was being made with any of the ideas under discussion, Nation improvised the format for a new science-fiction series. The slot up for grabs was that vacated by the police series *Softly Softly: Task Force*, which the BBC had decided to scrap.

Naturally, Nation's proposal displayed all of his recurring themes, with an unlawfully-convicted man fleeing the all-powerful Fascist forces of the Federation. *Blake's 7*'s view of the future was about as pessimistic as that of ***Survivors***, with the forces of good (who tended to be shades of grey) facing a seemingly impossible task in the fight against evil.

Nation delivered a pilot script, and went on to write the entire first season. It was premiered in the Christmas 1977 issue of the *Radio Times* with a colour spread depicting the stars of the show before their spacecraft, the *Liberator*. The actors were of a very high calibre, particularly Gareth Thomas, an RSC actor who went on to achieve further TV success in *The Citadel* and *Knights of God*. His solid presence as Blake, the exiled revolutionary who swears to return to the conformist Earth of the future, ensured that the series was gritty from the very start.

Things began slowly, Blake meeting only two of his seven in the first episode, and not finding his spacecraft until the second. His initial companions were Vila, the cowardly sneak-thief, and Jenna, the glamorous smuggler pilot. Soon to be added were the strongman Gan, unable to kill because of a limiter implanted in his brain, and the telepath Cally, a native of the planet Auron. However, the biggest impact on the series was to be made by Paul Darrow's Avon. Avon was a cynical computer expert who was only out for himself, with little time for Blake's heroics, and Darrow's initial performance was wonderfully understated. Completing the crew was Zen, the dour computer onboard the *Liberator*.

The first season was certainly gritty, if a trifle repetitive. Nation's interest in the mechanics of power resulted in some interesting episodes, like the snowbound resistance melodrama 'Project Avalon', but there was a lot of padding and frequent 'runaround' episodes, and stories like 'Duel', which were inspired by similar *Star Trek* episodes, did little to inspire confidence.

The main interest in the first season lay with Servalan, Supreme Commander of the Federation's space forces. Played to the verge of parody by former Hammer actress Jacqueline Pearce, Servalan was like a *Dynasty* cast member in space. Oozing evil in a white gown and cropped hairdo, she grew steadily more outrageous as the series progressed, backstabbing and seducing her junior officers in equal numbers. Her henchman was the brutal Travis, a one-eyed maverick space commander with a gun implanted in his hand. Travis only felt any trust towards mutoids, blood-drinking biological creations of the Federation.

At the end of the first season, Travis having pursued him across the galaxy in a battle to gain the tetchy super-computer Orac, Blake watched as the *Liberator* exploded on his viewscreen. Millions of children, and quite a few of their parents (the show being screened in the 'ironing board' slot), were dismayed. As it turned out, though, the explosion was just a projection of one possible future, and the start of a *Blake* tradition where every season would end with a cliffhanger.

The second season was, generally, much better than the first, with the introduction of a writer who was to stamp his mark on the series. Chris Boucher had been script editor of the show since the start, and brought to it a sense of realpolitik that was to result in many interesting stories. It was in this season that the first questions about the nature of revolution started creeping in, with Gan killed in a futile assault, and Travis going on trial as a scapegoat for Servalan's failings. Travis's defence was straight out of Nuremberg, and the political machinations around his escape were intriguing. The two best episodes of *Blake* were near the end of this season. Robert Holmes's 'Gambit' is, on the surface, a simple tale about Avon and Vila using Orac to beat a casino. However, two things elevated it to 50 minutes of astonishing television. First, the script resembled a Jacobean drama which cast good lines all around within the tightest of plots. Servalan played a game of tricks against the owner of the casino, and they charmed each other at the same time. The whole thing was a joy to watch.

The second vital element was the design. The staff and customers of the casino, the Big Wheel, were clad in a muddle of styles ranging forward from the Regency era, and Servalan was in red, out of white for the first time. Since *Blake*'s effects were so limited - largely due to the instantaneous nature of its creation, the first season also borrowing *Softly Softly*'s frugal budget - David Maloney had made an early decision to concentrate on character and script rather than try and match *Star Wars*' technology. However, the series had always had an economical but interesting visual tone, the designers, as in 'Gambit', often juxtaposing ancient styles to good effect. They made a virtue of the fact that the location filming for the series was limited to English quarries and woodlands, with the vintage car in 'Bounty' and the stately home in 'Rumours of Death' lending a strange aura of future shock to the series.

At the end of the second season came 'Star One', the height of the series, after which it would never be the same. Blake was about to launch an attack on the Federation's secret control centre, Star One. Typically, there was an argument amongst the crew, Avon, aware of the mass destruction that the raid will cause, telling Blake that he can 'wade in blood' if he likes, but that he wants out. As Chris Boucher said, 'the line between the freedom fighter and the terrorist is a fairly thin one'. As Blake goes ahead with the attack, Avon finally killing Travis, the crew discover that beyond Star One is an alien fleet, about to attack the Federation. Paradoxically, they find themselves fighting to defend the organization they sought to destroy. Injured, Blake wanders off the flight deck, telling Avon that he had always trusted him.

He was not to be seen again for a very long time. As Terry Wogan, an avid follower of the series, was fond of asking his radio listeners at the time, 'If it's called *Blake's 7*, why isn't there anybody called Blake in it?' Gareth Thomas left the show, and in his place were two new characters, the dashing Tarrant, a space captain who seemed to get most of Blake's lines, and Dayna, a weapons expert. With the defeat of the aliens and the collapse of the Federation, the crew were wandering a substantially less Fascist universe, one in which more traditional science-fiction adventures took place.

There was also a problem with the balance of the crew, Avon being clearly more in command than Tarrant, but still relegated to making quips from the sidelines. Some good episodes, however, stand out in this period. Science-fiction writer Tanith

Lee's 'Sarcophagus' saw Cally, the most under-used alien in telefantasy, finally getting to do something interesting. Boucher's 'City at the Edge of the World' (a Vila love story) and 'Rumours of Death' (where Avon tracked down the man who he thought had killed his lover) are also prime examples of good *Blake*. However, without a central theme, the crew seemed to have lost their way. When stranded on the planet Terminal, the *Liberator* having been destroyed by an organic parasite, the prospect of finding Blake exposed as a drug-induced mirage, it all seemed over for them.

And in a way, it was. The fourth season was to be very different from its predecessors, with an even lower budget. The move down-market was seemingly made quite consciously, the complex political intrigues of previous seasons giving way to adolescent power games. Paul Darrow's performance, in what seemed like resignation, turned into pure ham, Avon becoming a manic, power-mad anti-hero. A new character, Soolin, a gunfighter, proved to have virtually no character whatsoever. All in all, the show had quickly become what its critics had always accused it of being, a tacky space opera. Servalan, now in black (of course!) and going by the name of Sleer, would each week engage Avon in a contest to see who could go further over the top. The seven were now flying *Scorpio*, a dirty old freighter, and had only two different costumes each (a huge comedown from the clever design of the first three seasons).

However, two good points presented themselves: Tanith Lee's 'Sand', which was much deeper than the episodes around it, Servalan and Tarrant discussing their relationship while marooned together, and Robert Holmes's 'Orbit'. In this episode Avon found himself having to make a choice between death or killing Vila, a man who had been his foil and his friend. Although the bond between the two was the only throwback to previous seasons, Avon's decision surprised no one, and Keating put in a grand performance, curling up and sobbing as Avon hunted him down. The scene was almost a criticism of what the series had become - brutal and childish.

The final story, 'Blake', was another Boucher script. Avon locates Blake, who has become a bounty hunter with, as always, an unfeasible plan to destroy the Federation. The two men confront each other, and, misunderstanding or paranoid, Avon kills Blake. The skull-helmeted Federation guards move in, and the others are shot down in slow motion. Finally, only Avon stands, a smile on his face, for the end credits.

Ten million people tuned in for the death of Blake, a huge number considering the fact that the show was scheduled against ***Coronation Street***. There were protests, of course, on *Points of View*, that evil had defeated good, and a legendary letter-writing campaign that made *Blake* fans a major source of BBC irritation for years to come. There is a theory abroad that the series was too expensive, that the BBC's commitment to telefantasy was waning, and so the last season was deliberately lacklustre. Certainly, for a series that was once a showcase of commitment and intelligence, the final seasons were a sad parody.

Blake's death was a mercy killing.

First season *(2 Jan–27 Mar 78)*	**Second season** *(9 Jan–3 Apr 79)*	**Third season** *(7 Jan–31 Mar 80)*	**Fourth season** *(28 Sep–21 Dec 81)*
1 The Way Back	14 Redemption	27 Aftermath	40 Rescue
2 Space Fall	15 Shadow	28 Powerplay	41 Power
3 Cygnus Alpha	16 Weapon	29 Volcano	42 Traitor
4 Time Squad	17 Horizon	30 Dawn of the Gods	43 Stardrive
5 The Web	18 Pressure Point	31 The Harvest of Kairos	44 Animals
6 Seek – Locate – Destroy	19 Trial	32 City at the Edge of the World	45 Headhunter
7 Mission to Destiny	20 Killer	33 Children of Auron	46 Assassin
8 Duel	21 Hostage	34 Rumours of Death	47 Games
9 Project Avalon	22 Countdown	35 Sarcophagus	48 Sand
10 Breakdown	23 Voice from the Past	36 Ultraworld	49 Gold
11 Bounty	24 Gambit	37 Moloch	50 Orbit
12 Deliverance	25 The Keeper	38 Death-Watch	51 Warlord
13 Orac	26 Star One	39 Terminal	52 Blake

The Singing Detective

- **BBC Television** (BBC1) ◆ **Colour**
- **6 episodes** (60-80 minutes) ◆ **1986**
- **Writer:** Dennis Potter
- **Director:** Jon Amiel
- **Producers:** John Harris, Kenith Trodd

The Singing Detective is perhaps the greatest dramatic serial television has so far produced. One of the joys of this stunning drama is the difficulty the reviewer faces in pinning it down. To argue for the series' place in any one chapter in this book is tremendously difficult as, from the outset, Potter wanted to blur genres and cross borders. 'When I was working at MGM in Hollywood,' he explained, 'I realized that the studio based all narrative forms entirely upon category. At the beginning of a project they would ask what particular bag it was in. Was it a detective story? Was it a musical? Was it a romance? They saw it as a marketing problem, even before the first shot. That sort of thing throws a terrible carapace over the writer, and one of the things I wanted to do in *The Singing Detective* is break up the narrative tyranny.'

Potter began *The Singing Detective* as a response to what he saw as the death of the studio TV play, writing some scenes set in a hospital ward. The ensuing events grew out of that, but it is there that the story begins.

Philip Marlow, writer of trashy thrillers (his mother 'should have called me Christopher - I'd have written better'), is in Sherpa Tensing Ward (complete with a doctor named Finlay), suffering from psoriasis, a skin complaint that makes his temperature soar deliriously. He tries to cope with the treatment and Nurse Mills's administration of soothing cream ('Think boring! Think boring!'), but becomes increasingly paranoid that his ex-wife Nicola is scheming with her lover (Finney) to steal the film rights to the pulp thriller, *The Singing Detective*, that he wrote some time ago. His psychotherapist insists that the book is full of clues as to what is happening ('Doctors think like detectives. They always believe that they can come up with an answer or a cure.'), but Marlow slips further into his dreams and nightmares. He remembers his childhood - wasn't there a boy called Mark Finney? - and imagines events from the novel, with himself as the Singing Detective, Nurse Mills as nightclub singer Carlotta, and Binney as some sort of thug in the background. Two mysterious men haunt the action, and a woman's naked body is fished out of the Thames - she looks like his mother.

The levels of the script are astonishingly broad. Marlow, at times, seems to be writing the dialogue for all around him (Nicola and Finney add the punctuation verbally into their conspiratorial meetings). The boundaries of television naturalism are taken to an extreme - if not crossed completely - when the 'mysterious men' appear in the hospital and complain that Marlow hasn't even bothered to give them names. In another scene, Marlow and Dr Gibbon play a word game that stretches over five agonizingly intense minutes.

Starring: Michael Gambon (Philip Marlow) • Patrick Malahide (Raymond Binney/Mark Binney/Finney) • Joanne Whalley (Nurse Mills/Carlotta) • Bill Paterson (Dr Gibbon) • Lyndon Davies (Philip Marlow, aged ten) • Janet Suzman (Nicola) • Alison Steadman (Mrs Marlow/Lili) • Jim Carter (Mr Marlow) • Janet Henfrey (schoolteacher/scarecrow) • William Speakman (Mark Binney, aged ten) • Imelda Staunton (Staff Nurse White)

The Singing Detective knows that you always hurt the one you love

In trying to describe his uncategorizable serial, Potter claimed that it was basically about a man 'trying to deal with a situation which becomes increasingly hard to handle'. Potter succeeded in crafting a serial that, true to his word, mixed the detective story with the musical and the love story. It's a detective story of the mind, as fact and fiction blur (Is there really a plot against him? Was there really a Binney in the past?). It's a musical of dreaming surrealism where, as in Potter's *Pennies from Heaven*, the popular music of the 30s and 40s undercuts and comments on the action, with the ward round degenerating into a frantic performance of 'Dem Bones'. Even the old man, shaking in the bed next to Marlow, seems to join in. It's a romance of the heart, in the sense that the triumphant psychological finale (using 'We'll Meet Again', which would otherwise seem loaded with all the most obvious and boring connotations) sees Marlow emerging a stronger man than before, ready to walk down those mean streets.

Marlow not only shares aspects of the author's Forest of Dean childhood, but suffers from the same disease as Potter. But the intention was never to assault the viewer with feelings of anguish and rage. 'I've taken many different drugs, and they've been a help,' Dennis Potter commented. 'But their effectiveness has a limited span. After a while they cease to work and I know that for six weeks every year I'll be completely out of action. I used to believe my illness was a symptom of internal rage and disgust. But I no longer think that's true. It's just how the cards fall and the only consolation is that my place at the table may give me a view that is denied to the bloke who's collecting all the kings and aces.' Potter's own words reflect the resolution of the drama.

The sequences seen through the eyes of the young Marlow - first seen high atop a tree, the monarch of all he surveys - were some of the most impressive of the entire serial. The schoolteacher's relentless pursuit of the child who did the 'dirty deed' on her desk and - especially - the infamous 'bonking in the wood' scene drew much criticism. A selection of quotes from the letters page of the *Radio Times* captures the tone of rabid outrage at the series as a whole: 'Messy, fidgety, sadistic, semi-pornographic ... Absolute filth ... The scene in the woods ... appeared at 9.30 p.m. when many children and young people are still up and watching television. It would most certainly have been very distressing for elderly people ... ' And so on. Some even criticized Gambon's make-up.

(16 Nov–21 Dec 86)

1 Skin
2 Heat
3 Lovely Days
4 Clues
5 Pitter Patter
6 Who Done It

Mary Whitehouse's vile personal attack on Potter's mother proved that she did not comprehend the nature of fiction. Dennis Potter was honest enough to note that 'Everything that happens to a writer is bound to crop up in his work sooner or later... But although associations abound, the facts are not autobiographical at all.'

It's difficult to know how to respond to such indignation: pointing to *The Times*'s summation of the series as a work of genius would have no meaning for those too blind to see beyond their prejudices. However, when asked about the 'bad language', Potter pointed out that several expletives were removed, and stated that 'I don't actually mind censorship. I'm not in favour of total freedom of language that's made up of rhetorical four-letter words.'

Many would be surprised at such signs of constraint, but that's why Potter was such a great writer. The final irony, of course, is that *The Singing Detective* was passed over in favour of *The Life and Loves of a She Devil* when it came to the BAFTAs.

We think history will judge things a little differently.

By the time that Independent Television became a reality in September 1955, the BBC had already established the viability of telefantasy with the first two ***Quatermass*** serials. It was therefore unsurprising that the second channel's associated companies would continue the trend. While the early years of ITV are remembered for ITC's pioneering action series like *The Adventures of Robin Hood*, it should also be noted that two of the earliest productions by the fledgling ATV were the children's science-fiction series *The Strange World of Planet X* and the distinctly adult-flavoured *The Trollenberg Terror*.

This latter series, closely modelled on *The Thing from Another World*, was created by Peter Kay and produced and directed by Quentin Lawrence. Similar in its chilling nature to ***The Quatermass Experiment***, *The Trollenberg Terror*, like Nigel Kneale's series, was later adapted as a less successful film.

H.G. Wells' Invisible Man came from ATV in 1958. Although the series, produced by Ralph Smart, bore little relation to Wells's novel, it was enormously popular. Twenty-six episodes were made (several written by the likes of Ian Stuart Black and Brian Clemens), and the serial concerned a scientist, Peter Brady, who was rendered invisible when an experiment into optical density misfired. The gimmick of the series was that the identity of the actor who usually provided the voice for Brady wasn't disclosed at the time, although it later became common knowledge that the actor involved was Tim Turner. Lisa Daniely played Brady's sister, Deborah Watling his niece and Zena Marshall his girlfriend, whilst other actors involved in the series included Honor Blackman, Patrick Troughton, Anton Diffring, Barry Letts and Geoffrey Keen. The company also produced the 1958 serial *Time is the Enemy*.

ABC had recently acquired the creative flair of Canadian Sydney Newman. Newman's drama policy at ABC would produce *Armchair Theatre*, *Police Surgeon*, ***The Avengers*** and the ground-breaking children's series *Target Luna*. This was an adventure serial which began in April 1960, created and written by Malcolm Hulke and Eric Paice. By modern standards, the series was coy (three children spending their Easter hols at their father's secret rocket base); nevertheless, it was to have a direct effect on the genre, being the most quoted influence on the creation of *Doctor Who* (Hulke would later become one of the BBC series' most important writers). Such was the success of *Target Luna*, which starred David Markham, Frank Finlay, John Cairney and Annette Kerr, that three sequels were made, *Pathfinders in Space* and *Pathfinders to Mars* in 1960, and *Pathfinders to Venus* (1961), starring Peter Williams and Gerald Flood.

As with the BBC, occasional science fiction plays would be tried out on the network's drama anthology series. ATV's *Play of the Week*, in 1960, saw an interesting adaptation of John Lymington's *The Night of the Big Heat* featuring Bernard Cribbins, although the most successful one-off presentation of this kind, John Wyndham's *Dumb Martian* shown in *Armchair Theatre* in 1962, with a cast that included William Lucas, Ray Barrett and Hilda Schroder, was used as a taster for the company's *Out of This World* which began a week later. Other science-fiction plays tried out on *Armchair Theatre* include *I Can Destroy the Sun*, *The Others*, *Loop*, *The Invasion*, and the memorable 1958 production of *The Greatest Man in the World*.

ITC, later to become one of the most prolific and diverse producers of genre material, seemed to stumble across telefantasy by accident when it employed Gerry Anderson in 1961. Anderson had already been making puppet series for a variety of ITV companies for over four years, and when his proposal for a science-fiction series was rejected by Granada, he approached the film branch of Lew Grade's ATV and made *Supercar*, the first of his imaginative and influential projects.

While ITC initially held a monopoly on puppet-telefantasy, Associated Rediffusion was busy cornering the market in that other great 60s innovation, the telefantasy anthology. During 1961 they created one and contributed to another, giving the company the lead over the BBC's *Out of the Unknown* by some three years. Associated Rediffusion began contributing episodes to the American series *Allcoa Presents* (known as *One Step Beyond* in syndication) in its third and final season. The casts were mainly British, featuring Peter Wyngarde, Kenneth Cope, Andre Morell and Donald Pleasence.

However, it was *Tales of Mystery* that set the tone for much of what was to follow. Classic ghost stories by Algernon Blackwood were adapted by writers as varied as Giles Cooper and Philip Broadley and produced by Peter Graham Scott. Actor John Laurie introduced each of the episodes in the role of Blackwood, setting the scene for each of the twist-in-the-tale stories. Two further seasons were made before the series ended in 1963.

Although ABC's first venture into the territory, the Leonard White-produced *Out of This World* in 1962, had more in common with the later BBC series of this type (containing mainly adaptations of classic science fiction like Rog Phillips's 'The Yellow Pill'), the series was given the 'feel' of *Tales of Mystery* by having each episode introduced by Boris Karloff. Writers included Clive Exton, Leon Griffiths and Terry Nation (whose story *Botany Bay* was one of the few original screenplays *Out of This World* used).

ABC anticipated the BBC horror anthologies of the late 60s with *Mystery and Imagination*, which began in January 1966. Initially conceived as a 19th-century gothic, produced by Jonathan Alwyn and script-edited by Terence Feely, it included adaptations of Poe's *The Fall of the House of Usher* (with Susannah York) and Oscar Wilde's *The Canterville Ghost* (with Bruce Forsyth). Further episodes included appearances by Robert Hardy and Edward Woodward, and a memorable adaptation of M.R. James's *The Casting of the Runes*, starring Gordon Jackson. The concept went to Thames when it took over the ABC franchise in 1968. It featured adaptations of *Frankenstein*, starring Ian Holm and Richard Vernon, and *Dracula*, with Denholm Elliott, and was transmitted under the title *Playhouse: Mystery and Imagination*. A fifth season was produced in 1970, including an astonishing version of *Sweeney Todd* starring Freddie Jones and Russell Hunter.

Other ABC series of interest made during the early 60s included *Dimensions of Fear*, written by John Lucarotti in 1963, and Robert Banks Stewart's

Undermind, with Jeremy Wilkin, Rosemary Nicols, Jeremy Kemp, Denis Quilley, Peter Barkworth and George Baker, in 1965. A strange, gripping socio-political thriller with science-fiction overtones, *Undermind* featured scripts by David Whitaker and Robert Holmes. Granada's main drama-telefantasy offering of the era was Giles Cooper's psychological chiller *The Other Man*, a lavish play directed by Gordon Flemyng and starring Michael Caine, Sian Phillips and John Thaw, set on an alternative world in which Britain had sued for peace with Germany in 1941 and become a Nazi satellite. It was described by *The Times* as 'a major television event'.

Another strange entry into the genre was Edward Boyd's *The Corridor People*, a Granada series described by its producer Richard Everitt as 'an eccentric surrealist thriller', which is as apt a description as anything for this provocative and stylized series. Featuring one of the most disturbingly sexual performances of the 60s by Elisabeth Shepherd as the main villainess Syrie Van Epp, and further bizarre characters such as Gary Cockrell's Bogart-worshipping private detective, Alan Curtis as Inspector Blood and William Maxwell as Sergeant Hound, *The Corridor People* was the *Twin Peaks* of its day. Granada also produced Alan Garner's *The Owl Service*, a fine children's serial about mystical forces in the Welsh countryside. The series starred Edwin Richfield, Gillian Hills and Michael Holden.

Southern Television's adaptation of T.H. White's *The Master* was screened in early 1966, scripted by Rosemary Hill and starring Olaf Pooley and John Laurie. The company also created the long running *Freewheelers* in 1968, which spanned over five years and 104 episodes. Created and produced by Chris McMasters as a James Bond-type adventure series for older children, it featured an ever-changing trio of teenagers used by the laconic Colonel Buchan (Ronald Leigh-Hunt) to defeat evil villains, often the neo-Nazi von Gells (Geoffrey Toone). The kids in the first season were played by Tom Owen, Gregory Phillips and Mary Maude, whilst later years would feature Chris Chittell, Adrian Wright and Wendy Padbury.

The Champions, which began in the autumn of 1968, saw the teaming-up of two of the great names of the 60s ITC film-series, Monty Berman (producer of *The Baron*) and Dennis Spooner (co-creator of *Man in a Suitcase*). The pair would later produce ***Randall and Hopkirk (Deceased)***, ***Department S***, ***Jason King*** and *The Adventurer*. *The Champions* concerned a trio of agents (William Gaunt, Alexandra Bastedo and Stuart Damon) working for NEMESIS, who gain super-human powers after a plane crash in Tibet where they are rescued by a mysterious lost tribe, unbeknown to their boss Tremayne (Anthony Nicholls). The series was produced by Berman and written by many of the giants of the ITC film-series, including Donald James, Brian Clemens, Tony Williamson, Terry Nation, Philip Broadley and Dennis Spooner himself.

Some of the episodes, notably Clemens's tense 'Happening' (where Gaunt is stranded in the Australian outback suffering from amnesia with maverick Jack McGowan and assassin Michael Gough), Ralph Smart's 'To Trap a Rat' (an uncharacteristic look at the seamier side of 'Swinging London') and Spooner's 'The Interrogation' (an episode told mainly in flashback), are extremely good. Amongst the directors working on *The Champions* were Hammer regulars Freddie Francis, Roy Ward Baker and John Gilling, as well as ITC stalwart Cyril Frankel. Stephen Berkoff, Gerald Harper, Mike Pratt, John Woodvine, Donald Sutherland, Jeremy Brett, Gabrielle Drake, and Paul Eddington all appeared in the series, which remains a popular repeat item to this day.

Long before 1980's *Hammer House of Horror*, the film company had tried its hand at television, starting in the 50s with the pilot *Tales of Frankenstein*, then crafting its own supernatural anthology. *Journey to the Unknown* was a co-production with Twentieth Century Fox, produced by Anthony Hinds and Joan Harrison. Although shoddily treated by the ITV networks, the series proved to be a memorable one, especially its chilling deserted fairground opening sequence. *Psycho* author Robert Bloch wrote two episodes (*Girl of My Dreams* and *The Indian Spirit Guide*), while possibly the best episode was Michael J. Bird's chilling *Somewhere in a Crowd* (in which a TV commentator is disturbed by the recurring appearances of several faces in the crowd at major disasters). The series featured directors such as Michael Lindsay-Hogg, Peter Sasdy and Alan Gibson, and casts which were normally topped by an American star (David Hedison, Stephanie Powers, Joseph Cotton, Roddy McDowell or Barbara Bel Geddes) backed by strong support from British actors including Milo O'Shea, Dennis Waterman, Jane Asher, Edward Fox, Tom Adams and Michael Gough.

After a long and convoluted genesis, *Hammer House of Horror* proved to be a strange hybrid of old-style gothic and a more modern, graphic horror. The most obviously Hammer-like segment - Murray Smith's *Children of the Full Moon* - was one of the poorer episodes. A couple are forced to stay at a huge country house, dominated by the formidable presence of Mrs Ardoy (Diana Dors). A werewolf is seen at their window, and Sarah develops a taste for raw meat, while Tom comes to a sticky end under the axe of a suitably hairy woodcutter. Other obvious themes included witchcraft (*Witching Time*), cannibalism (*The Thirteenth Reunion*, where a sinister health farm is the backdrop to a group of air crash survivors who pander to their newfound taste for human flesh), and voodoo (*Charlie Boy*). Some tales were more unusual. *The Silent Scream* featured Peter Cushing as a concentration camp survivor and pet shop owner. The basement of his shop houses exotic animals, although, in an interesting update of Pavlov's experiments with dogs, the cages are replaced with cunningly-used electric force fields. The experiment is swiftly applied to human beings. In *Rude Awakening*, the central character (Denholm Elliott) has decided to murder his wife and marry his secretary (Lucy Gutteridge), but is plagued by on-going nightmares, each involving him coming to a grisly end. One of the most interesting and certainly most bizarre scripts was Don Shaw's *The Mark of Satan*, which closed the season, involving a strange disease 'cured' by drilling a hole in the head, and a mortuary attendant obsessed with numerology and the sounds of the police radio that he can hear when he looks towards the church weather vane.

Hammer House of Horror was reasonably popular, and the shocks it prompted are well remembered by many. The same cannot be said of the follow-up series, 1984's *Hammer House of Mystery and Suspense*. As with *Journey to the Unknown*, American backing (20th Century Fox) dictated at least one prominent American actor in every episode, and, like Hammer's first series, *Hammer House of Mystery and Suspense* was massacred by the schedulers. The horror element, as the title suggests, had been toned down, and yet the series was still shown late at night. The small, persistent audience, however, would be rewarded with a series every bit as interesting as *Hammer House of Horror*, although equally as variable (*Child's Play* has a family trapped in their home, which turns out - in an unbelievable twist-ending - to be a futuristic doll's house). In the neo-vampiric *The Late Nancy Irving* a famous female golfer, dependent on insulin injections, finds herself in a sinister country hospital. *Black Carrion* was an outrageously over-the-top Don Houghton story of a village from the 60s which had, effectively, disappeared along with its most famous occupants, a pair of now-forgotten rock and roll star brothers. Another fine episode was Dennis Spooner's *And the Walls Came Tumbling Down*, an old-style Hammer tale concerning the history of witchcraft surrounding an old church due for demolition, with a story that covered three centuries.

The 'Golden Age' of children's telefantasy began with the dawning of the 70s. Colour, and several companies devoting a large proportion of their budget to imaginative series, combined to produce a three-year period in the early 70s when LWT made *Jamie*, *Catweazle* and *The Guardians*, Thames created *Ace of Wands* and ***The Tomorrow People*** and ATV produced *Timeslip* and *Escape into Night*.

Catweazle, created by Richard Carpenter, concerned an eccentric 10th-century alchemist (Geoffrey Bayldon), transported into the 70s where he was befriended by a young boy (Robin Davies). Delightfully camp and silly, it ran for two seasons, and also starred Peter Butterworth. In 1971 it won the Writers Guild award for the Best Children's Drama Script. Both *Timeslip* and *Escape into Night* were the creations of Ruth Boswell, later a producer on ***The Tomorrow People*** and one of the most intelligent writers of children's television. *Timeslip*, co-created with her husband, James, was an ambitious look at the complexities of time travel, focusing on two teenagers, played by Spencer Banks and Cheryl Burfield. The series, produced by John Cooper, was in the form of four serials, 'The Wrong End of Time', 'The Time of the Ice Box' and 'The Year of the Burn Up', all by Bruce Stewart, and 'The Day of the Clone' by Victor Pemberton. The series also starred Denis Quilley and John Barron, with the first and eighth episodes introduced by ITN's science correspondent, Peter Fairley, which shows the kind of audience at which *Timeslip* was aimed. Although several of the later episodes were only recorded in black and white because of an ITV dispute, *Timeslip* remains a much-loved series.

Escape into Night was adapted by Boswell from Catherine Storr's novel *Marianne Dreams*, produced by Richard Bramwell, and starred Vikki Chambers as a young girl whose dreams involve a house (which she has drawn whilst awake) surrounded by monsters.

Trevor Preston's *Ace of Wands* was the story of Tarot, a brilliant magician and escapologist who spent most of his spare time solving mysteries and crimes (the more bizarre, the better). The title role was played by Michael MacKenzie, and the show also featured Tony Selby, Judy Loe and Donald Layne-Smith as his assistants. The first season, in 1970, had stories by Preston, William Emms and Don Houghton, and included outrageous supervillains (Hildegard Neil and Christopher Benjamin) and minor roles for the likes of Tim Curry and David Prowse. The show, produced by Pamela Lonsdale, proved to be one of the most popular in its slot that ITV had ever had. The second season began with Preston's 'Seven Serpents, Sulphur and Salt', which created one of the most memorable characters in children's television - Russell Hunter's Mr Stabs. The series' magical content was supervised by Ali Bongo. In 1972 both Selby and Loe were replaced by Roy Holder and Petra Markham.

Sadly, with a change of regime at Thames, the series was dropped soon afterwards, in favour of the longer-running but less imaginative ***Tomorrow People***. *Ace of Wands* did have spin-offs, however. Pamela Lonsdale's later series *Shadows* featured a Preston story entitled *Dutch Schlitz's Shoes* in which Russell Hunter reprised his Mr Stabs role, whilst in 1984 the character of Stabs was again revived by Preston for a one-off *Dramarama* episode which featured David Jason in the title role. This was also the era of such interesting serials as LWT's *The Adventures of Don Quick* (starring Ian Hendry), HTV's *The Clifton House Mystery*, Anglia's pseudo-documentary *Alternative 3*, and Thames's stunning one-off play *The Reaper*.

Thereafter, despite the success of ***The Tomorrow People***, most ITV companies seemed reluctant to make children's telefantasy. ABC's beautiful adaptation of *The Lion, The Witch and the Wardrobe* and series like Granada's *The Ghosts of Motley Hall* were notable exceptions. So too, were the productions of HTV, the Bristol-based region, who became brand leaders in the field, Leonard White producing first Bob Baker and Dave Martin's *Sky* (starring Marc Harrison) in 1975, then *The Georgian House* (with Adrienne Byrne and Spencer Banks) in 1976, and *King of the Castle* (Fulton Mackay, Milton Johns and Talfryn Thomas) in 1977. Patrick Dromgoole, the co-producer of these two series, was also involved, with Peter Graham Scott, in Jeremy Burnham and Trevor Ray's chilling *Children of the Stones* (filmed in Avebury, with Iain Cuthbertson and Gareth Thomas). Bob Baker's *Into the Labyrinth* (1981), starring Ron Moody and Pamela Salem, came from the same stable.

Despite the arrival of Nigel Kneale at ATV in 1976, to produce the excellent *Beasts*, the company's traditional support of telefantasy seemed to have dried up. After commissioning (and then bludgeoning) ***Sapphire & Steel*** and the imaginative children's series *Raven* (starring Phil Daniels and Shirley Cheriton) in 1977, ATV, the home of ***The Avengers*** and independent telefantasy, quietly forgot about science fiction and horror altogether.

This trend in the late 70s is perhaps best exemplified by the fate of *Star Maidens*, an (admittedly pretty awful) Anglo-German film series, created by Eric Paice, produced by James Gatward, and starring Judy Geeson and Gareth Thomas. The series, much of which was written by Ian Stuart Black, was directed by Freddie Francis. Most ITV regions showed the first few episodes then ditched the series, some didn't even bother to take it at all.

The early 80s saw ITV's telefantasy output reach its nadir, with only occasional science-fiction comedy series, such as Nigel Kneale's *Kinvig* and Graeme Garden and Bill Oddie's *Astronauts*, cropping up in the schedules. ATV's successor, Central, did produce Michael Dolenz's imaginative *Luna* (starring Patsy Kensit in one season) in 1983, but the only real development took place at Granada.

As early as 1974 Granada had seen the potential of supernatural drama, broadcasting two plays under the title *Haunted* that Christmas, both produced by Derek Granger. The Michael Apted-directed *Poor Girl* (starring Lynne Miller and Angela Thorne) was good but Julian Bond's adaptation of Kingsley Amis's *The Ferryman*, starring Jeremy Brett and Lesley Duncan, was a classic which gained huge viewing figures. In 1983, Granada did it again, June Wyndham-Davies producing *Shades of Darkness*, a series of supernatural plays. Included amongst these was Alan Plater's terrifying adaptation of L. P. Hartley's modern vampire play *Feet Foremost*, starring Jeremy Kemp and Carol Royle.

Thames, however, soldiered on with its policy of intelligent children's science fiction, Pamela Lonsdale producing Anthony Read's adaptation of John Wyndham's *Chocky* in 1984. Later came *The Gemini Factor*, *The Snow Spider*, and the dreadful *Time Riders* (starring Haydn Gwynne). HTV co-produced ***Robin of Sherwood***, whilst TVS also returned to its imaginative past with Richard Cooper's impressive and under-rated *Knights of God* in 1987, an epic serial of science fiction religious mania and Arthurian legend starring John Woodvine, Gareth Thomas, Don Henderson, Patrick Troughton, Nigel Stock and Anne Stallybrass alongside the young stars George Winter and Claire Parker. ATV's 1981 serial *Echoes of Louisa* was also worthy of praise.

In 1988 both Central and Granada tried to bring life back into the 'high drama' end of telefantasy with *The One Game* (starring Patrick Malahide) and *Wipe Out* (with Ian McElhinney) respectively. Both were tense and spooky, though *Wipe Out* featured a common fault amongst much telefantasy of the 80s in that it was about two episodes too long. *The One Game*, on the other hand, seemed to suddenly come to a halt rather than reach any sort of ending. Granada also produced *How To Be Cool* (1988), starring Roger Daltrey and Daniel Peacock which made much use of 60s/***Prisoner*** iconography in a story of a secret government department (the wonderfully named 'National Cool Board') which dictates fashion trends. Channel 4, too, was active in encouraging science-fiction development, as shown by the surreal *Max Headroom* (1987), *A Very British Coup* (1988), *Snakes and Ladders* (1989), *Centrepoint* (1990), the brilliant *Short and Curlies* play *Arcadia* (1990), the European co-production *Mission Eureka* (1991) and its 1995 sequel *The Sahara Project*, and U2's 1992 exercise in 'synthetic reality', the cyberpunk fantasy *Zoo TV*.

Even more than the BBC, ITV's future commitment to telefantasy remains uncertain, although 1991 was an encouraging year, with the Zenith/Anglia co-production of Steve Gallagher's *Chimera*, an extraordinary tale of genetic engineering that starred John Lynch, Christine Kavanagh, Kenneth Cranham and David Calder. 1995's anthology *Chiller*, which also featured the work of Gallagher, is a good reminder that the independent companies haven't lost the plot completely.

Gerry Anderson

The Adventures of Twizzle

- **APF/Associated Rediffusion** (ITV) ◆ B&W
- **52 episodes** (15 minutes) ◆ 1957-59
- **Creator/writer:** Roberta Leigh
- **Director:** Gerry Anderson

Torchy, The Battery Boy

- **Pelham Films/APF/ABC** (ITV) ◆ B&W
- **26 episodes** (15 minutes) ◆ 1959
- **Creator/writer:** Roberta Leigh
- **Director:** Gerry Anderson

Four Feather Falls

- **APF/Granada** (ITV) ◆ B&W
- **39 episodes** (15 minutes) ◆ 25 Feb–17 Nov 1960
- **Writers:** Barry Gray, Phil Wrestler, Jill Allgood, Mary Cathcart Bower
- **Producer:** Gerry Anderson
- **Directors include:** Gerry Anderson, David Elliot, Alan Pattillo

Voices: Nicholas Parsons • Kenneth Connor • David Graham • Denise Bryer

Supercar

- **APF/ATV/ITC** (ITV) ◆ B&W
- **39 episodes** (30 minutes) ◆ 1961-62
- **Writers:** Gerry Anderson, Sylvia Anderson, Hugh Woodhouse, Martin Woodhouse
- **Directors include:** David Elliot, Alan Pattillo, Desmond Saunders, Bill Harris
- **Producer:** Gerry Anderson

Voices: Graydon Gould • George Murcell • Sylvia Anderson • David Graham • Cyril Shaps

SUPERCAR
First season
(28 Jan–6 Aug 61)
1 Rescue
2 False Alarm
3 Talisman of Sargon
4 What Goes Up
5 Amazonian Adventure
6 Grounded
7 Keep it Cool
8 Jungle Hazard
9 High Tension
10 Island Incident
11 Ice-Fall
12 Phantom Piper
13 Pirate Plunder
14 A Little Art
15 Flight of Fancy
16 Deep Seven
17 Hostage
18 The Sunken Temple
19 The Lost City
20 Trapped in the Depths
21 Dragon of Ho Meng
22 Magic Carpet
23 Supercar Take One
24 Crash Landing
25 The Tracking of Masterspy
26 The White Line

Second season
(4 Feb–29 Apr 62)
27 The Runaway Train
28 Precious Cargo
29 Operation Superstork
30 Hi-Jack
31 Calling Charlie Queen
32 Space for Mitch
33 Atomic Witch Hunt
34 70-B-Low
35 The Sky's the Limit
36 Jail Break
37 The Day That Time Stood Still
38 Transatlantic Cable
39 King Kool

Fireball XL5

- **APF/ATV/ITC** (ITV) ◆ **B&W**
- **39 episodes** (30 minutes) ◆ **1962-63**
- **Writers:** Gerry Anderson, Sylvia Anderson, Alan Fennell, Anthony Marriott, Dennis Spooner
- **Directors:** Bill Harris, Alan Pattillo, Gerry Anderson, John Kelly, David Elliot
- **Producer:** Gerry Anderson
- **Associate producer:** Reg Hill

Voices: Paul Maxwell • David Graham • Sylvia Anderson • John Bluthal • Gerry Anderson (uncredited)

FIREBALL XL5
(28 Oct 62–23 Jun 63, 6–27 Oct 63)
1 Planet 46
2 The Doomed Planet
3 Space Immigrants
4 Plant Man from Space
5 Spy in Space
6 The Sun Temple
7 XL5 to H_2O
8 Space Pirates
9 Flying Zodiac
10 Space Pen
11 Space Monster
12 The Last of the Zanadus
13 Planet of Platonia
14 The Triads
15 Wings of Danger
16 Convict in Space
17 Space Vacation
18 Flight to Danger
19 Prisoner on the Lost Planet
20 The Forbidden Planet
21 Robert to the Rescue
22 Dangerous Cargo
23 Mystery of the TA2
24 Drama at Space City
25 1875
26 The Granatoid Tanks
27 The Robert Freighter Mystery
28 Whistle for Danger
29 Trial by Robot
30 A Day in the Life of a Space General
31 Invasion Earth
32 Faster than Light
33 The Day the Earth Froze
34 The Fire Fighters
35 Space City Special
36 Ghosts of Space
37 Hypnotic Sphere
38 Sabotage
39 Space Magnet

Stingray

- **APF/ATV/ITC** (ITV) ◆ **Colour**
- **39 episodes** (30 minutes) ◆ **1964-65**
- **Writers:** Gerry Anderson, Sylvia Anderson, Dennis Spooner, Alan Fennell
- **Directors include:** Alan Pattillo, David Elliott, John Kelly
- **Producer:** Gerry Anderson
- **Associate producer:** Reg Hill

Voices: Don Mason • Robert Easton • Lois Maxwell • Ray Barrett • David Graham

Most of Anderson's series for ITV were not networked. The episode listings derive from ATV (London) (*Supercar, Fireball XL5, Stingray, Thunderbirds*) and ATV (Midlands)

STINGRAY
(4 Oct 64–27 Jun 65)
1 [untitled]
2 Emergency Marineville
3 The Ghost Ship
4 Subterranean Sea
5 Loch Ness Monster
6 Set Sail for Adventure
7 The Man from the Navy
8 An Echo of Danger
9 Raptures of the Deep
10 Titan Goes Pop
11 In Search of the Tajmanon
12 A Christmas to Remember
13 Tune of Danger
14 The Ghost of the Sea
15 Rescue from the Skies
16 The Lighthouse Dwellers
17 The Big Gun
18 The Cool Caveman
19 Deep Heat
20 Star of the East
21 Invisible Enemy
22 Tom Thumb Tempest
23 Eastern Eclipse
24 Treasure Down Below
25 Stand By for Action
26 Pink Ice
27 The Disappearing Ships
28 Secret of the Giant Oyster
29 The Invaders
30 A Nut for Marineville
31 Trapped in the Depths
32 Count Down
33 Sea of Oil
34 Plant of Doom
35 The Master Plan
36 The Golden Sea
37 Hostages of the Deep
38 Marineville Traitor
39 Aquanaut of the Year

Thunderbirds

- **APF/ATV/ITC** (ITV) ◆ **Colour**
- **32 episodes** (50 minutes) ◆ **1965-66**
- **Writers:** Gerry Anderson, Sylvia Anderson, Alan Fennell, Alan Pattillo, Donald Robertson, Dennis Spooner, Martin Crump, Tony Barwick
- **Directors:** Desmond Saunders, David Lane, David Elliot, Brian Burgess, Alan Pattillo
- **Producers:** Gerry Anderson, Reg Hill, John Read

Voices: Peter Dyneley • Shane Rimmer • David Holliday • Matt Zimmerman • David Graham • Ray Barrett • Sylvia Anderson • Christine Finn • Jeremy Wilkin

THUNDERBIRDS
First season
(2 Oct 65–2 Apr 66)
1 Trapped in the Sky
2 Pit of Peril
3 The Perils of Penelope
4 Terror in New York City
5 Edge of Impact
6 Day of Disaster
7 Thirty Minutes after Noon
8 Desperate Intruder
9 End of the Road
10 The Uninvited
11 Sun Probe
12 Operation Crash-Dive
13 Vault of Death
14 The Mighty Atom
15 City of Fire
16 The Impostors
17 The Man from MI5
18 Cry Wolf
19 Danger at Ocean Deep
20 Move – and You're Dead
21 The Duchess Assignment
22 Brink of Disaster
23 Attack of the Alligators!
24 Martian Invasion
25 The Cham-Cham
26 Security Hazard

Second season
(2–30 Oct 66, 25 Dec 66)
27 Atlantic Inferno
28 Path of Destruction
29 Alias Mr Hackenbacker
30 Lord Parker's 'Oliday
31 Ricochet
32 Give or Take a Million

Captain Scarlet and the Mysterons

- **Century 21/ITC** (ITV) ◆ **Colour**
- **32 episodes** (30 minutes) ◆ **1967-68**
- **Creators:** Gerry and Sylvia Anderson
- **Writers include:** Gerry Anderson, Sylvia Anderson, Tony Barwick, Shane Rimmer, Peter Curran, David Williams, Alan Pattillo
- **Directors:** Desmond Saunders, David Lane, Brian Burgess, Alan Perry, Robert Lynn, Ken Turner, Leo Eaton
- **Producer:** Reg Hill
- **Associate producer:** John Read

Voices: Francis Matthews • Edward Bishop, Donald Gray • Paul Maxwell • Gary Files • Cy Grant • Charles Tingwell • Sylvia Anderson • Liz Morgan • David Healy • Janna Hill • Martin King • Lian-Shin • Jeremy Wilkin

CAPTAIN SCARLET AND THE MYSTERONS
(29 Sep 67–14 May 68)
1 The Mysterons
2 Winged Assassin
3 Big Ben Strikes Again
4 Manhunt
5 Avalanche
6 White as Snow
7 The Trap
8 Operation Time
9 Spectrum Strikes Back
10 Special Assignment
11 The Heart of New York
12 Lunarville 7
13 Point 783
14 Model Spy
15 Seek and Destroy
16 Traitor
17 Renegade Rocket
18 Crater 101
19 Shadow of Fear
20 Dangerous Rendezvous
21 Fire at Rig 15
22 Treble Cross
23 Flight 104
24 Place of Angels
25 Noose of Ice
26 Expo 2068
27 The Launching
28 Codename Europa
29 Inferno
30 Flight to Atlantica
31 Attack on Cloudbase
32 The Inquisition

Joe 90

- **Century 21/ITC** (ITV) ◆ **Colour**
- **30 episodes** (30 minutes) ◆ **1968-69**
- **Creators:** Gerry and Sylvia Anderson
- **Writers include:** Gerry Anderson, Sylvia Anderson, Tony Barwick, Shane Rimmer, Donald James, John Lucarotti
- **Directors include:** Desmond Saunders, Peter Anderson, Leo Eaton, Alan Perry
- **Producer:** David Lane
- **Executive producer:** Reg Hill

Voices: Len Jones • Rupert Davies • David Healy • Keith Alexander • Gary Files • Martin King • Jeremy Wilkin

JOE 90
(29 Sep 68–20 Apr 69)
1 Most Special Agent
2 Most Special Astronaut
3 Project 90
4 Hi-Jacked
5 Colonel McClaine
6 The Fortress
7 King for a Day
8 International Concerto
9 Splashdown
10 The Big Fish
11 Relative Danger
12 Operation McClaine
13 The Unorthodox Shepherd
14 Business Holiday
15 Arctic Adventure
16 Double Agent
17 Three's a Crowd
18 The Professional
19 The Race
20 Talkdown
21 Breakout
22 Child of the Sun God
23 See you down There
24 Lone-Handed 90
25 Attack of the Tiger
26 Viva Cordova
27 Mission X-41
28 Test Flight
29 Trial at Sea
30 The Birthday

The Secret Service

- **Century 21/ITC** (ITV) ◆ **Colour**
- **13 episodes** (30 minutes) ◆ **21 Sep-14 Dec 1969**
- **Creators:** Gerry and Sylvia Anderson
- **Writers:** Gerry Anderson, Sylvia Anderson, Donald James, Tony Barwick, Shane Rimmer, Pat Dunlop, Bob Keston
- **Directors include:** Alan Perry, Leo Eaton
- **Producer:** David Lane
- **Executive producer:** Reg Hill

Starring: Stanley Unwin
Voices: Stanley Unwin • Keith Alexander • Sylvia Anderson • Jeremy Wilkin • Gary Files • David Healy

UFO

- **Century 21/ITC** (ITV) ◆ **Colour**
- **26 episodes** (50 minutes) ◆ **1970-73**
- **Creators:** Gerry and Sylvia Anderson with Reg Hill
- **Writers include:** Gerry Anderson, Sylvia Anderson, Tony Barwick, David Tomblin, Alan Fennell, Donald James, Dennis Spooner, Alan Pattillo, Terence Feely
- **Directors:** Gerry Anderson, David Lane, Ken Turner, Alan Perry, Jeremy Summers, Cyril Frankel, David Tomblin, Ron Appleton
- **Producer:** Reg Hill

Starring: Ed Bishop (Ed Straker) • George Sewell (Alec Freeman) • Michael Billington (Paul Foster) • Wanda Ventham (Virginia Lake) • Vladek Sheybal (Dr Jackson) • Gabrielle Drake (Gay Ellis) • Antonia Ellis (Joan Harrington) • Dolorez Mantez (Nina Barry) • Peter Gordeno (Capt. Carlin) • Harry Baird (Mark Bradley) • Grant Taylor (General Henderson) • Gary Myers (Capt. Waterman)

UFO
(16 Sep 70–15 Mar 73)
1 Identified
2 Exposed
3 The Cat with Ten Lives
4 Conflict
5 A Question of Priorities
6 ESP
7 Kill Straker!
8 Sub-Smash
9 Destruction
10 The Square Triangle
11 Close Up
12 The Psychobombs
13 Survival
14 Mindbender
15 Flight Path
16 The Man who Came Back
17 The Dalotek Affair
18 Timelash
19 Ordeal
20 Court Martial
21 Computer Affair
22 Confetti Check A-OK
23 The Sound of Silence
24 Reflections in the Water
25 The Responsibility Seat
26 The Long Sleep

[In the ATV (Midlands) region episode 24 was scheduled for 8 May 71 (i.e. between episodes 20 and 21) but was postponed until 24 Jul 71.]

THE PROTECTORS
First season
(29 Sep 72–30 Mar 73)
Twenty-six episodes

Second season
(21 Sep 73–15 Mar 74)
Twenty-six episodes

The Protectors

- **Group Three Productions/ITC** (ITV) ◆ Colour
- **52 episodes** (30 minutes) ◆ 1972-74
- **Writers include:** Terence Feely, Brian Clemens, Donald James, Tony Barwick, John Goldsmith, Dennis Spooner, Sylvia Anderson, Jesse and Pat Lasky, Trevor Preston, Shane Rimmer, Robert Banks Stewart
- **Directors include:** Don Chaffey, Jeremy Summers, Cyril Frankel, Johnny Hough, Roy Ward Baker, Robert Vaughan, Michael Lindsay-Hogg, Charles Crichton, Don Leaver, David Tomblin
- **Producers:** Gerry Anderson, Reg Hill

Starring: Robert Vaughan (Harry Rule) • Nyree Dawn Porter (Contessa di Contini) • Tony Anholt (Paul Buchet) • Yasuko Nagazumi (Suki) • Anthony Chinn (Chino)

Space: 1999

- **Gerry Anderson Productions/RAI/Group Three/ITC** (ITV) ◆ Colour
- **48 episodes** (60 minutes) ◆ 1975-78
- **Creators:** Gerry and Sylvia Anderson
- **Writers include:** Johnny Byrne, Anthony Terpiloff, Christopher Penfold, David Weir, Edward de Lorenzo, Donald James, Tony Barwick, Pip Baker, Jane Baker
- **Directors include:** Lee H. Katzin, David Tomblin, Ray Austin, Charles Crichton, Bob Kellett, Val Guest, Tom Clegg
- **Producers:** Sylvia Anderson, Fred Frieberger

Starring: Martin Landau (John Koenig) • Barbara Bain (Helena Russell) • Barry Morse (Prof. Bergman) • Nick Tate (Alan Carter) • Tony Anholt (Tony Verdeschi) • Catherine Schnell (Maya) • Zienia Merton (Sandra Benes) • Yasuko Nagazumi (Yasko) • Prentis Hancock (Paul Morrow) • Clifton Jones (David Kano) • Anton Phillips (Dr Mathias) • John Hug (Bill Fraser) • Jeffrey Krissoon (Dr Ben Vincent)

SPACE 1999
First season
(4 Sep 75–19 Feb 76)
1 Breakaway
2 Force of Life
3 Collision Course
4 War Games
5 Death's other Dominion
6 Voyager's Return
7 Alpha Child
8 Dragon's Domain
9 Mission of the Darians
10 Black Sun
11 Guardian of Piri
12 End of Eternity
13 Matter of Life and Death
14 Earthbound
15 The Full Circle
16 Another Time, Another Place
17 The Last Sunset
18 The Infernal Machine
19 Ring around the Moon
20 Missing Link
21 Space Brain
22 The Troubled Spirit
23 The Testament of Arkadia
24 The Last Enemy

Second season
(4 Sep–23 Dec 76, 1 May 78, 8 Aug 78)
25 The Metamorph
26 The Exiles
27 Journey to Where
28 One Moment of Humanity
29 Brian the Brain
30 New Adam, New Eve
31 The Mark of Archanon
32 The Rules of Luton
33 All that Glisters
34 The Taybor
35 Seed of Destruction
36 The AB Chrysalis
37 Catacombs of the Moon
38 Space Warp
39 A Matter of Balance
40 The Beta Cloud
41 The Lambda Factor
42 The Bringers of Wonder (part one)
43 The Bringers of Wonder (part two)
44 The Seance Spectre
45 Dorzak
46 Devil's Planet
47 The Immunity Syndrome
48 The Dorcons

Terrahawks

- **Anderson Burr Pictures/LWT** (ITV) ◆ Colour
- **39 episodes** (30 minutes) ◆ 1983-86
- **Writers:** Gerry Anderson, Tony Barwick, Trevor Lansdown
- **Directors:** Alan Pattillo, Tony Lenny, Tony Bell, Desmond Saunders
- **Producers:** Gerry Anderson, Christopher Burr
- **Associate producer:** Bob Bell

Voices: Denise Bryer • Windsor Davies • Jeremy Hitchen • Anne Ridler • Ben Stevens

TERRAHAWKS	**First season**	**Second season**	**Third season**
	(8 Oct–31 Dec 83)	*(25 Sep–30 Dec 84)*	*(3 May–26 Jul 86)*
	Thirteen episodes	Thirteen episodes	Thirteen episodes

Dick Spanner P.I.

- **Virgin** (C4) ◆ Colour ◆ 1985

Space Precinct
[aka Space Precinct 2040]

- **Sky One** ◆ Colour
- **24 episodes** (50 minutes) ◆ 1995
- **Creator**: Gerry Anderson
- **Writers include**: Paul Mayhew-Archer, J. Larry Carroll, David Bennett Carren, Mark Harris, Sam Graham, Philip Morrow, Marc Scott Zicree, Nicholas Sagan
- **Directors include**: John Glen, Sidney Hayers, Alan Birkinshaw

Starring: Ted Shackelford (Brogan) • Rob Youngblood (Haldane) • Simone Bendix (Castle) • Nancy Paul (Sally Brogan)

SPACE PRECINCT
(18 Mar–26 Aug 95)
1 Protect and Survive
2 Enforcer
3 Body and Soul
4 Double Duty
5 The Snake
6 Time to Kill
7 Deadline
8 Seek and Destroy
9 The Power
10 Illegal
11 Divided we Stand
12 Two Against the Rock
13 Takeover
14 Predator and Prey
15 The Witness
16 Hate Street
17 Friends
18 Smelter Skelter
19 Flas h
20 The Fire Within (part one)
21 The Fire Within (part two)
22 Forever Beetle
23 Graveyard (part one)
24 Graveyard (part two)

Although Gerry Anderson made his name as producer of science-fiction puppet series in the early 60s, he actually began his TV career as a director. A job at the Ministry of Information during the 40s led to him joining the Gainsborough film unit, from where he set up Anderson/Povis Films with Arthur Povis, a film cameraman who was to become the first of Anderson's collaborators. The two worked together on Roberta Leigh's 1957 puppet series *The Adventures of Twizzle*. This led to ABC commissioning another series in the same vein. *Torchy, The Battery*

Thunderbirds: probably the most popular television programme in the world

Boy was the story of a young boy doll who lived in a fantasy world for toys called Topsy-Turvy-Land.

Seeing possibilities for puppet series, Anderson and Barry Gray created *Four Feather Falls*, the story of a western town centring on 'the nicest cowpoke you could ever meet', Tex Tucker (voiced by Nicholas Parsons), who would frequently burst into song (sung by Michael Holliday) and fight such contemptible critters as Pedro the Bandit and 'Big Bad' Ben. Anderson and Gray would work together on almost all of Anderson's future series, with Gray being responsible for the theme tunes for which Anderson's series were famous. Another regular colleague, Reg Hill, provided the special effects.

The creative team decided to concentrate on science fiction, and, after this proved too expensive for Granada, Anderson was headhunted by Lew Grade. The result was the successful *Supercar*, with its square-jawed mid-Atlantic hero Mike Mercury (the prototype for all future Anderson heroes).

The much-loved *Fireball XL5* came next. This was a space opera concerning the adventures of space pilot Steve Zodiac and his crew, Venus, Professor Matt Matic, and Robert the Robot (voiced by Anderson himself through an effects box). The special effects on the series, created by a new member of the team, Derek Meddings, ensured that *Fireball XL5* was a giant leap forward from *Supercar*. The memorable theme song was 'I Wish I was a Spaceman'.

Fireball XL5's sales around the world prompted a decision to film the next 'Supermarionation' series in colour. *Stingray* concerned the World Aquanaut Security Patrol, as represented by Troy Tempest, Phones, Commander Shore (whose 'Stand by for action. Anything can happen in the next half-hour!' opened each episode) and the mute mermaid, Marina. With Derek Meddings's effects now more realistic, and a series of outrageous villains, including Titan, the Aquaphibians and the Killer Fish, *Stingray* was Anderson's first truly groovy series. Though many of the plots were predictable and corny, there was a knowingness and a love of character that made the whole thing charming. The series introduced two standard elements of future Anderson series, a Christmas episode ('A Christmas to Remember') and a 'flashback' episode ('Aquanaut of the Year').

What happened next, however, was beyond all expectation. Anderson unveiled his most ambitious project, the series that was to write his name into history: *Thunderbirds*. The differences from its predecessors were immediately apparent. Its episodes were 50 minutes in length, and the hardware and effects were way beyond anything seen on television previously. The story concerned an ex-astronaut, Jeff Tracy, and his five sons (Scott, Virgil, Alan, Gordon and John - all named after Mercury astronauts) who formed the secret international rescue organization from their hi-tech island base. In their battles against the villainous

Hood or, more usually, natural disasters, the Tracy boys were aided by their genius house guest, Brains, their London agent, Lady Penelope Creighton-Ward, and her cockney ex-con chauffeur, 'Nosey' Parker.

The future world of *Thunderbirds* felt 'lived in', with the craft being dirtied down, and a coherent society portrayed. David Graham played both Parker and Brains, and Sylvia Anderson was the legendary husky whisperer, Lady Penelope. The show gave the nation a series of catchphrases ('FAB', 'Thunderbirds Are Go', 'Yus m'Lady', etc.).

What is often forgotten amid the hype is that the series was often as clichéd as previous Anderson series, the plots sometimes being woefully poor. Still, a further six episodes were transmitted in 1966. These were sometimes shown in two 30-minute segments on successive nights, a trick learned from American series such as *Batman*. Anderson spent much of 1966 shooting two feature films of the series, *Thunderbirds are Go* and *Thunderbird Six*.

Although *Thunderbirds* remains Anderson's best loved series, for many fans the pinnacle of his career came with *Captain Scarlet and the Mysterons* in 1967. *Captain Scarlet* portrays a future Earth at war, due to misunderstanding and xenophobia, with Mars. The Earth forces of Spectrum fought the faceless Mysterons and their human agents, notably Captain Black. The series had careful continuity with advantage in the conflict continually shifting.

The cast in the series included Francis Matthews doing, in Gerry Anderson's words, 'his Cary Grant voice' for Captain Scarlet, Ed Bishop (another actor who would have a long and fruitful association with the newly renamed Century 21 Productions) as his partner Captain Blue, and Donald Gray, whose velvet tones provided the voices not only of Colonel White, but also of the Mysterons and Captain Black. The puppets, unlike previous 'Supermarionation' series, were correctly scaled (i.e. their heads were proportionally the right size). The scripts, mostly by Tony Barwick, concentrated on the war of nerves between the protagonists rather than the all-action escapades of *Stingray* and *Thunderbirds*, and were neither as silly as previous Anderson efforts, nor as po-faced as later ones, even aspiring to the groovy frisson of the camper *Stingray* and *Thunderbirds* episodes on occasion. The stand out craft this time were the superb airships for Spectrum's pilots, the angels (Melody, Harmony, Rhapsody, Symphony and Destiny). Everyone remembers the episode where three new angel aircraft are 'Mysteronised', resulting in a dog-fight.

Several episodes were incredibly violent (Captain Brown literally explodes in the pilot), leading to the series being given a later time slot in some regions. Captain Scarlet's encounter with the

'Captain Scarlet is indestructible. You are not. Remember this'

Mysterons made him indestructible, and so many episodes began with a dire warning to children 'Captain Scarlet is indestructible. You are not. Remember this.'

Some episodes, such as 'White as Snow' (in which Scarlet loses confidence in Colonel White) and 'Crater 101' (which took the fight to the Moon) are amongst the finest pieces in the Anderson canon, although one or two - notably 'Manhunt' and 'Fire at Rig 15' - seem little more than left-over *Thunderbirds* scripts.

Anderson took several steps back with 1968's *Joe 90*, a series that was, at least in part, devised by Lew Grade. *Joe 90* was a severe disappointment after *Captain Scarlet*, telling the story of a nine-year-old boy, Joe McLaine, who could be programmed with the brain patterns of a range of experts. He worked as a special agent for the World Intelligence Network. The model work was pretty impressive, but the series lacked the quality of previous Anderson shows and the writing was a distinct throwback to tweeness.

After the live-action movie, *Doppleganger*, in 1968, Anderson's next series for ITC, *The Secret Service*, was a peculiar little spy spoof, mixing puppetry and live action, starring Stanley Unwin as an eccentric priest working for British Intelligence. It was a dismal flop, being disowned by Lew Grade, and cancelled after just 13 episodes. It was clearly time for a major rethink.

The result of this was *UFO*, Anderson's flawed masterpiece. It has been treated badly by British television, never having been networked and acquiring an undeserved reputation for being, in some way, 'dodgy', which has meant that several excellent (although perfectly harmless) episodes have never been shown terrestrially outside of a late night slot.

UFO was a live action series, Anderson's first. It benefited from some of Derek Meddings's most inspired effects work and a quality of writing which places the scripts of most other Anderson series in the shade. The series, set in 1980, concerned a secret military organization, SHADO, which was given the task of defending Earth from a nameless, green-skinned alien race. The aliens' aim seemed to be to steal human organs as spare parts to keep themselves alive. Ed Bishop's dour Commander Straker was in all of the episodes, but because of the curious filming schedule (*UFO* was filmed in two blocks, one of 17 episodes, then a further nine with a break in between), the cast was seldom the same two episodes running.

Among the most impressive elements in *UFO* was the series' hardware, including the submarine Skydiver and a superbly designed moonbase, complete with its own Interceptors. The best episodes made use of the series' sweeping, multi-character aspect, which gave *UFO* a filmic quality. David Tomblin's 'The Cat with Ten Lives' concentrated on a man controlled by the aliens via the strange conduit of the family cat. 'A Question of Priorities', 'The Square Triangle' (a murder mystery), 'Confetti Check A-OK', and 'The Sound of Silence' were almost soap opera, focusing on the effects of SHADO on individual lives, whilst Terence Feely's 'The Man who Came Back' and Tony Barwick's 'The Psychobombs' were strange, psychological studies of the techniques used by the aliens to disrupt and infiltrate Staker's organization.

UFO's reputation, however, was made by the four episodes given restricted time slots. 'Mindbender' was a surreal episode in which Straker touches a hallucinatory alien rock. He finds himself wandering around the *UFO* studio set, having his dialogue stopped by a shout of 'Cut!' from Sylvia Anderson, talking to Paul Foster, who tells him he is an actor called Michael, and watching 'rushes' of previous episodes. Feely's 'Timelash' was deemed to be risky after Bishop and Wanda Ventham injected themselves with drugs to counteract an alien device which was slowing down time. 'The Responsibility Seat', a straightforward tale of the isolation of command, contained scenes in which beautiful spy Jane Merrow seduced the SHADO chief. The last episode caused the most fuss. 'The Long Sleep', with its monochrome tinted hallucinatory dream sequences, plethora of drug speak, and an implied rape, was provocative enough to be totally banned in certain regions.

The episode has never been shown on terrestrial television before 10.30 p.m.

Anderson briefly toyed with the idea of making a second season, but soon he had another series underway, the glossy *The Protectors*, an international crime-fighting adventure series which, despite a quality cast, the cream of British TV writers and a huge hit single as a theme tune ('Avenues and Alleyways' by Tony Christie), was something of a disappointment, although it was given the benefit of a second season.

Next, Anderson returned to telefantasy (and to the moon) with *Space: 1999*, which, due to Anderson's wish to sell the series to the American market, starred Martin Landau, Barbara Bain and Barry Morse and cost more than all his other series put together. The premise was excellent, the Moon being blown out of Earth's orbit by a nuclear explosion. Unfortunately, despite a promising beginning, a clutch of guest stars including Anthony Valentine, Brian Blessed, Joan Collins, Christopher Lee, Peter Cushing and Leo McKern, and several well-remembered episodes - such as the extremely weird 'Black Sun' and the horrific 'Dragon's Domain' - the series was vacuous, slow-moving hippie drivel. A second season, made in 1976, tried to be a more standard adventure, and, in doing so, found new ways to be awful.

Anderson's next project was *Terrahawks*, a return to puppets, which, whilst it contained some mind-blowing effects, was, nevertheless, a huge disappointment to the many fans expecting a new *Thunderbirds*. As had often been proved before, Anderson seemed to think that there were only two ways to produce television: po-faced or childish. This was the latter, despite promising early in-jokes and the usual cool flirtations with the *Zeitgeist*. Anderson also created the detective spoof *Dick Spanner P.I.* in a co-production with Virgin and Channel 4. The episodes, blessed with a *Police Squad!* style of literalist humour, were originally shown as part of Channel 4's *Network 7* Sunday-morning series, but were popular enough to later be broadcast in their own right.

In 1991, the BBC, riding on the nostalgia boom which began in the mid-80s, bought *Thunderbirds* for BBC2. The publicity given to the series, both by the BBC and the press at large, suggested less a 25-year-old puppet series and more a significant event in the history of western civilization. *Stingray* and *Captain Scarlet* also proved to be huge hits, but even the BBC couldn't push *Joe 90* successfully.

Anderson's latest series is *Space Precinct*, a police procedural drama set in space, and sold directly to Sky Television, then the BBC. It suffers from the problems of much of his previous work: great effects let down by simplistic scripts and childish characterization. There may be something here that could, potentially, work out better than any of his previous shows, but it's going to take a second season to find out, and second seasons aren't something that the Anderson stable is good at.

The Avengers/The New Avengers

The Avengers

- **ABC Television** (ITV) ◆ B&W (1961-66); Colour (1967-69)
- **161 episodes** (50 minutes)
- **Creators:** Sydney Newman, Leonard White
- **Writers include:** Brian Clemens, Richard Harris, Terence Feely, Dennis Spooner, Peter Ling, James Mitchell, John Lucarotti, Eric Paice, Roger Marshall, Terrence Dicks, Malcolm Hulke, Martin Woodhouse, Philip Levene, Robert Banks Stewart, Tony Williamson, Jeremy Burnham, Terry Nation, Donald James
- **Directors include:** Don Leaver, Robert Tronson, Peter Hammond, Roger Jenkins, Jonathan Alwyn, Kim Mills, Raymond Menmuir, Bill Bain, Sidney Hayers, Charles Crichton, Peter Graham Scott, Roy Ward Baker, James Hill, Robert Day, John Hough, Cyril Frankel, Ray Austin, Don Chaffey, Robert Fuest, Don Sharp, Leslie Norman
- **Producers:** Leonard White, John Bryce, Julian Wintle, Albert Fennell, Brian Clemens

Starring: Patrick Macnee (John Steed) • Ian Hendry (Dr David Keel) • Ingrid Hafner (Carol Wilson) • Douglas Muir (One Ten) • Honor Blackman (Cathy Gale) • Julie Stevens (Venus Smith) • Jon Rollason (Dr Martin King) • Diana Rigg (Emma Peel) • Linda Thorson (Tara King) • Patrick Newell (Mother) • Rhonda Parker (Rhonda)

A series starring Ian Hendry as a doctor who is aided in his quest for justice by a shadowy figure from British Intelligence. Sound familiar? Probably not. *The Avengers* started life as something very different indeed.

In 1960, Ian Hendry was starring in an ABC series called *Police Surgeon*, a standard cops and robbers yarn which ran for 13 episodes. The series brought its star to the attention of Sydney Newman, head of drama. Newman, who had

THE AVENGERS
First season
(7 Jan–30 Dec 61)
1 Hot Snow
2 Brought to Book
3 Square Root of Evil
4 Nightmare
5 Crescent Moon
6 Girl on the Trapeze
7 Diamond Cut Diamond
8 The Radioactive Man
9 Ashes of Roses
10 Hunt the Man Down
11 Please Don't Feed the Animals
12 Dance with Death
13 One for the Mortuary
14 The Springers
15 The Frighteners
16 The Yellow Needle
17 Death on the Slipway
18 Double Danger
19 Toy Trap
20 The Tunnel of Fear
21 The Far Distant Dead
22 Kill the King
23 Dead of Winter
24 The Deadly Air
25 A Change of Bait
26 Dragonsfield

Second season
(29 Sep 62–23 Mar 63)
27 Mr Teddy Bear
28 Propellant 23
29 The Decapod
30 Bullseye
31 Mission to Montreal
32 The Removal Man
33 The Mauritius Penny
34 Death of a Great Dane
35 The Sell-Out
36 Death on the Rocks
37 Traitor in Zebra
38 The Big Thinker
39 Death Dispatch
40 Dead on Course
41 Intercrime
42 Immortal Clay
43 Box of Tricks
44 Warlock
45 The Golden Eggs
46 School for Traitors
47 The White Dwarf
48 Man in the Mirror
49 Conspiracy of Silence
50 A Chorus of Frogs
51 Six Hands across a Table
52 Killer Whale

Third season
(28 Sep 63–21 Mar 64)
53 Brief for Murder
54 The Undertakers
55 Man with Two Shadows
56 The Nutshell
57 Death of a Batman
58 November Five
59 The Gilded Cage
60 Second Sight
61 The Medicine Men
62 The Grandeur that was Rome
63 The Golden Fleece
64 Don't Look Behind You
65 Death à la Carte
66 Dressed to Kill
67 The White Elephant
68 The Little Wonders
69 The Wringer
70 Mandrake
71 The Secrets Broker
72 Trojan Horse
73 Build a Better Mousetrap
74 The Outside-In Man
75 The Charmers
76 Concerto
77 Esprit de Corps
78 Lobster Quadrille

Fourth season
(2 Oct 65–26 Mar 66)
79 The Town of No Return
80 The Grave-Diggers
81 The Cybernauts
82 Death at Bargain Prices
83 Castle De'ath
84 The Master Minds
85 The Murder Market
86 A Surfeit of H_2O
87 The Hour that Never Was
88 Dial a Deadly Number
89 Man-Eater of Surrey Green

The New Avengers

- **An Avengers (Film and TV) Production/IDTV Productions, Paris (ITV)**
- Colour
- **26 episodes** (50 minutes) ◆ 1976-77
- **Writers:** Brian Clemens, Dennis Spooner, Terence Feely, John Goldsmith
- **Directors include:** Ray Austin, Robert Fuest, James Hill, Sidney Hayers, Ernest Day, Don Thompson
- **Producers:** Albert Fennell, Brian Clemens
- **Associate producer** (episodes 14–18): Ron Fry

Starring: Patrick Macnee (John Steed) • Joanna Lumley (Purdey) • Gareth Hunt (Mike Gambit)

recently been asked by his boss, Howard Thomas, to produce something 'light-hearted', consulted *Police Surgeon*'s producer Leonard White, and between them they created a new series. Casting Hendry in the role of Dr David Keel, the pair developed a story that involved the death of Keel's girlfriend at the hands of a drugs ring. The devastated Keel, wanting to avenge her death, sought the aid of a mysterious undercover agent who in turn used Keel as a convenient cover for his covert activities. The agent's name was John Steed, the actor playing him, Patrick Macnee. The series' title came from Keel's perceived crusade to avenge the death of his lover and because Newman felt it was 'a great title'.

The Avengers proved to be a popular addition to the ITV schedules. Hendry and Macnee investigated a missing scientist in 'Nightmare', deadly isotopes in 'The Radioactive Man', a political assassination attempt in 'Kill the King' and the rise of a new Fascist party in 'Dead of Winter'. A strike by Equity in late 1961 delayed the first season mid-run and, during the six months before the second season began, Ian Hendry decided to leave. This should have been the end of *The Avengers* since the series was, essentially, Hendry's show. However, Leonard White, having several unfilmed scripts left over, elected to continue. Jon Rollason was hired to play Steed's new partner, another doctor, named Martin King, but he

90 Two's a Crowd
91 Too Many Christmas Trees
92 Silent Dust
93 Room without a View
94 Small Game for Big Hunters
95 The Girl from Auntie
96 The Thirteenth Hole
97 Quick-Quick Slow Death
98 The Danger Makers
99 A Touch of Brimstone
100 What the Butler Saw
101 The House that Jack Built
102 A Sense of History
103 How to Succeed…at Murder
104 Honey for the Prince

Fifth season
(14 Jan–6 May 67)
105 From Venus with Love
106 The Fear Merchants
107 Escape in Time
108 The See-Through Man
109 The Bird who Knew Too Much
110 The Winged Avenger
111 The Living Dead
112 The Hidden Tiger
113 The Correct Way to Kill
114 Never, Never Say Die
115 Epic
116 The Superlative Seven
117 A Funny Thing Happened on the Way to the Station
118 Something Nasty in the Nursery
119 The Joker
120 Who's Who???

Sixth season
(30 Sep–18 Nov 67)
121 Return of the Cybernauts
122 Death's Door
123 The £50,000 Breakfast
124 Dead Man's Treasure
125 You Have Just Been Murdered
126 The Positive Negative Man
127 Murdersville
128 Mission…Highly Improbable

Seventh season
(25 Sep 68–21 May 69)
129 The Forget-Me-Knot
130 Game
131 Super-Secret Cypher Snatch
132 You'll Catch Your Death
133 Split!
134 Whoever Shot Poor George Oblique Stroke XR40?
135 False Witness
136 All Done with Mirrors
137 Legacy of Death
138 Noon Doomsday
139 Look - (stop me if you've heard this one) But There Were These Two Fellers…
140 Have Guns - Will Haggle
141 They Keep Killing Steed
142 The Interrogators
143 The Rotters
144 Invasion of the Earthmen
145 Killer
146 The Morning After
147 The Curious Case of the Countless Clues
148 Wish you were Here
149 Love All
150 Stay Tuned
151 Take me to your Leader
152 Fog
153 Who was that Man I Saw you With?
154 Homicide and Old Lace
155 Thingumajig
156 My Wildest Dream
157 Requiem
158 Take-Over
159 Pandora
160 Get-A-Way!
161 Bizarre

[*The Avengers* transmission dates are as per ABC, which was almost the only region to broadcast all 26 episodes of the first season. An Equity strike caused a 13-week delay episodes 22 and 23. The second and third seasons were generally networked, as were the fourth, fifth and sixth, although Associated Rediffusion transmitted the episodes earlier in London and affiliated areas. Transmission details for the seventh season are as Thames. The season was partially networked until Dec 68, and there are extremely divergent transmission orders across the country. Episode 156 was broadcast in a late-night slot on 7 Apr 69 rather than prime-time 9 Apr. Episodes 23–26 of *The New Avengers*, entitled *The New Avengers in Canada*, were a co-production with Neilsen-Ferns, Toronto. *The New Avengers* transmission details are as per LWT. The first season was partially networked (until Dec 76); as was the second, with the exception of episode 26, which was scheduled for 25 Nov 77 but was replaced by episode 25. Episode 26 was therefore broadcast on different days in the various regions (e.g. 17 Dec 77 in LWT area).]

THE NEW AVENGERS
First season
(22 Oct 76–21 Jan 77)
1 The Eagle's Nest
2 House of Cards
3 The Last of the Cybernauts...??
4 The Midas Touch
5 Cat amongst the Pigeons
6 Target!
7 To Catch a Rat
8 The Tale of the Big Why
9 Faces
10 Gnaws
11 Dirtier by the Dozen
12 Sleeper
13 Three-Handed Game

Second season
(9 Sep–25 Nov 77)
14 Dead Men are Dangerous
15 Angels of Death
16 Medium Rare
17 The Lion and the Unicorn
18 Obsession
19 Trap
20 Hostage
21 K is for Kill - Part One: The Tiger Awakes
22 K is for Kill - Part Two: Tiger by the Tail
23 Complex
24 Forward Base
25 The Gladiators
26 Emily [not networked]

only appeared in three episodes. A new concept was also attempted. Honor Blackman became the first *Avengers* girl.

Cathy Gale was a television first, an intelligent, independent young woman of means. The arrival of Blackman, wearing the now legendary leather utility suits and the infamous 'kinky boots', and throwing villains about, had a profound effect on the series. It moved away from the dark, spy-orientated episodes of the first season towards the quirky and bizarre style for which the series became known. Because the episodes were now being pre-recorded, the Rollason stories were mixed in with the Cathy Gale ones, as were six stories made without Blackman but with another female partner, the singer Venus Smith (played by Julie Stevens, later a *Play School* presenter). However, it was the Cathy Gale episodes that really caught the public's imagination, keeping, according to one newspaper, 'the Bright Young Things of Belgravia and Chelsea at home on Saturday nights'.

The third season completed the transformation of Steed into the archetypal Englishman that we know today. During the filming of 'Mandrake', Blackman knocked wrestler Jackie Pallo unconscious during a fight sequence. The incident made the front pages of the national press.

Honor Blackman left in 1964, her immediate post-*Avengers* role being Pussy Galore in *Goldfinger*. (A reference is made to her presence at Fort Knox in the fourth season of *The Avengers*.) Changes took place behind the camera too, as Brain Clemens and his new partner Albert Fennell were given control of production. With an eye on the American market, the series also underwent a change of recording technique. The old videotaped episodes were replaced with expensive-looking filmed stories. Most important of all, however, was the casting of Diana Rigg as Emma Peel.

With her karate-influenced fighting technique, Emma Peel was TV's greatest feminist heroine, having a flirtatious but absolutely equal relationship with Steed. Dressed in crepe, PVC and lamé catsuits, thigh-length skirts or hipster pants, Emma Peel *was* the 60s. In her first season the show was at its height, walking the thin line between farce and seriousness, sharper, wittier, more liberal and groovier than anything before, or anything since. Writers such as Philip Levene and Malcolm Hulke were allowed to spin their wonderful fairy tales of espionage and friendship before Brian Clemens's over-intense, over-sexual, over-done vision of the series became all-encompassing.

'The Cybernauts' introduced the series' main bogey men, lumbering automatons, similar in menace to ***Doctor Who***'s Cybermen, and the legendary hellfire club story 'A Touch of Brimstone' brought the show headlines for the cuts demanded by the network, though Emma still got to whip-fight Cartney (Peter Wyngarde) in her 'Queen of Sin' garb.

The fifth season was made in colour, and *The Avengers* became the first British series to be screened on prime time American television. The offbeat humour of the show was best exemplified by the *Batman* spoof 'The Winged Avenger' and 'The Hidden Tiger', a story about killer cats. In 'Who's Who???' Steed and Emma have their minds transferred into the bodies of Freddie Jones and Patricia Haines. The Cybernauts returned (with Peter Cushing as their controller), and Emma was miniaturized in 'Mission... Highly Improbable'.

Diana Rigg quit *The Avengers* after the first two colour seasons, and, like Honor Blackman, went on to play the female lead in a Bond movie. For a short time, Fennell and Clemens were moved off the production team and, during this confusing period, Linda Thorson was cast as Steed's new partner, Tara King.

After the filming of a few disastrous episodes (later refilmed with additional footage), Fennell and Clemens returned to try to get the series back on course. It was a difficult job. Many of the decisions taken in their absence had a negative effect on the show, particularly the inclusion of the somewhat laboured comedy that surrounded the character of Mother, Steed and Tara's wheelchair-bound boss. Linda Thorson was quite inexperienced to begin with and, although she would later develop into a fine actress, her performances were not what might have been expected from Diana Rigg's replacement.

The season opened with 'The Forget-Me-Knot', which included a touching tag scene in which Emma and Tara meet in Steed's apartment. The Tara episodes had a self-conscious 'Englishness' which killed off any subtlety in the wit. The cool reception to the new season in America would eventually lead to the end of the series. The best episodes of the season were 'Game', a surreal revenge nightmare for Steed, and the slapstick 'Look - (stop me if you've heard this one), But There Were These Two Fellers...', which featured John Cleese. At the end of the last story, Steed and Tara were seen blasting off into space together. For a long time it seemed as though that was the end of *The Avengers*.

In 1975 a French champagne advert starring Patrick Macnee and Linda Thorson started the ball rolling again. Fennell and Clemens were approached by a French company (Canadian investment was also involved, hence the three episodes filmed in France and four in Canada), and *The New Avengers* was born. Whilst Steed was still the centre of attention, much of his 'running and jumping stuff' was taken by Mike Gambit (Gareth Hunt), whilst the new *Avenger* girl was Joanna Lumley as Purdey.

'Avenging is better than ever,' gushed the *Daily Mail*'s reviewer after the first

Emma Peel *was* the 60s

episode. 'Pay no attention to the title, *The New Avengers* are, thank goodness, the old *Avengers*, in fact, the very old ones in their 60s heyday.' That episode, 'The Eagle's Nest', upheld the elements that had made the old series so popular: a bizarre plot and location (Nazis hiding on an isolated Scottish island, masquerading as Trappist monks), a popular guest star (Peter Cushing), clever dialogue, and all-action stunts, preceded by a stunning new title sequence and an up-tempo arrangement of the theme music.

The first 13 episodes threw up several classics. 'The Last of the Cybernauts ... ??' brought back the monsters of old, whilst new menaces appeared in the form of a shooting range that fought back in 'Target!' and giant rats in the London underground in 'Gnaws'. If the first season had been passable, the second, not counting the wonderful 'Dead Men are Dangerous', was awful. 'K is for Kill', which featured footage of Emma Peel and was shot in France, and particularly the final four episodes shot in Canada, were especially bad. In an attempt to become more 'adult', the show only succeeded in becoming adolescent. At least Joanna Lumley managed to overcome the initial absurdity of her character to produce something charming and eccentric. Martin Shaw and Lewis Collins's appearances in the episode 'Obsession' doubtless gave Fennell and Clemens the idea of doing something different.

The various manifestations of *The Avengers* remain hugely popular today. Brian Clemens's notorious comment – 'If we did have a coloured man or a policeman, we would have the yardstick of social reality and that would make the whole thing ridiculous' – sounds incredibly naive now, but it was the bizarre world that *The Avengers* inhabited that has influenced generations of programme-makers since.

The Prisoner

- **ITC/Everyman Films (ITV)** ◆ Colour
- **17 episodes** (50 minutes) ◆ 1967-68
- **Creators:** Patrick McGoohan, David Tomblin (with George Markstein)
- **Writers:** David Tomblin, George Markstein, Terence Feely, Patrick McGoohan, Anthony Skene, Lewis Griefer, Michael Cramoy, Roger Parkes, Vincent Tilsley, Gerald Kelsey, Roger Woodis, Ian L. Rakoff
- **Directors:** Don Chaffey, Pat Jackson, Robert Asher, Roy Rossotti, Peter Graham Scott, David Tomblin, Parick McGoohan
- **Producer:** David Tomblin

Television is the business of compromise. If one person could do a series exactly how they wanted it would probably end up as either a work of genius or a meaningless mess. Patrick McGoohan, at exactly the right point in time, managed to do both.

The Prisoner starts with an immense title sequence: an angry secret agent driving into London under thundery skies, bursting into his boss' office, slamming down his resignation, and driving off again in his Lotus 7. But it's not so simple. At his home, an eerie undertaker walks up to the door. Gas hisses through the keyhole. Packing his bags for a holiday, the man collapses. When he wakes, he pulls back the curtains in alarm. He is in a strange village, a place of odd Italian design.

'Where am I?' 'In the Village.' 'What do you want?' 'Information. We want information.' 'You won't get it.' 'By hook or by crook, we will.' 'Who are you?' 'The new Number Two.' 'Who is Number One?' 'You are Number Six.' 'I am not a number. I am a free man!' The famous title sequence dissolves into laughter. In a matter of a minute we have had the format of the series explained, and been offered a series of visual set pieces, complimented by Ron Grainer's powerful theme music.

From the very start of the series there were two competing factions in the *Prisoner* production team. George Markstein, who had joined *Danger Man* as script editor at the end of the third season, had an idea based on a project devised in World War II, where dangerously burnt-out SOE operatives were held in beautiful surroundings in an attempt to pry their secrets out of them (Markstein is the man behind the desk in the title sequence). McGoohan, having just left the very successful role of *Danger Man*, was looking for something with some ideological and artistic meat to it. In effect, one man wanted a spy series, the other wanted an escape from a spy series. Between the two stood David Tomblin, a director and auteur very much part of the swinging art scene.

McGoohan had taken the idea to Lew Grade, and sold it to him on the strength of one meeting. McGoohan was the highest-paid television performer of his time, and had just completed two episodes of the first colour season of *Danger Man*. In effect, he was calling a halt to that concept, and it seems miraculous that Grade listened to him. Some of the ideas of the new series seemed almost a reaction to *Danger Man* concepts, although the episode 'Colony Three' in *Danger Man*, for instance, where spies train in an isolated village, and even the title song lyric,

Starring: Patrick McGoohan (The Prisoner) • Guy Doleman/George Baker/Leo McKern/Colin Gordon/Eric Portman/Anton Rodgers/Mary Morris/Peter Wyngarde/Patrick Cargill/Derren Nesbitt/John Sharpe/Clifford Evans/David Bauer/Georgina Cookson/Andre van Gysegham/Kenneth Griffith (Number Two) • Alexis Kanner (The Kid/Number 48) • Angelo Muscat (The Butler) • Peter Swanwick (The Supervisor) • Denis Shaw (Shopkeeper)

'They've given you a number and taken away your name', are hints towards *The Prisoner*. The new series was to be shot in two 13-episode batches. *Danger Man* was instantly dropped, an example of the authority that ITC gave McGoohan. (It is rumoured that some of the script material from the cancelled series found its way into *Man in a Suitcase*.)

The theme of *The Prisoner* was to be the individual against the community, with a background that meant that Number Six was never sure who was running the Village, where it was, or why the changing Number Twos wanted to know the answer to only one question: Why did he resign?

The Village itself was Portmeirion in Wales, an experimental architectural collection designed by Sir Clough Williams-Ellis. This information wasn't revealed to the audience until the final episode.

In most episodes, Number Six made an escape attempt, and the Village authorities foiled it. The final image of most episodes, which summed up the concept, was a pair of metal gates slamming in front of McGoohan's face.

Various writers approached the basic subject in different ways. In 'The Chimes of Big Ben' Leo McKern appears as a jazzy, intellectual Number Two. Number Six seems to have adapted to life in the Village, entering the art competition, with his sculpture, 'Escape'. It turns out that the sculpture is a boat, and he uses it in a bid for freedom. Going cross-country with an Estonian agent, Nadia, he eventually appears to reach London once more. However, when his former employers start asking him why he resigned he realizes that the chimes of Big Ben are just a tape-recording. He is back in the Village.

The episode demonstrates many of the show's best features. The Village was an idyllic community to live in, providing that one followed the rules: Western democracy in microcosm. There were references to current debates within the artistic community, but alongside the intellectual content, there was plenty of action. This basic format took us through 'A, B and C' (an attempt to electronically probe the Prisoner's brain), 'The Schizoid Man' (Terence Feely's ultimate reading of the original idea, a double of Number Six arriving to shake his sense of personal identity - the Prisoner typically reversed the roles in a brilliant escape attempt), and the rather brutal mind-control fable, 'The General'.

In between these episodes the first sign of militant strangeness arrived. McGoohan's own 'Free for All' (written under a pseudonym) has Number Six invited to run in a democratic election against the old Number Two (Eric Portman). He wins, and immediately orders that the gates be opened, telling the Villagers that they are all free. Against the format of the series, but perfectly in line with what the viewers know about their own democracies, the Villagers stay where they are. They know they aren't free, because the real power is far above the elected office which Number Six has aspired to.

Anthony Skene's three episodes were a little series in themselves. Two featured a black cat, who became a symbol for Number Six's endless pacing. In 'Many Happy Returns' we get a rehash of 'Big Ben', as Six escapes a deserted Village, and is probably betrayed by his superiors in London, being parachuted back into the Village. In 'Dance of the Dead' Mary Morris's Number Two stages a carnival, and everyone turns up in costume, but the Prisoner refuses to conform. Against a night-time backdrop he is taught a harsh lesson about laws, stark in such a baroque visual scene. Some of the dialogue, however, suggests that Skene had become caught up in the overall strangeness of the project. Things were getting odd for oddness' sake.

'Checkmate' took us back to the standard format, the Villagers' game of human chess disrupted by Six's refusal to obey. The question here, as in the early episodes, was who to trust in a very real escape bid, something akin to a prison camp movie. 'Hammer into Anvil' was the nadir of this real-

(29 Sep 67–2 Feb 68)
1 Arrival
2 The Chimes of Big Ben
3 A, B and C
4 Free for All
5 The Schizoid Man
6 The General
7 Many Happy Returns
8 Dance of the Dead
9 Checkmate

istic approach, a very straightforward tale of a vendetta Number Six pursues against an overtly sadistic Number Two (Patrick Cargill). 'It's your Funeral' sees Number Two (Derren Nesbitt) supposedly the subject of an assassination plot, and the by now politically-literate Number Six tries to stop it, for fear of reprisals. 'A Change of Mind' sees another brutal mind-control technique (lobotomization), the Village increasingly desperate in its efforts to make the Prisoner conform. It was becoming clear that he was the most important person in the place, that the Village was a place of the mind rather than a real location. Indeed, when Six escaped, each time he gave a different theory as to where he'd been held. In 'Big Ben', it is 'In Lithuania, on the Baltic, 30 miles from the Polish border', in 'Many Happy Returns', the best guess is an island off the coast of Morocco. Of course, in the end, it turned out to be much closer to home.

Here a division also took place. Markstein, who was becoming disenchanted by McGoohan's vision of what he took to be his own idea, left the project acrimoniously. Also, Grade decided that the series could not sustain two seasons. McGoohan was disappointed, but promised Grade that there would be an ending that would explain everything. From an ongoing 13-part drama season, *The Prisoner* became a complete 17-part series.

The episode that was to launch the second season was very exciting indeed, the timing of it being due to McGoohan securing a role in *Ice Station Zebra*. It meant that he wasn't there for an entire episode, but he was overseeing all aspects of production by this point, on an almost obsessional basis. It was left to David Tomblin to rewrite Vincent Tilsley's episode, one that threw an interesting light on many aspects of the series. 'Do Not Forsake Me Oh My Darling' has the Prisoner's mind transplanted into another man's body (an amazing performance from Nigel Stock). He travels to find Dr Seltzman, the scientist responsible for the process, in what is almost a standard back-projection version of *Danger Man* Europe. In this episode we discover that Number Six has a fiancée back in London, and discover what may be his (down-to-Earth) reason for resigning. The Seltzman project was one of the last cases he worked on, and the implications of mind-swapping went against the agent's independent turn of mind. Complete with dramatic pre-titles sequence, this episode relaunched the series on a spy-thriller basis. It was typical of the show that, contrary to all popular conceptions of a successful series, it only had the star in it for a couple of minutes. (Gay critics point out that *The Prisoner* can be seen as a gay fantasy, with the hero trying to maintain his lifestyle - McGoohan insisted that there was to be no romance for Six as this was a 'family show' - against the oppressive forces of conformity. When he went back to his girlfriend, he was literally wearing another man's face.)

From here, things got weird. Working with his own crew, and an agenda supplied by his artistic rather than populist leanings (McGoohan being the man who turned down both James Bond and ***The Saint***), the last four episodes of *The Prisoner* were a very personal creation.

'Living in Harmony' reformatted the show as a Western, with Six forced to be the sheriff in a small town, but refusing to wear a gun. The ending revealed it to be another Village plot, but it became clear that the concept was universal, and that issues of freedom and anarchy couldn't be tied down to one particular format. The episode was not shown in the American run of the series, perhaps because it involved the use of hallucinogenic drugs, or, more likely, because a 'hero' refusing to carry a gun in the era of Vietnam was too subversive.

10 Hammer into Anvil
11 It's your Funeral
12 A Change of Mind
13 Do Not Forsake Me Oh My Darling
14 Living in Harmony
15 The Girl who was Death
16 Once Upon a Time
17 Fall Out

The series was premiered on the ITV network while it was being filmed, and doubts were surfacing that *The Prisoner* would even be able to be screened as a single season. ***The Saint***'s first colour series had been backed up so much that repeats had been used to plug gaps, but, parallel to *The Prisoner* (and giving some idea of how different the show was to television around it) 30 episodes of *Man in a Suitcase* had just been completed without a hitch.

'The Girl who was Death' was another example of meddling with the format. With the Village scenes in 'Do Not Forsake Me' being mainly stock footage, viewers were starting to wonder if they'd ever see the full glory of the place again. The episode was a perfect parody of Bondian nonsense, resembling nothing more than one of the more grandiose episodes of *The Man from U.N.C.L.E.* It turned out that it was all a fairy tale, told by Six to an audience of children. It was almost an arrogant dismissal of McGoohan's past and the decadent nonsense that 'spy' movies had become.

The final episodes formed a two-part odyssey, Leo McKern's Number Two being returned to the Village in a final attempt to break Six's spirit. 'Once Upon a Time' was a confined Beckettian play, both men going back through their own histories, and the English psyche, in a test of willpower. The shouting match descends into Six asking Two 'Why don't you resign?' Number Two dies, and Six is released from the ultimate test, his prize: a meeting with Number One. This episode was originally designed to close the first season, filmed sixth out of the first 13. As such, it was so carefully-crafted that it has been performed as a companion piece to Beckett's *Endgame*. The rigours of the psychological warfare in the script helped push McKern towards a breakdown, and he was doubtful about returning, a year later, to film a conclusion.

'Fall Out' was apparently written in 36 hours in McGoohan's dressing-room. He arrived on the set to hand it out to a crew who had no idea what they were about to film. McKern returned, after a necessary shave, as a rebelliously-resurrected Number Two, in a surreal homage to Six. The President, a fawning figure in Judge's robes, praises the Prisoner's right to be himself, and his stand for the individual. He introduces Six, who has taken up position on a throne, to faces of rebellion. The voice of Youth is represented by Alexis Kanner in a hippie topper, to which McGoohan gives a nod of approval, and rebellion from within the system is personified by McKern. The President condemns both forms of revolt, saying only Six's revolt is pure. He asks the Prisoner to 'lead us or go'. He isn't sure he wants to do either, and tries to address the court, but each time he is silenced by the applause. The options are clear for a free spirit in a conformist society: join the élite or leave.

Six demands to see Number One and is taken to see a robed figure wearing a mask. Six rips off the mask, and finds another underneath: that of a chattering ape. He removes this, and finds that the face of Number One is his own, angry at having been exposed. Six of one, half a dozen of the other. Six's act of rebellion is still only part of the system.

Chaos erupts. Uniformed men run to and fro, in Bondian style. A missile is launched from within the Village (the real power is nuclear) and Six machine-guns down guards to the tune of 'All You Need is Love' (an ironic tilt of the head to what flower power failed to achieve). The Prisoner, Number Two, the Kid and the Butler (played silently throughout the series) escape by violence, and zoom off in a cage on the back of a lorry, finding themselves just outside London. They drive along the road, performing 'Dem Bones', the only final reality being the flesh. The Kid hops off to hitch-hike, Number Two returning to his function in Whitehall, and the Prisoner drives home to his flat. Each actor except McGoohan is given a namecheck as he leaves the cavalcade in an anarchistic nod to the friends that had kept him going thus far. The sequence reminds one these days of the last images of Julien Temple's *Great Rock'n'roll Swindle*, with the spiritual standing in for 'Frigging in the Rigging' (one wonders how McGoohan reacted to punk). When the Prisoner gets home, the door closes behind him in the same manner as the one in the Village did. Nobody ever escapes. By turns baffling and brilliant, the energetic final episode flooded the switchboard with complaints and, perhaps more satisfying for McGoohan, questions.

Much can be said about the iconography that *The Prisoner* established. It showed that a certain typeface (Albertus) can sum up everything about a society. Logos like the Penny Farthing bicycle and images of the ubiquitous rovers (balloons that served as roaring guards for the Village) became shorthand for a whole style. 'Be seeing you', with its chic hand gesture (similar to the Islamic 'Salaam', but probably inspired by the early Christian 'sign of the fish'), was a sign by which one knew that we are all still prisoners. If it is a Christian symbol, it's one of many discrete references to Christianity as the way out from domination that McGoohan presents us with ('Dem Bones', and the series, ends with 'Now hear the word of the Lord' echoing over London).

How much the Prisoner owes to John Drake, the *Danger Man*, is, to some, a very important question. Drake appears in Portmeirion in two episodes of the spy series. Also, almost as a joke, McGoohan employed an actor named John Drake in 'The Girl who was Death'. However, in 'Once Upon a Time', Number Two says 'In the morning break', rather than 'In the morning, Drake' as many fans believe. The question is only important because Markstein always believed the characters to be the same, while McGoohan saw Six as an Everyman figure. He'd initially agreed with Markstein, but might have been worried about infringing *Danger Man* creator Ralph Smart's rights. It takes a degree of anal-retentiveness to care about such trivia.

McGoohan has very forthright opinions on the show, stating that only seven episodes are the core material (the first, the last two, 'The Chimes of Big Ben', 'Free for All', 'Dance of the Dead', and 'Checkmate'). Of these, only 'Dance' is free of McGoohan's input as either director or writer, although much of his direction was uncredited on-screen. However, McGoohan has very rarely been drawn on the themes the show explored, leading people to wonder if it wasn't some strange kind of joke at their expense. When the *Prisoner* fan club asked him what they should name themselves, McGoohan replied 'Six of One ...'. One can only speculate as to whether this most active of fan societies shouldn't have been so literal and called themselves 'Half a Dozen of the Other'.

Whether *The Prisoner* signified anarchy, Christianity, or Marxism, it was certainly entertaining. Every episode was packed with not only the 60s concerns of brainwashing, high-technology and social engineering, but the adventure series staples of fist fights and chases. Finally, art and design turned the whole thing into another world, but one readily accessible from our own. If the look of the series persists today in car adverts, special editions of *The Tube* and McGoohan-directed, Emmy-winning *Columbo* episodes (notably a fairground sequence similar to that in 'The Girl who was Death'), then the message will also remain pertinent.

'I will not be pushed, stamped, filed, indexed, briefed, debriefed, or numbered. My life is my own.'

'Be seeing you.'

Randall and Hopkirk (Deceased)

- **ITC/Scoton** (ITV) ◆ **Colour**
- **26 episodes** (50 minutes) ◆ **1969-70**
- **Creator: Dennis Spooner**
- **Writers: Ralph Smart, Mike Pratt, Ian Wilson, Donald James, Ray Austin, Tony Williamson, Gerald Kelsey**
- **Directors include: Cyril Frankel, Ray Austin, Jeremy Summers, Roy Ward Baker, Leslie Norman, Robert Tronson, Paul Dickson**
- **Producer: Monty Berman**

'Before the sun shall rise on you, each ghost unto his grave must go.
Cursed the ghost who dares to stay, and face the awful light of day....'

With this charming piece of sub-Hammer hokum, ITC's Dennis Spooner and Monty Berman announced the arrival of their masterpiece. The title sequence begins with a hit and run, cuts to a graveyard and concludes with a sepia-tinted business sign, 'Randall and Hopkirk'. A thick white line is drawn through the second name and the word 'Deceased' written underneath.

From the start, *Randall and Hopkirk (Deceased)* announced itself as a series very different from those around it. One of the private eyes is a ghost.

Yes, it sounds stupid now - it sounded stupid then - but ITC usually allowed Spooner and Berman enough rope to hang themselves (they had previously produced *Man in a Suitcase* and *The Champions*). Spooner's basic premise was 'If a partnership is broken by death, does this automatically mean that it is ended?', and he wrote an outline about two detectives, one of whom is killed. Berman liked the idea and, together with director Cyril Frankel as creative consultant, the series entered production.

The role of Jeff Randall, originally written with then-ATV contract artist Dave Allen in mind, was given to Mike Pratt, a former member of Tommy Steele's Cavemen and a songwriter of some merit as well as a fine actor. Pratt was a regular at ITC in the 60s (working with Berman and Frankel on *The Baron* and *The Champions*). Kenneth Cope, already well known to audiences from *That Was the Week That Was* and **Coronation Street** was chosen to play his partner. The third member of the cast, Australian actress Annette Andre, played Marty's permanently bewildered widow, and the final regular was Ivor Dean who took the part of the gruff, ill-natured policeman so beloved by ITC.

The series debuted on Sunday 21 September 1969; the protests began not long afterwards. One reviewer raged 'the fact that there has been no massive protest against *Randall and Hopkirk* indicates to what depressing depths the tolerance level of the TV public has now been pushed'. The main problem with the series was that it never seemed able to make up its mind whether it wanted to be a comedy show or a serious private-eye series with an 'odd' element. Thus, while it gained a cult audience very quickly, many viewers were perplexed and switched over to something less demanding. The pilot episode is a useful indicator of these contradictions. 'My Late Lamented Friend and Partner' begins as an apparently run-of-the-mill crime drama episode and only turns strange when Marty Hopkirk bites the dust ten minutes in. The ghostly Marty appears to his partner (the only

Starring: Mike Pratt (Jeff Randall) • Kenneth Cope (Marty Hopkirk) • Annette Andre (Jean Hopkirk) • Ivor Dean (Inspector Large)

person who can see him) and helps him solve the crime of his murder, but, in doing so, falls foul of a curse which states that he must walk the earth for a hundred years.

Spooner, Berman and their writing team attempted to marry together the disparate elements into a workable format. Sometimes they leaned too heavily on traditional crime styles (as in Ralph Smart's 'But what a Sweet Little Room', the story of a John Christie-type lady-killer, or Donald James's 'Just for the Record', about a pretender to the throne). Occasionally the comedy would overstep the mark, notably in 'Murder Ain't What It Used to Be!', in which David Healy played a 30s-style gangster-ghost, complete with white violin case.

The series followed in the tradition of the other ITC series with a vaguely 'swinging London' feel, maintained by much use of location footage beside the strategically placed stock shots of Piccadilly Circus. And, as with ***The Avengers***, they contained car chases through the green-belt Hertfordshire backroads and glossy, colourful country houses with bizarre interiors.

Ray Austin's 'That's How Murder Snowballs' was a clever tale of a murder in a music-hall which allowed Jeff Randall the opportunity to go undercover as a mind-reading act. The episode, as with many in the series, provided work for a number of young, up-and-coming actors who would later achieve much wider fame, in this case a cameo role for David Jason. Another example was 'When did you Start to Stop Seeing Things?', which featured Keith Barron.

Other well-received episodes included 'Who Killed Cock Robin?', in which the pair have to save Jane Merrow from Cyril Luckham's evil solicitor, 'The Man from Nowhere', which had Ray Brooks appearing in Jean Randall's flat claiming to be the reincarnation of Marty, 'A Disturbing Case', a slapstick comedy episode co-written by Mike Pratt, and 'Vendetta for a Dead Man', wherein George Sewell provided a fine performance as a man jailed by Marty's evidence who turns up seeking vengeance.

'The Ghost who Saved the Bank at Monte Carlo', aside from a witty plot concerning Marty's strange aunt who believes she has discovered a system for winning at roulette, made great use of stock footage to turn Borehamwood film studios into the French Riviera. Its remarkable cast included Brian Blessed, Nicholas Courtney, Veronica Carlson and Roger Delgado. 'Somebody Just Walked Over My Grave' was an outrageous vision of late-60s counter-culture, best exemplified by Nigel Terry as an agoraphobic hippie painter who tells Jeff, 'I don't dig Rembrandt, man, he's a square!' The scenes in which Marty attempts to influence the result of an England/Germany football match were priceless.

Filming was not without its dilemmas: there were huge logistical problems on 'The Ghost Talks' after Mike Pratt broke his legs in an accident at his home, and

(21 Sep 69–13 Mar 70)

1 My Late Lamented Friend and Partner
2 A Disturbing Case
3 All Work and No Pay
4 Never Trust a Ghost
5 That's How Murder Snowballs
6 Just for the Record
7 Murder Ain't What It Used to Be!
8 Whoever Heard of a Ghost Dying?
9 The House on Haunted Hill
10 When did you Start to Stop Seeing Things?
11 The Ghost who Saved the Bank at Monte Carlo
12 For the Girl who has Everything
13 But what a Sweet Little Room
14 Who Killed Cock Robin?
15 The Man from Nowhere
16 When the Spirit Moves You
17 Somebody Just Walked Over My Grave
18 Could You Recognise the Man Again?
19 A Sentimental Journey
20 Money to Burn
21 The Ghost Talks
22 It's Supposed to be Thicker than Water
23 The Trouble with Women
24 Vendetta for a Dead Man
25 You Can Always Find a Fall Guy
26 The Smile Behind the Veil

[It is impossible to give an exact episode order for ***Randall and Hopkirk (Deceased)***. The series was not networked: whilst Midlands, LWT, Yorkshire and Granada began showing the series in the week commencing 21 Sep 69, in other regions the series didn't debut until as late as Nov 70. The above order is that adopted by London Weekend - the only company to broadcast all 26 episodes in one continuous run. In some regions, previously un-screened episodes would turn up in repeat runs well into the mid-70s.]

had to spend the episode in a hospital bed being told a story, in flashback, by Marty. At least it gave Kenneth Cope the rare chance to interact with other characters.

After the series ended, it was syndicated in the USA under the dreadful title *My Partner, The Ghost* in 1973 and, predictably perhaps, died a death. For several years, repeats were held up due to the untimely death of Mike Pratt; however, the series was resold to the networks in 1985 and has since enjoyed something of a renaissance as a new generation of fans discover the wacky world of *Randall and Hopkirk*. In 1994 the series was repeated highly successfully on BBC2.

This is not to imply that the series did not have deep faults: its best jokes (Marty interrupts Jeff whilst he's talking, and the onlooker is confronted by Jeff holding a conversation with the wall, or Marty's use of wind-power) were used to such an extent that the series seemed in danger of choking to death on them. And after about 20 episodes of Randall getting his face redesigned three times a week, the novelty began to wear thin. Still, the inventiveness and wit of *Randall and Hopkirk* are what sets it apart from many of its contemporaries.

A Mike Pratt line in 'A Sentimental Journey' seems to sum it all up: 'This is ridiculous,' says an anguished Jeff as one of Marty's stunts has gone drastically wrong again.

Wasn't it just, though?

The Tomorrow People

- **Thames Television** (ITV),
  Tetra Films/Reeves Entertainment Group/Nickelodeon/Thames (ITV)
- Colour
- **93 episodes** (*c.* 25 minutes) ◆ 1973-79, 1992–95
- **Creator:** Roger Price
- **Writers:** Roger Price, Brian Finch, John Watkins, Grant Cathro, Lee Pressman
- **Directors:** Paul Bernard, Roger Price, Stan Woodward, Vic Hughes, Leon Thau, Darrol Blake, Dennis Kirkland, Richard Mervyn, Peter Webb, Peter Yolland, Ron Oliver
- **Producers:** Ruth Boswell, Roger Price, Vic Hughes
- **Executive producer:** Alan Horrox (1992–95 only)

Starring: Nicholas Young (John) • Peter Vaughan-Clarke (Stephen) • Sammie Winmill (Carol) • Steve Salmon (Kenny) • Philip Gilbert (voice of TIM, Timus) • Elizabeth Adare (Elizabeth) • Dean Lawrence (Tyso) • Mike Holloway (Mike) • Nigel Rhodes (Andrew) • Misako Koba (Hsui Tai) • Kristian Schmid (Adam Neuman) • Kristen Ariza (Lisa Davies) • Adam Pearce (Kevin Wilson) • Christian Tessier (Marmaduke 'Megabyte' Damon) • Naomie Harris (Ami Jackson)

Stylish, intelligent, well-written ... *The Tomorrow People* was none of these. Thames's post-*Ace of Wands* attempt to muscle in on ***Doctor Who***'s 'family sci-fi' territory, the series was cheap, illogical, silly, and its 'special effects' made the BBC's attempts at colour separation overlay look state-of-the-art.

The series was the brainchild of writer/director/producer Roger Price. The opening story was a clever and surprisingly nasty tale about the 'breaking out' of children who represented the next stage of human evolution, homo superior. Stephen was the most recent addition to this select band. He joined the already-trained John, Kenny and Carol in their underground pad, where they were guided in their quest to benefit mankind by the computer TIM, entrusted to them by the oft-mentioned, but seldom seen, Galactic Trig.

The main things that *The Tomorrow People* had going for it were youthful energy, Nicholas Young's performance as John, and an extraordinary title sequence, which mixed memorable images with Dudley Simpson's tingling theme music. Unfortunately, the rest of the season fell back on children's series clichés which moved the series closer to Enid Blyton than ***Doctor Who***. The series' other characters, such as the grimly working-class youths, Ginge and Leftie, were abominably clichéd, and the only memorable thing about the early episodes was the evil shape-changing robot Jedikiah.

There was certainly a glam rock approach to the series, with cheap sets and tacky dialogue, laughable and yet, at the same time, gloriously kitsch. *Starburst* magazine said the series 'embodied images to be found in the lyrics of Bolan and Bowie. *The Tomorrow People* really were the children of the revolution.'

By the second season, Winmill and Salmon had left the series to be replaced by Elizabeth Adare. Her debut, 'The Blue and the Green', has claim to being the best *Tomorrow People* story. The plot revolved around aliens attempting to start a war amongst the youth of Earth by dividing them according to the colour of the new fashion craze for lapel badges. 'A Rift in Time' was also good, although some of the dialogue was hilarious. When Stephen asks 'Hey, why don't we just jaunt back in time to find out about the vase?', John's reply is 'You're forgetting, we haven't discovered time travel yet.' 'Oh yeah ... ' responds Stephen.

Flares, tank-tops, polo-necks ... It must be the Tomorrow People. And Jedikiah on a bike

The addition of the young gypsy Tyso, in the third season, added to the laboured comedy elements that had begun to creep into *The Tomorrow People*, which reached their height with 'A Man for Emily', in which Peter Davison played an alien whose notions of earth culture have been formed from cowboy movies. Davison met his future wife, Sandra Dickinson, on the show: she was playing the eponymous heroine. The season also featured an excellent new villain in Trevor Bannister's Colonel Masters, and finished with 'The Revenge of Jedikiah', which seemed to be a perfect way to end the series, concluding as it did with all of the Tomorrow People leaving Earth for Galactic Trig. Sadly, the show returned.

The 1976 series began with a new arrival, Mike, played by Mike Holloway. His claim to fame was as drummer with Flintlock, who had a residency on Roger Price's juvenile review show *You Must Be Joking*. The appearance of several future celebrities, such as Keith Chegwin as a rebel, Peter Duncan as a gladiator and Nicholas Lyndhurst as a stormtrooper, did not disguise the fact that camp humour was taking over. 'One Law', and, from the subsequent season, the surprisingly grim 'The Dirtiest Business' were passable drama, but the loss of Stephen at the end of the season, followed by the decision to make John and Elizabeth into parental figures, ensured that *The Tomorrow People* lost its edge completely.

'Hitler's Last Secret' revealed that the reincarnated Führer was an alien slug, 'The Thargon Menace' featured an outrageous parody of Idi Amin, and 'The Living

First season
(30 Apr–30 Jul 73)
- The Slaves of Jedikiah (Five episodes)
- The Medusa Strain (Four episodes)
- The Vanishing Earth (Four episodes)

Second season
(4 Feb–6 May 74)
- The Blue and the Green

14 An Apple for the Teacher
15 The Changing Picture
16 The Trojan Horse
17 Cuckoo in the Nest
18 The Swarming Season
- A Rift in Time

19 Vase of Mystery
20 Turn of the Thumb
21 From Little Acorns
22 Rise of the Roman Empire
- The Doomsday Men

23 Dressed to Kill
24 The Burning Sword
25 Run Rabbit Run
26 The Shuttlecock

Third season
(26 Feb–21 May 75)
- Secret Weapon

27 Lost and found
28 Not quite a Sleeping Beauty
29 Whose Side are you on Professor
30 A Present from Russia
- Worlds Away

31 Secret of the Pyramid
32 Hound of the Night
33 More for the Burning
- A Man for Emily

34 The Fastest Gun
35 Here We Go Round the Doozlum
36 A Man for Emily
- The Revenge of Jedikiah

37 Curse of the Mummy's Tomb
38 Last Chance
39 Farewell Performance

Fourth season
(28 Jan–10 Mar 76)
- One Law

40 One Law for the Poor
41 One Law for the Rich
42 Which Prohibits them Equally from Stealing Bread
- Into the Unknown

43 The Visitor
44 The Father-Ship
45 The Tunnel
46 The Circle

Fifth season
(28 Feb–4 Apr 77)
- The Dirtiest Business

47 A Spy is Born
48 A Spy Dies...
- A Much Needed Holiday

49 Spilled Porridge
50 Just Desserts
- The Heart of Sogguth

51 Beat the Drum
52 Devil in Disguise

Sixth season
(15 May–26 Jun 78)
- The Lost Gods

53 Flight of Fancy
54 Life before Death
- Hitler's Last Secret

55 Men Like Rats
56 Seeds of Destruction
- The Thargon Menace

57 Unexpected Guests
58 Playing with Fire

Seventh season
(9 Oct–13 Nov 78)
- Castle of Fear

59 Ghosts and Monsters
60 Fighting Spirit
- Achilles Heel

61 A Room at the Inn
62 Everything to Lose
- The Living Skins

63 A Harmless Fashion
64 Cold War

Eighth season
(29 Jan–19 Feb 79)
- War of the Empires

65 Close Encounter
66 Contact!
67 Standing Alone
68 All in the Mind

Ninth season
(18 Nov–16 Dec 92)
- The Tomorrow People (Five episodes)

Tenth season
(4 Jan–8 Mar 94)
- The Culex Experiment (Five episodes)
- Monsoon Man (Five episodes)

Eleventh season
(4 Jan–8 Mar 95)
- The Ramases Connection (Five episodes)
- The Living Stones (Five episodes)

Skins' had the world saved from an attack of balloons by the common cold. Worst of all was the final story, 'War of the Empires', which featured a peanut-eating US President. Subtle stuff.

The lengthy ITV strike of 1979 killed *The Tomorrow People*, and Price left to work in Canada. In 1992, however, he launched a new version of the show, starring ex-*Neighbours* actor Kristian Schmid. We wanted to be appalled. But Schmid was a revelation, and the series was miles better than the original. While no reference was made to the 70s series, the children this time teleporting (rather than jaunting) without the aid of a belt, the first story had the production values of modern action television alongside Price's humour, this time played just right. The best of the five effects-heavy and increasingly sophisticated stories were the last two, in which Christopher Lee played the reincarnated Rameses, and the youngsters fought off a full-scale alien invasion.

It's ironic to finally be able to say, after all these years, that it's a pity that *The Tomorrow People* was cancelled.

Sapphire & Steel

- **ATV** (ITV) ◆ Colour
- **34 episodes** (30 minutes) ◆ 1979-82
- **Creator:** P. J. Hammond
- **Writers:** P. J. Hammond, Don Houghton, Anthony Read
- **Directors:** David Foster, Shaun O'Riordan
- **Producer:** Shaun O'Riordan

Regular cast: David McCallum (Steel) • Joanna Lumley (Sapphire)

With: David Collings (Silver)

There are many methods of holding a television audience: interesting characters, intriguing plots, sparkling dialogue, stunning direction. Total lack of explanation is not generally regarded to be one of these methods. *Sapphire & Steel* never gave an inch to its audience, and that was why they loved it.

The characters of the title were 'elements', two of 115 of their kind, some of whom were named in the title sequence, who dealt with disturbances in the fabric of time, although sapphire and steel are not elements in the usual sense, and neither were several of the others mentioned.

The first two seasons each had two stories: a search for parents who had vanished while visiting a child's bedroom, a railway station inhabited by ghosts, a couple from the future who were attacked by the spirits of dead animals, and a battle against the faceless man who had appeared in every photograph ever taken. The remaining two stories involved a murder mystery at a nostalgia party which actually goes back in time, and a trap for our heroes at a time-shifting service station.

The plot summaries give some idea of how exotic the series was. Time is a vengeful force, continually trying to harm and disturb mankind. Rather than offering complex pseudoscientific explanations for the bizarre happenings, plots were explained through archetypal and mythic imagery. The dialogue was clipped and witty, and the characterization was as complex as that in any one-off play. Steel was a strong, silent man, able to block tremendous forces with his body and exert vast power. He spoke in quick, humourless, commands. However, he was not subtle. Only Sapphire could make time flow backwards (an effect achieved by making Lumley's eyes glow blue), convince humans of anything, and achieve instant trust in those they met. She was flirtatious, witty, and enjoyed the company of human beings far more than Steel did. Completing the trio was Silver, an expert in gadgets, who could open locks by rubbing his fingers together. He and Sapphire had a teasing relationship, which occasionally angered Steel.

The characterizations were achieved very quickly and expertly, never hinting at the elements' origins. The creator of the show, and writer of all but the murder mystery, was P.J. Hammond, an author with credits on *Hazell*, ***Z Cars*** and ***Dixon of Dock Green***. However, it was his work on the children's series *Ace of Wands* that indicated where his interests lay, magical opponents battling the occult adventurer Tarot in an ordinary English setting. Originally *Sapphire & Steel* was destined to fill the same slot. However, the idea was passed from Thames to ATV, where David Reid, the head of drama, was kept up all night by the disturbing format. The series, when

First season
(10 Jul–22 Nov 79)
Fourteen episodes

[Episodes 10–14 of the first season were originally scheduled for transmission between 9 and 23 Aug 79, but were delayed.]

it appeared, would be in an adult slot, ITV's only attempt to find the early-evening 'ironing board' group of older children and relaxing housewives with a fantasy series.

Second season
(6 Jan–5 Feb 81)
Ten episodes

Third season
(11–26 Aug 81)
Six episodes

Fourth season
(19–31 Aug 82)
Four episodes

The tone of the series was set by the first story: a claustrophobic environment (shot at ATV's Elstree studios), a small number of ordinary people, and a terrifying force that acted through everyday objects (in this case a nursery-rhyme book). There was no violence, but much confrontation and surreal action. There was also the merest hint of background as another element, Lead, arrived to help the menaced heroes.

Viewers quickly realized that they were watching a game: they didn't know the rules, but they liked the participants, and could recognize aspects of the game from the jargon. Besides, much of the mystical lore hinted at was pitched at the level of folk wisdom. It is tempting to think that *Sapphire & Steel* appealed to the female audience in much the same way that ***Blake's 7*** did: the male viewers were concerned with explanations, but the women just knew that the stories 'felt right'. For once, television had elected not to talk down to its audience.

The incidental music, by Cyril Ornadel, was a gentle mixture of mood pieces and recurring themes that subtly helped to establish the setting. The direction was extremely inventive, encouraging the actors to add shades of meaning to every speech, particularly when our heroes' silent telepathic conversations added ironic counterpoint to the speeches of humans around them.

Memorable moments of horror include Steel giving the ghosts of the wartime dead the soul of Tully, the innocent psychic investigator, to prevent further chaos, and George McDee, the beneficent scientist, begging his lover to shoot him rather than let him release a deadly virus. However, the most nightmarish images of all came from story four, concerning a blank-faced man who could free or trap anyone in photographs. Taken straight from Magritte, his initial appearance was horrifying, as was the moment when he set light to a picture containing the soul of a woman, whose dying screams were heard. Sapphire and Steel finally trapped him in a kaleidoscope, placed on a sinking ship which was to be encased in a glacier. However, Steel's final advice to the last survivor of the piece was chilling: to burn all photographs of herself, and never allow another one to be taken. Surrealistic, yes, but somehow resonant with folklore and truth.

Of course, it wasn't all as good as that. The third story was an unsubtle critique of meat-eating, involving a mobile fur coat and a hilarious assault by a feather pillow that very visibly used up David McCallum's ability to be earnest.

Sapphire & Steel was beset by poor scheduling and technical problems, the first season being interrupted by a strike which closed down the ITV regions completely, the last being shown by Central a long time after ATV had lost its franchise. It is, however, fondly remembered by both its audience and the actors involved. One can but hope that the situation in which we last saw Sapphire and Steel, trapped by their enemies, staring out of the window of what they thought was a café, into the endless void of space, was one that they escaped with their usual flair.

Robin of Sherwood

- **HTV/Goldcrest** (ITV) ◆ Colour
- **24 episodes** (standard length: 50 minutes) ◆ 1984-86
- **Creator**: Richard Carpenter
- **Writers**: Richard Carpenter, Anthony Horowitz, Andrew McCulloch, John Flanagan
- **Directors**: Ian Sharp, Robert Young, Alex Kirby, James Allen, Gerry Mill, Ben Bolt, Dennis Abey, Christopher King, Sid Robertson
- **Producers**: Paul Knight, Esta Charkham

Regular cast: Michael Praed/Jason Connery (Robin Hood) • Nickolas Grace (The Sheriff of Nottingham) • Judi Trott (Marion) • Clive Mantle (Little John) • Peter Llewellyn Williams (Much) • Robert Addie (Guy of Gisburne) • Ray Winstone (Will Scarlet) • Phil Rose (Tuck) • John Abineri (Herne the Hunter) • Mark Ryan (Nasir)

With: Philip Jackson (Abbot Hugo) • Martin West (Martin) • Steven Osborne (James) • Stuart Linden (Old Prisoner) • Claire Toeman (Meg) • Anthony Valentine (Simon De Belleme) • Jeremy Bulloch (Edward) • Richard O'Brien (Gulnar) • George Baker (Sir Richard of Leaford) • James Coombes (Grendal) • Philip Davis (Prince John) • Robbie Bulloch (Matthew)

Many television series have been criticized by Mary Whitehouse for their use of violence, but few have had accusations of paganism levelled against them. The show in question was the product of one man's attention to detail and his love for the subject matter.

Robin of Sherwood is set towards the end of the 12th century, a time when the Saxon peasantry are still dominated by Norman oppression. Robin and Much live at Loxley Mill, and when that is razed to the ground, Robin seeks vengeance with a motley collection of criminals, including the previously-enslaved Saracen, Nasir. (This development was not originally in the script, but director Ian Sharp pointed out what a superb character the Saracen was. Carpenter agreed, but kept Nasir's dialogue to a minimum, allowing Mark Ryan only some fun bits of body language and pithy comments. It shows how much influence the series had on the legend that the movie *Robin Hood: Prince of Thieves* (US 91) also included a Saracen hero.)

'The heroic figure is the man who takes on the world alone ... I think that if you can get a gut reaction from your audience, it's because deep, deep in their subconscious they are attracted to this idea of being your own man, in a society where very few people are ... I think there is an element of anarchy in all artists,' Carpenter said in *Timescreen*, adding that he paid particular attention to the work of Joseph Campbell, the folklore historian whose models of generic heroic myths had influenced, amongst others, George Lucas.

All these factors came together in *Robin*, a show conceived as the perfect heroic fable. Three things feature in the creation of the show: historical realism, a desire to at least touch upon previous interpretations of the Robin Hood story, and the influences of magic and myth. This was, if you like, the Complete Robin Hood, in much the same way as Granada's ***Sherlock Holmes*** was the ultimate modern reading of that text.

Historical realism is important in *Robin* in that it gives a grim foundation out of which to build the more wonderful elements. The Sheriff of Nottingham is a 'devious political animal', whose main reason for not winning against Robin is that he doesn't feel motivated to lose so many men in the forest. When he has got a good reason, he sets an efficient and ultimately deadly trap. King John may be insane, but he pauses to deliver a precise little speech on the complexities of the succession. His brother, Richard, is a wonderfully complex figure, charming the romantic Robin into thinking that his arrival restores everything the outlaw fought for. However, at his court, it becomes clear that Robin has become a political symbol, and won't be able to change the system from within. He rebels just as Richard orders him murdered.

The most terrifying thing about the villains in the show was their casual abuse of power. Gisburne, in 'The Children of Israel', having taken part in a purge of the Jews from Nottingham, actually says that he was 'only obeying orders'. Despite this, a series of convincing reasons were put forward as to why Robin was content to humiliate Gisburne and not, as Will kept urging, kill him. The best of these was that the people's hatred for Guy kept them supporting Robin, another good translation of folk tradition into political wisdom. Some of Robin's men are killed in 'Seven Poor Knights from Acre', and this both heightens our interest in the fate of the others and explains why Robin is content to lead a team of specialists. Time after time we see that Robin's men only survive because of the superiority of longbow to crossbow. Questions such as 'Isn't six men and one woman a recipe for trouble?' and 'How do the outlaws eat?' were actually addressed. The series took time out to convince the viewer that it could all be true.

Carpenter seemed determined to namecheck every facet of the Robin legend, apart from including new variations on the fight over the stream and turning the Lincoln Green of designer tights into highly-effective camouflage. The words 'Merry Men' are used, but only once, in a sarcastic speech from the Sheriff. Alan A Dale is a guest character, and Will Scarlet has darker reasons for his name than wearing a red hat.

The mythical power of *Robin of Sherwood* partly derived from its unblinking acceptance of magic. Herne was a shaman, acting as the Horned God of Celtic myth, but he still managed to travel effortlessly to wherever the outlaws went. In 'Lord of the Trees', the group attend the blessing ceremony for the woods, a purely pagan tradition. 'Blessed be,' says Robin. 'Aye, and Amen too,' replies Tuck. Gisburne is driven from the forest and back to the safety of his castle, an indication of how far the Norman tradition differed from the Saxon/Celtic surroundings.

The beauty of the forests around Bradford-on-Avon in Wiltshire, the impressionistic use of lighting, and the BAFTA award-winning Clannad soundtrack all helped to conjure up a mystical atmosphere. Lamenting their dead comrades at the end of 'Seven Poor Knights from Acre', Robin tells his people that they are now free, part of the green, and won't be tortured or hunted any more. The camera pans up to a startlingly beautiful forest scene, and, for a moment, the viewer is quite certain about what the outlaws are fighting for. As Robin says, 'Nothing's forgotten. Nothing is ever forgotten.'

When Carpenter was told that Praed had been offered a musical on Broadway, he decided to give Robin a hero's death, one that befitted the Hooded Man. Herne warns Robin of his fate, and so he makes sure Marion and Much are safe before standing alone on a hilltop, watching the Sheriff's men come forward. All the

First season
(28 Apr–26 May 84)
1 Robin Hood and the Sorcerer (100 minutes)
2 The Witch of Elsdon
3 Seven Poor Knights from Acre
4 Alan A Dale
5 The King's Fool

Second season
(9 Mar–13 Apr 85)
6 The Prophecy
7 The Children of Israel
8 Lord of the Trees
9 The Enchantment
10 The Swords of Wayland (100 minutes)
11 The Greatest Enemy

Third season
(5 Apr–28 Jun 86)
12 Herne's Son (part one)
13 Herne's Son (part two)
14 The Power of Albion
15 The Inheritance
16 The Sheriff of Nottingham
17 The Cross of St Ciricus
18 Cromm Cruac
19 The Betrayal
20 Adam Bell
21 The Pretender
22 Rutterkin
23 The Time of the Wolf (part one)
24 The Time of the Wolf (part two)

principals put in some great acting in 'The Greatest Enemy', but particularly Judi Trott, whose stoic 'Are we going to die?' is just one of the lines she invests with great strength.

Robin fires an arrow into the air, breaks his bow, and is shot down. The sequence is emotional and powerful, but full of hope. We never see the body. A new Hooded Man frees the captured outlaws, leading Mary Whitehouse to complain of a series that 'resurrected its hero'. *Robin* was always a problem for the NVLA, who complained about its violence (although the swordplay was strictly zero blood, and owed about as much to Errol Flynn as to Kung Fu movies) and its depiction of Lucifer in 'The Swords of Wayland'.

In the third season it was revealed that Herne's new Son was Robert of Huntingdon, a noble, Carpenter neatly using the other version of the Robin Hood legend (one more acceptable to courtly ears). Initially, Robert lives a double life, an interesting prospect until Guy suspects the truth. This happens in 'The Power of Albion', a great, simple adventure that plays on Connery's few strengths, and shows the way the third season could have gone.

Lewis Collins appeared in the episode 'The Sheriff of Nottingham' as Philip Mark, the would-be new Sheriff. With him came a 'Professional Beggar' by the name of Martin Shaw. This was typical of the in-jokes and camaraderie on what was, by all accounts, a very happy set.

In the episode 'The Cross of St Ciricus', Tuck discovers that Robin and Guy are actually brothers. Robin has, of course, fallen for Marion, but she fends him off until near the end of the season. Finally, in a mystical battle against the druid Gulnar (wonderfully played by Richard O'Brien), Robin kills a clay double of himself. Marion finds it, and, snapping with new grief, commits herself to a nunnery (Judi Trott having decided not to do the then-proposed fourth season). Unfortunately, with the collapse of Goldcrest, no funding was available for another season. As Carpenter says, if he'd known that, he'd have married them off.

There were problems with the third season. The length, for one thing, made the continual escapes and rescues seem more improbable, especially since the Sheriff now did seem to be doing his best to catch them. New writers were brought on to the show who didn't have the same feeling for archetypal content as Carpenter did, turning it into a standard action romp. The final problem was Robin himself. Jason Connery was positively wooden, not only in comparison to Michael Praed (who managed to be charismatic, mystical, and innocent all at the same time) but also compared to the cast around him. Particularly dreadful was the direct contrast between his bland stillness and Ray Winstone's mobile, angry, and always interesting Will Scarlet. All the intriguing plot developments in the world couldn't help an actor who was so out of his depth.

And so the series ended. Carpenter wrote the first of three book adaptations of the series' episodes, which has since become the definitive Puffin version of the subject. There were hopes of a feature film, until the bout of Robin mania that produced two features in the same year. Still, memories of sunlight, good triumphing over evil, and beautiful dialogue live on.

'Nothing's forgotten. Nothing is ever forgotten.'

HISTORICAL DRAMA

Historical drama proves to be a surprisingly detailed microcosm for TV as a whole: from *The Borgias* and *The Return of the Native* to ***Upstairs, Downstairs*** and *Brideshead Revisited*, it runs the gamut of emotions, popular affection and overall (in)competence.

The afternoon of the reopening of BBC Television after the war on 7 June 1946 saw a historical costume drama in the shape of George More O'Ferrall's production of Bernard Shaw's *The Dark Lady of the Sonnets*. However, given the nature of the embryonic medium, such a presentation was very much the exception rather than the rule during the late 40s and early 50s. Robert Louis Stevenson's *The Black Arrow* was adapted in 1951, with the author's unfinished *St Ives* being serialized four years later. Other historical classics of the era included Nigel Kneale's adaptation of *Wuthering Heights* (1953) and Rex Tucker's 1954 serial *The Three Musketeers* (starring Laurence Payne, Paul Whitsun-Jones, Paul Hansard and Roger Delgado).

Although the BBC had produced a six-part children's serial *Robin Hood* in 1953, with Patrick Troughton in the title role, ITC swept into a field it would come to dominate in 1955 with the immortal *The Adventures of Robin Hood*. The production had a certain class about it, as Lew Grade's eyes were pinned firmly on the American market, and it was blessed with excellent scripts (many written by refugees from the McCarthyite purges of Hollywood, who clearly identified with the outlaws), wonderful continuity, and much charm. The actors (Richard Greene as Robin, Alan Wheatley as the Sheriff, Paul Eddington as Will Scarlet) seemed to enjoy themselves nearly as much as the millions who watched every sword fight with bated breath. Notable directors included Lindsay Anderson and Hammer stalwart Terence Fisher.

In 1956 the same executive producer (Hannah Weinstein) and many of the same writers oversaw *The Adventures of Sir Lancelot* (starring William Russell) and *The Buccaneers* (with Robert Shaw's thigh-slapping pirate, Dan Tempest). ITC also scored with *The Count of Monte Cristo* (1956) and *The Adventures of William Tell* (1958, starring Conrad Phillips). Other ITV adventures of the era included *The Adventures of the Scarlet Pimpernel* (1955-56, starring Marius Goring), and *Ivanhoe*, starring Roger Moore, which began in 1958. Moore went on to become famous, but who now remembers ITC's 1958 offering *Sword of Freedom*, which detailed the 15th-century adventures of a swashbuckling Italian painter? *Zorro* it wasn't.

As the 50s drew to a close, the BBC's attitude to drama in a non-contemporary setting remained resolute in the face of ITC's simple action series. Peter R. Newman's *Yesterday's Enemy* (1958), set in the Burmese jungle in 1942, dared to suggest that British soldiers at war aren't always above reproach. Starring Gordon Jackson, the play became an equally controversial Hammer film the following year. In 1960, BBC producer Peter Dews adapted Shakespeare's *Richard II, Henry IV, Henry V, Henry VI* and *Richard III* under the collective heading *An Age of Kings*, followed some three years later by *The Spread of the Eagle*, which turned *Coriolanus, Antony and Cleopatra* and *Julius Caesar* into a nine-week serial. The BBC moved just a little closer to adventure mode with *The Splendid Spur* (1960), a Civil War serial starring Patrick Troughton, while the ITV companies were content to produce such simple twaddle as *Sir Francis Drake*, starring Terence Morgan, and *Richard the Lionheart* (1962).

In 1963, Granada brought some much needed class to ITV's historical output with *The Victorians*, a series of eight sixty-minute plays detailing life in the 19th century, produced by Philip Mackie. Two years later, a similar format was tried with *The Edwardians*, featuring four plays from the 1900s, produced by Philip Latham. Mackie also produced Granada's adaptations of Middleton and Rowley's *The Changeling* and Middleton's *Women Beware Women*, which were shown in 1965 under the not inaccurate umbrella title *Blood and Thunder*.

Despite such plays – and historical anthologies like the BBC's *Detective* (1964) and *Jury Room* (1965) – 60s television seemed to have little time for historical drama, its precise limits seemingly already established by the ITC adventure yarns. It was one thing to adapt the Jeeves and Wooster stories in *P. G. Wodehouse's The World of Wooster* (1965) and bring an Edwardian gent to swinging London (*Adam Adamant Lives!*), but quite another to expect a generation that TV executives rarely understood to enjoy anything as 'square' as history. The BBC bucked the trend, to great effect, with ***The Forsyte Saga***, and, to a lesser extent, with the 16th-century Anglo-Scottish adventure *The Borderers* (1968, starring Iain Cuthbertson, Michael Gambon and Joseph Brady). Thames followed the lives of British soldiers in India in the 1880s in *Frontier* (1968), while ATV seemed to be unsure what to make of Ted Willis's *Virgin of the Secret Service*, with a Bondian spy playing against a similar historical Indian milieu. 1969's interesting history of the Marlborough family, *The First Churchills*, prefigured later treatments of historical characters.

The 70s saw a revival of the historical drama's fortunes. There were adventures in the ITC mould, including HTV's *Arthur of the Britons* (1972), starring Oliver Tobias, which attempted to inject some brutality into an otherwise comfortable children's format. Southern's adaptation of Robert Louis Stevenson's *Black Arrow* is fondly remembered, as is *Kidnapped* (1979, starring David McCallum). Richard O'Sullivan's career took an exciting new twist when he played the title role in Richard Carpenter's *Dick Turpin* (also 1979). Imported and redubbed delights, intended for younger viewers, included *The Flashing Blade* ('It's better to have fought and lost/Than not have fought at all') and *The Water Margin*, the latter proving to be incredibly violent.

Lavish serials based on well-known novels included *The Pallisers* (1974), an attempt to do for Trollope what ***The Forsyte Saga*** had done for Galsworthy, and ***Poldark***. Yorkshire's adaptations included versions of Winifred Holtby's *South Riding* (1974), starring Dorothy Tutin as the 30s schoolmistress, *Raffles* (1977), starring Anthony Valentine and Christopher Strauli, and *Flambards* (1979). The BBC continued to work on slightly more high-brow productions, such as *Last of the Mohicans* (1971) and an epic serialization of *War and Peace* (1972).

There were some interesting cul-de-sacs along the way. The BBC's 1977 serial *The Eagle of the Ninth* and Thames's *Warrior Queen* (1978) both depicted the years of Roman rule. Much broader in scope was 1975's *Churchill's People*, a saga based on Churchill's *History of the English-Speaking Peoples*, which was a hugely-expensive flop. Normally, though, the BBC could be relied upon to produce dramas of the quality of ***The Six Wives of Henry VIII*** and ***Elizabeth R.*** In doing so they prompted a fascination with kings, queens and other historical figures that was to persist throughout much of the decade. 1974's *Fall of Eagles* was the BBC's 13-part depiction of the collapse of the Romanov, Hohenzollern and Hapsburg dynasties. 1975 saw ATV's *Edward the Seventh*, a visually stunning production that starred Timothy West, Robert Hardy, Sir John Gielgud, and Annette Crosbie as Victoria. Crosbie won a BAFTA award for her performance, and described Victoria as 'emotional, hysterical, obstinate, possessive and jealous. In fact, perfectly normal.'

Thames had already proved their class in the field of 'docu-drama' with *Jennie, Lady Randolph Churchill* and *Napoleon and Love* (both 1974). *Edward and Mrs Simpson*, in 1978, was, however, a revelation. The controversy it generated (the 82-year-old Duchess of Windsor managed to get it banned in France) is now forgotten, but memories of Edward Fox's astonishing performance live on. The same year saw John Mortimer's *Will Shakespeare* (starring Tim Curry, Ian McShane, John McEnery, André Morell and Simon MacCorkindale) and *Disraeli*, starring Ian McShane, both produced by ATV, and LWT's *Lillie* (with Francesca Annis as Lillie Langtry).

The 70s was also dominated by a series of productions that were simultaneously majestic acts of escapism and detailed critiques of the ever-present class system. The cycle began with the hugely successful ***Upstairs, Downstairs***, to which the BBC responded with *The Duchess of Duke Street*, a Saturday night staple for a couple of years. It starred Gemma Jones as Louisa 'Duchess' Trotter, who rose from maid to hotel manager in Edwardian London, and had the effortless quality of all the BBC's costume dramas. (1991's *The House of Elliot*, devised by ***Upstairs, Downstairs*** creators Eileen Atkins and Jean Marsh, was very much in this style.)

The other major focus was the 20th century's times of conflict, the engaging Great War aerial romp *Wings* proving an interesting adjunct to the usual concentration on World War II. The very popular *A Family at War*, which began in 1970, brought a soapy feel to proceedings. Although not dissimilar from the films of the war and immediate post-war era, series such as *Manhunt* (also 1970), ***Colditz*** and ***Secret Army*** tended to avoid jingoistic traps. All took time to portray the Nazis as thinking human beings, with the war itself often to blame for the changes in people's character.

This loose trend continued with Thames's drama-documentary *The Pathfinders* (1972), 1978's *Enemy at the Door*, concerning the German occupation of the Channel Islands, and Euston's hugely popular *Danger UXB* (1979). 1988's *Piece of Cake* concerned the often less-than-glamorous antics of young RAF pilots and excited much popular interest, but its uncompromising depiction of frightened, immature men did not endear itself to many who claimed that it was a far step from reality. The same year's *Wish Me Luck* was less controversial, and, almost as a consequence, much less interesting.

The 80s didn't just want to examine the 'old' themes like war, it wanted to create its own sub-genre, the historical sex-romp. The two strongest examples are the BBC's twin follies of 1981 and 1983, *The Borgias* and *The Cleopatras*. The former cost £2.4 million, had numerous orgy scenes and some terrible acting, and was loved by millions of pubescent schoolboys; the latter starred Richard Griffiths as Potbelly, various young actresses with little hair and clothing to match, and was just about as hopeless. It remains to be seen if the Beeb will ever try mining this little seam again.

Still, there *were* historical triumphs, the most obvious examples being Granada's gems *The Jewel in the Crown* and the earlier *Brideshead Revisited*. Anthony Burgess has described the latter as being 'the best piece of fictional television ever made'. Screenwriter John Mortimer injected playfulness and humour into Evelyn Waugh's novel, with Jeremy Irons playing narrator Charles Ryder, who tells of how he fell in love with both his teddy-carrying Oxford friend Sebastian Flyte (Anthony Andrews) and Flyte's sister, Julia (Diana Quick). The ITV strike held up production for so long that original director Michael Lindsay-Hogg had to leave, and junior director Charles Sturridge found himself in charge of a large crew, a £5 million budget, and Laurence Olivier (who played Lord Marchmain, Sebastian's father). The 11-part series gained nine million viewers, and broke barriers in terms of pace as well as subject matter. Anthony Andrews won the BAFTA for Best Actor, although his career has since been eclipsed by that of Irons.

If *Brideshead* proved anything, it was that the peak-time television audience in Britain was a good deal more open-minded than anyone had given them credit for. In 1981, the gates on budget and intellect were beginning to close, and it was just the right time for Granada (always the most adventurous of the independent companies in the field of drama) to reopen them, which it did, three years later, with its *tour de force*, *The Jewel in the Crown*. Its inception lay in the 1982 play *Staying On*, starring Trevor Howard and Celia Johnson. It concerned a couple remaining in India after the last days of the Raj, and producer Irene Shubik saw it as an experiment to test the viability of a much larger project. It was a useful time for 'Raj television', cast members of *Jewel* appearing in *Gandhi* (GB 82), *A Passage to India* (GB 84), and ITV's other Indian epic, *The Far Pavilions*. The latter was concerned with the adventurous myth of the Frontier, while *Jewel* was much more gritty from the start.

The plot concerned Daphne Manners (Susan Wooldridge), a British nurse, who falls in love with Hari Kumar (Art Malik), an Indian reporter. When Daphne is raped, Hari is arrested by security officer Ronald Merrick (Tim Piggot-Smith). However, screenwriter Ken Taylor fell foul of the problem that another wide-ranging drama, ***The Forsyte Saga***, had faced. Daphne died in childbirth, and Hari was imprisoned until the final episodes. After three episodes, the central characters had been reduced severely. Tim Piggot-Smith had to carry nearly the whole series. It is a mark of his acting skills that, as such a vicious villain, he was charismatic enough to do it. The reception was, as *The Daily Express* said, 'without equal', the programme triumphing at the Royal Television Society Awards (Best Actress for Peggy Ashcroft, the Design Award, and the Writer's Award) and the BAFTAs. The Asian Viewers and Listeners Award went to Susan Wooldridge.

The Jewel in the Crown had been run against the BBC's bought-in epic, *The Thorn Birds*, and beat it hollow in terms of quality, if not in ratings (the latter was possibly because of the Sunday repeats on Channel 4, the first arrangement of this kind, which meant that an astute viewer could watch both).

Granada wasn't alone in the field. In 1981 Euston filmed Elspeth Huxley's autobiography, *The Flame Trees of Thika*, but this was always going to be under *Brideshead*'s shadow. (Euston's best foray into historical mode was 1983's *Reilly – Ace of Spies*, blessed with superb scripts by Troy Kennedy Martin and a fine performance from Sam Neill.) *Thika*, however, proved a tad more interesting than the BBC's *Nanny*, created by and starring Wendy Craig, which began in 1981. More popular was *Tenko*, a wonderfully dirty vision of the reality of war that started the same year. Its splendidly-drawn characters, from a wide range of backgrounds, allowed the writers to examine and contrast the attitudes, fears and determination of women hurled into a Malayan POW camp in 1942. Despite the fact that some claimed that the Japanese guards were too 'nice', the public demanded that it return, which it did (twice). The grim fascination with the 20th century's most terrible moments of history was still unsatisfied, and, in 1987, the BBC finally aped the epic Granada productions with its own £6 million production of Olivia Manning's *Fortunes of War*, starring Kenneth Branagh and Emma Thompson.

Small wonder, then, that back in the mid-70s Lew Grade allowed himself to be convinced by his wife (a Christian) and the Pope to make something more positive, something set firmly in history that was about more than just political intrigue and murder (although there was a lot of that, too). *Jesus of Nazareth* was an epic in all senses of the word (apart from, apparently, Robert Powell's fee), costing over £9 million and taking three years to film. It is estimated that it has now been seen by 500 million people. Lew Grade was born on 25 December, 'but believe me,' he stressed, 'I'm not doing this to celebrate my birthday.'

An attractive recent trend for nostalgic post-war period drama encompasses such varied strands of television as *Heartbeat*, *Oranges are Not the Only Fruit*, *The Buddha of Suburbia*, *The Token King* and *Our Friends in the North*, showing that as television moves towards the millenium, what can be considered as historical drama (the 50s, 60s, 70s – and even the 80s) is moving with it.

1990 gave us the definitive *Jeeves and Wooster*, Stephen Fry and Hugh Laurie extracting every ounce of humour from Clive Exton's peerless adaptations, and the definitive *film noir*/World War II paranoid espionage drama (*Never Come Back*, written by David Pirie from John Mair's novel). Central's *Sharpe*, starring Sean Bean, which began in 1993, can in many ways be seen as the ultimate in ITV costume drama/adventure series, its lineage stretching back to the 80s Oliver Tobias vehicles *Smuggler* and *Adventurer* and the ITC serials of the 50s.

Despite this, the big budget travelogues are much thinner on the ground, 90s' offerings tending to concentrate on more recent (and thus, cheaper) eras, from BBC2's *Portrait of a Marriage* (memorably and salaciously trailed on the pilot episode of *The Mary Whitehouse Experience* an hour before) to Channel 4's equally randy *The Camomile Lawn*. In 1987 Leslie Megahy's outrageous *Screen Two*, *Cariani and the Courtesans*, starring Paul McGann, showed that it was possible to mix kinky sex and historical realism to critical acclaim. It was becoming clear, though, that much of the audience naturally attracted by historical drama wasn't keen on nudity and bonking, that the niche was there for costume drama as viewers remembered it, and as only the BBC could provide it.

The historical drama has therefore been crucial to the BBC's struggle to define itself in terms of quality and viewer appreciation. Series such as *Middlemarch*, *Martin Chuzzlewit* and *Pride and Prejudice* proved incredibly popular, reaffirming what the corporation does best and giving continual employment to Julia Sawalha. This trend has proved so successful that ITV recently stated its intention to re-enter the field.

The Six Wives of Henry VIII/Elizabeth R

- **BBC Television** (BBC2) ◆ **Colour**
- **12 episodes** (90 minutes) ◆ **1970, 1971**
- ***The Six Wives of Henry VIII*** **based on an idea by Maurice Cowan**
- **Writers: Rosemary Anne Sisson, Nick McCarty, Ian Thorne, Jean Morris, Beverley Cross, John Prebble, John Hale, Julian Mitchell, Hugh Whitemore, Ian Rodger**
- **Directors: John Glenister, Naomi Capon, Claude Whatham, Herbert Wise, Richard Martin, Roderick Graham, Donald McWhinnie**
- **Producers: Ronald Travers, Mark Shivas, Roderick Graham**

Starring: ***(The Six Wives of Henry VIII)*** – Keith Michell (Henry VIII) • Annette Crosbie (Catherine of Aragon) • Dorothy Tutin (Anne Boleyn) • Anne Stallybrass (Jane Seymour) • Elvi Hale (Anne of Cleves) • Angela Pleasence (Catherine Howard) • Rosalie Crutchley (Catherine Parr) • Patrick Troughton (Duke of Norfolk) • Sheila Burrell (Lady Rochford) • Bernard Hepton (Thomas Cranmer) • Wolfe Morris (Thomas Cromwell) • John Ronane (Sir Thomas Seymour) ***(Elizabeth R)*** – Glenda Jackson (Elizabeth I) • Robert Hardy (Robert Dudley) • Ronald Hines (William Cecil) • Daphne Slater (Mary Tudor) • Rachel Kempson (Kat Ashley) • Esmond Knight (Bishop de Quadra) • Leonard Sachs (Count de Feria) • John Cairney (Sir James Melville) • Vivian Pickles (Mary, Queen of Scots) • Stephen Murray (Sir Francis Walsingham) • Michael Williams (Duke of Alencon) • Margaretta Scott (Catherine de Medici) • David Collings (Sir Anthony Babington) • Peter Jeffrey (Phillip II of Spain) • Robin Ellis (Earl of Essex) • Paul Hardwick (Fr Robert Parsons) • John Woodvine (Sir Francis Drake) • John Nettleton (Francis Bacon) • Nicholas Selby (Sir Walter Raleigh) • Patrick O'Connell (O'Neill, Earl of Tyrone) • Peter Egan (Earl of Southampton) • Hugh Dickson (Sir Robert Cecil)

'Divorced, beheaded, died, divorced, beheaded, survived.' As any child knows, the life and wives of Henry VIII make for scandalous, racy reading, and so it was hardly surprising that 1970's *The Six Wives of Henry VIII* made contemporary controversies seem tame by comparison. To re-state history in tabloid-speak, Henry's first wife degenerated into flab and ugliness; his second was a sexy, scheming bitch, haunted by accusations of deformity and witchcraft; his third wife bore him the son he so desperately wanted, but died as a result of Henry's insistence that she attend the christening so soon after the birth; his fourth was unfashionable and smelly; his fifth was beautiful and had an affair with his best friend; and his sixth wife married and nursed him because the man she loved needed the money.

To begin by stressing the 'juicy' elements of Henry VIII's life and the resulting screenplay is not to imply that *Six Wives* was a forerunner of later over-blown sex-romps such as *The Borgias*; rather, that there is more than enough drama in Henry's life, properly handled, to enliven hours of wintry TV viewing.

Six Wives was one of the great successes of 70s television. During its initial BBC2 transmission it was watched by an average of four million people, setting new records for the second channel – the audience for the Catherine Howard episode was larger than that watching BBC1 at the time. The series won a record number of Society of Film and Television Arts awards, and was soon repeated on BBC1 to increased popular acclaim. It has now been transmitted in over 75 countries.

The construction of *Six Wives* was quite unusual, being a series of six plays, each examining the impact of one wife. Each play had a different writer, eschewing consistency of vision for vigorous development and change. Mark Shivas, one of the producers, felt that this was important: 'It meant that different facets of Henry's character were polished each week and, almost for the first time, we were able to start to understand this extraordinarily complicated man and his extraordinary wives.' The sets and the detailed costumes were of the quality associated with BBC productions of this sort and, for a time, were exhibited in the Victoria and Albert Museum.

The icing on the cake was the sterling performances from the actors, most obviously Keith Michell's portrayal of Henry, which was varied and powerful. With extra padding and clever make-up, the production coped well with Henry's colossal weight-increase over the years of his reign. Michell, an Australian Shakespearean actor, had previously played Henry for three years in the West End comedy *The King's Mare*, opposite Glynis Johns as Anne of Cleves. His aim for *Six Wives* was much more serious: to offer the public imagination an alternative vision of Henry VIII from that of the rutting, gross beast of Charles Laughton's film performance. 'What one never realizes,' he explained at the time, 'is that Henry VIII was only one king removed from Richard III. I mean, Richard was killed by Henry's father, Henry VII, and when Henry came to the throne all this bloodshed had been going on, this Wars of the Roses business, with kings killing each other right, left and centre, and princes being locked away in the Tower. Henry was the victim of violent times and violent men, but he emerged during a renaissance, and really became the first civilized king of England.'

Michell's rationale prompted a glowing performance, pulling constantly away from caricature, particularly in the first episode when Henry was seen, quite correctly, as a tall, handsome young man, with a strong sense of the romantic.

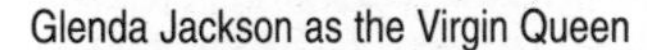
Glenda Jackson as the Virgin Queen

THE SIX WIVES OF HENRY VIII
(1 Jan–5 Feb 70)
1 Catherine of Aragon
2 Anne Boleyn
3 Jane Seymour
4 Anne of Cleves
5 Catherine Howard
6 Catherine Parr

Briefly a celebrity as a result of *Six Wives*, Michell later commented that 'I think we knew when we were making *Henry* that it was something rather special. Everyone got very excited about it and several times the camera crew gave us a round of applause at the end of a particular scene. But even so, I don't think any of us even dreamed it would have been quite so successful.' The series was adapted in 1973 as a film (*Henry VIII and His Six Wives*), with Michell reprising his role alongside Jane Asher and Charlotte Rampling. (He went on to give the world Captain Beaky. Enough said.)

Mark Shivas claimed that the series was a huge success because it 'exemplifies those things which the outside world always associates with the English – royalty and tradition. Plus, there is a bit of sex and violence in between.'

This style coursed through what virtually amounted to a sequel, the following year's *Elizabeth R*. Sharing the same construction and many of the same personnel with *Six Wives*, *Elizabeth R* was so popular that its initial transmission was followed by an immediate BBC1 repeat, a highly unusual and swift response to public and critical acclaim.

On the face of it, the life of Elizabeth I might lack the bloody sexuality of Henry's reign, but *Elizabeth R* was none the worse for that, its drama swinging towards the subtly psychological. At the core of the series was Glenda Jackson's return to television (fresh from winning an Oscar for Ken Russell's *Women in Love*). Her award-winning performance as the Virgin Queen drew greatly on the early events of Elizabeth's life: by the time Elizabeth was eight, she had seen her mother (Anne Boleyn) and her third stepmother (Catherine Howard) beheaded, both ostensibly for adultery; after Henry's death, she lived with Catherine Parr and Thomas Seymour, only to collapse with a nervous breakdown (at the age of 15½) when the former died in childbirth and the latter was beheaded for treason. Glenda Jackson commented, 'When you are young, these things go very deep. The fact that sex and sudden, violent, wilful death were so caught up together in the lives of the people who came close to this young girl must have marked her deeply; not just in her youth, but right up to her relationship with Essex, which also ended in violence and death.' Her performance – accentuated by the different writers – was that of the face-changing chameleon, 'altering to suit the circumstances and the people she was with, keeping her central self very much to herself'.

If Elizabeth suffered, it can fairly be said that Glenda Jackson suffered with her during the seven months of filming. Her hair was shaved back to the crown, and she wore a false straight nose that became bonier as the years passed. BBC make-up also took into account the scarring that resulted from Elizabeth's smallpox attack in the 1560s. By the final episode, her appearance was grotesque, with a deathly pale-white face: historians had said that this would be accurate because make-up was permanent and bathing was unfashionable. During the course of filming the series, Jackson mastered italic calligraphy, riding side-saddle, playing the virginal and dancing the Galliard, La Volta and the Pavane.

The episodes themselves were less obviously delineated than those of *Six Wives*: the first showed Elizabeth during the brief reign of Edward and Mary, flirting with Seymour and ultimately nearly suffering the same fate as him. In a marvellous piece of continuity, when Cranmer, Gardiner and Catherine Parr appeared, they were played by the same actors who had played the roles in *The Six Wives of Henry VIII*. The second episode saw the death of Mary, Elizabeth's succession to the throne, and the beginnings of her romance with Robert Dudley, Earl of Leicester. Intensely ambitious, Dudley came the closest to marrying Elizabeth, and Robert Hardy rightly highlighted the

ELIZABETH R
(17 Feb–24 Mar 71)
1 The Lion's Cub
2 The Marriage Game
3 Shadow in the Sun
4 Horrible Conspiracies
5 The Enterprise of England
6 Sweet England's Pride

awful quandary that Elizabeth's 'rejection' prompted: 'It was very difficult for a 16th-century man to live with the public and private knowledge that a woman had rejected him – even if she was the Queen.'

Subsequent plays dealt with Elizabeth's importance in the field of European diplomacy; her Machiavellian conflict with Mary Queen of Scots; her glorious pinnacle with the defeat of the Armada; and her sad decline into unpopularity and loneliness. 'Developing a character over this enormous width of canvas was a challenge I just couldn't resist', said Jackson.

The BBC effectively played up the historical accuracy of the series, claiming that – with one exception – the characters were based as much as possible on contemporary accounts, even going as far as directly deriving dialogue from actual recorded statements. (The exception was a fictional Devon sailor who brought news of the Armada's defeat.) Elizabeth's costumes were all based on contemporary portraits, her dresses becoming more extravagant as the years passed.

Elizabeth R was, like *The Six Wives of Henry VIII* before it, one of the great successes of its time, and doubtless gave Glenda Jackson an interesting insight into the workings and corruptions of high politics.

The Onedin Line

- **BBC Television** (BBC1) ◆ **Colour**
- **92 episodes** (50 minutes) ◆ **1970-80**
- **Creator:** Cyril Abraham
- **Writers:** Cyril Abraham, Ian Curteis, Ian Kennedy Martin, Michael J. Bird, Moris Fahri, John Lucarotti, Simon Masters, Allan Prior, Nick McCarty, Roger Parkes, Alun Richards, Peter Graham Scott, Roy Russell, Elaine Morgan, Bruce Stewart, Barry Thomas, Douglas Watkinson, David Weir, Mervyn Haisman, Martin Worth
- **Directors include:** David Sullivan Proudfoot, Jonathan Alwyn, David Cunliffe, Michael Hayes, Roger Jenkins, Gilchrist Calder, Lennie Mayne, Michael E. Briant, Geraint Morris, Ben Rea, David Reynolds, Gerald Blake, Pennant Roberts, Peter Graham Scott
- **Producers:** Peter Graham Scott, Peter Cregeen, Geraint Morris

Regular cast: Peter Gilmore (James Onedin) • Jessica Benton (Elizabeth Onedin/Lady Fogarty) • Howard Lang (Baines) • Anne Stallybrass (Anne Onedin) • Brian Rawlinson/James Garbutt (Robert Onedin) • Philip Bond (Albert Frazer) • Michael Billington/Tom Adams (Daniel Fogarty) • Mary Webster (Sarah Onedin) • Jill Gascoine (Letty Gaunt) • Laura Hartong (Charlotte Onedin) • Marc Harrison (William Frazer) • Christopher Douglas (Samuel Onedin)

With: James Hayter (Captain Webster) • Ken Hutchison (Matt Harvey) • Jane Seymour (Emma Callon) • Kate Nelligan (Leonora Biddulph) • Caroline Harris (Caroline Maudsley) • Cyril Shaps (Senor Braganza) • Warren Clarke (Josiah Beaumont) • Michael Walker (Seth Burgess) • Maurice Colbourne (Charles Marston) • Keith Jayne (Tom Arnold) • John Rapley (Dunwoody) • Roberta Iger (Margarita Onedin) • Frederick Jaeger (Max van der Rheede) • Jenny Twigge (Caroline Onedin)

Soviet composer Aram Khatchaturian would not be well known amongst television circles were it not for 'Spartacus', his piece which became the theme to *The Onedin Line*, BBC1's long-running saga of nautical folk. He couldn't have drawn much satisfaction from the fact, though, since the USSR had not signed the Berne Convention and he received no royalties for his work.

The music opened the story of James Onedin, the 28-year-old son of a Liverpool shopkeeper, in 1860. His father had just died, leaving the business to his older brother, Robert, and the cottage to his sister, Elizabeth. James had only £25 with which to make his fortune. He bought the schooner *Charlotte Rhodes* from Captain Webster, a bargain which included a strange condition, that he marry Webster's daughter, Anne. Of course, the man with 'ambition enough for an army of Napoleons' accepted. He set himself up as the owner of a shipping line, battling against his former employer, Callon. Onedin's Mate on the *Charlotte Rhodes* was Baines, a man with more of a heart than his ruthless boss. Initially illiterate, Anne (who was almost as much of an objector to her husband's methods as Baines was) taught the Mate to read and write. The two actors, Anne Stallybrass and Howard Lang (an ex-gunnery officer in the Navy who so identified with the part that he had cards made up with 'Captain Baines' on them), had a special relationship, Lang calling Stallybrass 'daughter' from their previous on-screen pairing, when Stallybrass had played Jane Seymour in ***The Six Wives of Henry VIII***.

Baines was to rise in rank to being Senior Captain on the Onedin Line, but his teacher wasn't so lucky. Anne died at the end of the second season, in the process of giving birth to the unfortunate Charlotte. In the usual way of historical series,

Onedin's daughter has a child of her own, Robert, by the bastard son, William, of Elizabeth's liaison with rival Captain Daniel Fogarty. She refuses to marry William, opting instead to become the wife of her other cousin, Samuel. He is from the safe side of the family, the son of worried shop-owner Robert and his abstinence-campaigner wife. Charlotte then runs off with villainous Seth Burgess, nearly giving him her Onedin Line shares, until James brings her back to Sam. Sam and Charlotte have a daughter, also called Anne, and, amazingly, stay together.

Meanwhile, Elizabeth has married Albert Frazer, a progressive steamship man with a line of his own. Theirs was a more friendly rivalry with James, especially after Albert died, and Elizabeth became owner of the line in her own right. Her lover, Daniel Fogarty, returns after 17 years' (or one season's) absence, and makes her Lady Fogarty. He is made Ambassador to Turkey, although he dies at sea before she can join him there.

James himself proved equally unlucky in love. Firstly, he is fought over by two women, Leonora Biddulph, a coal-merchant's daughter, and Mrs Caroline Maudsley, a rich, young widow. This was Peter Gilmore's own idea, a way to liven up a series of which he often seemed to grow tired. During the filming of the third season, he told the *Radio Times*: 'I like to clown around at rehearsals, get a bit of a laugh. I miss an audience ... ' These were to prove ominous words. Gilmore, at heart a serious actor with a fear of typecasting, toured the Continent with his song and dance act, and refused to do another season for some time. On returning, Onedin's character had not mellowed. The rivals in love had vanished, and he ended up marrying Charlotte's governess, Letty Gaunt. He lost her to illness, their only son also having died. It certainly didn't do his temper any good (conversation between two sailors: 'He is not God almighty!' 'No, the Almighty is merciful and forgiving... '). By the end of the series, James is once again married, to the exotic Margarita Juarez, a Spanish widow. Robert, his stay-at-home brother, is not so lucky. He manages, quite fittingly, to choke to death on a wishbone.

If the plots were complicated, the viewers were also confused by the typical soap-opera device of introducing a new actor as an old character. Thus, Michael Billington and Tom Adams both played Fogarty, Pamela Salem and Jane Seymour both appeared as Emma Callon, and Robert Onedin spent one season assuming a quite different face from that to which the viewers were accustomed. The steadfastness of Jessica Benton and Jill Gascoine gave the series some much-needed stability.

The series was always ambitious in its choice of settings: the Baltic (where Fogarty and James, in one of their never-ending races and wagers, were both stuck in the ice), the Amazon (where a mysterious woman was found floating in a canoe), excursions to run the Union blockade in the American Civil War, and just about every historical action zone in Africa and Asia. Most of these were simulated around Charlestown, in Devon, and Bayards Cove, near Dartmouth, also the setting for ***Poldark,*** a fact that gave the BBC's Sunday-night drama slot a great deal of visual continuity. The other series in this slot was *The Brothers*, and all three shows had something in common: maverick entrepreneurs, often denied their 'rightful' spoils, begging to be saved by a good woman.

Historically, *The Onedin Line* stretched from 1860 until 1886, the details looked after by Robin Craig, a nautical expert from University College, London. Onedin kept clippers going while his rivals invested in steam, a historically-accurate situation, and the business of life at sea was exact enough to keep Sir Francis Chichester at home on a Sunday night. Historical characters, including Samuel Plimsoll, appeared, Plimsoll himself initially helping Onedin save his ships from overloading, and then, typically, fighting with him over the universal application of the Plimsoll Line, and its restrictive effect on free trade. Onedin was the original Thatcherite, and objected to the Line as much as he objected to the emergent unions in the story 'The Hard Case'.

The show featured early displays of the talents of Ian Curteis and Ian Kennedy Martin, the latter's 'Mutiny' featuring John Thaw as a mutinous seaman. Apart

Drama Playhouse
(7 Dec 70)
1 The Wind Blows Free

First season
(15 Oct 71–21 Jan 72)
2 The Wind Blows Free
3 Plain Sailing
4 Other Points of the Compass
5 The High Price
6 Catch as Can
7 Salvage
8 Passage to Pernambuco
9 Homecoming
10 When My Ship Comes Home
11 A Very Important Passenger
12 Mutiny
13 Cry of the Blackbird
14 Shadow of Doubt
15 Blockade
16 Winner Take All

Second season
(17 Sep–31 Dec 72)
17 The Hard Case
18 Pound and Pint
19 A Woman Alone
20 Fetch and Carry
21 Yellow Jack
22 Survivor
23 Coffin Ship
24 'Frisco Bound
25 Beyond the Upper Sea
26 An Inch of Candle
27 Goodbye, Goodbye
28 Bloody Week
29 The Challenge
30 Race for Power

Third season
(21 Oct 73–27 Jan 74)
31 The Ship Devils
32 The Stranger
33 Echoes from Afar
34 Amazon Cargo
35 Danger Level
36 Black Gold
37 Law of the Fist
38 Ice and Fire
39 A Proposal of Marriage
40 Over the Horizon
41 The Silver Caddy
42 Port Out, Starboard Home
43 The Passenger

Fourth season
(25 Apr–27 Jun 76)
44 The Loss of the *Helen May*
45 A Cold Wind Blowing
46 Not Wanted on Voyage
47 Undercurrent
48 Quarantine
49 Uncharted Island
50 A Clear Conscience
51 Shipwreck
52 The Gamble
53 Month of the Albatross

Fifth season
(26 Jun–28 Aug 77)
54 When Troubles Come
55 Rescue
56 Coffin Ships
57 The Trade Wind
58 The Stowaway
59 Dead Man's Cargo
60 A Hard Life
61 The Hostage
62 Uncharted Waters
63 A Close Run Thing

Sixth season
(16 Jul–17 Sep 78)
64 No Smoke Without Fire
65 Collision Course
66 Double Dealers
67 Stand by to Go About
68 The Upright Man
69 The Reverend's Daughter
70 Highly Explosive
71 A Sea of Troubles
72 Men of Honour
73 The Fortune Hunters

Seventh season
(22 Jul–23 Sep 79)
74 Liverpool Bound
75 The Homecoming
76 The Paddy Westers
77 Dirty Cargo
78 To Honour and Obey
79 Running Free
80 The Suitor
81 Storm Clouds
82 Outward Bound
83 Homeward Bound

Eighth season
(31 Aug–26 Oct 80)
84 A Royal Return
85 Revenge
86 Blood Ties
87 The Honeymoon
88 Jonah's Luck
89 The Price of Pride
90 Vengeance
91 Guilty – In All Innocence
92 A Long Way Home

[As the episode titles indicate, the *Drama Playhouse* play was remade as the first episode of the first season. In the 'pilot' Sheila Allen played Anne.]

from such illustrious efforts, the writing was influenced mainly by Cyril Abraham, an old-time scripter who not only created the show but was still writing as late as the end of the seventh season. Much of the plotting was repetitive, apart from the Onedin family's complex domestic problems, and James seemed forever willing to risk his business on grandiose long shots (and at least once lost the whole thing doing it). Baines always objected to his employer's methods, at one point ordering lifeboats for the crew of an exploded petrol carrier, only to have Onedin belay the order, saying that the fog made the rescue too dangerous. However, there was a bond between the two men, Onedin insisting on rescuing Baines when he seemed lost to an iceberg. Other entrepreneurs were only slightly more rapacious than James was, but two particular foes took the biscuit: Josiah Beaumont, who blackmails young William over his debts, and the Dutch merchant Max van der Rheede, who became the sole threat to Onedin's livelihood in the even more internationally-inclined final season.

The Onedin Line was much loved by its audience (which at times reached 12 million), who flocked to see an exhibition of the costumes of the series at St Katharine's Dock in London. They followed with real-life anxiety the fate of the three-masted schooner *De Wadden* as she was beached and holed on the Ayrshire coast, and the *Charlotte Rhodes* herself as she was gutted by fire in Amsterdam in 1979. It could be seen as strange that, after a decade of the kind of historical drama that the BBC did best, the real star of *The Onedin Line* weighed 150 tonnes, was 100 ft long, and needed a crew of five to look after her. Compared to his ship, Peter Gilmore was hardly typecast at all.

Upstairs, Downstairs

- **LWT/Sagitta Productions** (ITV) ◆ **B&W** (1971), **Colour** (1972-75)
- **68 episodes** (50 minutes)
- **Creators:** Jean Marsh, Eileen Atkins
- **Writers:** Fay Weldon, Terence Brady, Charlotte Bingham, Jeremy Paul, Julian Bond, John Hawkesworth, Alfred Shaughnessy, Rosemary Anne Sisson, Anthony Skene
- **Directors include:** Derek Bennett, Raymond Menmuir, Herbert Wise, Bill Bain, Chris Hodgson, Cyril Coke
- **Producer:** John Hawkesworth
- **Executive producer:** Rex Firkin

Starring: Rachel Gurney (Lady Marjorie Bellamy) • David Langton (Richard Bellamy) • Simon Williams (James) • Nicola Pagett (Elizabeth) • Gordon Jackson (Hudson) • Angela Baddeley (Mrs Bridges) • Jean Marsh (Rose) • Pauline Collins (Sarah) • Evin Crowley (Emily) • George Innes (Alfred) • Patsy Smart (Roberts) • Brian Osborne (Pearce) • Christopher Beeny (Edward) • Ian Ogilvy (Laurence) • Jenny Tomasin (Ruby) • John Alderton (Thomas) • Meg Wynn Owen (Hazel) • Jacqueline Tong (Daisy) • Lesley Anne Down (Georgina Worsley) • Hannah Gordon (Virginia) • Anne Yarker (Alice) • Jonathan Seely (William) • Gareth Hunt (Frederick) • Karen Dotrice (Lily)

The cheerful inhabitants of 165 Eaton Place

It is commonly known that *Upstairs, Downstairs* was the brainchild of two actresses, Jean Marsh (who also starred in the series) and Eileen Atkins. Its development from script to screen, however, is a less well–documented saga.

Having been enchanted by the BBC's ***Forsyte Saga***, Marsh and Atkins were surprised that so little attention had been paid to the lives of the many servants of the Forsyte family. Marsh has since stated that the actresses' chief reasons for creating *Upstairs, Downstairs* were to provide themselves with good roles, but also to correct this glaring fault in British TV's portrayal of the class system. The concept, which started as a comedy, first called *Below Stairs*, and then *Behind the Green Baize Door*, finally landed on the desk of the head of the newly-created London Weekend Television company, John Whitney, a former producer who Jean Marsh had worked with in the past. The story of the Bellamy family and the servants with whom they shared their Eaton Place home would eventually become LWT's biggest worldwide seller.

By the time that producer John Hawkesworth and script-editor Alfred Shaughnessy became involved with the project, Eileen Atkins had moved on to perform in the West End run of *Vivat Regina*. The early production was dogged by bad luck, including a change in the hierarchy at LWT mere weeks after shooting began, which nearly resulted in the programme being scrapped. What saved *Upstairs, Downstairs*, in effect, was that it had been such a big investment for LWT, despite the fact that episodes were almost entirely studiobound. Additionally, a technician's strike meant that – as with LWT's other big new drama series, *Budgie* – although planned to be filmed in colour, the first six episodes had to be made in black and white. (To confuse matters even further, the pilot episode, Fay Weldon's 'On Trial', was later reshot in colour.)

A quality cast was assembled for the production, headed by character actor Gordon Jackson's commanding Scottish butler Hudson. Jean Marsh had created for herself the pivotal role of the housemaid, Rose, whilst the part originally intended for Eileen Atkins, the day-dreaming maid, Sarah, was taken by former ***Liver Bird*** Pauline Collins. Angela Baddeley's fire-breathing dragon, Mrs Bridges, would eventually become one of the series' most popular characters, whilst the roles of the 'upstairs' Bellamy family went to such distinguished theatrical talent as Rachel Gurney, David Langton, Nicola Pagett and Simon Williams.

A potentially disastrous slot of 10.30 p.m. on Sunday evenings was assigned to the series. Jean Marsh commented 'it could have been the kiss of death, but never in the history of TV has anything taken off so quickly. It rated immediately and what's more it got the thumbs up from critics.' The episodes had a gritty realism that was rare in TV of the era. The second episode, 'The Mistress and the Maids', written by feminist author Maureen Duffy, featured overtones of what critic Richard Marson called 'the lesbianism inherent in many relationships between female servants and carried the concurrent theme of sexual frustration and moral hypocrisy through the episode without a hint of sensationalism'. The first season also carried stories concerning a servant (Susan Penhaligon) made pregnant by a member of high society ('A Cry for Help'), the suicide of kitchen maid Emily ('I Dies for Love'), and the arrogance of the idle rich, as exemplified by the Bellamy's wayward daughter, Elizabeth ('The Key of the Door').

Significantly, the introduction of love interests for both Elizabeth and Sarah, in the form of poet Laurence and footman Thomas, had a negative effect on the storylines and the second season seemed in danger of drowning in its own sentimentality. Collins and Alderton (a husband and wife team whose subsequent careers included the *Upstairs, Downstairs* spin-off *Thomas and Sarah*, and the LWT comedy series *No – Honestly*) helped to give the series much publicity.

Probably the best-remembered episode of the series, 'Guest of Honour', concerned the King coming to dinner with the Bellamys. Sarah, heavily pregnant with James's child, turns up during the episode which was, apparently, based on a family story told to Alfred Shaughnessy during his childhood.

First season
(10 Oct 71–5 Mar 72)
1 On Trial
2 The Mistress and the Maids
3 Board Wages
4 The Path of Duty
5 A Suitable Marriage
6 A Cry for Help
7 Magic Casements
8 I Dies for Love
9 Why is Her Door Locked?
10 A Voice from the Past
11 The Swedish Tiger
12 The Key of the Door
13 For Love of Love

Second season
(22 Oct 72–19 Jan 73)
14 The New Man
15 A Pair of Exiles
16 Married Love
17 Whom God Has Joined...
18 Guest of Honour
19 The Property of a Lady
20 Your Obedient Servant
21 Out of the Everywhere
22 An Object of Value
23 A Special Mischief
24 The Fruits of Love
25 The Wages of Sin
26 A Family Gathering

Third season
(27 Oct 73–19 Jan 74)
27 Miss Forrest
28 A House Divided
29 A Change of Scene
30 A Family Secret
31 Rose's Pigeon
32 Desirous of Change
33 Word of Honour
34 The Bolter
35 Goodwill to All Men
36 What the Footman Saw
37 A Perfect Stranger
38 Distant Thunder
39 The Sudden Storm

Fourth season
(14 Sep–7 Dec 74)
40 A Patriotic Offering
41 News from the Front
42 The Beastly Hun
43 Women shall not Weep
44 Tug of War
45 Home Fires
46 If you were the Only Girl in the World
47 The Glorious Dead
48 Another Year
49 The Hero's Farewell
50 Missing: Believed Killed
51 Facing Fearful Odds
52 Peace out of Pain

Fifth season
(7 Sep–21 Dec 75)
53 On with the Dance
54 A Place in the World
55 Laugh a Little Louder, Please
56 The Joy Ride
57 Wanted – A Good Home
58 An Old Flame
59 Disillusion
60 Such a Lovely Man
61 The Nine Day Wonder
62 The Understudy
63 Alberto
64 Will Ye No' Come Back Again
65 Joke Over
66 Noblesse Oblige
67 All the King's Horses
68 Wither Shall I Wander?

[*Thomas and Sarah* ran for a single season of 13 episodes between 14 Jan and 8 Apr 79.]

Social comment reared its head in the form of the suffragette movement in 'A Special Mischief', whilst Lady Marjorie was blackmailed over an indiscretion in 'The Property of a Lady'. As the Great War approached, the third season had to contend with the loss of Nicola Pagett and Rachel Gurney (Lady Marjorie's planned trip to see her daughter was, inevitably, on board the *Titanic*). The spectre of war hung over the season, with Richard haunted by the death of his wife. James marries Hazel, a tempestuous and doomed relationship that obsessed the nation during the following year, whilst the final two episodes of the season were successful in evoking the jingoistic xenophobia that surrounded the outbreak of hostilities, but with a perception that undercut the false jollity of the characters.

Perhaps because of the accuracy with which the series displayed human emotions, the fourth season, which concerned the war years, was the most effective of all *Upstairs, Downstairs*. The series covered several storylines each week as news arrived from abroad concerning those who were actively involved in the war. As Richard and Hudson attempt to keep their respective worlds together in the face of the apocalypse, Edward leaves to fight in 'Women shall not Weep', Rose's fiancé, Gregory (Keith Barron), is killed in 'The Glorious Dead', and Edward comes home, shell-shocked, in the Emmy-nominated 'Another Year'. 'Peace out of Pain' sees the end of the war, and the tragic aftermath of the influenza epidemic of 1919, in which Hazel dies.

A final season moved the series into the 20s, covering post-war disillusionment ('On with the Dance'), James's entry into politics ('A Place in the World'), the terrorizing of the Bellamy grandchildren by a strict governess ('Wanted – A Good Home') and the 1926 General Strike ('The Nine Day Wonder'). Anthony Andrews, Robert Hardy and Nigel Havers made guest appearances, whilst the final two-part story centred on the Wall Street Crash, James's suicide, the loss of the Bellamy fortune and the sale of the house. The touching final scene had Rose as the last person to leave 165 Eaton Place, as the ghosts of the past echo around her.

Upstairs, Downstairs was a landmark in television history. A soap opera in construction, the series' peerless historical accuracy, continuity, attention to detail and gloss mark it down as much more. The series made for compelling viewing, yet in its time it achieved a critical acclaim perhaps matched only by ***When the Boat Comes In***. Like the BBC series, *Upstairs, Downstairs* concentrated on people's stories rather than the big issues of history. In reflecting the dichotomous face of British society in the early years of the 20th century, it showed a fine grasp of social history.

Colditz

- **BBC Television/Universal TV** (first season only) (BBC1) ◆ Colour
- **28 episodes** (50 minutes) ◆ 1972-74
- **Creators:** Brian Degas, Gerard Glaister
- **Writers:** Brian Degas, Troy Kennedy Martin, Arden Winch, N.J. Crisp, John Kruse, Marc Brandel, John Brason, Ian Kennedy Martin, Bryan Forbes, Thom Keyes, David Ambrose, Ken Hughes, Ivan Moffat, Robert Müller
- **Directors:** Michael Ferguson, Viktor Ritelis, Peter Cregeen, William Slater, Terence Dudley, Ken Hannam
- **Producer:** Gerard Glaister

Starring: Edward Hardwicke (Capt. Pat Grant) • David McCallum (Flt. Lt. Simon Carter) • Christopher Neame (Lt. Dick Player) • Robert Wagner (Flt. Lt. [later Major] Phil Carrington) • Jack Hedley (Lt. Col. Preston) • Bernard Hepton (Kommandant) • Hans Meyer (Hauptmann Ulmann) • Anthony Valentine (Major Mohn) • Richard Heffer (Capt. Tim Downing) • Paul Chapman (Capt. George Brent) • Dan O'Herlihy (Lt. Col. Dodd)

It is a strange fact of life that Major Pat Reid's books on the German POW camp at Colditz are now perhaps as well remembered for inspiring a children's board game as this superb example of BBC war-time drama. However, in its time *Colditz*, the series, provided drama of the highest quality, and, thanks to repeats that took it into the late 70s, it retains a stature that belies its comparative brevity.

When writer Brian Degas and producer Gerard Glaister began creating the series for the BBC, the story was already well known thanks to a British 1957 film *The Colditz Story*, starring John Mills. Much of the material in the film was later reused (in a vastly expanded form) in certain episodes of the TV series. However, Glaister wanted *Colditz* to be fiction based on the awful reality of Reid's books, and, having flown with the RAF during the war, he immediately recognized the potential pitfalls. 'A lot of values seem comic if you use the jargon of the day. Just because people said, "I say, old chap, I had a prang", they were not half-wits.' The dialogue was subtly brought up-to-date without forsaking period vernacular, stressing the dignity and bravery of the POWs whilst avoiding clichés and cardboard Nazis. Perceived reality played a role in shaping the series (actor Jack Hedley claimed that the reality of life at Colditz involved fine meals and 'Other Ranks' acting as servants), and the thrust of the series was the on-going escape plans of the men imprisoned in Castle Colditz, a dark fortress perched atop sheer cliffs from which escape was supposed to be impossible.

The action did not begin in Colditz straight away, but we were instead introduced to the lead characters before they moved to the castle in the fourth episode. Attention was focused on the stars: David McCallum as Flight Lieutenant Carter and Robert Wagner as Flight Lieutenant Carrington, an American flying for the Canadian air force who was absent from much of the second series. Carrington

First season
(19 Oct 72–25 Jan 73)
1 The Undefeated
2 Missing, Presumed Dead
3 Name, Rank and Number
4 Welcome to Colditz
5 Maximum Security
6 The Spirit of Freedom
7 Lord, Didn't it Rain
8 The Traitor
9 Bribery and Corruption
10 Tweedledum
11 Court Martial
12 Murder?
13 The Way Out
14 Gone Away (part one)
15 Gone Away (part two): With the Wild Geese

Second season
(7 Jan–1 Apr 74)
16 Arrival of a Hero
17 Ghosts
18 Odd Man In
19 The Guests
20 Frogs in the Well
21 Ace in the Hole
22 French Leave
23 The Gambler
24 Senior American Officer
25 Very Important Person
26 Chameleon
27 Death Sentence
28 Liberation

Preston, Player, Grant, Carrington and Carter: incarcerated within the walls of Colditz

eventually returned as a Major in the US forces. However, it was often the German characters who were the most popular with viewers, ranging from Bernard Hepton's civilized Kommandant to Hans Meyer's Hauptmann Ulmann and Anthony Valentine's ruthless Major Mohn. All characters had depth and pathos when they could so easily have become pale monsters.

The performances were excellent, as in the first season's notorious 'Tweedledum' episode, where it is decided that the only certain method of escape is repatriation on medical grounds. Michael Bryant played Wing Commander Marsh, who feigns madness, complete with toy plane, in a desperate attempt to get home, which he does, but only at the expense of his sanity. Such episodes were capable of staying in the minds of the viewer long after the 50 minutes elapsed.

The limited range of characters and locations ensured a strong emphasis on taut and complex plotting. The discovery of the body of a German corporal in the parcels office raises the temperature to such an extent that no one is convinced when the Kommandant treats it as suicide. Occasionally, there was conflict between the various groups trying to escape, as in 'Frogs in the Well', when the French begin using the same escape route as the Brits. There were encounters with the hideous SS, and, for a prison, a regular throughput of new characters (the first season alone saw Nigel Stock, Michael Gough, Peter Barkworth and Patrick Troughton in guest-starring roles).

Colditz also mirrored the war outside its walls as the series progressed, concluding with the German army in retreat and the threat of wholesale slaughter, followed by the glorious freedom of liberation. It remained, from start to finish, a dramatic and moving serial, seldom lapsing into gung-ho glorification of war. *Colditz* was one of the best examples of mid-70s popular television, proving that high drama and commercial and critical success can go hand-in-hand.

Poldark

- **BBC Television/London Film Productions** (BBC1) ◆ **Colour**
- **29 episodes** (50 minutes) ◆ **1975-77**
- **Based on:** novels by Winston Graham
- **Writers:** Jack Pulman, Paul Wheeler, Peter Draper, Jack Russell, Alexander Baron, John Wiles, Martin Worth
- **Directors:** Christopher Barry, Paul Annett, Kenneth Ives, Philip Dudley, Roger Jenkins
- **Producers:** Morris Barry, Tony Coburn, Richard Beynon, Colin Tucker

Regular cast: Robin Ellis (Ross Poldark) • Angharad Rees (Demelza Poldark) • Ralph Bates (George Warleggan) • Jill Townsend (Elizabeth Warleggan)

With: Clive Francis (Francis Poldark) • Frank Middlemass (Charles Poldark) • Mary Wimbush (Prudie) • Norma Streader (Verity Poldark) • Eileen Way (Agatha Poldark) • Paul Curran (Jud Paynter) • Don Henderson (Tom Carne) • Gillian Bailey (Jinny Carter) • Jonathan Newth (Captain Blamey) • Nicholas Selby (Nicholas Warleggan) • Judy Geeson (Caroline Penvenen) • Kevin McNally (Drake Carne)

Poldark was the BBC's attempt to continue its successful run of historical dramas such as ***The Forsyte Saga*** and *The Pallisers*, with a Sunday evening family audience in mind. Unlike the previous shows, however, it generated an audience that persists to this day, and – along with ***The Onedin Line*** – it had an influence on the direction historical drama took ever after.

The story concerns Ross Poldark, gloweringly played by the shy (and then largely unknown) actor Robin Ellis, who returns to his home, Nampara, in his native Cornwall in the 18th century, having fought in the American War of Independence. He finds his copper mine run down and in the process of being sold to evil industrialist George Warleggan by his weak cousin Francis, who has become engaged to Ross's ex-fiancée, Elizabeth, Ross having been presumed dead. Ross begins a campaign to regain his business and his love. However, the latter aim is complicated by the arrival of Demelza, the waif-like and dirty servant girl he weds because she's going to bear his child, just as Elizabeth has been persuaded to leave Francis.

The series was filmed around the preserved Georgian port of Charlestown near St Austell. Winston Graham, the author of the four books which were adapted into the first season, had grown up in Cornwall, and had done extensive research into the era of the mining barons. He was pleased with the casting (though Rees's elfin Demelza wasn't very like the rough creature of the novels), but occasionally appalled by the changes necessary to turn four books into the 16 episodes of the first season. Demelza's pregnancy, for instance, was a dramatic shorthand for long chapters of romance in the books, and the burning of Warleggan's home by irate miners that formed the climax to the first season was entirely the creation of the scriptwriters.

For the second season, commissioned by the BBC only after the first series had proved popular, Graham was much closer to the production. He wrote a new novel to allow the BBC to create the stories from the next three books, and he and his wife both appeared on screen: he as a gentleman at Drake Crane's wedding, she as a peasant.

Graham had named Demelza after a village in the area, the filmed locations often being exactly those the author envisaged, especially in the case of the old

First season
(5 Oct 75–18 Jan 76)
Sixteen episodes

Second season
(11 Sep–4 Dec 77)
Thirteen episodes

folly that was Dr Enys's cottage. Generally, the Cornish responded positively to the series, loving the authenticity of the customs and language depicted, if not the sometimes unconvincing RADA Cornish accents. As Jeffrey Bernard noted in *The Spectator*, this was a series where 'the bad were rotten and the good spoke like newsreaders'. He admitted, however, that he'd 'grown fonder and fonder of this load of old rubbish'.

The critics in general, accustomed to the BBC's historical drama being deadly sombre, were not kind. Alan Coren regarded the series as 'a step further into the cultural abyss ... not a vital remains unstapped nor a tush unpished', and compared it unfavourably to the more starched ***Upstairs, Downstairs*** on ITV, the series that *Poldark* had been designed to compete with. The thing was, in order to achieve that task, *Poldark* had been envisioned as a major break with the format of the BBC historical serial, being melodramatic, over the top, and full of action and passion. The shipwreck scene in the first season, for instance, utilized a large number of Cornish extras who ran into the sea and grabbed their booty with great gusto as one of Warleggan's ships ran aground. In season two, Ross had calmed down a bit, but still managed to be dragged in front of a French revolutionary firing squad, and was involved in a pistol duel with the angry Captain Monk Adderley.

Lofty it wasn't, but strike a chord it did, with 15 million viewers at its height, and sales to 45 countries. Ellis found himself recognized in Italy, Spain, and the USA, where the show was a big success as a segment of the prestigious *Masterpiece Theatre*. Alistair Cooke, then presenter of the showcase, famously didn't think much of the series, saying that he had very little historical detail to add to the melodrama. Christopher Biggins gained a cult following through his appearances as the lustful vicar, the Reverend Ossie Whitworth. The personality cult surrounding Robin Ellis reached its nadir when he performed in a Spanish TV advert in character, reading his lines phonetically, on the subject of underpants.

The second season began with Poldark returning from Holland, and took in war (Ross attempts to rescue Dr Emys from a French gaol); romance (the initial love quadrilateral becomes more complex); and Cornish mysticism (the drunken, toothless old goat Jud apparently returns from the dead). Similarly miraculous was Agatha, who was 98 at the start of the series and managed to hold on through 12 years of such adventures. The audience must also have been puzzled by the changing appearance of Dr Enys (Michael Cadman replacing Richard Morant) and Nampara itself (the location having moved).

The series ended with Elizabeth, having taken a potion to hasten her baby's birth, in order to lie about the identity of the father, losing the child. Ross had become a propserous MP, never having regained his true love.

Poldark helped to create the popular historical drama, opening the doors at the BBC for such successes as *The Duchess of Duke Street* and *The House of Elliot*. The full influence of the show didn't become clear until 1987, when the BBC showed a full repeat. The videos sold 200,000 copies. The Poldark Appreciation Society was formed two years later, gaining thousands of members worldwide, and forming a voice for a neglected subgroup of TV viewers, the lovers of romantic fiction. Rather as TV science fiction fandom became politicized by the cancellation of ***Blake's 7***, HTV's decision to replace Ellis and Rees with John Bowe and Mel Martin in the forthcoming TV movie sequel (a decision not caused by the passage of time, the latest book adapted being set 20 years later) caused a riot outside the production company's headquarters. There are four books left unadapted, and in post-*Middlemarch* television, there's a bounty to be enjoyed by bold broadcasters.

When the Boat Comes In

- **BBC Television** (BBC1) ◆ Colour
- **51 episodes** (50 minutes) ◆ 1976-81
- **Creator:** James Mitchell
- **Writers:** James Mitchell, Tom Hadaway, Alex Glasgow, Sid Chaplin, Jeremy Burnham, Colin Morris
- **Directors:** Gilchrist Calder, Paul Ciappesoni, Bill Hayes, Terence Williams, Michael Hayes, Vere Lorrimer, David Askey, Jonathan Alwyn
- **Producers:** Leonard Lewis, Andrew Osborn, David Maloney

Starring: James Bolam (Jack Ford) • Susan Jameson (Jessie Seaton) • James Garbutt (Bill Seaton) • Jean Heywood (Bella Seaton) • John Nightingale (Tom Seaton) • Edward Wilson (Billy) • Madelaine Newton (Dolly) • Malcolm Terris (Matt Headley) • Isla Blair/Lois Baxter (Lady Caroline) • William Fox (Duke of Bedlington) • Geoffrey Rose (Ashton) • Ian Cullen (Geordie Watson) • Martin Duncan (Roddy) • Basil Henson (Sir Horatio Manners) • Christopher Benjamin (Channing) • Rosalyn Bailey (Sarah)

One of the most popular songs of 1976 didn't find its way into the charts. It did, however, introduce the television audience to a new language. Alex Glasgow's rendition of the traditional Northern folk song 'Dance t'Thi Daddy' opened the first episode of *When the Boat Comes In* to a mixture of curiosity and disbelief.

When the Boat Comes In took absolutely no prisoners with its magnificent reconstruction of the 20s North East and, in doing so, dragged its audience into the world of the urban poor. This wasn't corny, socio-realist *Love on the Dole*-style drama, but featured shots of crumbling terraced slums so authentic you could feel the tuberculosis.

James Mitchell had grown up between the wars in South Shields where his father, a shipyard fitter, union activist and self-taught intellectual, became Mayor. Mitchell, using the tales of poverty and depression of his childhood, gave the television audience something they had never had before. 'Somebody who would never pick up a book of social history will watch without realizing he is watching social history,' said the writer, before adding, 'Of course he isn't, he's watching a play.' Though scorning any notion that the depressing poverty was something which people should remember with nostalgia, Mitchell did feel that his audience 'miss the working-class closeness. You can't have closeness in a high-rise.'

When the Boat Comes In was the BBC's equivalent of LWT's ***Upstairs, Downstairs***, both series carrying similar messages about the staggering inequality between the rich and poor in the early part of this century. But *When the Boat Comes In* did much more than draw on viewers' sympathy. It was funny too, and tragic, a love story that included large doses of politics and cynicism; and although the series was in some ways counter-productive and perpetuated the 'cloth cap' image of the Northerner, which still persists, *When the Boat Comes In* did much to capture the imagination of the nation.

James Bolam played Jack Ford: multi-talented rogue, working-class hero and snubber of the establishment. In the opening episode, Ford returns, decorated, from the Great War, to the 'land fit for heroes'. He becomes involved in union politics, helps with a lengthy miners' strike and, at the end of the season, goes to prison (secure in the knowledge that his actions will make him a martyr). He falls in love with the beautiful schoolteacher Jessie Seaton, and befriends her miner brother, Tom (the pair, and Jack's friend Matt, becoming poachers to feed strikers' families). Jessie's father is crippled in a mining accident, and Jack secures huge compensation, but, after making his other girlfriend, Dolly, pregnant, Ford and Seaton are torn apart.

One potential problem with the series, as noted by the *Radio Times*, was getting the Geordiesque right. Hyper-critical Tynesiders listened to each episode for the niceties of dialect. 'They haven't been able to prove us wrong yet,' said Mitchell, noting that the almost exclusive use of local actors had preserved linguistic purity. This can be seen in the many memorable guest appearances by noted North East actors during the first couple of seasons (Alan Browning as a union leader, John Woodvine as a conscientious objector, Bobby Pattison and Kevin Whately as miners). ***Z Cars***' Ian Cullen became a semi-regular as a Labour MP, while other guest stars (absolving the series of the claim of wholesale regional nepotism) included Paul Darrow and Bill Simpson.

When the Boat Comes In covered a greater range of subjects than simply the price of coal. 'Scabbing' (strike-breaking) was discussed at length, and there were entire episodes devoted to the *menage à trois* surrounding Jack, Jessie and Dolly. The youngest of the Seaton children, Billy, was studying at Edinburgh University to become a doctor. Later, he returns to the area and sets up a 'free surgery'. The landowning bogeymen of the first season (Sir Horatio Manners and the Duke of Bedlington) were introduced and Ford becomes friendly with both, having an affair with the Duke's daughter, Lady Caroline. As Jack's complex stepping-up the social ladder continues, old man Seaton becomes a capitalist shop owner, refusing his customers credit ('clocks tick, we don't'), Jessie marries her headmaster, Tom has a torrid affair with Dolly, and Jack becomes involved in politics, helping – through very dubious means – in the election of Geordie Watson.

Some episodes tackled more controversial subject matter, especially in the third season – made without Susan Jameson. Dolly miscarries and Jack, trapped in an unwanted marriage, organizes a divorce for himself. 'The Empire Builders'

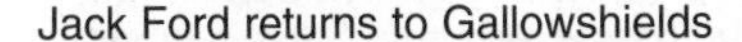

Jack Ford returns to Gallowshields

First season
(8 Jan–1 Apr 76)
1 A Land Fit for Heroes and Idiots
2 Say Hello... ...Say Tirra
3 Fish in Woolly Jumpers
4 Swords and Pickhandles
5 Coal Comfort
6 Empire Day on the Slagheap
7 A First Time for Everything
8 Paddy Boyle's Discharge
9 Angel on Horseback
10 King for a Day
11 Happy New Year, Some Say
12 Heads You Win, Tails I Lose
13 Kind-Hearted Rat with a Lifeboat

Second season
(29 Oct 76–4 Feb 77)
14 Ask for Tuppence, Take a Penny
15 Tram Ride to the Bluebell
16 A Pillowful of Buttercups
17 Roubles for the Promised Land
18 Bulbs to Keep the Garden Bright
19 God and Love and Wellesley Street
20 Whatever Made you Think the War was Over?
21 Ladies, Women, Sweethearts and Wives
22 After the Bonfire
23 A Wreath with our Names On
24 The Way it was in Murmansk
25 In the Front Line, You Get Shot At
26 The Simple Pleasure of the Rich

Third season
(8 Sep–15 Dec 77)
27 A House Divided
28 A Tiger, a Lamb and a Basket of Fruit
29 My Bonnie Lass, Goodbye
30 A Ticket to Care for the Wounded
31 Travel Light, Travel Far
32 Requiem for a Loser
33 Debts Owed, Debts Paid
34 The Empire Builders
35 Look up and See the Sky
36 Letters from Afar
37 The Father of Lies
38 Diamond Cut Diamond
39 A Marriage and a Massacre
40 High Life and Hunger
41 Please Say Goodbye Before You Go

Fourth season
(17 Feb–21 Apr 81)
42 Back to Dear Old Blighty
43 A Gift from Heaven
44 A Medal for the Argentine
45 Flies and Spiders
46 Oh, My Charming Billy Boy
47 Friends, Romans, Countrymen
48 The Bright Young Things
49 Action!
50 Comrades in Arms
51 Roll of Honour

sees Jack as a man of property and money, moving ever more quickly away from his working-class roots whilst the season (and apparently the series) ended with 'Please Say Goodbye Before You Go', in which Jack stops a deranged man from attacking Lady Caroline. He decides the time has come to move on and tells Matt that he is leaving for America. 'A land with prohibition,' Matt says incredulously, 'What are you going to do in a country without any alcohol?' 'Give them some,' replies Ford.

Four years later the series was resurrected by producer David Maloney. James Mitchell described the return of his hero: 'The survival of the individual has been his only political creed ... He's set up as a bootlegger on Park Avenue. I don't reckon he's given the North East a thought. He would have been too busy having a good time, or cheating someone.' Mitchell returned Ford, on the run from the FBI, to England in the mid-30s, in the middle of the Jarrow marches and a general air of depression. Some old faces turned up (Billy Seaton is now a society doctor with committed Communist sympathies, supplying arms to the Spanish Civil War fighters with the aid of his sister). James Bolam played Ford as a more worldly-wise figure, threatening to blackmail Watson unless he was given money, but only the £15 Ford believed he was owed from years before. The fourth season became something of a travelogue, with Ford a journeyman entrepreneur, looking at snapshots of 30s life.

Finally, he too becomes involved in the ominous events in Spain, attempting to use his manipulative skills to play the Communists and the Fascists off against each other, so that the Socialists ('My lot,' he says dryly) can achieve power. He fails, and is shot, dying in the arms of a Spanish rebel. ('You belong in a hospital,' he is told. 'I belong in a grave,' he replies.)

Ultimately, *When the Boat Comes In*, with its vintage cars and cobbled streets, was beautiful to look at and maybe that was the reason behind its long-lasting success, but the stories had a poetry of their own that shouldn't be overlooked. James Mitchell summed up his work on the series by saying that 'Being a professional writer means you deliver the goods on time, to the best of your ability and skill, for money. Craftsmanship and honesty are key words. It's my family tradition. My father was a skilled man who took pride in his craft. So am I.' In creating Jack Ford and the other characters whose dignity and lack of complaint under suffering was taken to the nation's heart, Mitchell went past mere craftsmanship, and brought the soul of the North East to television.

I, Claudius

- **BBC Television** (BBC2) ◆ **Colour**
- **12 episodes** (standard length: *c.* 50 minutes) ◆ **1976**
- **Adapted from:** novels by Robert Graves
- **Writer:** Jack Pulman
- **Director:** Herbert Wise
- **Producer:** Martin Lisemore

I, Claudius was a celebration of television and an acknowledgement of the medium's debt to literature and the theatrical stage. 1976 was the 40th anniversary of BBC television, and to mark this jubilee the corporation embarked upon a major adaptation of Robert Graves's black comedy. Whilst ostensibly similar to previous historical dramas, the series would be an epic 11-hour extravaganza, featuring the cream of Britain's Shakespearian theatre.

Jack Pulman's finely-judged script took most of its material from Graves's narrative, although the final three episodes, together with certain earlier plot-strands, notably Claudius's relationship with King of the Jews, Herod Agrippa, were drawn from the book's sequel, *Claudius the God*. The story had a staggering scope, covering the reigns of five Roman emperors. Risks were taken with the cast: while many of the supporting roles in the drama were taken by well-known character actors, key parts went to quality stage actors, virtually unknown on television. It is not unfair to say that *I, Claudius* was the series which first made the faces of Derek Jacobi, John Hurt, Sian Phillips and Patrick Stewart known to the man in the street.

The BBC concluded that such an obviously 'high-brow' presentation would not be the high-profile ratings success that *I, Claudius*' budget demanded. As a result, the series was not presented as an authentic, historically-accurate piece of BBC costume drama, but as a kind of Roman ***Forsyte Saga***. The audience warmed to the idea of an historical soap opera (with several buckets of blood at

Regular cast: Derek Jacobi (Claudius) • Brian Blessed (Augustus) • Sian Phillips (Livia) • George Baker (Tiberius) • John Hurt (Caligua) • Patrick Stewart (Sejanus) • Stratford Johns (Piso) • James Faulkner (Herod) • David Robb Germanicus) • Fiona Walker (Agrippina) • Sheila White (Messalina) • Beth Morris (Drusilla) • Margaret Tyzack (Antonia) • Ian Ogilvy (Drusus) • Kevin McNally (Castor) • John Rhys Davies (Macro) • Christopher Biggins (Nero) • Bernard Hill (Gratus) • Bernard Hepton (Pallus) • John Cater (Narcissus)

With: Christopher Guard (Marcellus) • John Paul (Agrippa) • Frances White (Julia) • Angela Morant (Octavia) • Sheila Ruskin (Vipsania) • Kevin Stoney (Thrasyllus) • Ashley Knight (Young Claudius) • Guy Siner (Pylades) • Denis Carey (Livy) • Darian Angadi (Plautius) • Patricia Quinn (Livilla) • Simon MacCorkindale (Lucius) • John Castle (Postumus) • Alan Thompson (Praxis) • Irene Hamilton (Placina) • Esmond Knight (Domitius) • Norman Rossington (Sergeant) • Edward Jewesbury (Titus) • Isabel Dean (Lollia) • James Bree (Monatanus) • Donald Eccles (Pollio) • Graham Rowe (Junius) • George Pravda (Gershom) • Roy Purcell (Vitellius) • Jo Rowbottom (Calpurnia) • Neal Arden (Cestius) • Patsy Byrne (Martina) • Bruce Purchase (Sabinus) • Karin Foley (Helen) • Charles Kay (Gallus) • Peter Williams (Silius Caecina) • Aubury Richards (Varro) • Sally Bazely (Poppaea) • Freda Dowie (Caesonia) • Lyndon Brook (Silanus) • James Fagan (Asprenas) • Norman Eshley (Marcus) • Moira Redmond (Domitia) • Roger Bizley (Plautius) • John Bennett (Xenophon) • Barbara Young (Agrippinilla) • Peter Bowles (Caractacus) • Graham Seed (Britannicus) • Cheryl Johnson (Octavia)

its disposal), and soon became embroiled in its tales of rivalry and murder. In America, where the series was syndicated on *Masterpiece Theatre*, *I, Claudius* gained a cult audience that ranged from history students to those who simply liked seeing lots of implied kinky sex on television.

I, Claudius concerns the corrupting influence of power. The story begins in Rome in 24BC, seven years after the Battle of Actium at which Augustus defeated Mark Antony and Cleopatra to become, in effect, ruler of the world. Augustus, played to perfection by Blessed, is an enlightened despot, although the power behind the throne is his wife, Livia, and in Sian Phillips's breathtaking performance one can fully perceive the reason for *I, Claudius*' success.

Livia's intentions are sighted early as she plots to keep the monarchy in place and ensure a succession for her son, Tiberius, ahead of more obvious candidates such as Augustus's nephew, Marcellus, and the Emperor's best friend, Marcus Agrippa. Despite her skilful manipulation of the family's affairs over the course of three decades (including poisoning just about everyone who stands in Tiberius's way), Livia also makes enemies, including her other son, Drusus, Agrippa's son, Postumus, and her grandchildren, Germanicus and Claudius. As the lame, stuttering, seemingly half-witted 'hero' of the piece, Derek Jacobi as Claudius won a BAFTA award for his performance full of comic pathos.

Finally, Livia poisons her husband. Blessed's famous death scene had the camera remaining on the actor for over four minutes, his eyes half-closed, whilst, out of shot, Livia delivered a beautiful soliloquy explaining her motives. 'It was extraordinary,' said Blessed afterwards. 'I felt my heartbeat going slower and slower. In a bizarre way, I thought I might die. Then we had to do a second take because all of the lights went out.'

George Baker's Tiberius was a strange and tormented character: a fine soldier at the story's beginning, his darker side is held in check only by Drusus, and his wife, Vipsania. Once Livia has succeeded in removing the latter, and the former had died of his wounds in battle, the new Emperor's descent into barbarism and tyranny began in earnest.

The middle episodes painted an atmosphere thick with perversion and death. The reign of terror orchestrated by the brutal head of the guards, Sejanus, carries thousands to their deaths whilst the royal family seem content to murder each other with abandon. Through it all, Claudius, taking the advice of those who wish him to live a long life, carries on playing the fool and is viewed as a threat by no one. Claudius states at one point that he has only three real friends, his cousin Postumus and brother Germanicus (who are both disposed of by the machinations of others) and Herod, the charismatic, roguish King of the Jews, who later becomes obsessed with the belief that he is the messiah.

In a key scene, Claudius is invited to dinner by his grandmother, the hideous poisoner who had been an all-seeing bogeywoman of the early episodes. Magnificently constructed, the scene allowed Livia to explain much of what had gone before (stating those deaths she is responsible for and those she is not), and placed the future of the series in context – by predicting what would come next including, much to his amusement, that Claudius would one day be emperor.

20 Sep–6 Dec 76
1 A Touch of Murder (100 minutes)
2 Waiting in the Wings
3 What Shall We Do About Claudius?
4 Poison is Queen
5 Some Justice
6 Queen of Heaven
7 Reign of Terror
8 Zeus, by Jove!
9 Hail Who?
10 Fool's Luck
11 A God in Colchester
12 Old King Log

By her death, in episode six, Livia was a woman of 80 and Phillips was smothered beneath layers of latex. Her then-husband, Peter O'Toole, was working at the time on the film version of *Caligula* (Ita/US 79). One day when she visited him on the set she was shocked to discover that the Roman armour used on the film was constructed from cheap plastic. 'All the good stuff is at the BBC,' she was told. The BBC spent their money wisely. Although *I,*

A grisly end for Claudius: Agrippinella, Nero and Claudius, from the final episode

Claudius was entirely studio-bound, the sets, costumes, music and lighting all captured the grandiose splendour of Imperial Rome.

By the time that the story reached the reign of Claudius's nephew, the notorious Caligula, the series was getting some of the highest viewing figures in the history of BBC2. John Hurt's deliciously camp, eye-rolling depiction of insanity and of absolute power, corrupting absolutely, seemed almost normal alongside the spectacle of Claudius's sister, Livilla, poisoning her husband, Castor, and casually discussing her sexual preferences with her lover, Sejanus, while her husband's body was still warm. The infamous ending of the eighth episode, in which Caligula attempts to prove his God-hood by cutting open his incestuously-pregnant sister's stomach and eating the embryo of their unborn child, was the only major departure from Graves's text (Drucilla dies of a fever in the book). The scene, with Caligula, his chin soaked in blood, staggering from the murder room and telling Claudius, quietly and sanely, not to go in, may be one of the most memorable images in television history.

The later assassination of Caligula led to a power vacuum. Thanks to the intervention of the palace guards (whose number included Bernard Hill and Norman Rossington), and with the cunning Herod and Claudius's manipulative wife, Messalina, making most of the decisions, Claudius the idiot, the last surviving member of the Julian family, becomes the emperor, much to his own dismay.

Most of the rest of the story concerned the internal politics of Claudius's years as ruler, the in-fighting between his aides, the ambitious Pallus and the pragmatic Narcissus, the Emperor's conquest of Britain and his eventual death at the hands of his fourth wife, Agrippinella, to be succeeded by his stepson, the tyrant Nero.

I, Claudius' legacy was huge. Intelligent, witty, dramatic and utterly absorbing, the series attracted many viewers to historical drama who would, otherwise, not have touched the genre with a bargepole. The series' dynamic performances and sweeping camera work (a testament to the skilful direction of Herbert Wise) were discussed at length in pubs up and down the country, in a way that few television series ever have been. Everything from the effective title music by Wilfred Josephs, and the titles themselves – a snake crawling across a tiled floor, as parodied by ***Blackadder*** – felt right. The affection with which the series is held by those it charmed and repulsed was proved in 1986 when it was repeated and again received enthusiastically.

Secret Army

- **BBC Television/BRT (Belgium)** (BBC1) ◆ Colour
- **43 episodes** (including 1 unbroadcast) (*c.* 55 minutes) ◆ 1977-79
- **Writers:** Willis Hall, John Brason, Arden Winch, James Andrew Hall, N. J. Crisp, Robert Barr, Simon Masters, Michael Chapman, David Crane, Paul Annett, Gerard Glaister, Lloyd Humphries, Allan Prior, Eric Paice
- **Directors:** Kenneth Ives, Viktor Ritelis, Paul Annett, Terence Dudley, Roger Jenkins, Michael E. Briant, Tristan de Vere Cole, Roger Cheveley, Andrew Morgan
- **Producer:** Gerard Glaister

Regular cast: Bernard Hepton (Albert Foiret) • Jan Francis (Lisa Colbert) • Christopher Neame (John Curtis) • Angela Richards (Monique Duchamps) • Clifford Rose (Sturmbahn-führer Kessler) • Michael Culver (Brandt) • Juliet Hammond-Hill (Natalie) • Stephen Yardley (Max Brocard) • Ron Pember (Alain) • Valentine Dyall (Dr Pascal Keldermans) • Nigel Williams (Francois) • Hazel McBride (Madelaine Duclos) • Terrence Hardiman (Reinhardt) • Ralph Bates (Paul Vercors) • Paul Shelley (Bradley) • Stephen Chase (Capt. Durnford)

With: Timothy Morand (Jacques) • James Bree (Gaston) • Maria Charles (Louise) • Ian McCulloch (Malaud) • Vivien Merchant (Mlle Gunet) • Peter Barkworth (Hugh Neville) • John Carson (Van Reijn) • Maurice Denham (Dom Girard) • Brewster Mason (Dom Pierre) • Gunnar Moller (Hans) • Marianne Stone (Lena) • Hilary Minster (Muller)

There was a time when many claimed that *Secret Army* was the best-ever example of the on-going drama serial. Its name might be less familiar now, but, when viewed in the 90s, *Secret Army* has lost little of its pace and tension, the strength of the performances and the quality of much of the writing still shining through. And how many serious programmes can boast of being the inspiration to an entire and hugely successful comedy spoof?

It does some disservice to the tone of the programme to mention its famous parody, but it is impossible to ignore the ***'Allo 'Allo!*** connection. Never has a sitcom so ruthlessly imitated another programme. With the exception of the location (the Café René is in France, not Belgium), almost all of the elements that made up *Secret Army* can be seen in Lloyd and Croft's sitcom, from the world-weary restaurateur to the beret-topped Communists. One *Secret Army* episode revolved around some old masters that were forged and taken by, respectively, Lifeline and the Gestapo, prefiguring ***'Allo 'Allo!***'s shenanigans with Van Clomp's most famous work. The sets were incredibly familiar, as were the actors, Hilary Minster, Gorden Kaye and Guy Siner having roles in both. *Secret Army* – like almost any war-time drama – did have its occasional fanciful moments (such as the rescue of Monique from Nazi-observed imprisonment in a nunnery by the others impersonating medical staff). However, the brooding, expansive theme music ('Nuages' by Django Reinhardt) implied the basic nature of *Secret Army* as clearly as the simple ditty that introduces ***'Allo 'Allo!*** The programmes are poles apart, but both provide interesting examples of popular television.

In fact, *Secret Army*'s title sequence is perhaps as well-remembered as the programme itself, with its railway lines and roads surrounded by trees fading into the distance, implying the course of Lifeline's escape route. Lifeline was a fictional amalgam of the various escape routes that were formulated in occupied Europe during World War II, allowing Allied aircrew shot down on bombing raids to return home. Between 1941 and 1945 some 3500 men were returned to their UK bases, grateful for the bravery of the huge range of contacts that saw them safely home. Indeed, the people who helped or controlled the escape routes were often in greater danger than the airmen, as *Secret Army* made clear: they were civilians resisting an occupying power, and could be tortured or executed. Such men and women were also completely untrained.

Lifeline's HQ is Le Candide in Brussels, a high-quality restaurant frequented by top German officers and run by the middle-aged Albert Foiret (Bernard Hepton, swapping sides after playing the Kommandant in ***Colditz***). Other key personnel at the outset are Lisa Colbert and John Curtis, an RAF man who acts as liaison with London. Lifeline controls safe houses, arranges for forged papers (particularly once Max Brocard joined the team), and runs a route south to Biarritz and over the Pyrenees.

Episodes would often begin with scenes showing the shooting-down of the Allied airmen, the ensuing drama dealing with matters of life and death and the ethics of human conflict. 'Prisoner of War' concerned London's insistence that Lifeline be used to transport a wounded Luftwaffe pilot to Britain, which, although furthering the Allies' war effort, might put the entire organization at risk. 'Good Friday' examined the collision between faith and patriotism as monks shelter an RAF man, a theme *Secret Army* was to examine on more than one occasion.

Secret Army devoted an equal amount of time to the people attempting to infiltrate Lifeline as to those running it. It portrayed the stresses in the Third Reich – between the old aristocrats and the new Nazis (such as Kessler) – and, in attempting to put a human face on Nazism, it was able to examine how far sane human beings can go in time of war.

Brandt, the head of the Luftwaffe, was the 'reasonable' face of Nazism, a man whose 'interrogation' tended away from the awful violence of Kessler and towards a no less sinister debriefing with coffee and cigars. He is utterly devastated when his wife and son are killed in an Allied bombing raid on Berlin, degenerating into physical violence when interviewing the man who could, feasibly, have dropped the fateful bomb. On the other hand, Kessler, the head of Gestapo, is the face of Fascism that countless war films had already portrayed, a cold and brutal man who frequently breaks the Geneva Convention, only granting prisoner of war status after information had been revealed. He is cool and analytical even when captured, and his stock response to the murder of German soldiers is to take and shoot innocent hostages until the culprit is revealed. Yet there is depth even to him: he is lonely, and actively pursues the civilized company of Madelaine Duclos. He is also dedicated to men in whom he has trust, striving to free Brandt from implication in an anti-Hitler

Kessler wants to be the first kid in his block to rule the world (from *'Lisa – codename Yvette'*)

First season
(7 Sep–29 Dec 77)
1 Lisa – Codename Yvette
2 Sergeant on the Run
3 Radishes with Butter
4 Child's Play
5 Second Chance
6 Growing Up
7 Lost Sheep
8 Guilt
9 Too Near Home
10 Identity in Doubt
11 A Question of Loyalty
12 Hymn to Freedom
13 Bait
14 Good Friday
15 Suspicions
16 Be the First Kid in Your Block to Rule the World

Second season
(27 Sep–20 Dec 78)
17 The Hostage
18 Russian Roulette
19 Lucky Piece
20 Trapped
21 Not According to Plan
22 Scorpion
23 Weekend
24 The Big One
25 Little Old Lady
26 Guests at God's Table
27 A Matter of Life and Death
28 Prisoner of War
29 Day of Wrath

Third season
(22 Sep–15 Dec 79)
30 The Last Run
31 Invasions
32 Revenge
33 A Safe Place
34 Ring of Rosies
35 Prisoner
36 Ambush
37 Just Light the Blue Touch-Paper
38 Sound of Thunder
39 Collaborator
40 Days of Judgement
41 Bridgehead
42 The Execution
43 What did You do in the war, Daddy? [unbroadcast]

[Although filmed, the final episode, written by John Brason and set some years after the war, was never transmitted. *Kessler* was broadcast between 13 Nov and 18 Dec 81 (six episodes).]

plot. However, when the order comes for Brandt's court-martial, he is as down-to-earth as ever. (Brandt's life lacks all meaning; he shoots himself rather than face this final disgrace.)

Secret Army showed members of Lifeline being forced to make difficult decisions by the nature of war and by the need for secrecy. Towards the end of the second season, when Monique and the others deliberately disobey Albert's orders, he is forced to remind her that there can only be one person in charge and that the lives of hundreds of people depend on him. He will not let anything – not even his love for her – put those lives at risk, and he will shoot her if she disobeys him again. When Lifeline is infiltrated by a German disguised as a crashed member of the RAF, Foiret's initial response is to want to kill all currently-held airmen for the sake of the entire organization. Max can show no mercy to the spy when he is eventually found, and Foiret's friend is just as brutal when he decides to take over Lifeline on behalf of the Communists. His betrayal leads to the death of Natalie's boyfriend, Francois, but Max is soon tracked down and killed. The Communists' desire to be seen to be the major force of resistance after the war is often in stark contrast to the selfless endeavours of the people of Lifeline.

The final season saw the war moving towards its conclusion, and paradoxically the threat to Lifeline increased day by day. The Allied advance is severing evasion lines, Communist vengeance is brewing for the death of Max, and Brandt's replacement (Reinhardt) turns out to be a formidable opponent. Albert is actually imprisoned at one point, but, given the nature of Le Candide and its clientele, this is not enough to save many of those working for Lifeline from the accusation of being Nazi sympathizers. Monique, captured by a mob and about to be lynched, has to be rescued by an American soldier.

These harrowing final episodes sum up much of *Secret Army*'s gritty approach and realistic attitude to warfare: the heroes were persecuted, the ostensible villains escaped. Kessler and Duclos flee from capture by the British, Kessler shooting a German soldier in the face so that he can assume his identity.

1981's spin-off, *Kessler*, depicted the former Nazi as a wealthy and respected businessman, complete with family. However, old faces return to haunt him, which forces 'Manfred Dorf' to flee to Britain and then to South America, where he hopes to link up with Martin Bormann. Set in modern times, *Kessler* was, depending on your point of view, either a sub-*Boys from Brazil* romp from the channel that produced *The Borgias*, or a shockingly plausible coda to one of the BBC's most important and thoroughly enjoyable dramatic serials.

The first BBC TV drama was broadcast live from Alexandra Palace on 6 November 1936. It was a stage play, *Marigold*, and was probably little more than a televised version of the theatre production. This was the pattern of all pre-war and much of the immediate post-war television – an extension of theatrical art, a static presentation in two dimensions. But the new form was growing fast. Drama output in 1936 consisted of four productions, the next year it leapt to 122, including *School for Scandal*, *Night Must Fall*, *Murder in the Cathedral*, *Anna Christie*, *Jane Eyre* and 14 Shakespeare plays.

Theatre Parade (1936-38) was the first umbrella drama series, featuring the talents of such early TV legends as George More O'Ferrell, Michael Barry, Royston Morley and Jan Bussell. There were few original plays – dramatists were more inclined to write for the cinema, radio or theatre than this new gimmicky medium. A ten-minute play called *The Underground Murder Mystery* by J. Bissel Thomas holds the distinction of being the first.

Post-war drama remained solidly theatrical with Shakespeare, Shaw and Dickens regulars, interrupted only by the occasional original work. However, there were the first social drama documentaries pioneered by Michael Barry, Robert Barr, Duncan Ross, Donald Wilson and Nigel Kneale. *Sunday Night Theatre* (1955-59) showcased the work of Rudolph Cartier, Andrew Osborn, Philip Mackie, Alvin Rakoff, Colin Morris, Stuart Burge, Gerard Glaister, Michael Elliott, Jack Pulman and Giles Cooper, whilst *The Sunday Night Play* (1960-63) continued the trend with David Mercer, John Osborne, Alun Owen, Naomi Capon, Don Taylor and Gilchrist Calder.

But the BBC was still, essentially, producing middle-class entertainment for a particular audience, as highlighted by the popularity of *Saturday Playhouse* (1958), a showcase for theatre-orientated works. At ABC, *Armchair Theatre* began in 1956 with similar aims and the same audience in mind. All that changed in 1958 when the company head-hunted Canadian TV executive Sydney Newman and encouraged him to come to England to make their television more 'modern'. Newman assembled a progressive young team (Peter Luke, Irene Shubik, Harry Moore, Verity Lambert) and effectively rewrote the book on what the TV play was supposed to be all about. The following years saw the TV debuts of Alun Owen, Harold Pinter, Angus Wilson, Ray Rigby and Robert Müller. *No Trams to Lime Street*, *A Night Out*, Rigby's *The Cupboard*, Robert Storey's *Dead Letter*, Ted Willis's *Hot Summer Night*, and John Bethune's adaptation of *The Picture of Dorian Gray* were TV history in the making. They took the trends of the 'working class heroes' of late-50s UK cinema and turned them into a form that became (sneeringly) known as 'the kitchen sink drama'.

By 1963 the BBC needed help with *its* drama output which, with the exception of ***Z Cars*** (itself dismissed by executives as mere prole entertainment) and the provincial thriller anthology *Suspense*, was desperately stale. So it head-hunted Sydney Newman... *Plus ça change, plus ça la même choice*. This wasn't a universally popular decision, even amongst the professionals (Don Taylor in *Days of Vision* describes the dismay within the BBC's drama ranks when this maker of 'tabloid journalism television' was appointed).

A two-pronged attack in 1963 produced *First Night* (to satisfy John Elliot's love of relevant, political drama, which spawned *The Road*, William Emms's *Sticks*, and David Turner's *The Bedmakers*) and *Festival* (for Peter Luke to adapt the classics). When both proved less than perfect, the two were married in *The Wednesday Play, the* television icon of the 60s. Initially, this contained productions orphaned from *Festival* (including Cartier's *The July Plot*), but when James MacTaggert brought Newman's wish for 'gusty, spontaneous contemporaneity' to the screen, the results were spectacular, the first play being *Tap on the Shoulder* by James O'Connor, who had once been convicted of murder. In 1965 alone, *The Wednesday Play* presented *Fable*, *Horror of Darkness*, *And Did Those Feet?*, *Ashes to Ashes* (Marc Brandel), *Campaign for One* (Marielaine Douglas and Anthony Church), *Three Clear Sundays* (O'Connor's remarkable exposé of death row), Michael Hastings's *For the West*, about the bloody Belgian Congo massacres, Dennis Potter's first four plays, and *Up the Junction*. Written by Nell Dunn, *Up the Junction*, with its pop song soundtrack, stark language, documentary direction (by ***Z Cars*** graduate Ken Loach) and a harrowing depiction of abortion, brought howls of protest, chiefly from Mary Whitehouse, who accused the play of 'presenting the working class woman as dirty and promiscuous'. Starring Carol White as the tragic heroine Sylvie, with Vickery Turner, Tony Selby and George Sewell, it was described by Tony Garnett as 'neither a play, a documentary or a musical. It is all three at once.' And when *Cathy Come Home* appeared six months later, it seemed the revolution was at hand!

The Wednesday Play, as Irene Shubik confessed, 'attempted a tabloid approach to the audience and succeeded in selling itself on sex, violence and the sensational'. Because of this it was as much a part of 60s culture as the Beatles. The intelligentsia loved the plays' exposure of British life, though it was loathed by many critics for its bourgeois trappings and pretentious smugness. What was undeniable was that it was perfectly suited for the age. Later producers included Shubik, Lionel Harris and Graeme McDonald. Philip Saville, Christopher Morahan, James Ferman, Gareth Davies, Waris Hussein, Alan Bridges, Herbert Wise and Charles Jarrott regularly directed plays. The series utilized the talents of every important dramatist of the 60s: Jim Allen, Andrew Davies, Julia Jones, Philip Purser (*Calf Love*), Charles Wood (*Drums Along the Avon*), Vickery Turner (*Kippers and Curtains*), Neville Smith and Gordon Honeycombe (*The Golden Vision*), Nigel Kneale (*Bam! Pow! Zap!*), Alan Gosling (*Happy*), Leon Whiteson (*Blood of the Lamb*) and Tony Parker (*Chariot of Fire*), along with Potter, Mercer, Plater, Rudkin and Terson.

BBC2 joined in the fun with *Story Parade*, *Out of the Unknown*, *Theatre 625*, and *Thirty Minute Theatre*. *625* was an important and prestigious avenue for writers like Arnold Wesker, David Turner, Giles Cooper, Pinter and Owen, though it was only when later plays like Cooper's *Kittens are Brave*, Nigel Kneale's *The Year of the Sex Olympics*, and Obi Egbuna's *Wind versus Polygamy* were repeated on BBC1 that most viewers began to realize it. *Thirty Minute Theatre*, on the other hand, began as a talent slot for writers new to the medium, a way of learning your trade before messing with the big boys on *The Wednesday Play*. Philip Levene, Peter van Greenaway, Peter J. Hammond and Dennis Potter wrote early plays, whilst writers like Dawn Pavitt and Terry Wale, Tom Stoppard, Rhys Adrian, Jack Trevor Story, Derrick Sherwin and Barry Bermange became regulars. The plays were often experimental (the works of Charlotte and Denis Plimmer, the 45-minute *Psychological Warfare*) or historical (Pat Flower's *The Tape Recorder* was British television's first colour drama production). Mini-series were attempted: *Something to Hide*, the biographical *These Men are Dangerous*, Arden Winch's *Waugh on Crime* or David Hodson's *Aggers and Torters*. MP Maurice Edelman wrote several plays, as did dramatist C.P. Taylor. Later contributors included John Mortimer, Roy Minton, Ian Curteis, Philip Martin, Jack Rosenthal and Susan Pleat (the surreal psychological nightmare *I Wouldn't Tell on You Miss*).

In response, various ITV companies tried to produce cutting-edge drama anthologies. Associated Rediffusion with *Half-Hour Story*, Yorkshire's *Seven Deadly Sins*, and Granada's *City 68* (all 1967) even got close to the quality of the BBC's output. However, it wasn't until 1969 when the various independent companies collaborated on *Saturday Night Theatre* that ITV began to win back some of the points lost to the BBC. Imaginative producers like Kenith Trodd, Peter Willis and Derek Bennett used the best of the BBC writers, but were discovering stars of their own, like Anthony Skene, Michael J. Bird and Colin Welland.

Short BBC drama series like *Biography* (1970), *Sextet* (1972), *Centre Play* (1974), and *Second City Firsts* also provided opportunites for both established and new talent, *Playhouse* replacing *Thirty Minute Theatre* as BBC2's major offering in 1974. The standard bearer for British TV drama in the 70s was, of course, *Play for Today*, the direct offspring of *The Wednesday Play*.

By the 80s, however, even *Play for Today* seemed jaded. ITV had, to all intents and purposes, given up producing one-off drama in favour of series and serials (even Thames's anthology *Storyboard* served as a trial run for potential series, spawning ***The Bill***, *Lytton's Diary*, and *Mr Palfrey of Westminster*). The BBC's attempts to keep the public occupied, like *Play of the Week* (1977), opened strongly (you can't get much stronger than *Professional Foul*) but ended in a dispiriting lack of interest. By the mid-80s, with *Play for Today*'s baby, *The Play on One*, seeming to have no real focus, the corporation diverted most of its time and energy into three new flagships for the filmed play, *Screen One*, *Screen Two*, and *Screenplay*. They found a few new masters: Steve Poliakoff, William Humble, Arthur Ellis, Stephen Volk, Meera Syall and Romain Gray. Sadly, as several writers (including J.C. Wilsher and Alan Plater) have noted, it is difficult to see where, exactly, other than in series TV, a writer new to the medium will get his first break these days. Pioneering 'new talent' slots like *Debut on Two* or Channel 4's *Fourplay* (and its various humorously-titled variants) are welcome. If only there were more of this kind of thing. *Performance*, meanwhile, has followed noble series like *The BBC Television Shakespeare* and *Theatre Night* in keeping the BBC's tradition of lavish, exotic costume drama going.

The history of British television drama mirrors the recent history of the nation. In putting the lives of their countrymen on film and videotape, successive generations of writers, directors, producers and actors have followed Hamlet's description of the play's purpose as to 'hold the mirror up to nature'.

Sometimes we need that mirror very badly.

Jim Allen Possibly the last man to include the word 'lard' in a British TV play, Allen is a former miner whose proud socialism has helped to shape his work, beginning with episodes of ***Coronation Street***. *The Hard Wood* (1966), *The Lump* (1967), and *The Big Flame* (1969) established Allen as a sympathetic writer of the working classes. After the radical *The Rank and File* ('quite obviously the man has gone too far', noted Barry Norman in *The Times*) came the even more controversial serial *Days of Hope* (1975), directed by Ken Loach, and starring Nikolas Simmonds and Pamela Brighton. This was intended as an early history of the Labour movement, from the Great War to the National Strike. However, it is probably now best remembered as the first BBC production to seriously challenge conventional attitudes to war, promoting pacifism as a tenable response to aggression. This was too much for Conservative critics, who lambasted its historical details and 'Communist Party' propaganda.

The Spongers (1978) was a heartfelt, if naive, attack on right-wing attitudes to Social Security, while *A United Kingdom* (1981) concerned a northern council rebelling against government cutbacks. Allen's more recent work includes *Willie's Last Stand* (1982), the post-war drama *The Gathering Seed* (1983), and, in the cinema, *Raining Stones* (GB 91) and *Land and Freedom* (GB 95), both with Ken Loach.

Alan Bennett Though often accused of 'professional northernism', Bennett's superb grasp of naturalistic dialogue and his flair for gentle observation continue to delight audiences.

Bennett's career began at Oxford University where his contributions to *Beyond the Fringe* earned him a place in comedy history. Major TV works include *My Father Knew Lloyd George* (1965), the sketch-based comedy series *On the Margin* (1966), *A Day Out* (1972), *Sunset Across the Bay* (1975), *One Fine Day* (1979), *Objects of Affection* (1982), *An Englishman Abroad* (1983), *The Insurance Man* (1986), and *Talking Heads* (1988). This latter series of intimate monologues, including Bennett as a homosexual still living with his mum, did much to attract people who would otherwise have run a mile from the word 'drama'. 1991's *A Question of Attribution* deservedly won a BAFTA award.

Film work, such as *A Private Function* (GB 84), *Prick Up Your Ears* (GB 87) and the Oscar-winning *The Madness of King George* (GB 95) hopefully won't keep Bennett away from producing more of the witty pieces of northern angst for which he is so loved.

Alan Bleasdale As the *Radio Times* noted, if Bleasdale's first ambition had been realized he would have been a winger running circles around the Everton defence. But Liverpool FC rejected Bleasdale as a 17-year-old and he became a teacher instead.

In 1975 his novel *Scully* was published. The book evolved into a series on local radio about the teenage hard case, Franny Scully. Later the characters would be used in his second BBC play, *Scully's New Year's Eve* (1978). His first, *Early to Bed*, was produced for *Second City Firsts* in 1975.

The Black Stuff was, prophetically, broadcast on the second day of the 80s, and followed the misadventures of an itinerant scouse Tarmac gang. At the time the play was written the unemployment figure was under a million, but to Bleasdale 'it was obvious that it would be the major problem of our times'. The 'boys' were led by Dixie Deans (Tom Georgeson) and the dignified socialist George Malone (Peter Kerrigan), whilst the other members included Chrissy (Michael Angelis), Loggo (Alan Igbon) and Yosser Hughes (Bernard Hill). Hill, who had previously appeared in *The Spongers*, *Professional Foul*, and Mike Stott's *Our Flesh and Blood*, would become synonymous with the role. The play mixed comedy with the brutality of their situation, far from home and on the verge of unemployment.

Such was the impact of *The Black Stuff* that the BBC asked Bleasdale to create a series of plays about the characters. A blood-relative of this, *The Muscle Market*, appeared in 1981, and was described by *Time Out* as 'a cracking contemporary comedy acutely sensitive to the problems of the 1980s'. It starred Pete Postlethwaite as the entrepreneur Danny Duggan.

The five-play *The Boys from the Blackstuff* (1982) saw the boys returning 'to farce, tragedy and tussles with the DoE'. Unlike other confrontational depic-

Yosser and kids, played by Timothy, Jamie and Tamantha Bleasedale (*The Boys from the Blackstuff*)

tions of the welfare state (notably that other Liverpool saga, *Bread*, with its sour-faced DSS clerks), *Jobs for the Boys* presented the young counter staff as bewildered and helpless. Chrissy and Loggo, together with George's son, Snowey, work illegally for the shady Irish builder Molloy. Then Yosser arrives, trailing his children with him, intoning lines that were soon to be national catchphrases: 'Gizza job' and 'Ah could do dat'. It was a remarkable performance from Hill which won him a BAFTA. Bleasdale, declaring himself apolitical, proved that whilst he was horrified by the Tory economic system, and the damage that it inflicted on people, he was as hostile to Militant as to the Monday Club.

The following *Blackstuff* plays were character studies of Dixie (*Moonlighter*), Chrissy (*Shop Thy Neighbour*), and Yosser. *Yosser's Story* began with a dream sequence in which Hughes's children drown. There was much humour, as when Yosser meets Liverpool captain Graeme Souness ('You look like me ... And Magnum'). Although Yosser's psychosis is more obvious, the portrayal of Chrissy, nagged by his wife (Julie Walters), slaughtering his pet geese was also memorable.

The final play was a sprawling dead-end, with no solutions to the tragedy. The scenes in a pub with eccentric characters such as 'Shake Hands' (Iggy Navaro) helped to place even Yosser into context. Maybe because of its critical acclaim ('Best British TV Drama of the Decade' for one), *Blackstuff* has become the object of parody ever since. Harry Enfield did it superbly in 'It's Grim Oop North' and 'The Scousers'; others, such as that by *Three of a Kind*, were unkind and desperately unfunny.

Moving to Channel 4, Bleasdale adapted *Scully* into a delightful series in 1984. Using many of the 'repertory company' of actors he enjoyed writing for (Tom Georgeson had a great role as a vicious police sergeant, and Andrew Schofield had appeared in *Blackstuff*), the young cast made Bleasdale's wry stories of adolescence into magical television. Schofield's performance as the hard-nut with a soft centre was tremendous, as were those of his friends Mooey (Ray Kingsley) and Mad Dog (Mark McGann). Another Liverpool icon, Kenny Dalglish, followed team mate Souness into acting (playing himself in Scully's daydreams), whilst Elvis Costello, who wrote the theme song ('Turning the Town Red'), also had a small part as Scully's retarded and railway-obsessed brother.

After Bleasdale's first *Film on Four* venture (the wry *No Surrender*), he returned to television, and controversy. *The Monocled Mutineer* was based on a book by William Allison and John Fairley concerning the Great War exploits of Percy Toplis, the soldier who led a coup at the Etaples training camp in 1917. Bleasdale, whose grandfather had fallen at Passchendaele, based his screenplay only loosely on fact, as we follow Toplis's encounters with authority (Timothy West's blustering General) and the mutiny, led by Toplis and Charles Strange (Matthew Marsh). In the mutiny's aftermath, as the deserters hide in the French hills, Toplis impersonates an officer, using his friends (Patrick Doyle and Billy Fellows) as his fags. He leads the rebels in the taking of a bridge, talking down a confrontation with a young captain who feels his duty is to stop them (the real-life officer, James Davis, by then in his nineties, stated that the scene was chillingly authentic). Eventually Percy returns home, falls in love with a widow (Cherie Lunghi) and lives as a fugitive before he is tracked down by the MI5 assassin Woodhall (Philip McGough), and dies in a hail of police bullets. Paul McGann (whose brothers, Mark and Joe, Bleasdale had previously worked with) gave an astonishing performance as the cynical Toplis.

Despite its quality, however, *The Monocled Mutineer* became the target of one of the most sustained hate campaigns waged against a television series. A BBC press release had stated that *The Monocled Mutineer* was historically accurate. It wasn't, although the fiction elements were incidental to the plot, notably a scene in which an officer (Nick Reding) is shot for cowardice. This had been inspired by the memories of Victor Sylvester, a 17-year-old conscript at Etaples. However, historians stated that this was inaccurate and the *Daily Mail* – already critical of the BBC over ***The Singing Detective*** – smeared *The Monocled Mutineer* as 'a tissue of lies'. Bleasdale was, rightly, horrified that his work had been used as someone else's political football and this spilled over into his next project.

G.B.H. started life as a film script, then became a novel and, finally, a 10½-hour series for Channel 4. Inspired, in part, by the political events in Liverpool during the 80s, *G.B.H.* cast Robert Lindsay as the ambitious council leader Michael Murray, whilst moderate schoolteacher Jim Nelson was played by Michael Palin. Other characters included the barbed, sexually-alluring Barbara Douglas (Lindsay Duncan) and Murray's senile mother (Julie Walters). There were also the, somewhat inevitable, appearances of Angelis, Schofield, Georgeson and Igbon. Controversially, *G.B.H.* was not chosen as 'best series' at the BAFTAs (a saga of alleged 'vote rigging' which gained almost as much press as the series itself). However, it did become a popular hit, *NME* describing it as 'jaundiced political satire laced with classic double-bluffs, highly-effective set-pieces, a touch of Tory evil and an abundance of food for thought'. 1995 saw Bleasdale reunited with Lindsay and Walters in *Jake's Progress*. 'I don't want to change society,' Bleasdale told the *Radio Times*, 'I want to reflect it.' Few writers reflect and delight society better than Alan Bleasdale.

Malcolm Bradbury Academic (Professor of American studies at the University of East Anglia) and novelist, Bradbury's original plays for TV include *The After Dinner Game* (1975) and *Standing in for Henry* (1980). Bradbury's superb adaptation of Tom Sharpe's *Blott on the Landscape*, in 1985, starred George Cole, Geraldine James, Simon Cadell, Julia McKenzie and David Suchet. He also wrote an award-winning adaptation of Sharpe's *Porterhouse Blue* in 1987 for Channel 4. Bradbury's novel of the sexual adventures of a left-wing university lecturer, *The History Man*, was, itself, adapted by Christopher Hamilton in 1981 to great acclaim (Anthony Sher playing the amoral Howard Kirk). In 1989 Bradbury's TV work returned to the campus with *Anything More Would Be Greedy*, whilst his 1990 adaptation of Kingsley Amis's *The Green Man* (starring Albert Finney) won praise for its surrealism, but was criticized for its sexual content. In 1996 Bradbury wrote one of the three BBC *Dalziel and Pascoe* films.

John Byrne Painter John Byrne began flexing his artistic imagination in other directions in 1977 when his play *Writer's Cramp* premiered at the Edinburgh Fringe. He followed this with

The Slab Boys, adapted for television in 1981.

Byrne came to most people's attention with 1987's *Tutti Frutti*. It concerned the 25th anniversary of Scotland's foremost rockers, the Majestics. Vocalist Big Jazza – the 'Beast of Rock' – dies in a car accident. His younger brother, Danny (Robbie Coltrane), is roped into the band, as is his girlfriend, Suzi Kettles (Emma Thompson). The rest of the band comprise Vince Diver (Maurice Roeves), Bomba (Stuart McGugan) and Fud (Jake D'Arcy). Under the dubious guidance of their uncool manager (Richard Wilson), the Majestics' tour becomes a disaster. Byrne described the ensuing events as 'funny in the way that life is funny; it's not all that funny when it's happening'.

In 1990 Byrne achieved similar success with *Your Cheatin' Heart*.

Rudolph Cartier Born in Austria in 1904, Cartier studied at the Vienna Academy of Music and Dramatic Art before embarking on a promising scriptwriting career in Berlin, working with Emeric Pressburger and Billy Wilder. Like his colleagues, the rise of the Nazis forced him to leave for Britain in 1935. After the war he was invited to join the BBC by Michael Barry. At their first meeting Cartier said he thought the whole approach to television drama was wrong, with too much emphasis on classics adaptations and the West End stage. The result of Cartier's new initiative was *Arrow to the Heart*, an adaptation of a German short story transmitted live on 20 July 1952, the first of over 120 productions Cartier would be responsible for.

In 1953 Barry commissioned Nigel Kneale (who had provided additional dialogue for *Arrow to the Heart*) to write an original drama series, and Cartier was chosen to direct it. ***The Quatermass Experiment*** was an instant hit and on its strength Cartier and Kneale began a ten-year collaboration that produced *Nineteen Eighty-Four*, two adaptations of *Wuthering Heights*, *The Creature*, ***Quatermass II***, and ***Quatermass and the Pit***. Like almost all BBC drama of the time, these were transmitted live, and yet the scale of production was epic even by modern standards, something which characterized all of Cartier's work (legend has it that on seeing a new script his first exclamation would always be 'I'll need a hundred extras'). Cartier never saw television as a medium which could not be as expensive or 'big' as the cinema, either in terms of subject or complexity. Thus he willingly tackled large-scale productions like *Clive of India* (1956), *A Midsummer Night's Dream* (1958), *Anna Karenina* (1961, with Sean Connery and Claire Bloom), and *Night Express* (1963).

Cartier chose to produce much European literature, such as Sartre's *The Respectful Prostitute* (1964), and his own origins were reflected in the number of German adaptations, often translated by Cartier himself, through which he did much to rehabilitate the image of the Germanic people in the eyes of the British public. He did this by confronting the crimes of the Third Reich – and the resistance to them – in a most direct way through plays like the surreal *Dr Korczak and the Children* (1962), *Stalingrad* (1963), *The July Plot* (1964, about the army conspiracy to assassinate Hitler in 1944), and *The Joel Brand Story* (1965). The latter focused on a bizarre deal between the Nazis and the Allies brokered by a Hungarian factory owner. *The Listener* remarked 'One's resistance to believing the ghastly story of Eichmann's offer of the lives of a million Jews for 10,000 lorries is justification enough for the production of this play.' With *The Joel Brand Story*, and *Lee Oswald – Assassin* (1966), Cartier virtually invented the concept of the modern drama-documentary.

His other passion in life was opera, which he was keen to bring to a wider audience with televised productions of *Saint of Bleecker Street* (1956), *A Tale of Two Cities* (1958), Verdi's *Otello* (1959), and *Tobias and the Angel* (1960).

Throughout his television career, Cartier worked only for the BBC, famously objecting to independent television by saying 'I hate the idea of my creative work being constantly interrupted for commercial reasons. I am an artist, not a salesman.' Like most BBC drama producers, Cartier was often required to work on episodes of series like *Maigret*, ***Z Cars***, and *Out of the Unknown*, and yet he applied the same exacting standards to this work as he would to a prestigious *Sunday Night Play*. He directed two pieces for *Out of the Unknown*, one of which (J.B. Priestley's *Level 7*) is widely regarded as the series' lost masterpiece. He also directed several plays for *Thirty Minute Theatre*, including the Hitler segment of Jean Benedetti's *These Men are Dangerous* trilogy, *Brainscrew* (1966), and *The News Benders* (1968), plus the *Late Night Horror* play *Triumph of Death* (1968), and episodes of *Fall of Eagles* (1972).

Like Dennis Potter, Cartier died on 7 June 1994. Although of different generations, in the same day were lost television's greatest dramatist, and the man who, in effect, created television drama as we know it. Characteristically modest, when interviewed in 1991 by BBC2's *The Late Show*, Cartier summed up his life's work thus: 'The public wants to be lifted out of their drab, dreary life, to look at this cold screen of glass, and look at another world. That is what the public expected of me.'

Alan Clarke In the late 60s and 70s, Clarke worked extensively on *The Wednesday Play* and *Play for Today*, directing the works of writers like Peter Terson (*The Last Train Through Harecastle Tunnel*), Don Shaw (*Sovereign's Company*), Alun Owen (*Joan*), and Colin Welland (*The Hallelujah Handshake*). A lighter effort was Douglas Livingstone's seaside-postcard tableau *I Can't See My Little Willie* (1970), and *Everybody Say Cheese* (1971).

In 1972 he directed the *Horatio Bottomley* episode of *The Edwardians* (with Timothy West), and David A. Yallop's dramatized reconstruction of the Craig/Bentley murder case, *To Encourage the Others*. For *Play for Today* he oversaw *A Life is Forever* by Tony Parker. Much of Clarke's work was firmly rooted in the realism of ordinary people's lives, yet he was also capable of a romantic intensity bordering on the mystical, especially on David Rudkin's *Penda's Fen* – ironically repeated by Channel 4 less than a week before Clarke's death in 1990.

In *Christine* and *Elephant* he turned his attention to the troubles in Northern Ireland, the latter being a remarkable dialogue-free rendering of a series of sectarian murders. *Contract* was an only slightly more wordy treatment of ex-Parachute Regiment officer A.F.N. Clarke's book based on his experiences in the Province, with a powerful near-silent performance by Sean Chapman effectively portraying the build-up of psychological pressure on the troops. Similar territory had been explored by Clarke in David Leland's *Psy Warriors* (1981), and he went on to direct *Made in Britain* for Leland's 1983 series *Birth of a Nation*. The same year saw Clarke directing a different portrait of youth-rebellion in Michael Hastings's Orwellian *Stars of the Roller State Disco*.

In 1988 Clarke directed Jim Cartwright's *Road*, an angry yet humorous picture of northern life on the poverty line, which was contrasted by Al Hunter's *The Firm* the following year, the story of a yuppie football hooligan Bex (Gary Oldman). The violence of Bex and his scum-mates has very little connection with the game itself, demonstrated by the fact that they were never shown actually watching a match, something which Clarke – with a life-long passion for football – was keen to reflect.

Apart from the genially dirty *Film on Four*, *Rita, Sue and Bob Too*, Clarke's most notorious work was Roy Minton's borstal drama *Scum*. Made for *Play for Today* in 1977, it was deemed unsuitable for transmission by BBC director general Alasdair Milne who doubted the veracity of the play, and also believed that Clarke had directed something so naturalistic it could easily be mistaken for a documentary. Coming so soon after Potter's *Brimstone and Treacle*, the BBC tried to suppress *Scum*, but Clarke and producer Margaret Matheson, and the critics they smuggled into television centre to view the play, were outspoken in its defence. Clarke directed a cinema treatment with much the same cast, but it was not until after his death that the original was eventually screened in a series of repeats in 1991, preceded by David Leland's impassioned introduction, which urged viewers to take advantage of probably their only chance to watch, and record, *Scum*.

Tom Clarke One of the major discoveries of BBC2's 'new talent' slot *Thirty Minute Theatre*, Clarke's witty slices of family life (*Everybody's Rich Except Us*, *A Brilliant Future Behind Him*, *Don't Go Down to Bingo Mother, Father's Coming to Tea!* and *Haven't You People Got Homes to Go To?*) were followed by the writer's best work in the early 70s. *Mad Jack*, the story of poet Siegfried Sassoon, starring Michael Jayston, was Clarke's first collaboration with Jack Gold, a partnership that would culminate in the magnificent *Stocker's Copper* (1971, starring Gareth Thomas). Clarke also wrote for less experimental areas of television, scripting an episode of ***The Troubleshooters*** in 1969 ('If He Hollers Let Him Go', directed by Ridley Scott).

Clarke's later work includes *The Moonlighters*, 1978's *Victims of Apartheid*, and *Muck and Brass* (1983), starring Mel Smith.

Brian Clemens Born in 1931, Clemens is the undisputed king of the ITV film series. His initial work was for the Danziger Brothers on *Mark Sabre*, *White Hunter* and *The Man from Interpol* in the 50s. Clemens then worked on *Danger Man*, and ***The Avengers*** at ABC, and it was on the latter series that he made his reputation, eventually becoming its celebrated associate producer with his partner Albert Fennell.

Away from crime drama, Clemens wrote for *Armchair Theatre* (1960's *Nest of Four*), *Sir Francis Drake* and the BBC's *Adam Adamant Lives!*, but it was his work at ITC on ***The Avengers***, *The Baron*, *The Champions*, *The Persuaders!* and *Man of the World* that is amongst the most highly regarded of the era.

Having script-edited *GS5*, Clemens created the anthology series *Thriller* for ATV. His first sitcom, *My Wife Next Door* (with John Alderton and Hannah Gordon), was a big success, whilst Clemens showed his versatility writing for *Quiller*, *Love Story* and ***Bergerac***. After creating *The* ***Professionals***, Clemens concentrated his attention on American television, although he was involved in the production of *Bugs*.

Giles Cooper A respected adapter of the works of others on mainstream drama series like *Maigret* (as script editor) and *Sherlock Holmes* (1965), as well as prestigious serials of Hemingway's *For Whom the Bell Tolls* (1965) and Waugh's *Sword of Honour* (1967 for *Theatre 625*), Cooper's original plays often walked more unconventional paths. Best described as dark comedies of middle-class behaviour, in many cases exact interpretation is open to debate, Cooper rarely discussing the meaning of his work, even when closely involved in the production process. He initially wrote for radio, with his first original television plays being *The No-Man* for Associated Rediffusion in 1955 and the BBC's *Liberty Hall* in 1958, although a version of his stageplay *Never Get Out* had been broadcast as early as 1952.

Much of Cooper's work centred on forced conflict between his characters leading to an unavoidable choice having to be made, as in *Where the Party Ended* (1960), where a wartime bomb disposal man turned robber discovers an unexploded bomb while tunnelling into a bank, and *Love and Penguins* (1961), in which a young bride is faced with the choice between her second husband or the companion of her first. *Point of Honour* (1960) had an Englishman in Spain attracted to the violent code of honour expressed by an outlaw waiting to kill the man who dishonoured his daughter. *The Power of Zero* (1961) and *Carried by Storm* (1964) trod similar territory, the latter in a Napoleonic War setting.

On a number of occasions, Cooper's scenarios were based more in the realms of telefantasy. *The Freewheelers* was a sub-*Clockwork Orange* analysis of rebellious youth, while *Loop* was a science fiction parable with the paradox of an invasion of the present from the future. *The Other Man* had Michael Caine as a British army officer speculating how his life might have been had the Germans won the last war. Other Cooper plays dealt with themes of modern alienation, such as *The Long House*, in which the inhabitants of a suburban terrace knock through all their interior walls to form a single commune, and *Kittens are Brave*, with a private nightmare hidden behind a conventional facade. Also produced for television were adaptations of Cooper's radio scripts *Unman, Wittering and Zigo* and *Seek Her Out* (both 1965), and plays like *The Double Doll* (1963), *A Wicked World* (1964) and *To The Frontier* (1968).

But for his tragic death falling from a train in December 1966, Giles Cooper would almost certainly have consolidated his existing successes with a career that seems only half-finished. Had he lived, it is conceivable that he would be remembered as a writer of the same calibre as David Mercer and Dennis Potter, although one lasting memorial is the annual Giles Cooper Award for new radio plays given in his honour.

Ian Curteis Originally an actor, Curteis graduated to BBC staff direction in 1963, and worked on episodes of ***Z Cars***, *Kipling*, *Out of the Unknown* (William Trevor's *Walk's End* in 1966), and *The Londoners* (John Betjeman's *Pity About the Abbey*). He turned to writing via 1969's *The Haunting*, series like ***Doomwatch*** and ***The Onedin Line*** and 1971's *Thirty Minute Theatre*, *A Distant Chill*.

Curteis's greatest talent is for historical and biographical reconstruction, as reflected in his contributions to *Biography*, *Beethoven* and *Sir Alexander Fleming* (both 1970), followed by the dreary three-part *Long Voyage Out of War* (1971). In 1972 he contributed to another biographical series, *The Edwardians* (*Mr Rolls and Mr Royce*).

Philby, Burgess and Maclean (1977) was the story of the three traitors, directed by Gordon Flemyng for Granada. This period also saw *People Like Us* and *Hess* (1978), the serial *Rough Justice*, *The Atom Spies* and *The Prince Regent* (1979). The epic *Churchill and the Generals* (1979) starred Timothy West as the prime minister and Ian Richardson as Montgomery. Later the same year, *Suez 1956*, about the failed Anglo-French military attempt to take over the Suez Canal after nationalization, was hailed as a television masterpiece.

In 1982 Curteis, in conversation with Alasdair Milne, was commissioned to write a similar play about the Falklands War. Curteis had a good working relationship with the BBC, having most recently written *Miss Morrison's Ghost*, but some within the Corporation were wary of the play's timing, the conflict having ended just months before. The BBC, already under attack for its news coverage of the war, shelved the project. Work recommenced in 1985, respected producer Cedric Messina being appointed and studio time booked. At the last moment, BBC head of drama Peter Goodchild suggested replacing Messina (who was working in Kenya on *The Happy Valley*) and demanded alterations to the script which would have ministers discussing the positive effect that winning the war would have on the next election. Curteis was adamant that there was no evidence that such discussions had taken place and, as his contract made him liable for the veracity of the play, he did not want to include such potentially libellous suggestions. The play was cancelled, with the resulting controversy made worse when production of Charles Wood's (unrelated) *Tumbledown* went ahead. To date the only transmission of any part of the play has been the reading of extracts in *The Liberal Conspiracy* in Channel 4's *Banned* season in 1991.

In recent years Curteis has worked on *The Nightmare Years* (1990) for American television, the Channel 4/European co-production *Mission Eureka* (1991), and – marking a return to the BBC under 'new management' – the adaptation of *The Choir*, from a novel by his wife, Joanna Trollope.

Andrew Davies A tutor at Warwick University, Davies began his TV-writing career in the 60s with *Who's Going to Take Me On?* (starring Richard O'Sullivan). Later work included one-off plays like *Is That Your Body, Boy?* (1970), *Fearless Frank* (1978, starring Leonard Rossiter as Edwardian adventurer Frank Harris) and the ITV children's series *Marmalade Atkins* (1980), about a pre-teen tearaway. *Marmalade Atkins in Space* won Davies his first TV award, a Pye Colour Television Award. (Davies co-created another fine children's series, the BBC's *The Boot Street Band*, in 1994).

Davies's next achievements were his adaptations of the works of R.F. Delderfield for the BBC. *To Serve Them All My Days* starred John Duttine as an idealistic young teacher at a repressed public school, and *Diana* featured both Patsy Kensit and Jenny Seagrove as the aristocratic paramour of the working-class Jan, played by Kevin MacNally. Jan courts the young Diana, having wandered into her family's estate. However, every time Jan seems to be getting close to marrying Diana, she runs away. The war takes her to France, where she marries a collaborator industrialist, who she kills when Jan, now working for British Intelligence, appears. Diana is wounded escaping from France, and later dies.

The serial evoked the awe of first love remarkably, Diana's acceptance of class barriers contrasting with Jan's heroic efforts to get over them. The breach of early innocence was compared to the British attitude to war, and both characters achieve redemption through working for a cause greater than themselves. Davies is possibly the only great television writer to include sexual material in the cause of true eroticism. Davies revels in 'vulnerable human bodies' as part of his humanistic world view, and has a tremendous romanticism that underlies his interest in the physical.

The most obvious example of this trend is Davies's two seasons of *A Very Peculiar Practice* (1986-88), which starred Peter Davison, Graham Crowden, David Troughton and Barbara Flynn. Stephen Daker (Davison) is a newly -divorced GP with a complex about being touched and a pile of other neuroses. He arrives to join the health centre team at Lowlands University. There he meets his superior, Jock (Crowden), who believes in homespun wisdom, is prone to whisky, and narrates his proposed book *The Sick University* into a portable recorder, Bob Buzzard (Troughton), an archetypal, amoral career doctor, and Rose Marie (Flynn), a radical feminist who isn't above using female guile to achieve power. Daker's innocence contrasts with the follies of his colleagues, but Davies doesn't want to vilify anyone. Jock is the possessor of real values, even if stuck in the past, Bob is a victim of his repressed career marriage and Rose Marie is a complex, not unsympathetic character who transcends the reactionary cliché that other writers would have made her. Daker falls for WPC Lyn Turtle (Amanda Hillwood), who is doing a course on body language. She teaches him the value of touching, and educates him to accept her polyamory. Davies's view is that men must shed their paternalistic attitudes, but to do so they need the sympathetic help of women. It's a liberal compromise that has earned him a lot of criticism, particularly for his first novel, *Getting Hurt*, but the fact that he straddles the divide produces some hopeful and life-affirming writing.

The university's vice-chancellor is prey to the forces of the market, and connives with the student union (a memorably dodgy bunch of hypocritical gangsters) to rob the students of what they need, particularly in the way of health care. A silent chorus to the action is provided by two nuns, who haunt the campus and take part in everything that is happening.

Daker has to deal with the angry Dr Furie (Timothy West), Bob's agreement to test an experimental drug (it turns students' ears blue) and, most memorably, an outbreak of non-specific urethritis. Following a feasibility study, Daker is promoted, and the series ends with happy authorial intervention, as, to save Stephen from leaving his lover, the university merges with Hendon Police College. Joe Melia appears as Davies's alter-ego, the creative writing fellow Ron Rust (the character would later reappear, ironically played by David Troughton, in Davies's 1994 telefantasy play *A Few Short Journeys of the Heart*). Along the way, the series had taken quick glimpses into poverty-stricken student life, religion and the life of the academic. Like a campus novel, it made Lowlands the world in microcosm, the place where liberal humanity fought Tory cynicism and radical dogma.

Lyn was gone in the second season, perhaps because she was too much of a fairy godmother to the innocent Stephen. He has to take on the problematic art historian Greta (Joanna Kanska), who was involved with Rose Marie as well as a violent French ex-lover. The university had been taken over by an American company, interested only in profit, and weapons technology takes precedence over art and literature. Bob finds himself attracted to a gay patient, a Geordie athlete, and one day wakes up without the will to live, eventually losing his wife to an old colleague. Professor Bunn is leading the resistance to change, a man with the habit of working at home naked. Rose Marie, who was using Greta in a cynical power game, tries to use this fact against Bunn and implicate Stephen, who she feels has taken Greta from her, in sexual misconduct. Greta herself solves the matter by delivering a lecture on the signifiers of the naked human body, almost an essay on Davies's work.

In 'Bad Vibrations' the divide between art and weapons culture is explored, as the work of an electronic noise band (Slab) is turned to military use. 'The Big Squeeze' has students living in cardboard boxes thanks to budget cuts. 'May the Force Be with You' combines a 'Reclaim the Night' march, Jock's freeing of a labful of experimental dogs, and Bob's efforts to start up a 'relaxation clinic'.

In the end, Jock dies, carrying a patient he misdiagnosed, Rose Marie runs off with the nuns, and Bob is left alone to guard a mechanised parody of a university. The Americans won. Daker is left with Greta. They vow to go to Poland, where something better is developing than the capitalist nightmare around them. The second season wasn't as popular with viewers as the first, the darker levels frustrating those who watched mainly for Bob's curt quips.

A Very Polish Practice appeared as a *Screen One* in 1992, and proved to be an empty tale of sexual and political despair. Other projects of this period included the plays *Ball-Trap on the Côte Sauvage*, *Inappropriate Behaviour* and *Filipina Dream Girls*, adaptations of *The Old Devils*, *Anglo-Saxon Attitudes* and *Middlemarch*, the pilot for *Anna Lee*, and the thriller *Mother Love*. This starred Diana Rigg and David McCallum, and showed off Davies's Jacobean influences, being constructed as something akin to tragedy. Davies's natural affinity with comedy also found an outlet with the 1995 sitcom *Game On*, which he co-created with Bernadette Davis.

House of Cards, starring Ian Richardson as Francis Urquhart, an aspiring Tory politician, and Susannah Harker as the journalist who becomes fascinated with him, is possibly Davies's best-known work. Concerning the ruthless methods that Urquhart employs to become prime minister, the series had the good fortune to be shown during the 1990 Tory leadership contest. Richardson's habit of speaking dramatic asides to camera underlined the Shakespearian nature of the project. In Michael Dobbs's novel the journalist uncovers the politician's schemes and he is exposed. In the adaptation, the more uneasy Davies has Urquhart lifting her up on to the wall of the Commons roof garden and pushing her over, before going on to gain the power he craves, in a perfect metaphor for the way the public allows their leaders to treat them. A highly controversial sequel, *To Play the King*, followed in 1993, with a liberal monarch played by Michael Kitchen causing problems for Urquhart. The trilogy concluded with *The Final Cut* in 1995. Urquhart – now a virtual pale-faced cadaver – was haunted by another ghost from his past, although most controversy was prompted by Davies's decision to fix the timing of the play firmly in the future by beginning with Lady Thatcher's funeral. Former Conservative party chief of staff Dobbs withdrew his name from the adaptation, but that seemed not to deter millions from tuning in.

Davies first adapted *Pride and Prejudice* for a 1980 production starring Daniel Day-Lewis. The 1995 version – starring Colin Firth, Jennifer Ehle, Alison Steadman and Julia Sawalha – was even more popular. Future work – the usual eclectic mix of adaptations and original dramas – seems set to confirm Davies as our most prolific and continually inventive TV writer.

John Elliot A veteran BBC producer (he was responsible for the spectacular 1954 documentary series *War in the Air*), Elliot emerged as a writer with the science-fiction serials *A for Andromeda* (1961) and *The Andromeda Breakthrough* (1962), which he co-created with Fred Hoyle. Elliot was an obvious recruit to Sydney Newman's drama revolution at the BBC, and was given the key task of producing *The Sunday Night Play* and *First Night* (both 1963), the latter series including two of Elliot's own plays, *The Youngest Profession* and *Hunt the Man*. Elliot also wrote for ***Z Cars*** in 1964, before developing his most famous creation ***Mogul*** (1965), which later became ***The Troubleshooters*** and ran for seven years.

A fine literary adapter, Elliot's productions of C.P. Snow's *Corridors of Power* and Chekhov's *Platonov* for *Play of the Month* show a writer of considerable depth and range. *Play for Today* also benefited from Elliot, with 1972's *Better Than the Movies*, *Child of Hope* (1975), and *The Chief Mourner* (1979) outstanding examples.

Elliot's 1972 biography of the poet *Shelley* starred Robert Powell, Jenny Agutter, Peter Bowles, Lalla Ward and Clifford Rose, in a beautiful co-production with Italian television. 'Adventurous, difficult, impressive and always lovely to watch,' noted Leonard Buckley in *The Times*. John Elliot's career described in a nutshell.

Clive Exton An author of tight, impressive stories for over three decades, Exton began writing for television in the late 50s with plays like *No Fixed Abode*, *Hold My Hand Soldier* and *The Big Eat* for *Armchair Theatre* and *The Close Prisoner* for *Studio 64*. He also worked on *Francis Durbridge Presents* before moving to the BBC where *Land of My Dreams* won considerable praise. *The Bone Yard*, produced by the future *Wednesday Play* team in 1964, was postponed due to alleged similarities with a real police corruption case and was eventually transmitted in January 1966. Exton also contributed adaptations to *Out of the Unknown* and *Play of the Month* (*The Moon and Sixpence*). Other plays include *Are You Ready for the Music?* and *The Rainbirds*.

Later Exton moved into series, creating *Conceptions of Murder* for LWT, *The Crezz* for Thames and *Dick Barton – Special Agent* for Southern, and contributing to ***Survivors*** and *A Ghost Story for Christmas* (the chilling *Stigma*). He was instrumental in the success of ***The Ruth Rendell Mysteries***, and continues in the 90s as a regular contributor to *Agatha Christie's Poirot* and *Jeeves and Wooster*. Exton has also written extensively for the cinema, his credits including *Isadora* (GB 69), *Entertaining Mr Sloane* (GB 70), *10 Rillington Place* (GB 71) and ***Doomwatch*** (GB 72).

Michael Frayn An outstanding columnist for *The Guardian* and *The Observer* during the 60s, Frayn's first two *Wednesday Plays*, *Jamie, On a Flying Visit* (1968) and *Birthday* (1969) brought him instant respect. Although most of his subsequent work has been in the theatre (notably award-winning plays like *Clouds*, *Alphabetical Order* and *Noises Off*), Frayn returned to TV in 1989 with *First and Last* for *Screen One*, winning an Emmy in the process. More recently, 1994 saw the production of the epic *A Landing on the Sun*.

Gerard Glaister A legendary producer of popular television, Glaister began as a director on *The Sunday Play*. His first series was the 1961 Rank/ATV co-production *Ghost Squad*. At the BBC, Glaister produced *The Dark Island*, Robert Barr's series *Moonstrike* (1963), the first of many of his productions set during World War II (Glaister had been a Spitfire pilot), and two years of ***Dr Finlay's Casebook***. *The Revenue Men* and the spy thriller *Codename* followed, whilst in the late-60s Glaister began a lengthy collaboration with writer Norman J. Crisp on *The Expert*. The pair would later co-create the long-running *The Brothers*, *Oil-Strike North*, and *Buccaneer*. Glaister's two most critically acclaimed successes were ***Colditz*** and ***Secret Army***. *Howards' Way* and *Trainer* are the latest additions to one of television's most impressive CVs.

Jack Gold A director of outstanding quality, Gold's early credits include the anti-fox hunting documentary *Death in the Morning*, Alan Bennett's *My Father Knew Lloyd George*, Jim Allen's *The Lump*, *The World of Coppard* for *Omnibus* (1968), Julia Jones's *Faith and Henry*, *Stocker's Copper*, *Mad Jack*, the series *Country Matters* and a jaundiced look at Hollywood, *Dowager in Hot Pants*. Although the cinema occasionally beckoned (*The Bofors Gun* (GB 68) and *Man Friday* (GB 75) foremost amongst his work in film), Gold's natural arena was television. Gold and Tony Garnett's realization of Brecht's *The Gangster Show: The Resistable Rise of Arturo Ui* (1972, starring Nicol Williamson as the Hitler-style Chicago gangster) won many awards, whilst the remarkable *Catholics: A Fable of the Future* (1974, for HTV) starring Trevor Howard, Martin Sheen and Cyril Cusack, is considered an authentic TV masterpiece.

God Bless Thee Jack Maddison (for *Centre Play*), *The Naked Civil Servant* and Keith Waterhouse's *Charlie Muffin* (starring David Hemmings) are amongst his later work.

Trevor Griffiths Manchester-born Griffiths worked as an education officer and wrote his first series, *Adam Smith*, under a pseudonym (Ben Rae). His later work included *Occupations* (1974), *Through the Night* (1975), the series *Bill Brand* (1976, starring Jack Shepherd), the cynical *Comedians* (1979, with Jonathan Pryce) and an adaptation of *Sons and Lovers* (1981). The same year saw *Country*, Griffiths's collaboration with Richard Eyre, starring Leo McKern and James Fox, whilst *Oi for England* (1982), about a skinhead band, was topically depressing. A proud socialist, *Bill Brand* remains Griffiths's most autobiographical work, detailing the problematic life of an idealistic left-wing MP, themes which continue to streak Griffiths's work in the 90s (*Hope in the Year Two*, *Thatcher's Children*).

David Hare The Royal Court's resident dramatist from 1969 to 1971, Hare's first TV play was the remarkable *Man Above Men* (1973). An award-winning theatre playwright, Hare's occasional TV plays are always dramatic, often controversial and usually breath-taking. 1978's *Licking Hitler* (starring Bill Paterson and

Kate Nelligan), which Hare directed himself, is all of these, and more. A vicious love story set in a wartime political research unit, *The Times* praised the play's 'unnerving brilliance'. Another self-directed *Play for Today*, *Dreams of Leaving*, followed in 1980. Hare spent most of the 80s as a main prop of the British cinema (*Paris By Night* (GB 89) and *Strapless* (GB 90)), though 1991's *Screen Two*, *Heading Home*, with Gary Oldman and Joely Richardson, was a magnificent return to the small screen.

Robert Holmes The tragedy of Holmes's career is that, because almost all of his work was in series television, he was never considered a first-division writer. As his friend Roger Marshall noted, 'in retrospect, he spent too much time tinkering around with lesser writers' work rather than getting on with his own'. Holmes collaborated with Marshall on the 1966 science-fiction film *Invasion*.

A former policeman and journalist, Holmes used his crime background to write for Granada's *Knight Errant* in the 50s. From there he moved to *Emergency – Ward 10*, *Ghost Squad*, *Intrigue*, *Undermind*, *Public Eye*, *Mr Rose*, and, for the BBC, ***Dr Finlay's Casebook***. A misdirected script had a profound effect on Holmes's career when an *Out of the Unknown* plot turned up in the ***Doctor Who*** production office. Holmes went on to write over 70 episodes for the telefantasy show, script-editing it between 1974 and 1977. He also wrote for ***The Saint***, ***Doomwatch***, ***Blakes' 7*** and contributed the play *Return Flight* to the anthology series *Dead of Night*.

Holmes continued to write for crime series like *Fraud Squad*, ***Dixon of Dock Green***, *Juliet Bravo*, ***Shoestring*** (which he also script-edited) and ***Bergerac***. Holmes's plays *The Brilliant New Testament* and *Mr X* (for *Trial*) were followed by series work on *The Regiment*, *Spy Trap* and *Warship* and the 1981 serial adaptation *The Nightmare Man*. Holmes died in 1986.

John Hopkins ***Z Cars***' initial script editor, Hopkins moved into single plays with *By Invitation Only* (1962), *Walk a Tight Circle* (1963), *Fable* (1965), *Horror of Darkness* (1966), and *A Game-Like-Only a Game* (1967), and the series *A Chance of Thunder*. His most extraordinary work was *Talking to a Stranger* (1967), concerning the break-up of a family as seen by its various members. It has been described by George Melly as 'television's first authentic masterpiece'. Later, he moved into cinema (writing *The Offence* (GB 72) and *Murder By Decree* (GB/Can 78)), though occasional TV plays like the Kafkaesque *Walk into the Dark* (1972), *A Story to Frighten the Children* (1976), *Codename Kyril* (1987), or the adaptation with John Le Carré of *Smiley's People* (1982) were always notable TV events.

William Humble The highest-rated British TV playwright discovered since the 70s, William Humble has been a mainstay of the BBC's big budget drama output since *On Giant's Shoulders*. *Poppylands*, an adaptation of P.D. James's *The Black Tower* (both 1985) and *Virtuoso* (1989) were vivid, intellectual *tours-de-force*. Humble's work in the 90s on *Screen One* has been of similar quality, including the remarkable *Hancock* (starring Alfred Molina), *Ex* (both 1991), and *Royal Celebration* (1993).

Julia Jones A television trailblazer, Jones, along with Irene Shubik, Verity Lambert and Fay Weldon, helped to define the role of women in television. *The Navigators*, *A Designing Woman*, *Up and Down*, the provocative *Tickle Times*, *Thirty Minute Theatre*'s *The Spoken Word*, and *Faith and Henry* combine articulate use of the erotic with a willingness to discuss sexual politics years before the term, or even its creative limits, had been defined. Jones's rants against Catholicism (1968's *A Bit of Crucifixion, Father*, or *The Quiet Hour* for 1973's *Away from It All* series), and her poetic hymn to ecology, *Still Waters* (1972), are just as impressive. A contributor to *Thirteen Against Fate* and *Home and Away* (1972), Jones stumbled into sitcom, with *Moody and Peg* (1973, co-created with Donald Churchill). *The Stretch*, about an ex-con's return home, was dubbed 'the worst play of 1973' by Alan Coren in *The Times*, who also called it '75 minutes of drivel' and 'pedestrian and pretentious'. Moving to ITV, Jones brilliantly adapted Antonia Fraser's Jemima Shore novel *Quiet as a Nun* in 1978, and later returned to the BBC to write *We, the Accused* and a *Miss Marple* in the 80s.

Ian Kennedy Martin If he were only remembered as the creator of ***The Sweeney***, Kennedy Martin's legacy would be enormous. But, like his brother, Troy, his greatest creation damns the writer with faint praise. 1963's adaptation of *The Prisoner*, starring Alan Badel and (significantly) Patrick McGoohan, was an awesome work. A noted contributor to ***The Troubleshooters***, *This Man Craig*, *Perkin's Patch*, ***The Onedin Line*** and ***Colditz***, it was probably Kennedy Martin's work as story editor on *Redcap* (1966), which starred John Thaw, that was to have the greatest effect on TV history. After ***The Sweeney*** took the police series to the brink, Kennedy Martin helped to redefine it once again with *Juliet Bravo* (1980), *The Chinese Detective* (1981), and the witty London drama *King and Castle* (1986).

Troy Kennedy Martin After serving with the Gordon Highlanders in Cyprus, Francis (Troy) Kennedy Martin wrote his first TV play, *Incident at Six Echo*, for the BBC in 1958. *The Interrogator* (1961) and *Man Without Papers* (1965) followed, and he created *Storyboard* in 1961, including a fine adaptation of John Wyndham's *The Long Spoon*. However, it is for his creation of television's first *noire* police series ***Z Cars*** (1962) that Kennedy Martin made his reputation. *Diary of a Young Man*, which he co-created with John McGrath in 1964, has been described as '***The Likely Lads*** meets Ken Loach', and was Nerys Hughes's first big TV break. Kennedy Martin also contributed to *Out of the Unknown*, a clever adaptation of 'The Midas Plague'. Though film work (*The Italian Job* (GB 69), *Kelly's Heroes* (US/Yug 70)) occupied much of his time, Kennedy Martin was always a popular name on television, writing episodes of ***Colditz*** and his brother Ian's ***The Sweeney***. The early 80s brought a magnificent return to mainstream TV with, in quick succession, *Reilly – Ace of Spies* (with Sam Neill, Leo McKern, Kenneth Cranham, and Tom Bell), *The Old Men at the Zoo* and the seminal ***Edge of Darkness***.

Nigel Kneale Manx writer Kneale began working for the BBC script department in 1952, collaborating with Rudolph Cartier on *Arrow to the Heart* (beginning a legendary partnership), Douglas Allen on *Mystery Story* and *The Cathedral* and Tony Richardson on *Curtain Down* (1953). Other early scripts include *The Affair at Assino*, *The Lake*, *The Commonplace Heart*, *Number Three*, and *Golden Rain*. It was ***The Quatermass Experiment*** (1953) which brought Kneale and Cartier television immortality.

Following a lavish version of *Wuthering Heights* (1953), with Richard Todd and Yvonne Mitchell, the pair produced the definitive adaptation of Orwell's *Nineteen Eighty-Four*. If ***The Quatermass Experiment*** shocked a nation, *Nineteen Eighty-Four* sent it into apoplexy. Five MPs tabled a bill that expressed outrage at the BBC's tendency to 'pander to sexual and sadistic tastes'. The legendary Room 101 scene as part of the torture of Peter Cushing by Andre Morell remains one of TV's most harrowing moments.

The Creature (1955), which again starred Cushing, was about a Himalayan expedition in search of the yeti, whilst further successes followed with ***Quatermass II*** and ***Quatermass and the Pit***, though Kneale also showed a more earthy side to his writing with *Mrs Wickens in the Fall* for *Sunday Night Theatre* in 1957.

The Road (1963) is one of Kneale's most overlooked works. In 1770, squire Hassell (James Maxwell) dabbles in 'natural philosophy' while his wife (Ann Bell) flirts with Gideon Cobb, sub-Johnsonian iconoclast of the London coffee-houses. Hassell is fascinated by the search for new knowledge, but is a prisoner of his age. Each Michaelmas Eve a local copse witnesses a visitation of screaming disembodied voices, which two years ago sent Sam Towler (Rodney Bewes) mad. Hassell thinks it is the ghost of some terrible past event, but the shocking conclusion shows it to be a pre-echo from a future 200 years hence, when a road has been built upon which thousands will flee a nuclear attack. Coming just months after the Cuban missile crisis, *The Road* maintained Kneale's habit of reflecting areas of current public concern. The spectre of the Bomb also featured in *The Crunch* (for *Studio 64*), in which Britain is threatened by a former colony with nuclear capability.

The Year of the Sex Olympics (1968), about a TV-obsessed future state, showed mankind's future as a race wallowing in pornography. It was actually Kneale's heartfelt acknowledgement of the permissive society, 'the new honesty' as the author described it in the *Radio Times*. However it also showed Kneale's abiding distrust of all forms of media, particularly (and ironically) television.

A pair of outstanding *Wednesday Plays*, *Bam! Pow! Zap!* (1969), with Clive Revill and Robert Powell, and *Wine of India* (1970), starring Brian Blessed and Annette Crosbie, along with his episode of *Out of the Unknown*, *The Chopper* (1971) and 1972's spine-chilling ghost story *The Stone Tape*, marked a golden period of creativity for Kneale. His last play of this period was a version of Jack and the Beanstalk for *Bedtime Stories* in 1974.

He moved to ATV in 1975 and, after *Murrain* for the *Against the Crowd* series, he produced *Beasts*, a series of six plays, each with animals as the protagonist. Some of these worked well, notably 'During Barty's Party', in which a couple are cut off in their house by a swarm of intelligent rats.

The sitcom *Kinvig* (1981) starred Tony Haygarth as a man who saw an alien around every corner, particularly in the form of Miss Griffin (Prunella Gee). Apart from Colin Jeavons's performance as a ufologist, this was a huge disappointment.

Kneale's recent TV work has included *Ladies' Night*, *Gentry* (with Roger Daltrey), adaptations of *The Woman in Black* and *Stanley and the Women* (with John Thaw), and *Sharpe's Gold* (1995).

Verity Lambert Roedean educated, Lambert worked as a typist at ABC before Sydney Newman made her his production assistant on *Armchair Theatre*. When Newman moved to the BBC in 1963 he gave Lambert his own creation, ***Doctor Who***, as her first production. Later involvement in *The Newcomers*, *Adam Adamant Lives!*, *Detective*, and *W. Somerset Maugham* furthered Lambert's reputation. She moved to LWT in 1971 to produce *Budgie*, and then to Thames as head of drama. An executive in Euston Films, Lambert was instrumental in the success of ***Minder***, *Rock Follies* and *Hazell*, also being involved in *The Norman Conquests*, ***Quatermass***, *Reilly – Ace of Spies* and *The Flame Trees of Thika*. Subsequently, she set up her own production company, Cinema Verity, which, to date, has produced television as diverse as *May to December*, *G.B.H.*, *Coasting*, *Boys from the Bush*, *Sleepers*, *A Class Act*, *She's Out* and *Eldorado*.

Mike Leigh Awarded an OBE in 1993 for his contribution to the British film industry, Leigh is famous for his observant, improvised texts and black comedy. Leigh's major television works include *Hard Labour* (1973), *The Birth of the 2001 FA Cup Final Goalie* (1975), *Nuts in May* (1976), the award-winning *Abigail's Party* (1977), *Who's Who?* (1979), and *Home Sweet Home* (1982). Leigh was also responsible for the charming Channel 4 series of short films, *Short and Curlies* (1987), before moving into the cinema with *High Hopes* and *Naked*. His frequent collaborator was his actress wife Alison Steadman.

David Leland An occasional actor, Leland wrote *Beloved Enemy* for *Play for Today* in 1981, starring Graham Crowden, Tony Doyle and Steven Berkoff. This was followed by *Psy Warriors*, in which supposed terrorists in army custody turn out to be soldiers undergoing anti-interrogation training. Directed by Alan Clarke, it featured John Duttine, Rosalind Ayres and Derrick O'Connor. *Birth of a Nation* is the generally accepted umbrella title for a series of four Leland plays for Channel 4 in 1983, all dealing with the failings of the current education system. The individual play *Birth of a Nation* had a run-down State comprehensive school falling apart before the viewer's eyes, with overworked and embattled teachers treating their pupils dispassionately, as well as more liberal-minded colleagues; *Flying in the Wind*, with uncharacteristic humour, argued the case for parental choice in teaching their own children; *RHINO* was a disturbing portrait of a persistent truant ('Really Here In Name Only') abandoned by the system, only to be picked-up and brutalized by it when her errant behaviour goes too far. The final play, *Made in Britain*, was a shocking look at the life of an intelligent but vicious skinhead (Tim Roth), spiralling towards a violent conclusion. More recently Leland has concentrated on the theatre and filmwork, co-writing *Mona Lisa* with Neil Jordan. In 1991 he introduced a posthumous BBC2 season including – *Made in Britain* – commemorating the work of his friend Alan Clarke.

Hugh Leonard Dublin playwright, Leonard first came to the BBC adapting his stage plays *Stephen D*, *My One True Love* and *A Time of Wolves and Tigers*. Original teleplays like *Silent Song* (1966), co-written with Frank O'Connor, and *The Late Arrival of Incoming Aircraft* (1968), were mixed with contributions to *Maupassant*, *Detective*, *The Liars* and *Thirteen Against Fate*. Leonard's love of gothic horror surfaced in *Late Night Horror* and a memorable adaptation for *The Hound of the Baskervilles* for Peter Cushing's *Sherlock Holmes* series. Less at home with comedy, 1969's lame series *Me Mammy* sprang from a Leonard *Comedy Playhouse*. His dramatized documentary *Insurrection – Easter Week 1916* celebrated the 50th anniversary of the Easter Uprising. The 1972 Granada series *Country Matters* saw the writer adapting H.E. Bates, and was followed by adaptations of *Nicholas Nickleby* and *Wuthering Heights*. *London Belongs to Me* and *Strumpet City* were as angry companion pieces as the late 70s produced, whilst Leonard's heritage showed itself in *Parnell and the Englishwoman* and episodes for the charming *The Irish RM* (1983), starring Peter Bowles and Bryan Murray.

Innes Lloyd Welsh-born Lloyd began his television career in the BBC's outside broadcast unit before moving to the drama department as a director on *United!* Appointed producer of ***Doctor Who***, then *Thirty Minute Theatre* (1968-71) and *Dead of Night*, Lloyd will be best remembered for his work in one-off drama. His chosen projects were often biographical, the subjects including *Order Wingate* (1972), *Reith* (1983), the spies *Wynne and Penkovsky* (1984), Donald Campbell in *Across the Lake* (1988, starring Anthony Hopkins), and the controversial *Bomber Harris* (1989, with John Thaw). Lloyd was a frequent collaborator with playwright Alan Bennett, producing his series *Objects of Affection* (1982) and *Talking Heads* (1989), and the plays *Sunset Across the Bay* (1975), *The Insurance Man* (1985), and *102 Boulevard Haussman* (1990).

An Englishman Abroad told the remarkable true story of the chance meeting between actress Coral Browne (playing herself) and spy Guy Burgess (Alan Bates) in Moscow in 1958, whilst *A Question of Attribution* (directed by John Schlesinger, completed shortly before Lloyd's death in 1991) was a logical sequel, showing the radically different fate of Anthony Blunt. James Fox played Blunt, and David Calder his MI5 interrogator, while initial controversy over the inclusion of a fictionalized meeting between Blunt and the Queen was rapidly dispelled by Prunella Scales's likeable performance.

Other Lloyd productions include *An Englishman's Castle*, the sentimental *Going Gently* (starring Norman Wisdom), Don Taylor's *Flayed*, *Speed King* (1979), David Turner's *C_2H_5OH* (1980), Tony Perrin's *The Union* (1981) and *East of Ipswich* (with Michael Palin).

Ken Loach If there is one director who is synonymous with *The Wednesday Play* then it is Ken Loach. Born in 1936, Loach joined the BBC as a trainee director in 1963, with his first assignment being the Troy Kennedy Martin/John McGrath serial *Diary of a Young Man*, followed by numerous episodes of ***Z Cars***. This was a good time to be a young innovative director at the BBC, Loach's first three *Wednesday Plays*, Eric Coltart's *Wear a Very Big Hat*, and James O'Connor's *Tap on the Shoulder* and *Three Clear Sundays*, appearing in rapid succession in early 1965. The O'Connor plays gained much attention at the time, the former an observation about society's disregard for different sorts of 'crook', whilst the latter was an impassioned tract against capital punishment (O'Connor had himself once been convicted of murder and was, according to Nancy Banks-Smith, 'One of the best writers to come out of prison since Bunyan').

Nell Dunn's *Up the Junction* was based on her book of dead-pan short stories from south London factories and pubs, which the vast majority of viewers were wholly unfamiliar with. In this respect (and in its depiction of a botched back-street abortion) it was probably a more accurate reflection of what life in 60s London was like for young working-class people than any other drama. Frederick Laws in *The Listener* remarked: 'Indignation about the frequency of tabooed words and at the scandalizing of the good name of Battersea was inevitable but not important.' A year later (after directing *The End of Arthur's Marriage*, and another angry James

O'Connor play *The Coming Out Party*), Loach directed the *Wednesday Play*, *Cathy Come Home*, on which he again used *Up the Junction*'s leading lady Carol White. Loach took the concept of naturalism (a new and powerful tool) to its ultimate end through the use of handheld 16-mm film cameras, making Jeremy Sandford's essay on the grim realities of homelessness look more like something from BBC news and current affairs than the drama department. In 1967, Loach's treatment of David Mercer's *In Two Minds* used similar techniques in a study of schizophrenia, which memorably inspired Anthony Burgess to threaten to drink himself insensible.

After Neville Smith and Gordon Honeycombe's immaculate football play *The Golden Vision* (1968), Loach turned to left-wing politics in Jim Allen's *The Big Flame*. In subsequent years Loach's collaboration with Allen would produce *The Rank and File* (1971) and *Days of Hope* (1975). After directing Barry Hines's feature film *Kes* (GB 69), Loach helped form Kestrel Films with Tony Garnett and Kenith Trodd to produce films for LWT, and his association with Hines continued with *The Price of Coal* (1977), *The Gamekeeper* (1979), and *Looks and Smiles* (1982). *A Question of Leadership* (1984) saw Loach working on a 'straight' documentary at last, based on Hines's research into the 1980 steelworkers' strike, but with such obviously pro-left sympathies the programme achieved only a limited network screening.

In recent years, Loach's television work has been almost wholly in the documentary field, including an edition of *Dispatches* for Channel 4 in 1991. A documentary about the 1984 miners' strike landed Loach in hot water when he overdubbed 'thuds' on to footage of a policeman truncheoning a picket. In the meantime, this great director has achieved critical success in the cinema, often producing material for *Film on Four*, including *Hidden Agenda* (1990), *Riff-Raff* (1991), *Ladybird, Ladybird* (1994), and *Land and Freedom* (1995).

Peter Luke A former Reuters newsman and wine expert, Luke joined Sydney Newman's ABC drama team in the late 50s as a story editor, then producer, on *Armchair Theatre*, where his own plays *Small Fish are Sweet*, *Pigs' Ears with Flowers*, and *Roll on Bloomin' Death* appeared. Moving, with Newman, to the BBC, Luke was given a huge say in the Corporation's drama output as producer of *Festival* (1963), *The Wednesday Play* (1964-66) and *Play of the Month* (1965). His production of *Hamlet at Elsinore* in 1963 was a landmark in broadcast technique, and in television's treatment of the classics, whilst his own plays, *A Man on Her Back* and *The Devil a Monk Wou'd Be*, were evocative and strong. He later became a freelance writer/director, working with Ken Russell on *Monitor*, before moving into the theatre with great success in the 70s.

Philip Mackie Along with Nigel Kneale and Donald Wilson, Philip Mackie was one of the first BBC contract writers, scripting *The Hole in the Wall*, *The Whole Truth*, *A Death in the Family* and *The Girl at the Next Table* during the 50s. He graduated into production and moved to Granada, where he became head of drama, his work including *Paris 1900*, *The Liars*, *The Caesars*, and *Mr Rose* and producing *Maupassant*, *Blood and Thunder*, and *The Victorians*. Mackie returned to freelance work in 1970 with the notorious sexually-explicit *Thérèse Ranquin*, starring Kate Nelligan, which was not shown for many years. *The Organisation*, a six-part series for Yorkshire, was followed by the *Conjugal Rights* trilogy and 1973's 'farce to end all farces' *Black and Blue* (starring Anthony Hopkins). In 1975 he adapted Quentin Crisp's autobiography *The Naked Civil Servant* for Thames. John Hurt won a BAFTA for his performance, and the play marks a turning point in television's treatment of homosexuality. Subsequent work included Yorkshire's wonderful series of *Raffles* adaptations (1975), *An Englishman's Castle* (1978) and the far less impressive *The Cleopatras* (1983). Mackie's final work before his death in 1985 was the two-part thriller for Channel 4, *Praying Mantis*.

Ian MacKintosh A former naval officer, MacKintosh used his previous occupation to great effect creating *Warship* for the BBC in 1973 with veteran Anthony Coburn. Telling the story of the frigate HMS *Hero* and its crew, the series was a popular one, running for four years, and marked a direct collaboration between the BBC and the Royal Navy. Moving to Yorkshire TV as a script-editor,

MacKintosh created the superb espionage series *The Sandbaggers* (starring Roy Marsden, Ray Lonnen and Diane Keen). As producer, he was responsible for the charming 1978 comedy-drama series *Wilde Alliance* (with John Stride and Julia Foster), and *Thundercloud*, a naval comedy set during World War II with Derek Waring. Whilst researching an episode of *The Sandbaggers*, MacKintosh went missing when his light aircraft disappeared over Alaska.

James MacTaggart Jim MacTaggart, as producer of *Storyboard*, *Teletale*, *First Night*, *Studio 64*, *The Four Seasons of Rosie Carr*, and *Diary of a Young Man*, was responsible for the development and production of much important television drama. When moving to *The Wednesday Play* in 1965 he was given the brief by Sydney Newman to produce plays that were 'gusty, spontaneous and contemporary'. His year as producer saw the first four Dennis Potter TV plays and *Horror of Darkness*, *Three Clear Sundays* and *Up the Junction*. Simultaneously, MacTaggart was also working as a director on *Suspense*, *Theatre 625*, ***Z Cars*** and *Corrigan Blake*. Going freelance, MacTaggart's career took twin courses, firstly as a writer/director of lavish *Play of the Month* adaptations like *Cyrano de Bergerac*, *Man and Superman*, *Candide*, *The Importance of Being Ernest* and *Robinson Crusoe* and episodes of *Churchill's People*. Secondly, as director of Potter's *Moonlight on the Highway* and writer of *Murders in the Rue Morgue* (1968, for *Detective*), *Boys and Girls Come Out to Play* (1973, for *Menace*) and *Scotch on the Rocks*, MacTaggart's mastery of tense, often surreal, fantasy was clearly seen.

John McGrath Television auteur McGrath, like his Oxford contemporary Don Taylor, began his work for the BBC as a director (his hard, cutting style being a major factor in the popularity of ***Z Cars***). His work with Troy Kennedy Martin continued in *Diary of a Young Man* in 1964. *Day of Ragnarok*, McGrath's contribution to *Six* (1965), established his writing credentials, though it was as a director of films such as *Billion Dollar Brain* (GB 67), *The Virgin Soldiers* (GB 69), and *The Reckoning* (GB 70) that McGrath made his name in the late 60s. Returning to the BBC with a trio of short pieces for *Play for Today*, *Orkney*, in 1971, McGrath followed this with *The Bouncing Boy* (1972) and *The Cheviot, the Stag and the Black, Black Oil* (1974, featuring a cast drawn from McGrath's 7:84 Theatre Company). 1980's *The Adventures of Frank* was a two-part musical *Play for Today*, starring Mike Ford.

Screenplays like *Blood Red Roses* (for Channel 4, 1986), and *The Long Roads* (for the BBC, 1993), continue to keep one of television's great innovators in the public eye.

Roger Marshall Leslie Halliwell's description of Roger Marshall as 'a writer of superior thrillers' is faint praise for one of television's most inventive and diverse writers. Marshall's introduction to TV was as an (often uncredited) member of Ralph Smart's writing team at ATV on film series like *The Adventures of William Tell*, *H.G. Wells' Invisible Man* and *Danger Man*. For a while he moved to America where he worked on Lloyd Bridges's *Sea Hunt*. Returning to England, Marshall wrote for *Knight Errant*, *No Hiding Place*, *Emergency – Ward 10* and ***The Avengers***, where his witty scripts and tight plotting were perfectly suited to the production. Marshall co-created ABC's long-running *Public Eye*, and became a regular contributor to Euston productions like *Special Branch* and ***The Sweeney***. His attempt to write an intelligent BBC variant was sabotaged by production follies, and he disowned the resulting *Target*. Marshall's scripts, even for moronic nonsense like ***The Professionals*** or *The Gentle Touch*, were always watchable. He also worked on ***Survivors*** for the BBC and then created a number of fine series during the 80s: Granada's *The Travelling Man* (1983), LWT's *Mitch* (1984, with John Thaw), the BBC's *Missing From Home* (1984), and Granada's *Floodtide* (1987). Marshall has also contributed to ***The Ruth Rendell Mysteries***.

David Mercer A socialist playwright who profoundly questioned the socialist states of the world, Mercer was a man who found himself, like the hero of his trilogy *The Generations* at his death, astride the Berlin Wall. It would be interesting to see what this 'rather battered Marxist' would have made of the events in Eastern Europe in the late 80s. Sadly, Mercer died in 1980.

Leaving school at 14, he joined the Merchant Navy, made it to Durham University and decided to become a painter. This took him to Paris, but failure in that career, and as a novelist, led to a nervous breakdown. After a course of analysis, he wrote *The Generations* which comprised *Where the Difference Begins* (1961), *A Climate of Fear* (1962), and *The Birth of a Private Man* (1963). The first play deals with a family reunion around the imminent death of the mother, and the way that the two Crowther brothers have progressed away from their train-driver father's traditional socialism, and across the class boundary.

Despite being rather verbose, the play brought aspects of the outside world crashing in on kitchen-sink drama. The second play, *A Climate of Fear*, begins with Colin Waring in the dock, sentenced to three months in prison for his part in a protest against nuclear weapons. His imprisonment is contrasted with a party scene, where fashionable socialist issues are discussed, and Freida (who had also been at the demo) describes her life with Leonard (Colin's father). Intercut with footage of Bertrand Russell, the play moved the private world even more into the public spotlight.

The last play, *The Birth of a Private Man*, begins at a funeral, Colin and Freida attending with their friends. It broadens to include Warsaw and finally centres, as it had to, on the Berlin Wall. It was as if Mercer was digging into the standard concerns of topical plays to consciously find the icon that lay under the kitchen sink. As Mercer told the *Radio Times*, 'All systems cripple their subjects almost from birth. There hasn't been a revolution in history which hasn't consumed itself.'

Apart from his political concerns, Mercer was interested in the dualities of the human mind. 1962's *A Suitable Case for Treatment* was a harrowing examination of psychiatric practice, and *In Two Minds* (1967) he explored the theories of R.D. Laing. In what may or may not have been a dramatization of actual Laing case material (Ken Loach's documentary-style direction blurring the point), Mercer explored the treatment of Kate, a schizophrenic. Laing's work asserts that schizophrenia is a political, rather than a physical, condition, anticipating the post-modern theorists, who tie in the schizoid state with the collapse of history and the growth of the moment, as the human state began to be defined by the impending closure of the atomic bomb. As a student of 'history' as a motivating force, schizophrenia must have seemed a great alternative for Mercer, the final acceptance of the duality that society seemed to expect. The play caused a storm of protest, notably from Anthony Burgess, who vitriolically attacked it in *The Listener*.

The Parachute (1968) was an examination of the contradictions implicit in pre-war German aristocracy, and *And Did Those Feet?* (1965) followed a pair of illegitimate twins, unwilling heirs to their aristocratic father, as they took refuge in the animal kingdom. *Let's Murder Vivaldi* (1968) was a middle-class drama of suppressed violence starring Glenda Jackson and Denholm Elliott. Philip Purser's review concluded 'if recordings of television programmes could be bought for private playback David Mercer's would be the sleeves you'd leave lying on the coffee table to impress people'. Sadly, by the time that home video became widely available, the BBC had, as Mercer memorably told *The Listener*, 'wiped the buggers!'

Robert Kelvin was the activist hero of Mercer's second trilogy, comprising *On the Eve of Publication* (1968), *The Cellar and the Almond Tree* and *Emma's Time* (both 1970). Kelvin was played by Leo McKern in the first play and Andrew Keir in the last, with Michelle Dotrice as Emma, the much younger woman who falls for the socialist writer in the first play and watches his life and death. The second play sees a friend of Kelvin's, Volubin, a former poet who had joined the Party in an unnamed Communist state, confronting an old countess in the palace flat the Party still allows her to occupy. He wants the keys to the wine cellar for an official gathering. She tells him of her memories of peasants and almond trees, he talks of the cellars he's been trapped in all his life. Mercer continued to explore the contradictions and compromises of post-modern life until just before history decided on a partial solution to the problem of the Bomb with the end of the Cold War. His work for Yorkshire TV included *An Afternoon at the Festival* (1973), *Huggy Bear* (1976), *A Superstition* (1977), and *Rod of Iron* (1979), for which he won an Emmy. On the way, he took on Thomas Hardy's Wessex ('Barbara of the House of Grebe', an episode of *Wessex Tales* in 1973) and the emptiness of its modern equivalent, the lives of the chattering classes. Television is weaker, and a good deal more compromised, without him.

Roy Minton An occasional writer for *The Wednesday Play* and *Play for Today*, Minton's first contribution was *Sling Your Hook* (1969), ostensibly a comedy about a group of Nottingham miners on holiday in Blackpool, but actually an allegory for the decline of the coal industry. The next year saw *The Hunting of Lionel Crane*, with Robert Powell and Michael Robbins, and *Ben* for *Thirty Minute Theatre*. After *Go For Gold* (1973), 1975's *Funny Farm* was set in a mental hospital, but it was a play based in another kind of state institution that would gain Minton lifelong notoriety. In *Scum*, tough young thug Carlin (Raymond Winston) is transferred to a stricter borstal after defending himself from a beating by two warders. Content to do his time quietly, his hand is forced by the toughest inmates, his only option being to be more vicious and take over effective control. The play's portrayal of the prison authorities' pragmatic acceptance of this power structure, along with the *de rigueur* racism and violence of both sides, and a shocking male rape scene, led to the BBC banning the play. Minton subsequently novelised the story, which was remade as a feature film in 1979 by the same director, Alan Clarke, after whose death the original was finally screened by the BBC in 1991. A gentler effort was the six-part *Horace* for Yorkshire TV in 1982, developed from a single BBC play about a mentally handicapped youth.

John Mortimer The most famous TV dramatist to have defended a murderer at the Old Bailey, Mortimer's career as a barrister not only supported his early writings, but also provided inspiration for his greatest creations. The radio play *The Dock Brief* was first transmitted in 1957, and was adapted for television with the same cast four months later. Ageing unsuccessful barrister Morganhall (Michael Hordern) is asked to represent Fowle (David Kossoff), who is accused of murdering his wife, and hopes a 'not guilty' verdict will bring him long-cherished fame. He constructs a masterly defence and subjects Fowle to an energetic dry run in his cell, but when they reach the courtroom his actual performance is so abysmal that the Home Secretary grants the convicted Fowle a reprieve. According to *The Times*, the performance 'touched that rare dramatic level at which comedy and tragedy are indistinguishable'. Mortimer's subsequent work includes *Too Late for the Mashed Potato* (1963), sketches for *BBC3*, *Desmond* (1968, for *A Touch of Venus*) and *Married Alive* (1970).

In the late 60s, Mortimer wrote two *Wednesday Plays*, *The Head Waiter* (starring Donald Pleasence) and *Infidelity Took Place*. The latter was another legal drama, starring John Nettleton as a fortysomething divorce lawyer determined to win his latest case for his female client (Judy Cornwall) and, hopefully, replace her husband with himself. In 1969 Mortimer contributed to ITV's *Play of Today* strand the autobiographical *A Voyage Round My Father*, with Ian Richardson and Mark Dignam. A remake in 1981 featured Alan Bates as Mortimer, with Laurence Olivier as his father. Mortimer also wrote the memorable six-part *Will Shakespeare* (1978) and the 1984 Channel 4 play *Edwin* and *Paradise Postponed* (1987). He also adapted the hugely successful 13-part *Brideshead Revisited* (1981) and John Fowles's *The Ebony Tower* for Granada (1984, starring Toyah Wilcox and Greta Scacchi).

BBC2's *Thirty Minute Theatre* produced a quintet of Mortimer's London plays in 1972, but the turning point in his career was a 1975 *Play for Today*. *Rumpole of the Bailey* centred on Horace Rumpole, one of what Mortimer calls the 'Old Bailey hacks' – barristers working for themselves rather than in a practice on whatever cases their chambers' clerks can scrimp for them. Played to perfection by the great Leo McKern, Rumpole has a weakness for cheap cigars and claret, quoting from *The Oxford Book of English Verse* and *Ackerman on Blood Stains*, whilst at the same time doing his best to keep his domineering wife Hilda ('She who must be obeyed', played initially by Joyce Heron, then Peggy Thorpe-Bates and Marion Mathie) in the manner in which she would like to be accustomed. To Hilda's not-so-secret shame, Rumpole is still a 'junior' barrister, never having become a Queen's Counsel (her father had been a judge by Rumpole's age!). Rumpole is asked to defend a West Indian youth accused of wounding, despite having signed a damning confession whilst in custody and seeming ready to plead guilty. Rumpole discovers the boy's illiteracy and proves his innocence. The play was an instant hit, Séan Day-Lewis remarking in *The Daily Telegraph* that Rumpole should be 'preserved for another day, and another play', but BBC drama stubbornly refused to countenance producer Irene Shubik's suggestion for a series on the grounds that it would have to be made by the 'rival' series department and that she could not be involved.

Incensed, Shubik resigned and she and Mortimer took the idea to Thames. The series began in 1978. Rather than a straight follow-on from the play, the episodes detailed six of Rumpole's past cases covering the years 1967 to the late 70s. 'Rumpole and the Younger Generation' had him defending a young member of the notorious Timson family accused of robbery when the youth was actually at a Rolling Stones gig. The episode introduced semi-regular characters like Uncle Tom (Richard Murdoch), an elderly barrister whom nobody could remember ever actually having a case, the overworked clerks Albert and Henry (Derek Benfield and Jonathan Coy), and Rumpole's most ambitious colleagues, often his opponents in court, Claude Erskine-Brown (Julian Curry), George Frobisher (Moray Watson) and Guthrie Featherstone QC MP (Peter Bowles), not to mention the latter's pushy wife Marigold (Joanna van Gyseghen).

Rumpole, as Frank Muir noted, 'embodied much of Mortimer's own compassionate liberal attitudes on what justice should be all about'. Perhaps Mortimer's most famous case was his (initially unsuccessful) defence of two of the three editors of the underground magazine *Oz* on obscenity charges in 1971 (a subsequent *Performance* dramatization of the case featured Simon Callow playing Mortimer), and shades of their lifestyle were no doubt the inspiration for 'Rumpole and the Alternative Society', with Jane Asher as a hippie commune member busted for cannabis dealing in a 1970 provincial town. Memorably, Rumpole flits between laid-back meals at the commune and the pub full of hostile locals run by an ex-RAF chum and, attracted more to the former, seems on the verge of joining the commune before his client admits her guilt to him. Rumpole persuades her to cop a plea and she gets three years!

In 'Rumpole and the Honourable Member', he aggressively defends an MP charged with rape and, in doing so, alienates his son's American fiancée (who doesn't seem to consider the possibility the man might be innocent). The season also introduced Rumpole's protégé, Philipa Trent (Patricia Hodge), who would go on to marry Erskine-Brown and end up far more successful than either.

The series continued for a further five seasons, finally ending in 1992. Later episodes introduced the jolly-hockey-sticks Fiona (Rosalyn Landor) and the so-PC-it-hurts Liz (initially Samantha Bond, then Abigail McKern). *Rumpole* over the years kept very much up to date with contemporary topics like racial tension ('Rumpole and the Fascist Beast'), whistle-blowing civil servants ('Rumpole and the Official Secret'), and even joy-riding ('Rumpole and the Family Pride'). If anyone should doubt the fame of John Mortimer's most famous creation, it is worth noting that the character was mentioned twice during the O.J. Simpson trial, with one defence attorney remarking that 'as Mr Rumpole would put it, I think we have a case of premature adjudication...'.

Robert Müller Müller, a German-born writer whose family escaped the Nazis in the 30s, initially used such themes as a direct inspiration for his work, with plays like *Afternoon of the Nymphs* and *Night Conspirators* (both for *Armchair Theatre*). *The Executioner* and *Death of a Private* brought Müller to the BBC, where his 1967 adaptation *Pirandello's Henry IV* for *Theatre 625* was an acclaimed success. He later developed into a brilliant writer of gothic horror, firstly for *Mystery and Imagination* (adaptations of *The Body Snatchers* and *Frankenstein*), then with his BBC series *Supernatural*. Along the way, Müller took on science fiction (producing three plays, *The Prophet*, *Beach Head* and *The Naked Sun* for *Out of the Unknown*). Müller, perhaps inevitably, contributed to ***Colditz***, and returned to his historical roots with *Russian Night 1941* (1981) and *Secrets* (1983).

Terry Nation One of the most famous names in broadcasting, his creation of the Daleks for ***Doctor Who*** has assured Welsh writer Terry Nation of television immortality.

A fine adapter of science fiction on *Out of this World*, Nation also walked Inspector Lockhart's beat on *No Hiding Place* and endured a frustrating period writing for Tony Hancock. Nation wrote extensively for ITC during the mid-60s on ***The Saint***, ***The Avengers*** (as script-editor), *The Persuaders!* and co-creating *The Baron*. His work at the BBC in the 70s, creating ***Survivors*** and ***Blake's 7***, and on the chilling *Drama Playhouse*, *The Incredible Robert Baldick*, was just as impressive. In the late 70s, Nation emigrated to Hollywood to work as a producer.

G. F. Newman A graduate of the 'all coppers are bastards' school, Newman came up with the almost definitive example of late-70s police drama, *Law and Order* (1978). Each of the four episodes concentrated on one aspect of the criminal justice system. Needless to say the police were outraged by 'The Detective's Tale', which featured the brutal Inspector Pyall (Derek Martin), who made the lads from ***The Sweeney*** look like boy scouts. Far from being 'the one bad apple', Pyall was presented as the terrible norm, his actions condoned and abetted by his colleagues because they got results. Interviewed in 1993, the writer observed 'The person who becomes a policeman has almost exactly the same pathology as the criminal.'

Billy (1979) saw Newman and director Charles Stewart tackle child-battering. Newman's next major target was the rundown of the NHS in 1983's *The Nation's Health*. Produced by Euston Films, it was one of the first major drama series for Channel 4, each of the four plays being accompanied by a studio discussion. *Here is the News* (1989) featured Richard E. Grant as an investigative journalist – with questionable sexual tendencies – attempting to find the truth behind various government conspiracies, only to have his sources betrayed by his editorial masters. The play landed the BBC in hot water when journalist Duncan Campbell sued, claiming that Grant's character was clearly based on him. *Nineteen 96* (1989) was a more circumspect interpretation of recent events in Northern Ireland, particularly the alleged shoot-to-kill policy by the security service and the claims of former MI5 officer Colin Wallace about sexual misconduct at an orphanage, but with the action transported to Wales seven years into the future. Keith Barron starred as the John Stalker-based Met officer assigned to look into the allegations, but undermined by MI5, MI6 and, possibly, the government. Newman elaborated on some of these themes in his 1991 three-play series, *For the Greater Good*.

Black and Blue (1991) was another collaboration with *Nineteen 96*'s producer Ruth Caleb, with a black West Country PC (Christopher John Hall) drafted into the Met to work undercover on a rundown council estate after the murder of a politician investigating the activities of the local CID. Most recently, *The Healer* was a more fantastical critique – almost a Christian parable – of the current state of the NHS, as a junior doctor with miraculous healing powers finds himself exploited by his Trust hospital.

It is somewhat surprising that while Newman continues to work, no comparable new writers have emerged to replace him as British TV's most 'angry' writer. During the late 80s it did seem that Arthur Ellis – with his surreal *The Black and Blue Lamp* and *The Police* examining both the image and the effects of police culture – was a likely candidate. In the meantime, Newman remains a considerable thorn in the side of the Establishment.

Sydney Newman Born in Toronto in 1917, Newman worked in the film industry, before joining the Canadian Broadcasting Corporation as television director of features and outside broadcasts, and later supervisor of drama. He came to Britain in 1958 after being appointed supervisor of drama at ABC television, where he produced *Armchair Theatre*, and devised *Police Surgeon*, ***The Avengers*** and *Out of this World*. His work on *Armchair Theatre* effectively changed the face of the television play, Newman being responsible for the first TV plays of Alun Owen, Harold Pinter and Robert Müller, amongst others. In 1963 he became head of drama at the BBC. Not so much a 'new broom' as a turbo-powered industrial vacuum cleaner, Newman restructured the whole department, dispensing with the old system whereby drama producers would also edit and direct their plays in favour of having separate producers and story editors, with directors chosen only after the scripts were commissioned. This had already worked on *Armchair Theatre*, but proved unpopular with many BBC directors of the old school.

Whilst at the BBC, Newman devised *First Night*, *The Wednesday Play*, ***Doctor Who*** and *Adam Adamant Lives!* He left the BBC in 1967, returning to Canada to following year. He was later director of CBC from 1972-75.

Peter Nichols A funny and inventive author, Nichols wrote many important plays for Granada, ATV and the BBC in the 60s, before a much publicized return to the theatre due to the restricting 'naturalism' of TV. Notable work includes *A Walk on the Grass* (1959), *Promenade* (1959), *Ben Spray* (1961), *The Big Boys* (1962), *The Continuity Man* (1963), *Ben Again* (1963), *The Hooded Terror* (1963), *The Gorge* (1968), *Hearts and Flowers* (1969), *The Common* (1973) and *Forget-Me-Not Lane* (1975). Having already established himself in film (writing the screenplays for *Catch Us If You Can* (GB/US 65), *Georgy Girl* (GB 66), *A Day in the Death of Joe Egg* (GB 72), and *Privates on Parade* (GB 82)), Nichols was one of the biggest influences on the development of television's 'new structures'. In 1991 Nichols made a welcome return to TV with an episode of ***Inspector Morse***.

Joe Orton Although better known for his theatre work, one of the great iconoclasts of the 60s and the playwright described by Richard Bryden as 'the Oscar Wilde of Welfare State gentility' began his career as a television dramatist. Leicester-born Orton, whose extraordinary life has been meticulously chronicled by author John Lahr, is most famous for his two masterpieces of black comedy, *Entertaining Mr Sloane* and *Loot*, his screenplay for the proposed third Beatles film (*Up Against It*), and his murder at the hands of his lover, Kenneth Halliwell, at the height of his fame in 1967.

The Erpingham Camp, Orton's TV debut, was produced by Peter Willes, the drama head at Rediffusion, as one of the *Seven Deadly Sins* series in 1966. The amoral nature of the series appealed to Orton and despite the inevitable criticism of the play's 'morbid fascination with sex', most critics noted the emergence of a major new talent.

When *The Good and Faithful Servant*, starring Donald Pleasence, appeared in 1967 he was already a media darling, *Loot* having taken the *Evening Standard*'s Drama award for 1966 and Orton having appeared as a guest of his friend Kenneth Williams on *Call My Bluff*. Television extracts of *Loot*, directed by Peter Moffatt and featuring the original theatre cast (Sheila Ballantine, Michael Bates, Kenneth Cranham and Simon Ward), appeared on the arts programme *Accolade*. (Moffatt also directed a posthumous adaptation of *Entertaining Mr Sloane* for *Playhouse* in 1968, which ensured that the normal naturalism of television did not intrude on Orton's surrealism. It starred Sheila Hancock and Edward Woodward.)

By the time *Funeral Games* was broadcast in 1968, Orton was dead. 'A ghoulish capriccio about faith and death,' wrote John Lahr, whilst *The Viewer*'s Anthony Shields called the play 'an absorbing portrait of a warped murderer', noting the great irony of Orton's own killing. The play juxtaposed the story of a defrocked priest (Bill Fraser) who had murdered his wife, with a religious charlatan (Michael Denison) seeking revenge on his wife for her suspected adultery, and a private detective (Ian McShane).

In 1973 Peter Willes remade Orton's radio play *The Ruffian on the Stairs* for TV, setting it in the early 60s as period drama. Orton, he noted, 'would have been amused' (significantly, it was broadcast on April Fool's Day). The BBC produced several documentaries on Orton, and, in 1986, Alan Bennett adapted *Prick Up Your Ears* as a film, starring Gary Oldman and Alfred Molina. In the wake of this, the BBC's *Theatre Night* in 1987 featured a performance of Orton's classic farce *What the Butler Saw*. It is interesting to note that the material that was, at the time of its stage debut, considered so shocking that the Lord Chamberlain demanded changes be made, had by this time become acceptable for prime-time television.

Alun Owen Liverpool-born Alun Owen's influence and popularity during the 60s was considerable, particularly via the landmark plays for *Armchair Theatre*,

No Trams to Lime Street (1959), *After the Funeral* (1960) and *Lena Oh My Lena* (1961). Owen's *Beauty and the Beast* variant, *The Rose Affair* (1961), was much criticized, though later work for the BBC like *The Stag*, the series *Corrigan Blake*, *A Local Boy* (all 1963), *Making of Jericho* (1966), *Shelter* (1967) and *Charlie* (1968) had critics drooling.

After writing the screenplay for *A Hard Day's Night* for the Beatles (for which he was Oscar nominated), Owen helped launch both *Theatre 625* (*Progress in the Park*, *A Little Winter Love*, both 1965) and *Thirty Minute Theatre* (*The Old Fella*, 1966) for BBC2. Owen next developed the trilogies *The Losers/The Winners/The Fantasist* for the BBC and *MacNeil/Cornelius/Emlyn* for ATV. He wrote the final *Wednesday Play*, *Joan*, in 1970, and remade *No Trams to Lime Street* as a musical with songs by Marty Wilde and Ronnie Scott. *Pal*, for *Play for Today*, along with plays like *Joy*, *Female of the Species*, *Giants and Ogres* and *Buttons* were popular successes in the early 70s.

Owen also wrote for *The Ronnie Barker Playhouse* (co-creating the Lord Rustless character), while his later work has included *Norma* (1974), *Forget-Me-Not* (1976, considered 'the piffling adventures of a girl reporter' by Philip Purser) and *Kisch, Kisch* (1983). The 1989 adaptation of *Unexplained Laughter* was another triumph for this wonderful writer.

Harold Pinter Born in Hackney, Pinter began publishing poetry and working in the theatre in the 50s, and married actress Vivien Merchant, who was to star in many of his television works. After his early theatre productions and radio stories received a mixed response, he wrote a TV play, *A Night Out*, for *Armchair Theatre* in 1960. Directed by Philip Saville, it starred Tom Bell as Albert Stokes, a young clerk. The play concerned Stokes's attempts to enjoy himself at an office party, despite the warnings of his nagging mother (Madge Ryan). Although he meets and picks up a chattering girl (played by Merchant), the evening ends in violence. Pinter's tragicomedy was the first play to top the weekly ratings.

Three months later, *Playhouse* transmitted *Night School*, which starred Milo O'Shea, Jane Eccles, Martin Miller and Vivien Merchant. Walter (O'Shea) returns home from prison to find that his two aunts had let his room to a schoolteacher (Merchant), and the wistful play revolves around his attempts to recover his 'territory'. The following years saw further plays for ITV: *The Collection* (1961) and 1963's *The Lover*, winner of the Prix Italia.

Pinter switched to the BBC in 1965, after being asked to write a play for the pan-European *The Largest Theatre in the World* series. *Tea Party* concerns the sudden unease that pervades the life of businessman Robert Disson (Leo McKern) after he engages a new secretary (Merchant) and marries for the second time. The play starred Jennifer Wright as his new wife, Diana, with supporting performances from John Le Mesurier and Charles Gray.

Theatre 625 produced a trio of Pinter plays in 1967: remakes of *A Night Out* (with Tony Selby, Anna Wing and Avril Elgar) and his radio play *A Slight Ache* (starring Maurice Denham, Hazel Hughes and Gordon Richardson), plus *The Basement*, originally conceived as a film script (it shares certain attributes with his screenplays for *The Servant* (GB 63), *The Quiller Memorandum* (GB 66) and *Accident* (GB 67)). The production foregrounded the work of director Charles Jarrott, who had directed *Tea Party*, and elevated the set to the status of major character. The location was a basement flat, but – despite Pinter's televisual trappings – the play echoed the territorial themes of *Night School*, concerning two men (Derek Godfrey and Pinter himself) battling for possession of a girl (Kika Markham).

Monologue (1973) was Pinter's first colour teleplay, starring Henry Woolf, whilst 1978 saw his *Play of the Week* adaptation of Aidan Higgin's *Langrishe, Go Down*, starring Jeremy Irons, Judi Dench and Annette Crosbie. *The Hothouse* (1982) was derived from a theatrical play he had written in 1958, and was directed by Pinter. This starred Derek Newark, James Grant and Angela Pleasence, and was set in a psychiatric hospital, where the comparative peace is disturbed by a mysterious death and an unknown birth.

These days, Pinter is more usually associated with the cinema (*The French Lieutenant's Woman* (GB 81), *The Handmaid's Tale* (US/W Ger 90)) though he is almost unique in being equally at home with theatre, radio, television and film as 1991's *Screen Two* adaptation of Kafka's *The Trial* (starring Kyle MacLachlan and Anthony Hopkins) ably proved.

Alan Plater Plater's early years were shaped by a simple class joke. His family moved to Hull when he was three, though his grandparents still lived in the North East. 'People would ask me where I was going for my holidays,' noted Plater. 'I would say Jarrow and I couldn't understand why they laughed.'

Plater served his writing apprenticeship working on ***Z Cars***. He wrote 18 episodes between 1963 and 1965, and a further 30 for its spin-off, *Softly Softly*. At one time he was writing an episode every three to four weeks with plays like *So Long, Charlie* (1963) or *Ted's Cathedral* (1964) and episodes of Granada's *The Villains* as a side-line.

In 1968 Plater produced his first trilogy for *Theatre 625*, *To See How Far It Is*. Having spent much of his time at Newcastle University involved in 'iconoclastic student journalism', Plater used his radio background to develop into a brilliant dialogue writer, something that still sees him in a league of his own. Plater was dissatisfied with television 'identikit drama', once stating 'If I see another play about a middle-aged menopausal businessman having an affair with his secretary, I shall kick the screen in!'

Popular successes followed in plays such as *The First Lady* (1968, starring Thora Hird), *Close the Coalhouse Door* (1969, co-written with Sid Chaplin), *Seventeen Per Cent Said Push Off* (1972: 'The northern yobbo taking the micky out of the college pudding is a time-honoured source of humour,' noted *The Times*, snobbishly) and *The Land of Green Ginger* (1974). *Green Ginger* especially, with its wistful evocation of northern aspirations and loss of innocence ('People from Hull have this mysterious northern mist behind their eyes,' says heroine Sally Brown), played alongside the broad comedy of another of Plater's recurring themes, the dream of advancement through sporting achievement. This climaxed in the 1975 series, *Trinity Tales*, which covered the lives of a group of Wakefield Trinity fans travelling to Wembley to watch the Rugby League Challenge Cup final. Plater's broad parody of Chaucer (episode titles include 'The Driver's Tale', 'The Man of Law's Tale' and 'The Wife of Batley's Tale') was a celebration of 'the collective joy of people doing daft things'. Plater drew on references to the media throughout. After a pie-eating contest, there is a parody of a *Match of the Day* summing-up, with a Brian Clough character saying 'It's a good result. It's good for the game. It's good for Derby, Brighton and Leeds. For Western European civilisation.' A competition in singing ribald songs became the 'Yorkovision song contest'.

Trinity Tales also spawned Plater's 1976 sitcom, *Oh No! It's Selwyn Froggitt* (Bill Maynard, who played Selwyn, had been Stan the Fryer in *Trinity Tales*). *Oh No!* centred on the life of a council labourer, who sees himself as an intellectual (reading the *Times Literary Supplement*). Selwyn's thumbs-up grinning visage helped to charm viewers, and the series, despite an occasional tendency towards abject silliness, is still fondly remembered.

Plater's other major TV work has included Granada's *The Stars Look Down* (1975), the BBC series *Middlemen* (1977), an adaptation of *The Barchester Chronicles* (1982), *Orwell on Jura* (1983), and *Get Lost!* (1980), a direct ancestor of *The Beiderbeck Affair*. The latter series concerned the misadventures of two school teachers (James Bolam and Barbara Flynn) who, whilst trying to obtain a set of rare records (by jazz trumpeter Bix Biederbeck), stumble across a local government conspiracy. Filled with excellent supporting characters (the man who hounds the police wanting to be a 'supergrass', or Terence Rigby's entrepreneur who responds to a question about who would want to smash a greenhouse with 'Somebody who doesn't like greenhouses?'), the series was a huge hit in 1985 and led to sequels, *The Beiderbeck Tapes* (1987) and *The Beiderbeck Connection* (1988).

Plater's recent work has included adaptations of the classic detective novels (*Miss Marple*, *Campion*, ***Sherlock Holmes***, *Maigret*), the award-winning *Fortunes of War* (1987), and Chris Mullin's *A Very British Coup* (1990), starring Ray McAnally, Allan MacNaughtan and Keith Allen. Despite his 1995 BBC comedy-thriller *Oliver's Travels* and his scripts for *Dalziel and Pascoe* (1996), Plater remains outspoken. He has attacked the BBC's reliance on independent production companies, stating that the system that gave rise to writers of his generation is being dismantled from within.

Charlotte and Denis Plimmer
Husband and wife team Charlotte and Denis Plimmer emerged on BBC2's *Thirty Minute Theatre* with a number of politically cynical and violent plays. Like their contemporaries, Dawn Pavitt and Terry Wale, the Plimmers's plays used elements of fantasy and allegory to produce a dazzling experimental mixture. And, with directors like Michael Hart and Chris Barry, the results were stunning if minimalist television. *Standing In for Santa Claus* (1968, starring Michael Gough) was an assured debut re-enacting a prison psychiatry session, and *The Chequers Manoeuvre* (also 1968, with Derek Newark and Geoffrey Palmer), concerning an apparent assassination plot by a fanatical military group, showed extraordinary talent. *Cause of Death* (1968) and *Where Have They Gone, All the Little Children* (1969, about the Biafra war) were jaundiced looks at 60s values. *... And Was Invited to Form a Government* and *A Formula for Treason* (both 1969) were further angry anarchic pieces, the television play used, for once, as a weapon rather than as a mirror. The pair later had a lengthy spell writing for *Hadleigh*.

Stephen Poliakoff Although primarily a writer for the theatre, Poliakoff has also contributed much fine television drama, beginning with the nuclear thriller *Stronger Than the Sun* (1977) and a classy pair of *Play for Todays*, *Caught on a Train* (1980) and *Soft Targets* (1983). The latter is a perfect example of Poliakoff's uncanny knack for presenting the intricacies of British social customs and locations – especially London – through the eyes of an outsider (in this case Ian Holm's homesick Russian journalist), giving the viewer a glimpse of the hidden, sometimes dangerous side of life we only occasionally connect with. 1980's *Bloody Kids*, directed by Stephen Frears, with Gary Holton, Nula Conwell, and Gwyneth Strong, was a manic study of urban anarchy (a low-budget, British *Warriors* in other words). Poliakoff has also adapted his own stage plays, *Hitting Town* and *Strawberry Fields*, for television, tackled senile dementia in *She's Been Away* (1989), and written a classic trio of *Film on Fours*, *Runners* (1982, with Kate Hardie, James Fox and Jane Asher), *Hidden City* (1990, starring Charles Dance), and *Close My Eyes* (1991, with Alan Rickman and Saskia Reeves).

Dennis Potter Fay Weldon has called Dennis Potter 'the best television playwright in the world'. The simple reason is that Dennis Potter loved television. He loved writing for it, commenting on it, and criticizing it. From his first appearance in the 1960 autobiographical documentary *Between Two Rivers* the love affair between Potter and TV continued until weeks before his death in 1994 when his final interview, a dignified, even life-affirming, head-to-head with Melvyn Bragg, was broadcast. The affair had its sticky moments, but the anger that Potter showed in his 1993 *Royal Television Society Memorial Lecture*, attacking those who sought to make television into a form without soul or poetry, will stand, alongside his exceptional work, as his epitaph.

In the early 60s Potter was TV critic for the *Daily Herald*, and wrote inserts for *Bookstand* and sketches for ***That Was the Week That Was***, often in partnership with David Nathan. He had already been a parliamentary candidate and a rejected ***Doctor Who*** writer (his story 'was about a schizophrenic who *thought* he was a time traveller', he told *The Times* years later). His early plays, beginning with *The Confidence Course* for *The Wednesday Play* in 1965, seemed to follow ***TW3***'s brief to discuss things society felt were best left unmentioned: the cynicism of politics (*Vote, Vote, Vote for Nigel Barton*), the complex relationships between adults and children (*Alice*), and the reality of historical figures (1967's *Message for Posterity*, prompted by tales of Churchill reluctantly sitting for his 80th-birthday portrait). Such interests, placed against a backdrop that derives from autobiography, can be seen throughout Potter's work.

Vote, with Keith Barron as the idealist working-class miner's son who has to stand (and lose) after a sitting MP is killed in a hunting accident, was scheduled for June 1965 but postponed by the BBC, who feared accusations of political bias. It was finally shown in December, a week after its 'prequel' *Stand Up, Nigel*

Barton, detailing his school-life, and featuring the wonderfully stern-faced Janet Henfrey playing virtually the same role as she would in ***The Singing Detective*** 20 years later. By the end of 1965, Potter had also written *Alice*, which starred George Baker and Deborah Watling. A simple theme was emerging: adults can be horrible, but childhood isn't any less complex and unpleasant. Potter dealt with this theme most brilliantly in 1979's *Blue Remembered Hills*, which had adults playing children to hammer home the point that, apart from scale, there is little to tell the two stages of development apart. It starred Colin Welland, Helen Mirren, Michael Elphick and Colin Jeavons, and deservedly won a BAFTA.

Potter clearly had an eye for the absurd (as in 1966's *Thirty Minute Theatre, Emergency Ward 9*), perhaps most shockingly shown in 1968's *A Beast with Two Backs*. Set in the Forest of Dean some 50 years before the writer's childhood there, it concerned what the *Radio Times* inexplicably described as a 'true legend': something has to be blamed for an attack on a woman in the forest, and a dancing bear seems a valid sacrifice. However, like a miniature *Twin Peaks*, even a rudimentary investigation began to uncover much that was rotten in the locality.

Potter was also fascinated with fantasy, as shown in 1966's *Where the Buffalo Roam* (with Hywel Bennett), *Shaggy Dog* (1968), and *Moonlight on the Highway* (1969), one of several Potter plays to focus on sexual loathing due to hideous childhood memories (*The Bonegrinder* is another). To many, Potter's plays were cynical or negative, including perhaps the man himself. In 1969 he announced that his twelfth play was the first that he was pleased with, and that it had helped him through a period of depression. His critics might have been excused for expecting a 'feel good' movie. To an extent, *Son of Man* was, but the fact that the central character was a very human Jesus ensured a largely vitriolic response, particularly as it was broadcast during Easter week.

Colin Blakely was a Jesus entirely shorn of divinity: 'I want to write a play about a man deluded with the thought that he might be Christ,' said Potter. 'It is much more marvellous to me that he should have been a man, who was born in the usual way, and died in the usual way.' Christian response was therefore going to be as negative as that which had greeted the publication of Nikos Kazantzakis's novel *The Last Temptation* in the 50s: the BBC was swamped with calls, and the majority of newspapers criticized the play. (Strangely, criticism largely revolved around the anger of Jesus, which was arguably the most biblical aspect of the production.) There are many commendable things about *Son of Man*, not least that it was a heartfelt attempt to rid Jesus of the 'meek and mild' image. Potter also saw the play as an attempt to bring Jesus to a modern audience: 'I tried to imagine the circumstances in which Jesus said "Love thy enemies". For he was saying that human love is the only thing of significance in a land occupied by vicious enemies. The thought behind that statement leaps two thousand years. We are still no nearer loving our enemies.' And it was Potter's most optimistic play: 'I had gone though a period of illness and depression before I wrote this play: in fact, it was written while I was in hospital. In a way it got me out of my depression. In my last *Wednesday Play*, *A Beast with Two Backs*, I was expressing what I felt to be the beast in man. Usually I see the beast. This play shows how we ought to behave to each other.'

Potter's next BBC play, 1970's *Angels are so Few*, can almost be seen as a deliberate attempt to court negative publicity, with its young married couple watching a TV film about the making of a porn movie. Certainly the violently anti-war *Lay Down Your Arms* (1970), the anti-politics *Traitor* (1971), and the anti-everything *Only Make Believe* (1973) show Potter's anger swinging out wildly (though often accurately) in many directions. *Only Make Believe* cast Keith Barron as a writer, scripting a TV play called *Angels are so Few*, getting dragged into the fantasy world he is creating. Other plays like *Follow the Yellow Brick Road* (1972), *Late Call* (1975) and the sexually explicit *Double Dare* (1976) also dealt with the nuts and bolts of television writing and production.

Casanova, a six-part serial, starred Frank Finlay as the famous womanizer and was even more controversial, Mary Whitehouse calling the production lewd and grossly indecent: Potter (rightly) insisted that the plays were strongly moralistic. Yet Potter could also be sensitive. *Joe's Ark* (1974) concerned the final days of a young Welsh girl dying of cancer, whilst *Schmoedipus* (1974) featured a sympathetic (if edgy) portrayal of a housewife's desire and guilt. 1976's *Where Adam Stood* was a magnificent tale of Victorian salvationism. Nevertheless, the BBC, doubtless stung by past criticism, chose to ban the infamous *Brimstone and Treacle* in 1976. Managing Director Alasdair Milne found the scene of the possessed man raping a brain-damaged girl too distressing for transmission, and so £70,000 of taxpayer's money went down the toilet. The play was finally broadcast in 1987.

1978 saw the six-part *Pennies from Heaven*, starring Bob Hoskins, Cheryl Campbell, Gemma Craven and Hywel Bennett. The plot concerned the travels and increasingly fraught private life of Arthur Parker, a sheet-music seller; controversy came in the form of extra-marital sex, abortion and prostitution; and televisual magic was created when the characters broke into the popular songs of the 30s. It wasn't subtle (Potter felt that the effect was better done in ***The Singing Detective***), but it was stunning, the 'banal and drivelling pop songs', as Potter put it, suddenly taking on a life of their own. The songs intruded into the drama like a drunken relative, underpinning and commentating on the action. The work gained a dedicated and enthusiastic audience. In 1993 Potter concluded his musical trilogy with *Lipstick on Your Collar*, starring Giles Thomas, Ewan McGregor, Louise Germaine, Douglas Henshall and Roy Hudd. The music of the 50s gave Potter more than ample opportunity to examine sexual mores and fantasies; unfortunately, television was again defending itself from charges of being a corrupting force, and a largely negative response was assured.

Potter seemed on safer ground when he preceded and followed ***The Singing Detective*** with adaptations of other people's work: F. Scott Fitzgerald's *Tender is the Night* (1985, starring Peter Strauss, Mary Steenburgen, Edward Asner, John Heard, Sean Young and Nancy Paul), and *Christabel* (1988). The former was breath-taking; the latter, with its true-life wartime bride forced to stay in Nazi Germany, was worthy but dull, despite the best efforts of Liz Hurley, Geoffrey Palmer, Ann Bell and Stephen Dillon.

Potter also tackled the horrors of growing old (*Cream in My Coffee*, 1980), and revelled in the joys of a larger stage when writing *Track 29* (GB 88) for Nicholas Roeg. His trio of TV films (*Visitors* (1987), *Secret Friends* (1992 for *Film on Four*) and the effects-laden *Midnight Movie* (broadcast posthumously in 1994)) are also worthy of praise. *Blackeyes* (1987), starring Gina Bellman, Michael Gough, Nigel Planer and Carol Royle, which Potter also directed and narrated, was a brave attempt to attack sexual exploitation. Unfortunately, Potter seemed unable to attack it without showing it, a problem that also afflicted *Midnight Movie*.

Potter's life was often painful, suffering from psoriasis and then cancer. However, by the end he had become a much-loved part of the medium he graced. His final wish was that his last two interconnected plays, *Karaoke* and *Cold Lazarus*, should be produced by the BBC and Channel 4 in co-operation. The plays were transmitted in 1996. In agreeing to cooperate in this way, Alan Yentob and Michael Grade have acknowledged a great writer and a great man.

Trevor Preston Equally at home with children's adaptations (1967's *The Lion, the Witch and the Wardrobe*) or the cynical, angry world of ***Callan***, Preston has been described by Troy Kennedy Martin as 'the best TV writer in the world'. Perhaps that's an over-statement, but there's no denying the quality of Preston's work. Creator of the legendary Thames children's fantasy *Ace of Wands* (1971), and with writing credits that included Gerry Anderson's *The Protectors*, Preston became a regular contributor to Euston's *Special Branch*, ***The Sweeney***, and ***Minder***. He also created two series of his own: 1978's *Out* (starring Tom Bell) and 1980's *Fox* (with Peter Vaughan). *The Racing Game* (1979) saw Preston adapting Dick Francis, and, in the 90s, he continued to provide great scripts for ***The Ruth Rendell Mysteries***.

Peter Ransley *Night Duty*, written for the experimental play series *Sextet* in 1972, was an early sign of Ransley's mastery of limited budgets and resources. *Bold Face Condemned*, his play for the provincial BBC drama unit's *Second City Firsts* (1974), and 1975's *The House on the Hill*, brought similar praise, along with *Bread or Blood* (1981) and *Shall I Be Mother?* (1983 for *Play for Today*).

The Price, a six-part serial for Channel 4 in 1985, was Ransley's masterpiece – a brilliant story of an IRA kidnap of an industrialist's wife and daughter starring Derek Thompson, Peter Barkworth and Harriet Walter. Later work includes 1986's *Inside Story* and *Sitting Targets* (1989).

Simon Raven Author, critic and dramatist, Raven's novelist career (1960's *Doctors Wear Scarlet* was the 20th century's first great vampire novel) has somewhat overshadowed a number of fine contributions to television. *Royal Foundation* (1961) and *The Scapegoat* (1964) were followed by a trio of startling, innovative *Wednesday Plays*: *Sir Jocelyn, The Minister Would Like a Word* (1965), *A Soirée at Bossom's Hotel*, and *A Pyre for Pvte. James* (both 1966). A superb adapter of others, Raven scripted Huxley's *Point Counterpoint* (1968), Iris Murdoch's *An Unofficial Rose* (1975), and *Sexton Blake and the Demon God* (1978). Two Trollope adaptations are of particular note – *The Way We Live Now* (1969), and *The Pallisers* (1974), a popular 26-part series starring Susan Hampshire and Philip Latham. In 1978, Raven's *Edward and Mrs Simpson* was both successful and controversial. More recently, Raven has adapted *Love in a Cold Climate* (1980) and the controversial *The Blackheath Poisonings* (1993).

Jack Rosenthal Of all television's great dramatists, none has produced a range of material as wide as Rosenthal, a writer whose work has covered soap opera, sitcom, historical-drama and crime series.

Rosenthal was born in Manchester, memories of his early life later becoming the basis for his celebrated play *The Evacuees*. After university, Rosenthal worked in advertising. In 1961 he began writing for the new Granada soap opera ***Coronation Street***. His first story was episode 30, in which Ena Sharples berated her daughter for working as a waitress in a café. It was the first of almost 200 episodes from Rosenthal over the course of the next eight years. He also worked as script editor and, in 1967, spent eight months as the show's producer.

Success led to work on another 60s icon, the BBC's ***That Was the Week That Was***. He also partnered ***Coronation Street*** colleague Harry Driver, the pair writing episodes for *The Odd Man* and plays for the BBC's *Comedy Playhouse* (*On the Knocker, A Picture of Innocence*, and the Elsie and Doris Waters vehicle, *The Chars*) in 1963. He also wrote for Granada's *The Villains* and the *Friday Night* series. *Pie in the Sky* (1963) was a fair stab at the generation gap, whilst *Green Rub* (also 1963) showed his ability to mix very funny dialogue with perfectly observed characters.

Although ***Coronation Street*** dominated Rosenthal's work in the 60s, occasional gems away from Weatherfield appeared. His contributions to *Playhouse* included *Your Name's Not God, It's Edgar* and *There's a Hole in Your Dustin, Delilah* (both 1968) about a group of Manchester dustbinmen with nicknames like Cheese and Egg, Heavy Breathing and inspector Bloody Delilah. With a cast that included Frank Windsor and Jack MacGowan, the play was funny, smutty and hugely enjoyable.

Granada asked Rosenthal to write (and produce) a series based on the characters. *The Dustbinmen* was a major part of the raging debate on taste and decency in 60s television. Like ***Till Death Us Do Part***, *The Dustbinmen*'s language came from the gutters. Graham Haberfield and John Barrett returned from the play, along with Bryan Pringle, John Woodvine and Trevor Bannister (Woodvine was later replaced by Brian Wilde). *The Dustbinmen*, loathed by purists and 'Clean up TV' campaigners, nevertheless became one of television's most successful sitcoms, with all six episodes of the first season topping the ratings. Rosenthal handed the series over to other writers after two seasons to set up *The Lovers*.

This was one of those great pieces of television that accurately captured a particular time and place as a young boy and girl took their first steps towards falling in love. The series helped to make its young stars, 20-year-old Richard Beckinsale and 17-year-old Paula Wilcox, household names. They were naive and charming, she the Paul McCartney-loving girl dreaming of marriage and trying to avoid the advances of 'Percy Filth', he the neo-George Best, desperate to get her knickers off. *The Lovers* was effective, timeless comedy, though again, following the initial success, Rosenthal left the project, and the series was never as successful or as accurate once Geoffrey

Lancashire took over writing it. With the exception of the bitter-sweet *Sadie, It's Cold Outside* (made for Thames in 1975), Rosenthal turned his back on sitcom.

Another Sunday and Sweet FA (1972) was the story of a Sunday park football game between two teams of psychos, refereed by the harassed David Swift ('What we are about to witness is called a football match. Not the beginning of World War Three'). It highlighted Rosenthal and director Michael Apted's eye for the absurd. *Polly Put the Kettle On*, in which Sylvia Kay makes the life of her soon-to-be-married daughter, Susan Penhaligon, utter misery, *Mr Ellis Versus the People* (Ron Moody's presiding officer watching a bewildering array of humanity on election day), and *There'll Almost Always Be an England* (where a street full of neighbours were evacuated due to a gas leak), all appeared in the summer of 1974, the latter two in Michael Dunlop's *Village Hall* (the series also included Kenneth Cope's football play *The Magic Sponge*). Other plays of the era include *Hot Fat* and the *Thirty Minute Theatre*, *And for My Next Trick*.

Rosenthal, who had recently married actress Maureen Lipman, won a BAFTA in 1975 for *The Evacuees*, which gave director Alan Parker his first big break and drew an evocative picture of wartime childhood. His next play, *Ready When You Are Mr McGill*, the amusing story of a film extra waiting to say his one line, became an industry favourite for its accurate picture of bickering crew members and bored actors filling in the *Daily Telegraph* crossword. Best of all was Jack Shepherd as a paranoid, manic-depressive director. Through it all, McGill (played with ironic detachment by Joe Belcher) appears as the one grain of sanity in the madness around him.

Later that year, another of Rosenthal's autobiographical pieces, *Bar Mitzvah Boy*, won another BAFTA award (*Spend, Spend, Spend*, the story of Pools winner Viv Nicholson, completed the hat-trick of awards in 1977). Other Rosenthal plays of the era include *Spaghetti Two-Step*, concerning the staff and customers of an Italian restaurant, and *The Knowledge*, about taxi drivers swotting for their qualification exam, only to be faced by Nigel Hawthorne's sadistic examiner. During the 80s he scored successes in the cinema, co-scripting *Yentl* (US 83) with its star Barbra Streisand, and with 1985's *The Chain* (GB). On television, his major work was *P'tang Yang Kipperbang* (a *First Love* film shown as part of Channel 4's opening night), a delightful story of a cricket-obsessed boy's discovery of girls. With excellent acting from the young cast, and the inspired use of the voice of John Arlott as the boy's imagination, *P'tang Yang Kipperbang* was charming, but heavily criticized for its lack of morality, whilst Philip Purser complained that school children of 1948 didn't say 'sod off', as if that really mattered.

Since then, Rosenthal's work has included *Fools on the Hill* (1986, a handsome portrayal of the early days of broadcasting at Alexandra Palace), *Day to Remember* (1986), *Bag Lady* (1989, for his wife's ambitious series of comedies *About Face*), *Mrs Capper's Birthday* (1985), the nostalgic *And a Nightingale Sang* (1989), *Sleeping Sickness* (1991), *Wide Eyed And Legless* (1993) and *Eskimo Day* (1996). The writer, who lists 'remembering how Manchester United used to play' among his hobbies, has also left the drama series a great legacy with his 1986 play *London's Burning*. Inspired by a friend, fireman Les Murphey, and by the horror and heroics of the Bradford City fire disaster, Rosenthal wrote a 100-minute screenplay focusing on the lives of Blue Watch at a London fire station, risking their lives every day in the public service, and yet undervalued by society. As Rosenthal said, 'Fire-fighters are unique in that they are civilians. They live at home with their families and go off to work like the rest of us. And there the similarity stops dead. Beyond that could be the nightmare of the fire at King's Cross.'

Rosenthal's crew were, as *Box of Delights* notes, 'lazy loafers, doing odd jobs, taking the mickey out of each other, cheating on their wives. But when the bell rang they were transformed into life-savers.' Rosenthal's group encompassed memorable characters with nicknames like Sicknote (always feeling ill) and Vaseline (a great performance from Mark Arden). Rosenthal even tackled potential cries of laddism by including a firewoman, the sexy-but-dangerous Josie (Katherine Rogers). *London's Burning* was a successful play and led to a series which, although not directly involving

Rosenthal, has carried his characters to a wider audience and, to date, eight seasons of humane, intelligent drama.

David Rudkin The author of complex, often mystical plays, Rudkin's interest in unnerving his audience can be seen in stage plays like *Afore Night Come*. His early TV work, like *The Stone Dance* (1966) and *Children Playing* (1967) used the medium to its fullest, though *House of Character* (1968) and *Blodwen, Home from Rachael's Marriage* (1969) could be said to follow the standard rules of late 60s *Wednesday Plays*. It was with two extraordinary *Thirty Minute Theatre* plays, *Bypass* (1972), and *Atrocity* (1973), that Rudkin found his niche. And, with the exception of *Pritan*, his first contribution to the notorious *Churchill's People*, Rudkin's subsequent work has been outstanding.

Penda's Fen (1974) – 'something that had beauty, imagination and depth', said *The Times* – is Rudkin's masterpiece, an eerie, disturbing and magnificent work, starring Spencer Banks and directed by Alan Clarke. His later work includes *The Ash Tree* (1975), a chilling Christmas ghost story, *Artemis 81* (1981), a surreal three-hour epic, and *Across the Water* (1983).

Jeremy Sandford *Cathy Come Home* shares, along with the other great *cause célèbre* of 60s TV drama, Nell Dunn's *Up the Junction*, a deep-rooted sense of outrage at a society that at once applauded the play's evocation of the welfare state gone wrong and yet allowed the reality to continue. *Cathy Come Home* made a profound impression on the housing minister Anthony Greenwood who said 'I would quite like it to be compulsory viewing once a month for the next five years.'

Cathy reunited *Up the Junction*'s director and star, Ken Loach and Carol White, with producer Tony Garnett (*Junction*'s script-editor). It was written by Jeremy Sandford, a campaigning journalist with an impressive series of books (*Prostitutes*, *In Search of the Magic Mushroom*, *Down and Out in Britain*) to his name. Sandford had grown up under the protection of the welfare state. His frustration stemmed not from the system itself, but from the way in which it creates outcasts. 'Our society is needlessly cruel,' he wrote in *Down and Out in Britain*. He acknowledged that *Cathy Come Home* was 'about Britain's intolerable housing lists. But it was about other, more important things. Compassion and the curious scheme of values which results in local authorities turning people out of "inadequate" accommodation.' Cathy hitch-hikes to London from her north country 'safe, ordinary' background, attracted by the permissive society (much as Sylvie had been in *Up the Junction*). She marries a driver (Ray Brooks) and they have two children. However, the problems of housing kill the marriage as the family move into a squalid tenement, then a dilapidated caravan, and finally into a hostel for the homeless, before being brutally (and publicly) evicted. Finally, Cathy has her children taken away from her and descends into the world of brutally-run 'refuges'.

Cathy was championed by the right-wing press as 'the truth behind socialism', but attacked by the Local Government Information Office which asked their members to watch repeats of the play and 'look out for blunders'. Sandford called this 'childish and mean-minded' and, in a celebrated counter-attack, wrote *Edna, the Inebriate Woman*, as his reply, which, after almost four years of false-starts and nervous twitches by the BBC, was produced in 1971, with Patricia Hayes in the title role.

Irene Shubik Originally an academic historian, Shubik worked as a story editor on *Armchair Theatre* and the science-fiction anthology *Out of this World* for ABC in 1962. Moving with her boss, Sydney Newman, to the BBC soon afterwards, she produced the similar *Out of the Unknown* for BBC2, utilizing a number of the same writers (and even some of the same scripts). Shubik also oversaw a series of Georges Simenon short-story adaptations, *Thirteen Against Fate*.

Moving to *The Wednesday Play* in 1967, she remained with the series through its transition to *Play for Today*, producing well over 50 plays, including Peter Terson's *The Last Train Through Harecastle Tunnel* (1969), Jeremy Sandford's *Edna, The Inebriate Woman* (1971) and John Mortimer's *Rumpole of the Bailey* (1975). At the same time she was also handling *Playhouse* for BBC2. Two supernatural plays in 1975 (*The Breakthrough* and William Trevor's *Mrs Aclands' Ghosts*) led directly to the series

Playhouse: The Mind Beyond the following year, with writers including Brian Hayles and Evan Jones.

In 1978 Shubik produced the first series of *Rumpole of the Bailey* for Thames. Moving to Granada in 1980, she produced Paul Scott's post-Indian independence drama *Staying On* (with Celia Johnson and Trevor Howard). Its success prompted Granada to make *Jewel in the Crown*, which Shubik helped to set-up. Her 1975 book *Play for Today: The Evolution of Television Drama* is a standard reference work.

Dennis Spooner Creator of some of the best remembered series of the 60s, Spooner's talent lay in producing well-paced, all-action television with a wry smile. Spooner's comic ability saw him working on the ATV ***Hancock*** series, before he spent a period script-editing ***Doctor Who*** and *The Baron*. At ITC, working first with Richard Harris and then producer Monty Berman, Spooner created a string of successful series (*Man in a Suitcase*, *The Champions*, ***Randall and Hopkirk (Deceased)*** and ***Department S***). Later, Spooner worked at the BBC on ***Doomwatch***, *Paul Temple* and ***Bergerac***, and for his friend Brian Clemens on *Thriller*, ***The New Avengers*** and ***The Professionals***. His final work before his death in 1986 was for *Hammer House of Mystery and Suspense* and a play for the children's anthology *Dramarama*.

Tom Stoppard Most famous for his work in theatre and films (*Rosencrantz and Guildenstern are Dead* and *Brazil* (GB 85)), Stoppard's early TV work included *A Separate Peace* (1966), *Teeth* (1967), a morbid black comedy about killer-dentists, the science-fiction play *Another Moon Called Earth* (1968, for *Thirty Minute Theatre*) and *Neutral Ground* (in collaboration with Clive Exton). His 1976 adaptation of *Three Men in a Boat* was followed in 1977 by the *Play of the Week*, *Professional Foul*, for which Peter Barkworth won a BAFTA. *The Telegraph* noted that the play 'pulled off the rare feat of being funny, engrossing and suspenseful, whether watched as an adventure of ideas, or as adventure with people'.

Later work includes the opera *Every Good Boy Deserves Favour* (1979) with Ian McKellen, and *Squaring the Circle* (1984), the first play concerning Solidarity, with Bernard Hill as Lech Walesa.

Don Taylor Born into a solid working-class background, Taylor studied at Oxford and joined the BBC in 1960. At the time, the old theatre-based practice of producers also directing and editing plays still held sway and it was in this multi-hatted capacity that – after episodes of *Scotland Yard* and an Arthur Swinson drama-documentary, *The Road to Carey Street* – Taylor produced N.J. Crisp's *The Dark Man* (1960) and David Turner's *The Train Set* (1961). Both appealed to Taylor's left-wing sensibilities, the first being a fable about racial prejudice set in a taxi firm, the latter about a factory owner desperate to buy a toy for his train-spotter son. Taylor then began to develop a group of writers he would direct almost exclusively over the next four years; Crisp, Turner, Hugh Whitemore and, especially, David Mercer, starting with *Where the Difference Begins* (1961).

Sydney Newman's restructuring of the BBC drama department in 1963 was anathema to Taylor, and following artistic differences with Newman and James MacTaggart over two plays he directed under the new system (George Target's *Workshop Limits* and Whitemore's *The Full Charter*, both 1963) he was moved off new plays. As an olive branch, Newman offered Taylor the initial producership of ***Doctor Who***, but the latter declined, directed Whitemore's *Dan, Dan the Charity Man*, and Mercer's *And Did Those Feet?* (both 1965) as a freelance and was then (he alleges in his book *Days of Vision*) effectively blacklisted from BBC drama.

Moving back to the theatre, with occasional work for the BBC arts features department, he returned to drama in 1972 to direct his own play *The Exorcism* for *Dead of Night*. *The Roses of Eyam* (1973) and *Dad* (1976) followed, whilst Taylor also worked for ATV, directing *Visitors* and *The Person Responsible* by his wife, Ellen Dryden, in 1974, and two plays in Nigel Kneale's *Beasts* series in 1976. Since then, with the exception of existing works such as Arthur Miller's *The Crucible* and Shakespeare's *Two Gentlemen of Verona*, all of Taylor's television work has been from his own scripts, including *When the Actors Come*, *Flayed* (both 1978), *In Hiding* (1980), and *A Last*

Visitor for Mr Hugh Peter (1981). He has also directed his own translations of Sophocles in a 1986 BBC trilogy.

Ken Taylor The author of the spectacular trilogy of plays, *The Seekers*, which opened BBC2's revolutionary *Theatre 625* series in 1964, Taylor was also involved in Stuart Burge's high profile *Studio 64* with *The Devil and John Brown*. Other plays included *The China Doll* (1960), *The Tin Whistle* (1962), and the prestigious 1966 adaptation of Wells's *Days to Come* for *Play of the Month*. *The Magicians* (1967) was another trilogy for *Theatre 625* which saw Taylor working with Jeremy Brett, Richard Todd, and Frank Finlay. In the 80s, Taylor became known as an impressive author of dramatic adaptations: 1984's *Jewel in the Crown*, episodes of *Miss Marple*, and the extraordinary *The Camomile Lawn* (*The Camomile Porn*, as *The Sun* wittily dubbed it), featuring Paul Eddington, Felicity Kendall and (rather a lot of) Jennifer Ehle.

Peter Terson The most remarkable thing about Terson's career is that it took so long to get going. A regular producer of stage plays, Newcastle-born Terson tried for years to break into television without success. It was only when a National Youth Theatre performance of his classic football play *Zigger Zagger* was televised in 1967 that Terson's work began to be accepted. Over the following years, he produced a string of exuberant, funny plays like *Mooney and his Caravan*, *The Apprentices*, *The Last Train Through Harecastle Tunnel* and *The Gregorian Chant*. His finest moments occurred in the early 70s with a trilogy of *Play for Todays*, *The Fishing Party* (1972), *Shakespeare – Or Bust* (1973), and *Three for the Fancy* (1974). These warm and hilarious plays concerned three Yorkshire miners (Brian Glover, Ray Mort and Douglas Livingstone), whose adventures in search of suitable leisure activities are thwarted by the forces of horrid conformity. These days Terson is, once again, a mainstay of the theatre, although a rare TV outing in 1983, *Atlantis*, for *Play for Today*, was welcomed by his many admirers.

William Trevor Irish author William Trevor was a prolific dramatist, notably for the BBC beginning with *The Babysitter* (for *The Wednesday Thriller*, 1965) and *Walk's End* for *Out of the Unknown* (1966). Trevor wrote *A Night with Mrs de Tanka* (1968), *The Mark-Two Wife* (1969) and *The Italian Table* (1970) for *The Wednesday Play*, and *The Penthouse Apartment* (1972) for *Thirty Minute Theatre*.

'William Trevor should perhaps get some sort of medal from the television actress' branch of Women's Lib, for he alone seems to specialize in writing big starring roles for women,' noted *The Times* when reviewing *O Fat White Woman*, his remarkable 1971 play of sexual repression starring Maureen Pryor and Peter Jeffrey. Amongst Trevor's other plays of the era are *The Grass Widow* (1971), *The General's Day* (1972), *Access to the Children* (1973), *Eleanor* (1974), *Mrs Acland's Ghost* (1975) and *Last Wishes* (1978). The trilogy *Matilda's England*, and *The Ballroom of Romance* (1980), concerning a faded Irish dance hall, were successful in the early 80s, as was Granada's *Secret Orchid* (1982), about a bigamist whose deception is revealed after he dies.

Later Trevor adapted his stage work for television with *The Children of Dynmouth* (1987) and *Beyond the Pale* (1989).

Kenith Trodd In 1968 Trodd founded Kestrel Films with Tony Garnett and Ken Loach to make plays for LWT, one of the first being Dennis Potter's *Moonlight on the Highway*. Trodd would produce much of Potter's subsequent work, including *Brimstone and Treacle*, *Blue Remembered Hills*, *Pennies from Heaven*, and ***The Singing Detective***. When the Kestrel contract was not renewed he moved to the BBC to work for *Play for Today*, his first production being Roger Smith's *The Operation*, with George Lazenby and Maurice Roeves in 1973. His association with the series continued until its end, taking in Roger Mahon's adaptation of *Shadows on Our Skin*, and Stephen Poliakoff's *Caught on a Train* and *Soft Targets*.

Of unswerving left-wing credentials, he also oversaw G.F. Newman's *Billy* (1979), Jim Allen's *United Kingdom*, *The Aerodrome* (1983) and *Here is the News* (1989). Often the subject of the attention of Mary Whitehouse and her people,

Trodd's work has included Michael Thomas's exceptionally rude *The MacGuffin*, and, more recently, Simon Gray's *Femme Fatale* for *Screen Two*.

Keith Waterhouse and Willis Hall Journalists Waterhouse and Hall met in Leeds in the 50s. During an era when the voice of young northern men was in great demand they created *Whistle Down the Wind* (GB 61), *A Kind of Loving* (GB 62) and *Billy Liar* (GB 63) in a golden age for the British cinema. Moving to television when similar voices were called for, the pair wrote for ***That Was the Week That Was***, then turned to drama. *The Sponge Room* (1964), *All Things Bright and Beautiful* (1964), *How Many Angels?* and *The Happy Moorings* (both 1965) were extensions of their stage and film work: witty yet grim depictions of northern life. Later, they would create the sitcom *Queenie's Castle* (1970), the cult comedy drama, *Budgie* (1971), *The Upchat Line* (1977, with John Alderton), 1973's series of their own *Billy Liar* (starring Jeff Rawle), and the children's favourite *Worzel Gummidge* (1979). Both writers have also worked individually, Hall writing plays like *They Don't All Open Men's Boutiques* (1972, about a dreadful lower league football team playing Leeds in the FA Cup), *The Railwayman's New Clothes* (1973) and *Song at Twilight* (1974); Waterhouse, with *Charlie Muffin* (1983), *Charters and Caldicott* (1985) and *Andy Capp* (1988). In 1988 the pair were reunited on the series *The Reluctant Dragon*.

Fay Weldon That a 24-year-old product of Hampstead Girls' school could break into the overwhelmingly male world of BBC drama doesn't seem so remarkable today – but in 1966 it was. Yet Fay Weldon's *Wife in a Blond Wig* (1966, for *Thirty Minute Theatre*), or *Wednesday Plays* like *Fall of the Goat* (1967) or *The Smoke Screen* (1969), were curios. Liberalism was all very well, but the sisters' place was still considered to be, as Stokeley Carmichael once noted, 'on your back, baby'. In this climate, it was Weldon's scripts for ***Upstairs, Downstairs*** that showed her ability to merge feminist concerns and exciting, demotic drama. Elsewhere, she continued to produce little gems like *A Load of Guilt* (1971 for *Trial*), *Hands*, *Splinter of Ice* (both 1972), the *Menace* play *Comfortable Words* and *In Memorium* for *Then and Now* (both 1973), a series written by and starring women.

It was 1986's *The Life and Loves of a She Devil* (starring Julie T. Wallace, Dennis Waterman, Patricia Hodge and Tom Baker) that brought Weldon to a mass audience. The production had a glossy schizophrenia, with a blazing mystical force that ITV tried to copy in 1991 with their own Weldon productions, *The Cloning of Joanna May* and *Growing Rich*, with varying degrees of success. The fact is, such texts walk a fine line between horror and the farce of masculine groin-thrusting. Other Weldon plays include the sinister *Zoe's Fever* (1986) and *Heart of the Country* (1987).

Colin Welland Coming to writing as a distraction from a successful acting career (notably in ***Z Cars***), Welland's early plays include *Bangelstein's Boys* (1969), *Slattery's Mounted Foot* (1970), *Roll on Four O'Clock* (also 1970, in which the author's past as a teacher was put to good use), *The Hallelujah Handshake*, and *Say Goodnight to Your Grandma* (both 1970). The touching *Kisses at Fifty* (1973) was the first sign of Welland's emerging greatness. *Jack Point* (1973), the harshly political *Leeds – United!* (1974) and *Your Man From the Six Counties* (1976) were critical successes, Welland being the first man to win the TV Writers Guild TV award three times. After the series *The Wild West Show* (1975), and a return to acting in *Cowboys* and Potter's *Blue Remembered Hills*, he moved into the cinema in the 70s, winning an Oscar for *Chariots of Fire* (GB 81), claiming that the British were coming (they weren't). He is still an occasional, and welcome, contributor to TV, as 1994's *Screen One*, *Bambino Mio*, proved.

Hugh Whitemore One of the most prolific playwrights of the 60s, Whitemore's work included *Dan, Dan the Charity Man*, *Application Form* (both 1965), *Final Demand*, *Girl of My Dreams* (both 1966), *Hello, Good Evening, and Welcome* (1968), *Party Games* (1970) and adaptations of Kafka's *Amerika*, *Don Quixote*, and *84 Charing Cross Road* (which he later scripted for the cinema). Whitemore's mastery of the chiller was highlighted in *Frankenstein Mark II*

(1966, *Out of the Unknown*), *The Bells of Hell* (*1968, Late Night Horror*) and *Deliver Us from Evil* (1973, *Menace*).

Act of Betrayal (1971), *Disappearing Trick* (1972) and *Goodbye* (1975), along with such award-winning fare as *Cider with Rosie* (1971) and an episode of ***Elizabeth R***, furthered his reputation as an author with a keen understanding of audiences. 1977's *Dummy* is a fine example of this, the story of a deaf and dumb girl forced into prostitution through an uncaring society. *I Remember Nelson*, the Emmy-winning *Concealed Enemies*, *The Final Days*, and *Utz* (co-written with Bruce Chatwin) are among his more recent plays.

Charles Wood Born into a working-class theatrical family, Wood enjoyed tasks behind the scenes but balked at an acting career, and so 'rebelled' by joining the army. Five years in the 17th & 21st Lancers was reflected in his first television plays, *Prisoner and Escort* (1963), and *Drill Pig* (1964) for ABC. He went on to write the film scripts for *The Knack* (GB 65), the Beatles' *Help!* (GB 65), *How I Won the War* (GB 67) and *The Charge of the Light Brigade* (GB 68).

Returning to television in 1969, *Drums Along the Avon* for *The Wednesday Play* was an essay in alienation starring Leonard Rossiter and Rafiq Anwar, whilst *A Bit of a Holiday* for Yorkshire Television's *The Root of All Evil* was a situation comedy which first introduced the character of Gordon Maple (George Cole), struggling writer, and his long-suffering wife (Gwen Watford), in Rome for the making of a film Gordon has written. Two years later, Wood used the premise again in another YTV series, *The Ten Commandments*, with Maple suffering his aged parents coming to live with them. It was not until 1977 that he managed to sell the concept as a series to the BBC, with two seasons of *Don't Forget to Write!*

In 1974 Wood returned to a military subject in the autobiographical three-part *Death or Glory Boy*, about a young recruit in the writer's old regiment, whilst 1977's *Love-Lies-Bleeding* started out as a dinner party comedy and ended with blood and bullets. *Mützen Ab!* (1974) for *Masquerade* and the *Play for Today*, *Do As I Say* were also notable successes. *Red Monarch*, a black comedy about the last days of Stalin for *Film on Four*, and the epic four-hour *Wagner* biography were both produced for Channel 4 in 1983. *Puccini* (1984) was a similar exercise, directed by Tony Palmer.

Tumbledown was originally to have been a film script, but the lack of American backing ruled this out. Based on the story of Robert Lawrence, a Scots Guards officer awarded the Military Cross for his bravery in one of the final battles of the Falklands, Wood and Richard Eyre finally sold it to the BBC.

More recently Wood – reflecting his interest in military history – adapted *Sharpe's Company* for ITV and *A Breed of Heroes* for the BBC. The latter, about a Parachute Regiment detachment in Belfast in the early stages of the troubles, underlined many of the points which *Tumbledown*'s critics overlooked, namely Wood's understandable empathy for the soldier in the midst of a situation into which politicians – his real target – have placed them.

Martin Worth A great writer of series television, Worth began writing in the 50s on *The Adventures of William Tell*, the Granada play *Shooting Star* and series like *Mrs Thursday*, *Sergeant Cork* and *Mr Rose*, as well as plays in *City '68*. At the BBC, Worth worked on *The Borderers*, ***Dr Finlay's Casebook*** and *Sutherland's Law*, also producing ***The Onedin Line***, as well as more adventurous areas like *Out of the Unknown* and *Menace*. A regular writer on *Public Eye*, Worth was also involved in the BBC telefantasy series ***Doomwatch*** (as script editor on the final season) and ***Survivors***, and on *The Regiment* and *Warship*. Worth's 80s work includes episodes of *Hammer House of Mystery and Suspense* and *C.A.T.S. Eyes*.

Bibliography

Alvarado, Manuel and John Stewart, *Made for Televison: Euston Films Ltd*, BFI Publishing, 1985

Attwood, Tony, *The Blake's 7 Programme Guide*, W.H. Allen, 1983

Baker, Simon and Olwen Terris, *A for Andromeda to Zoo Time - The TV Holdings of the National Film and Television Archive 1936-1979*, BFI Publishing, 1994

Ballantyne, James, *Researcher's Guide to British Film & Television Collections*, 4th ed., British Universities Film & Video Council, 1993

Barnett, Steven and Andrew Curry, *The Battle for the BBC*, Aurum, 1994

Benn, Tony, *Out of the Wilderness, Diaries 1963–67*, Arrow Books, 1987

Brake, Colin, *EastEnders - The First Ten Years*, BBC Books, 1994

Brandt, George W. (ed.), *British Television Drama*, Cambridge University Press, 1981

Brandt, George W. (ed.), *British Television Drama in the 80s*, Cambridge University Press, 1993

Brooke-Taylor, Tim, Graeme Garden and Bill Oddie, *The Goodies File*, Sphere Books, 1974

Bryant, Steve, *The Television Heritage*, BFI Publishing, 1989

Buckingham, David, *Public Secrets - EastEnders & its Audience*, BFI Publishing, 1987

Cain, John, *The BBC: 70 Years of Broadcasting*, BBC Books, 1992

Chapman, Graham, John Cleese, Terry Gilliam, Eric Idle, Terry Jones and Michael Palin, *Monty Python's Flying Circus: Just the Words*, vols 1 and 2, Methuen, 1989

Clark, Steve, *The British Television Location Guide*, 2nd ed., Seaspite Publishing, 1994

Clarke, Alan, '"This is Not the Boy Scouts": Television Police Series and Definitions of Law and Order', in Tony Bennett, Colin Mercer and Janet Woollacott (eds), *Popular Culture and Social Realism*, Open University Press, 1986

Cleese, John, and Connie Booth, *The Complete Fawlty Towers*, Methuen, 1988

Cook, Jim (ed.), *Television Sitcoms*, BFI Publishing, 1982

Cornell, Paul, Martin Day and Keith Topping, *The Avengers Programme Guide*, Virgin Publishing, 1994

Cornell, Paul, Martin Day and Keith Topping, *The Doctor Who Discontinuity Guide*, Virgin Publishing, 1995

Corrie, Andrew and John McCready, *Phil Redmond's Grange Hill - The Official Companion*, Weidenfeld & Nicolson, 1988

Curteis, Ian, *The Falklands Play*, Hutchinson, 1987

Davies, Russell (ed.), *The Kenneth Williams Diaries*, Harper Collins, 1994

Davis, Anthony, *Television: The First 40 Years*, Severn House Publishers, 1976

Davis, Anthony, *TV's Greatest Hits*, Boxtree, 1988

Davis, Anthony, *TV Laughtermakers*, Boxtree, 1989

Day-Lewis, Séan, *TV Heaven*, Channel 4/Broadcasting Support Services, 1992

Docherty, David, *Running the Show – 21 Years of London Weekend Television*, Boxtree, 1990

Down, Richard, *The New Improved Guide to Telefantasy Transmission Dates and Archive Holdings*, Kaleidoscope, 1993

Down, Richard and Chris Perry, *British Television Comedy and Light Entertainment Research Guide 1950-1995*, 2nd ed., Kaleidoscope, 1995

Down, Richard and Chris Perry, *British Television Drama Research Guide 1950 - 1995*, 2nd ed., Kaleidoscope, 1995

Dyja, Eddie, and (previous editions) Nick Thomas, David Leafe, Terry Ilott, Patience Costner, *et al.* (eds), *BFI Film and Television Handbook*, British Film Institute, annual publication

Elliot, John, *Mogul - The Making of a Myth*, Barrie & Jenkins, 1970

Ellis, Robin, *Making Poldark*, Bossiney Books, 1977

Frost, David and Ned Sherrin (eds), *That Was the Week That Was*, W.H. Allen, 1963

Fulton, Roger, *The Encyclopedia of TV Science Fiction*, 2nd ed., Boxtree, 1995

Gaiman, Neil, *Don't Panic – Douglas Adams & The Hitch-Hiker's Guide to the Galaxy*, Titan Books, 1988

Galton, Ray and Alan Simpson, *The Best of Steptoe and Son*, Robson Books, 1988

Gambaccini, Paul and Rod Taylor, *Television's Greatest Hits*, Network Books, 1993

Gilbert, W. Stephen, *Fight & Kick & Bite: The Life and Work of Dennis Potter*, Hodder, 1995

Green, Hugh Carleton, *The Third Floor Front: A View of Broadcasting in the Sixties*, Bodley Head, 1969

Haining, Peter, *The Television Sherlock Holmes*, W.H. Allen, 1986

Halliwell, Leslie, with Philip Purser, *Halliwell's Television Companion*, 3rd ed., Grafton, 1986

Harbord, Jane and Jeff Wright, *40 Years of British Television*, Boxtree, 1992

Harris, Kenneth, (with Michael Cox and Andrew Robinson (eds)), *A Centenary Celebration of Sherlock Holmes 1887-1987: A Granada Companion*, Karizzma, 1987

Haselden, John, *'Allo 'Allo! –The War Diaries of René Artois*, vols 1 and 2, BBC Books, 1988/1989

Hayward, Anthony, *The Who's Who of Soap Operas*, Guinness Publishing, 1991

Hayward, Anthony, *Who's Who on Television*, Boxtree, 1994

Heatley, Michael, *Emmerdale Farm Family Album – A Village Portrait*, Boxtree, 1994

Hill, Tim, *The Seventies*, Chapman Publishers, 1991

Home, Anna, *Into the Box of Delights*, BBC Books, 1993

Howarth, Chris and Steve Lyons, *The Red Dwarf Programme Guide*, Virgin Publishing, 1993

Howe, David J., Mark Stammers and Stephen James Walker, *Doctor Who – The Sixties*, Virgin Publishing, 1992

Hulke, Malcolm, *Writing for Television*, A & C Black, 1980

Hunt, Albert, *The Language of Television – Uses and Abuses*, Methuen, 1983

Hunter, Allan (ed.), *Chambers Film and TV Handbook*, Chambers, 1991

Isaacs, Jeremy, *Storm over Four*, Weidenfield & Nicholson, 1989

Jackson, Paul, 'T-T-T-Timing', in Phillippa Giles and Vicky Licorish (eds), *Debut on Two*, BBC Books, 1990

James, Clive, *Clive James on Television*, Picador, 1991

Jarvis, Peter, *Teletalk – A Directory of Broadcasting Terms*, BBC Print Unit, 1991

Kay, Graeme, *Coronation Street - Celebrating 30 Years*, Boxtree, 1991

Kelsey, Gerald, *Writing for Television*, A & C Black, 1990

Kingsley, Hilary, *Soap Box*, Macmillan, 1988

Kingsley, Hilary, *Casualty – The Inside Story*, rev. ed., Penguin/BBC Books, 1995

Kingsley, Hilary and Geoff Tibballs, *The Box of Delights*, Macmillan, 1990

Kneale, Nigel, *The Year of the Sex Olympics and Other TV Plays*, Ferret Fantasy, 1976

Lahr, John (ed.), *The Orton Diaries*, Methuen, 1986

Lawrence, John and Robert Lawrence MC, *When the Fighting is Over*, Bloomsbury, 1988

Leapman, Michael, *Last Days of the Beeb*, Allen & Urwin, 1986

Lewis, Jon E. and Penny Stempel, *Cult TV*, Pavilion Books, 1993

Lewisohn, Mark, *The Complete Beatles Chronicle*, Pyramid Books, 1992

Lofficier, Jean-Marc, *The Doctor Who Programme Guide*, 4th ed., Virgin Publishing, 1994

Lynch, Tony, *The Bill*, Boxtree, 1992

Lynn, Jonathan and Anthony Jay, *The Complete Yes Minister*, BBC Books, 1989

MacDonald, Ian, *Revolution in the Head*, Fourth Estate, 1994

Masterman, Len, *Teaching the Media*, Comedia, 1985

Milligan, Stephen, *What Shall We Do About the BBC?*, Tory Reform Group, 1991

Millington, Bob and Rob Nelson, *The Boys from the Blackstuff – The Making of TV Drama*, Comedia/Routledge, 1986

Moss, Nicholas, *BBC TV Presents: A Fiftieth Anniversary Celebration*, BBC Data Publications, 1986

Munro, Josephine, *The EastEnders Programme Guide*, Virgin Publishing, 1994

Newman, Kim, *Nightmare Movies*, Bloomsbury Publishing Ltd, 1984

Norden, Dennis, Sybil Harper and Norma Gilbert, *Coming to You Live!: Behind-the-Scenes Memories of Forties and Fifties Television*, Methuen, 1985

Paice, Eric, *The Way to Write for Television*, Elm Tree Books, 1981

Palmer, Tony, *The Trials of Oz*, Blond & Briggs, 1971

Passingham, Kenneth, *The Guinness Book of TV Facts and Feats*, Guinness Publishing, 1984
Perry, George, *Life of Python*, Pavilion Books, 1986
Pertwee, Bill, *Dad's Army*, David & Charles, 1989
Pike, Frank (ed.), *Ah! Mischief: The Writer and Television*, Faber and Faber, 1982
Poliakoff, Stephen, *Runners & Soft Targets*, Methuen, 1984
Potter, Dennis, *The Nigel Barton Plays*, Penguin, 1967
Potter, Dennis, *Waiting for the Boat*, Faber and Faber, 1984
Potter, Dennis, *The Singing Detective*, Faber and Faber, 1986
Potter, Dennis, *Seeing the Blossom*, Faber and Faber, 1994
Prior, Allan, *Z Cars*, Trust Books, 1963
Rogers, Dave, *The ITV Encyclopedia of Adventure*, Boxtree, 1988
Rogers, Dave, *The Prisoner & Danger Man*, Boxtree, 1988
Rogers, Dave, *The Complete Avengers*, Boxtree, 1989
Rosenthal, Jack, *Three Award-Winning TV Plays*, Penguin, 1978
Sanderson, Mark, *The Making of Inspector Morse*, Macmillan, 1991
Sangster, Jim, with Stephen O'Brien and Steve Lyons, *The Press Gang Programme Guide*, Leomac Publishing, 1995
Savage, Jon, *England's Dreaming*, Faber and Faber, 1992
Self, David, *Television Drama: An Introduction*, Macmillan, 1984
Shubik, Irene, *Play for Today: The Evolution of Television Drama*, Davis-Poynter, 1975
Shubik, Irene (ed.), *The Mind Beyond*, Penguin, 1976
Smith, Anthony, *British Broadcasting*, David & Charles, 1974
Stead, Peter, *Dennis Potter*, Seren Books, 1993
Sutton, Shaun, *The Largest Theatre in the World*, BBC Publications, 1982
Taylor, Don, *Days of Vision*, Methuen, 1990
Taylor, John Russell, *Anatomy of a Television Play*, Weidenfeld & Nicolson, 1962
Tibballs, Geoff, *The Golden Age of Children's Television*, Titan, 1991
Tibballs, Geoff, *The Boxtree Encyclopedia of TV Detectives*, Boxtree, 1992
Tibballs, Geoff, *Brookside – Life in the Close*, Boxtree, 1994
Tibballs, Geoff, *Randall and Hopkirk (Deceased)*, Boxtree, 1994
Tibballs, Geoff, *Brookside – The Early Years*, 1995
Tracey, Michael, *A Variety of Lives: A Biography of Sir Hugh Greene*, Bodley Head, 1983
Tulloch, John, *Television Drama: Agency, Audience & Myth*, Routledge, 1990
Tulloch, John and Manuel Alvarado, *Doctor Who – The Unfolding Text*, Macmillan, 1983
Tulloch, John and Henry Jenkins, *Science Fiction Audiences: Watching Doctor Who and Star Trek*, Routledge, 1995
Vahimagi, Tise, *British Television*, Oxford University Press, 1994
Wilmut, Roger, *Hancock, Artiste*, Queen Anne Press, 1983
Wilmut, Roger, *From Fringe to Flying Circus*, Queen Anne Press, 1985
Wilmut, Roger and Peter Rosengard, *Didn't You Kill My Mother-In-Law?*, Methuen, 1989
Wittrick, Rae (ed.), *The Patrick McGoohan Screenography*, Six of One Publications, 1984
Wood, Charles, *Tumbledown*, Penguin, 1987
Zukowska, Krystyna, *Between the Lines: Tony Clark's Dossier*, Boxtree, 1994

Terrestrial British Television Companies

(listed chronologically)

BBC Television 2 Nov 36-1 Sep 39
7 Jun 46 to date (BBC1 from 21 Apr 64)

Associated Rediffusion/Rediffusion (Jul 64 onwards);
London (weekday) franchise: 22 Sep 55-29 Jul 68
combined with ABC to form Thames: 30 Jul 68

ATV (Associated Television)
London (weekend) franchise: 24 Sep 55-28 Jul 68
Midlands (weekday) franchise: 17 Feb 56-31 Dec 81
Midlands (weekend) franchise: 2 Aug 68-31 Dec 81
1 Jan 82: became Central Independent Television

ABC Television (Associated British Picture Corporation)
Midlands (weekend) franchise: 18 Feb 56-28 Jul 68
Northern England (weekend) franchise: 5 May 56-28 Jul 68
combined with Rediffusion to form Thames: 30 Jul 68

Granada Television
North-west England (weekday) franchise: 3 May 56 to date
North-west England (weekend) franchise: 29 Jul 68 to date

Scottish Television Central Scotland franchise: 31 Aug 57 to date

TWW (Television West and Wales)
South Wales and West England franchise: 14 Jan 58-26 Jan 64
Wales and West England franchise: 27 Jan 64-3 Mar 68

Southern Television Southern England franchise: 30 Aug 58-31 Dec 81

Tyne Tees Television North-east England franchise: 15 Jan 59 to date

Anglia Television East England franchise: 27 Oct 59 to date

Ulster Television Northern Ireland franchise: 31 Oct 59 to date

Westward Television South-west England franchise: 29 Apr 61-11 Aug 81

Border Television Border franchise: 1 Sep 61 to date
Isle of Man franchise: 26 Mar 65 to date

Grampian Television Northern Scotland franchise: 30 Sep 61 to date

Channel Television Channel Islands franchise: 1 Sep 62 to date

Wales West and North: West and North Wales franchise: 14 Sep 62-26 Jan 64

BBC2 21 Apr 64 to date

HTV (Harlech Television) Wales and West England franchise: 4 Mar 68 to date

Yorkshire Television Northern England franchise: 29 Jul 68 to date

Thames Television London (weekday) franchise: 30 Jul 68-31 Dec 92

LWT (London Weekend Television) London (weekend) franchise: 2 Aug 68 to date

TSW (Television South West) South-west England franchise: 12 Aug 81-31 Dec 92

Central Independent Television Midlands franchise: 1 Jan 82 to date

TVS (Television South) Southern England franchise: 1 Jan 82-31 Dec 92

S4C (Sianel Pedwar Cymru) 1 Nov 82 to date

Channel 4 2 Nov 82 to date

TV-am Early morning franchise: 1 Feb 83-31 Dec 92

Carlton London (weekday) franchise: 1 Jan 93 to date

GMTV (Good Morning Television) Early morning franchise: 1 Jan 93 to date

Meridian Southern England franchise: 1 Jan 93 to date

Westcountry South-west England franchise: 1 Jan 93 to date

Index

PROGRAMME INDEX

Entries and page numbers in bold refer to the main entry for the relevant programme. Page numbers in italics refer to a page with an illustration.

D

E

F

NAME INDEX

C

D

E

F

Q

R

S

T

GENERAL INDEX